THE NEW TESTAMENT
with PSALMS & PROVERBS

Translation in the Oldest Tradition
The Traditional Text

Translated by:
Pastor Mark Spitsbergen, ThD, MS

The New Testament *with* Psalms & Proverbs
Translation in the Oldest Tradition

Paperback ISBN: 979-8-9944098-1-7

Address correspondence to:

Mark Spitsbergen
Abiding Place Ministries
2155 N Campo Truck Trail, Campo CA 91906
www.abidingplace.org
AwakeSD@me.com

Cover Design: Randy White & David Graham
Internal formatting: David Graham & April Flores
Date: January 25, 2026

Table of Contents

Also by Dr. Mark Spitsbergen

The Sequential Events in the life of Jesus Christ

Adam: From Glory to Shame

Man: Spirit, Soul, and Body

The NEW Creation that Brough Forth a New Man

The Unlimited Authority of the Believer

Alcohol in the Church

The Blood: The Power of Life and Purity

Ephesians: The Crown Jewel of the Epistles of Paul

The Miracles of Jesus Highlighted in the Gospel of John

Tongues: The Language of the Holy Spirit

Holiness– The Divine Life, The Forgotten Realm

The Last Two Kingdoms

The Last Trumpet

Nothing Can Harm You

ABOUT THE TRANSLATOR

Dr. Mark Spitsbergen is the Senior Pastor of the Abiding Place in San Diego, California where he and his wife Anne have pastored since 1985. He holds a Bachelor of Arts Degree (BA) in Biology/Chemistry from Point Loma Nazarene University, a Master of Science (MS) from the University of Saint Andrews, a Doctorate of Theology (ThD) from School of Bible Theology, as well as a Doctorate of Ministry (D. Min.) from Life Christian University. He has been studying Biblical languages since 1983. He began his study of biblical languages at PLNU and also studied at UCSD with Dr. David Noel Freedman.

THE NEW TESTAMENT

Translation in the Oldest Tradition
The Traditional Text

Translation comparing:

Greek: Byzantine Textform,
Stephen's Textus Receptus 1550;
Scrivener's Textus Receptus 1894

Eastern Aramaic: The Peshitta

English: The 1536 Tyndale Bible;
Geneva Bible, 1557;
King James, 1611 (1900)

PREFACE

We most certainly believe that the New Testament is the exact words of God delivered to us by God through His servants the apostles. The Word of God carries the highest importance and value for each one of us, as it is by the Word that we will be judged. Certainly, the Almighty God Who gave His Word to us has also watched over it to preserve its accuracy. The Greek and Aramaic New Testament have also been watched over and maintained by scribes who have valued it as the sacred and exact Word of God since the Apostle John presented it to the church.

Those who have worked to prepare the "Translation in the Oldest Tradition" have relied on those text types and translations that have been the most dominant in the church of Jesus Christ over the past 2,000 years. Most modern translations of the Bible rely heavily on a minority text type called the Alexandrian Text Type. This is one of the main differences of this translation: we completely ignore the Alexandrian Text Type and instead rely on all of those text types and translations into the English Language that were derived from the Byzantine Text Type, the Textus Receptus, and the Peshitta. The Byzantine and Peshitta texts are unique in that both have competing claims to the Priority Theory in which their respective text types best replicate the autograph (original). The Alexandrian Text Type however, was not given much value by the church until 1859.

Most modern-day translations not only give a priority to the Alexandrian Text Type, but also tend toward a thought-to-thought translation. We contend that the Greek New Testament can be accurately translated in an easy-to-understand word-for-word translation. We believe it is essential to know exactly what God has said and required of us. It is based on this certainty that we have worked since 2003 to provide this translation of the New Testament. In addition to all of the many resources made available to us, we also relied on every resource provided by Logos software.

The Byzantine Text Type/The Traditional Text

The Byzantine text, also known as the "Majority Text" and the "Traditional Textform," is a compilation of Greek New Testament Manuscripts that consists of the vast majority of all ancient Greek texts of the New Testament. It is strongly believed by many scholars that it is this text form that most accurately reflects the autograph (original) that was delivered to the church. The Byzantine Text Type reflects 80% of all existing Greek Manuscripts of the New Testament. The compilation of the Byzantine Text that was utilized for comparison in this translation was compiled and arranged by Maurice A. Robinson and William G. Pierpont, 2005.

The Textus Receptus:

Guided by the hand of God the Original Textus Receptus was arranged by Erasmus in 1516. We say guided because his Greek text of the Bible would result in the most profound event in history, the invention of the printing press. Stephanus completed an edited edition of the Erasmus Textus Receptus, which was followed by Scrivener's 1894 edition. The Textus Receptus and the Traditional Text have about 98% agreement.

The Peshitta:

The Peshitta is in the Syriac language, which is a form of Aramaic. It is believed that the Peshitta originated in the first century and has been used since then in the non-western church. Like the Greek Text forms of the Byzantine text, it is believed that the Peshitta is the oldest and most accurate witness of the original. Once again the Peshitta agrees closely with the Traditional text. This collection of Aramaic manuscripts is relied upon by the Syriac churches. Logos' edition of the Leiden Peshitta was used for this translation: "The Peshitta With Lexical and Morphological Tags by Dr. George Kiraz." Also, the English translations of the Peshitta by Drs. James Murdock, John W. Etheridge, and George Lamsa were compared.

English Translations:

Although earlier efforts were made to translate the Bible into English, the first complete translation of the New Testament from Greek texts was accomplished by William Tyndale and was first printed in 1526. His translation of the New Testament was made from the manuscripts compiled by Erasmus in 1516. His final edition was done in 1536 just prior to his death, where he was burned at the stake for his Bible translation. Much of his translation highly influenced the King James Version, which was completed in 1611.

The Geneva Bible was translated in Geneva, Switzerland by Protestant exiles who fled from the persecutions of Queen Mary. It was translated from Hebrew, Greek, and Aramiac manuscripts, as well as earlier English translations and contemporary German, French, Italian, Spanish, and Latin translations. It was first printed in 1560. The King James translation also relied heavily on the Geneva translation of the Bible. The great milestone of the Geneva Bible was that it was the first to use chapters and numbered verses.

The King James Bible, also called the Authorized Version, was translated by about 47 of the best scholars of their day that were appointed by King James in 1604. Prior to this, those who attempted to provide the Holy Scriptures to the common person were severely punished. In 1401, Henry IV outlawed the translation of the Bible. To translate it into the common language of the time was a crime, punishable by burning at the stake. It was King James that abolished this law. Although it was translated from Greek, it relied on the English translations that had already been completed. It is said that the King James Bible was shaped by Tyndale's translation, and the Geneva Bible. Yet at the same time there were the best scholars of the day who worked on the Translation of the King James Bible. However, the King James Bible emerged as the version that shaped the English Language of the period. It is, in the words of the famous skeptic H. L. Mencken, "a mine of lordly and incomparable poetry, at once the most stirring and the most touching ever heard of." Finally, the King James Version of 1900 is based off of the Pure Cambridge Tradition, which sought to more accurately reflect the original text.

Special thanks to the review and editing staff:

Dr. Stuart Graham M.D.
Dr. Joshua Spitsbergen Ph.D
Jeremiah Graham J.D.
Christopher Graham M.S.
David Graham M.A.T.
Randy White B.A. Ministry
Anne Spitsbergen B.A. Edu.

The Gospel of
Matthew

1 The book of the lineage of Jesus, the Messiah, the son of David, the son of Abraham.

2 Abraham begot Isaac, and Isaac begot Jacob, and Jacob begot Judah and his brethren.

3 And Judah begot Pheres and Zerah from Thamar, and Pheres begot Hezron, and Hezron begot Aram.

4 And Aram begot Aminadab, and Aminadab begot Nahshon, and Nahshon begot Salmon.

5 And Salmon begot Boaz by Rahab, and Boaz begot Obed by Ruth, and Obed begot Jesse.

6 And Jesse begot David the king, and David the king begot Solomon of the [wife] of Uriah.

7 And Solomon begot Rehoboam, and Rehoboam begot Abijah, and Abijah begot Asa.

8 And Asa begot Jehoshaphat, and Jehoshaphat begot Joram, and Joram begot Uzziah.

9 And Uzziah begot Jotham, and Jotham begot Ahaz, and Ahaz begot Hezekiah.

10 And Hezekiah begot Manasseh, and Manasseh begot Amos, and Amos begot Josiah.

11 And Josiah begot Jechoniah and his brothers at the time of deportation to Babylon.

12 And after the deportation, Jechoniah begot Salathiel, and Salathiel begot Zerubbabel.

13 And Zerubbabel begot Abiud, and Abiud begot Eliakim, and Eliakim begot Azor.

14 And Azor begot Zadok, and Zadok begot Achim, and Achim begot Eliud.

15 And Eliud begot Eleazar, and Eleazar begot Matthan, and Matthan begot Jacob.

16 And Jacob begot Joseph, the husband of Mary, of whom Jesus was born, Who is called Christ.

17 So all the generations from Abraham to David were fourteen generations, and from David until the deportation to Babylon were fourteen generations, and from the deportation of Babylon to Christ were fourteen generations.

18 Now the birth of Jesus the Christ was in this manner. When His mother Mary was engaged to Joseph, but before they were joined together, she was found to be with child from the Holy Spirit.

19 But her husband Joseph, being a righteous man, and not willing to make her a public example, thought to put her away secretly.

20 While he was considering these things, an angel from the Lord appeared unto him in a dream saying, "Joseph, son of David, do not be afraid to take Mary as your wife, for that which is in her is begotten of the Holy Spirit.

21 And she shall bring forth a Son, and you shall call His name 'Jesus,' and He shall save His people from their sins."

22 And all of this took place so that the words of the Lord that were spoken by the prophet might be fulfilled, saying,

23 "Behold, the virgin will conceive and she shall bring forth a Son, and they will call His name 'Emmanuel'" (which translated, means, "God is with us").

24 And being awakened out of his sleep, Joseph did as the angel of the Lord commanded him and took Mary to be his wife.

25 And he did not know her until she bore her first-born Son, and he called

His name "Jesus."

2 Now Jesus having been born in Bethlehem of Judea during the days of King Herod, Magi from the East came to Jerusalem,

2 saying, "Where is He that was born King of the Jews? For we saw His star in the East and have come to worship Him."

3 And King Herod, hearing this, was stirred, and all Jerusalem with him.

4 And he gathered together all of the Chief Priests and Scribes of the people and sought of them where Christ should be born.

5 And they said to him, "In Bethlehem of Judea, for thus it is written by the prophets,

6 'For you, Bethlehem of Judah, you are by no means least among the leaders of Israel, for out of you shall come a Captain Who will be the Shepherd of My people Israel.'"

7 Then Herod secretly called the Magi and sought to find out exactly what time the star appeared.

8 And sending them to Bethlehem, he said, "Go search diligently for the little child, and when you have found Him, send word back to me that I too may come and worship Him."

9 After hearing the king, they departed, and the star that they saw in the East went before them until it came and stood over where the little child was.

10 And seeing the star, they rejoiced with exceeding great joy!

11 And when they had come into the house, they saw the child with Mary, His mother, and fell down worshiping Him. And they opened up their treasures for Him: giving Him gifts of gold, frankincense, and myrrh.

12 And being divinely warned in a dream not to return to Herod they departed another way into their own country.

13 And after they had departed, an angel of the Lord appeared unto Joseph in a dream and said, "Get up, take the little child and His mother, and flee into Egypt, and stay there until I speak to you, for Herod is about to seek the little child to destroy Him."

14 And he got up and took the little child and His mother by night, and departed into Egypt.

15 And was there until the death of Herod, that what the Lord spoke through the prophet might be fulfilled, saying, "Out of Egypt have I called My Son."

16 Now Herod, knowing that he was mocked by the Magi, became full of rage, and sent and put to death all of the boys in Bethlehem and its borders, two years and younger, according to the time that he had precisely determined from the Magi.

17 Then was fulfilled that which was spoken by the prophet Jeremiah, saying,

18 "A voice in Rama was heard– lamentation and weeping and great mourning– Rachel weeping for her children, and would not be comforted because they are not."

19 But Herod having died, an angel of the Lord appeared in a dream to Joseph in Egypt,

20 saying, "Get up, and take the little child and His mother, and go into the land of Israel, for they are dead who sought to destroy the life of the little child."

21 And he got up, and took the little child and His mother, and came into the land of Israel.

22But having heard that Archelaus reigned over Judea in the place of his father, Herod, he was afraid to go there. And being divinely warned in a dream, he departed into the parts of Galilee.

23And he came and dwelt in a city called Nazareth; so that which was spoken by the prophets should be fulfilled, that He should be called a Nazarene.

3 John the Baptizer came in those days, preaching in the wilderness of Judea,

2saying, "Repent, for the Kingdom of Heaven has drawn near!"

3For this is the one that the prophet Isaiah spoke about, saying, "The voice of one crying out in the wilderness, 'Prepare the way of the Lord, make straight paths for Him.'"

4And John had camel's hair for his garment, and a leather girdle for a belt, and for food he ate locusts and wild honey.

5At that time, all Jerusalem and Judea and the country around Jordan went out to him

6and were baptized by him in the river Jordan, confessing their sins.

7Seeing many of the Pharisees and Sadducees coming to his baptism, he said, "You offspring of vipers, who forewarned you to flee from the coming wrath?

8Produce fruits worthy of repentance.

9And do not think, saying within yourselves, 'Abraham is our father,' because I tell you God is able to raise up children unto Abraham from these stones.

10For also the axe is already laid to the root of the trees, therefore every tree that does not bring forth good fruit is cut down and cast into the fire.

11I indeed baptize you with water unto repentance, but after me is coming One Who is mightier than myself, whose sandals I am not fit to carry. He will baptize you in the Holy Spirit and fire.

12The winnowing fork is in His hand, and He will thoroughly purge His floor. He will gather His wheat into His storehouse, but the chaff He will burn up with an unquenchable fire."

13At that time, Jesus came from Galilee to John at the Jordan to be baptized of him.

14But John was refusing Him, saying, "I need to be baptized by You, and yet You come to me?"

15But Jesus, answering, said to him, "You must allow it, for it is necessary for us to fulfill all righteousness," and he permitted it.

16When Jesus was baptized, as soon as He came up out of the water, then also were the heavens opened unto Him. And he saw the Spirit of God descending like a dove and coming upon Him.

17And there was a voice from out of Heaven saying, "This is My beloved Son in Whom I delight!"

4 And Jesus was led up into the wilderness by the Spirit to be tried by the Devil.

2And after having fasted forty days and forty nights, He was hungry.

3The Tempter came to Him and said, "If You are the Son of God, speak to these stones and make them bread."

4But He answering, said, "It is written, 'Man shall not live by bread alone, but by every word that goes out of the mouth of God.'"

5Then the Devil took Him to the holy

city and set Him on the top of the temple,
6 and said to Him, "If You are the Son
of God, cast Yourself down, for it is
written, 'He shall command His angels
to take care of you, and in their hands
they shall hold you up so that you do
not strike your foot against a stone.'"
7 Again Jesus said to him, "It is written, 'You shall not tempt the Lord your
God.'"
8 Again the Devil took Him into an
exceeding high mountain, and showed
Him all the kingdoms of the world and
their glory,
9 And he said to Him, "All these
things will I give You if You will fall
down and worship me."
10 Then Jesus said to him, "Get out of
here Satan! For it is written, 'You shall
worship the Lord your God, and Him
alone shall you serve!'"
11 At that time, the Devil left Him and
the angels came and ministered to
Him.
12 When Jesus heard that John was
arrested, He departed into Galilee.
13 And He left Nazareth and came and
dwelled in Capernaum, which is on the
seaside, in the borders of Zebulun and
Naphtali,
14 so that those things spoken by the
prophet Isaiah might be fulfilled, saying,
15 "The land of Zebulun and the land
of Naphtali by the way of the sea beyond Jordan, Galilee of the nations -
16 the people that sat in darkness have
seen a great light, and those who were
sitting in the region and the shadow of
darkness, to them light has sprung
forth."
17 From that time, Jesus began to announce and to say, "Repent, for the
Kingdom of Heaven is at hand!"
18 When Jesus was walking by the sea
of Galilee, He saw two brothers: Simon,
who is called "Peter," and Andrew, his
brother, casting a large net into the sea,
for they were fishermen.
19 And He said to them, "Come follow
me, and I will make you fishers of
men."
20 And they immediately left the nets
and followed Him.
21 And leaving there, He saw two
more brothers: James, the son of
Zebedee, and John, his brother, in the
boat with Zebedee, their father, mend-
ing their nets. And He called them.
22 And they immediately left the boat
and their father, and followed Him.
23 And they went throughout all of
Galilee, Jesus teaching in their synagogues, and announcing the good news
of the kingdom, and healing every disease and every sickness among the
people.
24 And His fame went out into all Syria, and they brought to Him everyone
who was ill with various diseases and
oppressing torments, possessed by
demons, lunatics and paralytics, and
He healed them.
25 And great crowds followed Him
from Galilee, Decapolis, Jerusalem,
Judea, and beyond Jordan.

5 But seeing the crowds, He went up
into the mountain and sat down,
and His disciples came to Him.
2 And He opened His mouth and
taught them, saying,
3 "Blessed are the poor in spirit, for
theirs is the Kingdom of Heaven.
4 Blessed are those that mourn, for
they will be comforted.
5 Blessed are the meek, for they shall
inherit the Earth.
6 Blessed are those who hunger and

thirst for righteousness, for they shall
be filled.
7Blessed are the merciful, for they
will receive mercy.
8Blessed are those whose hearts are
pure, for they will see God.
9Blessed are the peacemakers, for
they shall be called sons of God.
10Blessed are those persecuted for the
sake of righteousness, because theirs is
the Kingdom of Heaven.
11Blessed are you when you are
mocked and persecuted and have all
sorts of evil words uttered against you
falsely for my sake.
12Rejoice and be exceeding glad, for
great in number are your rewards in
Heaven, for in the same way, they persecuted the prophets who were before
you.
13You are the salt of the Earth, but if
the salt has become tasteless, with what
shall it be salted? For it has become
worthless, and should be cast out and
trampled on by men.
14You are the light of the world, a city
set upon a hill that cannot be hidden.
15Nor do they light a lamp and put it
under a basket– rather it is placed
upon the lamp stand, and it shines for
everyone in the house.
16Therefore let your light shine before men so that they may see your
good works and glorify your Father
Who is in Heaven.
17Do not suppose that I have come to
abolish the Law or the prophets. I did
not come to abolish, but to fulfill.
18I tell you for certain that until
Heaven and Earth shall pass away, not
one iota or even a letter of the Law
shall pass away until it all comes to
pass.
19Whoever then shall break one of
the least of these commandments and
shall teach men so shall be least in the
Kingdom of Heaven, but whoever shall
practice and teach them shall be called
great in the Kingdom of Heaven.
20For I tell you unless your righteousness exceeds that of the Scribes
and Pharisees, you shall in no way enter into the Kingdom of Heaven!
21You have heard that it was said to
the ancients, 'You shall not commit
murder,' and 'whoever commits
murder shall be in danger at the
judgment.'
22But I say to you that anyone angry
with his brother without cause will be
subject to the judgment, and if he
insults a brother, he will be subject to
the council, and if he says, 'You fool,' he
will be subject to the fire of Hell!
23Therefore, if you offer a gift at the
altar and remember that your brother
has something against you,
24leave your gift there before the altar
and go first and be reconciled to your
brother, and then come and offer your
gift.
25Agree with your adversary quickly
while you are being confronted, lest
your adversary delivers you over to the
judge, and the judge delivers you to the
officer and casts you into prison.
26I tell you with absolute certainty
you will not come out until you have
paid the last cent of debt.
27You have heard that it was said to
the ancients, 'You shall not commit
adultery,'
28but I tell you that everyone who
looks on a woman to lust after her has
already committed adultery with her in
his heart.
29And if your right eye causes you to
stumble, pluck it out and cast it from
you, for it is better that one of your
members perish instead of your whole

body being cast into Hell!

30 And if your right hand causes you to stumble, cut it off and cast it from you, for it is better that one of your members perish instead of your whole body being cast into Hell.

31 Also, it was said that whoever shall put away his wife, let him give to her a letter of divorce,

32 but I tell you that whoever shall put away his wife except on account of sexual immorality causes her to commit adultery, and whoever shall marry her afterwards commits adultery.

33 Again you have heard that it was said to the ancients, 'You shall not swear an oath, but you shall render to the Lord your oath,'

34 but I tell you: do not swear at all, neither by Heaven, for it is the throne of God,

35 nor by the Earth, because it is the footstool for His feet, or by Jerusalem, for it is the city of the great King!

36 Neither shall you swear by your head, because you are not able to make one hair white or black.

37 But let your word be 'yes, yes,' or 'no, no,' for what is more than these is evil.

38 You have heard that it was said, 'An eye for an eye, and a tooth for a tooth,'

39 But I tell you to not defend yourself from evil– but whoever strikes you on your cheek, turn to him the other also.

40 And to him who would take you to court to take away your shirt, give him your coat also.

41 And whoever would ask you to go a mile, go with him two.

42 To him who would ask you, give. And to him who would borrow from you, do not turn away.

43 You have heard that it was said, 'You shall love your neighbor and hate your enemy,'

44 but I tell you to love your enemies! Bless those who curse you, do right to those who hate you, and pray for those who despitefully use you and persecute you,

45 so that you may be sons of your Father Who is in Heaven: for His sun rises upon the evil and the good, and He sends rain upon the righteous and the unrighteous.

46 For if you love those who love you, what is your reward? Don't the tax collectors do as much?

47 And if you greet your brethren only, what do you do beyond others? Don't the tax collectors do as much?

48 Therefore, you be perfect, even as your Father in Heaven is perfect.

6 Be careful not to do your charitable giving before men in order to be seen by them, lest you get no reward from your Father in Heaven.

2 Therefore when you do your charitable giving, do not sound a trumpet before you as the hypocrites do in the synagogues and in the streets that they may have praise from men. I tell you for certain that they have their reward!

3 But when you give charitably, let not your left hand know what your right hand has done,

4 so that your charitable giving may be in secret, and then your Father, Who sees in secret, will reward you openly.

5 And when you pray, you shall not be as the hypocrites, for they love to pray standing in the synagogues, in the street corners, for appearance's sake before men. I tell you for certain: they have their reward!

6 But when you pray, enter into your

private chambers and shut the door. Pray to your Father Who is in secret. And your Father Who is in secret will reward you openly.

7 Now when you pray, do not babble like the pagans, for they think simply by doing a lot of talking they will be heard.

8 Therefore do not be like them, for your Father knows what you need before you even ask Him.

9 Therefore pray like this, 'Our Father, Who is in the heavens, sanctified is Your Name.

10 Your Kingdom come, Your will be done, on the Earth as it is in Heaven.

11 Give us today our daily bread,

12 and forgive us our trespasses as we forgive those who trespass against us.

13 And lead us not into temptation, but deliver us from the evil– for Yours is the Kingdom and the power and the glory forever. Amen!'

14 For if you forgive men their wrong-doings, your Father who is in Heaven will forgive you.

15 But if you do not forgive men for their wrong-doings, neither will your heavenly Father forgive you.

16 And when you fast, do not be as the hypocrites with a downcast countenance, for they disfigure their faces so that men will realize that they are fasting. I tell you for certain that they have their reward!

17 But when you fast, anoint your head and wash your face,

18 so that you will not appear to men as one fasting, but instead to your Father Who is in secret, and your Father Who sees you in secret will reward you openly.

19 Do not store up treasures upon the Earth where moth and rust will destroy and where thieves break in and steal.

20 But store up treasures for yourselves in Heaven where neither moth nor rust destroys and where thieves cannot break in and steal.

21 For where your treasure is, there your heart will be as well.

22 The light of the body is the eye– therefore if your eye is single, your whole body is full of light.

23 But if your eye is evil, your whole body will be dark. If, therefore, the light that is in you is darkness, how great is that darkness?

24 No one can serve two masters, for either he will hate the one and love the other, or he will hold to the one and despise the other. You are not able to serve God and riches.

25 Because of this, do not be concerned for your life as to what you shall eat or what you shall drink, nor for your body as to what you should wear. Isn't your life more than food, and your body more than clothing?

26 Look at the birds of heaven, for they do not sow or reap or gather into the storehouse, and your heavenly Father feeds them. Are you not much better than they?

27 But which of you, because of your concern for yourselves, can add to his height one cubit?

28 And why are you concerned about clothing? Look at how the lilies of the field grow– they labor not, neither do they spin.

29 But I tell you: not even Solomon in all of his glory was clothed like one of these!

30 But if God clothes the field, which today is and tomorrow is cast into the oven, how much more you, you of little faith?

31 Therefore do not be concerned, saying, 'What shall we eat?' or 'What

shall we drink?' or 'How shall we be clothed?',

32 for these are all the things that the nations seek after. For your heavenly Father knows that you have need of all these things.

33 But you seek first the Kingdom of God and His righteousness, and all these things will be added to you.

34 Therefore, do not be concerned about tomorrow, tomorrow will be concerned about the things of itself. Self-sufficient for the day is the evil thereof.

7 Do not judge, so that you will not be judged,

2 for with whatever judgment you judge, you shall be judged and the measure that you measure out shall in turn be measured to you.

3 But why would you look at the speck that is in your brother's eye while you do not realize that you have a log in your own eye?

4 Or how can you say to your brother, 'Allow me to pull the speck out of your eye,' while you have a log in your eye?

5 Hypocrite, first take the log out of your own eye, and then you will see clearly to remove the speck from your brother's eye.

6 Do not give that which is holy to the dogs, nor cast your pearls before swine, lest they should trample them under foot and then turn and attack you.

7 Ask, and it shall be given to you. Seek, and you shall find. Knock, and it shall be opened to you.

8 For everyone who asks, receives, and the one who seeks, finds, and to the one who knocks, it shall be opened.

9 Or what man among you, if his son should ask for bread, would give him a stone?

10 Also, if he should ask for a fish, would he give him a serpent?

11 If you then, being evil, know how to give good gifts to your children, how much more will your Father in Heaven give good things to them that ask Him?

12 Therefore, all things whatever you desire that men should do to you, do also to them, for this is the Law and the prophets.

13 Enter in through the narrow gate, for wide is the gate and broad is the way that leads to destruction, and there are many who go that way.

14 Because narrow is the gate, and restricted is the way that leads unto life, and there are few who find it.

15 But beware of false prophets who come to you in sheep's clothing but inwardly are ravening wolves.

16 By their fruits you shall know them. Do you gather grapes from a thorn bush, or figs from thistles?

17 So it is that every good tree produces good fruit, but a corrupt tree produces evil fruit.

18 A good tree cannot produce evil fruit, nor can a corrupt tree produce good fruit.

19 Every tree that does not produce good fruit is cut down and cast into the fire.

20 Therefore then, you shall know them by their fruits.

21 Not everyone who says to me, 'Lord, Lord,' shall enter into the Kingdom of Heaven, but he who does the will of My Father Who is in the heavens.

22 Many shall say to me in that day, 'Lord, Lord, have we not prophesied in Your Name, and in Your Name cast out demons, and in Your Name done many wonderful works?'

23 And then I will announce to them,

'I never knew you– get away from Me, you workers of iniquity!'

24 Everyone therefore who hears these words of Mine and does them, I will liken him to a wise man who built his house upon a rock.

25 And the rain came down, the floods came, the wind blew, and they beat upon that house– but it did not fall, for it was built upon the rock.

26 And every one who hears these words of Mine and does not do them shall be likened unto a foolish man who built his house upon the sand.

27 And the rain came down, the floods came, the wind blew, and they beat upon that house– and it fell, and great was the fall of it."

28 And after Jesus was finished speaking, the crowds were astonished at His teaching,

29 for His teaching was as one with authority, and not as the Scribes.

8

And when He had come down from the mountain, a great crowd followed Him.

2 And there was a leper who came and worshiped Him, saying, "If You are willing, You are able to cleanse me."

3 And Jesus stretched forth His hand and touched him, saying, "I will, be cleansed," and immediately his leprosy was cleansed.

4 And Jesus said to him, "See to it that you do not tell anyone, but go and show yourself to the priest and offer the gift which Moses commanded, for a testimony to them."

5 And Jesus entered into Capernaum, and a centurion came to Him, pleading

6 and saying, "Lord, my servant is lying at home paralyzed, in terrible distress."

7 Jesus said unto him, "I will come and heal him."

8 The centurion said, "Lord, I am not worthy that You should come under my roof, but speak the word only and I know that my servant shall be healed.

9 For I am also a man under authority, having soldiers under me; and I say to one, 'Go,' and he goes, and to another, 'Come,' and he comes, and to my servant, 'Do this,' and he does it."

10 When Jesus heard him, He was amazed and said to those who followed, "Truly I tell you, I have not found so great a faith in Israel!

11 I tell you that many shall come from the East and the West and shall sit at the table with Abraham, Isaac, and Jacob in the Kingdom of Heaven,

12 but the sons of the Kingdom shall be cast out into outer darkness– there shall be weeping and gnashing of teeth."

13 And Jesus said to the centurion, "Go, and be it unto you as you have believed." And his servant was healed in the same hour.

14 And when Jesus came to Peter's house, He saw his wife's mother down sick with a fever.

15 And He touched her hand, and the fever left her, and she got up and waited on them.

16 When evening came, they brought to Him all those possessed with demons, and He drove out the spirits with a word, and healed all who were sick.

17 In this way, He fulfilled what was spoken through the prophet Isaiah, saying, "He removed our sicknesses and carried away our diseases."

18 When Jesus saw the great crowds around Him, He gave a command to depart to the other side.

19 And a Scribe came unto Him and

said, "Teacher, I will follow You wherever You go."
20And Jesus said to him, "The foxes
have holes, and the birds of heaven
have nests, but the Son of Man has
nowhere to lay His head."
21Another one of His disciples said to
Him, "Lord, first let me go and bury
my father."
22But Jesus said to him, "Follow Me,
and leave the dead to bury their dead."
23And when He entered into the
boat, His disciples followed Him.
24And there arose a great shaking in
the sea, so that the boat was covered by
the waves, but He was sleeping.
25And His disciples came and woke
Him up, saying, "Lord, save us– for we
perish!"
26And He said to them, "Why are you
afraid, you of little faith?" Then He got
up and rebuked the wind and the
waves, and there became a great calm.
27And the men wondered, saying,
"What kind of man is this, that even
the winds and the lake obey Him?"
28And when He had come to the other side, into the country of the Gerge-
senes, there met Him two men possessed by demons, who came very violently out of the tombs so that no one
was able to pass by that way.
29And they cried out, saying, "What
have we to do with You, Jesus, Son of
God? Have You come here to torment
us before the appointed time?"
30Now there was a long way off from
them a herd of many swine feeding.
31And the demons pleaded with Him,
saying, "If you cast us out, allow us to
go into the herd of swine."
32And He said, "Go!" And when they
went out, they entered into the herd of
swine, and then all of the herd of swine
rushed down a steep place into the lake
and died in the waters.
33But those who fed them fled, and
went into the city, and reported all that
had happened to those possessed by
demons.
34And then all of the city came out to
meet Jesus, and when they saw Him,
pleaded with Him to leave their territory.

9 And He entered into the boat, and
crossed over and came into His
own city.
2And then they brought to Him a
paralytic lying on a bed. And Jesus,
seeing their faith, said to the paralytic,
"Child, be of good courage– your sins
have been forgiven."
3And then some of the Scribes said to
themselves, "This man blasphemes."
4And Jesus, perceiving their thoughts, said, "Why do you think evil in
your heart?
5For which is easier to say: 'Your sins
have been forgiven,' or to say, 'Arise and
walk?'
6But, that you may know that the Son
of Man has authority on Earth to forgive sins," He says to the paralytic,
"Arise, take up your bed and go to your
house."
7And he got up and went to his
house.
8And the crowds seeing this, were
astonished and glorified God, Who
had given such authority to men.
9When Jesus left there, He saw a man
sitting at the tax office, called Matthew,
and said to him, "Follow me," and he
rose up and followed Him.
10And while He was in the house, sitting at the table, the tax collectors and
sinners came and sat at the table with
Jesus and His disciples.
11And the Pharisees saw it and said

to His disciples, “Does your teacher eat with tax collectors and sinners?”

12 Now Jesus, hearing them, said, “The healthy are not in need of a physician, but they who are ill.

13 But go and learn what mercy is, for I do not desire sacrifice– for I came not to call the righteous, but rather sinners, to repentance.”

14 Then the disciples of John came to Him and said, “Why is it that both we and the Pharisees fast often, but Your disciples do not fast?”

15 And Jesus said to them, “Can the sons of the Bridegroom mourn while the Bridegroom is with them? But the days will come when the Bridegroom will be taken away, and then they will fast.

16 But no one puts a piece of unshrunk cloth on an old garment, because the patch will shrink and produce a worse tear.

17 Neither would they put new wine into old bottles, because the skins will burst, and the wine will pour out, and the skins will be destroyed. But rather, they put new wine into new skins and both are preserved.”

18 As He was speaking these things, a ruler came and worshiped Him, saying, “My daughter just now died, but come lay Your hand on her and she shall live.”

19 And Jesus and His disciples got up and followed him.

20 And there was a woman who had been hemorrhaging twelve years, and having come behind Him, touched the hem of His garment.

21 For she had said within herself, “If I shall only touch His garment, I shall be saved.”

22 But Jesus, turning and seeing her, said, “Be of good courage, daughter! Your faith has saved you,” and the woman was delivered from that moment.

23 And when Jesus came into the house of the ruler and saw the flute players and the crowd making a tumult,

24 He said to them, “Go away, the little girl is not dead, but sleeps.” And they laughed at Him.

25 But when He had sent the crowd out of the room, He entered and took hold of the little girl's hand, and she arose.

26 And the fame of this went out into all of that land.

27 And after Jesus left there, two blind men followed Him, crying out, saying, “Son of David, have mercy on us!”

28 After He came into the house, the blind men came to Him, and Jesus said to them, “Do you believe that I am able to do this?” And they said to Him, “Yes, Lord!”

29 Then He touched their eyes, saying, “According to your faith it shall be to you.”

30 And their eyes were opened, and Jesus sternly charged them, saying, “See to it that you let no one know.”

31 But they went out and made Him known in all the land.

32 And then as they were going out, they brought a man to Him who was mute, who was possessed by a demon.

33 And when the demon was cast out, the mute could speak, and the crowd was amazed, saying, “This has never been seen in Israel.”

34 But the Pharisees said, “By the prince of demons He cast out demons.”

35 And Jesus went about all of the cities and villages, teaching in their synagogues, and announcing the Good News of the Kingdom, and healing

every disease and sickness among the people.

36And seeing the crowds, He was moved with compassion for them, because they were faint and cast aside as sheep without a shepherd.

37Then He said to His disciples, "The harvest is indeed great, but the workmen are few.

38Therefore, beseech the Lord of the harvest that He may send out workmen into the harvest."

10 And having called His disciples, He gave them authority to drive out unclean spirits and to heal every disease and every sickness.

2Now these are the names of the twelve disciples: first Simon, who is called Peter, and Andrew, his brother, James of Zebedee, and John, his brother,

3Philip, and Bartholomew, Thomas, and Matthew the tax collector, James of Alphaeus, and Lebbaeus, who was surnamed Thaddaeus,

4Simon the Canaanite, and Judas Iscariot, who also betrayed Him.

5These twelve were sent out by Jesus, Who charged them, saying, "Go not into the way of the nations, and do not enter into the city of the Samaritans.

6But rather go to the lost sheep of Israel.

7Go and preach, saying, 'The kingdom of Heaven has come near.'

8Cure the sick, cleanse the lepers, raise the dead, cast out demons. Freely you received– freely give.

9Do not provide gold or silver or brass in your belts,

10nor a bag of provisions for the way, neither two tunics or sandals or a staff, for the workman is worthy of his food.

11And into whatever city or village that you enter, inquire who is worthy, and stay there until you depart.

12When you enter the house, greet it.

13And if indeed the house be worthy, let your peace come upon it, but if it is not worthy, let your peace return to you.

14And whoever will not receive you or hear your words, leave that house or city and shake off the dust from your feet.

15I tell you for certain: it will be more tolerable for the land of Sodom and Gomorrah on the day of judgment than for that city!

16Behold, I send you forth as sheep in the midst of wolves– be therefore wise as serpents and harmless as doves.

17But beware of men, for they will deliver you to the Sanhedrin, and they will whip you in their synagogues,

18and you shall be brought before governors and kings because of me, for a testimony to them and to the nations.

19But when you are delivered up, do not be concerned how or what you shall say, for it shall be given you in that moment what you shall speak.

20For you are not the one speaking, but the Spirit of your Father who speaks in you.

21For brother will betray brother to death, and the father the child, and the children will rise up against their parents and will put them to death.

22And you will be hated by everyone for my name's sake, but he who endures to the end shall be saved.

23But when they persecute you in one city, flee to another– for I tell you for certain: you will not finish with the cities of Israel until the Son of Man comes.

24A disciple is not above his teacher, nor a servant above his lord.

25 It is enough that the disciple be as his teacher, and the servant as his lord. If they call the Master of the house Beelzebub, how much more those of His household?

26 Therefore you should not fear them– for nothing is covered which shall not be revealed, and hidden which shall not be known.

27 What I tell you in darkness, speak in the light, and what you hear in the ear, proclaim upon the housetops.

28 And do not fear those who kill the body but are not able to kill the soul, but rather you should fear Him Who is able to destroy both soul and body in Hell.

29 Are not two sparrows sold for a coin, and not one of them shall fall to the ground without your Father?

30 But even the hairs of your head are all numbered.

31 Therefore you should not fear, for you are better than many sparrows.

32 Therefore, everyone who shall confess me before men, I will also confess him before My Father Who is in Heaven.

33 But whoever shall deny Me before men, him will I also deny before My Father in Heaven.

34 Think not that I am come to place peace on the Earth– I came not to place peace, but a sword!

35 I came to set a man at variance against his father, and a daughter against her mother, and a daughter-in-law against her mother-in-law.

36 And the enemies of a man shall be his household.

37 He who has more affection for father or mother than for Me is not worthy of Me, and he who has more affection for son or daughter than for Me is not worthy of Me.

38 And he that does not take his cross and follow after Me is not worthy of Me.

39 He that has found his life shall lose it, and he that has lost his life for My sake shall find it.

40 He that receives you receives Me, and he that receives Me receives Him Who sent Me.

41 He that receives a prophet in the name of a prophet receives a prophet's reward, and he that receives a righteous man in the name of a righteous man receives a righteous man's reward.

42 And whoever shall give one of these little ones a cup of cold water to drink only in the name of a disciple, I promise you, he will not lose his reward."

11 And it came to pass that when Jesus had finished giving instructions to His twelve disciples, He departed from there to teach and to preach in their cities.

2 When John heard in the prison the works of Christ, he sent two of his disciples,

3 who said to Him, "Are you the One to come, or do we wait for another?"

4 And Jesus answered, saying to them, "Go and tell John what you hear and see:

5 the blind receive their sight, and the crippled walk, the lepers are cleansed, and the deaf hear, the dead are raised, and the poor have the gospel preached to them.

6 And blessed is he who is not offended in Me."

7 Now, as these were leaving, Jesus began to say to the crowds concerning John, "What did you go out into the wilderness to see? A reed shaken by the wind?

8 But what did you go out to see? A man clothed in fine garments? Behold, those who are clothed in fine garments are in kings' houses.

9 But what did you go out to see? A prophet? Yes, and I tell you one more excellent than a prophet.

10 For this is he about whom it was written, 'Behold I send My messenger before Your face who shall prepare Your way before You.'

11 I tell you for certain that there has not risen among those born of women one greater than John the Baptizer, but he that is least in the Kingdom of Heaven is greater than he.

12 But from the days of John the Baptizer until now, the Kingdom of Heaven is taken by violence and the violent seize it.

13 For all of the prophets and the Law prophesied until John.

14 And if you will receive it, he is Elijah who is going to come.

15 He who has ears to hear, let him hear!

16 But to what shall I compare this generation? It is like little children in the markets, sitting and calling to their friends,

17 'We played the flute to you, but you did not dance. We mourned, but you did not wail.'

18 John came neither eating nor drinking, and they say, 'He has a demon.'

19 The Son of man came eating and drinking, and they say, 'Look, a Man Who is a glutton and a winebibber, a friend of tax collectors and sinners.' And wisdom was justified by her children."

20 Then He began to reproach those cities in which most of His deeds of power had been done, because they did not repent:

21 "Woe to you, Chorazin! Woe to you, Bethsaida! For if the works that have taken place in you had taken place in Tyre and Sidon, they would have repented long ago in sackcloth and ashes.

22 But I tell you it will be more tolerable for Tyre and Sidon on the day of judgment than for you!

23 And you, Capernaum, who has been exalted to Heaven, shall be brought down to Hell. For if the mighty works that were done in you had been done in Sodom, it would have remained until today.

24 But I tell you it shall be more tolerable for the land of Sodom on the day of judgment than for you!"

25 At that time Jesus continued, saying, "I praise You Father, Lord of Heaven and the Earth, that You have hidden these things from the wise and the prudent and revealed them to infants.

26 Yes, Father, for this was well pleasing in Your sight.

27 All things were delivered to Me by My Father, and no one knows the Son except the Father, and no one knows the Father except the Son, and to whomsoever the Son may reveal Him.

28 Come unto Me all you who labor and are heavy laden, and I will give you rest.

29 Take My yoke upon you and learn from Me, for I am meek and lowly in heart, and you shall find rest unto your soul.

30 For My yoke is easy and My burden is light."

12 At that time, Jesus went through the corn fields on the Sabbath day, and His disciples were hungry, and they began to pluck ears of corn to eat.

2 And when the Pharisees saw it, they

said, "Look what Your disciples are doing! This cannot be done on the Sabbath!"

3But He said to them, "Have you not read what David did when he and those with him were hungry?

4How he entered into the house of God and ate the loaves of presentation, which were not allowed for him, nor those with him, to eat?

5Or have you not read in the Law that on the Sabbath the priests in the temple profane the sabbath and are innocent?

6But I tell you: One that is greater than the temple is here.

7But if you would have known that I desire mercy and not sacrifice, you would not have condemned the innocent.

8For the Son of Man is also Lord of the Sabbath."

9And leaving there, He went into their synagogue.

10And there was a man who had a withered hand, and they asked Him, "Is it right to heal on the Sabbath day?" that they might accuse Him.

11But He said to them, "What man among you who has sheep, and if one of them falls into a pit on the Sabbath, will not take hold of it and pull it out?

12How much better then is a man than a sheep? So, it is right to do well on the Sabbath."

13Then He said to the man, "Stretch out your hand," and he stretched it out and it was restored, whole as the other.

14And the Pharisees left and held a counsel against Him, how they might destroy Him.

15But Jesus knew it and left there, and great crowds followed Him, and He healed them all.

16And He demanded of them that they should not make Him known,

17so that what the prophet Isaiah said might be fulfilled, saying,

18"Behold My Servant whom I have chosen, My Beloved in Whom My soul delights. I will put My Spirit upon Him, and He shall declare judgment to the nations.

19He will not argue or make a noise, and His voice will not be heard by anyone in the streets.

20He will not break a bruised reed, and He will not put out a smoking wick, until He brings forth judgment to victory.

21And in His name shall the nations trust."

22There was brought to Him one possessed by a demon, blind, and unable to speak, and He healed him so that the blind and the mute both saw and spoke.

23And all of the crowds were amazed and said, "Surely this is the Son of David!"

24But when the Pharisees heard this, they said, "This man casts out demons by Beelzebub, the Prince of demons."

25But Jesus, knowing what they were thinking, said to them, "Every kingdom divided against itself is destroyed, and every city or house divided against itself cannot stand.

26And if Satan casts out Satan, he is divided against himself. How therefore will his kingdom stand?

27And if I by Beelzebub cast out demons, by whom do your sons cast them out? Because of this, they shall be your judges.

28But if I by the Spirit of God cast out demons, then the Kingdom of God has come upon you.

29Or how can anyone enter into the house of a strongman and take his goods, unless he first binds the strongman? And then he can plunder his house.

30He who is not with Me is against Me, and he who does not gather with Me scatters.

31Because of this, I tell you that every sin and blasphemy shall be forgiven man, but men shall not be forgiven of blasphemy against the Spirit.

32And whoever speaks a word against the Son of Man, it shall be forgiven him– but whoever speaks against the Holy Spirit, it shall not be forgiven him, neither in this age or the one to come!

33Either make the tree good and its fruit good, or make the tree corrupt and its fruit corrupt, for the tree is known by its fruit.

34Offspring of vipers, how will you be able to speak good things? You are wicked beings, for out of the abundance of the heart the mouth speaks!

35The good man out of the good treasures of the heart produces good things, and the wicked man out of the wicked treasure produces wicked things.

36And I tell you that every useless word that men may speak, they shall give an account of it on the day of judgment.

37For by your words you shall be justified, and by your words you shall be condemned."

38Then some of the Scribes and the Pharisees responded, saying, "Teacher, we need to see a sign from You."

39But He answered them, saying, "An evil and adulterous generation seeks after a sign, and no sign shall be given except the sign of Jonah the prophet.

40For even as Jonah was in the belly of the great fish for three days and three nights, even so shall the Son of Man be in the heart of the Earth for three days and three nights.

41The men of Nineveh shall stand up in the judgment with this generation and shall condemn it– for they repented at the preaching of Jonah, and behold, someone greater than Jonah is here!

42The queen of the South shall rise up in the judgment with this generation and shall condemn it– for she came from the ends of the Earth to hear the wisdom of Solomon, and behold, One Who is greater than Solomon is here!

43But when the unclean spirit has gone out of a man, he goes through desert places seeking rest, but does not find it.

44Then he says, 'I will return to my house that I came out of,' and when he comes, he finds it unoccupied, swept, and decorated.

45Then he goes and brings along with himself seven spirits more wicked than himself, and they enter in and dwell there, and the final state of that man is worse than the first. Thus it shall be for this wicked generation."

46While He was still speaking to the crowds, His mother and brothers were standing outside, desiring to speak with Him.

47Then someone said to Him, "Your mother and brothers are standing outside, desiring to speak with you."

48But He replied to him who had spoken, "Who is My mother, and who are My brothers?"

49And stretching out His hand to His disciples, "Behold My mother and My brothers.

50For whoever shall do the will of My Father Who is in Heaven, the same is

My brother and sister and mother."

13 And on the same day, Jesus went
out of the house and sat down
by the sea.
2 And great crowds gathered together
to Him, so that He entered into a boat
and sat down while the crowds stood at
the shore.
3 And He spoke many things to them
in parables, saying, "Behold, a sower
went out to sow.
4 And as he sowed, some fell by the
road, and the birds came and devoured
them.
5 And some fell upon rocky places
where there was not much earth, and
immediately sprang up, because the
earth did not have much depth.
6 But as soon as the sun had risen,
they were scorched. And because they
had no root, they dried up.
7 And some fell among the thorns,
and the thorns grew up and choked
them.
8 But some fell upon the good
ground, and brought forth fruit– one a
hundred, another sixty, and yet another
thirty.
9 He that has ears to hear, let him
hear."
10 And the disciples came to Him and
said, "Why do you speak to them in
parables?"
11 And He answered them, saying,
"Because to you it is given to know the
mysteries of the Kingdom of Heaven,
but to them it is not given.
12 For whoever has, it shall be given to
him, and he shall have abundance– but
whoever does not have, even what he
has shall be taken away from him.
13 Because of this, I speak in parables
to them, that seeing they shall not see,
and hearing they shall not hear, nor
shall they understand.
14 And it is fulfilled in them that
which the prophet Isaiah said, 'In hearing you shall not hear nor understand,
and seeing you shall not see nor perceive.
15 For the heart of this people has
grown fat, and with dull ears they have
heard, and their eyes they have closed,
lest they should see with their eyes and
hear with their ears and understand
with their heart and should be convert-
ed, and I should heal them.'
16 But blessed are your eyes, because
they see, and your ears because they
hear.
17 For I tell you for certain that many
prophets and righteous men have desired to see what you have seen, but did
not see, and hear what you have heard,
but did not hear.
18 Therefore, hear the parable of the
sower.
19 When anyone hears the word of the
Kingdom and does not understand it,
the wicked one comes and steals what
was sown in his heart– this is what was
sown along the path.
20 And that which was sown upon the
rocky places is he who hears the word
and immediately receives it with joy,
21 but has no root in himself, but endures for a while, and as soon as tribulation or persecution arises, because of
the word, he is immediately offended.
22 And that which was sown among
thorns is he who hears the word, and
the cares of this age and the deceitfulness of riches choke the word, and it
becomes unfruitful.
23 But that which was sown on the
good ground is he who hears the word
and understands, and as a result brings
forth fruit– one a hundred, another
sixty, and another thirty."

24 Another parable He put forth to them, saying, “The Kingdom of Heaven has become like a man who sowed good seed in his field.

25 But while he slept, the men who were his enemies came and sowed weeds among them and went away.

26 And when the blade sprouted and the fruit was produced, then the weeds also appeared.

27 Then the servants came to the master of the house and said to him, ‘Master, didn't you sow good seed in your field? Where have these weeds come from?’

28 And he said to them, ‘A man that is my enemy did this.’ And his servants said to him, ‘Should we go out and gather them?’

29 But he said, ‘No, for perhaps in gathering the weeds you might also uproot the wheat with them.

30 Allow them to both grow together until the harvest, and in the time of the harvest I will say to the harvesters, “Gather first the weeds and bind them into bundles to burn them, but bring the wheat into my barn.”’”

31 He put forth another parable before them, saying, “The Kingdom of Heaven is like a mustard seed, which a man took and sowed in his field,

32 which is indeed smaller than all other seeds, but when it is grown is greater than all the herbs and becomes a tree, which all of the birds of heaven come and roost in its branches.”

33 He spoke another parable to them: “The Kingdom of Heaven is like leaven, which a woman took and hid in three measures of meal until the whole was leavened.”

34 Jesus spoke all these things in parables to the crowds, and He did not speak except by parables to them,

35 so that which was spoken by the prophet might be fulfilled, saying, “I will open My mouth in parables, I will utter things hidden from the overthrow of the world.”

36 Then Jesus, having dismissed the crowds, went into the house, and His disciples came unto Him, saying, “Explain to us the parable of the weeds of the field.”

37 And He answered and said to them, “He who sows the good seed is the Son of Man,

38 and the field is the world, and the good seed are the sons of the Kingdom, but the weeds are the sons of the evil one,

39 and the enemy who sowed them is the Devil, and the harvest is the end of the age, and the harvesters are the angels.

40 As therefore the weeds are gathered in the fire and consumed, thus it shall be at the end of the age.

41 The Son of Man will send His angels, and they will collect out of His Kingdom all causes of sin and those who do iniquity,

42 and they shall cast them into the furnace of the fire– there shall be weeping and gnashing of teeth!

43 Then shall the righteous shine as the sun in the Kingdom of their Father. He that has ears to hear, let him hear.

44 Again, the Kingdom of Heaven is like treasure hidden in the field, which a man found and hid, and then in his joy, he goes and sells all that he has and buys that field.

45 Again, the Kingdom of Heaven is like a merchant man seeking beautiful pearls,

46 who finds a very precious pearl, goes away and sells everything that he has, and buys it.

47 Again, the Kingdom of Heaven is
like a dragnet cast into the lake, which
gathers every kind.
48 When it was filled, it was drawn up
to the shore. And having sat down,
they collected the good ones into vessels, and the bad they cast away.
49 Thus shall it be at the end of the
age: the angels shall go out and separate the wicked from the midst of the
righteous
50 and shall cast them into the furnace
of fire– there shall be wailing and
gnashing of teeth!"
51 Jesus said to them, "Have you understood all these things?" They said,
"Yes, Lord."
52 And because of this, He said to
them, "Every scholar disciplined in the
Kingdom of Heaven is like a man who
is a master of a house that brings forth
out of his treasure things new and old."
53 Afterwards, when Jesus had finished these parables, He departed from
there.
54 And He came into His own country
and taught them in their synagogue, so
that they were amazed and said,
"Where did this wisdom and mighty
power come from?
55 Is not this the builder's son? Is not
His mother Mary, and His brethren
James, Joses, Simon, and Judas?
56 And are not all His sisters here with
us? Where then did all these things
come from?"
57 And they were offended by Him,
but Jesus said to them, "A prophet has
no honor in His own country and in
His own house."
58 And He did not do many deeds of
power there because of their unbelief.

14 At that time, Herod the tetrarch
heard of the fame of Jesus
2 and said to his servants, "This is
John the Baptizer! He is risen from the
dead, and because of this, works of
power operate in Him."
3 For Herod arrested John, bound
him, and put him in prison on account
of Herodias, the wife of Philip his
brother.
4 For John said, "It is not lawful for
you to have her."
5 And wanting to kill him, he feared
the multitude, because they regarded
him as a prophet.
6 But when Herod's birthday was cel-
ebrated, the daughter of Herodias
danced for Him, and it pleased Herod.
7 Whereupon he promised her with
an oath to give her whatever she asked.
8 But she was prompted by her mother to say, "Give me the head of John the
Baptizer on a platter."
9 And the king was distressed, but because of the oath and those that sat at
the table, he commanded it to be given.
10 And he sent and beheaded John in
the prison.
11 And his head was brought on a
platter and was given to the girl, and
she brought it to her mother.
12 And his disciples came and took his
body and buried it, and came and told
Jesus.
13 And hearing this, Jesus went away
by boat to a desert place, and the
crowds hearing of it, followed Him on
foot from the cities.
14 And when Jesus went out, He saw a
great crowd, and He had compassion
on them and healed their sick.
15 But when it was evening, His disciples came to Him, saying, "This is a
desert place, and the time is late. Send
the crowds away so that they can go
into the villages and buy food."
16 But Jesus said, "They have no need

to go away– you give them to eat."

17But they said, "We have nothing here except for five loaves and two fishes."

18And He said, "Bring them here to me."

19And He instructed the crowds to sit down on the grass. And taking the five loaves and the two fish, He looked up to Heaven and blessed it. And breaking it, He gave the loaves to the disciples, and the disciples to the crowds.

20And they all ate and were satisfied, and they took up the fragments that were left over: twelve baskets full.

21And those who ate were about five thousand men, besides women and children.

22And Jesus immediately compelled His disciples to enter into the boat and to go before Him to the other side while He dismissed the crowds.

23And having dismissed the crowds, He went away into the mountain to pray, and it was evening, and He was there alone.

24But the boat was in the midst of the lake, being tossed by the waves, because the wind was contrary to it.

25And in the fourth watch of the night, Jesus came to them, walking on the water.

26And the disciples, seeing Him walking on the lake, were troubled, saying, "It's a ghost!" and they cried out, being afraid.

27And Jesus responded immediately, saying to them, "Be of good courage, it is Me. Fear not."

28And Peter, answering Him, said, "Lord, if it is You, bid me to come to You upon the waters."

29And He said, "Come!" And having gotten out of the boat, Peter walked upon the waters to go to Jesus.

30But seeing the strong wind, he was afraid, and as he began to sink, he cried out, saying, "Save me, Lord!"

31And Jesus immediately stretched out His hand and took hold of him, saying, "O you of little faith, why did you doubt?"

32And entering into the boat, the wind ceased.

33And those in the boat came and worshiped Him, saying, "Surely You are the Son of God."

34And having passed over, they came to the land of Gennesaret.

35And when the men of that place recognized Him, they sent to all the surrounding country, and brought all those that were sick to Him.

36And they besought Him that they might only touch the hem of His garment, and as many as touched Him were made whole.

15 Then Scribes and Pharisees came to Jesus from Jerusalem, saying,

2"Why do Your disciples transgress the tradition of the elders? For they do not wash their hands before they eat bread."

3And He answered and said to them, "And why do you transgress the commandment of God by your traditions?

4For God commanded, saying, 'Honor your father and mother, and whoever speaks evil of their father or mother, let him die the death.'

5But you say, 'Whoever shall say to father or mother, "that whatever you might have profited from me it is Korban,"

6does not have to honor his father or mother'– making void the commandment of God by your tradition.

7Hypocrites! Well prophesied Isaiah

concerning you, saying,

8 ‘These people draw near to Me with their mouths, and with their lips they honor Me, but their heart is far from Me,

9 but in vain they worship Me, teaching for doctrines the instructions of men.’”

10 And He called the crowd to Himself. He said to them, “Hear and understand!

11 It is not that which enters into the mouth that defiles the man, but that which goes out of the mouth that defiles a man.”

12 Then His disciples came and said to Him, “You know that the Pharisees were offended when they heard the word.”

13 But Jesus said, “Every plant that was not planted by My heavenly Father shall be uprooted.

14 Leave them alone. They are blind leaders of the blind, and if the blind lead the blind, both will fall into a pit.”

15 And Peter, answering Him, said, “Explain this parable to us.”

16 But Jesus said, “Are you still without understanding?

17 Do you not understand that everything that enters the mouth goes into the belly and is cast out into the latrine?

18 But the things which go out of the mouth come from the heart, and these defile the man.

19 For out of the heart comes evil thoughts, murders, adulteries, sexual immoralities, thefts, false-witnessings, blasphemies–

20 these are the things that defile a man. But eating without washing your hands does not defile a man.”

21 And leaving there, Jesus went into parts of Tyre and Sidon.

22 And there was a Canaanite woman who came from that region, who cried out to Him, saying, “Have mercy on me Lord, Son of David, for my daughter is severely possessed by a demon.”

23 But He did not say a word to her. And His disciples came to Him, saying, “Send her away, for she cries out behind us.”

24 Then He replied, “I am not sent except to the lost sheep of the House of Israel.”

25 But she came and worshiped Him, saying, “Lord, help me!”

26 And He answering said, “It is not good to take the children’s bread and cast it to the dogs.”

27 But she said, “Yes Lord, for even the dogs eat of the crumbs that fall from their master’s table.”

28 Then Jesus replied and said to her, “O woman, great is your faith! Be it unto you as you desire.” And her daughter was healed from that hour.

29 And departing from there, Jesus went towards the sea of Galilee, and having gone up into the mountain, He sat down.

30 And great crowds came to Him, bringing with them the crippled, blind, mute, maimed, and many others, and laid them at the feet of Jesus, and He healed them.

31 So the crowd was amazed when they saw the mute speak, the maimed made whole, the crippled walk, and the blind seeing, and they glorified the God of Israel.

32 And Jesus called His disciples together and said, “I am moved with compassion for the crowd, because they have already continued here with Me for three days with nothing to eat, and I am not willing to send them away hungry, for they may faint on their

way."

33And His disciples said to Him, "Where can we find bread in the desert to satisfy such a great crowd?"

34And Jesus said to them, "How many loaves do you have?" And they said, "Seven, and a few small fish."

35And He commanded the crowd to sit down on the ground.

36And He took the seven loaves and the fishes, and giving thanks, He broke and gave them to His disciples, and the disciples to the crowd.

37And they all ate and were satisfied, and they took up the broken pieces that were left over: seven baskets full.

38And they who ate were four thousand men, besides women and children.

39And having sent away the crowds, He entered into the ship and came to the borders of Magdala.

16 And the Pharisees and Sadducees who came to Him, tempting Him, asked for a sign from Heaven to be shown to them.

2And He, answering, said to them, "When evening has come you say, 'It will be fair weather, for the sky is red.'

3And if the sky is red in the morning, then, 'There will be a storm today.' Hypocrites! You know how to discern the face of the sky, but not the signs of the times?

4A wicked and adulterous generation seeks a sign, and there shall be no sign given to it except the sign of Jonah the prophet." And He went away and left them.

5And His disciples, having come to the other side, forgot to bring bread.

6And Jesus said to them, "See and beware of the leaven of the Pharisees and Sadducees."

7And they reasoned among themselves, saying, "Because we did not bring bread."

8And Jesus, knowing this, said to them, "Why do you reason among yourselves because you did not bring bread? You of little faith!

9Do you still not understand or remember the five loaves for the five thousand, and how many baskets you collected?

10Or the seven loaves and the four thousand, and how many baskets you collected?

11How is it that you do not understand what I said concerning the leaven of the Pharisees and the Sadducees?"

12Then they understood that he was not referring to the leaven of bread, but of the doctrine of the Pharisees and the Sadducees.

13Now when Jesus arrived in the region of Caesarea Philippi, He questioned His disciples, saying, "Whom do men say that I, the Son of Man, Am?"

14And they said, "Some say John the Baptizer, and others Elijah, and others Jeremiah or one of the prophets."

15He said to them, "And who do you say that I Am?"

16And Simon Peter answered and said, "You are the Christ, the Son of the living God."

17Then Jesus said in reply to him, "You are blessed, Simon Bar Jonah, for flesh and blood has not revealed this to you, but My Father Who is in Heaven!

18Now I tell you that you are Peter, and upon this rock I will build My church, and the gates of Hades shall not prevail against it.

19And I will give you the keys of the Kingdom of Heaven, and whatever you bind on Earth will be bound in Heaven, and whatever you loose on Earth

will be loosed in Heaven."
20 Then He ordered His disciples not
to tell anyone that He is Jesus the
Christ.
21 From that time, Jesus began to
show His disciples that it would be
necessary for Him to go away to
Jerusalem and suffer many things of
the elders and the Chief Priests and
Scribes, and be killed, and then on the
third day be raised up.
22 But Peter took Him aside and began to rebuke Him, saying, "Favor to
you Lord, this shall never happen to
you!"
23 Then Jesus turned and said to Peter,
"Get away from Me, Satan! You are an
offense to Me, for your thoughts are
not after God, but after men!"
24 Then Jesus said to His disciples, "If
anyone will come after Me, let him
deny himself and take up his cross and
follow Me.
25 For whoever will save his life shall
lose it, but whoever will lose his life on
account of Me shall find it.
26 For what does it profit a man if he
gains the whole world but loses his
soul? Or what will a man give in exchange for his soul?
27 For the Son of man is about to
come with His angels in the glory of
His Father, and then He will render to
each one according to his doings.
28 Truly there are some who are
standing here who will not taste death
until they have seen the Son of Man
coming in His kingdom."

17 And six days later Jesus took
Peter, James, and John his
brother, and He led them to a high
mountain by themselves.
2 And He was transfigured before
them, and His face shone like the sun,
and His clothing became bright like the
light.
3 And suddenly, they saw Moses and
Elijah talking with Him.
4 And Peter answered and said to Jesus, "Lord, it is good for us to be here.
If You desire, I will make three tabernacles: one for You, and one for Moses,
and one for Elijah."
5 While he was still talking, suddenly
a radiant cloud overshadowed them,
and from the cloud a voice, saying,
"This is My dear Son, in whom I
delight– listen to Him!"
6 And hearing this, the disciples fell
upon the ground, being greatly afraid.
7 But Jesus came and touched them
and said, "Get up, and don't be afraid."
8 Then looking up, they saw no one
but Jesus alone.
9 And as they were coming down
from the mountain, Jesus commanded
them, saying, "Tell no one about the
vision, until the Son of Man is risen
from the dead."
10 And His disciples asked Him, saying, "Why do the Scribes say that Elijah
must come first?"
11 And Jesus answered and said to
them, "Elijah is coming first and will
restore all things.
12 But I tell you that Elijah has already
come, and they did not recognize him,
but they did to him what they desired.
Even so, the Son of Man is about to
suffer from them."
13 Then the disciples understood that
He was speaking of John the Baptizer.
14 When they came to the crowd, a
man came and knelt down before Him,
15 and he said, "Lord, have mercy on
my son. He is an epileptic and he suffers terribly. He often falls into the fire,
and into the water.
16 And I brought him to your disci-

ples, and they were not able to heal him."

17 And Jesus answered and said, "Oh faithless and perverse generation! How much longer must I be with you? How much longer must I put up with you? Bring Him here to Me!"

18 And Jesus rebuked it, and the demon went out of him, and the boy was healed from that time.

19 Then afterwards, the disciples, coming to Jesus, said, "Why were we unable to cast it out?"

20 And Jesus said to them, "Because of your unbelief. Truly I tell you that if you have faith as a grain of mustard, you can say to this mountain, 'Be removed,' and nothing shall be impossible for you!

21 But this kind will only go out by prayer and fasting."

22 And while they were in Galilee, Jesus said to them, "The Son of Man is about to be delivered into the hands of men,

23 and they will kill Him, and the third day He shall be raised up." And they were greatly distressed.

24 And when they came to Capernaum, those who collected the drachma came to Peter and said, "Does your teacher not pay the temple tax?"

25 He said, "Yes." And when he came into the house, Jesus, expecting him, said, "What do you think Simon? The kings of the Earth– from whom do they receive custom or tax: from their sons, or from strangers?"

26 Peter said, "From the strangers." Jesus said, "So then the sons are free.

27 But that we may not offend them, go to the lake and cast in a hook. And the first fish that you catch, take and open its mouth, and you shall find a stater. Give it to them for Me and for you."

18 At that time, the disciples came to Jesus, saying, "Who then is the greatest in the Kingdom of Heaven?"

2 And Jesus calling to Himself a little child, He set him in their midst,

3 and He said, "With certainty I tell you, unless you change and become like children, you will never enter into the Kingdom of Heaven.

4 Therefore, whoever humbles themselves as a little child, the same is the greatest in the Kingdom of Heaven.

5 And whoever receives a little child such as this one in My name receives Me.

6 But whoever shall cause one of these little ones who believes in Me to stumble, it would have been better for him to have hung a weighty millstone around his neck and be sunk into the depth of the sea.

7 Woe to the world because it causes stumbling, for it is necessary that those things that cause one to stumble come, but woe to that man by which the stumbling takes place!

8 And if your hand or your foot causes you to stumble, cut it off and cast it from you! For it is better to enter into life lame or maimed than to be cast into eternal fire with two hands and two feet.

9 And if your eye causes you to stumble, pluck it out and cast it away! For it is better to have one eye and enter into life, than having two eyes, to be cast into the fire of Gehenna.

10 See to it that you do not despise one of these little ones, for I tell you that their angels in Heaven continually behold the face of My Father Who is in Heaven.

11 For the Son of Man has come to save those who are lost.

12 What do you think: if there should be a man who had a hundred sheep, and one of them strayed off, would he not leave the ninety-nine on the mountain and go and seek the one that strayed?

13 And if he should find it, I tell you for sure that he would rejoice over it more than the ninety-nine that did not stray off.

14 So it is not the will of your Father Who is in Heaven that one of these little ones who are before Him perish.

15 But if your brother sin against you, go and reprove him between you and him alone. If he will hear you, then you have gained your brother.

16 But if he will not hear you, take along with you one or two witnesses, that by the mouth of two or three every word may be established.

17 But if he will not listen to them, tell it to the assembly. And if he fails to listen to the assembly, let him be to you as an unbeliever and a tax-gatherer.

18 I tell you the truth: whatever you bind on Earth shall be bound in Heaven, and whatever you set free upon the Earth shall be set free in Heaven.

19 I tell you the truth: if two of you agree upon the Earth concerning anything that they shall ask, it shall be done for them by My Father in Heaven–

20 for where there are two or three gathered in My name, there I will be in their midst."

21 Then Peter came to Him and said, "Lord, how often shall I forgive my brother if he sins against me, seven times?"

22 Jesus said to him, "I tell you not just seven times, but seven times seventy.

23 Because of this, the Kingdom of Heaven is likened unto a king which took account of his servants.

24 And when he had begun to take account, there was brought to him one who owed ten thousand talents.

25 But he did not have the ability to pay, so his lord commanded him to be sold, and his wife and children and all that he had, and payment be made.

26 Then the servant fell down and pleaded with him, saying, 'Lord, have patience with me and I will pay you everything!'

27 Then the lord, being moved with compassion for the servant, released him and forgave the debt.

28 But the servant went out and found one of his fellow servants who owed him a hundred denarii, and he seized him by the throat, saying, 'Pay me what you owe me!'

29 And his fellow servant fell down at his feet and pleaded with him, saying, 'Have patience with me and I will pay you everything.'

30 But he would not. Instead, he cast him into prison until he paid what he owed.

31 When his other fellow servants saw what he had done, they were very grieved and came and told their lord all that had taken place.

32 Then his lord called him and said to him, 'O you wicked servant! I forgave all that you owed because you pleaded with me.

33 Did it not also make it necessary that you should have had compassion on your fellow servant, as I also had compassion for you?'

34 And his lord was angry and delivered him to the tormentors, until he paid all that he owed him.

35 So also My heavenly Father will do

to you, unless each one of you forgive from your heart his brother their trespasses!"

19 And afterwards, when Jesus had finished these words, He departed from Galilee and He came to the borders of Judea beyond Jordan.

2 And great crowds followed Him, and He healed them there.

3 And the Pharisees came to Him, tempting Him, and saying to Him, "Is it lawful for a man to put away His wife for every reason?"

4 But He, answering, said to them, "Have you not read that He Who made them from the beginning made them male and female,

5 and on account of this shall a man leave his father and mother, and shall be joined unto his wife, and the two shall become one flesh,

6 so that they are no longer two, but one flesh? What therefore God has united together, let no man separate."

7 They said to Him, "Why then did Moses order that a bill of divorcement be granted to put her away?"

8 He said to them, "Because of your hardness of heart, Moses allowed you to put away your wives. However, this was not how it was to be from the beginning.

9 But I say to you that whoever puts away his wife– unless it is because of sexual immorality– and shall marry another, commits adultery. And her who he puts away, if she marries, commits adultery."

10 His disciples said to Him, "If this is the case of the man with the wife, then it is better not to marry!"

11 And Jesus said to them, "Not everyone can receive this word, but to those whom it is given.

12 For there are those who are born eunuchs, and there are eunuchs who were made eunuchs by men, and there are eunuchs who made themselves eunuchs for the Kingdom of Heaven. He who is able to receive it, let him receive it."

13 Then were brought to Him little children that He might lay His hands on them and pray, but His disciples rebuked them.

14 But Jesus said, "Allow the little children to come to Me and do not forbid them, because such is the Kingdom of Heaven."

15 And having laid His hands upon them, He departed from there.

16 And there came to Him one who said, "Good Teacher, what good thing must I do that I may have eternal life?"

17 But He said to him, "Why do you call Me good? No one is good except God. Now if you desire to enter into life, keep the commandments."

18 He said to Him, "Which ones?" And Jesus said, "You shall not commit murder, you shall not commit adultery, you shall not steal, you shall not bear false witness,

19 honor your father and mother, love your neighbor as yourself."

20 The young man said to Him, "All these things I have kept from my youth. What do I lack?"

21 Jesus said to him, "If you desire to be perfect, go and sell all your property and give it to the poor, and you shall have treasure in Heaven. And come and follow Me."

22 But the young man, having heard the word, went away grieved, for he had many possessions.

23 And Jesus said to His disciples, "With certainty I tell you that it is difficult for a rich man to enter into the

Kingdom of Heaven.

24 And again I tell you, it is easier for a camel to pass through the hole of a needle than a rich man to enter into the Kingdom of God."

25 But His disciples, having heard this, were astonished, saying, "Who can be saved?"

26 But Jesus, looking on them, said, "With men this is impossible, but with God all things are possible."

27 Then Peter, responding, said to Him, "You see that we have left all things and followed You. What shall there be for us?"

28 And Jesus said to him, "With absolute certainty I tell you that you who have followed Me, when the Son of Man shall sit down upon the throne of His glory in the regeneration, you shall also sit on twelve thrones, judging the twelve tribes of Israel.

29 And everyone who has left houses or brothers or sisters or father or mother or wife or children or lands, for My name's sake, shall receive a hundredfold, and shall inherit eternal life.

30 But many of the first shall be last, and the last shall be first.

20 For the Kingdom of Heaven is like a man, who was the master of the house, who went out in the morning to hire workmen for his vineyard.

2 And having agreed with the workman for a denarius for the day, he sent them into the vineyard.

3 And having gone out about the third hour, he saw others standing around in the marketplace.

4 And he said to them, 'Go also into the vineyard, and whatever may be just I will give you.' And they went.

5 Again having gone out about the sixth and ninth hour, he did the same.

6 And about the eleventh hour he went out and found others standing around, and he said to them, 'Why do you stand here idle all day?'

7 And they said to him, 'Because no one has hired us.' And he said to them, 'Go also into the vineyard, and whatever is just you will receive.'

8 When evening came, the lord of the vineyard said to his steward, 'Call the laborers and pay their wage, beginning at the last until you come to the first.'

9 And those hired at the eleventh hour came and received each a denarius.

10 Then came the first, supposing that they would receive more, and they also themselves received each a denarius.

11 And when they had received it, they murmured against the master of the house, saying,

12 'These last worked one hour, and you have made them equal to us who have borne the burden and heat of the day.'

13 But he responded to one of them, saying, 'Friend, I have done you no wrong. Didn't you agree with me for a denarius?

14 Take that which is yours and go, but I will give to this last one as I give also to you.

15 Is it not lawful for me to do as I will with that which is mine? Is your eye evil because I am good?'

16 So, the last shall be first and the first shall be last. For many are called, but few are chosen."

17 And Jesus, going up to Jerusalem, took the twelve disciples aside in the way and said to them,

18 "Behold, we go up to Jerusalem, and the Son of Man will be delivered to the Chief Priests and Scribes, and they

will condemn Him to death.
19 And they will deliver Him up to the
Gentiles to mock and scourge and to
crucify, and the third day He will rise
again."
20 Then the mother of the sons of
Zebedee came to Him with her sons,
worshiping, and desiring something of
Him.
21 And He said to her, "What would
you like?" She said to Him, "Say that
these, my two sons, may sit– one on
your right hand and one on your left–
in Your kingdom."
22 But Jesus answered and said, "You
don't know what you are asking. Are
you able to drink the cup which I am
going to drink, and to be baptized with
the baptism which I am baptized
with?" They said, "We are able."
23 And He said to them, "Indeed, you
shall drink My cup, and the baptism
which I am baptized with you shall be
baptized, but to sit on My right hand
and on My left is not Mine to give, but
for whom it has been prepared by My
Father."
24 And when the ten heard this, they
were angry at the two brothers.
25 But Jesus called them and said,
"You know that the rulers of the nations exercise lordship over them, and
the great ones exercise authority over
them.
26 But it shall not be so among you.
Rather, whoever would be great among
you, let him become your servant.
27 And whoever would be first among
you, let him be your slave.
28 Just as the Son of Man came not to
be served, but to serve, and to give His
life as a ransom for many."
29 And as they were going out of Jericho, a great crowd followed Him.
30 And behold, two blind men, sitting
beside the way, having heard that Jesus
is passing by, cried out, saying, "Lord,
Son of David, have mercy on us!"
31 But the crowd rebuked them that
they should be silent. But they cried
out even more, saying, "Lord, Son of
David, have mercy on us!"
32 And Jesus, having stopped, called
them and said, "What do you want Me
to do for you?"
33 They said to Him, "Lord, that our
eyes may be opened!"
34 And Jesus, being moved with compassion, touched their eyes, and they
immediately received sight in their eyes
and followed Him.

21 And when they drew near to
Jerusalem and came to Bethphage, towards the mount of Olives,
then Jesus sent two disciples,
2 saying to them, "Go into the village
that is opposite to you, and immediately you will find a donkey tied, and a
colt with her, untie them and bring
them to Me.
3 And if there is anyone that says anything to you, say, 'The Lord has need of
them,' and immediately he will send
them."
4 But this all happened that the the
things which were spoken by the
prophet might be fulfilled, saying,
5 "Say to the daughter of Zion, 'Behold, your King comes to you, meek,
and riding on a donkey, and a colt, the
foal of a beast of burden.'"
6 And the disciples went and did as
Jesus had ordered them.
7 And they brought the donkey and
the colt, and put their garments on
them, and He sat on them.
8 And a great crowd scattered their
garments on the way, and others cut
down branches from the trees and scat-

tered them on the way.

9 And the crowds that were going in front, and those that followed, cried out, saying, “Hosanna to the Son of David, blessed is He Who comes in the name of the Lord. Hosanna in the Highest!”

10 And as He entered into Jerusalem, all of the city was moved, saying, “Who is this?”

11 And the crowds said, “This is Jesus, the Prophet from Nazareth of Galilee.”

12 And Jesus entered into the temple of God and cast out all those selling and buying in the temple, and He turned over the tables of the money changers and the seats of those selling the doves.

13 And He said to them, “It is written: ‘My house shall be called a house of prayer,’ but you have made it a den of thieves.”

14 And the blind and lame came to Him in the temple, and He healed them.

15 But the Chief Priests and the Scribes– seeing the wonders which He did, and the children crying in the temple, saying, “Hosanna to the Son of David”– were angry.

16 And they said to Him, “Do you hear what they say?” And Jesus said, “Have you not read that out of the mouths of babes and sucklings You have perfected praise?”

17 And He left them and went out of the city and spent the night in Bethany.

18 Now early in the morning, coming back into the city, He was hungry.

19 And seeing a fig tree by the way, He came to it and found nothing on it except leaves only. And He said to it, “Let there be no more fruit from you for the age,” and immediately the fig tree dried up.

20 And seeing it, the disciples wondered, saying, “How immediately the fig tree dried up!”

21 And Jesus replied and said to them, “I tell you most absolutely, if you have faith and do not waver, then not only will you do what has been done to this fig tree, but even if you say to the mountain, ‘Be lifted up and thrown into the sea,’ it will be done!

22 Whatever you ask for in prayer, believing, you will receive.”

23 And when He came into the temple, the Chief Priests and the elders of the people came to Him while He was teaching, saying, “By what authority do You do these things, and who gave You this authority?”

24 And Jesus answered and said to them, “I will also ask you one thing, and if you tell Me, I will also tell you by what authority I do these things.

25 The baptism of John: where did it come from, Heaven or of men?” And they reasoned with themselves, saying, “If we should say, ‘From Heaven,’ He will say to us, ‘Why then didn't you believe him?’

26 But if we say, ‘From men,’ we fear the multitude, for all hold John as a prophet.”

27 And answering Jesus, they said, “We do not know.” He said to them, “Neither will I tell you by what authority I do these things.

28 But what do you think? A man had two children, and coming to the first, he said, ‘Child, go today and work in my vineyard.’

29 And he answered and said, ‘I will not,’ but afterwards, he regretted it and went.

30 And coming to the second one, he said likewise, and he, answering, said, ‘I will go, lord,’ but did not.

31 Which of the two did the will of the father?" They said to Him, "The first." Jesus said to them, "With absolute certainty I tell you that tax collectors and harlots will go into the Kingdom of God before you.

32 For John came to you in the way of righteousness and you did not believe him, but the tax collectors and the harlots believed him. But you, seeing it, did not afterwards repent and believe him.

33 Hear another parable: there was a certain man, a master of a house, who planted a vineyard, and placed a fence around it, and dug a winepress in it, and built a tower, and share-cropped it with husbandmen, and left the country.

34 And when the time of fruit drew near, he sent his servants to the husbandmen to receive his fruit.

35 And the husbandmen took the servants, and one they beat, and another they killed, and another they stoned.

36 And again, he sent more servants than the first, and they treated them in the same way.

37 Then finally he sent to them his son, saying, 'They will respect my son.'

38 But the husbandmen, seeing the son, said among themselves, 'This is the heir. Come, let us kill him and gain possession of his inheritance.'

39 And they took him and cast him out of the vineyard and killed him.

40 Therefore, when the lord comes to the vineyard, what will he do to those husbandmen?"

41 They said to Him, "He will destroy those extremely wicked men, and the vineyard he will lease to other husbandmen who will give to him the proper share of fruits in their season."

42 Jesus said to them, "Did you never read in the scripture, 'The stone which the builders rejected has become the head of the corner. This came to pass from the Lord and it is wonderful in our eyes'?

43 Therefore, I tell you that the Kingdom of God shall be taken from you and given to a nation that shall produce the fruits of it.

44 And he who falls on this stone shall be broken, but upon whoever it shall fall, it shall grind him to powder."

45 And the Chief Priests and the Pharisees, hearing His parable, knew that He was talking about them.

46 And earnestly desiring to take hold of Him, they feared the crowds, because they took Him for a prophet.

22 And Jesus, responding again, spoke to them in parables, saying,

2 "The Kingdom of Heaven is like a man, a king, who made a wedding feast for his son.

3 And he sent his servants to call those who had been invited to the wedding feast, and they would not come.

4 Again he sent other servants, saying, 'Say to those who have been invited, "Behold, my dinner is prepared. My oxen and fatted beasts are killed, and all things are ready. Come to the wedding feast!"

5 But they, being indifferent, departed, one to his own field, another to his business.

6 And the others, having laid hold on his servants, abused and killed them.

7 And hearing this, the king was angry, and he sent his forces to destroy those murderers and to burn their cities.

8 Then he said to his servants, 'The wedding feast is indeed ready, but

those who were invited were not worthy.
9 Go therefore into the thoroughfares
of the highways, and as many as you
find, invite them to the wedding feast.'
10 And the servants, going into the
highways, brought together all– as
many as were found, both the good and
the evil– and the wedding feast was full
of guests.
11 And when the king came to see the
wedding guests, he saw a man who was
not clothed with the wedding feast
garment.
12 And he said to him, 'Friend, how
did you get in here without having a
wedding garment?' But he was speechless.
13 Then said the king to his servants,
'Bind him, feet and hands, take him
away, and cast him out into outer
darkness. There shall be weeping and
gnashing of teeth!'
14 For many are called, but few are
chosen."
15 The Pharisees left and discussed
how they might snare Him by His
words.
16 And they sent their disciples, along
with the Herodians, to Him, saying,
"Teacher, we know that You are true,
and that You teach the way of God in
truth, and that You are not concerned
about, nor look upon, the appearances
of men.
17 Tell us then what You think: is it
lawful to give taxes to Caesar, or not?"
18 But Jesus, knowing their wickedness, said, "Why do you hypocrites put
Me on trial?
19 Show me the tax money." And they
handed Him a denarius.
20 And He said to them, "Whose image and inscription is this?"
21 They said to Him, "Caesar's." Then
He said to them, "Give to Caesar the
things that belong to Caesar, and the
things of God to God."
22 They were amazed at what they
heard, and they left Him and went
away.
23 On that same day, Sadducees, who
say there is no resurrection, came to
Him, and they questioned Him,
24 saying, "Teacher, Moses said if anyone should die without having children, that his brother should marry his
wife and raise up seed to his brother.
25 Now there were seven brothers
with us, and the first one who had
married died, and not having seed, left
his wife to his brother.
26 In like manner also the second,
then the third, unto the seventh.
27 And, last of all, the woman died
also.
28 Therefore, in the resurrection,
which of the seven shall she be wife to?
For all had her."
29 And Jesus answered them and said,
"You are in error, not knowing the
scriptures nor the power of God.
30 For in the resurrection, they neither
marry nor are they given in marriage,
but they are as the angels of God in
Heaven.
31 But concerning the resurrection of
the dead, have you not read what was
spoken to you by God, saying,
32 'I am the God of Abraham, and the
God of Isaac, and the God of Jacob'?
God is not the God of the dead, but of
the living."
33 And the crowds, hearing this, were
amazed at His teaching.
34 But the Pharisees, hearing that he
had silenced the Sadducees, gathered
unto Him.
35 And one of the doctors of the Law
questioned Him and said, testing Him,

36"Teacher, which commandment is
greatest in the Law?"
37And Jesus said to him, "You shall
love the Lord your God with all your
heart, and with all your soul, and with
all your mind.
38This is the first and the greatest
commandment.
39And the second is like it: you shall
love your neighbor as yourself.
40On these two commandments, all
of the Law and the prophets hang."
41And the Pharisees being assembled
together, Jesus questioned them,
42saying, "What do you think of the
Christ? Whose Son is He?" They said
to Him, "David's."
43He said to them, "How is it then
that David, being in the Spirit, called
Him Lord, saying,
44'The Lord said to my Lord, "Sit on
My right hand until I make Your enemies a footstool for Your feet."'
45If David called Him Lord, how is it
that He is his Son?"
46And no one was able to answer
Him a word, nor did anyone dare to
question Him anymore from that day.

23 Then Jesus spoke to the crowds
and to His disciples,
2saying, "The Scribes and the Pharisees sit on Moses's seat.
3Therefore, everything that they tell
you to keep, keep and do. But do not
do after their works, for they say and
do not.
4They bind heavy burdens that are
hard to bear, and lay them on the
shoulders of men, but they will not lift
a finger to move them.
5And all their works they do to be
seen by men: they make broad their
phylacteries and enlarge the borders of
their garments,
6they love their first-place positions
at supper and their front row seats in
the synagogues,
7and the salutations in the marketplace and to be called by men, 'Rabbi,
Rabbi.'
8But you shall not be called "Rabbi,"
for One is your Teacher, and that is
Christ, and you are all brethren.
9And you may not call anyone on the
Earth your father, for one is your Father, Who is in Heaven.
10Neither be called "Master," for One
is your Master, the Christ.
11But the greatest of you shall be
called servant.
12For whoever exalts himself shall be
humbled, and whoever humbles himself shall be exalted.
13Woe to you, Scribes and Pharisees,
hypocrites! For you devour the house
of the widow, and for a pretense make
long prayers. Because of this, you shall
receive more abundant judgment!
14But woe to you, Scribes and Pharisees, hypocrites! Because you shut up
the Kingdom of Heaven before men–
for you do not enter in, and those who
are entering in, you deny.
15Woe to you, Scribes and Pharisees,
hypocrites! For you traverse the sea
and land to make one convert, and
when he has become so, you make him
twice the son of Hell that you are!
16Woe to you, blind guides! You say,
'Whoever shall swear by the temple, it
is nothing, but whoever swears by the
gold of the temple is a debtor.'
17Fools and blind! For which is
greater: the gold, or the temple that
sanctifies the gold?
18And, 'Whoever swears by the altar,
it is nothing, but whoever swears by the
gift that is upon the altar is the debtor.'
19Fools and blind! For which is

greater: the gift, or the altar that sanctifies the gift?

20 He that swears by the altar swears by it and all things that are upon it.

21 And he that swears by the temple swears by it and by him who dwells in it.

22 And he who swears by Heaven swears by the throne of God and by Him Who sits upon it.

23 Woe to you, Scribes and Pharisees, hypocrites! For you pay tithes of mint and dill and cumin, and have put aside the more important issues of the Law: judgment and mercy and faith. These are the things you should have done, not neglecting the others.

24 Blind guides, who strain out the gnat and yet swallow a camel!

25 Woe to you, Scribes and Pharisees, hypocrites! Because you clean the outside of the cup and dish, but within, they are full of robbery and no self control.

26 Blind Pharisee! First cleanse the inside of the cup and dish, that the outside may become clean.

27 Woe to you, Scribes and Pharisees, hypocrites! For you are like white sepulchers, which outwardly appear really beautiful, but within are full of dead bones and all uncleanness.

28 Outwardly, you appear to men to truly be righteous, but within, you are full of hypocrisy and lawlessness!

29 Woe to you, Scribes and Pharisees, hypocrites! For you build the sepulchers of the prophets and adorn the tombs of the righteous,

30 and you say, 'If we had been in the days of our fathers, we would not have been partakers with them in the blood of the prophets.'

31 Therefore you bear witness to yourselves that you are sons of those who murdered the prophets,

32 and you fill up the measure of your fathers.

33 Serpents! Offspring of vipers! How shall you escape the judgment of Gehenna?

34 Behold, because of this, I send to you prophets and wise men and Scribes. And some of them you will kill and crucify, and some of them you will scourge in your synagogues and will persecute from city to city,

35 so that all of the righteous blood poured out upon the Earth should come upon you, from the blood of righteous Abel to the blood of Zechariah, son of Berechiah, whom you murdered between the temple and the altar.

36 I tell you for certain that all of these things shall come upon this generation.

37 Jerusalem, Jerusalem, who kills the prophets and stones those who have been sent to her! How often I would have gathered your children as a hen gathers her brood under her wings, but you would not.

38 Behold, your house is sent away desolate!

39 For I say to you, from now on you will not see Me until you say, 'Blessed is He Who comes in the name of the Lord.'"

24 And as Jesus was leaving and was going away from the temple, His disciples came to Him, pointing out the buildings of the temple.

2 But Jesus said to them, "Do you not see all these things? I tell you with absolute certainty, there shall not be one stone upon another stone which shall not be thrown down."

3 And as He was sitting upon the mount of Olives, the disciples came to Him, saying, "Tell us when these things

shall be, and what is the sign of Your coming and the end of the age?"

4 And Jesus, answering, said to them, "Beware that no one deceives you.

5 For many will come in My name, saying, 'I am the Christ,' and they will mislead many.

6 But you are about to hear of wars and rumors of wars– see that you are not disturbed, for it is necessary that all these things take place– but the end is not yet.

7 For nation shall rise up against nation, and kingdom against kingdom, and there shall be famine, and plagues, and earthquakes in different places.

8 For all of these are the beginning of labor pains.

9 Then they will deliver you up to be afflicted, and will kill you, and you will be hated by all nations for My name's sake.

10 And many will be offended, and will betray one another, and hate one another.

11 And many false prophets shall arise and lead many astray.

12 Because of the increase of iniquity, the love of many will grow cold.

13 But he who endures until the end, he will be saved.

14 And this good news of the Kingdom will be proclaimed throughout the whole world as a testimony to all the nations, and then the end will come.

15 Therefore, when you see the abomination of desolation, which was spoken of by the prophet Daniel, standing in the holy place (he who reads, let him understand),

16 at that time, those in Judea: run into the mountains!

17 He who is on the housetop, do not let him come down to take anything out of his house!

18 And he who is in the field, do not turn about to take his garment!

19 And woe to those that are with child and to those that are nursing in those days.

20 And pray that your flight will not be in the winter, nor on the sabbath.

21 For there shall be great tribulation, such as has not been from the beginning of the world until now, nor ever shall be!

22 And unless there had been a shortening of those days, there would have not been any flesh saved, but because of the elect, those days shall be shortened.

23 Then if anyone says, 'Behold, here is the Christ,' or, 'Over here,' do not believe it.

24 For there will arise false prophets and false Christs and will give great signs and wonders so as to mislead, if possible, even the elect.

25 Behold, I have foretold it to you!

26 Therefore, if they say, 'Behold, He is in the wilderness,' do not go there; 'Behold, He is in the chambers,' believe it not.

27 For as the lightning comes from the East and appears as far as the West, so shall the coming of the Son of Man be.

28 For wherever the carcass is, there the eagles will be gathered.

29 And immediately after the tribulation of those days, the sun shall be darkened, and the moon shall not give her light, and the stars shall fall from Heaven, and the powers of the heavens shall be shaken.

30 And then shall appear the sign of the Son of Man in Heaven, and then shall the tribes of the land wail, and they shall see the Son of Man coming on the clouds of Heaven with power and great glory.

31 And He will send His angels with a great sound of a trumpet, and they shall gather together His elect from the four winds, from the uttermost reaches of Heaven.

32 But learn a parable from the fig tree: when its branches become tender and it puts forth its leaves, you know that summer is near.

33 Even so also, when you shall see all these things, know that it is near– even at the doors.

34 Truly I say to you that this generation shall not pass away until all these things are fulfilled.

35 The heavens and the Earth shall pass away, but My words shall not pass away.

36 But concerning the day and the hour, no one knows, not even the angels in Heaven, but the Father only.

37 But as the days of Noah, so shall it also be of the coming of the Son of Man.

38 For as they were in the days before the flood– eating and drinking, marrying and giving in marriage, until the day that Noah entered into the ark,

39 and they knew it not until the flood came and took them all away– thus shall it also be at the coming of the Son of Man.

40 Then two will be in the field, the one shall be taken, and one shall be left.

41 Two women shall be grinding at the mill, one shall be taken, and one shall be left.

42 Therefore watch, for you know not what hour your Lord shall come.

43 But know this, that if the master of the house had known the time that the thief would come, he would have watched and not allowed his house to be broken into.

44 Therefore also, you be ready, for in the hour that does not seem likely, the Son of Man shall come.

45 Who then is the faithful and wise servant, whom the Lord has set over His household to give them food in season?

46 Blessed is the servant whom the Lord shall find so doing when He comes.

47 Truly I tell you that He will set him over all that belongs to Him.

48 But if the evil servant shall say in his heart, 'My Lord delays His coming,'

49 and shall begin to beat his fellow servants and to eat and drink with the drunken,

50 the Lord of that servant will come in a day which he does not expect and in an hour which he does not know,

51 and will cut him in two, and his portion will be with the hypocrites. There will be weeping and gnashing of teeth.

25 At that time, the Kingdom of Heaven will be like ten virgins who took their lamps and went to meet the bridegroom.

2 And five of them were wise, and five were foolish.

3 They who were foolish took their lamps, but did not take oil with them.

4 But the wise took oil in their vessels with their lamps.

5 And the bridegroom tarried, and they all became drowsy and slept.

6 But in the middle of the night there was a cry, 'Behold, the bridegroom comes! Go forth to meet him!'

7 Then all those virgins arose and trimmed their lamps.

8 And the foolish said to the wise, 'Give us some of your oil, for our lamps are going out.'

9 But the wise answered, saying, 'No, otherwise we will not have enough, but instead go to those who sell, and buy for yourselves.'

10 But as they went away to buy, the bridegroom came, and those that were ready went with him to the wedding feast, and the door was shut.

11 And afterwards, the other virgins came also, saying, 'Lord, lord, open to us!'

12 But he, answering, said, 'I tell you with the utmost certainty, I do not know you.'

13 Watch therefore, for you do not know the day nor the hour in which the Son of Man comes.

14 For it is like a man who goes away on a journey: he called his servants and gave to them his possessions.

15 And to one he gave five talents, and to another two, and to another one– to each according to his respective ability– and then immediately departed from the country.

16 And he who had received five talents went out and worked with them and made five other talents.

17 In like manner, he who had received the two gained another two.

18 But he who had received one went out and dug in the earth and hid his lord's money.

19 And after a long time, the lord of those servants came and settled accounts.

20 And he who had received five talents came and brought to him another five talents, saying, 'Lord, you delivered to me five talents. Behold, I have gained five other talents with them.'

21 And the lord said to him, 'Well done, good and faithful servant. You were faithful over a few things, I will set you over many things. Enter into the joy of your lord!'

22 And he who had received two talents, also coming to him, said, 'Lord, you delivered to me two talents. Behold, I have gained another two talents besides them.'

23 His lord said to him, 'Well done, good and faithful servant. You were faithful over a few things, I will set you over many things. Enter into the joy of your lord!'

24 And he who had received one talent also came to him, saying, 'Lord, I knew that you were a hard man, reaping where you did not sow, and gathering where you did not scatter.

25 And I was afraid, and went away and hid your talent in the earth. Behold, you may have your own.'

26 And his lord, answering him, said, 'You wicked and slothful servant! You knew that I reaped where I did not sow, and gathered where I did not scatter.

27 Therefore you should have put my money out to the money changers, so that I should have received my own with interest at my coming.

28 Therefore take from him the talent, and give it to him who has ten talents!

29 For everyone who has, to him shall be given, and he shall have great abundance. But to him who has not, even that which he has shall be taken from him!

30 And cast the useless servant into outer darkness, where there shall be weeping and gnashing of teeth!'

31 But when the Son of Man comes in His glory, and all the holy angels with Him, then He will sit upon the throne of His glory.

32 And all of the nations shall be gathered before Him, and He will separate them from one another as the shepherd separates the sheep from the goats.

33And He will set the sheep on His
right hand, but the goats on His left.
34Then will the King say to those on
His right hand, 'Come, blessed of My
Father, inherit the Kingdom that was
prepared for you from the overthrow of
the world.
35For I hungered, and you gave Me to
eat. I was thirsty, and you gave Me to
drink. I was a stranger, and you took
Me in,
36naked and you clothed Me. I was
sick and you visited Me, I was in prison
and you came to Me.'
37Then the righteous will answer,
saying, 'Lord, when did we see You
hungry and feed You, or thirsty, and
give You to drink?
38And when did we see You a
stranger and take You in, or naked, and
clothe You?
39And when did we see You sick, or
in prison, and come to You?'
40And the King will answer and say
to them, 'Truly I tell you that when you
did it to one of the least of these My
brethren, you did it to Me.'
41And then He shall say to those at
His left, 'Depart from Me, you cursed,
into the eternal fire that was prepared
for the Devil and his angels!
42For I was hungry, and you gave Me
nothing to eat. I was thirsty, and you
gave Me nothing to drink.
43I was a stranger, and you did not
take Me in, naked, and you did not
clothe me, sick and in prison, and you
did not visit Me.'
44Then they will answer Him and say,
'Lord, when did we see You thirsty, or a
stranger, or naked, or sick, or in prison,
and did not minister to You?'
45Then He will answer them, saying,
'I tell you truly, in that you did not do it
to one of the least, you did it not to
Me!'
46And these will go away into eternal
punishment, but the righteous into
eternal life."

26 And after Jesus had finished all
these sayings, He said to His
disciples,
2"You know that in two days the
Passover will take place, and the Son of
Man will be delivered up and
crucified."
3Then the Chief Priests were gathered together, along with the Scribes
and the elders of the people, in the
court of the High Priest, who was
called Caiaphas.
4And they took counsel together, in
order that they might by deception
seize Jesus and kill Him.
5But they said, "Not during the feast,
lest there should be an uproar among
the people."
6Now Jesus was in Bethany, in the
house of Simon, the leper.
7There came to Him a woman, having a very costly alabaster flask of
ointment, and poured it on His head
while He reclined at the table.
8But His disciples were very upset
when they saw it, saying, "What a
waste!
9For this ointment could have been
sold for much and been given to the
poor!"
10But Jesus, knowing this, said, "Why
do you cause trouble for this woman?
For what she has done for Me is a good
work.
11For you will always have the poor
with you, but you will not always have
Me.
12But when she poured this ointment
upon My body, she did it for My burial.
13I tell you for certain that wherever

this gospel shall be preached in all the world, what she has done shall also be spoken of for a memorial of her."

14 Then one of the twelve, who was called Judas Iscariot, went to the Chief Priests.

15 He said, "What will you give me, and I will deliver Him up to you?" And they offered him thirty pieces of silver.

16 And from that time, he sought the opportunity to betray Him.

17 Now on the first day of unleavened bread, the disciples came to Jesus, saying to Him, "Where do You want us to prepare for You to eat the Passover?"

18 And He said, "Go into the city unto a certain one, and say to him, 'The Teacher says, "My time is near, I will keep the Passover with you, with My disciples."

19 And the disciples did as Jesus had directed them, and prepared the Passover.

20 And the evening having come, He reclined at the table with the twelve.

21 And as they were eating, He said, "Truly I tell you that one of you will betray Me."

22 And being exceedingly grieved, each of them began to say to Him, "Is it me, Lord?"

23 But He, answering, said, "He who dips his hand with Me in the dish, he will betray Me.

24 Indeed, the Son of Man goes as it has been written concerning Him, but woe to that man by whom the Son of Man is betrayed! It would have been good if that man had not been born!"

25 And Judas, who was betraying Him, now responding, said, "Is it not me, Rabbi?" He said to him, "You have said."

26 And as they were eating, Jesus took the bread, and blessing it, broke and gave it to His disciples, and said, "Take, eat– this is My body."

27 And taking the cup, and giving thanks, He gave it to them, saying, "All of you drink,

28 for this is My blood of the New Testament, which is poured out for many for the removal of sins.

29 But I tell you that I will not drink the fruit of the vine from now on until the day when I drink it new with you in the Kingdom of My Father."

30 And having sung a hymn, they went out to the Mount of Olives.

31 At that time, Jesus said to them, "All of you shall go astray from Me tonight, because it is written: 'Smite the Shepherd, and the sheep of the flock shall be scattered.'

32 But after I am risen, I will go before you into Galilee."

33 And Peter, replying to Him, said, "Even if everyone is offended by You, I will never be offended."

34 Jesus said to him, "I tell you for certain that tonight, before the rooster crows, you will deny Me three times."

35 Peter said to Him, "Even if I should die with You, there is no way that I will deny You!" Likewise said also all of the disciples.

36 Then Jesus came with them to a place called Gethsemane, and he said to the disciples, "Sit here while I go over there and pray."

37 And, taking with Him Peter and the two sons of Zebedee, He began to be grieved and deeply distressed.

38 Then He said to them, "My soul is deeply grieved, even unto death! Remain here and watch with Me!"

39 And having gone a little ways, He fell upon His face, praying, and said, "My Father, if it is possible, let this cup pass from Me. But not as I will, rather

as you."
40 And He came to the disciples and
found them sleeping, and said to Peter,
"Were you unable to watch with Me for
just one hour?
41 Watch and pray so that you do not
enter into temptation– for indeed, the
spirit is willing, but the flesh is weak."
42 Again a second time He went away
and prayed, saying, "My Father, if this
cup cannot pass from Me except I
drink it, Your will be done."
43 And He came again and found
them sleeping, because their eyes were
heavy.
44 And He left them and went away
again, praying a third time, saying the
same thing.
45 Then He came to His disciples and
said to them, "Sleep on, rest and take
your rest, for now the hour has come,
and the Son of Man is betrayed into the
hands of sinners.
46 Rise up, let's go! For now he who
betrays Me is near."
47 And as He was still speaking, behold: Judas, one of the twelve, came,
and with him a great crowd from the
Chief Priests and elders with swords
and sticks.
48 And he who betrayed Him gave
them a sign, saying, "Whoever I kiss, it
is He– seize Him."
49 And he, quickly coming up to Jesus,
said, "Greetings, Rabbi," and kissed
Him.
50 But Jesus said to him, "Friend, for
what reason have you come?" Then
they came and laid hands on Jesus and
seized Him.
51 And behold, one of those with Jesus
drew a sword, stretched forth his hand,
and struck the servant of the High
Priest, and took off his ear.
52 Then Jesus said to him, "Put away
your sword, for everyone who uses the
sword shall die by the sword!
53 Don't you realize that I am now
able to call upon My Father, and He
will send Me more than twelve legions
of angels?
54 But then how should the scriptures
be fulfilled?"
55 At that time, Jesus said to the
crowds, "Are you coming out as against
a robber with swords and sticks to take
Me? I sat daily with you in the temple
teaching, and you did not seize Me.
56 But this has all come to pass that
the scriptures of the prophets might be
fulfilled." Then the disciples, forsaking
Him, ran away.
57 But they who had seized Jesus led
Him away to Caiaphas, the High Priest,
where the Scribes and elders were
gathered together.
58 And Peter followed Him from afar
unto the court of the High Priest, and
entered in and sat with the officers to
see the end.
59 And the Chief Priests and the
elders and the whole Sanhedrin sought
false evidence against Jesus so that they
might put Him to death,
60 but found none. Even though many
false witnesses came forward, they
found none. Then at last, two false witnesses came forward:
61 "This One said, 'I am able to destroy the temple of God and in three
days build it.'"
62 And the High Priest stood up and
said to Him, "Have You no response to
what these witnesses say against You?"
63 But Jesus was silent, and the High
Priest, responding, said to Him, "I
command You by the living God that
You tell us if You are the Christ, the
Son of God!"
64 Jesus said to him, "You have said it.

Moreover I tell you that after this you shall see the Son of Man sitting at the right hand of the Power, and coming with the clouds of Heaven."

65 Then the High Priest rent his garments, saying, "He has blasphemed! Why would we have any more need for witnesses? For now you have heard His blasphemy!

66 What do you think?" And they, answering, said, "He deserves to be put to death!"

67 Then they spat in His face and beat Him, and some struck Him with the palm of their hands,

68 saying, "Prophesy to us, Christ: who is it that struck you?"

69 But Peter was sitting in the court, and a maid came to him, saying, "You were also with Jesus the Galilean."

70 But he denied it before them all, saying, "I do not know what you are talking about."

71 And when he went out onto the porch, another maid saw him and said to those who were there, "This man was also with Jesus the Nazarene."

72 And again, he denied with an oath: "I know not the man!"

73 But after a little while those who stood by, having come, said to Peter, "Truly you are also of them, for even your speech reveals it."

74 Then he began to curse and to swear, "I do not know the man!" And immediately a rooster crowed.

75 And Peter remembered the word of Jesus, Who had said to him, "Before the rooster crows, you will deny Me three times," and he went out and wept bitterly.

27 When the morning came, the Chief Priests and the elders took counsel of the people against Jesus so that they might put Him to death.

2 And binding Him, they led Him away and delivered Him up to Pontius Pilate, the governor.

3 Then Judas, who betrayed Him, seeing that He was condemned, regretted what he had done and returned the thirty pieces of silver to the Chief Priests and elders,

4 saying, "I sinned, betraying innocent blood." But they said, "What is that to us? You keep it!"

5 And throwing down the silver in the temple, he departed and went away and hung himself.

6 And the Chief Priests, taking the silver, said, "It is not lawful to put it into the treasury, since it is blood money."

7 And having taken counsel, they bought with it the field of the potter for a burial ground for strangers.

8 As a result, the field was called the Field of Blood unto this day.

9 Then that which was spoken by Jeremiah the prophet was fulfilled, saying, "And I took the thirty pieces of silver, the price of Him on whom a price was set, the price set of the sons of Israel,

10 and gave them for the field of the potter, according as the Lord directed me."

11 But Jesus stood before the governor, and the governor questioned Him, saying, "Are You the King of the Jews?" And Jesus said to Him, "You said it."

12 And when He was accused by the Chief Priests and the elders, He said nothing.

13 Then Pilate said to Him, "Don't You hear these many things that they have witnessed against You?"

14 And He did not even answer him one word, so that the governor was ex-

ceedingly amazed.
15 Now at the feast, it was customary
for the governor to release one prisoner
desired by the multitude.
16 And they had a notable prisoner
called Barabbas.
17 Therefore, being gathered together,
Pilate said to them, "Whom do you
want me to release to you? Barabbas, or
Jesus, Who is called 'Christ'?"
18 He knew that because of envy they
had handed Him over.
19 Now as he was sitting on the judgment seat, his wife sent a message, saying, "Let there be nothing between you
and this righteous man, for I have experienced many things in a dream today because of Him."
20 But the Chief Priests and the elders
had persuaded the crowds that they
should beg for Barabbas and should
destroy Jesus.
21 And the governor, answering them,
said, "Which of the two do you want
me to release to you?" And they said,
"Barabbas!"
22 Pilate said to them, "What then
should I do with Jesus, Who is called
Christ?" They all said to him, "Let Him
be crucified!"
23 And the governor said, "Why?
What evil did He commit?" But they
cried out more, saying, "Let Him be
crucified!"
24 Now Pilate, seeing that he availed
nothing, but rather an uproar grew, he
took water and washed his hands before the crowd, saying, "I am innocent
of the blood of this righteous Man– it's
your responsibility!"
25 And all the people replied, saying,
"His blood be on us and on our children!"
26 Then he released Barabbas to them.
But Jesus, having been scourged, was
handed over to be crucified.
27 Then the governor's soldiers took
Jesus to the praetorium, and all the
companies gathered against Him.
28 And they stripped Him and put a
scarlet robe around Him.
29 And having woven a crown of
thorns, they put it on His head, and a
reed in His right hand. And bowing
before Him, they mocked Him, saying,
"Hail, King of the Jews!"
30 And they spit on Him, and took the
reed and struck Him on His head.
31 And when they had mocked Him,
they took off the robe, and put His own
garments back on Him, and led Him
away to crucify Him.
32 And as they went, they found a
man, a Cyrenaean by the name of Simon, they compelled him to carry His
cross.
33 And having come to a place called
Golgotha, which is called "The Place of
the Skull,"
34 they gave Him vinegar mixed with
gall to drink. But tasting it, He refused
to drink it.
35 And having crucified Him, they
divided His garment and cast a lot so
that which the prophet said might be
fulfilled: "They divided My garments
among themselves, and for My apparel
they cast a lot."
36 And they sat down and kept a
watch over Him there.
37 And they put in writing over His
head His accusation: "This is Jesus, the
King of the Jews."
38 Then two thieves were crucified
with Him, one at the right, and one at
the left.
39 And those passing by blasphemed
Him, shaking their heads
40 and saying, "You Who can destroy
the temple and in three days build it,

save yourself! If You are the Son of God, come down from the cross!"

41And also in like manner the Chief Priests, mocking Him, along with the Scribes and the elders, said,

42"He saved others, but He is not able to save Himself. If He is the King of Israel, let Him come down now from the cross, and we will believe Him.

43He trusted in God, so if He would have Him, let Him deliver Him now, for He said, 'I am the Son of God.'"

44And in the same way, the robbers who were crucified with Him reproached Him.

45Now from the sixth hour, darkness was over all of the land until the ninth hour.

46And about the ninth hour, Jesus cried out with a loud voice, saying, "Eli, Eli, lama sabachthani"– which is to say, "My God, My God, why have You forsaken Me?"

47Then some of those who were standing there who heard this said, "He calls for Elijah."

48And immediately, one of them ran and took a sponge, and filled it with vinegar, and put it on a reed, and gave Him to drink.

49But the others said, "Leave it. Let's see if Elijah will come and save Him."

50And Jesus cried out again with a loud voice and yielded up His spirit.

51And behold, the veil of the temple was torn in two, from the top to the bottom, and the earth quaked, and the rocks exploded.

52And the tombs were opened, and many bodies of the saints who had fallen asleep arose.

53And after He had arisen, they went forth out of the tombs, and entered into the holy city and appeared to many.

54But the centurion and those who kept the watch over Jesus, having seen the earthquake and the things that took place, feared greatly, saying, "Truly this was the Son of God!"

55Now there were many women who had followed Jesus and ministered to Him from Galilee, looking on from far away,

56among whom was Mary Magdalene, and Mary the mother of James and Joseph, and the mother of the sons of Zebedee.

57And when evening had come, a rich man came, Joseph by name, from Arimathea, who himself was a disciple of Jesus.

58He had gone to Pilate and begged the body of Jesus– then Pilate commanded that the body be given to him.

59And Joseph took that body and wrapped it in a clean linen cloth.

60And he placed it in his new tomb, which he had hewn in a rock, and rolled a great stone to the door of the tomb and went away.

61And there was Mary Magdalene and the other Mary, sitting opposite of the sepulcher.

62Now on the day after the preparation, the Chief Priests and the Pharisees were gathered to Pilate,

63saying, "Lord, we remember what the Deceiver said while He was living: that after three days, 'I will arise.'

64Command therefore that the sepulchre be secured until the third day, lest His disciples come by night and steal Him and say to the people, 'He is risen from the dead,' and the final deception be worse than the first."

65And Pilate said to them, "You have a guard. Go and make it as secure as you know."

66And they went and secured the

sepulcher, sealing the stone with a guard.

28 Now late on the Sabbath, at dawn, towards the first day of the week, Mary Magdalene and the other Mary came to see the sepulcher.

2 And behold, there was a great earthquake, for an angel of the Lord descended, coming out of Heaven, rolled away the stone from the door, and was sitting upon it.

3 His appearance was like lightning, and his clothing white like snow.

4 And those who kept guard trembled from fear of him and were as dead men.

5 And the angel responded to the women and said, "Fear not, I know you seek Jesus, Who was crucified.

6 He is not here, for He is risen!" And also he said, "Come see the place where the Lord laid.

7 Go now quickly, and say to His disciples that He has risen from the dead. And He goes before you into Galilee, there you shall see Him. Behold, I have told you."

8 And quickly, leaving the tomb with fear and great joy, they ran to tell the disciples.

9 Now as they were going to tell it to His disciples, then suddenly Jesus met them, saying, "Rejoice!" And they came to Him and hugged His feet and worshiped Him.

10 Then Jesus said to them, "Fear not. Go and tell My brethren that they are to go into Galilee, and they shall see Me there."

11 And as they left, some of the guards went into the city and reported to the Chief Priests everything that happened.

12 And they were assembled with the elders and counsel, who took and gave a lot of money to the soldiers,

13 saying, "Say that His disciples came and stole Him at night while we were asleep.

14 And if the governor hears about this, we will win him over and make you safe."

15 And they took the money and did as they were told, and the report spread among the Jews until this present time.

16 But the eleven disciples went into Galilee, to the mountain where Jesus had appointed.

17 And seeing Him, they worshiped Him– but some doubted.

18 And Jesus came, speaking to them, saying: "All authority has been given to Me in Heaven and on Earth.

19 Go make disciples of all the nations, baptizing them in the name of the Father and the Son and the Holy Spirit.

20 Teach them to obey everything that I have commanded you. And realize that I am with you every day, until the end of the age." Amen!

The Gospel of
Mark

1 The beginning of the good news of Jesus Christ, the Son of God.

2 As it is written in the prophets, "Behold, I send my messenger before your face, who will prepare your way before you.

3 The voice of one crying in the wilderness, 'Prepare the way of the Lord, make straight a highway for Him.'"

4 John came baptizing in the wilderness and proclaiming the baptism of repentance for forgiveness of sins.

5 And the whole region of Judea came out to him, and those of Jerusalem and were baptized by him in the river Jordan, confessing their sins.

6 And John was clothed with camel's hair and with a leather belt around his waist. And he ate locusts and wild honey.

7 And he proclaimed, saying, "One mightier than I is coming behind me. I am not worthy to stoop down and loosen the straps of His sandals.

8 I have baptized you with water, but He will baptize you with the Holy Spirit."

9 And it came to pass in those days that Jesus came from Nazareth of Galilee and was baptized by John in the Jordan.

10 And just as He was coming up from the water, He saw the heavens split apart, and the Spirit, as a dove, descending upon Him.

11 And a voice came from Heaven: "You are My beloved Son, in whom I am well pleased."

12 And immediately the Spirit drove Him into the wilderness.

13 And He was in the wilderness forty days, tempted by Satan, and was with the wild beasts, and the angels took care of Him.

14 Now after John was arrested, Jesus came into Galilee, proclaiming the good news of the Kingdom of God,

15 and saying, "The time is fulfilled, and the Kingdom of God has come–repent and believe in the good news!"

16 And passing along the Sea of Galilee, He saw Simon, and Andrew, his brother, casting a net into the Sea, for they were fishermen.

17 And Jesus said to them, "Come, follow Me, and I will cause you to become fishers of men."

18 And immediately, they forsook their nets and followed after Him.

19 And as He went a little further from there, He saw James, of Zebedee, and John, his brother, and they were in their boat repairing their nets.

20 And immediately He called them. And they forsook their father, Zebedee, in the boat with the hired help and followed after Him.

21 And they went into Capernaum, and immediately, on the Sabbath, having entered into the synagogue, He taught.

22 And they were amazed at His teaching, for His teaching was as one having authority, and not as the Scribes.

23 And there was in their synagogue a man with an unclean spirit, and he cried out,

24 saying, "What have You to do with us, Jesus of Nazareth? Have You come to destroy us? I know Who You are: the Holy One of God!"

25 And Jesus rebuked him, saying, "Be quiet, and come out of him!"

26 And the unclean spirit, convulsing and crying out with a loud voice, came out of him.

27 And they were all astonished, so they were asking each other, saying,

"What is this? What new doctrine of
authority is it that even the unclean
spirits obey Him?"
28And the report of Him immediately
spread into the surrounding areas of
Galilee.
29And they, immediately having left
the synagogue, entered into the house
of Simon and Andrew, along with
James and John.
30Now Simon's mother-in-law was in
bed with a fever, and immediately they
told Him about her.
31And having come to her, He took
her hand and raised her up, and immediately the fever left her and she began
to serve them.
32And when it was evening, at sunset,
they brought to Him all who were sick
and those possessed with demons.
33And the whole city was gathered
around the door.
34And He healed many that were ill
of various diseases and cast out many
demons, and did not allow them to
speak, because they knew Him.
35And very early, while still dark, He
rose up and went out and departed into
a desert place, and there He prayed.
36And Simon and those with Him
searched for Him.
37And finding Him, they said,
"Everyone seeks for You."
38And He said to them, "Let's go into
the neighboring towns, so that I might
also preach there, for because of this I
have come."
39And He was preaching in their synagogues in all of Galilee, and casting
out demons.
40And a leper came to Him, pleading
with Him and kneeling down to Him,
and saying to Him, "If You are willing,
You can make me clean."
41And Jesus, moved with compassion, reached out with His hand,
touched Him, and said, "I will. Be
made clean."
42And as soon as He had spoken,
immediately the leprosy departed from
him, and he was cleansed.
43And He strictly instructed him, and
immediately sent him away,
44and He said to him, "Make sure
that you say nothing to anyone, but go,
show yourself to the priest, and offer
for your cleansing what Moses commanded, for a witness to them."
45-But he, having gone out, began to
preach and spread the word, so that He
could no longer publicly enter into the
city, but was outside in desert places.
And they came to Him from all
around.

2 And again He entered into Capernaum after some days, and it was
reported that He was in a house.
2And immediately, so many gathered
that there was no room, not even in
front of the door– and He spoke the
word to them.
3And there came to Him one paralyzed, carried by four of them.
4And not being able to come near to
Him through the crowd, they removed
the roof above Him and dug through,
lowering the mat upon which the paralyzed was laid.
5Then Jesus, seeing their faith, said to
the one paralyzed, "Child, you are released from your sins."
6Now some of the Scribes were sitting there, questioning in their hearts,
7"Why does this One speak blasphemy in this manner? Who can forgive
sins but God alone?"
8And immediately, Jesus knowing
this in His Spirit– that they were reasoning this way within themselves–

said to them, "Why do you reason
these things in your hearts?
9Which is easier to say to the paralytic, 'Your sins are forgiven,' or to say,
'Arise, take up your bed and walk'?
10But that you may know that the
Son of Man has authority on Earth to
forgive sins," He said to the paralytic,
11"I say to you, 'Arise and take up
your bed, and go to your house.'"
12And immediately, he arose and
took up his bed and went out before
them all so that they were all amazed
and glorified God, saying, "We have
never seen anything like this!"
13And He went out again beside the
sea, and the whole crowd came to Him,
and He taught them.
14And walking along, he saw Levi of
Alphaeus sitting at the tax booth, and
he said to him, "Come follow me." And
he arose and followed Him.
15And as He sat at dinner in the
house, many tax collectors and sinners
were eating with Jesus and His disciples, for there were many following
Him.
16And the Scribes and the Pharisees,
seeing Him eating with the tax
collectors and sinners, said to his
disciples, "Why does He eat and drink
with the tax collectors and the
sinners?"
17And Jesus, hearing this, said to
them, "The healthy have no need of a
physician, but those who have sickness.
I have not come to call the righteous,
but sinners, to repentance."
18Now the disciples of John and the
Pharisees were fasting, and they came
to Him and said, "Why do John's disciples and those of the Pharisees fast, but
Your disciples do not fast?"
19And Jesus said to them, "Can the
sons of the bridal chamber fast while
the bridegroom is with them? As long
as the bridegroom is with them, they
cannot fast.
20But the days will come when the
bridegroom will be taken from them,
and they will fast in those days.
21And no one sews a piece of unshrunk cloth on an old garment, otherwise the patch pulls away from it–
the new from the old– and a worse tear
is made.
22And no one puts new wine into old
wineskins, otherwise the new wine will
burst the skins and the wine pours out
and the wineskin is destroyed. But one
puts new wine into new wineskins."
23And it came to pass on the Sabbath
He went through the grain fields, and
as they made their way, His disciples
began to pick the grain.
24And the Pharisees said, "Why are
they doing on the Sabbath that which is
not lawful?"
25And He said to them, "Have you
not read what David did, when he was
in need and was hungry, and those
with him?
26How he entered into the house of
God, when Abiathar was High Priest,
and ate the loaves of the showbread,
which is not right to eat except for the
priest, and gave also to those that were
with him?"
27And He said to them, "The Sabbath
was made for man, and not man for the
Sabbath.
28Therefore the Son of Man is Lord
also of the Sabbath."

3 And He entered again into the synagogue, and a man was there who
had a withered hand.
2And they watched Him, whether He
would heal him on the Sabbath, so that
they might accuse Him.

3And He said to the man who had
the withered hand, “Come into the
middle.”
4Then He said to them, “Is it right on
the Sabbaths to do good, or to do evil–
to save a life, or to kill?” But they said
nothing.
5And He looked around at them with
anger, being grieved at their hardness
of heart. He said to the man, “Stretch
out your hand.” And he stretched it out,
and his hand was restored as healthy as
the other.
6And the Pharisees went out immediately and conspired with the Herodians about how to destroy Him.
7And Jesus departed with His disciples to the sea, and a great multitude
from Galilee and from Judea followed
Him.
8And from Jerusalem, and from
Idumea, and from Jordan, and from
Tyre and Sidon, a great multitude came
to Him, hearing of all that He was doing.
9And He told His disciples to have a
boat waiting for Him because of the
crowd, so that He might not be pressed
upon,
10for many were cured. Therefore,
everyone who had a plague threw
themselves on Him so that they might
touch Him.
11And when the unclean spirits saw
Him, they fell down at His feet and
cried out, saying, “You are the Son of
God.”
12And He sternly rebuked them not
to make Him known.
13And He went up into a mountain
and called those He desired, and they
came to Him.
14And He appointed twelve which
were with Him, that He might also
send them to preach,
15and He gave them authority to cure
sickness and to cast out demons:
16And He gave Simon the name “Peter,”
17and upon James, the one of
Zebedee, and John, the brother of
James, He laid the name “Boanerges,”
which is, “Sons of Thunder,”
18and Andrew, and Philip, and
Bartholomew, and Matthew, and
Thomas, and James, the son of Alphaeus, and Thaddaeus, and Simon the
Canaanite,
19and Judas Iscariot, who betrayed
Him. And they came to a house,
20and the crowd assembled again, so
that they were not able to eat any
bread.
21And when those of Him heard this,
they went to restrain Him, for they
said, “He is beside himself.”
22And the Scribes who came down
from Jerusalem said, “He has Beelzebub, and so by the ruler of the demons
He casts out demons.”
23And calling them, He spoke in a
parable to them, “How can Satan cast
out Satan?
24But if a kingdom is divided against
itself, that kingdom cannot stand.
25And if a house is divided, that
house cannot stand.
26And if Satan has risen up against
himself and is divided, he cannot
stand, but his end has come.
27No one can enter into the strong
one's house, plundering his goods, unless first the strong one is bound, and
then his house may be plundered.
28I tell you for certain that every one
of the sins of the sons of men will be
forgiven, and blasphemies of whatever
they shall have blasphemed,
29but whoever blasphemes against
the Holy Spirit shall not have forgive-

ness forever, but is subject to eternal judgment!"

30 Because they said, "He has an unclean spirit."

31 Then His brothers and mother came, and being outside, sent to Him, calling to Him.

32 And a crowd was sitting around Him, and said to Him, "Look, Your mother and Your brothers are outside seeking You."

33 And He replied to them, saying, "Who are My mother and My brothers?"

34 And looking around at those who sat around Him, He said, "Behold My mother and My brothers!

35 For whoever does the will of God, the same is My brother and My sister and My mother."

4 And again He began to teach by the sea. And a large crowd gathered to Him, so that He entered into a boat on the sea and sat down, while the crowd was beside the sea on the land.

2 And He taught them by many parables, and said to them in His doctrine:

3 "Listen! Behold, there went out a sower to sow.

4 And it came to pass in the sowing that some fell on the road, and the fowls of heaven came and consumed it.

5 And another fell on stony ground, where it had not much earth, and immediately it sprang up, because it had not much depth of earth.

6 But when the sun rose, it was scorched. And because it had no root, it withered.

7 And some fell upon thorns, and the thorns grew up and choked it, and it produced no fruit.

8 And some fell on good ground and produced fruit that came forth and increased and brought forth: some thirty, and some sixty, and some a hundred."

9 And He said to them, "He that has ears to hear, hear!"

10 And when He was alone, the twelve that were with Him asked Him about the parable.

11 And he said unto them, "To you it is given to know the mystery of the Kingdom of God. But unto them that are without shall all things be done in parables,

12 that when they see, they shall see and not discern, and when they hear, they shall hear and not understand, lest at any time they should turn back, and their sins should be forgiven them."

13 And He said unto them, "Do you not understand this parable? How then should you understand all other parables?

14 The sower sows the word.

15 And these are they by the wayside, where the word is sown. And when they hear it, Satan immediately comes and takes away the word that was sown in their hearts.

16 And likewise, they that are sown on the stony ground are they that, when they have heard the word, at once received it with gladness,

17 yet they have no roots, and so endure but a time. And as soon as trouble and persecution arise for the word's sake, they immediately fall away.

18 And these are those that were sown among thorns, that hear the word,

19 and the cares of this age and pleasure of wealth and the desire for other things come in and choke the word, and it brings forth no fruit.

20 And those that were sown in the good ground are they that hear the word and receive it and bring forth fruit, some thirty, some sixty, some a

hundred."
21And He said to them, "Is a lamp
brought in to be placed under a container, or under a bed? No– but so that
it may be set upon a lampstand!
22For nothing is hidden except it be
revealed. Nor is anything concealed,
rather it shall be made visible.
23If anyone has ears to hear, listen!"
24And He said to them, "Consider
what you hear! With what measurement you measure, it shall be measured
to you, and more added to you who
hear.
25For whoever has, more will be giv-
en to him. And he who has not, even
that which he has will be taken away."
26And he said, "The Kingdom of God
is as if a man should sow seed in the
ground,
27and should sleep and rise up night
and day, and the seed should spring
and grow up (he knows not how).
28For the Earth brings forth fruit of
herself: first the blade, then the ears,
then the full corn in the ear.
29And as soon as the fruit is brought
forth, he thrusts in the sickle, because
the harvest has come."
30And He said, "To what shall we
liken the Kingdom of God? Or what
kind of parable may we use for it?
31It is like a mustard seed that, when
sown upon the Earth, is the smallest of
all seeds that are upon the Earth,
32yet when sown, grows and becomes
the greatest of all herbs, and it puts
forth large branches, so that the birds
of heaven can nest under its shade."
33And with many such parables He
spoke the word to them, as they were
able to hear.
34But He did not speak to them without a parable. But when they were
alone, He expounded all things to His
disciples.
35And the same day, when the
evening came, He said unto them, "Let
us pass over unto the other side."
36And they dismissed the crowd and
took Him with them, as He was, in the
boat. And there were also other small
boats with Him.
37And a great wind storm came up
and threw the waves into the boat, so
that it was full.
38And He was in the stern, asleep on
a headrest. And they woke Him up,
saying, "Master, do You not even care
that we perish?"
39And He got up and rebuked the
wind and said unto the sea, "Be still! Be
silent!" And the wind stopped, and a
great calm came.
40And he said to them, "Why are you
such cowards? How is it that you have
no faith?"
41And they feared exceedingly, and
said one to another, "What manner of
man is this, for both the wind and the
sea obey Him?"

5 And they came to the other side of
the sea, to the country of the
Gadarenes.
2And when He stepped out of the
boat, immediately a man from the
tombs with an unclean spirit met Him,
3who lived among the tombs. And no
one was able to bind him with chains,
4for he had often been shackled and
bound with chains. But he tore the
chains, and the shackles he shattered.
And no one had the strength to subdue
him.
5And continually each day and night,
in the mountains and in the tombs, he
was crying out and cutting himself
with stones.
6But when he saw Jesus from a dis-

tance, he ran and bowed down before Him.

7And he screamed with a loud voice, saying, “Why do You bother me, Jesus, Son of the Most High God? I demand You by God, do not torment me!”

8For he had said to the unclean spirit, "Come out of the man, you unclean spirit!"

9And He asked him, “What is your name?” And he answered, saying, “My name is Legion, for we are many.”

10And he begged Him earnestly not to send them out from the region.

11Now there was on the hillside a great herd of swine feeding,

12and all of the demons begged Him, saying, “Send us into the swine, that we may enter into them!”

13And Jesus immediately gave them permission, and the unclean spirits went out and entered into the swine, and the herd rushed down the steep slope into the sea. Now there were about two thousand, and they drowned in the sea.

14But the keepers of the swine fled and told it to the city and to those in the countryside. And they came to see what was done.

15And they came to Jesus and saw the one possessed with demons sitting and clothed and in his right mind, who had the Legion, and they were afraid.

16And they that saw it described to them what happened to the one possessed with the demons, and also concerning the swine.

17And they began to plead with Him that He would leave their territory.

18And when He got into the ship, the one who had the demons pleaded with Him that he might be with Him.

19But Jesus would not allow him, but said to him, “Go home into your own house and to your friends and show them what great things the Lord has done for you and how He had compassion on you.”

20And he departed and began to publish in the ten cities what great things Jesus had done for him, and everyone marveled.

21And when Jesus had crossed over again by boat unto the other side, many people gathered to Him, and He was near the sea.

22And there came one of the rulers of the Synagogue, whose name was Jairus, and when he saw Him, he fell down at His feet

23and pleaded intensely with Him, saying, “My little girl has come to the end. Come lay Your hands on her, so that she may be saved and live!”

24And He went with him. And many people followed Him and pressed against Him.

25And there was a certain woman who was diseased with an issue of blood for twelve years,

26and had suffered many things from many physicians, and had spent all that she had and yet felt no better at all, but grew worse.

27Having heard of Jesus, she came into the crowd behind Him and touched His garment,

28for she said, “If I can only touch His garment, I shall be whole.”

29And immediately her fountain of blood was dried up, and she felt in her body that she was healed of the plague.

30And Jesus immediately felt within Himself the power that went out of Him, and He turned around in the crowd and said, “Who touched My garment?”

31And His disciples said to Him, “The people press against You, and yet

You ask, 'Who touched Me?'"

32 And he looked around to see the one who had done this thing.

33 The woman feared and trembled (for she knew what was done within her), and she came and fell down before Him and told Him the truth of everything.

34 And He said to her, "Daughter, your faith has made you whole. Go in peace, and be whole of your plague."

35 While He was still speaking, there came from the ruler of the synagogue, saying, "Your daughter is dead. Why trouble the teacher any further?"

36 But Jesus, immediately hearing the word that was spoken, said to the ruler of the synagogue, "Do not fear, only believe!"

37 And no one was released to follow Him, except Peter and James and John, the brother of James.

38 And when He came to the house of the ruler of the synagogue and saw an uproar, weeping and much wailing,

39 and entering, He said to them, "Why do you make the uproar and weep? The child is not dead, but sleeps."

40 And they laughed at Him. Then He drove them all out and took the father and the mother of the child, and them that were with Him, and entered in where the child laid.

41 And He took the child by the hand and said to her, "Talitha Koumi," which is by interpretation: "Girl, I say to you: 'Arise.'"

42 And immediately the child arose to her feet, for she was twelve years of age, and they were greatly amazed with great amazement.

43 And He immediately charged them that no man should know of it, and He commanded them to give her something to eat.

6 And He left from there and came to His hometown, and His disciples accompanied Him.

2 And being on the Sabbath, He began to teach in the synagogue. And many who heard Him were amazed, saying, "What is this? Who has given Him this wisdom, and such power that has been done through His hands?

3 Is not this the carpenter, the son of Mary and brother of James, Joses, Judas, and Simon? And are not His sisters here with us?" And they took offense at Him.

4 And Jesus said to them, "A prophet is not without honor, except in his own hometown, and among his own kin, and in his own house."

5 And in that place He could not do any works of power, except for a few sick, who He laid His hands on and cured.

6 And He was amazed at their unbelief. And He went to the different villages, teaching.

7 And He called the twelve and began to send them out two by two, and He gave them authority over the unclean spirits.

8 And He commanded them that they should take nothing for their journey except a staff only– no bag, no bread, no money in their belts–

9 but to wear sandals and to not put on two tunics.

10 And He said to them, "Wherever you enter into a house, remain there until you leave that place.

11 And as many places as will not receive you or hear you, when you leave there, shake off the dust from under your feet as a testimony to them, for truly I tell you, it shall be more tolera-

ble for Sodom and Gomorrah on the
day of judgment than for that city."
12 And they went out proclaiming that
all should repent.
13 And they cast out many demons
and anointed with oil many who were
sick and they were cured.
14 And King Herod heard of Him, for
His name became known, and he said,
"John the Baptizer is risen from death,
and therefore miracles are worked by
him."
15 Others said, "It is Elijah." And some
said, "It is a prophet, or as one of the
prophets."
16 But when Herod heard of Him, he
said, "It is John, whom I beheaded– he
is risen from the dead."
17 (For Herod himself had sent and
seized John and bound him and cast
him into prison on account of Herodias, which was his brother Philip's
wife, for he had married her.
18 John said to Herod, "It is not lawful
for you to have your brother's wife."
19 Herodias held it against him and
would have killed him, but she could
not.
20 For Herod feared John, knowing
that he was a righteous and holy man,
and kept him safe. And when he heard
Him, he did many things, and heard
him gladly.
21 But when a convenient day came,
Herod made a supper on his birthday
for the high-ranking captains, and the
prominent of Galilee.
22 And the daughter of Herodias came
in and danced and pleased Herod and
them that sat at the table. Then the
king said unto the girl, "Ask me what
you will, and I will give it to you."
23 And he swore unto her, "Whatever
you shall ask of me, I will give it to you,
even unto half of my kingdom."
24 And she went out and said to her
mother, "What shall I ask?" And she
said, "The head of John the Baptizer."
25 And she quickly returned with
haste to the king and asked, saying, "I
want you to give me, on a plate, the
head of John the Baptizer."
26 And the king was grieved, but for
his oath's sake and also for their sake
which sat at supper, he would not deny
her.
27 And immediately the king sent the
executioner and ordered him to bring
his head. And he went and beheaded
him in the prison.
28 And he brought his head on a platter and gave it to the girl, and the girl
gave it to her mother.
29 And when his disciples heard of it,
they came and took up his body and
put it in a tomb.)
30 And the apostles gathered themselves to Jesus and told him all things,
both what they had done and taught.
31 And He said to them, "Come away
to an isolated place all by yourselves
and rest a little," for many were coming
and going, and they had no opportunity to eat.
32 And they departed into an isolated
place by boat.
33 And the people saw them departing, and many knew Him and ran there
on foot from all the cities, arriving
ahead of them, and came together unto
Him.
34 And Jesus went out and saw a great
crowd and had compassion on them,
because they were like sheep that had
no shepherd. And He began to teach
them many things.
35 And it being already a late hour, his
disciples came to Him, saying, "This is
a desert place, and it is a late hour.
36 Let them depart so that they may

go into the country and villages and buy for themselves bread, for they have nothing to eat."

37 He answered and said to them, "You give them food." And they said to Him, "Shall we go and buy 200 denarii of bread and give them food?"

38 He said to them, "How many loaves do you have? Go and look." And when they had searched, they said, "Five loaves and two fish."

39 And He commanded them to make them all sit down by companies on the green grass.

40 And they sat down group by group, by hundreds and by fifties.

41 And He took the five loaves and the two fish, and looked up to heaven, and blessed and broke the loaves, and gave them to His disciples to put before them. And He divided the two fish among them all.

42 And they all ate and were satisfied.

43 And they took up twelve baskets full of the fragments and of the fish.

44 And those who ate of the loaves were about five thousand men.

45 And right after this, He had His disciples go into the boat and go before Him to the other side, to Bethsaida, while He sent the people away.

46 And as soon as He had sent them away, He departed into a mountain to pray.

47 And when evening had come, the boat was in the midst of the sea, and He was alone on the land.

48 And He saw them laboring in the rowing, for the wind was contrary to them. And about the fourth quarter of the night, He came unto them, walking on the sea, and would have passed by them.

49 When they saw Him walking upon the sea, they supposed it was a phantom and cried out;

50 for they all saw Him and were afraid. And immediately He talked with them, and said unto them, "Be encouraged, it is Me! Be not afraid."

51 And He went up unto them into the ship, and the wind ceased. And they were overwhelmed in themselves beyond measure, and marveled,

52 for they did not consider the loaves, because their hearts were hardened.

53 And they crossed over and went into the land of Gennesaret, and came up to the shore.

54 And as soon as they came out of the boat, He was recognized right away.

55 And, running throughout all the surrounding country, they began to carry all that were sick on beds to the place where they heard that He was.

56 And wherever He entered, into towns or villages or fields, they laid their sick in the streets and asked Him if they might touch only the border of His garment. And as many as touched Him were healed.

7 And the Pharisees came to Him, and some of the Scribes that came from Jerusalem,

2 and when they saw some of His disciples eat bread with defiled hands (that is, without washing their hands), they complained.

3 For the Pharisees and all the Jews, except they wash their hands often, will not eat, observing the traditions of the elders.

4 And when they come from the market, except they wash, they will not eat. And many other things which they have taken upon them to observe, as the washing of cups and cruses and of brazen vessels and of tables.

5 Then the Pharisees and the Scribes

asked Him, "Why do Your disciples not walk according to the traditions of the elders, but eat bread without washing their hands?"

6And He replied, saying to them, "Isaiah prophesied correctly concerning you hypocrites, as it is written, 'This people honors Me with their lips, but their hearts are far from Me.

7In vain they worship Me, teaching human concepts as doctrines.'

8For you lay aside the commandments of God and observe the traditions of men, as the washing of cruses and of cups and many other such things you do."

9And He said to them, "You cast aside the commandment of God to observe your own traditions.

10For Moses said, 'Honor your father and mother,' and, 'Whoever curses father or mother, let him die for it.'

11But you say, 'If a man shall say to father or mother, "Whatever you would have gained from me is Corban (that is, a gift),"'

12and so you do not require him to do anything more for his father or his mother,

13making void the word of God through your own traditions, which ye have ordained. And many things like this you do.

14And He called all the people unto Him, and said to them, "Listen to Me, every one of you, and understand.

15There is nothing outside of a man that can defile him when it enters into him, but the things which proceed out of him is what defiles the man.

16If any man has ears to hear, let him hear."

17And when He went into the house away from the people, His disciples asked Him about the parable.

18And He said to them, "Are you still without understanding? Do you still not perceive that whatever enters into a man from without cannot defile him,

19because it enters not into his heart, but into the belly, and then goes out into the waste that purges out all foods?"

20And He said, "That which defiles a man comes out of a man.

21For from within, even out of the heart of men, proceeds evil thoughts, adultery, sexual immorality, murder,

22theft, covetousness, wickedness, deceit, uncleanness and a wicked eye, blasphemy, pride, foolishness–

23all these evil things come from within and defile a man."

24And from there He got up and went into the borders of Tyre and Sidon, and entered into a house and desired that no one would know about it– but He could not be hidden.

25For a certain woman, whose daughter had an unclean spirit, heard of Him, and came and fell at His feet.

26The woman was a Greek out of Syrophoenicia, and she asked Him if He would cast the demon out of her daughter.

27Jesus said to her, "Let the children be filled first, for it is not right to take the children's bread and throw it to the dogs."

28She answered and said to Him, "This is true, Master. But still, the dogs also eat the children's crumbs from under the table."

29And He said to her, "For this saying, go your way. The demon has gone out of your daughter."

30And when she had come home to her house, she found that the demon had departed, and her daughter was lying on the bed.

31And He departed again from the coasts of Tyre and Sidon, and came unto the Sea of Galilee, through the midst of the coasts of Decapolis.

32And they brought to Him one who was deaf, having a speech impediment, and they appealed to Him to lay His hand on him.

33And He took him away from the crowd to be alone, and He thrust His fingers into his ears and spit, taking hold of his tongue.

34And looking up into heaven, He groaned, and He said, "EPH-PH-A-THA" (that is, "Be opened").

35And immediately his ears were opened, and the bond of his tongue was loosed, and he spoke plainly.

36And He commanded them that they should tell no man. But the more He charged them, even more abundantly they proclaimed.

37And they were astonished beyond measure, saying, "He has done all things well, and has made both the deaf to hear and the mute to speak!"

8 In those days, there was a very great company. And having nothing to eat, Jesus called His disciples to Him and said to them,

2"I have compassion on these people, because they have now been with Me three days and have had nothing to eat.

3And if I should send them away fasting to their own houses, they will faint by the way, for some of them came from far away."

4And His disciples answered Him, "Where should anyone find bread here in the desert to satisfy these?"

5And He asked them, "How many loaves do you have?" They said, "Seven."

6And He commanded the people to sit down on the ground. And He took the seven loaves, gave thanks, broke it, and gave to His disciples to set before them. And they did set them before the people.

7And they had a few small fishes, and He blessed them and commanded them also to be set before them.

8And they ate and were satisfied. And they took up seven baskets full of the broken fragments that were left.

9And they who had eaten were about four thousand. And He sent them away.

10And right after, He entered into a boat with his disciples and came into the parts of Dalmanutha.

11And the Pharisees came there and began to argue with him, seeking from Him a sign from Heaven and tempting Him.

12And He groaned in His spirit and said, "Why does this generation seek a sign? Truly I tell you, there shall be no sign given to this generation."

13And He left them, went into a boat again, and went to the other side.

14And they had forgotten to take bread with them. They did not have more than one loaf with them in the boat.

15And He charged them saying, "Take heed, and beware of the leaven of the Pharisees and of the leaven of Herod."

16And they reasoned among themselves, saying, "It's because we have no bread."

17And when Jesus knew it, He said to them, "Why are you reasoning about having no loaves? Do you still not perceive nor understand? Have you hardened your hearts?

18Have you eyes, and see not? And have you ears, and hear not? Do you not remember?

19 When I broke five loaves among the five thousand, how many baskets full of broken food did you take up?" They said unto Him, "Twelve."

20 "When I broke seven among four thousand, how many baskets of the fragments of broken food did you take up?" They said, "Seven."

21 And He said unto them, "How is it that you do not understand?"

22 And He came to Bethsaida. And they brought a blind man unto Him and desired Him to touch him.

23 And He took hold of his hand, and led him out of the town, and spat in his eyes, and put His hands upon him, and asked him whether he could see anything.

24 And he looked up and said, "I see men– for I see them walking as if they were trees."

25 Again He put His hands on his eyes and made him see. And his sight was restored, and he saw every man clearly.

26 And He sent him home to his house, saying, "Neither go into the village, nor tell it to anyone in the village."

27 And Jesus went out, and His disciples, into the villages of Caesarea Philippi. And on the way, He asked His disciples, "Whom do men say that I am?"

28 And they answered, "Some say that You are John the Baptizer, some say Elijah, and some, one of the prophets."

29 And He said to them, "But who do you say that I am?" Peter answered and said unto Him, "You are the Christ."

30 And He charged them that they should tell no man about it.

31 And He began to teach them how that the Son of Man must suffer many things, and should be reproved of the elders, and of the high priests and Scribes, and be killed, and after three days arise again.

32 And He spoke that saying openly. And Peter took Him aside and began to rebuke Him.

33 Then He turned about and, seeing His disciples, rebuked Peter, saying, "Get behind Me, Satan! For you are not thinking after the things of God, but the things of men."

34 And He called the crowd with His disciples, saying to them, "Whoever desires to follow after Me must deny himself and take up his cross and follow Me.

35 For whosoever will save his life will lose it. But whosoever shall lose his life, for My sake and for the gospel, the same shall save it.

36 What shall it profit a man if he should gain all the world but lose his own soul?

37 Or what shall a man give in exchange for his soul?

38 Whosoever therefore shall be ashamed of Me and of My words among this adulterous and sinful generation, of him shall the Son of Man be ashamed when He comes in the glory of His Father with the holy angels."

9 And He said to them, "Truly I tell you, there are some that stand here who shall not taste of death until they have seen the Kingdom of God come with power."

2 And after six days, Jesus took Peter, James, and John and led them up into a high mountain out of the way, alone, and He was transfigured before them.

3 And His garments began to shine, and were made very white, even as snow– so white as no fuller can make upon the Earth.

4 And there appeared unto them Eli-

jah with Moses, and they talked with Jesus.

5 And Peter answered and said unto Jesus, “Master, it is good for us to be here. Let us make three tabernacles: one for You, one for Moses, and one for Elijah.”

6 For he didn’t know what to say, because they were terrified.

7 And there was a cloud overshadowing them, and a Voice came out of the cloud, saying, “This is My dear Son, hear Him!”

8 And suddenly, they looked around and saw no one with them but Jesus only.

9 And as they came down from the mountain, He charged them that they should tell no man what they had seen, until the Son of Man was risen from the dead.

10 And they kept that saying among themselves, questioning what the rising from the dead should mean.

11 And they asked Him, saying, “Why then say the Scribes that Elijah must first come?”

12 He answered and said to them, “Elijah certainly shall come first and restore all things. And also the Son of Man, as it is written, shall suffer many things and be treated with contempt.

13 But I also tell you that Elijah has come, and they have done to him whatsoever they desired, as it is written of him.”

14 And He came to His disciples, and saw many people around them, and the Scribes arguing with them.

15 And immediately when the people saw Him, they were surprised, and ran to Him and greeted Him.

16 And He said to the Scribes, “Why are you debating with them?”

17 And one from the company answered and said, “Master, I have brought my son to You, who has a demon spirit.

18 And whenever it takes him, it tears him, and he foams and gnashes with his teeth, and pines away. And I spoke to your disciples that they should cast it out, and they had no power.”

19 He answered him and said, “O generation without faith, how long shall I be with you? How long shall I suffer you? Bring him to Me.”

20 And they brought him to Him. And as soon as the spirit saw Him, he threw him into convulsions, and he fell down on the ground, wallowing and foaming.

21 And He asked his father, “How long has this been happening to him?” And he said, “Since he was a child.

22 And it often cast him into the fire, and also into the water, to destroy him. But if you can do anything, have mercy on us and help us!”

23 But Jesus said to him, “If you are able to believe, all things are possible to him that believes.”

24 And immediately the father of the child cried out with tears, saying, “Lord, I believe! Help my unbelief!”

25 When Jesus saw that the people came running together unto Him, He rebuked the foul spirit, saying unto him, “You dumb and deaf spirit, I command you to come out of him and enter no more into him!”

26 And crying out and being thrown into a great convulsion, it came out. And he was as one that had been dead, insomuch that many said he was dead.

27 But Jesus grabbed his hand and lifted him up, and he rose up.

28 And when He came into the house, His disciples asked Him privately, “Why couldn't we cast it out?”

29 And He said, “This kind can only

come out by prayer and fasting."

30 And they departed from there and took their journey through Galilee, and He didn't want anyone to know it.

31 For He was instructing His disciples, and said to them, "The Son of Man shall be delivered into the hands of men, and they shall kill Him. And after that He is killed, He shall arise on the third day."

32 But they did not understand what He was saying, and were afraid to ask Him.

33 And He came to Capernaum. And when He came to the house, He asked them, "What were you discussing on the way?"

34 And they did not respond, for on the way they reasoned among themselves who should be the greatest.

35 And He sat down and called the twelve to Him, and said to them, "If any man desires to be first, the same shall be last of all and servant of all."

36- And He took a child and set him in the midst of them, and took him in his arms, and said to them,

37 "Whoever receives any such child in My name receives Me. And whoever receives Me receives not Me, but Him that sent Me."

38 Then John replied, saying, "Teacher, we saw one casting out demons in Your name, but he was not following us, so we tried to stop him, because he did not follow us."

39 But Jesus said, "Don't forbid Him! For there is no one that shall do a miracle in My name that can easily speak evil of Me.

40 Whoever is not against you is on your side.

41 For whosoever shall give you a cup of water to drink in My name because you belong to Christ, I tell you with certainty, he shall not lose his reward.

42 And whoever shall offend one of these little ones that believe in Me, it would be better for him that a millstone were about his neck and that he be cast into the sea.

43 Wherefore if your hand offends you, cut it off! It is better for you to enter into life maimed, than having two hands, to go into Hell– into the fire that never shall be put out,

44 where their worm does not die, and the fire shall never go out.

45 Likewise if your foot offends you, cut it off! For it is better for you to go lame into life, than having two feet to be cast into Hell– into fire that shall never be put out,

46 where their worm does not die, and the fire never goes out.

47 And if your eye offends you, pluck it out! It is better for you to go into the Kingdom of God with one eye, than having two eyes, to be cast into Hell fire,

48 where their worm does not die, and the fire never goes out.

49 Every man therefore shall be salted with fire, and every sacrifice shall be seasoned with salt.

50 Salt is good, but if salt has lost its saltiness, with what shall it be seasoned? See that you have salt in yourselves, and have peace with one another."

10 And He left from there and went into the coasts of Judea, through the region that is beyond Jordan, and the people came to Him again. And just like before, He taught them again.

2 And the Pharisees came and asked Him a question, whether it were lawful for a man to put away his wife, to tempt

Him.
3And He answered and said to them,
“What did Moses tell you to do?”
4And they said, “Moses allowed us to
write a letter of divorcement and to put
her away.”
5And Jesus answered and said to
them, “Because of the hardness of your
hearts, he wrote this precept to you.
6But at the beginning of creation,
God made them male and female.
7And for this reason shall a man
leave his father and mother and shall
be joined to his wife,
8and the two shall be one flesh. So
then, they are not two, but one flesh.
9Therefore what God has joined together, let not man separate.”
10And in the house, His disciples
asked Him again of that matter.
11And He said to them, “Whoever
puts away his wife and marries another
commits adultery against her.
12And if a woman forsakes her husband and is married to another, she
commits adultery.”
13And they brought children unto
Him that He should touch them. And
His disciples rebuked those that
brought them.
14When Jesus saw it, He was dis-
pleased, and said to them, “Allow the
children to come to Me and forbid
them not, for of such is the Kingdom of
God.
15I assure you of this: unless you receive the Kingdom of God as a little
child, you will never enter in.”
16And He took them up in His arms,
put His hands upon them, and blessed
them.
17And when He had come to the
road, there came one running and
kneeled down to Him and asked Him,
“Good Master, what shall I do that I
may inherit eternal life?”
18Jesus said to him, “Why do you call
Me good? There is no one good but
One, which is God.
19You know the commandments: you
shall not commit adultery, you shall
not murder, you shall not steal, you
shall not bear false witness, you shall
not defraud, honor thy father and
mother.”
20He answered and said to Him,
“Master, all these I have observed from
my youth.”
21But Jesus, looking at him, loved
him and said, “You lack one thing: go
sell what you own, and give it to the
poor, and you will have treasure in
Heaven. Then take up the cross, and
come follow Me.”
22But he was sad with that word and
went away grieved, for he had great
possessions.
23And Jesus, looking around, said to
His disciples, “What a hard thing it is
for those who have riches to enter into
the Kingdom of God.”
24And His disciples were shocked by
His words. But Jesus continued, and
said unto them, “Children, how hard is
it for them that trust in riches to enter
into the Kingdom of God!
25It is easier for a camel to go
through the hole of a needle than for a
rich man to enter into the Kingdom of
God.”
26And they were beyond astonished,
saying between themselves, “Who then
can be saved?”
27Jesus looked at them and said,
“With men it is impossible, but not
with God. For with God all things are
possible.”
28And Peter began to say unto Him,
“You see, we have forsaken all and have
followed you.”

[29]Jesus replied and said, "With certainty I tell you, there is no one who
has left house, or brethren, or sisters, or
father, or mother, or wife, or their children, or lands, for My sake and the
gospel's,
[30]who will not receive a hundredfold
now in this life– houses, and brethren,
and sisters, and mother, and children,
and lands, with persecutions– and in
the age to come, eternal life.
[31]Many that are first shall be last, and
the last, first."
[32]And they were on the road going
up to Jerusalem, and Jesus went before
them. And they were amazed, and as
they followed, were afraid. And Jesus
took the twelve again and began to tell
them what things should happen to
Him:
[33]"You see that we are going up to
Jerusalem, and the Son of Man shall be
delivered unto the Chief Priests and
unto the Scribes, and they shall condemn Him to death and shall deliver
Him to the gentiles.
[34]And they shall mock Him and
scourge Him and spit upon Him and
kill Him, and the third day He shall
rise again."
[35]And then James and John, the sons
of Zebedee, came to Him, saying,
"Master, we desire that whatever we ask
that You will do it for us."
[36]He said to them, "What do you
want Me to do for you?"
[37]They said to Him, "Grant unto us
that we may sit– one on Your right
hand, and the other on Your left hand–
in Your glory."
[38]But Jesus said unto them, "You do
not know what you ask. Can you drink
of the cup that I shall drink of and be
baptized in the baptism that I shall be
baptized with?"
[39]And they said to Him, "We are
able." Jesus said to them, "You shall
drink of the cup that I shall drink, and
be baptized with the baptism that I
shall be baptized with,
[40]but to sit on My right hand and on
My left hand is not Mine to give, but to
them for whom it has been prepared."
[41]And when the ten heard that, they
began to be indignant towards James
and John.
[42]But Jesus called them unto Him
and said to them, "You know that they
who bear rule among the gentiles reign
as lords over them, and they that are
great among them exercise authority
over them.
[43]However, it shall not be this way
among you. But whoever desires to be
great among you shall be your servant,
[44]and whoever desires to be chief
shall be servant unto all.
[45]For even the Son of Man came not
to be served, but to serve, and to give
His life a ransom for many."
[46]And they came to Jericho. And as
He was going out of Jericho with His
disciples and a great number of people,
Bartimaeus, the son of Timaeus, who
was blind, sat by the roadside, begging.
[47]And when he heard that it was Jesus the Nazarene, he began to cry and
to say, "Jesus, Son of David, have mercy
on me!"
[48]And many rebuked him that he
should be quiet. But he cried out even
more, "Son of David, have mercy on
me!"
[49]And Jesus stood still and asked for
him to be called. And they called the
blind, saying to him, "Be comforted.
Get up, He is calling you!"
[50]And he threw away his garment,
got up, and came to Jesus.
[51]And Jesus replied and said to him,

"What do you want Me to do for you?" The blind said to him, "Rabbi, that I might see."

52 Jesus said to him, "Go your way. Your faith has saved you." And instantly, he received his sight and followed Jesus on the road.

11 And when they came near to Jerusalem, to Bethphage and Bethany, towards the mount of Olives, He sent out two of His disciples,

2 and said to them, "Go into the town that is before you, and as soon as you enter into it, you shall find a colt tied, which no man has ever sat on. Loose him and bring him.

3 And if anyone shall say to you, 'What are you doing?' say that the Lord has need of him, and he will not hesitate to send him here."

4 And they went their way and found a colt tied by the door, outside in a place where two roads met, and they untied him.

5 And some of them that stood there said to them, "What are you doing untying the colt?"

6 And they said unto them just as Jesus had commanded them, and they let them go.

7 And they brought the colt to Jesus, and placed their garments on him, and He sat upon him.

8 And many spread their garments in the way. Others cut down branches of the trees and placed them in the way.

9 And they that went before and they that followed cried out, saying, "Hosanna! Blessed be He that comes in the Name of the Lord!

10 Blessed be the coming Kingdom of our father David! In the Name of the Lord, Hosanna in the Highest!"

11 And Jesus entered into Jerusalem and into the temple. And when He had looked around on all things, the hour being late, He went out to Bethany with the twelve.

12 And the next morning, when they had come out from Bethany, He was hungry.

13 And He saw a fig tree in the distance with leaves, and went to see if He might find anything on it. But when He came there, He found nothing but leaves, for it was not yet the time for figs.

14 And Jesus responded and said to it, "No one shall eat fruit from you for the age." And His disciples heard it.

15 And they came to Jerusalem. And Jesus went into the temple and began to cast out the sellers and the buyers in the temple, and overthrew the tables of the money changers and the seats of them that sold doves,

16 and would not allow anyone to carry a vessel through the Temple.

17 And He taught them, saying, "Is it not written: 'My house shall be called the House of Prayer for all nations?'– but you have made it a den of thieves!"

18 And the Scribes and the Chief Priests heard it, and sought how to destroy Him– for they feared Him, because all the people were captivated by His doctrine.

19 And when the evening came, He went out of the city.

20 And in the morning, as they passed by, they saw the fig tree dried up by the roots.

21 And Peter remembered and said to Him, "Rabbi, behold! The fig tree which you cursed: it is withered away."

22 And Jesus answered them, "Have God's faith.

23 I tell you with certainty that whoever shall say to this mountain, 'Be re-

moved and cast into the sea,' and shall not waver in his heart, but shall believe that those things which he has said shall take place– whatever he says shall be done for him!

24 Because of this I tell you, anything you ask when you pray, believe that you have received it, and it will be yours.

25 And when you stand and pray, forgive, if you have anything against anyone, that your Father also Who is in Heaven may forgive you your trespasses.

26 But if you do not forgive, then neither will your Father Who is in Heaven forgive you of your trespasses."

27 And He came again to Jerusalem. And as He walked in the Temple there came to Him the Chief Priests, and the Scribes, and the elders.

28 And they said to Him, "By what authority do You do these things, and who gave you this authority to do these things?"

29 Jesus replied to them, "I will also ask you a certain thing. If you answer Me, I will also tell you by what authority I do these things.

30 The baptism of John: was it from Heaven or of men? Answer Me."

31 And they reasoned among themselves, saying, "If we shall say, 'From Heaven,' He will say, 'Why then didn't you believe him?'

32 But if we shall say, 'Of men...'"– then they feared the people. For all men counted John that he was truly a prophet.

33 And they answered and said unto Jesus, "We cannot tell." And Jesus answered and said to them, "Neither will I tell you by what authority I do these things."

12 And He began to speak to them in parables. "A man planted a vineyard, and surrounded it with a fence, and dug a wine-vat, and built a tower, and leased it to farmers, and left the country.

2 And when the time came, he sent to the tenants a servant, that he might receive of the fruit of the vineyard from the tenants.

3 But they took him and beat him, and sent him away with nothing.

4 And again, he sent unto them another servant, and they threw stones and struck his head, and having assaulted him, sent him away.

5 And again he sent another, and they killed him. And many others, some they beat, and some they killed.

6 Still therefore having his one beloved son, he also sent him to them last, saying, 'They will respect my son.'

7 But the tenants said among themselves, 'This is the heir. Come, let us kill him, and the inheritance shall be ours.'

8 And they took him and killed him and cast him out of the vineyard.

9 What then shall the lord of the vineyard do? He will come and destroy the tenants, and lease out the vineyard to others.

10 Have you not read this scripture: 'The Stone which the builders rejected has become the Head Stone of the corner.

11 This was from the Lord, and it is marvelous in our eyes.'"

12 And they wanted to lay hold on Him, but they feared the crowd, for they knew that He spoke the parable against them. And they left Him and went away.

13 And they sent unto Him some of the Pharisees and Herodians to trap

Him in His words.
14 And when they had come, they
said, "Teacher, we know that You are
true and do not regard nor consider
the status of men, but teach the way of
God in truth. Is it lawful to pay taxes to
Caesar or not?
15 Should we give or should we not
give?" But knowing their hypocrisy, He
said to them, "Why do you test Me?
Bring me a denarius, that I may see it."
16 And they brought it. And He said
to them, "Whose image and inscription
is this?" And they said to Him, "Caesar's."
17 And Jesus answered and said to
them, "Then give to Caesar that which
belongs to Caesar, and to God that
which belongs to God." And they were
amazed at Him.
18 Then came the Sadducees to Him,
who say there is no resurrection. And
they asked Him, saying,
19 "Teacher, Moses wrote unto us if
any man's brother dies and leaves his
wife behind, and leaves no children,
that his brother should take his wife
and raise up seed unto his brother.
20 There were seven brothers. The
first took a wife and, dying, left no
seed.
21 And the second took her and died,
and neither left her any seed. And the
third likewise.
22 And seven had her and left no seed.
Last of all, the woman also died.
23 Therefore, in the resurrection,
when they shall rise again, whose wife
shall she be? For the seven had her as
wife."
24 Jesus answered and said to them,
"Do you not therefore err, not knowing
the scriptures nor the power of God?
25 For when they shall rise again from
the dead, they neither marry nor are
given in marriage, but are as the angels
that are in Heaven.
26 As concerning the dead, that they
shall rise again, have you not read in
the book of Moses, how in the bush
God spoke to him, saying, 'I am the
God of Abraham, and the God of Isaac,
and the God of Jacob.'?
27 He is not the God of the dead, but
the God of the living. You are therefore
greatly deceived!"
28 And there came one of the Scribes,
who had heard them reasoning together. Knowing that He had answered
them well, he questioned Him, "Which
is the first of all the commandments?"
29 Jesus answered him, "The first of all
the commandments is: 'Hear, Israel: the
Lord our God, the Lord is One!
30 And you shall love the Lord your
God with all your heart, and with all
your soul, and with all your mind, and
with all your strength.' This is the first
commandment.
31 And the second is like unto this:
'You shall love your neighbor as yourself.' There is no other commandment
greater than these."
32 And the Scribe said to Him, "Well
said, Teacher. You have spoken according to the truth. There is One God, and
there is not another besides Him.
33 And to love Him with all of the
heart, and all the understanding, and
with all the soul, and with all the
strength, and to love one's neighbor as
oneself, is more than all burnt offerings
and sacrifices."
34 And when Jesus saw that he answered thoughtfully, He said to him,
"You are not far from the Kingdom of
God." And no man after that dared to
ask Him any question.
35 And Jesus responded and said,
teaching in the temple, "Why do the

Scribes say that Christ is the Son of
David?
36For David himself, inspired by the
Holy Spirit, said, 'The Lord said to My
Lord, "Sit on My right hand until I
make Your enemies Your footstool for
Your feet."'
37Therefore David himself called
Him 'Lord'– how is He then his son?"
And the great crowd heard Him gladly.
38And He said to them in His doctrine, "Beware of the Scribes, who love
to go in long robes, and love salutations
in the marketplaces,
39and the chief seats in the synagogues, and to sit in the uppermost
rooms at feasts,
40and devour widows' houses, and for
a pretense make long prayers. These
shall receive greater damnation!"
41And Jesus, having sat down across
from the treasury, saw how the crowd
put money into the treasury. And many
rich were putting in much.
42And there came a certain poor
widow, and she threw in two lepta,
which makes a kodrantes.
43And He called unto Himself His
disciples and said to them, "I tell you
with certainty that this poor widow has
put in more than all of them who have
put into the treasury.
44For they all put in out of their
abundance, but she, out of her poverty,
put in all that she had– even all her living."

13 And as He was going out of the
temple, one of His disciples said
unto him, "Teacher, see what stones
and what buildings are here."
2And Jesus answered and said to him,
"You see these great buildings? There
shall not be left one stone upon another that shall not be thrown down."
3And as He sat on the Mount of
Olives across from the temple, Peter,
James, John and Andrew asked Him
privately,
4"Tell us: when shall these things be,
and what is the sign when all these
things shall take place?"
5And Jesus answered them and began
to say, "Take heed lest anyone deceive
you.
6For many shall come in My name,
saying, 'I am He,' and shall deceive
many.
7But when you shall hear of wars and
tidings of war, don't be troubled– for
such things must be, but the end is not
yet.
8For nation shall rise against nation,
and kingdom against kingdom, and
there shall be earthquakes in many
places, and there shall be famines and
troubles. These are the beginning of
the birth pains.
9But take heed to yourselves, for they
shall deliver you up to the Sanhedrin
and to the synagogues. And you shall
be beaten and shall be brought before
rulers and kings for My sake, for a testimony unto them.
10And the gospel must first be
preached among all nations.
11But when they shall bring you and
hand you over, do not be concerned
nor premeditate what you will say, but
speak that which shall be given you at
that time, for it is not you who speaks,
but the Holy Spirit.
12The brother shall deliver up the
brother to death, and the father, the
son, and the children shall rise up
against their parents and shall put
them to death.
13And you shall be hated by all on
account of My name. But whoever shall
endure unto the end, the same shall be

saved.

14 But when you shall see the abomination of the desolation, which was spoken by Daniel the prophet, standing where it should not– let him that reads understand– then let them that are in Judea flee to the mountains.

15 And let him that is on the housetop not go down into the house nor go in to take anything out of his house.

16 And he that is in the field, let him not return to the things behind to take his garment.

17 But woe to those who are with child and to those who give suck in those days!

18 And pray that your flight is not in the winter.

19 For there shall be in those days such tribulation as was not from the beginning of creation that God created until now, nor shall be.

20 And except that the Lord should shorten those days, no flesh would be saved. But for the elect's sake, whom He has chosen, He has shortened those days.

21 And then if anyone says to you, 'Look, here is the Christ!' or, 'Look, He is there!' you shall not believe it.

22 For false christs shall rise up, and false prophets, and shall show miracles and wonders to deceive, if possible, even the elect.

23 Now take heed! Behold, I have told you all things beforehand.

24 But in those days, after that tribulation, the sun shall be darkened, and the moon shall not give her light,

25 and the stars of heaven shall fall, and the powers which are in heaven shall be shaken.

26 And then shall they see the Son of Man coming in the clouds with great power and glory.

27 And then shall He send His angels and shall gather together His elect from the four winds, and from the extremity of Earth to the extremity of Heaven.

28 But learn a parable from the fig tree: when its branches are yet tender and have brought forth leaves, you know that summer is near.

29 So in like manner, when you see these things come to pass, understand that it is near, even at the doors!

30 I tell you with certainty, that generation shall not pass away until all these things shall take place.

31 Heaven and Earth shall pass away, but My words shall not pass away.

32 But of the day and the hour, no man knows– no, not the angels that are in Heaven, nor the Son– only the Father.

33 Beware! Watch and pray, for you do not know when the time is!

34 It is as a man going away from his home on a journey gives to his servants authority, and to each one his work, and commands the door-keeper to keep a watch.

35 Therefore be watchful, for you do not know when the Lord of the house will come: in the evening or at midnight, at the crowing of the rooster or at dawn.

36 Lest, suddenly coming, He should find you sleeping.

37 And what I say unto you, I say unto all: watch!"

14 Now after two days was the Passover and Unleavened Bread, and the High Priests and the Scribes were seeking how they might deceitfully take Him and put Him to death.

2 But they said, "Not on the feast, lest there be unrest among the people."

3 And He being in Bethany, in the

house of Simon the leper, as He was
reclining, there came a woman having
an alabaster box of ointment, of pure
nard that was costly. And she broke
open the box and poured it on his
head.
4And there were some that were angry in themselves and said, "What was
the need to waste this ointment?
5For it might have been sold for more
than three hundred denarii and been
given to the poor!" And they scolded
her.
6But Jesus said, "Leave her alone.
Why do you cause her trouble? She has
done something good for Me.
7For you shall always have the poor
with you, and whenever you desire, you
may do something good for them. But
you will not always have Me.
8What she could do, she did. She has
come beforehand to anoint My body
for the burial.
9I tell you with certainty, wherever
this gospel shall be preached throughout the whole world, this also that she
has done shall be spoken of in her remembrance."
10And Judas Iscariot, one of the
twelve, went away to the Chief Priests
to betray Him to them.
11When they heard that, they were
glad and promised that they would give
him money. And he sought how he
might conveniently betray Him.
12And on the first day of Unleavened
Bread, when they kill the Passover, His
disciples said to Him, "Where do You
want us to go and prepare, that You
may eat the Passover?"
13And He sent out two of His disciples and said to them, "Go into the city
and you will meet a man carrying a
pitcher of water. Follow him.
14And whenever he goes in, say to
the master of the house, 'The Teacher
asks, "Where is the chamber where I
shall eat the Passover with My disciples?"'
15And he will show you a large furnished upper room made ready. Prepare for us there."
16And His disciples went out and
came to the city and found as He had
told them, and they prepared the
Passover.
17And coming in the evening, He
came with the twelve.
18And as they were reclining and eating, Jesus said, "With certainty I tell
you that one of you who is eating with
Me shall betray Me."
19Now they began to be grieved and
said to Him one by one, "Is it me?"
And another, "Is it me?"
20But He, replying, said to them, "It is
one of the twelve, who is dipping with
Me in the platter.
21Indeed, the Son of Man will go as it
has been written about Him, but woe
to that man by whom the Son of Man is
betrayed! It would have been good for
him if that man had never been born!"
22And as they were eating, Jesus,
having blessed, took a loaf of bread,
broke it, and gave it to them, and said,
"Take, eat– this is My body."
23And taking the cup, having given
thanks, He gave it to them, and they all
drank of it.
24And he said to them, "This is My
blood of the New Covenant, which is
poured out for many.
25I tell you with certainty, I will drink
no more of this fruit of the vine until
that day when I drink it new in the
Kingdom of God."
26And having sung a hymn, they
went out to the Mount of Olives.
27And Jesus said to them, "All of you

shall be offended in Me tonight. For it is written, I will smite the Shepherd and the sheep shall be scattered.

28 But after I arise, I will go before you into Galilee."

29 But Peter said to Him, "Even if everyone shall be offended, I will not be!"

30 And Jesus said to Him, "I tell you with certainty that today, even tonight, before the rooster crows twice, you will deny Me three times."

31 But he spoke more insistently, "If it is necessary for me to die with You, I will never deny You!" In like manner also they all said.

32 And they came into a place called Gethsemane. And He said to His disciples, "Sit here while I shall pray."

33 And He took with Him Peter, James, and John, and He began to be overwhelmed and in agony.

34 And said unto them, "My soul is deeply grieved, even unto death! Remain here and watch!"

35 And having gone a little further, He fell down on the ground and prayed, that if it were possible, the hour might pass from Him.

36 And He said, "Abba, Father, all things are possible for You! Take away this cup from Me! But not what I will, but what You will."

37 And He came and found them sleeping, and said to Peter, "Simon, are you sleeping? Couldn't you watch one hour with Me?

38 Watch and pray, so that you do not enter into temptation. Surely the spirit is willing, but the flesh is weak."

39 And again He went away and prayed and spoke the same words.

40 And He returned and found them asleep again, for their eyes were heavy, neither did they know what to say to Him.

41 And He came the third time, and said to them, "Sleep now and take your rest, it is enough! The hour has come! Behold, the Son of Man is delivered into the hands of sinners!

42 Get up, let's go! Behold, he who betrays Me approaches."

43 And immediately, while He was speaking, Judas, one of the twelve, came up, and with him a great crowd with swords and clubs from the Chief Priests and Scribes and elders.

44 Now he that betrayed Him had given them a signal, saying, "The One I kiss, He is the One. Take Him and lead Him away safely."

45 And as soon as he had come, he went straight to Him and said, "Rabbi, Rabbi!" and kissed Him.

46 And they laid their hands on Him and arrested Him.

47 And one of those who stood by drew out a sword and smote a servant of the High Priest, and cut off his ear.

48 And Jesus, responding, said to them, "Have you come out against a thief, with swords and clubs to take Me?

49 I was daily with you in the temple, teaching, and you did not arrest Me–but that the Scriptures should be fulfilled."

50 And they all ran away and left Him.

51 And one certain young man followed Him, having a linen cloth on his naked body, and the young men grabbed him,

52 but he left the linen cloth, running away from them naked.

53 And they led Jesus away to the High Priest. And to Him came all the Chief Priests, and the elders, and the Scribes.

54 And Peter followed Him from a far

distance to within the court of the High Priest, and sat with the officers and warmed himself at the fire.

55 And the Chief Priests and all of the Sanhedrin sought for witnesses against Jesus to put Him to death, and found none.

56 For many bore false witness against Him, but their witnesses did not agree with each other.

57 And some came forth bearing false witness against Him, saying,

58 "We heard Him say, 'I will destroy this temple made with hands, and within three days I will build another made without hands.'"

59 But their witness did not agree.

60 And the High Priest stood up among them and questioned Jesus, saying, "Have You no answer to what they testify against You?"

61 And He was silent and answered nothing. Again, the High Priest questioned Him and said to Him, "Are you the Christ, the Son of the Blessed?"

62 And Jesus said, "I am. And you shall see the Son of Man sitting on the right hand of power and coming in the clouds of Heaven."

63 Then the High Priest tore his clothes and said, "What need do we have of any further witnesses?

64 You have heard the blasphemy! What is your decision?" And they all condemned Him to be worthy of death.

65 And some began to spit on Him, and to cover His face, and to beat Him, and say to Him, "Prophesy!" And the officers struck Him with the palms of their hands.

66 And Peter being in the court below, there came one of the maids of the High Priest.

67 And when she saw Peter warming himself, she looked at him, saying, "You were also with Jesus the Nazarene."

68 But he denied it, saying, "I do not know Him, neither do I understand what you are saying." And he went out onto the porch, and the rooster crowed.

69 And the maid, seeing him again, began to say to them that stood by, "This is one of them."

70 And again he denied it. And again after a little while those that stood by said to Peter, "Surely, you are one of them– for you are of Galilee, and your speech confirms it!"

71 But He began to curse and to swear, saying, "I do not know this Man of Whom you speak!"

72 And again the rooster crowed. And Peter remembered the word that Jesus spoke to him: "Before the rooster crows twice, you shall deny Me three times," And thinking about it, he wept.

15 And first thing in the morning, the Sanhedrin, having convened with the elders and the Scribes and the whole Sanhedrin, bound Jesus and led Him away and delivered Him to Pilate.

2 And Pilate questioned Him, "Are You the King of the Jews?" And He answered and said to him, "You have said it."

3 And the Chief Priests accused Him of many things.

4 But Pilate questioned Him, saying, "Are You not going to answer? Consider how many things they witness against You."

5 But Jesus did not say anything, so that Pilate marveled.

6 Now at that feast he would release to them any one prisoner they requested.

7 And there was one named Barrabas, who was imprisoned with those that made insurrection, and in the insurrec-

tion committed murder.

8 And the crowd called unto him and began to desire that he do as he had always done.

9 Pilate answered them and said, “Do you want me to release the King of the Jews?”

10 For he knew that the Chief Priests had delivered Him out of envy.

11 But the Chief Priests had moved the people that he should rather deliver Barrabas unto them.

12 And Pilate answered again and said to them, “What do you want me to do with Him Whom you call the King of the Jews?”

13 But they cried again, “Crucify Him!”

14 Pilate said unto them, “What evil has He done?” But they cried out all the more, “Crucify Him!”

15 But Pilate, desiring to please the crowd, released to them Barabbas and delivered Jesus, when He had scourged Him, to be crucified.

16 And the soldiers led Him away into the court, which is the praetorium, and called together the whole military unit.

17 And they clothed Him with purple, and they wove a thorny crown and placed it on Him.

18 And they began to greet Him, “Hail, King of the Jews!”

19 And they struck Him on the head with a reed and spit on Him, and kneeled down and worshiped Him.

20 And when they had mocked Him, they took the purple off of Him and put His own clothes on Him and led Him out to crucify Him.

21 And they compelled one that passed by, called Simon, a Cyrenian (who came out of the field, and was the father of Alexander and Rufus), to carry His cross.

22 And they brought Him to a place named Golgotha (which is by interpretation: “the place of a skull”).

23 And they gave Him wine mingled with myrrh to drink, but He did not take it.

24 And when they had crucified Him, they divided His garments, casting lots for who would get what part to take.

25 And it was about the third hour, and they crucified Him.

26 And there was the inscription written of what He was accused of: “The King of the Jews”.

27 And with Him they crucified two thieves– the one on the right hand, and the other on His left.

28 And the scripture was fulfilled, which says, “He was counted among the wicked.”

29 And they that went by slandered Him, wagging their heads and saying, “Aha! You Who would destroy the temple and then build it in three days,

30 save yourself and come down from the cross!”

31 Likewise the Chief Priests also mocked Him among themselves, with the Scribes, and said, “He saved others– Himself, He cannot save!

32 Let Christ, the King of Israel, descend now from the cross that we may see and believe!” And they that were crucified with Him heaped insults on Him.

33 And when the sixth hour had come, darkness came over all the Earth until the ninth hour.

34 And at the ninth hour Jesus cried with a loud voice, saying, “Eloi, Eloi, lama sabachthani,” which, being interpreted is: “My God, My God, why have You forsaken Me?”

35 And some of them that stood by, when they heard it, said, “Listen, He

calls for Elijah."
36And one ran and filled a sponge
full of vinegar and put it on a reed so
that He could drink, saying, "Leave
Him alone. Let's see if Elijah will come
and take Him down."
37But Jesus cried with a loud voice
and expired.
38And the veil of the temple was torn
in two pieces, from the top to the bottom.
39And when the centurion who stood
across from Him saw that He so cried
out and expired, he said, "Truly this
Man was the Son of God!"
40There were also women looking on
from a distance, among whom were
Mary Magdalene, and Mary the mother of James the little, and Joses, and Salome,
41who also, when He was in Galilee,
followed Him and ministered unto
Him, and many other women who
came up with Him to Jerusalem.
42And evening having now come, because it was preparation (that is, before
the Sabbath),
43Joseph of Arimathea, a noble counselor, came– who also himself was
waiting for the Kingdom of God– and
went boldly to Pilate, and begged the
body of Jesus.
44And Pilate was surprised that he
was already dead, and called unto him
the centurion, and asked him how long
He had been dead.
45And when he knew it from the centurion, he gave the body to Joseph.
46And he bought a linen cloth, and
took Him down, and wrapped Him in
the linen cloth and laid Him in a tomb
that was cut out of a rock, and rolled a
stone before the entrance of the tomb.
47And Mary Magdalene and Mary of
Joses saw where He was laid.

16

And when the Sabbath Day was
past, Mary Magdalene, and
Mary of James, and Salome, bought
fragrances, that they might come and
anoint Him.
2And early in the morning, the next
day after the Sabbath Day, they came to
the tomb when the sun had come up.
3And they said one to another, "Who
shall roll away the stone from the entrance of the tomb for us?"
4And when they looked, they saw
how the stone had been rolled away–
for it was a very great stone.
5And they went into the tomb and
saw a young man sitting on the right
side, clothed in a long white robe. And
they were very surprised.
6And he said unto them, "Don't be
alarmed! You seek Jesus of Nazareth,
Who was crucified. He is risen. He is
not here. Behold the place where they
laid Him.
7But go and tell His disciples and Peter. He will go before you into Galilee–
there shall you see Him, just as He told
you."
8And they went out quickly and fled
from the tomb, for they trembled and
were overwhelmed with amazement.
And they said nothing to anyone, for
they were afraid.
9When Jesus was risen early on the
first day of the week, He appeared first
to Mary Magdalene, out of whom He
had cast seven demons.
10She went and told it to those who
had been with Him, who were grieving
and weeping.
11And when they heard that He was
alive and had been seen by her, they
did not believe.
12After that, He appeared in another
form to two of them as they walked,
going into the country.

13 And they went and told it to the
rest, and neither did they believe them.
14 After that, He appeared unto the
eleven as they were reclining, and He
reproached their unbelief and hardness
of heart, because they did not believe
them who had seen Him after He was
risen.
15 And He said to them, "Go into all
the world, and proclaim the gospel
unto all the creation.
16 The one who believes and is baptized shall be saved, but the one that
does not believe shall be damned.
17 And these miracles will follow
those who believe: in My name they
will drive out demons and speak with
new tongues.
18 They shall take up serpents, and if
they drink something deadly, they shall
not be hurt. They shall lay hands on
the sick, and they shall recover."
19 So then after the Lord had spoken
to them, He was taken up into Heaven
and sat down at the right hand of God.
20 And they went out everywhere,
preaching, the Lord working with them
and establishing the Word through the
miracles that followed. Amen!

THE GOSPEL OF
LUKE

1 Since indeed many have endeavored to compose an account concerning those things which are most certainly believed among us,

2as they were from the beginning eyewitnesses and ministers of the Word who delivered them to us,

3it seemed right to me also, having followed faithfully, observing everything, to write an orderly account of these things for you, most excellent Theophilus,

4that you may know with certainty those things that you have been instructed in.

5In the days of Herod, the king of Judea, there was a priest named Zechariah, of the course of Abijah. And he had a wife from the daughters of Aaron, and her name was Elizabeth.

6And they were both righteous before God, walking blameless in all of the commandments and statutes of the Lord.

7And they had no children, because Elizabeth was barren, and they were both old.

8And it came to pass in serving his priestly duty, in the order of his course before God,

9according to the custom of the priesthood, he was chosen to enter into the temple of the Lord to burn incense.

10And the entire multitude of people were praying outside during the time of incense.

11And an angel of the Lord appeared to him, standing on the right of the altar of incense.

12And seeing him, Zechariah was troubled, and fear fell on him.

13But the angel said to him, "Be not afraid, Zechariah, for your request has been heard, and your wife Elizabeth will bear a son, and you will call his name 'John.'

14And you shall have joy and gladness, and many shall rejoice at his birth.

15He will be great before the Lord, and he will absolutely not drink wine or strong drink, and he will be filled with the Holy Spirit, even from his mother's womb.

16And he will turn many of the sons of Israel to the Lord their God.

17And he shall go forth before Him in the spirit and power of Elijah, and shall turn the hearts of the children to the fathers, and the disobedient to the wisdom of the righteous, to make ready a people prepared for the Lord."

18And Zechariah said to the angel, "By what shall I know this? For I am old, and my wife is advanced in her days."

19And the angel answered him and said, "I am Gabriel, who stands before God. I was sent here to speak to you and announce this good news.

20And so now you will be silent and not able to speak until the day that these things take place, because you did not believe my words, which shall be fulfilled in their time."

21And the people were waiting for Zechariah, and wondered why he was being delayed in the temple.

22But when he came out, he was not able to speak to them, and they recognized that he had seen a vision in the temple. And he was making signs to them and remained unable to speak.

23And when the days of his service were fulfilled, he departed to his house.

24Now after these days, his wife Elizabeth conceived, and she hid herself five months, saying,

25"This is what the Lord has done for me in the days when He looked upon

me, to take away my reproach from
among men."
26And in the sixth month, the angel
Gabriel was sent by God to a city of
Galilee named Nazareth,
27to a virgin engaged to a man named
Joseph, of the house of David. And the
virgin's name was Mary.
28And when the angel came to her,
He said, "Rejoice, highly favored one!
The Lord is with you! You are blessed
among women!"
29But when she saw him, she was
greatly perplexed by what he said, and
tried to figure out what kind of greeting this was.
30And the angel said, "Don't be
afraid, Mary– you have found favor
with God!
31And behold, you will conceive in
your womb and bear a son, and you
shall call His name 'Jesus.'
32He will be great, and will be called
the Son of the Most High. And the
Lord God will give Him the throne of
His father David,
33and He shall reign over the house
of Jacob forever. And of His kingdom
there shall be no end!"
34Then Mary said to the angel, "How
can these things be, seeing as I have not
known a man?"
35And the angel, answering, said to
her, "The Holy Spirit shall come upon
you, and the power of the Most High
will overshadow you. Therefore, the
Holy One Who shall be born shall be
called 'The Son of God.'
36And behold, your cousin Elizabeth,
she has also conceived a son in her old
age. And this is her sixth month,
though she was called barren.
37For with God, nothing shall be impossible."
38And Mary said, "Behold the handmaiden of the Lord! May it happen to
me according to your word!" And the
angel departed from her.
39And Mary arose in those days and
went quickly into the hill country, into
a city of Judah,
40and entered into the house of
Zechariah, and greeted Elizabeth.
41And when Elizabeth heard the
greeting of Mary, the babe leaped in
her womb, and Elizabeth was filled
with the Holy Spirit.
42And she cried out with a loud voice
and said, "Blessed are you among
women, and blessed is the fruit of your
womb!
43And why has this happened to me,
that the mother of my Lord should
come to me?
44For behold, as soon as the voice of
your greeting came into my ears, the
babe leaped in my womb for joy!
45And you are blessed because you
believed, for those things shall be performed which you were told from the
Lord."
46And Mary said, "My soul magnifies
the Lord,
47and my spirit rejoices in God my
Savior,
48for He has looked on the lowly degree of His handmaiden. Behold, from
now on all generations shall call me
blessed,
49for He that is mighty has done great
things to me, and holy is His name.
50And His mercy is upon them that
fear Him, from generation to generation.
51He shows strength with His arm.
He scatters those that are proud in the
imagination of their hearts.
52He puts down the mighty from
their thrones, and exalts the humble.

53 He fills the hungry with good things, and sends the rich away empty.

54 He remembers mercy, and helps His servant Israel,

55 just as He promised to our fathers– to Abraham and to his seed forever."

56 And Mary stayed with her about three months, and returned home again to her own house.

57 Elizabeth's time had come that she should give birth, and she brought forth a son.

58 And her neighbors and her cousins heard how the Lord had shown great mercy upon her, and they rejoiced with her.

59 And it came to pass on the eighth day, they came to circumcise the child, and called his name "Zechariah," after the name of his father.

60 And his mother answered and said, "Not so, but he shall be called John."

61 And they said unto her, "There is none of your kin that is called by this name."

62 And they made signs to his father, how he would have him called.

63 And he asked for a writing tablet and wrote, saying, "His name is John." And they marveled.

64 And immediately his mouth was opened, and his tongue, and he spoke, blessing God.

65 And fear came on all of them that dwelt near to them. And all these sayings were being talked about throughout all the hill country of Judea.

66 And all that heard them laid them up in their hearts, saying, "What manner of child shall this be?" And the hand of the Lord was with him.

67 And his father Zechariah was filled with the Holy Spirit, and prophesied, saying,

68 "Blessed be the Lord God of Israel, for He has looked upon and redeemed His people,

69 and has raised up a horn of salvation unto us in the house of His servant David,

70 even as He spoke by the mouth of His holy prophets since the age began,

71 that we should be saved from our enemies and from the hands of all that hate us,

72 that He would show mercy to our fathers, and remember His holy covenant,

73 and to perform the oath which He swore to our father Abraham,

74 to grant us that we, being delivered out of the hands of our enemies, might serve Him without fear,

75 in holiness and righteousness in His sight all the days of our lives.

76 And you, child, shall be called the prophet of the Most High, for you shall go before the face of the Lord to prepare His ways,

77 and to give knowledge of salvation unto His people by the forgiveness of their sins,

78 through the tender mercy of our God, whereby the Day-Spring from on high has visited us–

79 to give light to those who sit in darkness and the shadow of death, to guide our feet into the way of peace."

80 And the child grew and waxed strong in spirit, and was in the wilderness until the day came when he should show himself unto Israel.

2 And it happened in those days that there went out a decree from Augustus the Emperor that all the world should be registered.

2 This was the first registration executed when Cyrenius was governor in Syria.

3 And every man went to his own city to be registered.

4 And Joseph also went up from Galilee, out of a city called Nazareth, into Judah, unto a city of David that is called Bethlehem, because he was of the house and lineage of David,

5 to be registered with Mary, his espoused wife, who was with child.

6 And it happened while they were there, her time came that she should give birth.

7 And she gave birth to her firstborn Son, and wrapped Him in swaddling clothes, and laid Him in a feeding trough, because there was no room for them within the inn.

8 And there were, in the same region, shepherds abiding in the field and watching their flock by night.

9 And behold, the angel of the Lord stood by them, and the glory of the Lord shone all around them, and they were exceedingly afraid.

10 But the angel said unto them, "Don't be afraid! For behold, I bring you tidings of great joy, which shall be to all the people.

11 For unto you is born this day, in the city of David, a Savior, Who is Christ the Lord.

12 And this is the sign for you: You shall find the child wrapped in swaddling clothes and laid in a feeding trough."

13 And suddenly there was with the angel a multitude of heavenly hosts praising God and saying,

14 "Glory to God in the highest! Peace on Earth! Good will toward men!"

15 And it came to pass as the angels were gone away from them into Heaven, the shepherds said one to another, "Let us go into Bethlehem and see this thing that has happened, which the Lord has shown unto us!"

16 And they came with haste and found Mary and Joseph, and the Babe lying in a feeding trough.

17 And when they had seen it, they went all around and made known what had been told to them about the Child.

18 And everyone who heard it wondered at those things which were told to them by the shepherds.

19 But Mary kept all these sayings and pondered them in her heart.

20 And the shepherds returned, glorifying and praising God for all that they had heard and seen, even as it was told unto them.

21 And when eight days were completed that the child should be circumcised, His name was called "Jesus," which the angel called Him before He was conceived in the womb.

22 And when the time of their purification was completed according to the Law of Moses, they brought Him to Jerusalem to present Him to the Lord,

23 as it is written in the Law of the Lord, "Every male that first opens the matrix shall be called holy to the Lord,"

24 and to offer a sacrifice, as it is said in the Law of the Lord, "A pair of turtledoves, or two young pigeons."

25 And behold there was a man in Jerusalem whose name was Simeon. And this man was righteous and devout, and longed for the consolation of Israel, and the Holy Spirit was upon him.

26 And it was revealed to him of the Holy Spirit that he would not see death before he had seen the Lord's Christ.

27 And he came by the Spirit into the temple. And when the parents of the little child Jesus brought Him in, after the custom of the law,

28 then he took Him up in his arms

and blessed God and said,

29 “Master, now let Your servant depart in peace, according to Your word,

30 for my eyes have seen Your salvation,

31 which You have prepared before the face of all people.

32 A light of revelation to the Gentiles and the glory of Your people Israel.”

33 And Joseph and His mother were overwhelmed by those things that were spoken of Him.

34 And Simeon blessed them and said to Mary His mother, “Behold, this child shall be for the fall and rising again of many in Israel and a sign which shall be spoken against,

35 and also a sword shall go through your soul, that the thoughts of many hearts may be revealed.”

36 And there was Anna, a prophetess, the daughter of Phanuel of the tribe of Asher. She was of a great age, and had lived with her husband seven years from her virginity.

37 But she had been a widow for about eighty-four years, who never went out of the temple, serving God with fasting and supplication night and day.

38 And at the same hour she came up and gave thanks to the Lord and spoke of Him to all that looked for redemption in Jerusalem.

39 And when they had performed all things according to the Law of the Lord, they returned into Galilee, to their own city, Nazareth.

40 And the Child grew and became strong in spirit, and was filled with wisdom, and the grace of God was upon Him.

41 And His parents went to Jerusalem every year at the feast of Passover.

42 And when He was twelve years old, they went up to Jerusalem after the custom of the feast.

43 And when they had completed the days, as they returned home, the child Jesus remained in Jerusalem. And Joseph and His mother did not know it,

44 but, supposing He was in the company, went a day's journey and looked for Him among their relatives and acquaintances.

45 Now when they did not find Him, they returned to Jerusalem, looking for Him.

46 And then after three days they found Him in the temple, sitting in the midst of the doctors, both hearing them and questioning them.

47 And all that heard Him were amazed at His understanding and answers.

48 And when they saw Him, they were shocked. And His mother said to Him, “Child, why have You done this to us? Look, your father and I were distressed looking for You.”

49 And He said to them, “Why were you looking for Me? Did you not know that I must be about My Father's business?”

50 And they did not understand the word which He spoke to them.

51 And He went down with them and came to Nazareth, and was subject to them. And His mother kept all these things in her heart.

52 And Jesus increased in wisdom and stature, and in favor with God and man.

3 In the fifteenth year of the reign of Tiberius the Emperor, Pontius Pilate being governor of Judea, and Herod being Tetrarch of Galilee, and his brother Philip Tetrarch in Iturea and in the region of Trachonitis, and Lysanias being the Tetrarch of Abilene,

[2]when Annas and Caiaphas were the
High Priests, the word of God came
upon John the son of Zechariah in the
wilderness.
[3]And he went into all the country
around Jordan, preaching the baptism
of repentance for the remission of sins.
[4]As it has been written in the book of
the words of Isaiah the prophet, saying,
"The voice of one crying in the wilderness: 'Prepare the way of the Lord,
make His paths straight.
[5]Every valley shall be filled and every
mountain and hill shall be brought low.
And the crooked things shall be made
straight, and the rough ways smooth.
[6]And all flesh shall see the salvation
of God.'"
[7]Then he said to the crowd that had
come to be baptized by him, "O generation of vipers! Who has forewarned
you to flee from the wrath to come?
[8]Produce therefore fruits worthy of
repentance, and do not begin to say in
yourselves, 'We have Abraham as our
father.' For I say to you, God is able of
these stones to raise up children to
Abraham.
[9]But the ax is already laid to the root
of the trees so that every tree which
does not produce good fruit is cut
down and cast into the fire."
[10]And the people asked him, saying,
"What shall we do then?"
[11]He answered and said to them, "He
that has two coats, let him give to him
that has none. And he that has food, let
him do the same."
[12]And then came also tax collectors
to be baptized, and said to him,
"Teacher, what shall we do?"
[13]And he said to them, "Require no
more than that which is appointed to
you."
[14]The soldiers also asked him, saying,
"What shall we do?" And he said to
them, "Do not oppress anyone, nor
falsely accuse, and be satisfied with
your wages."
[15]As the people were in expectation
and were reasoning in their hearts concerning John, whether or not he might
be the Christ,
[16]John answered and said to them all,
"I indeed baptize you with water, but
One mightier than I is coming after
me, Whose shoe's latchet I am not worthy to unloose. He will baptize you
with the Holy Spirit and with fire,
[17]Who has a winnowing fan in His
hand, and He will purge His floor and
will gather the wheat into His barn, but
the chaff He will burn with unquenchable fire."
[18]And so with many other things he
exhorted, preaching glad tidings to the
people.
[19]Then Herod the Tetrarch, being rebuked by him because of Herodias, his
brother Philip's wife, and for all the
evils which Herod had done,
[20]also added to all this by shutting
John up in prison.
[21]Now it came to pass, when all of the
people had been baptized, that also Jesus was baptized, and praying, the
Heaven was opened,
[22]and the Holy Spirit came down in a
bodily form like a dove upon Him, and
a voice came from Heaven, saying,
"You are My dear Son, in Whom I delight."
[23]And Jesus Himself began, being
about thirty years old, as it was supposed, the son of Joseph, who was the
son of Eli,
[24]of Matthat, of Levi. of Melchi, of
Janna, of Joseph,
[25]of Mattathias, of Amos, of Nahum,
of Esli, of Naggai,

26of Maath, of Mattathias, of Semei,
of Joseph, of Judah,
27of Joannes, of Rhesa, of Zerubbabel, of Shealtiel, of Neri,
28of Melchi, of Addi, of Cosam, of
Elmodam, of Er,
29of Joses, of Eliezer, of Jorim, of
Matthat, of Levi,
30of Simeon, of Judah, of Joseph, of
Jonan, of Eliakim,
31of Meleas, of Menna, of Mattatha,
of Nathan, of David,
32of Jesse, of Obed, of Boaz, of
Salmon, of Naasson,
33of Aminadab, of Aram, of Esrom,
of Perez, of Judah,
34of Jacob, of Isaac, of Abraham, of
Terah, of Nahor,
35of Serug, of Ragau, of Peleg, of
Eber, of Sala,
36of Cainan, of Arphaxad, of Shem,
of Noah, of Lamech,
37of Methusaleh, of Enoch, of Jared,
of Mahalalel, of Cainan,
38of Enosh, of Seth, of Adam, of God.

4 Jesus then, full of the Holy Spirit,
returned from Jordan and was led
by the Spirit into the wilderness,
2being tempted by the Devil for forty
days. And in those days, He ate nothing. And after those days were over, He
was hungry.
3And the Devil said to Him, "If you
are the Son of God, speak to this stone
that it becomes bread."
4And Jesus answered him saying, "It
is written, 'Man shall not live by bread
alone, but by every word of God.'"
5And the Devil took Him up into a
high mountain and showed him all the
kingdoms of the inhabited world in a
moment.
6And the Devil said to Him, "I will
give You all this authority and the
splendor of them, for it has been handed over to me, and I give it to anyone I
please.
7Therefore, if you worship me, all
these things will be Yours."
8Jesus answered him and said, "Get
behind Me, Satan! For it is written,
'You shall worship the Lord your God,
and Him only shall you serve.'"
9And he led Him to Jerusalem, and
set Him on a pinnacle of the temple,
and said to Him, "If You are the Son of
God, cast Yourself down from here.
10For it is written, 'He shall give His
angels charge over you, to keep you,'
11and, 'With their hands they shall
hold you up, so that you do not strike
your foot against a stone.'"
12Jesus answered and said to him, "It
is said, 'You shall not tempt the Lord
your God.'"
13And all of the temptations of the
Devil being finished, he withdrew from
Him for a time.
14And Jesus returned in the power of
the Spirit into Galilee, and there went
out news concerning Him throughout
all the surrounding country.
15And He taught in their synagogues,
being glorified by all.
16And He came to Nazareth, where
He was brought up, and according to
His custom, He went into the synagogue on the Sabbath day and stood up
to read.
17And there was given to Him the
book of the prophet Isaiah. And when
He had rolled open the book, He found
the place where it was written:
18"The Spirit of the Lord is upon me,
because He has anointed me to proclaim good news to the poor. He has
sent me to heal the shattered hearts, to
announce freedom to the captives, re-
covery of sight to the blind, to release

the oppressed,

19 and to proclaim the acceptable year of the Lord."

20 And He rolled up the book, and gave it again to the minister, and sat down. And the eyes of all that were in the synagogue were fastened on Him.

21 And He began to say to them, "Today this scripture is fulfilled in your ears."

22 And everyone witnessed this and wondered at the gracious words that came out of His mouth, and said, "Isn't this Joseph's son?"

23 And He said to them, "You may very well say to me this parable: 'Physician, heal yourself. Whatever we have heard that You did in Capernaum, do also here in Your own country.'"

24 And he said, "With certainty I tell you, no prophet is accepted in his own country.

25 But I tell you of a truth, many widows were in Israel in the days of Elijah, when the heavens were shut up for three years and six months, when there was a great famine upon all the land.

26 And Elijah was not sent to any of them except to Sarepta of Sidonia, to a widow woman.

27 And many lepers were in Israel in the time of Elisha the prophet. And yet, none of them were healed except Naaman the Syrian."

28 And hearing these things, everyone in the synagogue was filled with indignation.

29 And they got up and threw Him out of the city and led Him to the edge of the mountain upon which their city was built, to throw Him down headfirst.

30 But He, passing through their midst, went away.

31 And He went down to Capernaum, a city of Galilee, and there taught them on the sabbaths.

32 And they were amazed at His doctrine, for His word was with authority.

33 And in the synagogue there was a man who had an unclean demon spirit. And He cried with a loud voice,

34 saying, "Ah! What do You have to do with us, Jesus of Nazareth? Have You come to destroy us? I know who You are: the Holy One of God!"

35 And Jesus rebuked him, saying, "Shut up, and come out of him!" And the demon threw him into the midst, coming out of him, and did not hurt him.

36 And there came an awe upon them, and they spoke among themselves, saying, "What manner of word is this? For with authority and power He commands the unclean spirits, and they come out!"

37 And a rumor about Him went out into every place of the surrounding country.

38 And He rose up and came out of the synagogue and He entered into Simon's house. Simon's mother-in-law was oppressed with a severe fever, and they interceded to Him for her.

39 And He stood over her and He rebuked the fever, and it left her. And immediately, she got up quickly and served them.

40 Now as the sun was going down, everyone who had those sick with various diseases brought them to Him. And He laid His hands on every one of them and healed them.

41 And also demons went out of many of them, crying out, saying, "You are the Christ, the Son of God!" And He rebuked them and did not allow them to speak, for they knew that He was the Christ.

42Now that the sun had risen, He left
and went into a desert place. And the
crowds sought Him out and came to
Him and restrained Him, so that He
would not leave them.
43But He said to them, “I must also
go to other cities to announce the glad
tidings of the Kingdom of God. It was
for this reason that I was sent.”
44And He preached in the synagogues of Galilee.

5 It came to pass, as the crowd
pressed upon Him to hear the word
of God, that He was standing by the
lake of Gennesaret.
2And He saw two boats positioned by
the lake, but the fishermen were gone
out of them and were washing their
nets.
3And He entered into one of the
boats, which was Simon’s, and asked
him to thrust out from the land a little.
And He sat down and taught the crowd
from the boat.
4When He had finished speaking, He
said to Simon, “Launch out into the
deep and let down your nets for a
catch.”
5And Simon answered and said to
Him, “Rabbi, we have labored all night
and have taken nothing. Nevertheless,
at Your word I will let down the net.”
6And when they had done so, they
enclosed a great multitude of fish, and
their net was breaking.
7And they beckoned to their partners, who were in another boat, that
they should come and help them. And
they came and filled both the boats, so
that they were sinking.
8When Simon Peter saw it, he fell
down at Jesus’ knees, saying, “Lord,
depart from me, for I am a sinful man.”
9For awe had laid hold on him and
those with him at the catch of fish
which they had taken.
10And it was the same also for James
and John, the sons of Zebedee, who
were partners with Simon. And Jesus
said to Simon, “Fear not, for from now
on you will catch men.”
11And they brought the boats to land,
and they left everything to follow Him.
12Now, while He was in one of the
cities, there came a man full of leprosy.
And when he saw Jesus, he fell on his
face and pleaded with Him, saying,
“Lord, if You are willing, You can make
me clean.”
13And He reached out His hand and
touched him, saying, “I will. Be made
clean.” And immediately the leprosy
departed from him.
14And He instructed him that he
should tell no man, “But go and show
yourself to the priest and offer for your
cleansing, as Moses commanded, as a
witness to them.”
15But so much the more there went
out a report regarding Him. And great
crowds came together to hear and to be
healed of their infirmities by Him.
16But He would withdraw into the
wilderness and pray.
17And while He was teaching, on one
of the days, there were Pharisees and
doctors of law sitting by, who had come
out of every village of Galilee, Judea,
and Jerusalem. And the power of the
Lord was there to heal them.
18And, behold, men were carrying on
a cot a man who was paralyzed. And
they looked for a place to bring him in
to lay before Him.
19And when they could not find a
way to bring him in, because of the
crowd, they went up on the roof of the
house and lowered his cot down
through the tile into the midst before

Jesus.

20 And seeing their faith, He said unto him, "Man, your sins have been forgiven."

21 And the Scribes and Pharisees began to reason, saying, "Who is this that speaks blasphemies? Who can forgive sins but God alone?"

22 But Jesus, knowing their thoughts, responded and said to them, "Why are you reasoning in your hearts?

23 Which is easier to say, 'Your sins are forgiven,' or to say, 'Arise and walk'?

24 But that you may know that the Son of Man has power on Earth to forgive sins," He said to the one paralyzed, "I tell you: arise, take up your cot, and go to your house."

25 And immediately he stood up before them, and took up that which he was laying on, and departed to his house, glorifying God.

26 And they were all ecstatic, and glorified God, and were filled with fear, saying, "We have seen strange things today!"

27 And after that, He went out and saw a tax collector named Levi sitting at the tax office, and said to him, "Follow Me."

28 And leaving everything, he got up and followed Him.

29 And Levi made for Him a great feast in his house. And there was a great company of tax collectors and of others that were at the table.

30 And the Scribes and Pharisees murmured against His disciples, saying, "Why do you eat and drink with tax collectors and sinners?"

31 And Jesus answered them and said, "Those who are healthy do not need a physician, but those who are sick.

32 I have not come to call the righteous, but sinners, to repentance."

33 Then they said to Him, "Why do the disciples of John fast often and make supplication, and the disciples of the Pharisees also, but yours eat and drink?"

34 And He said unto them, "Can you make the sons of the bridechamber fast as long as the Bridegroom is with them?

35 But the days will come when the Bridegroom shall be taken away from them, then shall they fast in those days."

36 Then He spoke again to them in a parable, "No one puts a new piece of garment on an old, for if they do, the new will tear the old, for the piece that is new will not agree.

37 And no one puts new wine into old skins, for if you do, the new wine will burst the skins, and it will run out and the skin will be destroyed.

38 But new wine is put into new skins, and both are preserved.

39 And no one that drinks old wine immediately desires new, for he says, 'The old is better.'"

6 It came about on the next Sabbath, while He was passing through the grain fields, that His disciples plucked the ears of grain and were eating, rubbing them in their hands.

2 But some of the Pharisees said to them, "Why are you doing that which is not lawful to do on the Sabbaths?"

3 And Jesus replied to them and said, "Have you not read what David did when he was hungry, and those who were with him?

4 How he went into the house of God and took the bread of the presence and ate, and gave to those who were with him, which was not lawful to eat except for the priests only?"

5 And He said to them, "The Son of
Man is Lord of the Sabbath."
6 And it came about on another Sabbath that He again went into a synagogue and taught. And there was a
man whose right hand was paralyzed.
7 And the Scribes and Pharisees
watched Him to see whether He would
heal on the Sabbath, that they might
find an accusation against Him.
8 But He knew their thoughts and said
to the man who had the paralyzed
hand, "Arise and stand in the midst."
And he got up and stood.
9 Then Jesus said to them, "I have a
question for you: is it lawful to do good
or to do evil on the Sabbath, to save life
or destroy it?"
10 And looking around at them all, He
said to the man, "Stretch out your
hand." And he did so. And it was
restored and made whole like the other.
11 But they were filled with madness
and consulted with one another what
they might do to Jesus.
12 And it came about in those days
that He went out into a mountain to
pray, and spent the night in prayer to
God.
13 And when the day had come, He
called His disciples and He chose from
them twelve, whom He also called
apostles:
14 Simon, whom He named Peter, and
Andrew his brother, James and John,
Philip and Bartholomew,
15 Matthew and Thomas, James the
son of Alphaeus, and Simon called
Zealot, and
16 Judas of James, and Judas Iscariote,
who also became a betrayer.
17 And He came down with them and
stood on a level place, and a crowd of
His disciples and a great multitude of
people from all of Judea and Jerusalem,
and the sea coasts of Tyre and Sidon,
who came to hear Him and to be
healed of their diseases.
18 And those tormented by unclean
spirits were also healed.
19 And the whole crowd was trying to
touch Him, because power came out of
Him and healed them all.
20 And He lifted up His eyes upon the
disciples and said, "Blessed are the
poor, for yours is the Kingdom of God.
21 Blessed are the hungry, for you
shall be filled. Blessed are you who
weep, for you shall laugh.
22 Blessed are you when men shall
hate you, and shall cut you off and reproach you, and cast out your name as
wicked, because of the Son of Man.
23 Rejoice on that day, and leap for
joy– for behold, your reward is great in
Heaven! After this manner did their
fathers to the prophets.
24 But woe to you that are rich, for
you are receiving your comfort.
25 Woe to you who have been filled,
for you shall hunger. Woe to you who
laugh now, for you shall mourn and
weep.
26 Woe to you when all men speak
well of you, for so did their fathers to
the false prophets.
27 But I say to you who hear: Love
your enemies, do well to them who
hate you,
28 bless those who curse you, and pray
for those who spitefully use you.
29 To him who strikes you on the
cheek, also offer the other. And to him
who takes away your coat, also do not
hold back your shirt.
30 Give to everyone that asks of you.
And the one who takes what is yours,
don't ask for it back.
31 And as you desire men should do
to you, do also to them likewise.

32 If you love those who love you,
what praise is it to you? For sinners
love those who love them.
33 And if you do right to them that do
right to you, what praise is it to you?
For sinners do the same.
34 And if you lend to those of whom
you expect to receive, what praise is it
to you? For sinners lend to sinners, that
they may receive the equivalent.
35 But you shall love your enemies, do
right and lend, expecting nothing
again. And your reward shall be great,
and you shall be the sons of the Highest, for He is kind to the unthankful
and the wicked.
36 Therefore be compassionate, as also
your Father is compassionate.
37 And do not judge, and you shall
not be judged. Do not condemn, and
you shall not be condemned. Pardon,
and you shall be pardoned.
38 Give, and good measure will be
given to you– pressed down, shaken
together and running over, they will
give into your bosom. For the same
measure that you measure will be measured back to you."
39 And He spoke a parable to them,
"Can the blind lead the blind? Will
they not both fall into a ditch?
40 The disciple is not above his
teacher, but everyone shall be perfected
as his teacher.
41 But why do you look at the mote in
your brother's eye, but do not perceive
the beam that is in your own eye?
42 Or how can you say to your brother, 'Brother let me pull the mote out
that is in your eye,' when you do not
perceive the beam that is in your own
eye? Hypocrite! Cast the beam out of
your own eye first, then you will see
clearly to pull out the mote out of your
brother's eye.
43 For a good tree does not bring forth
evil fruit, nor does an evil tree bring
forth good fruit.
44 For every tree is known by its fruit.
For no one gathers figs from thorns,
nor gathers grapes from a thornbush.
45 The good man out of the good treasure of his heart brings forth that
which is good, and the wicked man out
of the wicked treasure of his heart
brings forth that which is wicked– for
out of the abundance of the heart his
mouth speaks.
46 And why do you call Me, 'Lord,
Lord,' but do not do what I say?
47 Whoever comes to Me and hears
My words and does them, I will show
you to whom he is like:
48 He is like a man who built a house,
and dug deep, and laid the foundation
on a rock. And the waters rose, and the
streams burst against the house, but
could not move it, for it was established
upon the rock.
49 But he that hears and does nothing
is like a man that built a house on the
earth without a foundation, on which
the stream burst against, and the house
collapsed, and the fall of that house was
great."

7 When He had completed all of His
words in the ears of the people, He
entered into Capernaum.
2 Now there was a centurion's servant,
who was precious to him, who was sick
and ready to die.
3 And having heard about Jesus, he
sent the elders of the Jews to Him,
earnestly requesting Him to come save
his servant.
4 And they came to Jesus and encouraged Him earnestly, saying, "He is worthy that You should do this for him,
5 for he loves our nation and has built

us a synagogue."

6 And Jesus went with them. And when He was not far from the house, the centurion sent friends to Him, saying to Him, "Lord, trouble not Yourself, for I am not worthy that You should enter under my roof.

7 Neither did I count myself worthy to come to You. But say a word, and my servant shall be healed.

8 For I also am a man set under authority, having under myself soldiers. And I say to one, 'Go,' and he goes, and to another, 'Come,' and he comes, and to my servant, 'Do this,' and he does it."

9 When Jesus heard this, He was amazed by him, and turning to the crowd following Him, said, "I have not found such great faith in Israel!"

10 And those that were sent, returning to the house, found the sick servant healthy.

11 And it was after that, on the next day, that He went into a city called Nain, and many of His disciples went with Him, along with a great crowd.

12 But when He came near to the city gate, behold, there was a dead man carried out, who was the only son of his mother, and she was a widow. And a considerable crowd from the city was with her.

13 And when the Lord saw her, He had compassion on her and said to her, "Do not weep."

14 And He went and touched the coffin, and they that bore him stood still. And He said, "Young man, I say to you: arise."

15 And he that was dead sat up and began to speak. And He gave him to his mother.

16 And they were all seized by fear, and they glorified God, saying, "A great prophet has risen up among us!" and, "God has visited His people!"

17 And this report of Him went throughout all Judah and in all the surrounding country.

18 And the disciples of John reported all these things to him.

19 And, calling for two of his disciples, John sent them to Jesus, saying, "Are You the coming One, or do we wait for another?"

20 And coming to Him, the men said, "John the Baptizer sent us to You to ask You: 'Are You the coming One, or do we wait for another?'"

21 And right at that time, He healed many from diseases, and plagues, and evil spirits, and had given sight to many that were blind.

22 And Jesus answered, saying, "Go tell John what you see and what you hear. Because the blind receive their sight, the crippled walk, lepers are cleansed, the deaf hear, the dead are raised up, and the poor have the gospel preached to them.

23 And blessed is the one who is not offended in Me."

24 And the messengers of John having gone, He began to speak to the crowd about John, "What did you go out into the wilderness to look at? A reed being shaken by the wind?

25 Rather, what did you go out to see? A man in soft apparel? Look, those in splendid apparel and living in luxury are in royal palaces.

26 But what did you go out to see? A prophet? Yes, I say to you: an extraordinary prophet.

27 This is he concerning whom it was written, 'Behold, I am sending My messenger before You, who will prepare Your way before You.'

28 Also, I tell you, there is no greater prophet of those born among women

than John the Baptizer, yet the lesser one in the Kingdom of God is greater than he is."

29 And all the people who heard, and the tax collectors, declared God righteous, having been baptized by John's baptism.

30 But the Pharisees and the lawyers had rejected God's plan for them, refusing to be baptized by him.

31 And the Lord said, "To what then will I compare the men of this generation? And what are they like?

32 They are like children sitting in the marketplace, calling to each other and saying, 'We played the flute for you, but you did not dance. We sang a mournful song, but you did not weep.'

33 For John the Baptizer came neither eating bread nor drinking wine, and you say, 'He has a demon.'

34 The Son of Man came eating and drinking, and you say, 'Behold, a glutton and a drunkard, a friend of tax collectors and sinners.'

35 But wisdom is justified by all her children."

36 And one of the Pharisees asked Him to eat with him. And He came into the house of the Pharisee and reclined to eat.

37 And behold, in the city, a woman who was a sinner, having learned that He was dining in the house of the Pharisee, brought an alabaster box of ointment,

38 and standing behind His feet, weeping, began to bathe His feet with her tears and dry them with her hair, and continued to kiss His feet and anoint them with oil.

39 And seeing this, the Pharisee who invited Him said to himself, "If this were a prophet, He would know what sort of woman this is who touches Him, for she is a sinner."

40 And Jesus answered, saying to him, "Simon, I have something to say to you." And he said, "Speak, Teacher."

41 "A certain creditor had two debtors: one owed five hundred denarii, and the other five.

42 But when they could not pay, He canceled both of their debts. Now, which one will love him the most?"

43 And Simon replied, saying, "I suppose the one for whom He canceled the greater debt." And He said, "You have judged rightly."

44 And turning toward the woman, he said to Simon, "See this woman? I entered your house. You did not give me water for My feet, but she has bathed My feet with her tears and dried them with her hair.

45 You gave Me no kiss, but she, from my coming in, has not stopped kissing My feet.

46 You did not anoint My head with oil, but she anointed My feet with perfume.

47 For this reason, I tell you, her sins, which are many, are forgiven, because she has shown great love. But the one who is forgiven little loves little."

48 Then He said to her, "Your sins are forgiven."

49 And those reclining with Him began to say within themselves, "Who is this Who even forgives sin?"

50 But He said to the woman, "Your faith has saved you– go in peace."

8 And it came to pass, afterwards, He went through cities and villages, proclaiming and bringing the good news of the Kingdom of God. And the twelve were with Him,

2 and some of the women who had been cured of evil spirits and diseases:

Mary, called Magdalene, from whom seven demons went out,

3 also Joanna, the wife of Chuza, Herod's steward, and Susanna, and many others, who provided for Him from their resources.

4 When a great crowd gathered, and those from the city came to Him, He spoke through a parable:

5 "A sower went out to sow his seed. And as he sowed, some fell upon the road and were trampled, and the birds of heaven devoured it.

6 And some fell upon the rock, and as it grew, it withered, because it did not have moisture.

7 And some fell in the midst of thorns, and the thorns grew and choked it.

8 And some fell into the good ground and produced fruit, a hundredfold." Saying these things, He cried out, "He who has ears to hear, listen!"

9 Then His disciples asked Him, saying, "What does this parable mean?"

10 And He said, "To you it has been given to know the mysteries of the Kingdom of God, but to others by parables, that seeing they shall not see, and hearing they shall not understand.

11 This is the parable: the seed is the Word of God.

12 And those on the road are those who hear, then the Devil comes and takes away the word from their heart, unless having believed they should be saved.

13 And those upon the rocks, when they hear, receive the word with joy. But these have no root, who believe for a while, but in time of trial fall away.

14 And those which fell among thorns are those that hear, and along the way the cares and wealth and pleasures of this life choke it, and no fruit matures.

15 But those in the good ground are those who hear the word, hold it fast in an honorable and good heart, and bring forth fruit by persistence.

16 For no one lights a candle and covers it under a vessel, nor puts it under the table, but sets it on a candlestick, that they who enter may see the light.

17 For nothing is hidden which shall not be manifested, nor anything secret that shall not be known and come to light.

18 Take heed therefore how you hear. For whoever has, to him shall it be given. And whoever does not have, from him shall be taken even that which he seems to have."

19 Then His mother and His brethren came to Him, and couldn't get to Him because of the crowd.

20 And it was told to Him, saying, "Your mother and your brothers are standing outside, desiring to see You."

21 But He, replying, said to them, "My mother and My brothers are those who hear the Word of God and do it."

22 And it took place on a certain day that He went into a boat, and His disciples, and He said to them, "Let's go over to the other side of the lake." And they launched out.

23 And as they sailed, He fell asleep. And a wind storm came up on the lake, and they were being flooded, and were in danger.

24 And they went to Him and woke Him up, saying, "Master, Master, we are perishing!" Then He got up, rebuked the wind and the raging of the water, and they ceased. And there was a calm.

25 And He said to them, "Where is your faith?" And being afraid, they were amazed, saying to one another, "Who is this that commands even the wind and the waves, and they obey

Him?"

26And they sailed to the region of the Gadarenes, which is opposite Galilee.

27And having gone out upon the land, there was a man who met him from the city, who had demons for a long time, and who wore no clothes, neither lived in a house, but in the tombs.

28When he saw Jesus, he cried out and fell down before Him, and said with a loud voice, "What have I to do with You, Jesus, the Son of the Most High God? I plead with You, don't torment me!"

29For He was commanding the unclean spirit to come out of the man. For many times it would seize him while he was being kept bound with chains and shackles, and he would break the bonds and be driven by the demons into the wilderness.

30And Jesus asked him, saying, "What is your name?" And he said, "Legion," because many demons had entered into him.

31And he appealed to Him that He would not command them to go out into the abyss.

32Now there was a herd of many swine feeding on a hill. And they appealed to Him that He would allow them to enter into them. And He allowed them.

33Then the demons went out of the man and entered into the swine. And the herd rushed down the cliff into the lake and drowned.

34When those who fed them saw what happened, they took off and fled into the city and into the country, announcing what had taken place.

35And they came out to see what had taken place, and came to Jesus, and found the man out of whom the demons had gone out clothed and in his right mind, sitting at the feet of Jesus. And they were afraid.

36For those who had seen it also related to them by what means he that was possessed of the demons was made whole.

37And all the multitude of the country of the Gadarenes asked Him to depart from them, for they were taken with great fear. And He got into the boat and returned.

38Then the man, out of whom the demons departed, begged Him to go along with Him. But Jesus sent him away, saying,

39"Go home again and show all that God has done for you." And he went his way and preached throughout all the city what Jesus had done for him.

40Now it followed, that when Jesus returned, that the crowd welcomed Him, for they were all looking for Him.

41And behold, there came a man named Jairus– He was a ruler of the synagogue– and he fell down at Jesus's feet and besought Him that He would come to his house,

42because he had an only daughter, who was about twelve years of age, and she was dying. And as He went, the crowds pressed against Him.

43And a woman having an issue of blood for twelve years, who had spent all her money on physicians, neither could anyone cure her,

44came behind Him and touched the hem of His garment. And immediately her issue of blood stopped.

45And Jesus said, "Who touched Me?" But everyone denied it. Peter, and those that were with Him, said, "Master, the crowds thrust against You and press, and You say, 'Who touched Me?'"

46And Jesus said, "Somebody touched

Me, for I know power went out of Me."

47When the woman saw that she was not hidden, she came trembling and fell at His feet and told Him why she had touched Him, and declared to Him before all of the people how that she was instantly healed.

48And He said to her, "Daughter, be blessed, your faith has made you whole. Go in peace."

49While He was still speaking, there came one from the ruler of the synagogue's house, who said to him, "Your daughter is dead, don't trouble the Teacher."

50When Jesus heard that, He responded to the father, saying, "Fear not, only believe, and she shall be made whole."

51And when He came to the house, He did not allow anyone to go in except Peter, James, and John, and the father and mother of the child.

52Now they were all bewailing for her, but He said, "Do not weep, she is not dead, but is sleeping."

53And they laughed at Him, knowing she was dead.

54But He put them all out and took hold of her and cried out, saying, "Child, arise."

55And her spirit came into her again, and she immediately got up. And He directed them to give her something to eat.

56And her parents were ecstatic, But He charged them that they should tell no one what had happened.

9 Then He called the twelve together and gave them power and authority over all demons and to heal diseases.

2And He sent them to preach the Kingdom of God and to cure the sick.

3And He said to them, "Take nothing for your journey: neither staff, nor traveler's bag, nor bread, nor money, nor have two coats.

4And whatever house you enter into: there remain, and from there depart.

5And whoever will not receive you, when you go out of that city, shake off the very dust from your feet for a testimony against them."

6And they went out and went through the towns, preaching the gospel and healing everywhere.

7And Herod the Tetrarch heard of all that was done by Him, and was greatly perplexed, because it was said of some that John was risen again from the dead,

8also, by some, that Elijah had appeared, and also, by others, that one of the old prophets was risen again.

9And Herod said, "I have beheaded John. But who is this of Whom I hear such things?" And he desired to see Him.

10And the apostles returned and told Him what things they had done. And He took them and went aside into a solitary place near to a city called Bethsaida.

11And the crowds knew of it, and followed Him. And He received them and spoke unto them of the Kingdom of God, and He healed those in need of healing.

12And when the day began to wear away, then came the twelve and said to Him, "Send the people away, that they may go into the towns and villages in the area and lodge and find provision, for we are here in a solitary place."

13But He said to them, "You give them food." And they said, "We have no more, but five loaves and two fish, unless we should go and buy food for

all these people."
14And they were about five thousand
men. And He said to his disciples,
"Have them sit down in groups of fifty."
15And they did so, and made them all
sit down.
16And he took the five loaves and the
two fish and looked up to Heaven and
blessed them, and broke, and gave to
the disciples to set before the crowd.
17And they ate and were all satisfied.
And there was taken up of that which
remained twelve baskets full of broken
fragments.
18And it took place that, as He was
alone praying, His disciples were with
Him. And He asked them, saying,
"Who do the crowds say that I am?"
19They answered and said, "John the
Baptizer, others Elijah, and others that
one of the old prophets is risen again."
20Then He said to them, "But who do
you say that I am?" Peter answered and
said, "You are the Christ of God."
21And He warned and commanded
them that they should tell no one,
22saying, "It is necessary for the Son
of Man to suffer many things, and be
rejected by the elders and the high
priests and Scribes, and be put to
death, and the third day rise again."
23And He said to them all, "If anyone
will come and follow Me, he must deny
himself and take up his cross daily, and
follow Me.
24For whoever desires to save his life
will destroy it, but whoever shall lose
his life because of Me shall save it.
25For what advantage is it if a man
were to win the whole world, if he destroys or suffers the loss of himself?
26For whoever is ashamed of Me and
of My words, of him shall the Son of
Man be ashamed when He comes in
His own glory and of the Father and of
the holy angels.
27But I tell you the truth, there are
some of those standing here who shall
not taste death until they see the Kingdom of God."
28And it followed, about eight days
after He spoke these things, that He
took Peter, John, and James, and went
up into a mountain to pray.
29And it took place that, as He
prayed, the appearance of His face
changed and His garment began to
shine bright.
30And behold, two men talked with
Him, who were Moses and Elijah,
31who, appearing in glory, spoke of
His departure, which He would accomplish at Jerusalem."
32But Peter and those with Him were
oppressed with sleep. And when they
woke up, they saw His glory, and two
men standing with Him.
33And it happened, as they parted
from Him, Peter said to Jesus, "Master,
it is good for us to be here. Let us make
three tabernacles: one for You, one for
Moses, and one for Elijah," for they did
not know what to say.
34But as he was saying these things, a
cloud came and overshadowed them,
and they were afraid as they entered
into the cloud.
35And there came a voice out of the
cloud, saying, "This is My dear Son,
hear Him."
36And as soon as the voice came, Jesus was found alone. And they were
silent and told no one in those days
anything about what they had seen.
37And it took place on the next day,
as they came down from the mountain,
a great crowd met Him.
38And behold a man of the crowd
cried out, saying, "Teacher, I plead with
You, look upon my son, for he is my

only child!

39 And a spirit takes him, and suddenly he cries out, and it throws him into convulsions, foaming, and with difficulty departs from him, bruising him.

40 And I begged your disciples to cast him out, and they could not!"

41 Jesus answered and said, "O faithless generation, and perverted, how long shall I be with you and bear with you? Bring your son here."

42 And as he was still coming near, the demon threw him down and threw him into convulsions. And Jesus rebuked the unclean spirit, and healed the child, and gave him back to his father.

43 And they were all overwhelmed at the majesty of God. While they all wondered at all the things which He did, Jesus said to His disciples,

44 "Let these words sink down into your ears, for the Son of Man is about to be delivered into the hands of men."

45 But they did not understand the word, for it was veiled from them, that they should not perceive it. And they were afraid to ask Him about this word.

46 Then there came up a discussion among them: who might be the greatest.

47 When Jesus perceived the thoughts of their hearts, He took a child and set it by Him.

48 And said to them, "Whoever receives this child in My name receives Me, and whoever receives Me receives Him that sent Me. For he that is least among you all, the same shall be great."

49 And John replied and said, "Master, we saw one casting out demons in Your name and we forbade him, because he did not follow with us."

50 And Jesus said unto him, "You should not forbid him, for he that is not against us is with us."

51 And it followed, when the time came that He should be received up, that He firmly set His face to go to Jerusalem.

52 And He sent messengers before His face. And traveling, they entered into a village of the Samaritans, so as to make ready for Him.

53 And they would not receive Him, because His face was going toward Jerusalem.

54 When His disciples James and John saw it, they said, "Lord, do You want us to command that fire come down from Heaven and consume them, even as Elijah did?"

55 But Jesus turned and rebuked them, saying, "You do not know what spirit you are of!

56 The Son of Man has not come to destroy men's lives, but to save them!" And they went to another village.

57 And it happened, as He went in the way, someone said to Him, "Lord, I will follow You wherever You go."

58 But Jesus said to him, "Foxes have holes and the birds of the air have nests, but the Son of Man has nowhere to lay His head."

59 And He said to another, "Follow Me." But he said, "Lord, allow me first to go and bury my father."

60 Then Jesus said to him, "Let the dead bury their dead, but you go and preach the Kingdom of God."

61 And another also said, "I will follow You, Lord, but let me bid them farewell who are at my house."

62 But Jesus said to him, "No one that puts his hand to the plow and looks back is fit for the Kingdom of God."

10 After these things, the Lord appointed seventy others also, and sent them out two by two before Him into every city and place where He was about to go.

2And He said to them, "The harvest is great, but the laborers are few. Pray therefore that the Lord of the harvest send forth laborers into His harvest.

3Go. Behold, I send you out as lambs among wolves.

4Carry no purse, nor provision bag, nor sandals, and greet no one on the way.

5Into whatever house you enter, first say, 'Peace be to this house.'

6And if the son of peace is there, your peace shall rest upon it, but if not, it shall return to you again.

7Then in the same house remain, eating and drinking that which is supplied by them, for a laborer is worthy of his wages. Go not from house to house.

8And into whatever city you enter and they receive you, eat the things set before you.

9And heal the sick that are in it, and say to them, 'The Kingdom of God has come near to you.'

10But into whatever city you shall enter, and they do not receive you, go out into the streets and say,

11-Even the dust which has stuck to us out of this city, we wipe off against you! Furthermore, know this: that the Kingdom of God has come near to you.'

12But I say to you that it shall be more bearable on that day for Sodom than for that city!

13Woe be to you, Chorazin! Woe to you, Bethsaida! For if the miracles that were done in you had taken place in Tyre and Sidon, they would have repented long ago, sitting in sackcloth and ashes!

14Still it will be more bearable for Tyre and Sidon at the judgment than for you!

15And you Capernaum, who are exalted to Heaven, shall be thrust down to Hell!

16He that hears you, hears Me, and he that rejects you, rejects Me, and he that rejects Me, rejects Him that sent Me."

17And the seventy returned with joy, saying, "Lord, even the demons are subject to us in Your name."

18And He said unto them, "I saw Satan as lightning falling out of Heaven.

19See, I have given you the authority to tread on snakes and scorpions and over every power of the enemy, and absolutely nothing can harm you.

20Only do not rejoice in that the spirits are subject to you, but rejoice more in that your names are written in Heaven."

21In that same hour Jesus rejoiced in the Spirit and said, "I praise You, Father, Lord of Heaven and Earth, that You have hidden these things from the wise and prudent and have revealed them to the infants. For yes, Father, this was well pleasing in Your sight."

22And turning to His disciples, He said, "All things are given to Me by My Father. And no man knows Who the Son is but the Father, neither Who the Father is except the Son, and he to whom the Son will reveal Him."

23And having turned to His own disciples, he said, "Blessed are the eyes that see what you see.

24For I tell you that many prophets and kings have desired to see what you see, but did not, and to hear what you have heard, but did not hear."

25And behold, there stood a lawyer and tempting Him, saying, "Teacher, what shall I do to inherit eternal life?"

26He said to him, "What is written in

the Law? How do you read it?"
27And He answered and said, "You
shall love the Lord your God with all of
your heart, and with all of your soul,
and with all of your strength, and with
all of your mind, and your neighbor as
yourself."
28And He said to him, "You have answered correctly. Do this and you shall
live."
29But he, desiring to justify himself,
said to Jesus, "Who then is my neighbor?"
30Jesus replied and said, "There was a
man who went down from Jerusalem
to Jericho, and fell into the hands of
thieves, who stripped him and inflicted
wounds on him, and went away, leaving him half-dead.
31But then, by chance, one of the
Priests went on the road and saw him,
and passed by on the opposite side.
32Likewise also, when a Levite came
to the same place and he saw him, he
passed by on the opposite side.
33But one of the Samaritans, traveling, came to him and, having seen him,
was moved with compassion.
34And went to him and bound up his
wounds and poured in oil and wine,
and put him on his own beast, and
brought him to an inn and took care of
him.
35And on the next day, when he departed, he took out two denarii, gave
them to the innkeeper, and said to him,
'Take care of him. And whatever you
spend more, when I come again, I will
repay you.'
36Now, to him that fell among the
bandits, which of these three does it
seem to you was a neighbor?"
37And he said, "The one who showed
compassion towards him." Therefore,
Jesus said to him, "Go and do likewise."
38Now it happened, that as they went
on, He entered into one of the villages.
And a woman named Martha welcomed Him into her house.
39And this woman had a sister called
Mary, who sat at Jesus's feet and listened to His message.
40And Martha was overburdened
with a lot of serving. And coming up,
she said, "Lord, don't You care that my
sister has left me alone to serve? Therefore speak to her to help me."
41And Jesus replied and said to her,
"Martha, Martha, you care for and
worry about too many things
42when one thing is necessary. Mary
has chosen the good part, which shall
not be taken away from her."

11 And it took place while He was
in one place praying, when He
finished, one of His disciples said to
Him, "Lord, teach us to pray, as also
John taught his disciples."
2And He said to them, "When you
pray, say, 'Our Father, Who is in Heav-
en, sanctified is Your name. Let Your
kingdom come. Let Your will be done,
even on the earth as it is in heaven.
3Give us our daily bread today.
4And forgive us our sins, for we also
ourselves forgive everyone that trespasses against us. And lead us not into
temptation, but deliver us from evil.'"
5And He said to them, "Who among
you shall have a friend and shall go to
him at midnight and say to him,
'Friend, lend me three loaves,
6for a friend of mine has come to me
from a journey, and I have nothing to
set before him.'
7And he should answer and say, 'Do
not trouble me, because the door is already shut and my children are with
me in bed, I cannot get up and give it

to you.'
8I tell you, even though he would not
get up to give because he was a friend,
but because of his shameless insistence,
he wakes up to give him whatever he
needs.
9And I tell you to ask, and it will be
given to you. Seek, and you shall find.
Knock, and it shall be opened unto
you.
10For everyone that asks, receives,
and he that seeks, finds, and to him
that knocks, it will be opened.
11Now which of you, who is a father,
shall have a son who asks for bread–
would you give him a stone? Also, if he
asks for fish, instead of a fish will he
give him a serpent?
12Or also, if he asks for an egg, will he
give him a scorpion?
13If you then who are evil know how
to give good gifts to your children, how
much more will the heavenly Father
give the Holy Spirit to those who ask
Him?"
14And He was casting out a demon
that was deaf and mute. And it followed, when the demon was gone out,
the mute spoke, and the crowds were
amazed.
15But some of them said, "He casts
out demons by the power of Beelzebub,
the prince of demons."
16And others tempted Him, seeking a
sign from Heaven.
17But He knew their thoughts, and
said to them, "Every kingdom divided
against itself is made desolate, and a
house against a house falls.
18So also if Satan is divided against
himself, how shall his kingdom stand?
Because you say I cast out demons by
Beelzebub.
19And if I by Beelzebub cast out
demons, by whom do your sons cast
them out? Therefore, they shall be your
judges.
20But if I by the finger of God cast
out demons, know then the Kingdom
of God is come upon you.
21When a strong man is armed, he
keeps his own dwelling, and his goods
are secure.
22But when a stronger one than he
comes and overcomes him, he takes
from him his armor, in which he trusted, and divides his goods.
23He that is not with Me is against
Me. And he that gathers not with me,
scatters.
24When the unclean spirit is gone out
of a man, he walks through waterless
places seeking rest. And finding none,
he says, 'I will return to my house,
where I came out.'
25And when he comes, he finds it
swept and decorated.
26Then he goes and takes seven other
spirits more wicked than himself, and
they enter in and dwell there, and the
last state of that man is worse than the
first."
27And it happened that, as He spoke
those things, there was a woman from
the crowd who lifted up her voice and
said to Him, "Blessed is the womb that
carried you and the breast that nursed
you!"
28But He said, "Yes, rather blessed are
they that hear the Word of God and
keep it!"
29But the crowds being gathered
thickly together, He began to say, "This
is a wicked generation that seeks after a
sign, and there shall be no sign given it,
except the sign of Jonah the Prophet!
30For as Jonah was a sign to the
Ninevites, so shall the Son of Man be to
this generation.
31The Queen of the South shall rise

up in the judgment with the men of
this generation and condemn them, for
she came from the ends of the world to
hear the wisdom of Solomon, and behold, a greater-than-Solomon is here!
32The men of Nineveh shall rise up in
the judgment with this generation and
shall condemn it, because they repented at the preaching of Jonah, and behold, a greater-than-Jonah is here!
33Now, no one lights a lamp to set it
in a hidden place, or under a basket,
but upon a lampstand, that they who
enter may see the light.
34The eye is the lamp of the body.
Therefore when the eye is single, the
whole body is also light. But when it is
evil, the body is also dark.
35Beware therefore, lest the light that
is in you be darkness.
36If therefore your whole body is
light, without having any part dark,
everything shall be lit up, as when a
lamp with its brightness lights things
up for you."
37And as He spoke, a Pharisee asked
Him to dine with him. And He went in
and sat down to eat.
38But the Pharisee, seeing it, was
amazed that He did not first wash before dinner.
39And the Lord said to him, "Now do
you Pharisees make clean the outside
of the cup and the platter, but your inward parts are full of plunder and
wickedness.
40You fools! Did not He who made
the outside also make the inside?
41But of the things that are within,
give as alms, and behold all things will
be clean to you.
42But woe to you, Pharisees! For you
tithe the mint and rue and all manner
of herbs, and pass over judgment and
the love of God. These you should have
done and yet not left the other undone.
43Woe to you, Pharisees! For you love
the uppermost seats in the synagogues
and greetings in the markets.
44Woe to you, Scribes and Pharisees,
hypocrites! For you are as graves that
are unseen, and the men that walk over
them do not know it."
45Then one of the doctors of the law
responded and said to him, "Teacher,
saying these things, You reproach us
also."
46And He said, "Woe to you also,
lawyers! For you burden men with
burdens heavy to bear, and you yourselves do not touch the burden with
one finger.
47Woe to you! For you built the sepulchers of the prophets, but your fathers killed them.
48So then you bear witness and consent to the deeds of your fathers, for
they killed them, and you build their
sepulchers.
49Because of this, the wisdom of God
said, 'I will send them prophets and
apostles, and some of them they shall
kill and persecute,
50that I may require the blood of all
the prophets, which was shed from the
overthrow of the world, of this generation–
51from the blood of Abel unto the
blood of Zechariah, who perished between the altar and the house.' Yes, I
tell you, it shall be required of this generation.
52Woe to you, lawyers! For you have
taken away the key of knowledge. You
did not enter in yourselves, and those
who would have entered, you hindered."
53And as He was saying these things
to them, the Scribes and the Pharisees
began to urgently press Him to speak

about many things,

54 watching Him, and seeking to catch something from His mouth, that they might accuse Him.

12

As there gathered together an innumerable multitude, in so much that they trampled on one another, He began to say to His disciples, "First of all, beware of the leaven of the Pharisees, which is hypocrisy.

2 For there is nothing covered that shall not be uncovered, neither hidden that shall not be known.

3 Because whatever you have spoken in darkness, the same shall be heard in the light. And that which you have spoken in the ear in secret places shall be proclaimed on the housetops.

4 But I'm telling you, My friends, be not afraid of those who kill the body, and after that have no more that they can do.

5 But I will show you Whom you shall fear. Fear Him Who, after He has killed, has authority to cast into Hell. I tell you, fear Him.

6 Are not five sparrows sold for two assaria? And not one of them is forgotten by God.

7 But even the hairs of your head have all been numbered. Fear not therefore, for you are worth more than many sparrows.

8 But I tell you, whoever confesses Me before men, him shall the Son of Man confess before the angels of God.

9 And he that denies Me before men shall be denied before the angels of God.

10 And whoever speaks a word against the Son of Man, it shall be forgiven him. But unto him that blasphemes the Holy Spirit, it shall not be forgiven.

11 But when they bring you unto the synagogues and unto the rulers and the authorities, take no thought how or what things you shall reply in defense, or what you shall speak.

12 For the Holy Spirit shall teach you in the same hour what you should say."

13 And someone in the crowd said, "Teacher, tell my brother to divide the family inheritance with me."

14 And He said to him, "Man, who appointed Me to be a judge or arbitrator over you?"

15 And He said to them, "Be watchful and on guard against covetousness, because one's life is not about the abundance of his possessions."

16 Then He spoke a parable to them, "The ground of one rich man brought forth an abundance.

17 And he thought to himself, saying, 'What shall I do? Because I have no more room to store my fruit.'

18 And he said, 'This is what I will do: I will take down my barns and build bigger ones to store all of my produce and my goods.

19 And I will say to my soul, "Soul, you have many goods stored up for many years. Take your rest. Eat, drink, and be merry."'

20 But God said to him, 'You fool, this night your soul is required of you! Now then, who shall these things belong to that you have prepared?'

21 So it is for the one who stores up for himself, and is not rich towards God."

22 And He spoke to His disciples, "Because of this, I tell you: take no thought for your life, what you shall eat, neither for your body, what you shall put on.

23 The life is more than food, and the body is more than clothing.

24 Consider the ravens: they neither sow nor reap, which neither have a

storehouse nor barn, and yet God feeds them. How much better are you than the birds?

25 Which of you by taking thought can add to his stature one cubit?

26 If then you are not able to do that thing which is least, why do you take thought for the rest?

27 Consider the lilies, how they grow. They do not labor, they do not spin. But I say to you that not even Solomon in all his glory was clothed as one of these.

28 But if God clothed the field with grass– which is today and shall be cast into the furnace tomorrow– how much more will He clothe you of little faith?

29 And seek not what you shall eat or what you shall drink, neither be anxious.

30 For all of the nations of the world seek after these things, but your Father knows that you have need of these things.

31 Only seek the Kingdom of God, and all these things shall be added to you.

32 Do not fear, little flock, for it is your Father's delight to give you the Kingdom.

33 Sell your possessions and give charitably, making for yourself a purse that does not grow old, a treasure in Heaven that does not fail, where thief cannot approach, nor moth destroy.

34 For where your treasure is, there will your heart be also.

35 Let your loins be girded up and your lamps burning,

36 and be like men waiting for their lord to return from the wedding, so that when he comes, they may immediately open the door when he knocks.

37 Blessed are those servants whom the lord shall find watching when he comes. I tell you with certainty, he will gird himself and make them sit down to eat, and will come and serve them.

38 And if he comes in the second watch, and if he comes in the third watch, and shall find them so, blessed are those servants.

39 But know this: if the master of the house had known what hour the thief should come, he would have watched, and not allowed his house to be broken into.

40 Therefore, you also should be ready, for the Son of Man will come in an hour that you had not considered."

41 Then Peter said to him, "Lord, are You telling this parable for us, or for everyone?"

42 And the Lord said, "Who then is the faithful and wise steward, whom his Lord shall make ruler over His household, to give them their portion in the appointed time?

43 That servant is blessed, whom his Lord shall find so doing when He comes.

44 Truly, I tell you that He will set him over all that He possesses.

45 But if that servant shall say in his heart, 'My Lord has delayed His coming,' and shall begin to beat his men-servants and maid-servants, and to eat and drink, and to be drunk,

46 the Lord will come for that servant in a day when he does not expect it, and at an hour which he has not considered, and will cut him in two and will appoint his portion with the unbelievers.

47 But that servant who knew the will of his Lord and did not prepare, nor did according to His will, shall be beaten much.

48 But he that did not know and did things worthy of stripes shall be beaten

with few. For unto whom much is giv-
en, much shall be required of him. And
to whom much was committed, that
much more they will ask of him.
49I came to cast fire into the Earth,
and wish that it were already kindled!
50But I have a baptism to be baptized
with, and how am I pressed until it is
finished!
51Do you think that I have come to
provide peace in the Earth? I tell you:
no, but rather division!
52For from now on there shall be five
in one house divided, three against two
and two against three.
53The father shall be divided against
the son, and the son against the father–
the mother against the daughter, and
the daughter against the mother– the
mother-in-law against the daughter-in-
law, and the daughter-in-law against
her mother-in-law."
54Then He also said to the crowd,
"When you see a cloud arise out of the
West, immediately you say, 'A shower is
coming,' and so it is.
55And when a south wind is blowing,
you say, 'There will be heat,' and it
comes to pass.
56Hypocrites! You know how to discern the fashion of the Earth and of the
sky, but how is it that you do not discern the time now?
57But also, why do you not judge for
yourselves what is right?
58For while you go with your adversary to the magistrate, along the way
give diligence to be released from him,
unless he drags you to the judge, and
the judge should deliver you to the officer, and the officer should cast you
into prison.
59I tell you, you will in no way come
out until you have also paid the last
coin."

13 Now there were present at the
same time some who spoke to
Him of the Galileans, whose blood Pilate mingled with their own sacrifices.
2And Jesus, answering them, said,
"Do you think that these Galileans
were sinners beyond all the other
Galileans, because they suffered such
things?
3I tell you: no! But unless you repent,
you all shall likewise perish.
4Or those eighteen, upon whom the
tower in Siloam fell and killed them, do
you think that they were sinners above
all men that dwelt in Jerusalem?
5I tell you: no! But unless you repent,
you all shall likewise perish."
6He spoke this parable: "There was
one who had a fig tree planted in his
vineyard, and he came seeking fruit on
it but found none.
7Then he said to his gardener, 'I have
come for three years seeking fruit from
this fig tree, and there has been none.
Cut it down! Why does it render the
ground useless?'
8But he answered and said to him,
'Lord, leave it alone this year also, until
I dig around it and fertilize it
9and see if it will bear fruit. And if
not, then afterwards, cut it down.'"
10Now He was teaching in one of the
synagogues on the Sabbath.
11And there was a woman who had a
spirit of infirmity for eighteen years,
and she was doubled over and not able
to stand up straight.
12When Jesus saw her, He called her
to Him and said to her, "Woman, you
are delivered from your disease."
13And He laid His hands on her, and
immediately she was made straight and
glorified God.
14But the ruler of the synagogue responded with indignation, because Je-

sus had healed on the Sabbath day, and said to the people, “There are six days in which it is necessary to work. In them, come and be healed, and not on the Sabbath.”

15 Then the Lord replied and said to him, “Hypocrite! Doesn't each one of you on the Sabbath loose his ox or his donkey from the stall and lead him to the water?

16 And ought not this daughter of Abraham, whom Satan has bound for eighteen years, be loosed from this bond on the Sabbath day?”

17 And when He said this, all his adversaries were ashamed. And the whole crowd rejoiced over all the excellent deeds that were done by Him.

18 Then He said, “What is the Kingdom of God like? Or what shall I compare it to?

19 It is like a grain of mustard seed, which a man took and sowed in his garden. And it grew and became a great tree, and the birds of heaven lodged in its branches.”

20 And again He said, “To what shall I liken the Kingdom of God?

21 It’s like leaven, which a woman took and hid in three measures of flour until all was leavened.”

22 And He went through the cities and towns, teaching and making progress toward Jerusalem.

23 And someone asked Him, “Lord, are there few being saved?” And He said to them,

24 “Agonize to enter in at the narrow gate. For I tell you: many will try to get in, but they will not be able to.

25 When the Master of the house rises up and shuts the door, and you stand outside and begin to knock at the door, saying, ‘Lord, Lord, open unto us!’ and He shall answer and say to you, ‘I do not know where you are from,’

26 then you will begin to say, ‘We have eaten and drunk in your presence, and You taught in our streets.’

27 And He shall say, ‘I tell you, I do not know you or where you are from! Depart from me, all you workers of unrighteousness!’

28 There shall be weeping and gnashing of teeth when you shall see Abraham, and Isaac, and Jacob, and all the prophets in the Kingdom of God, and yourselves cast out.

29 And they shall come from the east and west and from the north and south and shall sit down in the Kingdom of God.

30 And behold, there are those who are last who shall be first, and first who shall be last.”

31 On that same day, some of the Pharisees came to Him and said to Him, “Go and leave this place, for Herod wants to kill You.”

32 And He said to them, “Go and tell that fox, ‘Behold, I cast out demons and perform cures today and tomorrow, and the third day I make an end.’

33 Nevertheless, I must walk today and tomorrow and the day following. For it cannot be that a prophet perishes outside of Jerusalem.

34 Jerusalem, Jerusalem, who kills the prophets and stones those who were sent to her! How often would I have gathered your children together as the hen gathers her brood under her wings, but you would not!

35 Behold, your house shall be left desolate unto you. For I tell you, you shall not see Me until the time comes that you shall say, ‘Blessed is He that comes in the name of the Lord.’”

14 And it took place that He went into the house of one of the rulers of the Pharisees to eat bread on a Sabbath, and they watched Him.

2And behold, there was a man before Him who had edema.

3And Jesus responded and spoke to the lawyers and Pharisees, saying, “Is it lawful to heal on the Sabbath?”

4But they were silent. And He took hold, healed him, and let him go.

5And responding to them, He said, “Which of you shall have a donkey or an ox fall into a pit and he would not immediately pull him out on the Sabbath day?”

6And they were not able to reply to Him as to these things.

7And He spoke a parable to the guests, remarking how they chose the chief places, saying to them,

8“When you are invited by anyone to a wedding, do not recline in the chief place, lest a more respected one than you has been invited by him,

9and he that invited both him and you shall say to you, ‘Come, and give place to this one,’ then you shall be ashamed when you take the lowest place.

10Instead, when you are invited, go and sit in the lowest place, that when he comes that invited you he may say, ‘Friend, come up higher.’ Then you shall have glory before those who recline with you.

11Because whoever exalts himself shall be humbled, and he that humbles himself shall be exalted.”

12Then He also said to him who had invited Him to dinner, “When you make dinner or a supper, do not invite your friends or your brothers, nor your kinsmen or rich neighbors, lest they then invite you in return, and a repayment is made.

13But when you make a feast, call the poor, crippled, lame, and blind,

14and you shall be blessed, for they cannot repay you. For you shall be repaid in the resurrection of the righteous.”

15Then one of them that sat at the table, hearing this, said to Him, “Blessed is he who shall eat bread in the Kingdom of God.”

16But He said to him, “There was a man who made a great supper and invited many.

17And he sent his servant at the hour of supper to say to those who were invited, ‘Come, everything is now ready.’

18And they all began to make excuses. The first said to him, ‘I have bought a field, and I need to go and see it. Please have me excused.’

19And another said, ‘I have bought five pairs of oxen, and I am going to prove them. Please have me excused.’

20Then another said, ‘I have married a wife, and therefore I cannot come.’

21And the servant came and reported these things to his lord. Then the master of the house, being angry, said to his servant, ‘Go out quickly into the streets and lanes of the city, and bring the poor, and crippled, and lame, and blind.’

22And the servant said, ‘Lord, it has been done as you commanded, and there is still room.’

23And the lord said to the servant, ‘Go out into the highways and hedges, and compel them to come, that my house may be filled.’

24For I tell you that none of those men who were invited shall taste my supper.”

25There went a great crowd with Him. And He turned to them and said,

26“If anyone comes to Me and hates not his father, and his mother, and wife, and children, and brothers, and sisters, and his own life also, he cannot be My disciple.

27And whoever does not carry his cross and come after Me cannot be My disciple.

28For which of you, desiring to build a tower, would not first sit down and count the cost, whether he has enough to complete it?

29Lest, after that he laid the foundation, he should not be able to finish it. Then all that see it would begin to mock him,

30saying, ‘This man began to build and was not able to finish.’

31Or what king would go to make war against another king without first sitting down to take counsel whether he is able with ten thousand to meet him that comes against him with twenty thousand.

32And if not, then while he is still far off, he sends an ambassador and asks for terms of peace.

33Therefore, every one of you that does not forsake all that he has cannot be My disciple.

34Salt is good, but if the salt shall become tasteless, with what shall it be seasoned?

35It is fit for neither land nor manure, so they cast it out. He that has ears to hear, let him hear!”

15 Then all the tax-collectors and sinners drew near to Him to hear Him.

2And the Pharisees and Scribes murmured, saying, “He receives sinners and eats with them.”

3Then He spoke to them a parable, saying,

4“What man of you having a hundred sheep, and losing one of them, would not leave the ninety-nine in the wilderness and go after that which is lost until he finds it?

5And when he has found it, lays it on his shoulder, rejoicing.

6And coming to the house, he calls together his friends and neighbors, saying to them, ‘Rejoice with me, for I have found my sheep that was lost!’

7I tell you, that even so there shall be joy in Heaven over one sinner repenting, more than over ninety-nine righteous persons who did not need to repent.

8Or what woman having ten silver coins, if she loses one, does not light a candle, and sweep the house, and seek diligently until she finds it?

9And having found it, she calls together her friends and her neighbors, saying, ‘Rejoice with me, for I have found the silver coin which I had lost!’

10Even so, I tell you: there is joy before the angels of God over one sinner repenting.”

11Then He said, “A man had two sons.

12And the younger of them said to his father, ‘Father, give me my part of the wealth that belongs to me.’ And he divided his substance with them.

13And not many days after, the younger son gathered all that he had together, and went into a distant country, and there he wasted his wealth with riotous living.

14And when he had spent all that he had, there arose a great famine throughout all that country, and he began to be needy.

15And he went and bound himself to a citizen of that same country, who sent him into his fields to feed pigs.

16And he longed to fill his belly with
the husks that the pigs were eating, but
no one gave it to him.
17Then he came to himself and said,
'How many of my father's hired servants have an abundance of bread, and
I am dying of hunger?
18I will get up and go to my father
and will say to him, "Father, I have
sinned against Heaven and before you.
19I'm no longer worthy to be called
your son. Make me as one of your
hired servants."'
20And he arose and went to his father. But when he was still a long way
off, his father saw him and had compassion, and ran and fell on his neck
and kissed him.
21And the son said to him, 'Father, I
have sinned against Heaven and before
you, and I am no longer worthy to be
called your son.'
22But his father said to his servants,
'Bring out the best robe, and clothe
him, and put a ring on his hand and
sandals on his feet.
23And bring the fatted calf and kill it,
and let us eat and celebrate!
24For this, my son was dead and is
alive again! He was lost and is found!'
And they began to celebrate.
25But the elder son was in the field.
And when he came and drew near to
the house, he heard music and dancing.
26And he called one of his servants
and asked what these things meant.
27And he said to him, 'Your brother
has come, and your father has killed
the fatted calf, because he has received
him safe and well.'
28And he was angry and would not
go in. Then his father came out and encouraged him.
29He answered and said to his father,
'Look, these many years I have served
you. I have never transgressed your
commandments, and you never gave
me a goat to celebrate with my friends.
30But when your son who has devoured your living with harlots came,
you killed the fatted calf for him.'
31And he said unto him, 'Son, you are
always with me, and all that I have is
yours.
32But to celebrate and rejoice was
right, because your brother was dead,
and is alive! And was lost, and is
found!'"

16 And He said also to His disciples, "There was a rich man
who had a steward that was accused
unto him that he had wasted his goods.
2And he called him and said to him.
'How is it that I hear this of you? Give
an account of your stewardship, for you
can no longer be steward.'
3The steward said within himself,
'What shall I do– for my lord will take
away from me the stewardship? I cannot dig, and I am too ashamed to beg.
4I know what I will do when I am put
out of the stewardship, that they may
receive me into their houses.'
5Then he called each one of his lord's
debtors, saying to the first, 'How much
do you owe my lord?'
6And he said, 'A hundred measures of
oil.' And he said to him, 'Take your bill
and sit down quickly and write fifty.'
7Then he said to another, 'How much
do you owe?' And he said, 'A hundred
measures of wheat.' He said to him,
'Take your bill, and write eighty.'
8And the lord praised the unrighteous steward, because he had done
prudently. For the sons of this age, in
their generation, are more prudent
than the sons of light.
9And I say to you, make friends of

the unrighteous mammon, that when you shall depart, they may receive you into everlasting dwellings.

10 He that is faithful in that which is least, the same is faithful in much. And he that is unfaithful in the least is unfaithful also in much.

11 Therefore, if you have not been faithful in the unrighteous mammon, who will entrust to you the true riches?

12 And if you have not been faithful in that which is another's, who will give you your own?

13 No servant can serve two lords, for either he shall hate the one and love the other, or he shall lean to the one and despise the other. You cannot serve God and mammon."

14 The Pharisees heard all these things, who were also covetous, and they mocked Him.

15 And He said to them, "You are those who justify yourselves before men, but God knows your hearts. For that which is highly esteemed among men is an abomination before God.

16 The Law and the Prophets were until John. From that time, the Kingdom of God is preached, and everyone presses into it.

17 But it is easier for Heaven and Earth to pass away than for a letter of the Law to fail.

18 Whoever puts away his wife and marries another commits adultery. And everyone who marries her that is put away from her husband commits adultery.

19 Now there was this rich man who was clothed in purple and fine linen, daily feasting sumptuously.

20 But there was this beggar named Lazarus who laid at the gate, full of sores.

21 And he longed to be filled with the crumbs that fell from the rich man's table. Also, dogs came and licked his sores.

22 And it came to pass that the beggar died and was carried by the angels into Abraham's bosom. The rich man also died and was buried.

23 And being in torment, in Hell, he lifted up his eyes and saw Abraham from far away and Lazarus in his bosom.

24 And he, crying out, said, 'Father Abraham, have mercy on me, and send Lazarus that he may dip the tip of his finger in water and cool my tongue, for I am suffering in this flame!'

25 But Abraham said to him, 'Son, remember that in your lifetime you received your good things, but Lazarus likewise evil things. But now he is comforted and you are suffering.

26 And besides all of these things, there is a great chasm fixed between us and you, so that those who would pass from here to you cannot, neither can they pass from you to us.'

27 Then he said, 'I pray therefore, Father: send him to my father's house,

28 for I have five brothers, so that he might witness to them, that they might not come to this place of torment.'

29 Abraham said to him, 'They have Moses and the Prophets– let them hear them!'

30 And he said, 'No, father Abraham! But if one came unto them from the dead, they would repent!'

31 But he said to him, 'If they will not hear Moses and the Prophets, neither will they believe though one rose from dead.'"

17 Then He said to the disciples, "It is impossible that offenses will not come, but woe to him through

whom they come!
2 It would be better for him that a
weighty millstone were hung about his
neck and he be cast into the sea, than
that he should offend one of these little
ones.
3 Take heed to yourselves. If your
brother sins against you, rebuke him.
And if he repents, forgive him.
4 And if he sins against you seven
times in a day, and seven times a day
should return to you, saying, 'I repent,'
you should forgive him."
5 And the apostles said to the Lord,
"Increase our faith."
6 The Lord replied, "If you have faith
as a mustard seed, you would say to
this mulberry tree, 'Be uprooted and
planted in the sea,' and it would obey
you.
7 But which of you, having a servant
plowing or shepherding, would say to
him when he had come from the field,
'Come at once and sit at the table.'?
8 But will he not say to him, 'Prepare
my supper, and put on your apron, and
serve me while I eat and drink, and afterward you eat and drink'?
9 Does he thank that servant because
he did the things commanded of him? I
think not!
10 So you also, when you have done all
you were commanded, say, 'We are servants not deserving of praise, for we
have done that which was our duty.'"
11 And it took place, as He went to
Jerusalem, that He passed through
Samaria and Galilee.
12 And as He entered into one of the
towns, ten leprous men met Him, who
stood at a distance
13 and lifted up their voices and said,
"Jesus, Master, have mercy on us!"
14 When He saw them, He said to
them, "Go and show yourselves to the
priests." And it happened that as they
went, they were made clean.
15 And one of them, when he saw that
he was healed, turned back, and with a
loud voice glorified God,
16 and fell down on his face at His feet
and gave Him thanks. And he was a
Samaritan.
17 And Jesus responded and said,
"Were there not ten cleansed? But
where are the nine?
18 Was no one found to return to give
glory to God except this stranger?"
19 And He said to him, "Arise and go
your way. Your faith has made you
whole."
20 Now the Pharisees asked, "When is
the Kingdom of God coming?" And He
answered and said, "The Kingdom of
God does not come with observation.
21 They shall not say, 'Behold, over
here!', or 'Behold, over there!', for the
Kingdom of God is in the midst of
you!"
22 And he said to the disciples, "The
days will come when you shall desire to
see one of the days of the Son of Man,
but you will not see it.
23 And they shall say to you, 'Behold,
here!', or 'Behold, there!'– do not go
forth, nor follow.
24 For as the lightning lights from one
end of heaven and shines unto the other part of heaven, so will also the Son
of Man be in His days.
25 But first, He must suffer many
things and be rejected by this generation.
26 And as it happened in the time of
Noah, so shall it also be in the time of
the Son of Man.
27 They were eating and drinking, and
were marrying and being given in marriage, until that same day that Noah
entered into the ark, and the flood

came and destroyed them all.
28Likewise also, as it was in the days
of Lot– they were eating and drinking,
they were buying and they were selling,
they were planting and they were
building.
29And even the same day that Lot
went out of Sodom, it rained fire and
brimstone from heaven and destroyed
them all.
30In the same way shall it be on the
day the Son of Man is revealed.
31On that day, the one who is on the
housetop, let him not come down to
take his goods, and the one who is in
the field not turn back to the things left
behind.
32Remember Lot's wife.
33Whoever will seek to save his life
will lose it, and whoever shall lose his
life shall save it.
34I tell you, in that night there shall
be two in one bed; the one shall be tak-
en and the other left.
35Two shall be grinding together; the
one shall be taken and the other left.
36Two men shall be in the field; the
one shall be taken and the other left."
37And they responded and said to
Him, "Where, Lord?" And He said
unto them, "Wherever the body is,
there shall the vultures gather."

18 And then He told them a parable about why it is necessary to
always pray and not to be discouraged.
2He said, "There was a judge in a certain city who did not fear God and did
not respect man.
3And there was a widow in that city
who also kept coming to him, saying,
'Grant me justice against my accuser.'
4And he was unwilling for a while.
But afterwards he said to himself, 'Even
though I do not fear God, and have no
respect for man,
5yet because this widow will not give
up bothering me, I will grant her justice, unless her continual coming wears
me out!'"
6Then the Lord said, "Listen to what
the unjust judge said.
7And will God not execute vengeance
for His elect, who cry to Him day and
night, and be long-suffering to them?
8I tell you that He will execute
vengeance for them quickly. And yet,
when the Son of Man comes, will He
find faith upon the Earth?"
9And He spoke this parable to some
who trusted in themselves that they
were righteous, and despised others:
10"Two men went up into the temple
to pray, the one a Pharisee and the other a tax-collector.
11The Pharisee stood and prayed
these things within himself, 'God, I
thank you that I am not as the other
men– extortioners, unrighteous, adulterers– or as this tax-collector!
12I fast twice in the week. I tithe of all
that I gain.'
13And the tax-collector stood afar off
and would not lift up his eyes to Heav-
en, but smote his breast, saying, 'God,
be merciful to me, a sinner!'
14I tell you, this man departed home
to his house declared more righteous
than the other. For every one that exalts himself shall be humbled, and he
that humbles himself shall be exalted."
15Then they brought unto Him also
infants that He should touch them. But
when His disciples saw it, they rebuked
them.
16But Jesus called to them, saying,
"Allow the little children to come to
Me, and do not forbid them. For such
is the Kingdom of God.
17For certainly I tell you: whoever

does not receive the Kingdom of God
as a little child shall in no way enter in."
18 And this one ruler asked Him, saying, "Good Teacher, what must I do to
inherit eternal life?"
19 Jesus said to him, "Why do you call
Me good? No one is good, except God
alone.
20 You know the commandments: you
shall not commit adultery, you shall
not kill, you shall not steal, you shall
not bear false witness, honor your father and your mother."
21 And he said, "All these have I kept
from my youth."
22 When Jesus heard that, He said to
him, "Yet you are lacking one thing: sell
all that you have and distribute it to the
poor, and you shall have treasure in
Heaven. And come, follow Me."
23 When he heard that, he was deeply
grieved, for he was very rich.
24 When Jesus saw him grieved, He
said, "How hard is it for those who
have riches to enter into the Kingdom
of God!
25 It is easier for a camel to go
through the hole of a needle than for a
rich man to enter into the Kingdom of
God."
26 Then those that heard it said, "Who
then is able to be saved?"
27 And He said, "The things impossible with men are possible with God."
28 Then Peter said, "Behold, we have
left all to follow You."
29 And He said to them, "I tell you for
certain, there is no one who has left
house or father and mother or brethren
or wife or children, for the sake of the
Kingdom of God,
30 who shall not receive much more in
this time, and in the age to come, life
everlasting."
31 Then having taken the twelve, He
said to them, "Behold, we go up to
Jerusalem, and all things shall be fulfilled that have been Written by the
Prophets about the Son of Man.
32 For He will be delivered to the
Gentiles, and will be mocked, and will
be insulted, and shall be spit upon.
33 And having scourged Him, they
will kill Him. And on the third day, He
will rise again."
34 And they did not understand these
things that He was saying. These things
were hidden from them, and they did
not know what He said.
35 Now it came to pass, as they came
near Jericho, there was one blind who
sat by the way, begging.
36 And when he heard the crowd pass
by, he asked what it meant.
37 Then they told him that Jesus the
Nazarene is passing by.
38 And he cried out, saying, "Jesus,
Son of David, have mercy on me!"
39 And they that went before rebuked
him that he should be silent. But he
cried out so much more: "Son of David,
have mercy on me!"
40 Then Jesus stopped and commanded him to be brought to Him. And
when he was coming near, He asked
him,
41 saying, "What do you want Me to
do for you?" And he said, "Lord, that I
might receive my sight."
42 And Jesus said to him, "Receive
your sight. Your faith has saved you."
43 And immediately, he received his
sight and followed Him, glorifying
God. And all the people, when they
saw it, gave praise to God.

19 And he entered in and passed
through Jericho.
2 And behold, there was a man named
Zacchaeus who was chief among the

tax-collectors, and he was rich.
3And he was seeking to see who Jesus
is, and could not, because of the crowd,
for he was of small stature.
4And running out in front, he went
up into a sycamore tree, that he might
see Him when He passed by.
5And when Jesus came to that place,
He looked up and saw him, and said to
him, "Zacchaeus, come down quickly,
for today I must abide in your house."
6And responding quickly, he came
down and joyfully received Him.
7And all of them murmured when
they saw it, saying, "He stays with a
man who is a sinner."
8But Zaccheaus, standing up, said to
the Lord, "Behold, Lord, the half of my
wealth I give to the poor. And if I have
taken anything from anyone by false
accusation, I restore fourfold."
9Then Jesus said to him, "Today, salvation has come to this house, inasmuch as he also is a son of Abraham.
10For the Son of Man has come to
seek and save the lost."
11As they heard these things, He
spoke, adding a parable because He
was near Jerusalem and they thought
that the Kingdom of God was about to
appear.
12Therefore, He said, "There was this
noble man who went into a distant
land to receive for himself a kingdom
and to return.
13And he called ten of his servants
and gave to them ten minas, saying
unto them, 'Trade until I come.'
14But his citizens hated him and sent
messengers after him, saying, 'We will
not have this man to reign over us!'
15And it came to pass when he returned, having received the kingdom,
that he commanded those servants to
be called to him, to whom he gave the
money, so that he might know what
each one gained by trading.
16Then came the first, saying, 'Lord,
your mina has produced ten minas.'
17And he said to him, 'Well done,
good servant! Because you were faithful in a very little thing, have authority
over ten cities.'
18And the second came, saying,
'Lord, your mina has made five minas.'
19Then he said to that one also, 'Be
over five cities.'
20And another came and said, 'Lord,
behold here is your mina, which I have
kept laid up in a handkerchief,
21for I was afraid of you, because you
are a harsh man. You take up what you
did not lay down, and reap where you
did not sow.'
22But he said to him, 'Out of your
own mouth I will judge you, wicked
servant! You knew that I am a harsh
man, taking up what I did not lay
down, and reaping what I did not sow.
23And so why didn't you give my
money to the bank, that I might have
received interest at my coming?'
24And he said to those that stood by,
'Take the mina from him and give it to
him that has ten minas.'
25And they said to him, 'Lord, he has
ten minas.'
26'For I tell you, that everyone who
has, it shall be given. But from him
who has not, even that which he has
shall be taken from him.
27Moreover, those enemies of mine
who were not willing for me to reign
over them, bring them here, and slay
them before me.'"
28And having said these things, He
continued on toward Jerusalem.
29And it took place when He came
near to Bethphage and Bethany, near
the mount of Olives, He sent two of his

disciples,
30saying, "Go into the village that is
before you. When you enter, you will
find a colt tied, on which no man has
ever sat. Untie him and bring him.
31And if anyone asks you why you
untie it, you shall say to him, 'Because
the Lord has need of him.'"
32Those who had been sent, departing, found it just as He had spoken to
them.
33And as they were untying the colt,
the owners said to them, "Why are you
untying the colt?"
34And they said, "The Lord has need
of him."
35And they led him to Jesus. And
having cast their garments on the colt,
they put Jesus on.
36And as He went, they spread their
garments in the way.
37And as He drew near to the descent
of the Mount of Olives, the multitude
of His disciples praised God, rejoicing
with a loud voice, for they had all seen
the works of power,
38saying, "Blessed is the King that
comes in the name of the Lord! Peace
in Heaven, and glory in the Most
High!"
39And some of the Pharisees from the
crowd said to Him, "Teacher, rebuke
your disciples!"
40He answered them and said, "I tell
you, if these should remain silent, the
rocks would cry out."
41And when He had come near to the
city, He wept over her,
42saying, "If you had known in this–
your day– the things that belonged to
your peace! But now they are hidden
from your eyes.
43For the days shall come upon you
that your enemies shall cast a rampart
and surround you, and keep you in on
every side,
44and shall level the ground with you
and your children in it. And they shall
not leave in you one stone upon another, because you did not recognize the
time of your visitation."
45And He went into the temple and
began to cast out those who were selling and buying in it,
46saying to them, "It is written, 'My
house is the house of prayer,' but you
have made it a den of thieves!"
47And He taught daily in the temple.
And the Chief Priests, and Scribes, and
the first of the people were seeking to
destroy Him,
48and could not discover what to do,
because the people were hanging on
him, listening.

20 And it took place on one of
those days, as he taught the
people in the temple and preached the
gospel, the Chief Priests and the
Scribes came with the Elders
2and spoke to Him, saying, "Tell us:
by what authority do You do these
things, or who gave You this authority?"
3And, answering them, He said, "I
also will ask you one thing, and you tell
Me:
4the baptism of John– was it from
Heaven or men?"
5And they reasoned among themselves, saying, "If we shall say, 'From
Heaven,' He will say, 'Why then didn't
you believe him?'
6But if we shall say, 'Of men,' all the
people wll stone us, for they are persuaded that John was a prophet."
7And they answered that they did not
know the source.
8And Jesus said to them, "Neither
will I tell you by what authority I do

these things."

9Then He began to speak this parable to the people: "There was a man who planted a vineyard, and leased it out to farmers, and left the country for a long time.

10And when the season had come, he sent a servant to the farmers that they should give him the fruits of the vineyard. But the farmers beat him and sent him away with nothing.

11And again he sent yet another servant, but they beat him and dishonored him and sent him away with nothing.

12And again he sent a third to the vineyard, but they also wounded him and cast him out.

13Then the lord of the vineyard said, 'What shall I do? I will send my beloved son; perhaps they will respect him when they see him.'

14But when the farmers saw him, they reasoned among themselves, saying, 'This is the heir. Come, let us kill him, that the inheritance may be ours!'

15And they cast him out of the vineyard and killed him. What then will the lord of the vineyard do to them?

16He will come and destroy these farmers and will give his vineyard to others." But when they heard this, they said, "May it not be!"

17And He looked at them and said, "What then does it mean that is written: 'The stone that the builders rejected has become the head of the corner?'

18Everyone who falls on that stone shall be broken. But on whoever it falls, it will grind him to powder!"

19And the Chief Priests and the Scribes in the same hour sought to lay hands on Him, but they feared the people, for they knew that He had spoken this parable against them.

20And they watched Him, and sent spies who disguised themselves to be righteous, that they might trap Him with words, so as to deliver Him unto the power and authority of the governor.

21And they questioned Him, saying, "Teacher, we know that You say and teach what is right, neither regard any man's person, but you teach the way of God in truth.

22Is it lawful for us to give Caesar tribute, or not?"

23But, perceiving their craftiness, He said to them, "Why do you test Me?

24Show me a denarius. Whose image and inscription is it?" Then they answered and said, "Caesar's."

25And he said to them, "Give then unto Caesar that which belongs to Caesar, and to God that which belongs to God."

26And they could not catch Him in His speech before the people. And they marveled at His answers and could say nothing.

27Then some of the Sadducees came to Him, who deny that there is resurrection, and they questioned Him,

28saying, "Teacher, Moses wrote unto us: if any man's brother dies having a wife, and the same dies childless, that his brother should take his wife and raise up seed unto his brother.

29There were seven brethren. And the first took a wife and died childless.

30And the second took the wife, and he died childless.

31And the third took her, and likewise also the seven, and left no children behind them and died.

32Last of all, the woman also died.

33Therefore, in the resurrection, whose wife of them shall she be? For seven had her as a wife."

34Jesus answered and said to them,

"The sons of this age marry and are given in marriage.

35But those who are accounted worthy of that age, to obtain the resurrection from the dead, neither marry nor are given in marriage.

36For neither can they die anymore, for they are like the angels, for they are also sons of God, being sons of the resurrection.

37But that the dead are raised, even Moses showed at the bush, when he called the Lord: 'The God of Abraham, and the God of Isaac, and the God of Jacob.'

38For He is not the God of the dead, but of the living, for all live to Him!"

39Then some of the Scribes responded and said, "Well spoken, Teacher."

40And after that no one dared ask Him anything.

41Then He said to them, "How do they say that Christ is David's Son?

42And David himself said in the book of the Psalms, 'The Lord said to my Lord, "Sit on My right hand,

43until I make Your enemies a footstool for Your feet."'

44David therefore called Him "Lord"– how is He then his son?"

45Now as all the people were listening, He said to His disciples,

46"Beware of the Scribes, who like to walk in robes and love salutations in the market-place and the first seats in the synagogues and first place in the suppers,

47who devour widows' houses and out of wrong motives make long prayers! These shall receive a greater damnation!"

21 As He looked up, He saw the rich casting their offerings into the treasury.

2And He saw this poor widow casting in two small coins.

3And He said, "Of a truth I tell you that this poor widow has put in more than them all.

4For they have all cast in the gifts to God out of their abundance. But she has cast in– out of her poverty– all of her substance."

5And as some were speaking about the temple, how that with goodly stones and consecrated gifts it was adorned, He said,

6"The days will come when these things that you look upon: there shall not be left a stone upon a stone that shall not be thrown down!"

7Then they asked Him, saying, "Teacher, when shall these things be, and what sign will there be when these things are about to take place?"

8Then He said, "Beware that you are not deceived. For many will come in My name saying, 'I am he, and the time draws near,' but do not follow them.

9But when you shall hear of wars and sedition, do not be afraid. For these things must take place first, but the end is not immediate."

10Then He said to them, "Nation shall rise against nation, and kingdom against kingdom.

11Great earthquakes shall be in different places, and famines, and plagues, and fearful things. And there shall be great signs from Heaven.

12But before all these things, they shall lay their hands on you and persecute you, delivering you up to the synagogues and into prison, and bring you before kings and governors for My name's sake.

13But it shall turn to you for a testimony.

14Therefore settle it in your hearts

that you do not premeditate a defense,

15 for I will give you a mouth and wisdom that all your adversaries will not be able to speak against nor resist.

16 Yes, you shall be betrayed by your parents, and by your brethren, and relatives, and friends. And some of you they shall put to death.

17 And you shall be hated of all men for My name's sake.

18 Yet, not one hair of your heads shall perish.

19 By your patience, possess your souls.

20 And when you shall see Jerusalem surrounded by armies, then understand that the desolation is near.

21 Then let them who are in Judea flee to the mountains. And those which are in the midst, get out! And those in the countryside, do not enter into her.

22 For these are the days of vengeance, to fulfill all things that have been written.

23 But woe to them that are with child and to those that are nursing in those days, for there shall be great trouble in the land and wrath among these people.

24 And they shall fall by the edge of the sword and shall be led captive into all nations. And Jerusalem shall be trodden under foot by the nations until the time of the nations be fulfilled.

25 And there shall be signs in the sun, and moon, and stars. And in the Earth, distress of nations with perplexity, roaring seas and waves.

26 Men's hearts shall faint from fear and expectation of those things that are coming on the inhabitants of the Earth. For the powers of Heaven shall be shaken.

27 And then shall they see the Son of Man come in a cloud with power and great glory.

28 But when these things begin to come to pass, look up and lift up your heads, because your redemption draws near."

29 And He spoke a parable to them, "Behold the fig tree and all trees.

30 When you have already seen them sprout, you know of yourself that summer is already near.

31 So also, when you see these things come to pass, know that the Kingdom of God is near.

32 I tell you for certain that this generation will not pass away until all these things are done.

33 Heaven and Earth shall pass away, but My words shall not pass away.

34 But pay attention to yourselves, lest your hearts be overcome with drinking bouts and intoxication and cares of this life, and that day should suddenly come upon you.

35 For as a snare it shall come on all them sitting on the face of the Earth.

36 Watch therefore continually, and pray that you may be counted worthy to escape all these things that are about to come to pass, and to stand before the Son of Man."

37 And He taught in the temple by day, and at night He went out and lodged on the mount called "Olives."

38 And all the people came early in the morning to Him in the temple, to hear Him.

22 The Feast of Unleavened Bread drew near, which is called Passover.

2 And the Chief Priests and Scribes sought how they might kill Him, for they feared the people.

3 Then Satan entered into Judas, who is surnamed Iscariot, being of the

number of the twelve.

4And he went his way and discussed with the Chief Priests and captains how he might deliver Him up to them.

5And they were very happy and agreed to give him money.

6And he promised and sought an opportunity to deliver Him to them away from the crowd.

7Then came the Day of Unleavened Bread, in which it was essential to kill the Passover.

8And He sent Peter and John, saying, "Go and prepare us the Passover, that we may eat."

9But they said to Him, "Where do You want us to prepare it?"

10And He said to them, "Look, when you enter into the city, a man will meet you with a pitcher of water. Follow him into the house where he enters,

11and say to the master of the house, 'The Teacher says to you, "Where is the guest-chamber where I shall eat the Passover with My disciples?"'

12And he will show you a large furnished upper room. There, make ready."

13Then they went and found just as He had said to them, and they prepared the Passover.

14And when the hour came, He reclined, and the twelve apostles with Him.

15And He said to them, "I have earnestly desired to eat this Passover with you before I suffer.

16For I tell you, I will no more eat of it until it is fulfilled in the Kingdom of God."

17And He took the cup and gave thanks and said, "Take this and share it among yourselves.

18For I tell you, I will not drink of the fruit of the vine until the Kingdom of God comes."

19And He took the bread, and giving thanks, He broke it and gave it to them, saying, "This is My body, which is given for you. Do this in remembrance of Me."

20And after they had eaten, in like manner He took the cup, saying, "This is the New Covenant in My blood, which is poured out for you.

21Yet behold, the hand of him that will deliver Me up is with Me on the table.

22And indeed, the Son of Man goes just as it has been determined, but woe to that man by whom He is betrayed!"

23And they began to inquire among themselves who it might be among them that would do this.

24Then there was also strife among them, which of them should be thought the greatest.

25And He said to them, "The kings of the nations rule over them, and those who exercise authority over them are called benefactors.

26But not you. Rather, the greatest among you shall be as the least, and he that leads as he who serves.

27For who is greater: he that sits at the table, or he that serves? Is it not he that sits at the table? But I am among you as He that serves.

28But you are those who have remained with Me in My trial.

29And I appoint to you a kingdom, just as My Father appointed to Me,

30that you may eat and drink at My table in My kingdom, and may sit on thrones judging the twelve tribes of Israel."

31And the Lord said, "Dear Simon, understand: Satan has demanded to sift you as wheat.

32But I have prayed for you that your

faith will not fail. And when you return
again, strengthen your brothers."
33And He said to him, "Lord, I am
ready to go with you to prison and to
death."
34And He said, "I tell you, Peter, that
before the rooster crows this day, you
will have denied that you know Me
three times."
35And He said to them, "When I sent
you without wallet, suitcase, and sandals, did you lack anything?" And they
said, "No."
36And then He said to them, "However, now, he who has a purse, let him
take it, and also a suitcase. And he that
has no sword, let him sell his coat and
buy one.
37For I tell you, that which is written
must be fulfilled in Me, 'And with the
lawless was He numbered.' For those
things which are written of Me have an
end."
38And they said "Lord, look, here are
two swords." And He said to them, "It
is enough."
39And He came out and went to the
Mount of Olives, as was His custom.
And His disciples followed Him.
40And when He came to the place,
He said to them, "Pray that you do not
enter into temptation."
41And He withdrew from them about
a stone's throw, and falling on His
knees, prayed,
42saying, "Father, if You are willing,
take away this cup from Me. But not
My will, rather Yours, be done."
43And there appeared to Him an angel from Heaven, strengthening Him.
44And He was in agony, and prayed
more fervently. And His sweat became
as great drops of blood falling down to
the Earth.
45And He rose up from prayer and
came to His disciples. He found them
sleeping from grief,
46and He said to them, "Why do you
sleep? Get up and pray, that you may
not enter into temptation."
47But while He was still talking, behold there came a crowd. And he that
was called Judas, one of the twelve, was
leading them and drew near to Jesus to
kiss Him.
48And Jesus said to him, "Judas, do
you betray the Son of Man with a kiss?"
49But those around Him, seeing what
was about to happen, said to Him,
"Lord, shall we strike with the sword?"
50And one of them struck a servant
of the High Priest and took off his right
ear.
51And Jesus responded and said, "Allow this to happen!" And He touched
his ear and healed him.
52Then Jesus said to the Chief Priests,
and rulers of the temple, and the elders
that had come to Him, "Have you come
out against a robber with swords and
clubs?
53When I was daily with you in the
temple, you did not stretch out your
hand against Me. But this is your hour
and the power of darkness."
54Then they seized Him, and led Him
away, and brought Him to the house of
the High Priest. And Peter was following afar off.
55Now, they had kindled a fire in the
midst of the court and sat down together. Peter sat down to warm himself
among them.
56And one of the maids saw him as
he sat by the light, and staring at him,
said, "This one was with Him."
57But he denied Him, saying,
"Woman, I do not know Him."
58And after a while, another saw him
and said, "You also are of them." But

Peter said, "Man, I am not!"

59 And after about an hour, another one said strongly, "Certainly, this one was with Him, for he is also a Galilean!"

60 And Peter said, "Man, I do not know what you are talking about!" And immediately, as he was speaking, the rooster crowed.

61 And the Lord turned back and looked at Peter. And Peter remembered the word of the Lord, how He said to him, "Before the rooster crows, you will deny Me three times."

62 And Peter went out and wept bitterly.

63 And the men that were guarding Jesus mocked Him and beat Him.

64 And, having blindfolded Him, they were hitting Him in the face and asking Him, "Who is it that hit You?" saying, "Prophesy!"

65 And many other blasphemous things they said to Him.

66 And when it was day, the elders of the people, both the High Priests and Scribes, came together and led Him to the Sanhedrin, saying,

67 "If You are the Christ, tell us." And He said, "If I were to tell you, you would not believe.

68 And if also I should ask, you would not answer Me or let Me go.

69 From now on shall the Son of Man sit at the right hand of the power of God."

70 Then they all said, "Then You are the Son of God?" He said to them, "You say that I am."

71 Then they said, "What further need do we have of any more witnesses? We ourselves have heard from His own mouth."

23 And the whole multitude of them arose and led Him unto Pilate.

2 And they began to accuse Him, saying, "This One we have found perverting the people and forbidding to pay tribute to Caesar, saying that He is Christ, a King!"

3 And Pilate questioned Him, saying, "Are You the King of the Jews?" Then He answered him and said, "You have said it."

4 Then said Pilate to the Chief Priests and the people, "I find no fault in this Man."

5 But they persisted, saying, "He stirs up the people, teaching throughout the whole of Judea, and beginning from Galilee, even to this place."

6 But Pilate, hearing Galilee, asked whether the Man was a Galilean;

7 and knowing that He was from Herod's jurisdiction, sent Him to Herod, who was also at Jerusalem in those days.

8 And when Herod saw Jesus, he was exceedingly glad, for he had been wishing for a long time to see Him, because he had heard many things concerning Him and was looking forward to seeing Him do a miracle.

9 Then he questioned Him about many things, but He did not answer him.

10 The Chief Priests and Scribes stood by, violently accusing Him.

11 Then Herod with his troops made Him nothing, and mocked Him, and put splendid apparel on Him, and sent Him back to Pilate.

12 And the same day Pilate and Herod were made friends with one another, for before they were hostile to each other.

13 And Pilate called together the Chief

Priests and the rulers and the people,
14and said to them, "You have
brought this Man to me as One Who
misleads the people, and look, I have
examined Him before you and have
found no fault in this Man regarding
the accusations against Him.
15Also, neither has Herod. For I sent
you to him and, lo, nothing worthy of
death has been done by Him.
16I will therefore chasten Him and
release Him."
17Now it was necessary to release one
of them at the feast.
18But all the multitude cried out at
once, saying, "Away with Him, but release Barabbas to us!"
19who had been cast into prison on
account of an insurrection and murder
that was made in the city.
20Therefore Pilate called to them
again, desiring to release Jesus.
21But they were crying out saying,
"Crucify Him! Crucify Him!"
22He said to them the third time,
"What evil has He done? I find no
cause of death in Him. Therefore, having chastised Him, I will release Him."
23But they cried out with boisterous
voices, demanding that He be crucified. And their voices and those of the
Chief Priests prevailed.
24And Pilate gave the sentence that
their request should be done.
25Then he released to them the one
who had been cast into prison because
of insurrection and murder, whom
they desired, and delivered Jesus to
their will.
26And as they led Him away, they laid
hold on Simon, a Cyrenian who was
coming from the field. They put the
cross upon him to bear it after Jesus.
27And a great multitude followed
Him of the people, and women who
were mourning and lamenting Him.
28But Jesus turned to them and said,
"Daughters of Jerusalem, do not weep
for Me, but weep for yourselves and for
your children.
29For behold, the days will come
when men shall say, 'Blessed are the
barren and the wombs that never bore
and the breasts that never nursed.'
30Then shall they begin to say to the
mountains, 'Fall on us,' and to the hills,
'Cover us.'
31For if they do these things in the
green tree, what shall take place in the
dry?"
32And there were led with Him two
evildoers to be put to death.
33And when they came to the place
which is called "A Skull," there they
crucified Him and the evildoers, one
on the right, and the other on the left.
34Then Jesus said, "Father, forgive
them, for they do not know what they
are doing." Then, dividing His garments, they cast lots.
35And the people stood, and as spec-
tators, were sneering along with their
rulers, saying, "He saved others. Let
Him save Himself if this is the Christ,
the chosen of God!"
36The soldiers also ridiculed Him
and came offering Him vinegar,
37and said, "If You are the King of the
Jews, save Yourself!"
38Now, there was also an inscription
written over Him, written in Greek,
Latin, and Hebrew: "This is the King of
the Jews."
39And one of the evildoers that had
been hanged railed on Him, saying, "If
You are the Christ, save Yourself and
us."
40But the other one responded and
rebuked him, saying, "Don't you even
fear God, since you are under this same

judgment?

41 For we indeed justly receive what we deserve for what we did. But this Man has done nothing wrong."

42 And he said to Jesus, "Lord, remember me when You come into Your Kingdom."

43 And Jesus said to him, "With certainty, I tell you, today you will be with Me in Paradise."

44 And it was about the sixth hour of the day, and there came a darkness over all the Earth until the ninth hour.

45 And the sun was darkened. And the veil of the temple was torn in the middle.

46 And Jesus cried out with a loud voice and said, "Father, into Your hands I commit My spirit!" And when He said this, He expired.

47 When the Centurion saw what had happened, he glorified God, saying, "Indeed this was a righteous Man!"

48 And all of the crowd, who came together to see this spectacle that took place, returned home, beating their breasts.

49 And all of those who knew Him and the women who followed Him from Galilee stood afar off, watching these things.

50 And behold there was a man named Joseph, a counselor, who was a good and righteous man,

51 who had not consented to the counsel and actions of them, who was of Arimathea, a city of the Jews, who was also himself waiting for the Kingdom of God.

52 He went to Pilate and begged for the body of Jesus,

53 and took it down, and wrapped it in a linen cloth, and placed it in a tomb hewn from a rock, in which no one had ever laid.

54 And it was the Day of Preparation, and the Sabbath was coming.

55 Now also the women followed, who had come with Him from Galilee, saw the tomb and how his body was laid,

56 and having returned, they prepared perfumes and ointments, and rested on the Sabbath day according to the commandment.

24 But on the first day of the week, at early dawn, they came to the tomb, bringing the perfumes that they had prepared and some others with them.

2 And they found the stone rolled away from the tomb

3 and went in, but did not find the body of the Lord Jesus.

4 And it happened, as they were perplexed about this, that behold, two men stood by them in shining garments.

5 But they became terrified and bowed their faces to the earth. They said to them, "Why do you seek the living among the dead?

6 He is not here, but is risen! Remember how He told you when He was with you in Galilee,

7 saying, 'the Son of Man must be delivered into the hands of sinful men, and be crucified, and the third day arise'?"

8 And they remembered His words.

9 And having returned from the tomb, they told all these things to the eleven and to all the rest.

10 Now, it was Mary Magdalene and Joanna, and Mary of James, and the rest with them, who told these things to the apostles.

11 And their words seemed to them as idle tales, and they did not believe them.

12 Then Peter got up and ran to the

tomb and stooped down and saw the
linen clothes lying alone, and went
home wondering at what had happened.
13And behold, two of them were going on that same day to a village called
Emmaus, about sixty stadia from
Jerusalem.
14And they were talking with one another about all the things that had tak-
en place.
15And it happened, as they talked
and reasoned, that Jesus Himself came
near and went with them.
16But their eyes were restrained from
recognizing Him.
17And He said to them, "What are
these things that you are talking about
as you walk and are so sad?"
18And Cleopas answered and said to
Him, "Are You alone a stranger in
Jerusalem and have not known the
things which have come to pass in it in
these days?"
19And He said to them, "What
things?" And they said to Him, "The
things concerning Jesus the Nazarene,
who was a Man, a Prophet, mighty in
deed and word before God and all of
the people.
20And how the Chief Priests and our
rulers delivered Him to be condemned
to death and crucified Him.
21But we were trusting that He was
about to redeem Israel. And also, with
regards to all of these things, today is
the third day since these things happened.
22And also some of the women
among us shocked us, having gone early to the tomb,
23and having not found His body,
came announcing also that they had
seen a vision of angels, who said He
was alive.
24And some of those who were with
us went to the tomb and found it as
also the woman had described, but
they did not see Him."
25And He said to them, "O foolish,
and slow of heart to believe upon all
that the Prophets Spoke!
26Was it not necessary for Christ to
suffer these things and enter into His
glory?"
27And beginning from Moses and
from all of the Prophets, He explained
all of the scriptures concerning Himself.
28And they drew near to the village
where they were going, and He appeared to be continuing on farther.
29And they constrained Him, saying,
"Abide with us, for evening is near and
the day is almost over." And He went in
to abide with them.
30And it came to pass as He reclined
with them, taking the bread, He blessed
it and, having broken, He gave it to
them.
31And their eyes were opened, and
they recognized Him. And He disap-
peared from them.
32And they said between themselves,
"Did not our hearts burn within us
while He talked with us by the way and
as He opened to us the scriptures?"
33And they rose up the same hour
and returned again to Jerusalem and
found the eleven gathered together and
those that were with them,
34saying, "The Lord is risen indeed,
and has appeared to Simon!"
35And they told what things were
done in the way, and how they knew
Him by the breaking of bread.
36As they were telling these things,
Jesus Himself stood in their midst and
said to them, "Peace be with you."
37But terrified and filled with fear,

they thought they were looking at a
spirit.
38And He said to them, "Why are you
so troubled, and why do such thoughts
arise in your hearts?
39See My hands and My feet, that I
am He. Handle Me and see, for a spirit
does not have flesh and bones as you
see that I have."
40And having said this, He showed
them His hands and feet.
41And while they still were in disbe-
lief for joy and wonder, He said to
them, "Have you anything to eat?"
42And they gave Him a piece of a
broiled fish and honeycomb.
43And He took it and ate it before
them.
44And He said to them, "These are
the things that I spoke to you while I
was still with you: all that has been
written in the Law of Moses and in the
Prophets and in the Psalms concerning
Me must be fulfilled."
45Then He opened up their minds to
understand the scriptures.
46And said to them, "Thus is it written, and thus it behooved Christ to suffer and to rise again from the dead on
the third day,
47and that repentance and forgiveness of sins should be proclaimed in
His name to all nations, beginning at
Jerusalem.
48And you are witnesses of these
things.
49And behold, I send the promise of
My Father upon you. But wait in the
city of Jerusalem until you are endued
with power from on high."
50And He led them out to Bethany,
and lifted up His hands and blessed
them.
51And it happened that, as He blessed
them, He departed from them and was
carried up into Heaven.
52And they worshiped Him and returned to Jerusalem with great joy,
53and were continually in the temple,
praising and blessing God. Amen.

THE GOSPEL OF JOHN

1 In the beginning was the Word, and the Word was with God, and the Word was God.

2 He was in the beginning with God.

3 All things came into being by Him, and without Him not even one thing came into being unless He made it.

4 In Him was life, and the life was the light of man.

5 And the light shines in the darkness, and the darkness cannot overcome it.

6 A man rose up who was sent from God– his name was John.

7 He came to witness that he might testify concerning the light, that through Him everyone might believe.

8 He was not the light, but that he might witness concerning the light–

9 the true light that gives light to every man that comes into the world.

10 He was in the world, and through Him the world came into being, yet the world failed to recognize Him.

11 He came unto His own, and His own did not receive Him.

12 But as many as would receive Him, who would believe in His name, to them He gave authority to be children of God,

13 who were begotten not of blood, neither of the will of the flesh, nor of man's will, but of God.

14 And the Word was made flesh and came and tabernacled among us, and we saw His glory: the glory of the only begotten of the Father, full of grace and truth.

15 John testified concerning Him and spoke with a loud voice, saying, "This is He who was to come after me, the One I told you about, the One Who was first, Who existed before me."

16 And of His fullness we have all received, and grace upon grace.

17 For the law was given by Moses, but grace and truth came by Jesus Christ.

18 No one has ever seen God. The only begotten Son of the Father, Who dwells intimately with Him, has come to make him known.

19 And this is the testimony of John, when the Jews sent unto him Priests and Levites from Jerusalem to ask him, "Who are you?"

20 And he declared openly and did not refuse to say who he was, and he declared, saying, "I am not the Christ."

21 And they asked him, "Who are you then? Are you Elijah?" And he said, "I am not." "Are you the Prophet?" And he answered, "No."

22 Then they said to him, "Tell us who you are. What do you say about yourself? So that we may provide the information to those who sent us."

23 He said, "I am a voice crying in the wilderness, 'Make straight the way of the Lord,' as the prophet Isaiah spoke."

24 And it was the Pharisees who had sent them.

25 And they asked him and said to him, "Why then do you baptize, if you are not the Christ, nor Elijah, nor the Prophet?"

26 John answered them, saying, "I baptize in water, but there is One standing among you that is not known by you.

27 He it is, Who coming after me, is preferred before me, Whose sandal straps I am not worthy to untie."

28 These things happened in Bethany, beyond the Jordan, where John was baptizing.

29 The next day, John saw Jesus coming toward him, and he said, "Behold! The Lamb of God Who takes away the sin of the world!

30 This is the One I told you about Who would come after me, the One

Who is preferred before me because He was before me.

31 And I did not know Him, but so that He could be revealed to Israel, I came baptizing in water."

32 And John was able to make Him known, pointing out that he was able to see with his eyes the Spirit come down upon Him as a dove out of Heaven and remain upon Him.

33 "I did not know Him, but the One Who sent me to baptize in water, He said to me, 'The One that you see the Spirit come down on and remain upon, He is the One that will baptize in the Holy Spirit.'

34 And I saw with my eyes and gave testimony to the event that declared Him to be the Son of God."

35 Again the next day, John and two of his disciples were standing together,

36 and looking at Jesus passing by, he said, "Behold, the Lamb of God!"

37 And two of his disciples heard what he said, and they followed Jesus.

38 Then Jesus turned around and saw them following Him. He said to them, "What do you want?" Then they said, "Rabbi," (which means "teacher"), "where do You live?"

39 He said to them, "Come and see." They went and saw where He lived and they stayed with Him, for it was the tenth hour of the day.

40 One of the two who had followed Him after hearing John was Andrew, Simon Peter's brother.

41 The first thing He did was to find his own brother Simon and tell him, "We have found the Messiah," which being interpreted means "The Christ."

42 And he led him to Jesus. Now when Jesus looked up and saw him, he said, "You are Simon, the son of Jonah– you shall be called 'Cephas,'" which being interpreted means "Peter."

43 The next day, He resolved to go to Galilee. And Jesus found Philip, and said to him, "Follow Me."

44 Now Philip was from Bethsaida, which was the city of Andrew and Peter.

45 Philip found Nathaniel and said to him, "We have found the One Who Moses wrote about in the Law and in the Prophets: Jesus the son of Joseph, Who is from Nazareth."

46 And Nathaniel said, "Can any good thing come from Nazareth?" And Philip said, "Come quickly and see."

47 Jesus saw Nathaniel coming toward Him and said concerning him, "Look, an Israelite in whom there is truly no deceit."

48 Nathaniel said to Him, "Where do You know me from?" Jesus answered him and said, "Before Philip called you, while you were still under the fig tree, I saw you."

49 Then Nathaniel responded to Him and said, "Rabbi, You are the Son of God! You are the King of Israel!"

50 Jesus replied to Him and said, "You believe because I was able to tell you that I saw you under the fig tree? You will see greater things than this."

51 And He said to him, "I tell you for certain, from now on you will see Heaven open and the angels of God ascending and descending upon the Son of Man."

2 And on the third day a marriage took place in Cana, which is in Galilee. And the mother of Jesus was there.

2 Now Jesus was also invited, and His disciples, to the marriage.

3 And having a shortage of wine, the mother of Jesus said to Him, "They are

out of wine."

4 Jesus said to her, "Woman, what is this to Me and to you? My time has not come."

5 His mother said to the servants, "If He says something, whatever it is, do it."

6 Now there were six stone water pots sitting out, according to the purification ritual of the Jews, containing two or three measures each.

7 Jesus said to them, "Fill the water pots with water." And they filled them up to the top.

8 And He said to them, "Now draw out, and carry it to the ruler of the feast." And they carried it.

9 Now the ruler of the feast tasted the water that became wine and did not know where it had come from, but the servants knew who had drawn the water. The ruler of the feast called the bridegroom,

10 and he said to him, "Every man sets out the best wine first, and then the inferior after everyone has drunk well, but you have kept the best wine until now!"

11 This Jesus did as the beginning of His miracles in Cana of Galilee, and manifested His glory, and His disciples believed in Him.

12 After this, He and His mother, His brothers, and His disciples went down to Capernaum, and there they remained a few days.

13 And the Passover of the Jews was near, and Jesus went up to Jerusalem.

14 And He found those selling oxen, and sheep, and doves, and the moneychangers sitting in the temple.

15 And having made a whip of cords, He drove all of them out of the temple, both the sheep and the oxen and the moneychangers, pouring out the coins and turning over the tables.

16 And He said to them that sold the doves, "Take these things out of here! Do not make My Father's house a house of merchandise!"

17 His disciples remembered that it was written, "The zeal of Your house has consumed me."

18 The Jews then answered and said to Him, "What miracle do You show us, since You have done these things?"

19 Jesus replied and said to them, "Destroy this temple, and in three days I will raise it up."

20 The Jews then said, "This temple has been being built for forty-six years, and will You raise it up in three days?"

21 But the temple that He spoke about was His body.

22 When He was raised from the dead, then His disciples remembered that He had said this, and they believed the scriptures and the word that Jesus had spoken.

23 And as He was at the Passover in Jerusalem, at the feast, many of them believed on His name, beholding the signs that He did.

24 But because Jesus knew everything, He did not entrust Himself to them,

25 because He knew what was in man, and He had no need for anyone to give Him a testimony of man.

3 There was a man from the Pharisees named Nicodemus– he was a ruler of the Jews.

2 He came to Jesus at night and said to Him, "Rabbi, we know that You are a Teacher that has come from God. For unless God is with him, no one is able to perform the miracles that You perform."

3 Jesus answered and said to him, "With absolute certainty, I assure you,

without being born again, no one is
able to see the Kingdom of God."
4 Nicodemus said to Him, "How can a
man be born once he is old? Can he
enter a second time into his mother's
belly and be born?"
5 Jesus answered, "With absolute certainty, I assure you, unless one is born
of water and of Spirit, he cannot enter
into the Kingdom of God.
6 What is begotten of the flesh is flesh,
and what is begotten of the Spirit is
spirit.
7 Do not be surprised because I told
you it is necessary to be born again.
8 The wind blows where it wills, and
its sound you hear, but you do not
know where it comes from and where
it is going. So it is with everyone that
has been born of the Spirit."
9 Nicodemus answered Him and said,
"How can these things be?"
10 Jesus answered him and said, " You
are the teacher of Israel and do not
know these things?
11 With absolute certainty, I assure
you, that which We know We speak,
and We bear witness of that which We
have seen, but you do not receive Our
witness.
12 If you do not believe when I tell
you about earthly things, how will you
believe if I tell you about heavenly
things?
13 Now, no one has gone up into
Heaven except the Son of Man that
came down out of Heaven, Who is in
Heaven.
14 And just as Moses lifted up the serpent in the wilderness, likewise it is
necessary that the Son of Man be lifted
up,
15 so that everyone that believes in
Him should not perish, but have eternal life.
16 For God loved the world so much
that He gave His only begotten Son,
that everyone who believes in Him
should not perish, but have eternal life.
17 For God did not send His Son into
the world to condemn the world, but
that the world might be saved through
Him.
18 Whoever believes in Him is not
condemned. But whoever does not believe has already been condemned because he has not believed in the name
of the only begotten Son of God.
19 Now this is the condemnation: that
Light has come into the world, but men
loved the darkness more than the
Light, because their deeds were evil.
20 For everyone who practices
wickedness hates the light and will not
come to the light, so that his works are
not exposed.
21 But he who does the truth comes to
the light, so that it may be shown that
his deeds are performed by God."
22 After these things, Jesus and His
disciples came into the land of Judea,
and there He stayed with them and was
baptizing.
23 Now John was also baptizing in
Aenon near Salim, because the water
was plentiful there. And people were
constantly arriving and were being
baptized.
24 For John was not yet thrown into
prison.
25 Then a controversy about purification arose with the disciples of John
and the Jews.
26 So they came to John and said to
him, "Rabbi, He Who was with you
across the Jordan, Who you bore witness of, now He is baptizing, and
everyone is coming to Him."
27 John answered and said, "A man is
not able to receive anything unless it is

given to him from Heaven.

28 You yourselves are my witnesses that I said I am not the Messiah, but that I am sent before Him.

29 It is the bridegroom who gets the bride. But the friend of the groom, who stands and listens for him, rejoices with joy because of the voice of the bridegroom. Therefore, my joy is fulfilled.

30 He must increase, while I decrease.

31 The One Who comes from above is above all. The one who is of the Earth is earthly and speaks from the Earth. The One Who comes from Heaven is above all,

32 and He testifies of what He has seen and heard, and no one accepts His testimony.

33 Whoever accepts His testimony has confirmed that God is true.

34 He who God has sent speaks the words of God, for God gives the Spirit to Him without limit.

35 The Father loves the Son and has placed all things in His hand.

36 Whoever believes in the Son has eternal life, but he who does not obey the Son will not see life– instead, God's wrath remains on him."

4 Now when the Lord had learned that the Pharisees had heard that Jesus had baptized and made more disciples than John–

2 and certainly Jesus Himself did not baptize, rather His disciples–

3 He left Judea and went back again into Galilee.

4 It was necessary for Him to pass through Samaria.

5 He then came to a Samaritan city called Sycar, near to the property that Jacob gave to his son Joseph.

6 Now Jacob's well was there, and Jesus, being tired from the journey, sat down on the well at about the sixth hour.

7 A woman from Samaria came to draw water. Jesus said to her, "Give Me a drink,"

8 for His disciples had gone into the city in order to buy food.

9 Then the Samaritan woman said to Him, "How is it that You, being a Jew, ask of me, a Samaritan woman, for a drink?" for the Jews do not associate with the Samaritans.

10 Jesus replied and said to her, "If you knew about the gift of God, and Who it is that is saying to you, 'Give Me a drink,' you would have asked Him and He would give you living water."

11 The woman said, "Sir, You have no container and the well is deep– where then would this living water come from?

12 Are You greater than our father Jacob who gave us this well, who drank from it along with his sons and his cattle?"

13 Jesus answered and said, "Everyone who drinks from this water will thirst again,

14 but whoever drinks from the water that I give will never ever thirst. But the water that I give will become in him a fountain of water springing up into eternal life."

15 The woman said, "Sir, give me this water so that I will not thirst, nor come here to draw water."

16 Jesus said to her, "Go, call your husband, and come here."

17 The woman answered and said, "I do not have a husband." Jesus said, "You have spoken correctly in that you have said, 'I have no husband,'

18 for you have had five husbands, and the one that you have now is not your husband. What you have said is true."

19And the woman said, "Sir, I perceive that You are a prophet.
20Our fathers worshiped on this
mountain, and You say that in
Jerusalem is the place where it is necessary to worship."
21Jesus said to her, "Woman, believe
Me, an hour is coming that neither in
this mountain nor in Jerusalem will
you worship the Father.
22You worship what you do not know.
We know Whom we worship, because
salvation is of the Jews.
23But an hour is coming, and now is,
when the true worshippers will worship the Father in Spirit and in truth,
for the Father seeks those who worship
Him.
24God is Spirit, and those who worship Him must worship Him in Spirit
and Truth."
25The woman said to Him, "I know
that the Messiah is coming, Who is
called Christ. Whenever He comes, He
will tell us all things."
26Jesus said to her, "I am that One,
speaking to you."
27And upon this His disciples came
and were shocked that He was speaking with a woman, yet no one said,
"What do you want?" or, "Why are you
talking with her?"
28The woman then left her water pot,
and went away into the city, and said to
the men,
29"Come, see a man that told me
everything that I have done. Is this not
the Christ?"
30Then they went out of the city and
came to Him.
31In the meantime the disciples asked
Him, saying, "Rabbi, eat?"
32But He said to them, "I have food
to eat that you do not know about."
33Then the disciples said one to another, "Has anyone brought Him
food?"
34Jesus said to them, "My food is to
do the will of Him that sent Me, and to
fulfill His work.
35You should not say that there are
still four months until the harvest
comes. I tell you: behold, lift up your
eyes and see, the fields are already
white to harvest!
36And he that reaps receives wages,
and gathers fruit to eternal life, so that
both he that sows and he that reaps
may rejoice together.
37For indeed this is a true saying, that
there is one that sows and another that
reaps.
38I send you to reap that which you
did not toil for– others toiled, and you
enter into their labors."
39From out of that city of the Samaritans, many of them believed in Him
because of the word of her testimony,
saying, "He told me everything that I
had done."
40Then when the Samaritans came to
Him, they asked Him to stay with
them. And He stayed there two days.
41And many more of them believed
through His word.
42And they said to the woman, "It is
no longer because of what you have
said that we believe, for we ourselves
hear and we have seen that this is truly
the Savior of the world, the Christ."
43Now after the two days He came
out from there and went into Galilee.
44Jesus himself testified that indeed a
prophet has no honor in his own native
land.
45When He had then come to Galilee,
the Galileans received Him, for they
had seen everything that He did in
Jerusalem at the feast, for they were
also at the feast.

46 Jesus then came again to Cana of Galilee where He had made the water wine. Now at Capernaum there was a royal official whose son was ill.

47 When he had heard that Jesus had come from Judea into Galilee, he went out to meet Him and asked Him to come and heal his son who was indeed about to die.

48 Then Jesus said to him, "If you do not see miracles and wonders, surely you will not believe."

49 The ruler said to Him, "Master, come before my young child dies."

50 Jesus said to him, "Go, for your son lives." And the man departed, for he believed the word that Jesus spoke to him.

51 Now, as he was returning, his servants came to meet him and reported to him saying, "Your child lives!"

52 Then he asked them at what time he had gotten better and they said to him, "The fever left him yesterday at the seventh hour."

53 The father knew then that it was at the same time in which Jesus said to him, 'Your son lives,' and he and his whole household believed.

54 This is the second miracle that Jesus did when he had come again into Galilee from Judea.

5

After this there was a feast of the Jews, and Jesus went up to Jerusalem.

2 And at Jerusalem there is a pool at the Sheep Gate, called in Hebrew: "Bethesda," which has five porches.

3 In these porches were laying a great number of those who were sick, blind, lame, and paralytic, awaiting the stirring of the water.

4 For an angel descended from time to time into the pool and stirred up the water. He who first entered the water after the agitation of the water became whole of whatever disease had taken hold of him.

5 Now there was a man who had an illness for thirty-eight years.

6 Jesus, seeing this and knowing that he had laid there for a long time, said to him, "Do you desire to be whole?"

7 The infirmed answered Him, "Lord, I do not have a man to cast me into the pool whenever the water is stirred up, so while I am coming another steps in before me."

8 Jesus said to him, "Rise up and take up your cot and walk."

9 And the man was immediately cured and took up his bed and walked. But that day was on a Sabbath.

10 Then said the Jews to the one that was cured, "It is not lawful for you to carry your cot on the Sabbath."

11 He answered them, "He that made me whole said to me, 'Take up your cot and walk.'"

12 They asked him, "Who is the Man that told you to take up your cot and walk?"

13 But he that was cured did not know who it was, for Jesus slipped out since there was a crowd in that place.

14 After this Jesus found him in the temple, and He said to him, "See now! You have become well. Sin no more so that a worse thing does not come upon you."

15 The man went away and reported to the Jews that Jesus was the One that made him whole.

16 And because of this, the Jews persecuted Jesus and looked for an opportunity to kill Him, because this was done on a Sabbath.

17 But Jesus answered them, "My Father is always at work, and so I work."

18 Therefore, because of this, the Jews desired even more to kill Him, because He not only broke the Sabbath, but He also called God His own Father, making Himself equal with God.

19 Jesus therefore replied and said to them, “With absolute certainty, I tell you: the Son does not have the ability to do anything of Himself, for whatever He sees the Father doing, all these things the Son may also do likewise.

20 For the Father loves the Son and shows Him everything that He Himself is doing, and will show Him greater works so that you may be astonished.

21 For even as the Father raises up the dead and gives life, so also the Son gives life to whom He wills.

22 The Father does not judge anyone, but has given all judgment to the Son,

23 so that all may honor the Son, just as they honor the Father. He who does not honor the Son does not honor the Father Who sent Him.

24 With absolute certainty, I tell you, those who hear My word and believe in the One Who has sent Me have eternal life and shall not come into judgment, but have passed from death into life.

25 With absolute certainty, I tell you that the time is coming, and now is, when the dead shall hear the voice of the Son of God, and they who hear shall live.

26 Just as certainly as the Father has life in Himself, even so He has given the Son also to have life in Himself.

27 And He also gave Him authority to execute judgment, because He is a Son of man.

28 Do not marvel at this. For an hour is coming in which all those in the graves will hear His voice,

29 and they will come out– those who have done good to a resurrection of life, but those who practiced wickedness to a resurrection of judgment.

30 I do not have power to do anything of Myself. Accordingly as I hear, I judge. And My judgment is righteous, because I seek not My will, but the will of the Father Who sent Me.

31 If I testify of Myself, My testimony is not true.

32 Another testifies of Me, and I know that the testimony is true which He testified of Me.

33 You sent to John, and he testified of the truth.

34 Now I do not receive the testimony of man, but these words of Mine can save you.

35 He was the lamp burning and shining, and for a time you were willing to rejoice in his light.

36 But I have the greater witness than that of John. For the works Father has given Me to finish, these works themselves which I do, testify on My behalf that the Father has sent Me.

37 And the Father who sent Me has Himself provided the proof concerning Me. You have never heard His voice, nor have you seen His outward appearance.

38 And you do not have His word abiding in you, because you do not believe the One Whom He sent.

39 Search the Scriptures, for you think in them you have eternal life, for they also testify concerning Me.

40 But you will not come to Me so that you may have life.

41 I do not receive glory from men.

42 Nevertheless, I have known that you do not have the love of God in yourselves.

43 I come in the name of My Father, and you do not receive Me. If another one comes in his own name, that one

you will receive.

44 How are you able to believe, when you seek glory from one another and you do not seek the glory that only comes from God?

45 You should not think that I will accuse you to the Father. Moses, in whom you have believed, will accuse you.

46 If indeed you believe Moses, then you should believe Me, for it was about Me that he wrote.

47 But if you do not believe his writings, how will you believe My words?"

6

After these things Jesus went across the Sea of Galilee, which is the Sea of Tiberias.

2 And a great crowd followed Him, because they saw the miracles which He performed upon the sick.

3 And Jesus went up into the mountain, and there He sat among His disciples.

4 Now the Passover, the feast of the Jews, was near.

5 When Jesus lifted up His eyes and saw that a large crowd had come to Him, He said to Philip, "Where is there a market place, so we may buy bread so these may eat?"

6 But He said this testing him, for He knew what He was about to do.

7 Philip replied to Him, "Two hundred denarii would not buy enough bread. Even then, each of them would only receive a little."

8 One of His disciples, Andrew, the brother of Simon Peter, said to Him,

9 "A lad is here who has five barley cakes and two fish. But what are these among so many?"

10 But Jesus said, "Make these men sit down." Now, there was thick grass in that place, so about five thousand men in number sat down.

11 Jesus took the cakes, and having given thanks, He distributed them to the disciples, and the disciples to those seated– also the fish in the same way, as much as they desired.

12 And when they had enough, He told His disciples, "Collect the broken pieces that are left over, so that nothing is lost."

13 Then they gathered the fragments, and they filled twelve baskets from the leftovers of the five cakes of barley that were eaten by them.

14 Therefore the men, seeing the miracle that Jesus had performed, said, "Surely this is the Prophet Who is to come into the world."

15 Jesus then, knowing that they were about to come and seize Him in order to make Him king, withdrew again alone into the mountain by Himself.

16 When evening came, His disciples went down to the sea.

17 And they entered into the boat, for they were going to Capernaum on the other side of the sea. Now it was already dark, and Jesus had not come unto them.

18 The sea became rough because a strong wind began to blow.

19 And having rowed about three to four miles, they beheld Jesus walking on the Sea. As He came near the boat, they were terrified.

20 But He said to them, "It is I! Do not be afraid!"

21 Then they willingly received Him into the boat, and instantly the boat came to the land where they were going.

22 The next day, the crowd was standing on the other side of the sea. They saw that no other boat was there except the one that His disciples entered into, because Jesus had not entered along

with them into the small boat, for His
disciples had gone away alone.
23 But other small boats came from
Tiberias near to the place where they
ate the Lord's bread of thanksgiving.
24 Then, when the multitude saw that
Jesus was not there nor His disciples,
they also entered themselves into the
boats and came to Capernaum, seeking
Jesus.
25 And finding Him on the other side
of the sea, they said, "Rabbi, when did
You come here?"
26 Jesus answered them and said,
"With absolute certainty, I tell you, that
you do not seek Me because you saw a
miracle, but because you ate the bread
and were filled.
27 Labor not for the food that is consumed, but for the food which remains
unto eternal life, which the Son of Man
will give you. For the Father God has
sealed Him."
28 Then they said to Him, "What shall
we do that we may work the works of
God?"
29 Jesus answered them and said,
"This is the work of God: that you believe in the One He sent."
30 They said to Him, "What miracle
will You do that we may see and believe
You– what work?
31 Our fathers ate manna in the
wilderness, according as it is written,
'He gave them bread out of Heaven to
eat.'"
32 Then Jesus said to them, "With absolute certainty, I tell you, Moses did
not give you the bread from Heaven,
but My Father has given you the True
Bread from Heaven.
33 For the Bread of God is He Who
comes down from Heaven and gives
life to the world."
34 Then they said to Him, "Lord, give
us this Bread from now on."
35 But Jesus said to them, "I am the
Bread of Life. Those who come to Me
will in no way hunger, and those who
believe in Me will in no way ever thirst.
36 But I said to you that you have also
seen Me, and have not believed.
37 All that the Father gives Me shall
come to Me, and he that comes to Me
will in no way be cast outside.
38 For I have come down out of Heav-
en, not that I may do My own will, but
the will of Him Who sent Me.
39 And this is the will of the Father
Who sent Me, that of all He has given
Me, I shall lose none, but shall raise it
up on the last day.
40 And this is the will of Him who
sent Me, that all who look upon the
Son and believe in Him should have
eternal life, and I shall raise him up at
the last day."
41 Then the Jews murmured about
him, because He said, "I am the Bread
that came down from Heaven."
42 And they said, "Is this not Jesus, the
son of Joseph? Do we not know His father and mother? How can He say, 'I
came down from Heaven'?"
43 And Jesus answered them and said
to them, "Do not murmur to each other,
44 for no one is able to come to Me
unless the Father Who sent Me draws
him. And I shall raise him up on the
last day.
45 It is written in the prophets, 'And
they shall all be taught of God.' Everyone that has heard from the Father and
learned shall come to Me.
46 Not that anyone has seen the Father, except He Who is from God– He
has seen the Father.
47 With absolute certainty, I tell you,
those believing in Me have eternal life.

48 I am the Bread of Life.

49 Your fathers ate manna in the wilderness and died.

50 This is the Bread that came down out of Heaven, that anyone may eat of it and not die.

51 I am the Living Bread that came down from Heaven– if anyone eats of this Bread, he will live forever. And indeed, the Bread that I give is My flesh, which I give for the life of the world."

52 Then the Jews argued with one another, saying, "How can He give us His flesh to eat?"

53 Then Jesus said to them, "With absolute certainty, I tell you, if you do not eat the flesh of the Son of Man and drink of His blood, you do not have life in yourself.

54 He who eats of My flesh and drinks of My blood has eternal life, and I will raise him up on the last day.

55 For My flesh truly is food, and My blood truly is drink.

56 He who eats of My flesh and drinks of My blood dwells in Me, and I in him.

57 Just as the Living Father sent Me, and I live through the Father, also he who partakes of Me shall also live through Me.

58 This is the Bread that came down out of Heaven, not as your fathers ate manna and died. He who partakes of this Bread shall live forever."

59 He said these things while teaching in the synagogue in Capernaum.

60 Many of His disciples who heard Him said, "This is a hard saying. Who is able to hear it?"

61 But Jesus knowing in Himself that His disciples murmured about this said to them, "Does this offend you?

62 What if you should see the Son of Man ascending up where He was at first?

63 It is the Spirit that makes alive, the flesh is of no benefit. The words which I speak to you are Spirit and they are life.

64 But there are some of you who do not believe." For Jesus knew from the beginning who they were that did not believe, and who it was that would betray Him.

65 And then He said, "I tell you that no one is able to come to Me unless it is given to him from My Father."

66 At this many of His disciples went away and they walked no longer after Him.

67 Then said Jesus to the twelve, "Are you also desiring to go away?"

68 Then Simon Peter answered Him, "Master, to whom shall we go? You have the words of eternal life.

69 And we have believed and we have known that You are the Christ, the Son of the Living God."

70 Jesus answered them. "Did not I choose twelve of you, and one of you is a Devil?"

71 He said this of Judas Iscariot, of Simon, for he was about to betray Him, being one of the twelve.

7 And after these things Jesus walked in Galilee, for He did not desire to walk in Judea, because the Jews sought to kill Him.

2 Now the Jewish Feast of Tabernacles was near.

3 Then His brothers said to Him, "Depart from here and go to Judea, so that Your disciples will also see Your works that You do.

4 For no one does anything in secret who himself seeks to be known openly. If You do these things, reveal Yourself to the world."

5For even His brothers did not believe in Him.
6Jesus then said to them, "My time
has not yet come, but your time is
whenever you are ready.
7The world is not able to hate you.
But it hates Me, because I testify about
it, that its works are evil.
8You go up to the feast. I am not going to this feast, because My time is not
yet fulfilled."
9And saying these things to them, He
remained in Galilee.
10But when His brothers went up,
then He also went up to the feast– not
openly, but as in secret.
11Then the Jews sought Him in the
feast and said, "Where is He?"
12And there was much whispering
about Him among the crowds. Some
said that He was good, but others
replied, "No, rather He deceives the
multitudes."
13However, no one spoke publicly
about Him because they feared the
Jews.
14But, the feast now being half over,
Jesus went up to the temple and taught.
15And the Jews were amazed, saying,
"How is it that He knows the writings,
having not been taught?"
16Jesus answered them and said, "My
teaching is not My own, but of the One
Who sent Me.
17If anyone desires to do His will, he
will know about the teaching– whether
it is from God or if I speak on My own.
18The one who speaks of himself
seeks his own glory. But He who seeks
the glory of the One sending Him, this
One is true and there is no unrighteousness in Him.
19Has not Moses given you the Law?
Yet none of you keep the Law. Why do
you seek to kill Me?"
20The crowd answered and said, "You
have a demon. Who seeks to kill You?"
21Jesus answered and said to them, "I
have done one work, and all of you are
shocked.
22Yet because Moses gave you circumcision, even though it is not from
Moses but from the fathers, you circumcise a man on a Sabbath.
23If a man can be circumcised on a
Sabbath so that the Law of Moses is not
broken, are you angry because I made a
man completely whole on Sabbath?
24Stop judging according to appearances, rather judge righteous judgment."
25Some of them from Jerusalem said,
"Is not this the One they seek to kill?
26For here He is speaking freely, and
no one says anything to Him. Have the
rulers recognized that this is truly the
Christ?
27Now, we know where this Man is
from. But when the Christ comes, no
one will know where He is from."
28Then Jesus, teaching in the temple,
cried out and said, "Now you know Me
and you know where I am from. And I
have not come of myself, but the One
Who has sent Me is true. That One you
do not know.
29But I know Him, because I am
from Him, and He sent Me."
30Then they sought to seize Him, but
no one laid a hand on Him, because
His hour had not yet come.
31Now many of the crowd believed in
Him and said, "When the Christ
comes, will he do more miracles than
these that are done?"
32The Pharisees heard the crowd
murmuring these things about Him.
And the high priests and the Pharisees
sent temple guards to seize Him.
33Then Jesus said, "I am with you for

a little more time, then I shall go to the
One Who sent Me.
34You shall seek Me and shall not
find Me. And where I am, you will not
be able to come."
35Then the Jews said among themselves, "Where is He about to go so that
we shall not find him? Will He go to
the dispersed among the Greeks and
teach those Greeks?
36What is this word that is spoken:
'You will seek Me and not find Me.
And where I am, you will not be able to
come'?"
37Now in the last great day of the
feast, Jesus stood and cried out, saying,
"If anyone is thirsty, let him come to
Me and drink.
38He who believes in Me, just as the
Scriptures said, out of his belly shall
flow rivers of living water."
39Now this He spoke concerning the
Spirit, Whom they who believe in Him
were about to receive. For the Holy
Spirit was not yet given, because Jesus
was not yet glorified.
40Some of the crowd then, hearing
this word, said, "Truly, this is the
Prophet."
41Others said, "This is the Christ,"
but others said, "What? The Christ will
not come from Galilee.
42Have not the Scriptures said that
the Christ shall come from the seed of
David, and from Bethlehem, the city of
David?"
43A division therefore arose in the
crowd because of Him.
44Now some of them desired to seize
Him, but no one laid their hands on
Him.
45Then the temple guards came to
the high priests and Pharisees. And
they said to them, "Why didn't you
bring Him?"
46The temple guards answered, "Never has a man spoken like this Man."
47Then the Pharisees answered them,
"Have you not also been deceived?
48Have any of the rulers or the Pharisees believed in Him?
49No! But this crowd, which does not
know the Law, is cursed."
50Nicodemus said to them, (he who
came to Him at night, being one of
them),
51"Does our Law judge the man, unless it hears him first and knows what
he is doing?"
52They answered and said to him,
"Are you also of Galilee? Search and
see, for that Prophet will not arise out
of Galilee."
53Then every one of them went to his
own house.

8 But Jesus went to the Mount of
Olives.
2And again, in the morning, He arrived back at the temple. And all the
people came to Him, and He sat down
to teach them.
3But the Scribes and the Pharisees
brought to Him a woman having been
taken in adultery, and stood her in
their midst.
4They said to Him, "Teacher, this
woman was taken in the very act of
adultery.
5Now Moses commanded us in the
Law that such a person should be
stoned. Therefore, what do You say?"
6Now this they said, tempting Him,
in order to be able to accuse Him. But
Jesus stooped down and wrote with His
finger in the dirt.
7And as they continued to question
Him, He rose up and said to them,
"The one who is without sin among
you– throw a stone at her first."

8 And again He bent down and wrote in the dirt.

9 But hearing, and being convicted by their conscience, they went out one by one, beginning from the eldest unto the last. And Jesus was left alone, and the woman standing in the midst.

10 And Jesus rose up and, seeing no one but the woman, He said to her, "Woman, where are your accusers? Has no one condemned you?"

11 And she said, "No one, Master." And Jesus said to her, "Neither do I condemn you, go and sin no more."

12 Then Jesus again spoke to them, saying, "I am the Light of the World, he who follows Me will in no way walk in darkness, but will have the Light of Life."

13 Then the Pharisees said to Him, "You testify about Yourself– Your testimony is not true."

14 Jesus answered them and said, "Even if I testify about Myself, My witness is true, because I know where I came from and where I am going. But you do not know where I came from, nor where I am going.

15 You judge according to the flesh. I judge no one.

16 But even if I judge, My judgment is true, because I am not alone. But the Father who sent Me is with Me.

17 And in your Law it is written that the testimony of two men is true.

18 I am One Who witnesses about Myself. And the Father Who sent Me, He witnesses concerning Me."

19 They said to Him, "Where is Your Father?" Jesus answered, "You have not recognized Me, nor My Father. If you had recognized Me, you would have also recognized My Father."

20 These words were spoken in the treasury, as He taught in the temple. And no one seized Him, because His hour had not yet come.

21 Then He said to them again, "I go away, and you will seek Me, but you will die in your sin. Where I go, you are not able to come."

22 Then the Jews said, "Will He kill Himself? Because He says, 'Where I go, you are not able to come.'"

23 But He said to them, "You are from below– I am from above. You are of this world– I am not of this world.

24 Therefore I said to you that you will die in your sins. For if you do not believe who I am, you shall die in your sins."

25 Then they said to Him, "Who are You?" Jesus said to them, "That which I told you even from the beginning.

26 I have many things to say and to judge concerning you, but He who sent Me is true. And what I have heard from Him, these things I speak to the world."

27 They did not understand that He spoke to them of the Father.

28 Then Jesus said to them, "When you lift up the Son of Man, then you will know Who I am, and that of Myself I do nothing. But as My Father taught Me, I speak these things.

29 And He that sent Me is with Me. The Father has not left Me alone, for I always do those things that please Him."

30 As He spoke these things, many believed in Him.

31 Then Jesus said to the Jews who believed in Him, "If you remain in My Word, then you are truly My disciples.

32 And you shall know the truth, and the truth will set you free."

33 They answered Him, "We are the seed of Abraham, and we have never been enslaved to anyone. How can You say, 'You will become free'?"

34Jesus answered them, "With absolute certainty, I tell you that everyone who commits sin is a slave of sin.

35But the slave will not remain in the house forever– the Son remains forever.

36If then the Son shall set you free, you are really free.

37I know that you are the seed of Abraham. But you seek to kill Me, because My word has no place in you.

38I speak what I have seen with My Father, and you therefore do what you have seen with your father."

39They answered and said to Him, "Abraham is our father." Jesus said to them, "If you were the children of Abraham, you would do the works of Abraham.

40But now you seek to kill Me, a Man Who has spoken the truth to you, which I heard from God. Abraham would not do this.

41You do the works of your father." Then they said to Him, "We were not born of sexual immorality. We have one father: God."

42Then Jesus said to them, "If God were your father, you would love Me. For I came forth from God, and have come; and neither of Myself have I come, but He sent Me.

43Why do you not understand My speech? Because you are not able to hear My Word.

44You are of your father the Devil, and the lust of your father you will do. He was a murderer from the beginning, and remained not in the truth, because the truth was not in him. When he speaks a lie, he speaks of his own, because he is also the father of the lie.

45And because I speak the truth, you do not believe Me.

46Who of you convinces Me of sin? And if I tell you the truth, why do you not believe Me?

47The one who is of God hears the words of God. Therefore, you do not hear, because you are not of God."

48Then the Jews answered and said to Him, "Do we not say well that You are a Samaritan, and You have a demon?"

49Jesus answered, "I do not have a demon. But I honor My Father, and you dishonor Me.

50And I do not seek My glory. There is One that seeks and judges.

51With absolute certainty, I tell you, if anyone keeps My word, he will never ever behold death."

52Then the Jews said to Him, "Now we know that You have a demon. Abraham died, and the prophets, and you say, 'If anyone keeps My word, he shall never ever taste of death.'

53Are You greater than our father Abraham, who died? And the prophets, who died? Whom do You make Yourself?"

54Jesus answered, "If I glorify Myself, My glory is nothing. It is My Father Who glorifies Me, Whom you say is your God.

55And you do not know Him, but I know Him. And if I say that I do not know Him, I shall be like you: a liar. But I know Him, and I keep His Word.

56Your father Abraham leaped for joy that he should see My day. And he saw it and was glad."

57Then the Jews said to Him, "You are not yet fifty years old, and have You seen Abraham?"

58Jesus said to them, "With absolute certainty, I tell you, before Abraham came into being, I Am."

59Then they took up stones, that they might throw at Him. But Jesus was hidden from them and went out of the

temple, going through the midst of
them, and so passed by.

9 And, passing by, He saw a man
blind from birth.
2 And His disciples asked Him, saying, “Rabbi, who sinned: this one, or
his parents, that he was born blind?”
3 Jesus answered, “Neither this one
sinned, nor his parents. But that the
work of God might be revealed in Him.
4 It is necessary for Me to work the
works of the One Who sent Me while it
is day. The night comes when no one
will be able to work.
5 While I am in the world, I am the
Light of the world.”
6 Saying these things, He spat on the
ground and made clay out of the spittle
and smeared the clay upon the blind
one’s eyes,
7 and said to him, “Go, wash in the
pool of Siloam” (which is translated
“sent”). Then he went and washed, and
came seeing.
8 Then the neighbors and those who
had seen him before when he was blind
said, “Is this not the one who sat and
begged?”
9 Some said, “It is him,” and others,
“He is like him.” He said, “I am the
one.”
10 Then they said to him, “How were
your eyes opened?”
11 He answered and said, “A man
called Jesus made clay and anointed my
eyes, and said to me, ‘Go to the pool of
Siloam and wash.’ And, going and
washing, I received sight.”
12 Then they said to him, “Where is
He?” He said, “I do not know.”
13 And they brought him who was
once blind to the Pharisees.
14 Now it was a Sabbath when Jesus
made clay and opened his eyes.
15 Then the Pharisees asked him again
how he received his sight. And he said
to them, “He put clay on my eyes, and I
washed, and I see.”
16 Then said some of the Pharisees,
“This Man is not from God, because
He does not keep the Sabbath.” Others
said, “How is a Man Who is a sinner
able to do such miracles?” And there
was a division among them.
17 Then they said again to the blind
one, “What do you say about Him, in
that He opened your eyes?” And he
said, “He is a prophet.”
18 But the Jews did not believe concerning him, that he was blind and received his sight, until they called the
parents of him who had received his
sight.
19 And they asked them, saying, “Is
this your son whom you say was born
blind? How then does he now see?”
20 Then his parents answered them,
and said, “We know that this is our son
and that he was born blind.
21 But how he now sees, we do not
know– or who opened his eyes, we do
not know. He is old enough, ask him–
he will speak for himself.”
22 His parents said these things because they feared the Jews, for the Jews
had already agreed that if anyone
should confess Him as Christ, he
would be expelled from the congregation.
23 Because of this, his parents said,
“He is of age, ask him.”
24 Then they called the man who was
blind a second time, and said to him,
“Give glory to God, for we know that
this Man is a sinner.”
25 Then he answered and said, “I do
not know if He is a sinner. One thing I
know: I was blind– now I see!”
26 And they said to him again, “What

did He do to you? How did He open your eyes?”

27 He answered them, “I told you already, and you have not heard. Why do you wish to hear it again? Do you also wish to become His disciples?”

28 And then they scorned him and said, “You’re one of His disciples, but we are Moses’s disciples.

29 We know that God has spoken by Moses. But as for this One, we do not know where He is from.”

30 The man answered them and said, “Indeed, this is a marvel! In that you do not know where He is from, and yet He has opened my eyes.

31 We know that God will not hear a sinner. But if anyone fears God and does His will, He hears that one.

32 From the age, it was not heard that anyone opened the eyes of one that was born blind.

33 If He was not from God, He would not be able to do anything.”

34 They answered and said to him, “You were altogether born in sin, and do you teach us?” And they threw him out.

35 Jesus heard that they threw him out and, finding him, He said to him, “Do you believe in the Son of God?”

36 And he answered and said, “Who is He, Sir, that I may believe in Him?”

37 And Jesus said to him, “You have both seen Him, and it is He that is speaking with you.”

38 And he said, “I believe, Lord!” and he worshiped Him.

39 And Jesus said, “For judgment I have come into the world, that the ones who do not see may see, and those who see may become blind.”

40 And those of the Pharisees who were with Him heard these things, and said to Him, “Are we also blind?”

41 Jesus said to them, “If you were blind, you would have no sin. But now you say, ‘We see.’ Therefore, your sin remains.”

10 “I tell you, with absolute certainty, he one who does not enter through the door into the sheep pen, but climbs up some other way, the same is a thief and a robber.

2 But the one entering by the door is the shepherd of the sheep.

3 The door-keeper will open for him, and the sheep hear his voice. He calls his own sheep by name, and leads them out.

4 When he sends out his own sheep, he goes in front of them. And the sheep follow him, because they know his voice.

5 But they will never follow a stranger, but shall flee away from him, because they do not know the voice of a stranger.”

6 Jesus told them this allegory, but they did not understand what was spoken to them.

7 Jesus therefore said again to them, “With absolute certainty, I tell you that I am the Door of the sheep.

8 Everyone who came before Me are thieves and robbers, but the sheep did not hear them.

9 I am the Door. If anyone enters through Me, he will be saved and shall go in and out and shall find pasture.

10 The thief does not come, except that he may steal, kill, and destroy. I came that they may have life, and might have it abundantly.

11 I am the Good Shepherd! The Good Shepherd lays down His soul for the sheep.

12 But the hired servant, not even being a shepherd, who does not own the

sheep, will see the wolf coming, and will leave the sheep, and run away! And the wolf seizes them and scatters the sheep.

13 But the hired servant runs away because he is a hired servant and has no concern for the sheep.

14 I am the Good Shepherd, and I know Mine and am known by Mine,

15 just as the Father knows Me and I also know the Father. Now I lay down My soul for the sheep.

16 And I have other sheep that are not of this fold. I must also bring them, and they will hear My voice, and they will become one flock with one Shepherd.

17 Because of this the Father loves Me, because I lay down My soul that I may take it up again.

18 No one takes it from Me, but I lay it down of Myself. I have authority to lay it down, and I have authority to take it up again. I received this command from My Father."

19 Then again a division occurred among the Jews because of these words.

20 And many of them said, "He has a demon and is uttering madness. Why listen to Him?"

21 Others said, "These are not the words of one who is possessed by a demon. Is a demon able to open the eyes of the blind?"

22 And the Feast of Dedication took place in Jerusalem, and it was winter.

23 And Jesus was walking in the temple in Solomon's porch.

24 Then the Jews, encircling Him, said to Him, "How long will You keep our soul in suspense? If You are the Christ, tell us publicly."

25 Jesus answered them, "I told you, and you did not believe. The works that I do in the name of My Father, these bear witness of Me.

26 But you do not believe, because you are not of My sheep. As I said to you,

27 My sheep hear My voice, and I know them, and they follow Me.

28 And I give eternal life to them, and they shall never ever perish, and no one shall snatch them from My hand.

29 My Father, who gave them to Me, is greater than all. And no one has authority to snatch them out of My Father's hand.

30 I and the Father are One."

31 Then the Jews took up stones again that they might stone Him.

32 Jesus answered them, "I have shown you many awesome works from My Father– for which of these works do you stone Me?"

33 The Jews answered Him, saying, "We do not stone You because of an awesome work, but because of blasphemy, and that You, being a man, make Yourself God."

34 Jesus answered them, "Is it not written in your Law, 'I said you are gods'?

35 If He called them gods to whom the word of God came, and the Scriptures cannot be broken,

36 why do you say of Him, whom the Father sanctified
and sent into the world, 'You blaspheme,' because I said, 'I am the Son of God'?

37 If I do not do the works of My Father, do not believe Me.

38 But if I do, even if you do not believe Me, believe the works, so that you may know and believe that the Father is in Me, and I am in the Father."

39 Then they attempted again to seize Him, but He passed out of their hands.

40 And He went away again to the other side of the Jordan to the place

where John first baptized, and stayed there.

41 And many came to Him and said, "John did not do any miracles, but all that John spoke concerning this one is true."

42 And many believed in Him there.

11 Now Lazarus was sick, who was of Bethany, the town of Mary and her sister Martha.

2 And it was Mary, who anointed the Lord with ointment and dried His feet with her hair, whose brother Lazarus was sick.

3 Therefore the sisters went to Him, saying, "Lord, behold, the one You love is sick."

4 And hearing it, Jesus said to her, "This sickness is not unto death, but rather for the glory of God, that the Son of God may be glorified through it."

5 Now Jesus loved Martha, and her sister, and Lazarus.

6 Therefore when He heard that he was sick, He still remained in the place where He was for two days.

7 Then after this He said to the disciples, "Let's go into Judea again."

8 The disciples said to him, "Rabbi, the Jews have sought to stone You, and are You going there again?"

9 Jesus answered, "Are there not twelve hours in a day? If anyone walks in the day, he does not stumble, because he sees the light of the world.

10 But if anyone walks in the night, he stumbles, because the light is not in him."

11 These things He said, and after this He said to them, "Our friend Lazarus has fallen asleep. But I am going that I may wake him up."

12 Then the disciples said to him, "Lord, if he has fallen asleep, he does well."

13 But Jesus had spoken about his death. But they thought He spoke of the sleep of rest.

14 Therefore, at that time, Jesus said unto them plainly, "Lazarus is dead.

15 And I rejoice for your sake that I was not there, so that you may believe. Now let us go to him."

16 Then Thomas, who is called "Didymus," said to the other disciples, "Let's go, so that we may die with Him."

17 Then when Jesus came, He found that he had already been four days in the grave.

18 Now Bethany was near Jerusalem, about two miles.

19 And many of the Jews came to Martha and Mary in order to comfort them concerning their brother.

20 Then when Martha had heard that Jesus was coming, she met Him. But Mary was sitting in the house.

21 Then Martha said to Jesus, "Master, if You had been here, my brother would not be dead.

22 But even now I know that whatever You ask God, God will give You."

23 Jesus said to her, "Your brother will rise again."

24 Martha said to Him, "I know that he will rise again in the resurrection on the last day."

25 Jesus said to her, "I am the Resurrection and the Life. The one who believes in Me, even if he dies, he shall live.

26 And everyone living and believing in Me shall never die. Do you believe this?"

27 She said to Him, "Yes, Master, I have believed that You are the Christ, the Son of God Who is come into the world."

28 And saying these things, she went away and called her sister Mary secretly, saying, "The Teacher is here and He calls for you."

29 And when she heard this, she rose up quickly and came to Him.

30 Now Jesus had not yet come into the village, but was in the place where Martha had met Him.

31 Then those Jews that were with her in the house and consoling her, seeing that Mary rose up quickly and went out, followed her, saying, "She is going to the tomb that she may weep there."

32 Then Mary, when she came where Jesus was, seeing Him, she fell at His feet, saying, "Master, if You had been here, my brother would not have died."

33 Then when Jesus saw her weeping, and the Jews weeping who came down with her, He groaned in the spirit and was stirred Himself.

34 And He said, "Where have you put him?" And they said, "Master, come and see."

35 Jesus wept.

36 Then the Jews said, "See how He loved him."

37 But some of them said, "Could not He, Who was able to open the eyes of the blind, have caused that this one should not have died?"

38 Then, groaning again within Himself, Jesus came to the tomb. Now it was a cave, and a stone was laid against it.

39 Jesus said, "Remove the stone." Martha, the sister of the one who died, said, "Master, he stinks by now, for it is the fourth day."

40 Jesus said to her, "Didn't I tell you that if you would believe, you would see the glory of God?"

41 Therefore, they took away the stone where the dead one was laid. And Jesus lifted His eyes upward and said, "Father, I thank You that You have heard Me.

42 And I knew that You always hear Me, but for the sake of the crowd standing here I have said this, so that they might believe that You have sent Me."

43 And then He cried out with a strong voice, "Lazarus, come out here!"

44 And the one who had died came out, his feet and hands having been bound with grave clothes, and his face being wrapped with a cloth. Jesus said to them, "Untie him, and let him go."

45 Then many of the Jews that came to Mary, now beholding what was done, believed in Him.

46 But some of them went to the Pharisees and told them what Jesus had done.

47 Then the Chief Priests and the Pharisees assembled a Sanhedrin and said, "What are we to do? For this man is doing many miracles.

48 If we leave him alone, many will believe in Him, and the Romans will come and take away our place and nation."

49 But one of them, Caiaphas, who was the high priest that year, said to them, "You definitely do not understand.

50 You have not considered that it is profitable for us that one man dies on behalf of the people, and not that the whole nation perish."

51 But this that he said went forth not of himself, but being the high priest that year, he prophesied that Jesus was about to die for the nation.

52 And not for the nation only, but also that He may gather together into one the children of God that were scattered.

53 Then from that day they resolved to
kill Him.
54 Then Jesus no longer walked about
freely among the Jews, but went from
there into a place near the desert, into a
city called Ephraim, and there remained with His disciples.
55 And the Passover of the Jews was
near. And many came out of the country into Jerusalem before the Passover
in order to purify themselves.
56 Then they sought Jesus and said to
each other as they stood in the temple,
"What do you think? Surely He will not
come to the feast?"
57 Now all the Chief Priests and the
Pharisees gave an order that if anyone
knew where He was, they were to report it, so that they might arrest Him.

12 Then six days before the Passover, Jesus came into Bethany,
where Lazarus was, who had died,
whom He had raised from the dead.
2 Then they made Him supper. And
Martha served, but Lazarus was one of
them which reclined with Him.
3 Then Mary took a pound of pure
spikenard ointment, very expensive, to
anoint the feet of Jesus, and she wiped
His feet with her hair. And the house
was filled from the fragrance of the
ointment.
4 Now Simon's son, Judas Iscariot, one
of His disciples, who was about to hand
Him over, said,
5 "Why was this ointment not sold for
three hundred denarii, and given to the
poor?"
6 But he said this, not because he was
concerned for the poor, but because he
was a thief, and had the case and carried that which was put in it.
7 Then Jesus said, "Leave her alone,
for she has kept it for the day of My
burial.
8 For you will always have the poor
among you, but you will not always
have Me."
9 Then a large crowd of the Jews
learned that He was there. And they
came not only because of Jesus, but because they wanted to also see Lazarus,
whom He raised from the dead.
10 But the Chief Priests had resolved
that Lazarus also should be killed.
11 Because of him many of the Jews
went away and believed in Jesus.
12 The next day many people came to
the feast because they had heard that
Jesus was coming to Jerusalem.
13 They took palm branches and came
out to meet Him, and they cried out,
"Hosanna! Blessed is He who comes in
the name of the Lord, the king of
Israel!"
14 Now Jesus had found a young donkey, and He sat on it, just as it is written:
15 "Be not afraid, daughter of Zion.
Behold, your King comes, sitting upon
a foal of a donkey."
16 But His disciples did not know
these things at first. But when Jesus was
glorified, then they remembered that
these things were written of Him, and
that they did these things to Him.
17 Now then, the crowd that was with
Him testified that He had called
Lazarus out of the grave and raised
Him from the dead.
18 Because of this also the multitudes
went to meet Him, because they heard
of the miracle that He had done.
19 Then the Pharisees said among
themselves, "You see we have not done
any good! Look, the world goes after
Him!"
20 Now there were some Greeks
among those coming up, so that they

might worship at the Feast.

21 Then these came to Philip, who was of Bethsaida of Galilee, and asked him, saying, "Sir, we desire to see Jesus."

22 Philip came and told Andrew, and again Andrew and Philip came and told Jesus.

23 But Jesus answered them, saying, "The hour has come that the Son of Man should be glorified.

24 With absolute certainty, I tell you, unless the grain of wheat that falls into the ground dies, it abides alone. But if it dies, it brings forth much fruit.

25 The one who loves His life shall ruin it. And he who hates his life in this world, this one shall keep it to eternal life.

26 Whoever serves Me must follow Me. And where I am, there My servant will also be. And if anyone serves Me, the Father will honor him.

27 Now My soul is troubled, and what shall I say, 'Father, deliver Me from this hour'? But for this hour I have come.

28 Father, glorify Your name." Then came a voice from Heaven, "I have glorified it, and I will also glorify it again."

29 Then the multitude that stood by also heard, saying, "It thundered!" Others said, "An angel spoke to Him!"

30 Jesus answered and said, "This voice did not come for My sake, but for you.

31 Now is the judgment of this world. Now is the ruler of this world driven out.

32 And if I am lifted up from the Earth, I will draw everyone to Myself."

33 Now this He spoke to make known the death that He was about to die.

34 Then the people answered Him, "We heard from the Law that Christ will abide with us forever. And why do you say that it is necessary that the Son of Man be lifted up? Who is the Son of Man?"

35 Then Jesus said to them, "Yet a little while the Light is with you. Walk while you have the Light, so that the darkness does not seize you. And the one walking in darkness does not know where he is going.

36 While you have the Light, believe in the Light, that you may become the sons of Light." Jesus said these things, and then went away and hid from them.

37 And so many were the miracles that He did in front of them, yet they did not believe in Him,

38 that the Word of Isaiah the prophet might be fulfilled, saying, "Lord, who has believed our report, and to whom is the arm of the Lord revealed?"

39 On account of this they were not able to believe, because again Isaiah said,

40 "He has blinded their eyes and hardened their heart, so that their eyes cannot see and their hearts understand and change, and I should heal them."

41 Isaiah said this because he saw His glory and spoke concerning Him.

42 Yet still, many among the chief rulers believed in Him. But because of the Pharisees they did not confess Him, lest they should be put out of the congregation.

43 For they loved the glory of men more than the glory of God.

44 But Jesus cried out and said, "Those who believe in Me do not believe in Me, but in the One Who sent Me.

45 And he who sees Me sees the One Who sent Me.

46 I have come as a Light into the world, so that all who believe in Me shall not remain in darkness.

47 And if anyone hears My words and

believes not, I will not judge him. For I
did not come that I might judge the
world, but that I might save the world.

48 He who rejects Me, and receives
not My words, has one who judges
him: the word that I speak will judge
him on the last day.

49 Because I have not spoken from
Myself, but the Father Who sent Me–
He gave Me a command, what I should
say and what I should speak.

50 And I know that His command is
eternal life. Therefore, whatever I
speak, as the Father has said to Me, so I
speak."

13 And before the feast of Passover,
Jesus, knowing that His hour
had come that He should depart from
this world to the Father, having loved
His own who were in this world, He
loved them to the end.

2 The Devil had already put into the
heart of Judas Iscariot, Simon's son, to
betray Him. Now that supper was over,

3 Jesus– knowing that the Father had
placed all things into His hand, and
that He had come forth from God, and
returned to God–

4 He rose up from supper, and laid
down His mantle and, taking a towel,
He tied it around Himself.

5 Then He poured water into a pitcher
and began to wash the disciples' feet,
and to dry them with the towel that He
had around Him.

6 Then He came to Simon Peter. And
he said to Him, "Master, shall You wash
my feet?"

7 Jesus answered and said to him,
"You do not know what I am doing
now, but you shall understand these
things later."

8 Peter said to Him, "No! You will
never wash my feet!" Jesus replied, "If I
do not wash you, then you shall have
no part with Me."

9 Simon Peter said to Him, "Master,
not my feet only, but also my hands
and head!"

10 Jesus said to him, "He who is
washed has no need except to have his
feet washed, but is completely clean.
And you are clean, but not all of you."

11 For He knew who would betray
Him. Because of this He said, "Not all
of you are clean."

12 Then when He had washed their
feet and had taken His mantle and reclined again, He said to them, "Do you
understand what I have done for you?

13 You call Me, 'Teacher,' and 'Lord,'
and what you say is correct, for I am.

14 Therefore, if I– your Lord and
Teacher– washed your feet, you owe it
to wash one another's feet.

15 For I gave you an example, as I have
done for you, you also should do.

16 With absolute certainty, I assure
you, the slave is not greater than his
Lord, neither is the messenger greater
than the one who sent him.

17 If you know these things, then happy are you if you do them.

18 I am not speaking concerning all of
you. I know whom I have chosen, but
that the scriptures might be fulfilled,
'The one who eats bread with Me lifted
up his heel against Me.'

19 I tell you of this now, before it happens, so that when it happens, you may
believe that I am He.

20 With absolute certainty, I assure
you, whoever receives the one I send
receives Me. And the one who receives
Me receives the One Who sent Me."

21 Saying these things, Jesus was troubled in the Spirit, and testified and
said, "With absolute certainty, I assure
you, one of you will betray Me."

22Then the disciples looked at one
another, perplexed about what was
said.
23Now there was one of His disciples
reclining in the bosom of Jesus, whom
Jesus loved.
24Then Simon Peter signaled him to
ask who it was that He spoke this
about.
25Then he leaned back upon the
chest of Jesus, saying to Him, "Lord
who is it?"
26Jesus said to him, "It is he who I
give the bread after it is dipped." And
then He dipped the bread, and gave it
to Judas Iscariot, of Simon.
27And then after the bread, Satan entered into him. Then Jesus said to him,
"What you do, do quickly."
28But no one who was reclining understood why this was spoken.
29For some were of the opinion that
because Judas carried the case that Jesus said to him, "Buy what we need to
have for the feast," or to give something
to the poor.
30So, having received the bread he
immediately went out. And it was
night.
31Then, when he was gone, Jesus said,
"Now is the Son of Man glorified, and
God is glorified in Him.
32If God is glorified in Him, God
shall also glorify Him in Himself and
shall glorify Him right away.
33Children, I am with you for just a
little while. You shall seek Me, and just
as I said to the Jews– that where I go,
you are not able to come– so also I tell
you now.
34I give to you a new commandment:
that you love one another. Just as I have
loved you, that you also love one another.
35By this shall everyone know that
you are My disciples, if you have love
one for another."
36Simon Peter said to Him, "Lord,
where are You going?" Jesus answered
him, "Where I am going, you are not
able to follow now. But you shall follow
Me later."
37Peter said to Him, "Lord, why am I
not able to follow You now? I will lay
down my soul for You!"
38Jesus said, "Will you lay down your
soul for Me? With absolute certainty, I
tell you, before the rooster crows you
will deny Me three times."

14 "Do not allow your heart to be
troubled. You believe in God,
also believe in Me.
2In My Father's house there are many
dwellings. Now if it were not so, I
would have told you. I go to prepare a
place for you.
3And if I go away and prepare a place
for you, I will come again and receive
you to Myself, that where I am you may
also be.
4And where I go you know, and the
way you know."
5Thomas said, "Lord, we do not
know where you are going. How can
we know the way?"
6Jesus answered him, "I am the Way,
and the Truth, and the Life. No one
comes to the Father except through
Me.
7If you know Me, then you know My
Father also. And from now on you
know Him, and have seen Him."
8Philip said to Him, "Lord, show us
the Father, and satisfy us."
9Jesus answered him, "Have I been
with you for so long a time and you do
not know Me, Philip? To see Me is to
see the Father! So why do you say,
'Show us the Father?'

10 Do you not believe that I am in the Father and that the Father is in Me? The words that I say to you I do not speak on My own. But the Father dwelling in Me performs the works.

11 Believe Me that I am in the Father, and the Father is in Me. Otherwise believe because of the works.

12 With absolute certainty, I tell you, that he who believes in Me will also do the works that I do. Also, he will do greater than these, because I am going to the Father.

13 Now whatever you ask in My name, I will do it, so that the Father may be glorified in the Son.

14 If you ask anything of Me in My name, I will do it.

15 If you love Me, keep My commandments.

16 And I will ask the Father, and He will give you another Paraclete, Who will dwell with you forever.

17 He is the Spirit of Truth, Whom the world will not be able to receive, because it neither sees Him nor recognizes Him. You know Him, because He dwells beside you and shall be in you.

18 I will not leave you orphans– I am coming to you.

19 Yet a little while and the world will not see me any more; but you will see Me. Because I live, you also will live.

20 On that day you shall know that I am in the Father, and you are in Me, and I am in you.

21 He that has My commandments and keeps them is the one that loves Me. And he who loves Me shall be loved by My Father, and I shall love him and reveal Myself to him."

22 Judas said to Him, not Iscariot, "Lord, what has happened that You are about to reveal Yourself to us and not to the world?"

23 Jesus answered and said to him, "If anyone loves Me, he will keep My words, and My Father will love him, and We shall come to him and make Our dwelling place with him.

24 Whoever does not love Me does not keep My words; and the word that you hear is not My own, but My Father's who sent Me.

25 I have said these things to you while I remain with you.

26 But the Paraclete, Who is the Holy Spirit, Whom the Father will send in My name, He is the One Who will teach you everything and remind you of everything that I have spoken to you.

27 I leave you with Peace. My Peace I give to you. I give it to you not as the world gives it to you. Do not let your heart be troubled, and do not be afraid.

28 You have heard Me tell you that I am going away and coming again to you. If you loved Me, you would rejoice that I said I am going to the Father, because the Father is greater than Me.

29 And now I have told you this before it happens so that, when it happens, you may believe.

30 I shall no longer speak much with you, for the ruler of this world is coming, and he has nothing in Me–

31 but that the world may know that I love the Father and that I do exactly as the Father has commanded me. Get up! Let us go from here."

15 "I am the True Vine, and My Father is the Husbandman.

2 He takes away every branch in Me that does not bear fruit. And everyone that bears fruit, He prunes so that it can bear more fruit.

3 You are already clean through the word that I have spoken to you.

4 Dwell in Me, and I in you. Just as

the branch has no power to bring forth fruit by itself, unless it dwells in the vine, so neither can you, unless you dwell in Me.

5 I am the Vine, you are the branches. He who dwells in Me, and I in him, is the one who bears much fruit, for without Me you can do nothing.

6 If one does not remain in Me, he is cast out as the branch and is dried up; and they collect and cast them into a fire, and they are burned.

7 If you dwell in Me, and My words dwell in you, then you may ask what you desire, and it shall be done for you.

8 My Father is glorified in this: that you bring forth much fruit, and be My disciples.

9 As the Father has loved Me, I have also loved you. Dwell in My love.

10 If you keep My commandments, then you will dwell in My love, just as I have kept My Father's commandments and dwell in His love.

11 These things I have spoken to you, that My joy may be in you, and that your joy may be full.

12 This is My commandment: that you love one another, as I have loved you.

13 No one has greater love than this: that he lay down his soul for his friends.

14 You are My friends if you do as I command you.

15 I no longer call you servants, for the servant does not know what his master does. Now you are My friends, for I have made known to you everything that I have heard from My Father.

16 You have not chosen Me, but I have chosen you. And I appointed you that you should go and bring forth fruit, and that your fruit should remain– so that whatever you ask the Father in My name, He will give it to you.

17 This is My commandment, that you love one another.

18 If the world hates you, know that it hated Me before you.

19 If you were of the world, the world would be fond of its own. On account of this, the world hates you, because you are not of the world, for I have chosen you out of the world.

20 Remember the words that I told you: No servant is greater than his master. If they persecute Me, even so they will persecute you. If they keep My word, even so they will keep yours.

21 But they will do all these things to you because of My name, because they do not know the One Who sent Me.

22 If I had not come and spoken to them, they would not have sin. But now they have no excuse for their sin.

23 To hate Me is to also hate My Father.

24 If I had not done these works among them that no one else has done, they would not have sinned. But now they have seen, and they have hated both Me and My Father.

25 But this is the fulfillment of that which is written in their Law: They hated Me without cause.

26 When the Paraclete comes, Whom I will send to you from the Father, the Spirit of Truth Who comes from the Father, He will bear witness of Me.

27 And you will bear witness of Me, because you are with Me from the beginning."

16 "I have spoken these things to you so that you will not be caused to stumble.

2 They are going to cast you out of the synagogue. In fact, the hour is coming that everyone who kills you will think that he is offering worship to God.

3 And they will do these things to you, because they have not known the Father, nor Me.

4 However, I have spoken these things to you, that when the hour comes, you will remember that I told you so. I did not tell you this at the beginning, because I was with you.

5 And now I return to the One Who sent Me; and none of you ask Me, 'Where are You going?'

6 But because I said these things to you, grief has filled your heart.

7 But I have told you the truth: It is expedient for you that I go away, for if I do not go away, the Paraclete will not come to you. But if I go, I will send Him to you.

8 And when He comes, He will convince the world of sin, and of righteousness, and of judgment.

9 About sin, because they do not believe in Me.

10 About righteousness, because I now go to My Father, and you no longer see Me.

11 And about judgment, because the ruler of this world has been judged.

12 I still have many things to tell you, but you are not able to bear them now.

13 But when the Spirit of Truth comes, He will guide you into all truth, for indeed He will not speak on His own, but whatever He hears, He will speak, and He will announce to you what is coming.

14 He will glorify Me, because He will receive from Me, and will announce it to you.

15 Everything that the Father has is Mine. For this reason I said that He shall receive from Me, and announce it to you.

16 A little while, and you will look on Me no more. And again, a little while, and you will see Me, because I go away to the Father."

17 Then His disciples said to one another, "What is this that He says to us, 'A little while and you will no longer look at Me; and again, a little while and you see Me' and, 'Because I go to the Father'?"

18 Then they said, "What is this that He says, 'A little while?' We do not understand what He says."

19 Now Jesus knew what they desired to ask Him, and He said to them, "Why do you seek the meaning of this saying from each other, 'A little while, and you will look on Me no more and again, a little while, and you see Me'?

20 With absolute certainty, I tell you, that you shall weep, and lament, but the world will rejoice. And you shall be sorrowful, but your sorrow shall turn into joy.

21 When the woman brings forth she has sorrow, because her hour has come. But when she brings forth the young child, she no longer remembers the tribulation, because of the joy that she has brought forth a man into the world.

22 And now then, indeed you have sorrow. But I will see you again, and your heart will rejoice, and no one can take your joy from you.

23 And in that day you shall not ask anything of Me. With absolute certainty, I tell you, whatever you may request of the Father in My name, He will give it to you.

24 Until now you have not requested anything in My name. Ask, and you will receive, so that your joy may be fulfilled.

25 I have spoken these things to you in allegories. An hour comes when I will no longer speak to you in allegories, but I will tell you plainly of the Father.

26In that day you will ask in My
name, and I tell you I will not ask the
Father for you.
27For the Father Himself cares for
you, because you have cared for Me,
and you have believed that I came forth
from God.
28I came forth from the Father, and I
have come into the world. Again, I
leave the world, and return to the Father."
29His disciples said to Him, "Behold,
now You speak plainly, and are not
speaking an allegory.
30Now we know that You know all
things, and no one should question
You. By this we believe that You came
from the Father."
31Jesus answered them, "Do you believe now?
32Behold, an hour is coming, and
now has come, that you will be scattered, everyone to His own place, and
you will leave Me alone. Yet I am not
alone, because the Father is with Me.
33I have told you these things, so that
you may have peace in Me. In the
world you shall have tribulation: but be
of good courage– I have conquered the
world."

17 Jesus said these things, and lifted up His eyes to Heaven, saying, "Father, the hour has come. Glorify
the Son, that the Son may glorify You.
2Inasmuch as you have given Him
authority over all flesh, so that He
might give eternal life to all those that
You have given Him.
3Now this is eternal life, that they
know You, the one true God, and Jesus
Christ, Whom You sent.
4I have glorified You upon the Earth.
I have finished the work that You gave
Me to do.
5And now Father, glorify Me with
Yourself, with the glory I had with You
before the world existed.
6I manifest Your name to the men
you gave Me out of the world. They
were Yours, and You gave them to Me,
and they have kept Your Word.
7Now they know that all You have
given Me is from You.
8Because the words You gave to Me, I
have given them; and they received,
and have known truly that I came from
You, and they believed You have sent
Me.
9I pray for them– I do not pray for
the world, but for those whom You
have given Me, for they are Yours.
10And all that is Mine is Yours, and
all that is Yours is Mine; and I have
been glorified in them.
11And I am no longer in the world,
but these are in the world, and I come
to You. Holy Father, keep them in Your
name, those whom You gave to Me, so
that they may be one, as We are.
12When I was with them, I kept them
in Your name. You gave them to Me,
and I guarded them and none of them
were destroyed– except the son of destruction, that the scriptures may be
fulfilled.
13But now I come to You, and I speak
this in the world, that they may have
My joy fulfilled in them.
14I have given them Your Word, and
the world hates them because they are
not of the world, even as I am not of
the world.
15I do not ask You to take them out of
the world, but that You would keep
them from the Evil One.
16They are not of the world, even as I
am not of the world.
17Make them holy in Your truth–
Your Word is truth.

[18]Just as You sent Me into the world,
I also sent them into the world.
[19]And I sanctify Myself for them, so
that they may also truly be made holy.
[20]I do not ask concerning them
alone, but also concerning those who
will believe in Me through their word.
[21]So that all may be one, just as You
are in Me, Father, and I am in You, that
they also may be one in Us, that the
world may believe that You have sent
Me.
[22]And I have given them the glory
that You have given Me, so that they
may be one, just as We are one.
[23]I in them, and You in Me, so that
they may be perfect in one, so that the
world may know that You have sent
Me, and loved them, just as You have
loved Me.
[24]Father, I desire that those who You
have given Me, that where I am, that
they may also be with Me, that they
may look on the glory that You gave
Me, because You loved Me before the
overthrow of the world.
[25]Righteous Father, indeed the world
does not know You, but I know You,
and these know that You have sent Me.
[26]And I have made Your name
known to them, and I will continue to
make it known, that the love with
which You loved Me may be in them,
and I am in them."

18 Jesus said these things, and He
went out with His disciples
across the brook Kidron, to where
there was a garden, into which He and
His disciples entered.
[2]And Judas, who betrayed Him, also
knew the place, because Jesus often re-
sorted there with His disciples.
[3]So Judas, receiving a cohort and police from the Chief Priests and from
the Pharisees, came there with lamps
and torches and weapons.
[4]Then Jesus, knowing all things that
were coming upon Him, came out and
said to them, "Whom do you seek?"
[5]They answered Him, "Jesus the Nazarene." He said to them, "I am He".
And Judas, who handed him over, also
stood there with them.
[6]Then as He said, "I am," they
stepped back and fell to the ground.
[7]Then again He inquired of them,
"Whom do you seek?" And they said,
"Jesus the Nazarene."
[8]Jesus answered, "I told you that I
am. If then you seek Me, let these go."
[9]That the word may be fulfilled
which was spoken, "Of those whom
You gave Me I have lost not one of
them."
[10]Then Simon Peter, who had a dagger, pulled it out and struck the servant
of the High Priest, and cut off his right
ear, and the name of the servant was
Malchus.
[11]Then Jesus said to Peter, "Put back
your dagger into the sheath. The cup
which the Father has given Me, should
I not drink it?"
[12]Then the cohort, and the commander, and the soldiers of the Jews took
Jesus and bound Him.
[13]And they led Him away first to Annas, for he was the father-in-law of Caiaphas, who was the High Priest that
year.
[14]Now it was Caiaphas who advised
the Jews that it was profitable for one
man to die for the sake of the people.
[15]Now Simon Peter followed Jesus,
and another disciple (and that disciple
was known to the High Priest), and entered together with Jesus into the court
of the High Priest.
[16]Now Peter stood at the door out-

side. Then the other disciple that was known to the High Priest went out and spoke to the doorkeeper and brought in Peter.

17 Then the young girl, who was the doorkeeper, said to Peter, "Are you not also of the disciples of this Man?" He said, "I am not."

18 And a servant and an officer stood and warmed themselves by a fire, because it was cold. And Peter also stood with them and warmed himself.

19 Then the High Priest questioned Jesus about His disciples and about His teaching.

20 Jesus answered him, "I spoke openly to the world. I always taught in the synagogue and in the temple precincts, where the Jews always come together, and I spoke nothing in secret.

21 Why do you question Me? Question those who heard what was spoken. Behold, these know what I said."

22 Now having said this, one of the officers standing by gave Jesus a blow with the palm of his hand, saying, "Is that how You answer the High Priest?"

23 Jesus answered him, "If I have said anything wrong, then produce some evidence of the evil, but if well, why do you hit Me?"

24 Then Annas sent Him away bound to Caiaphas the High Priest.

25 And Simon Peter was standing and warming himself, then they said to him, "Are you not also one of His disciples?" He denied it and said, "I am not!"

26 The servant of the High Priest, who was a relative of the one whose ear Peter had cut off, said, "Did I not see you in the garden with Him?"

27 Then Peter denied it again, and immediately a rooster crowed.

28 Then they led Jesus from Caiaphas to the Praetorium. Now it was early and they did not enter into the Praetorium, so that they would not be defiled, that they may eat the Passover.

29 Then Pilate came outside and declared to them, "What accusation do you bring against this Man?"

30 They answered and said to him, "If this Fellow was not an evildoer, then we would not have handed Him over to you."

31 Then Pilate said to them, "You take Him and judge Him according to your law." The Jews said to him, "It is not lawful for us to put anyone to death,"

32 that the word of Jesus might be fulfilled which He said, signifying what death He would die.

33 Then Pilate entered again into the Praetorium, and called Jesus and said to Him, "Are You the King of the Jews?"

34 Jesus answered, "Do you ask this on your own, or did others tell you about Me?"

35 Pilate answered, "Am I a Jew? Your nation and the High Priest handed You over to me. What did You do?"

36 Jesus answered, "My Kingdom is not of this world. If My Kingdom were from this world, My servants would fight, so that I would not be handed over to the Jews. But now My Kingdom is not from here."

37 Then Pilate said to Him, "So then You are a King?" Jesus answered, "You say that I am a King. For this I was born, and for this I came into the world, that I may bear witness of the truth. All those of the truth hear My voice."

38 Pilate said to Him, "What is truth?" And saying this, he went out again to the Jews and said to them, "I have not found any fault in Him.

39 Now it is a custom for you that one be released at the Passover. You decide then: should I release the King of the Jews to you?"

40 Then they all cried out again, saying, "Not this one, but Barabbas!" Now Barabbas was a bandit.

19 Then at that time, Pilate took Jesus and scourged Him.

2 And the soldiers braided thorns into a crown and put it on His head, and threw a robe of purple around Him.

3 Now they came to Him, saying, "Hail, King of the Jews!" and they gave Him blows with the palms of their hands.

4 And Pilate came outside again and said to them, "Behold, I bring Him out to you, that you may know that I do not find any fault in Him."

5 Then Jesus came out wearing the crown of thorns and the purple robe, and he said, "Behold the Man."

6 Therefore, when the Chief Priests and the temple police saw Him, they cried out, saying, "Crucify Him! Crucify Him!" Pilate said to them, "You take Him and crucify Him. Indeed, I find no fault in Him."

7 The Jews answered and said, "We have our Law, and according to the Law He must die, because He made Himself the Son of God."

8 Then when Pilate heard this word, he became more afraid.

9 And he entered into the Praetorium, and said to Jesus, "Where are You from?" But Jesus did not give him an answer.

10 Then Pilate said to Him, "Will You not speak to me? Do You not know that I have authority to set You free, and I have authority to crucify You?"

11 Jesus answered him, "You would have no authority over Me at all, if it were not given to you from above. Because of this, he who betrayed Me has the greater sin."

12 As a result of this Pilate sought to release Him. But the Jews cried out, saying, "If you release this fellow, you are not a friend of Caesar! Anyone who makes himself a king speaks against Caesar!"

13 When Pilate heard this word, he brought Him out and caused Him to sit down on the judge's bench in the place called the Stone Pavement, but in Hebrew: 'Gabbatha.'

14 Now it was the Day of Preparation for the Passover, being the sixth hour, and he said, "Behold your king!"

15 Then they cried out, "Away! Away! Crucify Him!" Pilate said to them, "Shall I crucify your King?" The Chief Priests answered, "We have no king but Caesar."

16 Then finally, he handed Him over to them so that they could crucify Him. Then they led Jesus away.

17 And He went out, carrying His cross. He went out to what was called the Place of the Skull, called 'Golgotha' in Hebrew.

18 There they crucified Him. And with Him were two others on either side, and Jesus was in the middle.

19 And Pilate also wrote a title and put it on the cross and it was written, "Jesus the Nazarene, The King of the Jews."

20 Therefore many of the Jews read this title, because the city was near to the place where Jesus was crucified, and it was inscribed in Hebrew, Greek, and Latin.

21 Then the Chief Priests of the Jews said to Pilate, "Do not write, 'King of the Jews,' but that this man said, 'I am King of the Jews.'"

22 Pilate answered, “What I have written, I have written.”
23 When the soldiers had crucified
Jesus, they took His clothes and made
four parts, a part for each soldier. Also
there was a robe. Now the robe did not
have a seam– it was woven from the
top throughout.
24 Therefore they said to one another,
“Let’s not divide it, but roll the dice for
it to see whose it will be,” that the scripture might be fulfilled which said,
“They divided My garments among
them, and they cast a lot for My clothing.” So then the soldiers did these
things.
25 Now standing by the cross of Jesus
was His mother, and His mother’s sister, Mary of Clopas, and Mary Magdalene.
26 Then Jesus saw His mother, and the
disciple that He loved standing by. He
said to His mother, “Woman, behold
your son.”
27 Then He said to the disciple, “Behold your mother,” and from that hour,
the disciple took her into his care.
28 After these things, Jesus, knowing
that everything was finished so that the
scriptures might be fulfilled, He said, “I
thirst.”
29 There was a vessel there full of
vinegar and they filled a sponge with
vinegar and, putting around it hyssop,
they brought it to His mouth.
30 Then when Jesus took the vinegar,
He said, “It is finished.” And bowing
his head, He yielded up His Spirit.
31 Therefore since it was the Day of
Preparation, the Jews did not want the
bodies to remain upon the cross during
the Sabbath, for that was a High Sabbath day. They asked Pilate that their
legs be broken, and they be taken away.
32 Then the soldiers came and broke
the legs of the first and then of the other one who was crucified with Him.
33 But coming to Jesus, when they saw
that He was dead, they did not break
His legs.
34 But one of the soldiers pierced His
side with a spear. And immediately
there came out blood and water.
35 And this testimony was by an eye-
witness, and his testimony is true, and
what he is telling he knows to be true,
that you might also believe.
36 For indeed these things happened
that the scriptures might be fulfilled,
‘Not a bone is to be broken.’
37 And again another scripture said,
‘They shall look on Him whom they
have pierced.’
38 Now after these things, Joseph of
Arimathea– being a disciple of Jesus,
but secretly, because of fear of the
Jews– asked Pilate if he could take His
body. And Pilate gave permission.
Then he came and took the body of Jesus.
39 And Nicodemus also came, the one
who came to Him first at night, carrying about one hundred pounds of a
mixture of myrrh and aloes.
40 Then they took the body of Jesus
and bound Him in fine linen with the
spices, according to the burial custom
of the Jews.
41 Now in the place where He was
crucified was a garden, and in the garden a tomb in which no one had ever
been laid.
42 So then, because of the Jewish Day
of Preparation, they laid Jesus in that
tomb, because it was nearby.

20 And early on the first of the
week, it still being dark, Mary
Magdalene came to the tomb. And she
saw that the stone had been removed

from the tomb.

2 Then she ran and came to Simon Peter and to the other disciple whom Jesus loved, and said to them, “They have taken away the Lord from the tomb, and we do not know where they put Him.”

3 Then Peter and the other disciple went out and came into the tomb.

4 And the two of them ran together, and the other disciple ran faster than Peter and came first into the tomb.

5 And, stooping down, he saw the linen lying there, yet he did not enter.

6 And then came Simon Peter, following him, and he went into the tomb and saw the linen lying there.

7 And the cloth which was on His head, was not lying with the linen, but wrapped up separately in its own place.

8 Then the other disciple came in also, who had come first into the tomb, and saw and believed.

9 For they did not yet know the Scripture, that it was necessary for Him to rise from the dead.

10 Then the disciples returned again to their own.

11 Now Mary stood outside by the tomb weeping. Then, as she wept, she stooped down into the tomb.

12 And she saw two angels in white, one sitting at the head and one at the feet, where the body of Jesus had lain.

13 And they said to her, “Woman, why do you weep?” She said to them, “Because they took away my Lord, and I do not know where they put Him.”

14 And, saying these things, she turned around and saw Jesus standing, and did not know that it was Jesus.

15 Jesus said to her, “Woman, why do you weep? Whom do you seek?” Supposing that One to be the gardener, she said to Him, “Sir, if You carried Him away, tell me where You put Him, and I will take Him away.”

16 Jesus said to her, “Mary!” She turned to Him saying, “Rabboni!” that is to say, “Teacher.”

17 Jesus said to her, “Do not touch Me, for I have not yet ascended to My Father,

but go to My brothers and tell them, ‘I ascend to My Father and your Father, and My God and your God.’”

18 Mary Magdalene came reporting to the disciples that she had seen the Lord and that He told her these things.

19 Now it was the evening of the first day of that week, and the door was shut where the disciples were assembled, because of fear of the Jews. Jesus came and stood in their midst, and said to them, “Peace to you.”

20 And when He said these things, He showed them His hands and His side. Then the disciples rejoiced, having seen the Lord.

21 Then Jesus said to them again, “Peace to you. Just as My Father sent Me, I also send you.”

22 And saying these things, He breathed on them and said, “Receive the Holy Spirit.

23 Anyone’s sins you release, they shall be released; and anyone’s you may retain, are retained.”

24 Now Thomas, one of the twelve, who is called Didymus, was not with them when Jesus came.

25 Then the other disciples kept telling him, “We have seen the Lord.” But he said to them, “Unless I see the mark of the nails in His hands, and put my finger into that mark of the nails, and put my hand into His side, I will not believe!”

26 And after eight days His disciples were inside again, and Thomas was

with them. Jesus came, the door having been shut, and stood in their midst and said, “Peace to you.”

27 He then told Thomas, “Bring your finger here, and see My hands, and bring your hand here and put it right into My side, and be no longer unbelieving, rather believe.”

28 Thomas replied, and said to Him, “My Lord and my God!”

29 Jesus said to him, “Because you have seen Me, Thomas, you have believed. Blessed are those who have not seen Me, and have believed.”

30 Jesus did many other miracles in the presence of His disciples, that are not written in this book.

31 But these things were written so that you may believe that Jesus is the Christ, the Son of God, and that believing you may have life in His name.

21 After these things, Jesus showed Himself again to the disciples on the sea of Tiberias and He appeared in this way:

2 Simon Peter, and Thomas, who is called Didymus, and Nathanael from Cana of Galilee, were together with those of Zebedee, and two of His other disciples.

3 Simon Peter said to them, “I am going fishing.” The others said, “We are coming with you.” They immediately went and entered into the boat, and that night they caught nothing.

4 Now it was already early in the morning, and Jesus stood toward the seashore. However, the disciples did not know that it was Jesus.

5 Jesus said to them, “Little children, do you have anything to eat?” They answered Him, “No!”

6 And He said to them, “Cast the net toward the right side of the boat, and you will find.” Then they cast, and they were no longer able to draw it because of the great number of fish.

7 Then the disciple whom Jesus loved said to Peter, “It is the Lord.” When Simon Peter heard that it was the Lord, he girded himself with an outer tunic, for he was naked, and he cast himself into the sea.

8 But the other disciples came in the boat– for it was not far to the land, but about two hundred cubits– dragging the net of fish.

9 Then, as they went up on the land, they saw hot coals and fish laying on it, and bread.

10 Jesus said to them, “Now bring of the fish that you have caught.”

11 Simon Peter went up and dragged the net full of large fish to the land. The catch was one-hundred-and-fifty-three, yet the net was not torn, though there were so many.

12 Jesus said to them, “Come, have breakfast.” None of the disciples dared to question Him, “Who are You?” They recognized that it was the Lord.

13 Then Jesus came and took the bread and gave it to them, and the fish in like manner.

14 This is the third time that Jesus was revealed to His disciples after being raised from the dead.

15 Then, when breakfast was ended, Jesus said to Simon Peter, “Simon of Jonah, do you love Me more than these?” He said, “Yes Lord, You know that I care for You.” He said to him, “Feed My little lambs.”

16 He said to him the second time, “Simon, Jonah, do you love Me?” He said to Him, “Yes, Lord, You know that I care for You.” He said to him, “Pastor My flock.”

17 He said to him the third time, “Si-

mon, Jonah, do you care for Me?” Peter was grieved that He said the third time, “Do you care for Me.” And he said to Him, “Lord, You know all things. You know that I care for You.” Jesus said to him, “Feed My flock.”

18 “With absolute certainty, I tell you, when you were younger, you girded yourself and walked where you desired. But when you are old, you shall extend your hands, and another shall gird and shall carry you where you do not want.”

19 But He said these things describing by what death he would glorify God. And having said these things He told him, “Follow Me.”

20 And Peter turned and saw the disciple that Jesus loved following, who also leaned upon His chest at supper, and said, “Lord, who is it that will betray You?”

21 Then Peter, seeing him, said to Jesus, “Lord, what about this one?”

22 Jesus said to him, “If I desire him to remain until I come, what is that to you? You follow Me!”

23 Then this word went out from the brethren that this disciple would not die. But Jesus did not say that he would not die, but, “If I desire him to remain until I come, what is that to you?”

24 This is the disciple who bore witness concerning these things, wrote these things, and we know that his testimony is true.

25 And there are also many things which Jesus did, that if they were written down, I suppose that the world itself could not contain the books that should be written. Amen.

THE ACTS OF THE APOSTLES

1 O Theophilus, it was I who made the first report concerning all the things which Jesus began both to do and to teach,

2 until the day He was taken up, having given commandments by the Holy Spirit to the apostles whom He had chosen.

3 To whom He also presented Himself alive by many convincing proofs, after He had suffered, being seen by them for forty days, and speaking concerning the Kingdom of God.

4 And, after being assembled with them, He ordered them not to depart from Jerusalem, but to wait for the promise of the Father, “Which you heard from Me.

5 For John indeed baptized with water, but you shall be baptized with the Holy Spirit not many days from now.”

6 So therefore, having come together, they asked Him, saying, “Lord, will You restore the Kingdom to Israel at this time?”

7 But He said to them, “It is not for you to know the times and seasons, which the Father has placed in His own authority;

8 but you will receive power when the Holy Spirit comes upon you, and you shall be My witnesses both in Jerusalem, and in all Judea and Samaria, and unto the farthest reaches of the Earth.”

9 And having said these things, as they were looking on Him, He was taken up and a cloud received Him up out of their sight.

10 And as they were gazing into Heaven as He went, also behold two men appeared to them in bright clothing.

11 And they said, “Men of Galilee, why do you stand looking into heaven? This same Jesus, Who was taken up from you into Heaven, shall certainly come in the same way as you watched Him go into Heaven.”

12 Then they returned into Jerusalem from the mount called Olives, which is near Jerusalem, being the distance of a Sabbath's journey.

13 And when they had entered, they went up to the upper chamber, where Peter, and James, John, Andrew, Philip, Thomas, Bartholomew, Matthew, James of Alphaeus, Simon the Zealot, and Jude of James were staying.

14 All of these were devoted intensely to one purpose in prayer and supplication, with the women and Mary, the mother of Jesus, and with His brethren.

15 And in those days, Peter, having stood up in the midst of the disciples, said (the number of names together being about 120),

16 “Men, brethren, it was necessary that this scripture be fulfilled, which the Holy Spirit spoke before by the mouth of David concerning Judas, who became guide to those who took Jesus.

17 For he was numbered with us and obtained the lot in this ministry.”

18 This one indeed therefore obtained a field out of the wages of unrighteousness, and having fallen headfirst, burst in the midst, and all his inward parts gushed out.

19 And it became known to all those dwelling in Jerusalem, so that the field was called in their own language, “Akeldama,” that is: “a field of blood.”

20 For it was written in the book of Psalms, “Let his habitation become desolate, and let no one dwell in it,” and “Let another one take his position of oversight.”

21 “It is necessary, therefore, that from those men who have accompanied us during all the time that the Lord Jesus

came in and went out among us,
22beginning from the Baptism of
John until the day in which He was
taken up from us, one of these should
become a witness with us of His resurrection."
23And they set forth two: Joseph,
called Barsabas, who was surnamed
Justus, and Matthias.
24And, praying, they said, "You, Lord,
knower of the hearts of everyone,
choose from one of these two
25to take the place of the ministry
and apostleship, from which Judas fell
away to go to his own place."
26And they gave their lots, and the lot
fell on Matthias, and he was numbered
with the eleven apostles.

2 And on the day that Pentecost
came, they were all of one purpose
in the same place.
2And suddenly there came out of
Heaven the sound of a violent rushing
wind and it filled the whole house
where they were seated.
3And there appeared cloven tongues
like fire, and they set down upon each
one of them.
4And they were all filled with the
Holy Spirit and began to speak with
other tongues, as the Spirit spoke forth
from them.
5Now there were sojourning in
Jerusalem devout men, Jews, from
every nation under Heaven.
6And it came to pass that, at this
noise, the multitude came together and
were confounded, because each one
heard them speaking in his own dialect.
7But they stood and wondered, saying, "Are not all of these speaking
Galileans?
8How then do each of us hear in our
own dialect in which we were born?
9Parthians, Medes, Elamites, inhabitants of Mesopotamia, Judea and also
Cappadocia, of Pontus and Asia,
10Phrygia, Pamphylia, Egypt and the
regions of Libya about Cyrene, and vis-
itors of Rome, both Jews and proselytes,
11Cretans and Arabians, we hear
them speak in our own tongues the
great things of God."
12They were all amazed, and perplexed, saying one to another. "What
does this mean?"
13But others mocked, saying, "These
are all filled with new wine."
14But Peter, standing with the eleven,
lifted up his voice and spoke to them,
"Men of Judea, and all you inhabitants
of Jerusalem, be this known unto you,
and give heed unto my words.
15For these are not drunk, as you
suppose, for it is the third hour of the
day.
16But this is that spoken through the
prophet Joel:
17'And it shall be, in the last days,'
says God, 'I will pour out My Spirit
upon all flesh; and your sons and your
daughters shall prophesy, and your
young men shall see visions, and your
old men shall dream dreams.
18And upon My male and female servants, I will pour out My Spirit in those
days, and they shall prophesy.
19And I will give wonders in the
heavens above and miracles upon the
earth below, blood and fire, and a cloud
of smoke.
20The sun shall turn to darkness, and
the moon to blood, before the great
and wonderful day of the Lord comes.
21And it shall be that whoever shall
call upon the name of the Lord shall be
saved.'

22Men of Israel, listen to these words:
Jesus the Nazarene, a Man approved by
God to you through works of power
and wonders and miracles– which God
did through Him in your midst, as you
yourselves know–
23He Who was given over through
the determinate counsel and foreknowledge of God, you having taken
by wicked hands did nail Him up and
put to death.
24Whom God raised up, loosing the
pains of death, because it was not possible for Him to be held by it.
25David also said concerning Him, 'I
always saw the Lord before me, for He
is on my right hand, that I should not
be shaken:
26Therefore did my heart rejoice, and
my tongue rejoiced greatly– moreover
also my flesh shall rest in expectation,
27because You will not leave my soul
in Hades, neither will You allow Your
Faithful One to see corruption.
28You have made known to me the
ways of life– You shall make me full of
joy with Your presence.'
29Men and brethren, let me speak
confidently to you concerning the patriarch David, for also he is dead and is
buried, and his sepulcher is with us
even until this day.
30Therefore, being a prophet, and
knowing that God had sworn with an
oath, that from the fruit of his loins,
according to the flesh, He would raise
up Christ to sit on His throne–
31foreseeing this, He spoke concerning the resurrection of Christ, that His
soul was not left in Hades, neither
would His flesh see corruption.
32This Jesus has God raised up, of
which we are all witnesses.
33Therefore God exalted Him to His
right hand. And having received from
the Father the promise of the Holy
Spirit, He has poured out this, which
you now see and hear.
34For David is not ascended into the
heavens, but he says himself: 'The Lord
said unto my Lord, "Sit on My right
hand
35until I make your enemies a footstool for your feet."'
36Therefore, let all the house of Israel
know for certain that God has made
this same Jesus, whom you have crucified, both Lord and Christ."
37Now when they heard this, they
were pierced to their heart, and said
unto Peter and to the other apostles,
"Men and brethren, what shall we do?"
38Then Peter said unto them, "Repent
and be baptized, each of you, in the
name of Jesus Christ for the removal of
sins, and you shall receive the gift of
the Holy Spirit.
39For the promise is unto you, and to
your children, and to all that are far off,
as many as the Lord our God shall call."
40And with many other words he
earnestly testified and exhorted, saying,
"Save yourselves from this crooked
generation."
41Therefore, those that gladly welcomed his word were baptized, and
there were added that day about three
thousand souls.
42And they continued steadfastly in
the apostles' doctrine and fellowship,
and in breaking of bread, and in
prayers.
43And fear came upon every soul,
and many wonders and miracles were
done by the apostles.
44And all that believed were together,
and had all things in common.
45And they sold their possessions and
goods, and divided them to everyone,
according as anyone had need.

46And they, continuing daily with
one accord in the temple, and breaking
bread in their houses, partook of food
with gladness and simplicity of heart,
47praising God and having favor with
all the people. And the Lord added to
the church daily such as should be
saved.

3 Peter and John went up together
into the temple at the ninth hour of
prayer.
2And a man who was lame from his
mother's belly was carried– whom they
placed daily at the gate of the temple
called Beautiful, to ask alms from those
who were going into the temple–
3Who, seeing Peter and John being
about to enter into the temple, asked to
receive alms.
4And Peter, gazing upon him with
John, said, "Look on us."
5And he gave attention to them, expecting to receive something from
them.
6But Peter said, "I do not have silver
and gold, but what I have, this I will
give to you: in the name of Jesus Christ
the Nazarene, rise up and walk."
7And taking him by the right hand,
he raised him up. And instantly his feet
and ankle bones were strengthened.
8And leaping up, he stood and
walked and entered with them into the
temple, walking and leaping and praising God.
9And all the people saw him walking
and praising God.
10For they knew him, that it was he
who for alms was sitting at the Beautiful gate of the temple, and they were
filled with awe and amazement at what
had happened to him.
11And as the lame man who was
healed tightly held Peter and John, all
the people ran together unto them, utterly amazed, into the porch called
Solomon's.
12Now Peter, beholding it, responded
to the people, "Men! Israelites! Why do
you marvel at this? Why do you stare at
us as if our own power or piety had
made this man walk?
13The God of our fathers, Abraham
and Isaac and Jacob, has glorified His
Servant, Jesus, Him whom you handed
over and denied in the presence of Pilate, when he had decided to release
Him.
14But you have denied the Holy and
Righteous One and begged that a man,
a murderer, be given over to you.
15And you have killed the Author of
Life, Whom God raised up from
among the dead, of which we are witnesses.
16And by the faith in His Name this
one was made strong, whom you see
and know. His Name and the faith that
is by Him gave to him this complete
wholeness before you all.
17And now, brethren, I know that you
acted in ignorance, as also your rulers.
18But in this way, what God announced beforehand by the mouth of
all His prophets, that Christ should suffer, He has fulfilled.
19Repent, therefore, and be convert-
ed, that your sins may be wiped out, so
that times of refreshing may come
from the presence of the Lord.
20And He shall send Jesus Christ,
Who before was proclaimed to you,
21Whom Heaven must certainly receive until the times of restoration of
all things, which God spoke by the
mouth of His Holy Prophets from an
age.
22For certainly, Moses said to the fathers, 'The Lord God will raise up to

you a Prophet like me from among
your brethren. You shall hear Him in
all things whatsoever He may tell you.
23 And it shall be: every soul who
shall not listen to that Prophet shall be
utterly destroyed from among the people.'
24 And certainly, all of the prophets,
from Samuel and those who came after,
as many as spoke, announced these
days.
25 You are the sons of the prophets
and of the covenant that God appointed to our fathers, saying to Abraham,
'And in your seed shall all the families
of the Earth be blessed.'
26 To you first, God has raised up His
Child, Jesus. He has sent Him, blessing
you by turning each of you away from
your wickedness."

4 Now, as they were speaking to the
people, the priests, the captain of
the temple, and the Sadducees came
upon them,
2 being distressed that they taught the
people and proclaimed in Jesus the
resurrection from the dead.
3 And they laid hands on them and
put them in holding until the next day,
for it was already evening.
4 But many of those who had heard
the word believed, and the number of
the men came to about five thousand.
5 And it came to pass, on the next day,
the rulers and the elders and the
Scribes were gathered together in
Jerusalem–
6 also Annas, the High Priest, Caiaphas, John and Alexander, and as
many as were of a High Priestly family–
7 and, standing them in their midst,
inquired, "In what power or in what
name did you do this?"
8 Then Peter, filled with the Holy
Spirit, said to them, "Rulers of the people, and elders of Israel,
9 if we are examined this day about a
good work, in which a crippled man
has been healed,
10 be it known to all of you, and to all
the people of Israel, that in the name of
Jesus Christ the Nazarene, Whom you
crucified, Whom God raised from the
dead, by Him this one stands before
you whole.
11 This is the stone that has been rejected by you builders, which has become head of the corner.
12 And there is no salvation by any
other means, for there is not another
name given under Heaven unto men by
which we must be saved."
13 But observing the boldness of Peter
and John and realizing that they were
illiterate and uneducated, they marveled, recognizing that they had been
with Jesus.
14 And beholding the man standing
with them who had been healed, they
could say nothing against it.
15 And, having commanded them to
go outside the Sanhedrin, they conferred with one another,
16 saying, "What shall we do to these
men? For it is certain that an obvious
miracle has taken place through them,
which is evident to all those living in
Jerusalem, and we are unable to deny
it.
17 So that it spread no further among
the people, let us severely threaten
them to no longer speak in this name
to any man."
18 And, having called them, they
charged them not to speak or teach in
the name of Jesus.
19 But Peter and John, responding to
them, said, "Whether it is right before

God to listen to you rather than God,
you judge.
20For we cannot but speak of what we
have seen and heard."
21But they threatened them, letting
them go, finding no way as to how they
might punish them on account of the
people, because all were glorifying God
on account of what happened,
22for the man was more than forty
years old on whom this miracle of healing had taken place.
23And, being released, they came to
their own and reported everything to
them that the High Priest and the Elders had said.
24And hearing this, they lifted up
their voices with one accord to God
and said, "O Master, You are the God
Who made Heaven and the Earth, and
the sea and all that are in them,
25Who by the mouth of Your servant
David said, 'Why did the nations rage,
and the people plot folly?
26The kings of the Earth stood up,
and the rulers were gathered together
against the Lord and against His
Christ.'
27Who indeed were gathered together against Your holy child Jesus–
Whom You anointed– both Herod and
Pontius Pilate, with the Gentiles and
people of Israel,
28to do whatever Your hand and
counsel predetermined to happen.
29And now, Lord, look upon their
threats and give to Your servants all
boldness to speak Your word,
30by stretching out Your hand to heal
and perform miracles and wonders
through the name of Your holy child
Jesus."
31And having prayed, the place was
shaken in which they were assembled,
and they were all filled with the Holy
Spirit and spoke the Word of God with
boldness.
32Now the multitude of those that
believed were of one heart and soul,
and no one said of anything which he
possessed that it was his own, but
everything they had was communal.
33And with great power the Apostles
gave witness to the resurrection of the
Lord Jesus, and great grace was upon
all of them.
34Neither was anyone among them
impoverished, for as many as were
owners of estates or houses sold them
and brought the value of the sale,
35and laid it at the Apostles' feet. And
distribution was made to each according as anyone had need.
36And Joses– who was surnamed
Barnabas by the Apostles, which being
interpreted is "son of consolation," a
Levite, of Cyprus by birth–
37had an available field. Having sold
it, he brought the money and laid it at
the Apostles' feet.

5 But a man, who was named Ananias, with Sapphira his wife, sold a
possession,
2and he kept back some of the price–
his wife also being aware of it– and
having brought a portion of it, laid it at
the Apostles' feet.
3But Peter said, "Ananias, why did
Satan fill your heart to lie to the Holy
Spirit and to keep back from the price
of the estate?
4While it remained with you, did it
not remain yours? And having sold it,
wasn't it in your own authority? Why
did you establish this deed in your
heart? You have not lied to man, but to
God!"
5Now Ananias, hearing these words,
falling down, died. And great fear came

upon all those who heard these things.

6 And the younger ones arose and wrapped him up and, having carried him out, buried him.

7 And it came to pass after about three hours his wife also came in, not knowing what had happened.

8 And Peter responded to her, “Tell me if you sold the estate for so much?” And she said, “Yes, for so much.”

9 And Peter said, “Why did you agree together to tempt the Spirit of the Lord? Behold, the feet of those who buried your husband are at the door, and they shall carry you out.”

10 And she immediately fell down at his feet and died. And the young men came in and found her dead and carried her out and buried her by her husband.

11 And great fear came upon the whole assembly and upon all who heard these things.

12 And by the hands of the Apostles many miracles and wonders took place among the people. And they were all with one purpose in Solomon's porch.

13 And none of the rest had the courage to join them, but the people magnified them.

14 And more believers were added to the Lord, multitudes of both men and women,

15 insomuch that they brought the sick out into the streets and laid them on beds and cots, that at least at the coming of Peter his shadow might overshadow some of them.

16 And also the multitude came together from the cities around Jerusalem to bring those sick and tormented by unclean spirits, who were all healed.

17 And the High Priest, having raised up, and all those with him, which is the sect of the Sadducees, were filled with anger,

18 and laid their hands on the Apostles and put them in a public jail.

19 But an angel of the Lord opened the doors of the prison during the night, and having brought them out, said,

20 “Go, and stand in the temple and speak to the people all the words of this life.”

21 Then, hearing this, they entered into the temple at dawn and were teaching. Now the High Priest having come (and those with him), they called together the Sanhedrin and all the council of elders of the sons of Israel and sent to the prison to have them brought.

22 But when the officers came they did not find them in the prison. They returned and reported it,

23 saying, “Indeed we found the prison shut with all security, and the keepers standing outside before the doors. But when we opened it, we found no one inside.”

24 And when they heard these words, both the priest, and the captain of the temple, and the High Priest, were at a loss concerning them and what had happened.

25 Then came one who reported to them, saying, “Behold, the men whom you put in prison are standing in the temple teaching the people.”

26 Then the captain, having gone with the officers, brought them, without force, for they feared the people lest they should be stoned.

27 And, having brought them, they set them in the Sanhedrin. And the High Priest asked them,

28 saying, “Did we not severely command you not to teach in this name? And, behold, you have filled Jerusalem

with your teaching, and have purposed
to bring this Man's blood upon us."
29 But Peter and the Apostles, answering, said, "It is necessary to obey God
rather than man.
30 The God of our Fathers raised up
Jesus, Whom you killed, having hanged
on a tree.
31 Him has God exalted by His right
hand as a Prince and Savior, to give repentance to Israel and forgiveness of
sins.
32 And we are His witnesses of these
things, and also the Holy Spirit, Which
God gave to those who obey Him."
33 Now, having heard this, they were
cut to the heart and took counsel to put
them to death.
34 But a certain one of the Sanhedrin
having risen up, a Pharisee, Gamaliel
by name, a teacher of the Law honored
by all of the people, commanded to put
the Apostles out for a little while,
35 and said to them, "Men, Israelites,
take heed to yourselves concerning
what you are about to do to these men.
36 For before these days Theudas rose
up, declaring himself to be somebody,
to whom were joined a number of men,
about four hundred, who were put to
death, and all as many as were persuaded by him were dispersed and it
came to nothing.
37 After this, Judas the Galilean rose
up in the days of the census and led
away the people after him. And he was
destroyed, and those who had confidence in him were scattered.
38 And now I say to you: stay away
from these men. Leave them alone. Because if this counsel or work is of man,
it will be overthrown.
39 But if it is from God, you cannot
overthrow it, without also finding
yourselves fighting against God."
40 And they were persuaded by him.
And they called the Apostles, and beat
them, and charged them not to speak
in the name of Jesus, and they were released.
41 Then they departed from the presence of the Sanhedrin, rejoicing that
they were counted worthy to be dishonored for the Name.
42 And daily in the temple, and in
every house, they did not cease teaching and preaching Jesus Christ.

6 And in those days, the disciples
multiplying, there arose a murmuring of the Hellenists against the
Hebrews, because their widows were
overlooked in the daily service.
2 And the twelve called the multitude
of disciples together, saying, "It is not
right that we should leave the Word of
God to minister to tables.
3 Now brethren, search out from
among yourselves seven men of good
report, full of the Holy Spirit and wisdom, whom we shall appoint over this
need.
4 And we will give ourselves continually to prayer and the ministry of the
Word."
5 And the word was pleasing in the
sight of all the multitude. And they
chose Stephen, a man full of faith and
the Holy Spirit, and Philip, and Pro-
chorus, and Nicanor, and Timon, and
Parmenas, and Nicolas, a proselyte
from Antioch,
6 who stood before the Apostles. And
they laid their hands on them, and
prayed.
7 And the Word of God grew, and the
number of the disciples in Jerusalem
increased greatly. A great number of
the Priests obeyed the faith.
8 And Stephen, full of faith and pow-

er, did wonders and great miracles
among the people.
9But some of those from the synagogue called Freedmen rose up, disputing with Stephen, also Cyrenians and
Alexandrians and those from Cilicia
and Asia,
10and they had no ability to oppose
the wisdom and the Spirit by which he
spoke.
11Then they instigated men to say,
“We have heard him speak blasphemous words against Moses and God.”
12They stirred up the people and the
elders and the Scribes, and they came
upon him, seized him, and led him to
the Sanhedrin.
13And false witnesses stood up, saying. “This man has not ceased to speak
blasphemous words against this holy
place and the law.
14For we have heard him say that Jesus the Nazarene will destroy this
place, and change the customs Moses
delivered to us.”
15And all those who sat in the Sanhedrin, staring at him, saw his face as if
it were the face of an angel.

7 And the High Priest asked, “Are
these things so?”
2And he said, “Men, brothers and fathers, listen! The God of Glory was
seen by our father Abraham, being in
Mesopotamia, before he lived in Haran.
3And said to him, ‘Come out from
your country and from your relatives,
and come here into the country that I
will show you.’
4Then he came out from the country
of the Chaldeans and settled in Haran.
And after that his father died, he was
made to move into this country where
you now dwell.
5But He did not give him his inheritance, not even a foot of ground, but
He promised to give it to him to possess and to his seed after him, for he
himself had no child.
6And God said this, that his seed was
to dwell in land belonging to another,
and they would be slaves and ill-treated
for four hundred years.
7And God said, ‘Then I will judge the
nation to which you will be a slave, and
after this they will come out to serve
Me in this place.’
8And He gave him a covenant of circumcision. And so he begat Isaac and
circumcised him the eighth day. And
Isaac, Jacob. And Jacob, the twelve patriarchs.
9And the patriarchs, being jealous,
gave Joseph over to Egypt, but God was
with him.
10And He delivered him from all his
tribulation, and gave him grace and
wisdom before Pharaoh, the king of
Egypt, and appointed him leader over
Egypt and his whole household.
11But a famine came upon the whole
of Egypt and Canaan, and great tribulation. And our fathers could not find
food.
12But Jacob, hearing that bread was in
Egypt, sent forth our fathers first.
13And at the second time, Joseph was
made known to his brothers, and
Joseph's race became known to
Pharaoh.
14Then Joseph, sending, called for
Jacob, his father, and the relatives– sev-
enty-five souls in all.
15And Jacob went down into Egypt
and died, he and our fathers.
16And they were carried to Shechem
and were placed in the tomb, which
Abraham bought for a price of silver
from the sons of Hamor of Shechem.
17And as the time of the promise

drew near, which God swore to Abraham, the people increased and multiplied in Egypt,

18until another king rose up who did not know Joseph.

19He took advantage of our race, ill-treating our fathers, and made them abandon their babies, so they would not live.

20In that time, Moses was born, and was well-pleasing to God, who was nursed three months in his father's house.

21And he was set forth, and the daughter of Pharaoh took him up and nursed him for her own son.

22And Moses was trained in all of the wisdom of Egypt and was powerful in his words and deeds.

23And when a period of forty years was fulfilled, it came into his heart to look on his brothers, the sons of Israel.

24And seeing one being wronged, he retaliated and took vengeance for the oppressed, striking down the Egyptian.

25And he presumed that his brothers understood that God would grant them deliverance by his hand, but they did not understand.

26And on the following day he saw them fighting and he tried to reconcile them peacefully, saying, 'Men, you are brothers. Why do you wrong each other?'

27But the one wronging his neighbor thrust him away, saying, 'Who appointed you ruler and judge over us?

28Do you wish to do away with me just as you did away with the Egyptian yesterday?'

29And Moses fled at these words. And he dwelt in the land of Midian, and fathered two sons.

30And forty years being completed, he saw in the wilderness of Mount Sinai the Angel of the Lord, in a flame of fire in a bush.

31And seeing this sight, Moses marveled. And as he came near to look, there was the Lord's voice:

32'I am the God of your father, the God of Abraham and the God of Isaac and the God of Jacob.' And Moses became terrified and dared not look.

33And the Lord said to him, 'Loose the sandal from your feet, for the place on which you stand is holy ground.

34I have surely seen the affliction of My people in Egypt, and I have heard their groans, and I have come down to deliver them. And now, come here, I will send you into Egypt.'

35This Moses, whom they denied, saying, 'Who appointed you ruler and judge?' God sent as a ruler and deliverer by the hand of the Angel that appeared to him in the bush.

36This one led them out doing wonders and signs in the land of Egypt and in the Red Sea, and forty years in the wilderness.

37This is the Moses that said to the sons of Israel, 'The Lord your God shall raise up a prophet from your brothers just like me– you shall hear Him!'

38This is he who was in the church in the wilderness with the Angel that spoke to him in Mount Sinai, and with our fathers, who received the living oracles to give to us,

39to whom our fathers did not wish to obey, but thrust away and turned their hearts back to Egypt,

40saying to Aaron, 'Make gods for us to go before us. For this Moses, who led us from the land of Egypt, we do not know what has happened to him.'

41And they made a calf on that day, and offered up a sacrifice to the idol, and rejoiced in the works of their

hands.
42But God turned and handed them
over to serve the host of heaven, just as
it is written in the book of the
prophets, 'O House of Israel, did you
offer to Me slain animals and sacrifices
for forty years in the wilderness?
43And you raised up the tent of
Moloch, and the star of your god Rem-
phan, the images that you made to
worship them. And I will remove you
beyond Babylon.'
44And the Tabernacle of Witness was
with our fathers in the wilderness, just
as He Who talked with Moses commanded, to make it according to the
pattern that he had seen.
45And our fathers, having received it,
brought it in with Joshua in taking possession of the nations, who God drove
out from before our fathers until the
days of David,
46who found grace before God and
asked to find a tabernacle for the God
of Jacob–
47but Solomon built Him a house.
48But the Most High does not dwell
in temples made with hands, as the
prophet says,
49"'The Heaven is My throne, and the
Earth is a footstool for My feet. What
kind of house will you build Me?" says
the Lord, "Or what place for My rest?
50Did not My hands make all these
things?"'
51You stiff-necked and uncircumcised of heart and ears! You unceasing-
ly oppose the Holy Spirit, as your fathers also did.
52Which of the prophets did your fathers not persecute? And they killed
those who announced beforehand the
coming of the Righteous One, Who
now you have betrayed and murdered,
53who received the Law by the direction of angels, and did not keep it."
54And hearing these things, they
were cut to their heart, and they
gnashed their teeth at him.
55But being full of the Holy Spirit, he
gazed into Heaven. He saw the glory of
God, and Jesus standing at the right of
God,
56and said, "Look, I see the heavens
open and the Son of Man standing at
the right of God!"
57And screaming with a loud voice,
they held their ears, and with one purpose rushed upon him.
58And driving him out of the city,
they stoned him. And the witnesses
took off their garments and laid them
at the feet of a young man called Saul.
59And they stoned Steven, as he was
calling out and saying, "Lord Jesus, receive my spirit."
60And, kneeling down, he cried out
with a loud voice, "Lord, do not hold
them accountable for this sin!" And,
saying that, he fell asleep.

8 And Saul was there approving of
his execution. And on that day a
great persecution came upon the
church in Jerusalem. And everyone except the Apostles were scattered
throughout the areas of Judea and
Samaria.
2And devout men buried Steven and
made a great expression of sorrow over
him.
3And Saul was raging against the
church, entering house by house and
dragging out men and women, handing them over to imprisonment.
4Then those who were scattered went
about preaching the Word.
5And Philip went down into a city of
Samaria, proclaiming Christ to them.
6And the multitudes, with one mind,

paid attention to what Philip said, hearing and beholding the miracles that he did.

7For indeed unclean spirits, crying out with a loud voice, came out of many. And many paralyzed and lame were healed.

8And there was great joy in that city.

9And a man named Simon had been in the city before, practicing magic, astonishing the people of Samaria, saying he was someone great,

10who everyone paid attention to, from the least to the greatest, saying, "This is the great power of God!"

11And they paid attention to him, because he astounded them for a considerable time with his magic arts.

12But when Philip preached about the Kingdom of God and the name of Jesus Christ, they believed and were baptized, both men and women.

13And Simon also himself believed and was baptized, and attended constantly to Philip, being astonished, beholding the miracles and great power.

14When the Apostles heard in Jerusalem that the Samaritans had received the Word of God, they sent Peter and John,

15who went down to pray that they might receive the Holy Spirit,

16for He was not yet fallen on any of them, but they had only been baptized into the name of the Lord Jesus.

17At that time they laid their hands upon them, and they received the Holy Spirit.

18When Simon saw that through the laying on of hands of the Apostles the Holy Spirit was given, he offered them money,

19saying, "Give me also this authority, so that anyone whom I lay hands on shall receive the Holy Spirit."

20But Peter said to him, "May your silver perish with you, because you considered that money could acquire the gift of God!

21You have neither a part nor a share in this thing, for indeed your heart is not right before God!

22Repent then from this wickedness of yours, and beg the Lord– perhaps He will pardon the thought of your heart!

23For indeed I perceive you are in the gall of bitterness and shackles of iniquity."

24And Simon replied, saying, "Pray on my behalf to the Lord that these things that you have said do not come upon me."

25Then when they had borne witness and spoke the Word of the Lord, they returned to Jerusalem preaching the gospel to many villages of the Samaritans.

26And an angel of the Lord spoke unto Philip, saying, "Arise and go down to the South on the road that goes down from Jerusalem to Gaza," which is desert.

27And he got up and went. And behold, a man, an Ethiopian eunuch, a ruler of Candace, queen of Ethiopia, who was over all of her treasure, who had come to worship in Jerusalem,

28who was returning, seated on his chariot. And he was reading the prophet Isaiah.

29And the Spirit said to Philip, "Go near and join that chariot."

30And Philip, running over, heard him reading the prophet Isaiah, and said, "Do you understand what you are reading?"

31And he said, "How shall I be able to unless someone guides me?" And he called Philip to come up and sit with

him.
32And the portion of scripture which
he read was, "He was led like a sheep to
the slaughter, and as a lamb before his
shearer is silent, so he opened not His
mouth.
33In His humiliation His judgment
was taken away. Who shall make
known His generation? For His life is
taken away from the Earth."
34And the eunuch, answering Philip,
said, "I ask you, Who is the prophet
speaking about? Himself, or someone
else?"
35And Philip opened his mouth and
began from this scripture, preaching
Jesus to Him.
36And as they traveled down the
road, they came upon some water. And
the Eunuch said, "Look, water. What
hinders me from being baptized?"
37And Philip said, "If you believe
with all your heart, you may." And he
answered and said, "I believe that Jesus
Christ is the Son of God."
38And he commanded the chariot to
stand still. And both of them went
down into the water, Philip and the
Eunuch, and he baptized him.
39And when they came up from the
water, the Spirit of the Lord snatched
Philip away. And the Eunuch saw him
no more, so he went on his way rejoicing.
40However, Philip found himself at
Azotus. And he went about preaching
to all the cities until he reached Caesarea.

9 But Saul, still breathing out threats
and murder against the disciples of
the Lord, approached the High Priest,
2desiring from him letters to the synagogues in Damascus, that if he found
any man or woman belonging to the
Way, he might bring them bound to
Jerusalem.
3But as he was traveling, it happened
as he drew near to Damascus, suddenly
a light from Heaven flashed around
him.
4And, falling upon the ground, he
heard a voice saying unto him, "Saul,
Saul, why do you persecute Me?"
5And he said, "Who are You, Lord?"
And the Lord said, "I am Jesus, Whom
you persecute. It's hard for you to kick
against the spurs."
6Trembling and astonished, he said,
"Lord, what would You have me do?"
And the Lord said, "Arise and go into
the city, and you will be told what you
must do."
7And the men who were traveling
with him stood speechless, hearing the
voice, but seeing nothing.
8And Saul got up from the ground.
But when he opened his eyes, he could
not see. And they led him by the hand
to bring him to Damascus.
9And he was three days without
sight, and he neither ate nor drank.
10And there was a disciple in Damascus named Ananias. And the Lord said
to him in a vision, "Ananias." And he
said, "Here am I, Lord."
11And the Lord continued, "Arise,
and go to the street called Straight, and
seek Saul of Tarsus, in the house of Judas. He is there praying,
12and he has seen, in a vision, a man
named Ananias coming and laying his
hand on him, that he may see."
13But Ananias replied, "Lord, I have
heard from many concerning this man,
how he has done much evil to your
saints in Jerusalem.
14And he is here with authority from
the High Priest to arrest all that call
upon your name."

15 But the Lord said to him, "Go, for this is My chosen vessel, to carry My name before nations and kings, and the sons of Israel.

16 I Myself will show him how much he will have to suffer for My name."

17 And Ananias went and entered into the house and laid his hands upon him, saying, "Brother Saul, the Lord Jesus sent me, Whom you saw on the road as you were coming, so that you may recover your sight and be filled with the Holy Spirit."

18 And immediately, recovering his sight, there fell from his eyes something like scales. And he arose and was baptized.

19 And when he had taken some food, he was strengthened. And Saul stayed with the disciples that were in Damascus.

20 And right away, he preached Christ in the synagogues, that this is the Son of God.

21 But everyone that heard him was confused and said, "Is this not the one who destroyed those who called upon this name in Jerusalem, and came here to bind them to bring them to the High Priests?"

22 But Saul greatly increased in power and confounded those Jews who lived in Damascus, proving that this is the Christ.

23 But when many days were fulfilled, the Jews conspired to do away with him.

24 But the plan against him became known to Saul, and also that they closely watched the gate day and night so that they might destroy him.

25 And the disciples took him at night, lowering him down the wall in a basket.

26 And Saul arrived in Jerusalem, attempting to join the disciples, and they were all afraid, not believing that he was a disciple.

27 But Barnabas, taking charge, brought him to the Apostles, and explained to them how that in the way he encountered the Lord, and that He spoke to him, and how in Damascus he spoke fearlessly in the name of Jesus.

28 And he was with them coming in and going out in Jerusalem.

29 And he spoke fearlessly in the name of the Lord Jesus, and he talked and also debated with the Hellenists. And they endeavored to kill him.

30 When the brothers learned of this, they brought him to Caesarea, and sent him away to Tarsus.

31 Then all of the churches had peace throughout Judea, Galilee, and Samaria. Being built up and moving in the fear of the Lord and in the encouragement of the Holy Spirit, they multiplied.

32 And it happened that Peter, passing throughout the area, went down also to the saints dwelling at Lydda.

33 And he found there a man whose name was Aeneas, who for eight years lay upon a bed with paralysis.

34 And Peter said to him, "Aeneas, Jesus the Christ heals you. Arise and make your bed." And he rose up immediately.

35 And all the inhabitants of Lydda and Sharon who saw him turned to the Lord.

36 And in Joppa there was a disciple named Tabitha, which translated means Dorcas. She was full of good works and almsgiving.

37 And it came to pass in those days that she, becoming sick, died. And they washed her and laid her in an upper room.

38 And Joppa was near to Lydda. The disciples, hearing that Peter was there, sent two men to call him, to come without delay unto them.

39 And Peter rose up and accompanied them. When he had arrived, they brought him into the upper room and all of the widows stood by him weeping, and showing the coats and garments that Dorcas made while she was with them.

40 And Peter sent all of them outside and he knelt down and prayed. And, turning to the body, he said, "Tabitha, arise." And she opened her eyes and saw Peter and sat up.

41 And giving her his hand, he lifted her up and called the saints and the widows, and presented her alive.

42 And it was known throughout all Joppa, and many believed upon the Lord.

43 And Peter happened to remain many days in Joppa with one Simon, a tanner.

10 There was a man in Caesarea named Cornelius, a centurion of the band called Italic,

2 devout and God-fearing with his whole household, who gave much alms to the people and prayed always to God.

3 He saw in an open vision, around the ninth hour of the day, an angel of God coming to him, and he said, "Cornelius."

4 But he stared at him in fear and said, "What is it, Lord?" And he said, "Your prayers and your alms have ascended as a memorial before God.

5 And now send some men to Joppa, and summon Simon, who is called Peter.

6 He is staying with Simon the Tanner, whose house is by the sea. He will tell you what you should do."

7 And when the angel that spoke to Cornelius had departed, he called two of his household servants and a devout servant who attended constantly to him,

8 and recounting everything to them, sent them to Joppa.

9 And the next day, as they traveled and came near the city, at about the sixth hour, Peter went up upon the housetop to pray.

10 And he became hungry and wanted to eat. And while they made ready, ecstasy came upon him.

11 And he saw the heavens open and a vessel which was like a great sheet, coming down, being lowered to the earth by its four corners.

12 On it were all of the four-footed creatures of the Earth and wild beasts and creeping things and birds of the heavens.

13 And a voice said to him, "Peter, arise, kill, and eat."

14 But Peter said, "This can't be Lord, for I have not eaten anything common and unclean."

15 And the voice came again to him a second time, "What God has cleansed, you shall not call common."

16 And this happened three times, and suddenly the vessel was snatched up into Heaven.

17 Now as Peter was thinking through what he had seen in the vision, the men who were sent by Cornelius to find the house of Simon stood at the porch.

18 And they called out asking if Simon, called Peter, was staying there.

19 As Peter was still thinking about the vision, the Spirit said to him, "Behold, three men are looking for you.

20 Get up now, go down, and travel

with them. Do not hesitate, because I
have sent them."
21 And Peter, going down to the men,
said, "Behold, I am the one you are
looking for. What is the reason you
have come?"
22 And they answered, "The centurion
Cornelius, a righteous and God-fearing
man, to which all the Jewish nation will
bear witness, was instructed by a holy
angel to summon you to his house and
to listen to your words."
23 Then he invited them in as guests.
And the next day he rose up and went
with them, and also the brethren that
were from Joppa accompanied him.
24 And the next day, he entered Caesarea, and Cornelius, who was waiting
for them, called together his family and
close friends.
25 And as Peter came in, Cornelius
went to meet him, falling down at his
feet to worship.
26 But Peter pulled him up, saying,
"Arise! I also am a man."
27 And talking with him, he went in
and found many gathered together.
28 He said to them, "You know how it
is unlawful for a Jewish man to join or
come unto another race. However, God
has shown me not to call a man common or unclean.
29 And for this reason I have come at
your request without objection. Let me
ask, then, for what purpose have you
sent for me?"
30 And Cornelius proclaimed, "Four
days ago, at this very hour, I was fasting
and praying at the ninth hour in my
house, and behold, a man stood before
me in bright clothing
31 and said, 'Cornelius, your prayer
has been heard, and your alms were
remembered before God.
32 Therefore, send to Joppa and call
for Simon, who is called Peter. He is a
guest in a tanner's, Simon's, seaside
house.'
33 Then I immediately sent for you,
and you have done well by coming.
Now therefore we are all gathered before God, having come to hear all that
God has commanded you."
34 And Peter opened his mouth, and
said, "Of truth, I realize that God is no
respecter of persons,
35 but in every nation, he who fears
Him and practices righteousness is acceptable.
36 The word that He sent to the sons
of Israel– announcing the Gospel of
peace through Jesus Christ, Who is
Lord of all–
37 you know the word that came
throughout all Judea, beginning from
Galilee after the baptism that John
preached,
38 how that God anointed Jesus of
Nazareth with the Holy Spirit and
power, Who went about doing good
and healing all who were oppressed by
the Devil, because God was with Him.
39 And we are witnesses of all that He
did in the country of Judea and
Jerusalem. And, hanging Him upon a
tree, they put Him to death.
40 This One, God raised up on the
third day and caused Him to be seen–
41 not to all the people, but to witnesses chosen by God beforehand, who
ate and drank with Him after He arose
from the dead.
42 And He commanded us to preach
to the people and to bear witness that
this is the One appointed by God to
judge the living and the dead.
43 To Him all the prophets bear witness that all who believe in Him receive
forgiveness of sins through His name."
44 While Peter was speaking these

words, the Holy Spirit fell upon all of them who heard the word.

45 And those from the circumcised believers who accompanied Peter were amazed that the gift of the Holy Spirit was also poured out upon the Gentiles.

46 For they heard them speaking with tongues and magnifying God. Then Peter replied,

47 "Can anyone refuse them water? Should not these be baptized, who have also received the Holy Spirit just like us?"

48 And he commanded them to be baptized in the name of the Lord. Then they asked him to remain some days.

11 Now the apostles and the brethren that were in Jerusalem heard that the Gentiles had also received the Word of God.

2 And when Peter went up to Jerusalem, those of the circumcision disputed with him,

3 saying, "You went in– to uncircumcised men– and ate with them."

4 But Peter began to explain to them the sequence of events, saying,

5 "I was in the city of Joppa praying, and in ecstasy I had a vision. A vessel came down from Heaven, which was a large sheet let down by four corners, and it came to me.

6 I looked into it closely and I saw four-footed creatures of the Earth, and wild beasts, and creeping things, and the birds of heaven.

7 And I heard a voice saying to me, 'Arise, Peter, kill and eat.'

8 But I said, 'By no means, Lord, because nothing common or unclean has ever entered into my mouth.'

9 And the voice replied a second time from Heaven, 'What God has cleansed, you shall not make common.'

10 And this happened three times, and was drawn back again into Heaven.

11 And behold, immediately three men stood at the house where I was, who were sent from Caesarea to me.

12 And the Spirit told me to go with them, doubting nothing. And also with me were these six brethren, and we entered into this man's house.

13 And he explained to us how he had seen an angel in his house, who stood and said, 'Send men to Joppa and find Simon, who is called Peter,

14 who shall speak to you words by which you and all your house will be saved.'

15 And as I began to speak, the Holy Spirit fell on them just as on us at first.

16 Then I remembered the words of the Lord when He said, 'John certainly baptized you with water, but you shall be baptized in the Holy Spirit.'

17 If God then also gave them the same gift as us, who believe in the Lord Jesus Christ, who was I to be able to hinder God?"

18 And when they heard these things, they grew silent, and glorified God, saying, "Also unto the Gentiles has God given repentance unto life."

19 Now those who were scattered by the tribulation that took place upon Stephen spread out as far as Phoenicia, and Cyprus, and Antioch, speaking the word to none but Jews only.

20 But some of them were men from Cyprus and Cyrene, who came to Antioch and spoke to the Greeks, proclaiming to them the Lord Jesus.

21 And the hand of the Lord was with them, and many of them believed and turned unto the Lord.

22 And the report about them was heard in the ears of the church in Jerusalem, and they sent out Barnabas

to go as far as Antioch,
23who arrived, and seeing the grace
of God, rejoiced and encouraged them
all that with purpose of heart they
would cleave to the Lord–
24for he was a good man, and full of
the Holy Spirit and faith. And a multitude of people were added unto the
Lord.
25Then Barnabas departed to Tarsus
to look for Saul.
26And having found him, he brought
him to Antioch. And it happened that
they were gathered together a whole
year in the church and taught a large
crowd. And the disciples were called
Christians first in Antioch.
27In these days prophets came down
from Jerusalem to Antioch.
28And there rose up among them one
named Agabus, who through the Spirit
showed clearly that a great famine was
about to come on all the inhabitants,
which happened under Claudius.
29And the disciples determined to
send support to the brethren of Judea
according as each one had prospered.
30Which also they did, sending it to
the elders by the hands of Barnabas
and Paul.

12 And at that time King Herod
laid hands on some of the
church to harm them.
2And he put James, the brother of
John, to the sword.
3And perceiving that it pleased the
Jews, he set out to take Peter too. Now
this was in the days of Unleavened
Bread.
4And he seized him, putting him into
prison, handing him over to four sets
of four soldiers to guard him, intending
at the Passover to bring him out to the
people.
5Peter was therefore kept in prison.
And the church prayed fervently to
God for him.
6And that very night, before Herod
was about to bring him forth, Peter fell
asleep between two soldiers, bound by
two chains. And prison guards stood
before the door of the prison.
7And behold, an angel of the Lord
stood by him, and a light shone in the
cell. And he tapped Peter's side and
woke him, saying, "Rise up, quickly."
And the chains fell off of his hands.
8And the angel said to him, "Gird
yourself and bind your sandals." And
he did so. And he said, "Put on your
mantle and follow me."
9And he went out, following him,
and he was uncertain that it was truly
happening, because of the angel, but
thought he was seeing a vision.
10And he went by the first guard and
the second, and they came to the iron
gate leading into the city– which
opened automatically by itself– and
moved along through the street. And
suddenly the angel departed from him.
11And Peter came to himself, and
said, "Now I know for certain that the
Lord sent His angel and delivered me
from the hand of Herod and all of the
expectation of the Jewish people."
12And realizing this, he went to the
house of Mary, the mother of John,
who is called Mark, where a group was
gathered together and prayed.
13And he knocked at the door of the
gate, and a young girl named Rhoda
came to answer it.
14And recognizing the voice of Peter,
she did not open the gate, because of
her delight, but ran in and reported
that Peter stood at the gate.
15But they said to her, "You are
crazy!" But she insisted that it was so.

Then they said, "It is his angel."
16 Now Peter continued to knock.
Then they opened, and seeing him,
were amazed,
17 but he motioned with his hand for
them to be quiet. He explained to them
how the Lord led him out of the prison.
And he said, "Tell this to James and the
brethren." And he departed and went
off to another place.
18 And when it was day, there was not
just a little confusion among the soldiers of what had happened to Peter.
19 When Herod inquired of him and
he was not found, he examined the
guards and had them led away. And he
went down from Judea to Caesarea, to
spend some time.
20 Now Herod was furiously angry
with Tyre and Sidon. But they came to
him with one passion, and having won
over Blastus, the king's chamberlain,
they begged for peace, because their
country was nourished by the king's
country.
21 And on an appointed day, Herod,
clothed with royal garments, also sitting down upon his throne, gave a public address to them.
22 And the people cried out, "It's a
voice of a god, and not man!"
23 Then the angel of the Lord immediately struck him, because he did not
give God the glory. And he died, having been eaten by worms.
24 But the word of God grew and multiplied.
25 Now Paul and Barnabas returned
from Jerusalem when they had fulfilled
their ministry, bringing with them
John, who was called Mark.

13 Now there were also in the
church that was at Antioch
some prophets and teachers: Barnabas,
and Simon, also called Niger, and Lucius of Cyrene, and Manaen who had
been raised with Herod the Tetrarch,
and Saul.
2 And while they performed the service of the Lord and fasted, the Holy
Spirit said, "Set apart now Barnabas
and Saul unto the work to which I have
called them."
3 Then, having fasted and prayed,
they laid their hands on them, releasing
them.
4 They then, having been sent forth
by the Holy Spirit, went down to Seleu-
cia and from there they sailed to
Cyprus.
5 And arriving in Salamis, they proclaimed the Word of God in the synagogue of the Jews. And they also had
John as an assistant.
6 And having gone through the whole
island as far as Paphos, they found a
man who was a magician, a Jewish false
prophet, named Bar-Jesus,
7 who was with the proconsul, Sergius
Paulus, an intelligent man, who invited
Barnabas and Paul, seeking to hear the
Word of God.
8 But Elymas the magician withstood
them, for this is another way to interpret his name, seeking to pervert the
proconsul from the faith.
9 But Saul, who is also Paul, full of the
Holy Spirit, staring at him,
10 said, "O full of deceit and all vil-
lainy, son of the Devil, enemy of all
righteousness, will you never cease to
make crooked the straight ways of the
Lord?
11 And now, behold! The hand of the
Lord is upon you, and you shall be
blind, not seeing the sun for a season."
And instantly there fell upon him a
mist and a darkness, and he went grop-
ing about looking for someone to lead

him by the hand.

12 When the proconsul saw what had happened, he believed, being amazed at the doctrine of the Lord.

13 Now Paul and those around him put out to sea from Paphos, they came to Perga in Pamphylia. And John departed from them, returning to Jerusalem.

14 And they passed through Perga, arriving in Antioch-Pisidia, and they entered into the synagogue on the Sabbath day and sat down.

15 And after the reading of the Law and the Prophets, the rulers of the synagogue sent to them, saying, "Men, brethren, if you have a word of exhortation for the people, speak."

16 And Paul stood up, and gestured with his hands, saying, "Men, Israelites, and those who fear God, listen.

17 The God of this people Israel chose our fathers, and exalted the people in their sojourn in the land of Egypt, and with a high arm He brought them out of it.

18 And for a period of forty years He put up with them in the wilderness.

19 And he pulled down seven nations in the land of Canaan, and distributed the land by lot to them.

20 And after this, for about four hundred and fifty years, He gave judges until the time of Samuel the prophet.

21 And after this they asked for a king. And God gave them Saul, son of Kish, a man from the tribe of Benjamin, for forty years.

22 And after removing him, He raised up unto them David as king, and testified, saying, 'I found David of Jesse, a man after My heart, who will do all of My will.'

23 From this seed, according to the promise to Israel, God brought forth a Savior, Jesus.

24 John, going before his face, preached the baptizing of repentance to all the people of Israel.

25 And as John fulfilled his course, he said, 'I am not who you think I am. But, behold, He comes after me, whose sandals I am not worthy to take off His feet.'

26 Men, brethren, sons of the race of Abraham, and those among you who fear God, to you the word of this salvation was sent.

27 For indeed those dwelling in Jerusalem, and their rulers, because they did not know Him, they, having condemned Him, fulfilled the voice of the prophets, which are read every Sabbath.

28 And finding no reason for death, they demanded Pilate to execute Him.

29 And when they fulfilled all that had been written about Him, they took Him down from the tree and placed Him in a tomb.

30 But God raised Him from the dead,

31 Who was seen many days by those who came up with Him from Galilee to Jerusalem, who are His witnesses to the people.

32 And we announce good news to you, the promise made to the fathers,

33 God has fulfilled to us their children, raising up Jesus, as also it has been written in the second Psalm, 'You are My Son, today I have begotten You.'

34 And that He raised Him from the dead, never again to return to corruption, therefore He has said, 'I will give you the holy things of faithful David.'

35 So He also said in another place, 'You will not give your Holy One to see corruption.'

36 For David, having truly served his own generation through the counsel of

God, fell asleep, was laid with his fathers, and saw corruption.

37 But He whom God raised up did not see corruption.

38 Therefore, be it known to you men, brethren, that through this One forgiveness of sins are announced,

39 and from all things which you could not by the law of Moses be justified, in Him everyone who believes is made righteous.

40 Therefore beware lest what is said by the prophets comes upon you,

41 'Behold, you scoffers, and wonder and perish, because I work a work in your day, a work that you would not believe, if it were told to you in detail.'"

42 But the Jews having gone out of the synagogue, the Gentiles begged that these words be spoken to them the next Sabbath.

43 And the synagogue being broken up, many of the Jews and the devout proselytes followed Paul and Barnabas, who, speaking to them, persuaded them to continue in the grace of God.

44 And on the coming Sabbath, nearly all of the town came together to hear the word of God.

45 And the Jews, seeing the multitudes, were filled with jealousy, and spoke against the things spoken by Paul, contradicting and blaspheming.

46 But Paul and Barnabas boldly said, "It was necessary to first speak to you the Word of God, but since you have rejected it, and have judged yourselves unworthy of eternal life, behold, we turn unto the Gentiles!

47 For so has the Lord commanded us, 'I have set you for a light of the Gentiles, that you should be for salvation unto the uttermost part of the Earth.'"

48 And the Gentiles, hearing this, rejoiced and glorified the Word of the Lord and believed, as many as were appointed unto eternal life.

49 And the word of the Lord was carried through the whole country.

50 But the Jews stirred up the devout and honorable women and the chief ones of the city, and raised up a persecution against Paul and Barnabas, and cast them out of their district.

51 But they, shaking off the dust of their feet against them, went to Iconium.

52 And the disciples were filled with joy and the Holy Spirit.

14

And in Iconium it came to pass that they went together into the synagogue of the Jews and spoke in such a way that a large number of both Jews and Greeks believed.

2 But the disobedient Jews stirred up and infected the souls of the Gentiles against the brethren.

3 So then they stayed a long time, speaking boldly in the Lord, who bore witness to His Word of Grace, granting miracles and wonders to be done through their hands.

4 But the multitude of the city was divided, and part held with the Jews, and part held with the apostles.

5 And when an assault was made by the Gentiles and also the Jews, together with their rulers, to mistreat and stone them,

6 being aware, they fled to Lystra and Derbe, cities of Lycaonia, and those neighboring,

7 and there they preached the gospel.

8 And there sat a man in Lystra, powerless in his feet, lame from his mother's belly, who had never walked.

9 The same heard Paul speak, who, gazing at him and observing that he had faith to be healed,

10 said with a loud voice, "Stand up on
your feet." And he leaped up and
walked.
11 And the crowds, seeing what Paul
had done, lifted up their voices, speaking Lycaonian, "The gods, having become like men, have come down to
us!"
12 And they called Barnabas "Zeus,"
and Paul "Hermes," seeing that he was
the chief speaker.
13 And the priest of Zeus, who was
before the city, brought a bull and
wreaths to the gates, for the multitude
desired to offer a sacrifice.
14 When the apostles Barnabas and
Paul heard it, they tore their garments
and rushed into the crowd, shouting
15 and saying, "Men, why do you do
this? For we also are men, who have
the same kind of feelings as you,
preaching this: that you should turn
away from such folly unto the Living
God, Who made Heaven, and the
Earth, and the sea, and all that are in
them,
16 Who in past generations allowed all
the nations to go in their own ways.
17 And yet He did not leave Himself
without a witness, doing good, giving
you rain from heaven and seasons of
fruitfulness, filling your hearts with
food and gladness."
18 And with this statement they barely
restrained the crowd from offering a
sacrifice to them.
19 And there came Jews from Antioch
and Iconium, and persuading the
crowd and having stoned Paul, they
dragged him from the city, considering
him dead.
20 But when his disciples gathered
around, he rose up and came into the
city and the next day he departed with
Barnabas to Derbe.
21 Having preached the gospel to that
city and having made many disciples,
they returned to Lystra, and into Iconium, and into Antioch.
22 They strengthened the souls of the
disciples, encouraging them to abide in
the faith, and that through many tribulations we enter into the Kingdom of
God.
23 And when they had appointed elders in every church, they prayed with
fasting, setting them before the Lord
on whom they had believed.
24 And passing through Pisidia, they
came into Pamphylia.
25 And when they had preached the
Word in Perga, they came down into
Attalia.
26 And from there they sailed to Antioch, from where they had been given
over to the grace of God unto the work
that they fulfilled.
27 And when they arrived, they
brought the church together. They rehearsed all that God had done with
them and how He opened the door of
faith to the Gentiles.
28 And they spent a long time there
with the disciples.

15 And there came down from
Judea those teaching the brethren, "Unless you are circumcised after the custom of Moses, you cannot be
saved."
2 But this caused dissension and no
small controversy with them, and Paul,
and Barnabas. And it was arranged that
Paul and Barnabas, and some of the
others from them, should go up to
Jerusalem to the apostles and elders
concerning this issue.
3 Therefore those sent forth from the
church went through Phoenicia and
Samaria, telling in detail the conversion

of the nations, and caused great joy for
all the brethren.
4 And arriving in Jerusalem, they
were received by the church and the
apostles and the elders, and they related how much God had done through
them.
5 But some, who had come to believe
from the sect of the Pharisees, rose up,
saying, "It is necessary to circumcise
them, and order them to keep the Law
of Moses."
6 Now the apostles and elders had
come together to look into this issue.
7 And after a lot of controversy, Peter
stood up, saying to them, "Men,
brethren, you know that from the first
day God chose among us, that by my
mouth the Gentiles should hear the
word of the gospel and believe.
8 And God, Who knows the hearts,
gave them witness, giving them the
Holy Spirit just like us,
9 and made no distinction between us
and them, purifying their hearts by the
faith.
10 Now then, why tempt God by
putting a yoke upon the neck of the
disciples, which neither our fathers nor
we had strength to bear?
11 For we believe that we are saved
through the grace of the Lord Jesus
Christ in the same manner also."
12 But the whole crowd kept silent and
listened to Barnabas and Paul, who
made known how many miracles and
wonders God performed among the
Gentiles through them.
13 And after they had kept silent,
James responded, "Men and brethren,
listen to me.
14 Just as Simon had first made
known that God visited the Gentiles to
take from them a people for His name.
15 Also this harmonizes according to
the word the prophets wrote:
16 "'After this I will return, and rebuild
the tent of David that has fallen, and
from its ruins, I will rebuild and set it
up again.
17 So that the remnant of men might
seek the Lord and upon all of the nations who have called upon My name,"
says the Lord who does all of this.'
18 Known to God are all of His works
from the age.
19 Therefore, I judge that we should
not trouble those from the nations who
are turning unto God,
20 rather send this message to them:
that they abstain from pollutions of
idols, and sexual immorality, and
things strangled, and blood.
21 For Moses from ancient generations has had those that preach him in
every city, being read in the synagogues
every Sabbath."
22 Then the opinion of the apostles
and the elders, along with the whole
church, was to choose men from
among them to send to Antioch along
with Paul and Barnabas: Judas, called
Barsabas, and Silas, leading men with
the brethren.
23 By their hand they wrote this, "The
apostles and the elders and brethren, to
those at Antioch, and Syria, and Cilicia– brethren from out of the nations:
Greetings.
24 Since we heard that some coming
out from us have troubled you with
words, subverting your souls, to whom
we gave no commandment, saying,
'You must be circumcised and keep the
Law,'
25 having come into agreement, our
opinion was to send chosen men for
your sake, with our beloved Barnabas
and Paul,
26 men having given up their souls for

the name of our Lord Jesus Christ.
27Therefore, we have sent Judas and
Silas, and they shall communicate the
same thing by word.
28The Holy Spirit's opinion, and ours,
was not to lay upon you a greater
weight except these necessary things:
29abstain from sacrifices to idols, and
blood, and things strangled, and sexual
immorality, from which carefully keeping yourselves, you will do well.
Farewell."
30Therefore, being released, they
came to Antioch. And having brought
together the multitude, they handed
over the epistle.
31And having read it, they rejoiced
over the consolation.
32Judas, and also Silas, themselves
also being prophets, exhorted the
brethren through much speaking and
strengthened them.
33And continuing for a time, they
were released with peace from the
brothers to those who had sent them.
34But Silas decided to stay.
35And Paul and Barnabas decided to
stay in Antioch, teaching and preaching the Word of the Lord, among many
others also.
36And after some days, Paul said to
Barnabas, "We should return now to
look after those brethren in every city
that we have proclaimed the Word of
the Lord, to see how they are."
37And Barnabas desired to also take
along John, being called Mark.
38But Paul felt that he would not be
worthy to take along, for he departed
from them from Pamphylia and did
not accompany them unto the work.
39And there became a sharp dis-
agreement, so that they departed from
one another. And Barnabas, taking
Mark, sailed away into Cyprus.
40And Paul, having chosen for himself Silas, went out, being handed over
to the grace of God by the brethren.
41And he went through Syria and
Cilicia, strengthening the churches.

16 And he arrived at Derbe and
Lystra, and behold, a disciple
was there named Timothy, a son of a
believing Jewish woman, but of a Greek
father.
2The brethren in Lystra and Iconium
testified in support of him.
3Paul, desiring to take this one with
him, took him and circumcised him
because of the Jews who were in those
places, for they all knew that his father
was a Greek.
4As they traveled through the cities,
they delivered to them the decrees to
keep, that had been decided on by the
apostles and the elders in Jerusalem.
5Therefore, the churches were
strengthened in the faith, and their
number increased day by day.
6And they went through Phrygia and
the country of the Galatians, being for-
bidden by the Holy Spirit to speak the
Word in Asia.
7But having come to Mysia, they attempted to travel through Bithynia, but
the Spirit would not allow them.
8And having passed by Mysia they
went down into Troas.
9And Paul saw, by a vision of the
night, a man of Macedonia who was
standing, and calling him, and saying,
"Come over into Macedonia and help
us!"
10And so then, seeing the vision, we
immediately sought to go into Macedonia, concluding that the Lord had
called us to preach the gospel to them.
11Therefore, sailing from Troas, we
ran a straight course to Samothracia

and afterward to Neapolis,

12 and from there into Philippi, which is a colony, the first city of that part of Macedonia. And we spent some days in this city.

13 And on the day of the Sabbath we went outside the city by a river, where it was customary to pray. And having sat down, we talked with the women who came together.

14 And a certain woman named Lydia, from a city of Thyatira, a seller of purple, a worshiper of God, listened– whose heart the Lord opened up to respond to what was spoken by Paul.

15 And when she was baptized– and her house– she made a request, saying, "If you have judged me to be faithful to the Lord, come stay in my house." And she compelled us.

16 And it happened, as we were going to pray, a certain young girl having a spirit of divination met us, whose prophesying supplied much gain for her masters.

17 She followed after Paul and us, and cried out, saying, "These men are the servants of the Most High God, who are proclaiming to us a way of salvation!"

18 And this she did for many days. But Paul, being provoked, turned to the spirit and said, "I command you in the name of Jesus Christ to come out of her!" And it left her that same hour.

19 But her masters, seeing that their expectation of gain was gone, took hold of Paul and Silas, and dragged them into the marketplace before the rulers,

20 and bringing them to the chief magistrate, said, "These men, being Jews, have stirred up our city,

21 and they proclaim customs which are not lawful for us to receive nor do, being Romans."

22 And the multitude and the chief magistrate rose up together against them, tearing off their garments, commanding them to be beaten with rods.

23 And having laid many stripes on them, they threw them into prison, ordering the jailor to keep them secure,

24 who having received such an order, threw them into the inner prison and locked their feet into the stocks.

25 Now at about midnight, Paul and Silas were praying, singing praise to God, and the prisoners listened to them.

26 And suddenly there was a great earthquake, which shook the foundation of the prison, and instantly all of the doors were open and all the chains were unfastened.

27 And the jailor, being awakened from his sleep and seeing the doors of the prison opened, drew his sword and was about to put himself to death, thinking that the prisoners had escaped.

28 But Paul called out with a loud voice, saying, "Do no harm to yourself, we are all here!"

29 And asking for lights, he rushed in, and fell down before Paul and Silas, trembling.

30 And he led them outside, saying, "What must I do to be saved?"

31 And they said, "Believe upon the Lord Jesus Christ, and you will be saved, and your house."

32 And they spoke to him the Word of the Lord along with all those in his house.

33 And taking them in that same hour of the night, he washed their stripes, and right afterward was baptized, he and all of his household.

34 And having brought them into the house, he set a table for them and re-

joiced with all his house, having believed in God.
35 And when it was day, the chief
magistrates sent the sergeants, saying, "
Release those men."
36 And the jailor reported these words
to Paul, "The chief magistrate has sent
for you to be released. Now then, go
out– leave in peace."
37 But Paul said to them, "They beat
us publicly, being uncondemned Roman men, and they threw us into
prison. And now do they drive us out
secretly? No! But rather let them come
themselves and lead us out."
38 And the sergeants reported these
words to the chief magistrates, and
they were frightened when they heard
that they were Romans.
39 And they came and appealed to
them, and having brought them out,
asked them to go out of the city.
40 And leaving the prison, they came
to Lydia, and having seen the brethren,
they comforted them and went away.

17 And traveling through Am-
phipolis and Apollonia, they
came to Thessalonica, where there was
a synagogue of the Jews.
2 And according to Paul's custom, he
went to them and preached the Word
to them for three Sabbaths–
3 and opening up and setting before
them the necessity for Christ to have
suffered and to have risen from the
dead, and saying, "This is the Christ,
Jesus, Whom I proclaim to you."
4 And some of them were obedient
and joined themselves to Paul and
Silas, and a great many of the God-
fearing Greeks, and some of the princi-
pal women not a few.
5 But the disobedient Jews, becoming
jealous, also took in addition some agi-
tators who were wicked men, and gathered a crowd, causing a city uprising,
and setting out for the house of Jason,
sought to bring them into the mob.
6 But not finding them, they drug Jason and some of the brethren to the
ruler of the city, crying out, "Those
turning the inhabited world upside
down have also come here,
7 whom Jason has received as guests,
and these all act contrary to the decrees
of Caesar, saying there is another King:
Jesus."
8 And hearing these things, they
stirred up the crowd and the rulers of
the city.
9 And taking a bond from Jason and
the others, they set them free.
10 But at night, the brethren quickly
sent both Paul and Silas away to Berea,
who having arrived, went into the synagogue of the Jews.
11 And these were more noble than
those in Thessalonica, who received
the word with all eagerness, daily ex-
amining the scriptures, if these things
were so.
12 Then indeed many of them believed, and of the honorable Greek
women and men not a few.
13 But when the Jews from Thessalonica came to know that the Word of
God was also proclaimed by Paul in
Berea, they came there, harassing and
stirring up the crowds.
14 And immediately the brethren sent
Paul away to go to the sea. And Silas
and Timothy remained there.
15 And those accompanying Paul
brought him to Athens, and having received orders for Silas and Timothy
that they should come quickly to him,
they departed.
16 But as Paul was waiting for them in
Athens, his spirit was provoked in him,

beholding the city, which was full of idols.

17 He therefore reasoned with the Jews in the synagogue, and those who were God-fearing, and those being present in the marketplace, every day.

18 And some of the Epicurean and Stoic philosophers met with him. And some said, “What does this chatterer desire to communicate? Now, he seems to be a preacher of good news about a foreign demon, this Jesus, and the resurrection.”

19 And they took hold of him, bringing him to the hill of Mars saying, “We desire to know what new teaching this is by which you speak.

20 For you have brought some surprising ideas to our ears– we therefore desire to know what these things mean.”

21 And all the Athenians and the visiting strangers spent their time in nothing other than to tell or hear something new.

22 And Paul, standing in the midst of Mars hill, said, “Men, Athenians, I see you all as very religious.

23 For passing through and looking up at the objects of your worship, I also found an altar on which was written, ‘To an unknown God.’ Whom then you ignorantly worship, this One I proclaim to you:

24 the God Who made the world and everything in it. This One, being Lord of Heaven and Earth, dwells not in temples made by hands,

25 nor served by men’s hands, for He has need of nothing. He gave everything life and breath and all things,

26 and He made from one blood every nation of men to dwell upon the face of the whole Earth, setting appointed seasons and the boundaries of their dwellings,

27 that they should seek the Lord. Perhaps they might feel after and find Him, even though he is not far from each one of us.

28 For in Him we live, and move, and exist. As also some of the poets among you have said, ‘Indeed, we are His offspring.’

29 Being then offspring of God, we should not consider gold, or silver, or stone impressions crafted and thought up of men to be the resemblance of the divine.

30 Therefore God, disregarding the time of your ignorance, now commands all men everywhere, to repent!

31 Because He has set a day in which He is going to judge the inhabitants of the Earth in righteousness by the Man Whom He has appointed, having provided everyone with faith by His resurrection from death.”

32 But when they heard the resurrection of the dead, they mocked and said, “We will hear more later from you about this.”

33 Thus Paul came out from their midst.

34 But some of the men, joining themselves to him, believed. Among them were Dionysius– an Areopagite– and a woman named Damaris, and others with them.

18 After these things, departing from Athens, he came to Corinth.

2 And finding a Jew of Pontus named Aquila, and Priscilla his wife (his family recently coming from Italy because Claudius had arranged that all Jews were to depart from Rome), came to them,

3 and because he was of the same trade, he remained with them and

worked, for they were tentmakers by trade.

4 And he preached in the synagogue on every Sabbath, persuading both Jews and Gentiles.

5 But when Silas and Timothy came down from Macedonia, Paul was pressed by the Spirit to testify of Christ Jesus to those Jews.

6 But they set themselves against him and blasphemed. Shaking off his garments he said, "Your blood upon your heads! I am clean. From now on I will go to the Gentiles."

7 And departing from there, he came to a house of one named Justus, a worshiper of God, whose house was joined to the synagogue.

8 And Crispus, the ruler of the synagogue, believed the Lord, together with his whole house. And many of the Corinthians, hearing, believed and were baptized.

9 And the Lord said in the night through a vision to Paul, "Fear not, but speak and be not silent,

10 because I am with you, and no one shall take hold of you to hurt you, because I have many people in this city."

11 And he remained for a year and six months, teaching them the Word of God.

12 Now Gallio was proconsul of Achaia, and the Jews with one mind rose up against Paul and led him to the tribunal,

13 saying, "This one persuades men to worship God contrary to the Law."

14 And Paul being about to open his mouth, Gallio said to the Jews, "If indeed then it was some wrong or some bad crime, oh Jews, according to reason I would listen to you.

15 But if it is a question about a word and names and law that concerns you, then you see to it– I will not be a judge of these things."

16 And he drove them from the tribunal.

17 And all the Greeks took hold of Sosthenes, the ruler of the synagogue. They beat him before the tribunal. And not one of these things mattered to Gallio.

18 And Paul, having remained for many more days, took leave of the brothers sailing to Syria. Also, Priscilla and Aquila went along with him, having shaved his head in Cenchrea because he had a vow.

19 And coming down into Ephesus, he left them there while he went into the synagogue to preach to the Jews.

20 And they asked him to stay for a longer time, but he refused,

21 rather taking leave of them, and saying, "I must by all means keep the feast at Jerusalem. God willing, I will return to you." And he sailed from Ephesus.

22 And coming down to Caesarea, having gone up, he greeted the church and went down to Antioch.

23 And spending some time, he successively went out through the land of Galatia and Phrygia, confirming all the disciples.

24 And a certain Jew named Apollos, born in Alexandria, an eloquent man, came to Ephesus, being skillful in the scriptures.

25 This one was instructed in the way of the Lord and, being fervent in the Spirit, he spoke and taught accurately the things concerning Jesus, understanding only the Baptism of John.

26 And this one began to speak boldly in the synagogue. And Priscilla and Aquila heard him, and took him and explained the way of God more per-

fectly.
27And being desirous to depart to
Achaia, they wrote the brethren urging
the disciples to welcome him, who,
having arrived, was of much help to
those who believed through grace.
28For he vigorously proved the Jews
wrong publicly, proving through the
scriptures Jesus to be the Christ.

19 Then it came to pass that while
Apollos was in Corinth, Paul,
passing through the upper parts, came
down into Ephesus and found some
disciples.
2And he said to them, "Did you receive the Holy Spirit when you believed?" And they said to him, "We
have not so much as heard that there is
a Holy Spirit."
3And he said, "What were you baptized unto then?" And they said, "Unto
the baptism of John."
4But Paul said, "John baptized with a
baptism of repentance, telling the people about the One coming after him, so
that they may believe in Him– that is,
Jesus."
5And hearing this, they were baptized in the name of the Lord Jesus.
6And Paul laying his hands on them,
the Holy Spirit came upon them and
they spoke with tongues and prophesied.
7And there were about twelve men in
all.
8And he went into the synagogue,
speaking boldly for three months, exhorting and persuading them concerning the Kingdom of God.
9And as some were hardened and
disobeyed, speaking evil of the Way before the multitudes, he departed from
them, setting apart the disciples, and
reasoning daily in the school of Tyran-
nus.
10And this he continued for two
years, so that all of the inhabitants of
Asia heard the Word of the Lord, both
Jews and Greeks.
11And God performed extraordinary
works of power by the hands of Paul.
12So that also from his body were
brought to the sick handkerchiefs and
aprons, and the diseases departed, and
the evil spirits went out.
13And some traveling Jewish exor-
cists also attempted to name the name
of the Lord Jesus over them who had
evil spirits, saying, "I charge you by Jesus, Who Paul preaches."
14And they were seven sons of Sceva,
a Jewish High Priest, that did this.
15But the evil spirit answered, saying
to them, "Jesus I know, and Paul I recognize, but who are you?"
16And the man in whom the evil
spirit was leaped upon them and both
overcame and overpowered them, so
that they fled away from that one's
house naked and wounded.
17And this became known to all Jews
and also Greeks who inhabited Ephesus, and fear fell upon all of them, and
the name of the Lord Jesus was magnified.
18And many of those who believed
came confessing and disclosing their
practices.
19And a large number of them that
practiced curious arts brought together
their books to burn before everyone.
And an accounting of the value of
them was also determined to be 50,000
pieces of silver.
20So with might the Word of the Lord
increased and prevailed.
21And when these things were fulfilled, having passed through Macedonia and Achaia, Paul purposed in the

Spirit to go to Jerusalem, saying, "After I have come there, I must also see Rome."

22 And sending into Macedonia two that ministered to him, Timothy and Erastus, he stayed a time in Asia.

23 And about that time there was no small disturbance concerning the Way.

24 For a certain silversmith, named Demetrius, was making silver shrines for Artemis, providing those craftsmen with no little trade.

25 And gathering the workmen together concerning these things, he said, "Men, you know that from this trade is our wealth.

26 Also we see and hear that not only in Ephesus, but nearly all of Asia, that this Paul has persuasively turned away a great multitude, saying that they are not gods that are made with hands.

27 And not only does this endanger our business to be brought into contempt, but also the temple of the great goddess Artemis to be considered nothing– and her magnificence, whom the whole of Asia and its inhabitants worship, is also about to be destroyed."

28 And having heard this, and having become full of anger, they cried out, saying, "Great is Artemis of the Ephesians!"

29 And the whole city being filled with confusion, they rushed with one mind into the theater, having seized Gaius and Aristarchus, Macedonians traveling with Paul.

30 Though Paul wanted to go in before the people, the disciples would not let him.

31 And some of the Asian officials, who were also His friends, sent to him encouraging him not to venture himself to the theater.

32 Therefore some cried one thing and others another, for the assembly was confused and the multitude did not know why they had come together.

33 But they brought Alexander from the crowd, the Jews pushing him forward. And Alexander, waving his hands, desired to defend himself before the assembly.

34 But knowing that he is a Jew, they became as one voice, everyone crying out over two hours, "Great is Artemis of the Ephesians!"

35 But the town clerk quieted the multitude down, saying, "Men, Ephesians, for what man is there that does not know the city of Ephesus to be the temple-keeper of Artemis and of that image fallen from Zeus?

36 Therefore, these things being undeniable, you are to calm down and do nothing rash.

37 For you brought these men who are neither temple robbers nor blasphemers of your goddess.

38 If then indeed Demetrius and those craftsmen together with him have a matter against anyone, the courts are open and there are proconsuls– let them accuse one another.

39 And if anything concerning other matters, solve it in a lawful assembly.

40 For we are also in danger of being accused of insurrection concerning this. There being no cause for it, how will we be able to give an account concerning this conspiracy?"

41 And saying these things, he dismissed the assembly.

20 And after the uproar ceased, Paul sent for the disciples, and having taken leave of them, he departed, traveling to Macedonia.

2 And when he had gone over those parts and comforted them with many

words, he came into Greece.

3And having spent three months, it happened that the Jews plotted against him as he was about to sail for Syria, so he made the decision to return through Macedonia.

4And Sopater, a Berean, and Aristarchus and Secundus, Thessalonians, and Gaius of Derbe, and Timotheus, and Tychicus, and Trophimus of Asia, accompanied him to Asia.

5And these, going ahead, waited for us in Troas.

6And we sailed away to Philippi after the days of unleavened bread, and we came to them in Troas after five days, where we stayed seven days.

7And on the first of the week, the disciples having come together to break bread, Paul addressed them, being about to depart the next morning, and continued to speak until midnight.

8And many lamps were in the upper room where they were gathered together.

9And a young man named Eutychus, sitting down in the window, sinking into a deep sleep, Paul preaching for a long time, fell from the window, falling down from the third floor, and he was taken up dead.

10And Paul went down and embraced him, and taking him into his arms, said, "Do not be concerned, for his soul is in him."

11And going up and breaking bread, and having eaten sufficiently, and conversing until morning, then he departed.

12And they brought the boy alive and were not a little comforted.

13But going ahead to the ship, we set sail to Assos, intending to take Paul on there, for so it had been arranged, himself having purposed to go on foot.

14And when he met us in Assos, we took him in and came into Mitylene.

15And sailing away from there, afterward we came near Chios, and the next day we crossed Samos. And remaining by Trogyllium, next we came to Miletus.

16For Paul decided to sail by Ephesus, so that he might not come to spend time in Asia. For he hurried, if it were possible, for him to be in Jerusalem for the day of Pentecost.

17And from Miletus he sent to Ephesus and called for the elders of the church.

18And when they came to him, he said to them, "You know from the first day when I arrived in Asia, how I was with you all the time,

19serving the Lord with all humility and tears, and trials, which came to me by the plots of the Jews,

20how that I did not draw back from declaring to you anything that was profitable, and taught you publicly and from house to house,

21testifying to Jews, and also to Greeks, repentance to God and faith in our Lord Jesus Christ.

22And now, behold, being bound in the Spirit, I go to Jerusalem, not knowing what shall happen to me in it,

23except that the Holy Spirit testifies of me in every city saying that bonds and tribulations await me.

24But I make no account of myself, nor hold my soul precious, so that I might finish my race with joy, and the ministry, which I received from the Lord Jesus, to testify of the gospel of the grace of God.

25And now, behold, I know that all of you will see my face no more, among whom I have gone about proclaiming the Kingdom of God.

26 Because of this, I testify on this parting day that I am pure from the blood of all,

27 for I did not keep back from you all the counsel of God.

28 Take heed therefore to yourselves and to all the flock, in which the Holy Spirit has placed you as overseers, to shepherd the church of God, which He purchased with His own blood.

29 For I know that after my departure, grievous wolves will come in among you, not sparing the flock.

30 And from you yourselves shall arise men speaking distorted things, to draw away disciples after themselves.

31 Therefore watch, remembering that for three years I did not cease warning each one of you with tears night and day.

32 And now brethren, I commit you to God and the Word of His grace, which is able to build you up and give you an inheritance with all those who have been made holy.

33 I have desired no one's silver, gold, or clothing.

34 But you yourselves know that these hands of mine did minister to my needs and those with me.

35 I have shown every one of you how, laboring, you should give aid to the weak, and remember the words of the Lord Jesus, that He Himself said, 'It is more blessed to give than to receive.'"

36 And saying these things, he knelt down and prayed for them all.

37 And there was a lot of weeping, and falling upon the neck of Paul, they kissed him,

38 sorrowing much over the word that he spoke, that they would see his face no more. And they went with him to the boat.

21 And it came to pass, departing from them, we set sail with a straight course to come to Cos, and then next to Rhodes, and from there to Patara.

2 Finding a boat crossing over to Phoenicia, we boarded and sailed.

3 And sighting Cyprus and leaving it on the left, we sailed to Syria, and we landed in Tyre as the ship was unloading its cargo there.

4 And having found disciples, who told Paul through the Spirit not to go up to Jerusalem, we remained there seven days.

5 But when our days there were completed, setting out, we traveled, everyone with their wives, and the children accompanied us until we were outside the city. And kneeling down on the seashore, we prayed.

6 We took leave of one another, and went up into the ship, and they returned to their homes.

7 And when we had finished our voyage from Tyre, we came to Ptolemais, and greeted the brethren, and stayed with them for one day.

8 And the next day we departed with Paul and came to Caesarea, and we entered into the house of Philip the Evangelist, being of the seven, staying with him.

9 And he had four virgin daughters who prophesied.

10 And we remained many days. Then a prophet came down from Judea named Agabus.

11 And when he came to us, and had taken Paul's belt, he bound his own feet and hands, saying, "This is what the Holy Spirit says, 'The man who owns this belt shall be bound in this way by the Jews in Jerusalem and given over into the hands of Gentiles.'"

12 And when we heard this, we, and those that were there, urged him not to go up to Jerusalem.

13 Then Paul replied, “Why are you making me cry and breaking my heart? I am not only ready to be bound, but also to die in Jerusalem, which I do eagerly for the name of the Lord Jesus.”

14 But not persuading him, we were silent, saying, “The Lord’s will be done.”

15 And after those days we prepared to go up to Jerusalem.

16 And disciples from Caesarea went with us, bringing us to Mnason– a Cypriot, an old disciple– with whom we might lodge.

17 And when we came to Jerusalem, the brethren received us gladly.

18 And afterward, Paul met with James, along with all of the elders.

19 And having greeted them, he related one by one what things God had done for the nations through his ministry,

20 which also having heard, they glorified God and said to him, “You see, brother, how many thousands of Jews there are who have believed, and all are zealous for the Law.

21 And they have learned about you– that you teach all of the Jews among the nations to forsake Moses, telling them not to circumcise their children, nor to walk in the customs.

22 What is to be done? A multitude will come together, for they will hear that you have come.

23 Therefore do this that we say to you: We have four men who have a vow on themselves.

24 Take these, be purified along with them, and pay their expenses, that they may shave their heads and everyone will know that all that they have learned of you is nothing, but you yourself walk orderly and keep the Law.

25 And concerning the believing nations, we have written deciding that they keep no such thing, except to keep themselves from both idol sacrifices, and blood, and a thing strangled, and sexual immorality.”

26 Then Paul, taking the men the next day, having been purified with them, entered into the temple, declaring the completion of the days of purification until the offering should be offered for each one of them.

27 Now the seven days were about to be complete. The Jews from Asia, having seen him in the temple, stirred up the multitude, and they grabbed hold of him with their hands,

28 crying out, “Men, Israelites, help! This is the man who is teaching everyone everywhere against the people and the Law and this place– and even more, he also brought Greeks into the temple and has defiled this holy place!”

29 For they had before seen Trophimus the Ephesian in the city with him, whom they supposed Paul had brought into the temple.

30 And the whole city was moved, and the people came running together. And having laid hold on Paul, they dragged him outside of the temple and quickly shut the door.

31 And as they sought to kill him, information came up to the commander of the soldiers that all of Jerusalem was in an uproar,

32 who, immediately taking soldiers and centurions, ran down upon them, and seeing the commander and the soldiers, they stopped beating Paul.

33 Then the commander, coming near, took and commanded that he be bound with two chains, and inquired who he

might be and what he was doing.

34 But in the crowd, some cried out one thing, and others something else, and being unable to know with certainty because of the uproar, he commanded him to be brought into the fortress.

35 Now when they came to the stairs, the soldiers were carrying him because of the violence of the crowd.

36 For the multitude of the people were following, crying out, "Away with Him!"

37 And being about to be brought into the fortress, Paul said to the commander, "Is it permitted for me to say something to you?" And he said, "Do you know Greek?

38 Are you not that Egyptian, who before these days caused a riot and led out four thousand men of the assassins into the wilderness?"

39 But Paul said, "I am indeed a Jew, of Tarsus in Cilicia, a citizen of no insignificant city. I beg you, permit me to speak to the people."

40 And allowing him, Paul, standing on the stairs, waved his hand to the people and it became very quiet as he spoke in the Hebrew language, saying,

22 "Men, brethren, and fathers, hear my defense to you now."

2 And having heard that he addressed them in the Hebrew language, they became even more quiet, and he said,

3 "I am indeed a Jewish man, born in Tarsus of Cilicia, but brought up in this city at the feet of Gamaliel, having been instructed according to the exactness of the Law of the fathers, and was zealous for God, even as all of you are this day,

4 who persecuted this Way unto death, binding men and women, and delivering them up to prison,

5 as also the high priest can bear witness of me and all of the elders, from whom also having received letters for the brethren, I went to Damascus to also bring those who were there bound to Jerusalem so that they might be punished.

6 And while I was on my journey and coming near to Damascus, about noon, suddenly a bright light shone about me from Heaven.

7 And I fell to the ground and heard a voice saying to me, 'Saul, Saul, why do you persecute Me?'

8 And I replied, 'Who are You, Lord?' And He said to me, 'Jesus the Nazarene, Whom you are persecuting.'

9 And those who were with me definitely saw the light and were terrified, but they did not hear His voice speaking to me.

10 And I said, 'What shall I do, Lord?' And the Lord said to me, 'Rise up and go to Damascus, and there you shall be told about everything that has been appointed for you to do.'

11 But since I could not see, because of the glory of that light, those who were with me took my hand and led me to Damascus.

12 And one Ananias, a devout man according to the Law, well-spoken of by all the Jews living there,

13 came to me, and standing beside me, he said, 'Brother Saul, look up!' In that very hour I looked upon him.

14 Then he said, 'The God of our fathers has appointed you to know His will and to see the Righteous One and hear His voice from His mouth,

15 because you will be His witness to all men of what you have seen and heard.

16 And now, why delay? Rise up, be baptized, and wash away your sins,

calling on the name of the Lord.'

17 And after I returned to Jerusalem and while I was praying in the temple, I came into an ecstasy,

18 and saw Him saying to me, 'Hurry and get out of Jerusalem quickly, because they will not receive your testimony concerning Me.'

19 And I said, 'Lord, they realize that I imprisoned and beat in the synagogues those who believed in You,

20 and while the blood of your witness Stephen was poured out, I myself was standing by and approving also of his murder, and keeping the coats of those men who killed him.'

21 And He said to me, 'Go, for I will send you unto the nations far away.'"

22 Up to this point they listened to his words, but they lifted up their voice, saying, "Away from the Earth with such a person– it is not right that he should live!"

23 And they were shouting and throwing off their coats and tossing dust into the air.

24 The tribune commanded that he be led to the barracks, saying that he should be examined by flogging to know the reason for the outcry against him.

25 But when they stretched him out with straps, Paul said to the centurion standing by, "Is it legal for you to whip a man who is a Roman and not condemned?"

26 When the centurion heard this, he went to the tribune, and said, "What are you about to do? For this man is a Roman."

27 And the tribune came, asking him, "Tell me, are you a Roman?" And he said, "Yes."

28 The tribune answered, "With a large sum I got my citizenship." Paul said, "I was born one."

29 Immediately then, those about to examine him drew back from him. And the tribune also was afraid, for he realized that he was a Roman and that he had bound him.

30 Since he wanted to know what he was being accused of by the Jews, the next day he released him and ordered the Chief Priests and the entire Sanhedrin to meet. He brought Paul down and stood before them.

23

And Paul, looking intensely at the Sanhedrin said, "Men, brothers, I have lived with all good conscience before God up to this day."

2 Then the High Priest commanded those standing by him to hit him in the mouth.

3 At this Paul said to him, "God will strike you, you whitewashed wall! And are you sitting there judging me according to the Law, and ordering that I should be hit contrary to the Law?"

4 And those standing by said, "You insult the High Priest of God?"

5 And Paul declared, "Brethren, I did not know that he was High Priest, for it is written, 'For you shall not speak evil of the ruler of your people.'"

6 When Paul noticed that part were Sadducees, but the others Pharisees, he called out to the council, "Men, brethren, I am a Pharisee, the son of a Pharisee. Concerning the confidence and resurrection of the dead, I am on trial."

7 When he said this, a dissension began with the Pharisees and the Sadducees, and the multitude was divided.

8 For the Sadducees say that there is no resurrection, nor angel, nor spirit, but Pharisees agree with all three.

9 But a loud cry arose. And part of the

Scribes of the Pharisees stood up in protest, saying, “We find nothing evil in this man. But if a spirit has spoken to him, or an angel, let us not fight against God.”

10 But when the dissension became so great, the tribune, being concerned lest they tear Paul apart, ordered the soldiers to go down and take him from their midst and bring him to the barracks.

11 And then that night the Lord came near and stood by him, saying, “Be courageous, Paul. For just as you testified concerning Me in Jerusalem, even so you shall also bear witness in Rome.”

12 And when it was day, certain of the Jews conspired together, and put themselves under a curse, saying that they would not eat or drink until they had killed Paul.

13 And there were more than forty that made this plot.

14 And they came to the high priest and elders, saying, “We have bound ourselves under a curse of curses: we will eat nothing until we have slain Paul.

15 Now therefore, you, with the council, make known to the chief captain that you want him to bring him down tomorrow, as though you had more questions to ask him, and we will be ready to kill him when he comes.”

16 When Paul’s sister’s son heard of their lying in wait, he went and entered into the castle and told Paul.

17 And Paul, having called one of the centurions, said, “Take this young man unto the chief captain, for he has something to report to him.”

18 And he took him and said, “Paul the prisoner called me and asked me to bring this young man to you, who has something to tell you.”

19 Then the chief captain took him by the hand and went away, and asked him, “What is it that you have to report to me?”

20 And he said, “The Jews agreed to request that you bring Paul to the Sanhedrin tomorrow, as though they would enquire about something more accurately of him.

21 You should not be convinced by them, for more than forty men lie in wait for him, who have put themselves under a curse neither to eat or drink until they put him to death, and now are ready, waiting for a promise from you.”

22 Then the chief captain dismissed the young man and charged him, “Tell no one that you made these things known to me.”

23 And having called two of the centurions, he said, “Make ready two hundred soldiers to go to Caesarea, and seventy horsemen, and two hundred spearmen– at the third hour of the night.”

24 And they provided mounts to set Paul on, to bring him safely to Felix the governor,

25 having written a letter to this effect:

26 “Claudius Lysias, unto the most excellent governor Felix, greetings.

27 This man was seized by the Jews, and they were about to put him to death. I came up with a troop and rescued him, having learned that he was a Roman.

28 And desiring to know the charge for which they accused him, I brought him down to their Sanhedrin,

29 whom I found to be accused of questions concerning their Law, but having no accusation worthy of death or of bonds.

30 Then having been informed of a

plot about to be carried out by the Jews
against this man, I immediately sent
him to you, having also charged the
accusers to speak what they may
against him before you. Farewell."
31Therefore the soldiers, according to
their orders, took Paul by night and
brought him to Antipatris.
32Then the next day, they left the
horsemen to go with him and returned
to the castle.
33When they came to Cesarea, they
delivered the epistle to the governor,
and presented Paul before him.
34When the governor had read it, he
asked what province he was from. And
understanding that he was from Cilicia,
35he said, "I will hear you when your
accusers have arrived." And he commanded
that he should be kept in the
praetorium of Herod.

24 Then after five days Ananias
the High Priest came down
with the elders, and with an Orator
named Tertullus, made a representation
to the governor against Paul.
2When Paul was called, Tertullus began
to bring charges, saying, "Through
your forethought, great peace is being
experienced through you, and many
good things are done for this nation,
3both in every way and everywhere
we gladly accept this with all thankfulness,
most excellent Felix.
4But that I may not be a hindrance
any longer, I beseech you to briefly
hear us in your clemency.
5We have found this man a pest, and
a mover of insurrection among all the
Jews throughout the world, and a
leader of the sect of the Nazarenes,
6who also attempted to profane the
temple, whom also we seized, and according
to our Law desired to judge.
7But the chief captain, Lysias, came
up, and, with great force took him out
of our hands,
8having commanded his accusers to
come to you– from whom you may be
able yourself to examine concerning all
of these things, to know what we accuse
him of."
9Then the Jews also agreed, declaring
these things to be so.
10But Paul answered, after the governor
motioned to him to speak, "Knowing
that you have been the judge of this
nation for many years, I more cheerfully
make a defense for the things concerning
myself.
11You can verify that there are no
more than twelve days since I went up
to worship at Jerusalem,
12and that they neither found me in
the temple disputing with any man or
gathering a mob, neither in the synagogues
nor in the city.
13Neither can they prove the things
that they accuse me of.
14But this I confess to you, that after
the Way, which they call a sect, so I
serve the God of my fathers, believing
all things that have been written in the
Law and the Prophets,
15and have confidence in God that
there is about to be the resurrection of
the dead, both of the righteous and the
unrighteous, which they themselves
also await.
16Because of this then, I continually
exercise myself to have a blameless
conscience before God and man.
17But after many years, I came and
brought alms and offerings to my nation.
18in which they found me purified in
the temple, neither with multitude, nor
with unquietness– but it was Jews from

Asia
19 who ought to appear here before
you and accuse me if they have anything against me.
20 Or these themselves, let them say if
they have found any unrighteousness
in me when I stood before the Sanhedrin,
21 except for this one voice which I
cried standing among them, 'Concerning the resurrection of the dead, I am
judged this day by you.'"
22 When Felix heard these things, he
deferred them, for he knew the things
concerning the Way, saying, "When
Lysias the chief captain has come, I will
examine you as to these things."
23 He ordered the centurion to keep
Paul, to let him rest, and not forbid any
of his acquaintances to minister or to
come to him.
24 And after some days, Felix and his
wife Drusilla arrived, who was a Jew-
ess. He sent for Paul and heard him
concerning his faith in Christ.
25 And as he discussed righteousness,
and dominion over oneself, and the
coming judgment, Felix became terrified, saying "Go away until another
time, then I will send for you and receive you."
26 He hoped also that money might be
given to him by Paul, so that he might
release him. For this reason he fre-
quently sent for him to converse with
him.
27 But after two years, Festus Porcius
became the successor of Felix. And Felix, desiring to acquire favor with the
Jews, left Paul bound.

25 When Festus came into the
province after three days, he
went up to Jerusalem from Caesarea.
2 Then the High Priest and the chief
of the Jews made a representation
against Paul, and appealed to him,
3 asking a favor against him: that he
would send him to Jerusalem, forming
an ambush to put him to death on the
way.
4 Festus answered that Paul should be
kept at Caesarea, for he himself would
soon leave.
5 Therefore he said, "Those among
you in power, let them go down with
me. If there is anything in this man, let
them accuse him."
6 When he had spent more than ten
days among them, he departed to Cesarea, and the next day sat down on the
judgment seat and commanded Paul to
be brought.
7 When he had come, the Jews who
had come from Jerusalem came around
him and laid many grievous charges
against Paul that they could not prove.
8 He said in his defense, "Neither
against the Law of the Jews, nor against
the temple, nor against Caesar, have I
sinned."
9 But Festus, willing to do the Jews a
pleasure, answered Paul and said, "Will
you go to Jerusalem and there be
judged of these things before me?"
10 Then Paul said, "I stand before the
judgment seat of Caesar, where I ought
to be judged. To the Jews I have done
nothing wrong, as also you know very
well.
11 If I have hurt them or committed
anything worthy of death, I do not
refuse to die. But if there is nothing to
these things whereof they accuse me,
no man ought to deliver me to them. I
appeal to Caesar."
12 Then Festus, having conferred with
the council, answered, "You have appealed to Caesar. To Caesar you shall
go!"

13 Then after some days had passed, King Agrippa and Bernice came to Caesarea to salute Festus.

14 And when they had been there many days, Festus related the things of Paul to the King, saying, “There is a man left in prison by Felix,

15 about whom, when I came to Jerusalem, the high priests and elders of the Jews asked judgment against him,

16 to whom I answered, ‘It is not the manner of the Romans to deliver up any man who is accused before he has the opportunity to face his accusers to offer a defense concerning the accusation.’

17 Therefore– they having come together here– without delay, the next day, I sat on the judgment seat commanding the man to be brought forth,

18 concerning whom, when the accusers stood up, they brought no charges of such things as I supposed,

19 but had certain questions against him of their own superstition and of one Jesus, Who was dead, Who Paul affirmed to be alive.

20 But being perplexed concerning this inquiry, I asked him whether he would be willing to go to Jerusalem and there be judged concerning these things.

21 But Paul– himself having appealed to be kept for the decision of Caesar– I commanded him to be kept until I might send him to Caesar.”

22 Agrippa said unto Festus, “I would also like to hear the man myself.” Then he said, “Tomorrow you shall hear him.”

23 Therefore, on the next day, when Agrippa and Bernice came with great pomp and had entered into the hall with the captains and chief men of the city at Festus’s command, Paul was brought forth.

24 And Festus said, “King Agrippa and all men that are here present with us, you see this man, about whom all the multitude of the Jews have pleaded with me, both at Jerusalem and also here, crying that he ought not to live any longer.

25 Yet I found that he has committed nothing worthy of death. Yet because he has appealed to Augustus, I have determined to send him,

26 of whom I have no certain thing to write unto my lord. Therefore I have brought him unto you, and especially before you, king Agrippa, that after examination I might have something to write.

27 For I think it is unreasonable to send a prisoner and not to signify the charges that are laid against him.”

26 Agrippa said to Paul, “You are permitted to speak for yourself.” Then Paul, stretching out his hand, made a defense:

2 “I think myself happy, King Agrippa, because I shall make a defense this day before you of all the things that I am accused of by the Jews,

3 being that you are an expert in all customs and questions that are among the Jews. Therefore I beseech you to hear me patiently.

4 Certainly then, my manner of life from my youth, which was at the first among my own nation at Jerusalem– all of the Jews know,

5 who knew me from the beginning, if they would testify of it– that according to the strictest sect of our religion I lived a Pharisee.

6 And now I stand, being judged for the hope of the promise made to our

fathers by God,
7 to which our twelve tribes, earnestly
serving God day and night, hope to
come. For which hope I am accused by
the Jews, O King Agrippa.
8 Why should it be considered an in-
credible thing to you that God should
raise the dead?
9 I also indeed thought of myself that
I should do many things against the
name of Jesus the Nazarene,
10 which I also did in Jerusalem, and
having received authority from the
Chief Priests, I shut up many of the
saints in prison. And they being put to
death, I gave my vote against them.
11 And I punished them often in every
synagogue and compelled them to
blaspheme. And being exceedingly furious against them, I persecuted them
even unto foreign cities,
12 in which also, as I went to Damascus with authority and a commission
from the Chief Priests,
13 at midday, O King, I saw in the way
a light from Heaven, beyond the
brightness of the sun, shining around
me and them that journeyed with me.
14 And all of us having fallen down to
the ground, I heard a voice speaking to
me and saying in the Hebrew tongue,
'Saul, Saul, why do you persecute Me?
It is hard for you to kick against the
spurs.'
15 And I said, 'Who are You, Lord?'
And He said, 'I am Jesus, Whom you
persecute.
16 But rise and stand on your feet, for
I have appeared to you for this purpose, to appoint you an assistant and a
witness both of what you have seen and
of what I shall show to you,
17 taking you out from the people and
from the nations to which I now send
you,
18 to open their eyes that they might
turn from darkness to light, and from
the authority of Satan unto God, that
they may receive forgiveness of sins
and inheritance among them that have
been made holy by that faith in Me.'
19 After this, King Agrippa, I was not
disobedient to the heavenly vision,
20 but showed first to them of Damascus, and at Jerusalem, and throughout
the coast of Judea, and to the nations,
declaring that they should repent and
turn to God and do works worthy of
repentance.
21 For this cause, the Jews caught and
tried to kill me in the temple.
22 Nevertheless, having obtained help
from God, unto this day, I have stood
witnessing both to small and to great,
saying nothing else than what both the
Prophets and Moses said should take
place:
23 that Christ should suffer, and that
He should be the first that should rise
from the dead, and will show light to
the people and to the nations."
24 While speaking these things in his
defense, Festus said with a loud voice,
"Paul, you are crazy! Much learning
has made you crazy!"
25 Then Paul said, "I am not crazy,
most noble Festus, but speak the words
of truth and soundness of mind.
26 The king knows of these things, before whom I speak boldly, for I am persuaded that none of these things are
hidden from him, for this thing was
not done in a corner.
27 King Agrippa, do you believe the
prophets? I know that you believe."
28 Agrippa said to Paul, "You almost
persuade me to become a Christian."
29 And Paul said, "I pray to God that
not only you were almost, but altogether such as I am, and also all that hear

me today, except these bonds."
30 And he having said these things,
the king rose up, and the governor,
along with Bernice, and they that sat
with them.
31 And when they were gone, they
talked between themselves, saying,
"This man has done nothing worthy of
death or bonds."
32 Then Agrippa said to Festus, "This
man might have been let go if he had
not appealed to Caesar."

27 Now when it was decided that
we should sail to Italy, they delivered Paul and some other prisoners
to a centurion named Julius, of the
band of Caesar.
2 And having gone on board a ship to
Adramyttium, which would navigate
along the districts of Asia, we set sail
with Aristarchus, a Macedonian of
Thessalonica.
3 Then the next day, we came to
Sidon. And Julius treated Paul kindly
and gave him liberty to go to his
friends and receive care.
4 From there we set sail. We sailed by
Cyprus, because the winds were contrary.
5 Then we sailed along the sea coast
of Cilicia and Pamphylia, and came to
Myra, of Lycia.
6 And there the centurion found a
ship of Alexandria sailing to Italy, and
he put us on it.
7 But sailing slowly for many days,
and barely having come over against
Cnidus, because the wind withstood
us, we sailed close to the coasts of Crete
beside Salmone.
8 And barely coasting along, we came
to a place called Fair Havens, near to a
city called Lasaea.
9 But when much time had passed,
and the voyage being already danger-
ous, also because the fast had already
passed, Paul exhorted them,
10 saying, "Men, I perceive that this
voyage is about to be met with disaster
and much loss, not only of the cargo
and of the ship, but also of our lives."
11 But the centurion was persuaded
more by the steersmen and the
shipowner than what Paul had spoken.
12 And the port being unfavorable to
winter in, the majority counseled to set
sail from there, so that they might be
able to arrive at Phoenice, a port of
Crete which serves to the southwest
and northwest, to winter.
13 When the south wind blew gently,
supposing that they achieved their
purpose, they weighed anchor and
coasted close by Crete.
14 But not long afterward arose a hurricane wind, called Euroclydon.
15 But when the ship was caught and
could not be brought around, we let
her go and were driven along.
16 And we came to a small island
named Clauda, and we were hardly
able to become masters of the boat,
17 which they took up, and used helps,
undergirding the boat. Fearing lest they
should have fallen into quicksand, they
let down the gear, so they were driven.
18 The next day, when we were violently tossed with a storm, they cast out
all the cargo.
19 And the third day we cast out with
our own hands the tackling of the ship.
20 And seeing neither sun nor stars
for many days, and no small tempest
laying on us, all hope was taken away
that we should be saved.
21 Then after there had been a long
abstinence, Paul stood up in the midst
of them and said, "Men, you should
have been obedient to me and not set

sail from Crete to have gained this disaster and loss.
22And now I exhort you to be of good
cheer, for there shall be no loss of any
man's life from among you, only of the
ship.
23For there stood by me this night an
angel of God, Whose I am, Whom I
serve,
24saying, 'Fear not, Paul. For you
must be brought before Caesar. And,
behold! God has given to you all that
sail with you.'
25Therefore, men, be of good cheer,
for I believe God that it shall be even as
it was told me.
26But we must run aground onto an
island."
27But when the fourteenth night had
come, and we were being driven about
in the Adriatic, toward the middle of
the night, some of the sailers supposed
we were nearing some country.
28And having sounded, they found
twenty fathoms. And when they had
gone a little further, they sounded
again and found fifteen fathoms.
29Then fearing lest they should have
run upon some rocky places, they cast
four anchors out of the stern and
wished for the day to come.
30But the sailors, desiring to flee out
of the ship, had let down the boat into
the sea, with the excuse that they
would have cast out anchors from the
bow.
31Paul said unto the centurion, "Except these abide in the ship, you cannot
be saved."
32Then the soldiers cut away the
ropes of the boat and let it fall.
33Now until day was about to come,
Paul encouraged all of them to have
some food, saying, "This is the fourteenth day that you have been watching
and continued without food, having
taken nothing.
34Therefore, I appeal to you to take
some food, for this is for your safety.
For there shall not fall a hair of the
head from one of you."
35And when he had said these things,
he took bread and gave thanks to God
in the presence of them all, and broke it
and began to eat.
36Then also all of them became
cheerful, and they also took food.
37We were all together in the ship,
two hundred seventy-six souls.
38And when they had eaten and were
satisfied, they lightened the ship and
cast the wheat into the sea.
39When it was day, they did not know
the land. But they perceived a bay with
a shore, which they proposed to try to
drive the ship onto.
40And when they had cut away the
anchors, they committed themselves to
the sea, at the same time losing the
bands of the rudders and hoisting the
foresail to the wind, they made for the
shore.
41But falling into a place where two
seas met, the vessel ran aground and
the bow stuck hard, remaining unmovable. Then the stern was broken by the
violence of the waves.
42Then the soldiers' counsel was that
the prisoners should be killed, lest any
of them escape by swimming away.
43But the centurion, desiring to save
Paul, kept them from their plan and
commanded those being able to swim
to cast themselves overboard first and
go for the land.
44And the others he commanded to
go, some on boards and some on things
from the ship. And so it came to pass
that they were all brought safely to the
land.

28 And then, being saved, they
knew that the island was called
Melita.
2And the barbarians of the country
showed us no little kindness, for they
kindled a fire and received every one of
us, because of the rain that was present
and because of the cold.
3And when Paul had gathered a bun-
dle of sticks and put them into the fire,
there came a viper out of the heat and
fastened on his hand.
4When the barbarians saw the beast
hanging from his hand, they said to
one another, "This man must certainly
be a murderer, whom having been
saved from the sea, justice would not
permit to live!"
5He, having then shaken the beast off
into the fire, indeed suffered no injury.
6Now they were expecting him to become swollen and to be about to fall
down dead. But after they had been
expecting for a long time, and seeing
nothing bad happening to him, they
changed their minds and said that he
was a god.
7Now in the same parts were lands
belonging to the chief of the island,
whose name was Publius, who received
us in a friendly way and lodged us for
three days.
8And it happened that the father of
Publius laid oppressed with fevers and
dysentery, whom Paul went in to and
prayed, and laid his hands on him, and
healed him.
9This therefore having taken place,
the rest also that had diseases in the
island came and were healed,
10who also honored us with many
honors. And when we were departing,
they provided us with the necessary
things.
11After three months, we sailed in an
Alexandrian ship, which had wintered
in the island, whose ensign was of the
sons of Zeus.
12And having been brought to Syra-
cuse, we remained there three days.
13From there, having gone around,
we arrived at Rhegium. And after one
day, the south wind blew. On the second day, we came to Puteoli
14where, having found brethren, we
were urged to remain with them for
seven days. And then we came to
Rome.
15And from there, when the brethren
heard of us, they came to meet us as far
as the marketplace of Appius and
Three Taverns. When Paul saw them,
he took great courage, giving thanks to
God.
16Then when we came to Rome, the
centurion delivered the prisoners to the
camp commander. But Paul was allowed to remain by himself with the
soldier who kept him.
17And it happened, after three days,
Paul called together those who were
the chief ones of the Jews. And when
they had come, he said to them, "Men
and brethren, though I have done
nothing against the people or customs
of our fathers, yet I was delivered as a
prisoner from Jerusalem into the hands
of the Romans,
18who, when they had examined me,
would have let me go, because they
found no cause of death in me.
19But when the Jews cried out against
it, I was compelled to appeal to Caesar,
not because I had anything to accuse
my nation of.
20For this cause have I called for you,
even to see and to speak to you, for because of the hope of Israel I am bound
with this chain."
21But they said to him, "We neither

received letters out of Judea concerning
you, nor has any of the brethren reported or come saying anything evil of
you.

22 But we will hear from you what you
think concerning this sect, for we know
that it is spoken against everywhere."

23 And they arranged a day to meet
with him. Many came to his lodging, to
whom he expounded, fully testifying of
the Kingdom of God and persuading
them of the things concerning Jesus,
both from the Law of Moses and the
Prophets, from morning until evening.

24 And some believed the things that
were spoken, and some did not believe.

25 When they agreed not among
themselves, they departed, Paul having
spoken one word: "Well spoke the Holy
Spirit by the Prophet Isaiah unto our
Fathers,

26 saying, 'Go to this people and say,
"With your ears shall you hear, and
shall not understand; and with your
eyes shall you see, and not perceive.

27 For the heart of this people has
grown fat, and their ears are hard of
hearing, and their eyes have they
closed, lest they should see with their
eyes, and hear with their ears, and understand with their hearts, and should
be turned back, and I should heal
them."'

28 Therefore, be it known to you that
this salvation of God is sent to the nations and they will hear!"

29 And when he had said these things,
the Jews departed and had much discussion among themselves.

30 And Paul dwelt two whole years in
his own hired house and received all
who came to him,

31 preaching the Kingdom of God and
teaching those things concerning the
Lord Jesus, unhindered with all boldness.

The Epistle of Paul the Apostle to the

Romans

1 Paul, a servant of Jesus Christ,
called an apostle, separated unto the
gospel of God,
2 which was promised before by His
prophets in the holy scriptures,
3 concerning His Son, Who came
from the seed of David according to
the flesh,
4 Who was shown to be the Son of
God in power according to the Spirit of
Holiness by the resurrection from the
dead of Jesus Christ our Lord,
5 by Whom we have received grace
and apostleship, for obedience in the
faith among all the nations, for His
name,
6 In Whom also you are called of Jesus Christ.
7 To all those who are in Rome,
beloved of God, called holy ones: grace
to you, and peace from God our Father
and from the Lord Jesus Christ.
8 First, I thank my God through Jesus
Christ for you all, because your faith is
published throughout all the world.
9 For God is my witness, Whom I
serve with my spirit in the gospel of
His Son, that without ceasing I make
mention of you
10 always in my prayers, asking if by
any means somehow now by the will of
God I might succeed in coming to you.
11 For I desire to see you, that I may
impart some spiritual gift to you to
strengthen you.
12 That I might be comforted together
with you through the common faith,
both yours and mine.
13 But I do not want you to be unaware, brethren, that many times I
proposed to come to you (and was
hindered even until now), that I might
have some fruit among you, as I have
also among other nations.
14 For I am debtor both to the Greeks
and barbarians, and to the wise and
unlearned.
15 So, as for me, I am also eager to
preach the gospel to you who are in
Rome.
16 For I am not ashamed of the gospel
of Christ, for it is the power of God
unto salvation to everyone who believes, to the Jew first and to the Greek.
17 For in it the righteousness of God is
revealed from faith to faith, as it has
been written, "But the righteous shall
live by faith."
18 For the wrath of God is revealed
from Heaven against all ungodliness
and unrighteousness of men who hold
the truth in unrighteousness.
19 For that which may be known of
God is revealed among them, for God
showed it to them.
20 For from the creation of the world,
the invisible things of Him are perceived, being understood by the things
created, both His eternal power and
divinity, so that they are without excuse.
21 Yet, knowing God, they glorified
Him not as God, nor were thankful,
but became vain by their imaginations,
and their foolish heart was darkened.
22 Professing to be wise, they became
fools.
23 And turned the glory of the immortal God unto the similitude of the
image of mortal man, and of birds, and
four-footed beasts, and of serpents.
24 Therefore, God also gave them up
to the desires of their hearts: unto uncleanness, to defile their own bodies
between themselves,
25 who turned the truth of God into a
lie, and reverenced and served the created things more than Him Who created it, Who is blessed forever. Amen.
26 For this reason, God gave them up

unto shameful passions, for also their
females changed the natural use into
that which was contrary to nature.
27 And in like manner also the males,
leaving the natural use of the female,
were inflamed in their lust towards one
another, males with males doing that
which is shameful, and receiving in
themselves the retribution of their deception.
28 And just as they did not approve of
having God in their knowledge, God
gave them up to a worthless mind to do
improper things,
29 being filled with all unrighteousness, sexual immorality, wickedness,
covetousness, malice, full of envy,
murder, strife, guile, evil disposition,
whisperers,
30 slanderers, hateful to God, disre-
spectful, proud, boastful, inventors of
evil things, disobedient to parents,
31 without understanding, those who
do not keep their word, without natural
affection, unappeasable, unmerciful–
32 who, knowing the righteous judgment of God, that those who practice
such things are worthy of death, not
only do them but also applaud those
who practice them.

2 Therefore you are inexcusable, O
man, anyone who judges, for that
in which you judge another, you condemn yourself, for you who judge do
the same things.
2 But we know that the judgment of
God is according to truth upon those
that do such things.
3 O man who judges those who practice such things and does them yourself, do you think that you shall escape
the judgment of God?
4 Or do you despise the riches of His
kindness and forbearance and longsuffering, not knowing that the kindness
of God leads you to repentance?
5 But according to your hardness and
unrepentant heart you store up for
yourself wrath in the day of wrath and
revelation of the righteous judgment of
God,
6 Who will repay everyone according
to his works:
7 to those who, by persistence in good
works, seek glory and honor and immortality– eternal life,
8 but to those who, from selfish ambi-
tions, obey not the truth but obey unrighteousness– wrath and anger,
9 anguish and distress upon every
soul of man that does evil– the Jew
first, and the Greeks–
10 but glory and honor and peace
upon all that do good, the Jew and the
Greeks.
11 For there is no respect of persons
with God.
12 For as many as sinned without law
shall also perish without the Law, and
as many as have sinned with the Law
shall be judged by the Law.
13 For the hearers of the Law are not
righteous with God, but the doers of
the Law shall be shown to be righteous.
14 For when the nations, who do not
have a law, do by nature the Law, they,
not having a law, are a law unto themselves,
15 who show the works of the law
written in their hearts, their conscience
bearing witness and their thoughts between each other either accusing or ex-
cusing them,
16 on that day when God shall judge
the secrets of men by Jesus Christ, according to my gospel.
17 Behold, you are called a Jew, and
trust in the Law, and rejoice in God,
18 and you know His will, and ap-

prove the things that are more excellent, being instructed out of the Law,
19and also are persuaded that you are
called a guide unto the blind, a light to
those in darkness,
20an instructor to the ignorant, a
teacher of babes, having a formal instruction of knowledge and of the truth
in the Law.
21You then who teach others, do you
not teach yourself? You declare, "Do
not steal," do you steal?
22You say, "Do not commit adultery,"
do you commit adultery? You that abhor idols, do you commit irreverent
acts?
23You who boast in the Law through
the transgression of the Law dishonor
God.
24For the name of God is blasphemed
by you among the nations, as it is written.
25Circumcision is truly profitable if
you do the Law, but if you are a transgressor of the Law, your circumcision
has become uncircumcision.
26If then the uncircumcised keeps the
requirements of the Law, will not his
uncircumcision be considered circumcision?
27And the uncircumcised, by nature
fulfilling the Law, shall judge you who
with the letter of circumcision break
the Law.
28For a Jew is not one outwardly, nor
is circumcision outwardly in the flesh.
29But a Jew is one inwardly, and circumcision is of the heart, by the Spirit,
not in a letter, his praise is not from
men, but from God.

3 What advantage then does the Jew
have? Or what is the value of circumcision?
2Much in every way, because the
words of God were first committed to
them.
3What if some were unfaithful? Will
their unbelief cancel the faith of God?
4By no means! But let God be true
and every man false, as it is also written, "So that you may be shown to be
righteous in Your words, and prevail in
Your judgments."
5And if our unrighteousness is met
by the righteousness of God, what shall
we say? Is God unrighteous who in-
flicts wrath? I speak like a man.
6By no means! For then how shall
God judge the world?
7For if in my untruthfulness, the
truth of God abounded unto His glory,
why am I being condemned as a sinner?
8And why not say, as some slander us
and report us to say, "Let us do evil that
good may come?" Their condemnation
is deserved.
9What then? Are we any better off?
Not at all. For we have already concluded that both Jews and Greeks are
all under sin.
10As it is written: "There is none
righteous, not one.
11There is no one who understands.
There is no one who earnestly desires
God.
12All have turned aside. Together
they have become worthless. There is
no one who shows kindness– there is
not even one.
13Their throats are an open grave,
with their tongues they deceive, the
venom of vipers
is under their lips,
14their mouths are full of cursing and
bitterness,
15their feet are swift to shed blood,
16destruction and wretchedness are
in their ways,

17 and the way of peace they did not know.

18 There is no fear of God before their eyes."

19 Now we know that whatever the Law says, it speaks to those in the Law, that every mouth may be stopped and all the world be under judgment to God.

20 Therefore, by the works of the Law no flesh shall be shown righteous in His sight. The knowledge of sin is through the Law.

21 But now the righteousness of God is manifested separately from the Law–although the Law and the Prophets bear witness of it–

22 even the righteousness of God through the faith of Jesus Christ to all and upon all those who believe. For there is no difference,

23 for all have sinned and come short of the glory of God.

24 Being made righteous as a gift by His grace through the redemption in Christ Jesus,

25 Whom God set forth as the mercy seat through faith in His blood, to reveal His righteousness by the passing over of the sins that had before taken place,

26 by the forbearance of God, for the demonstration of His righteousness in this present time, He being just and the One who makes righteous through the faith of Jesus.

27 Where is boasting? It was excluded. By what law? Of works? No, but by the law of faith.

28 We conclude that a man is made righteous by faith without the works of the law.

29 Is He the God of the Jews only and not also of the nations? Yes, also of the nations,

30 since it is indeed one God who will make the circumcision righteous out of faith, and the uncircumcised through faith.

31 Do we then invalidate the Law through faith? No way! On the contrary, we establish it.

4 What then shall we say that Abraham, our father according to the flesh, obtained?

2 If Abraham were made righteous by works, then he has reason to boast, but not with God.

3 For what does the Scripture say? "Abraham believed God, and it was counted to him for righteousness."

4 To him that works, the reward is not counted of grace, but of debt.

5 To him that does not work, but believes on Him that makes the ungodly righteous, his faith is counted for righteousness.

6 Even as David described the blessedness of the man unto whom God ascribed righteousness without works:

7 "Blessed are they whose iniquities are forgiven, and whose sins are covered.

8 Blessed is that man to whom the Lord does not consider his sin."

9 Came this blessedness then upon the circumcised, or also upon the uncircumcised? For we say that faith was accounted to Abraham for righteousness.

10 How was it counted? Being in circumcision or in uncircumcision? Not in circumcision, but in uncircumcision.

11 And he received the sign of circumcision, a seal of the righteousness of faith, which he had still in uncircumcision, that he should be the father of all them that believe, though they be

uncircumcised, that righteousness
might also be counted to them.
12 And he is the father of the circumcision, not only to those of the circumcision, but also to those who walk in
the steps of the faith of our father
Abraham being uncircumcised.
13 For the promise, that he should be
the heir of the world, was not given to
Abraham or to his seed through the
Law, but through the righteousness of
faith.
14 For if they who are of the Law be
heirs, then faith has been made void
and the promise of no effect,
15 for the Law brings about wrath, for
where there is no Law, there is no
transgression.
16 Wherefore it is of faith, that it
might be by grace, that the promise
might be to all the seed, not to those of
the Law only, but also to those of the
faith of Abraham, who is the father of
us all,
17 as also it is written, "I have made
you a father of many nations," before
God whom he believed: Who gives life
to those that are dead, and calls into
existence the things that do not exist.
18 Who against any expectation, yet in
expectation, he believed that he should
become the father of many nations according to that which was spoken, "So
shall your seed be."
19 And not being weak in faith, he did
not consider his own body already
dead--being about 100 years old--and
the deadness of Sarah's womb.
20 For he did not waver at the promises of God through unbelief, but was
strong in faith, giving glory to God,
21 and being fully persuaded that what
God had promised, He was also able to
do.
22 And therefore it was counted to
him for righteousness.
23 It is not written because of him
only that it was counted to him,
24 but also because of us, to whom it is
going to be counted, to those who believe in Him Who raised Jesus our
Lord from the dead.
25 He was handed over for our trespasses, and was raised up in order to
make us righteous.

5 Therefore, having been made
righteous by faith, we have peace
with God through Jesus Christ our
Lord.
2 By Whom also we have access by
faith into this grace in which we stand,
and boast in expectation of the glory of
God.
3 And not only that, but we also boast
in hardships, knowing that hardship
works endurance,
4 and endurance, proven character,
and proven character, expectation.
5 And the expectation will not be dis-
appointed, because the love of God is
poured into our hearts by the Holy
Spirit given to us.
6 For when we were without strength,
in due time, Christ died for the ungodly.
7 For rarely would anyone die for a
righteous man. On the behalf of one
good some might even dare to die.
8 But God demonstrates His love for
us, in that while we were still sinners,
Christ died for us.
9 Much more then, being now made
righteous by His blood, we shall be
saved by Him from the wrath.
10 For if being enemies we were reconciled to God through the death of
His Son, much more now, being
changed, we shall be saved by His life.
11 And not only this, but we also boast

in God through our Lord Jesus Christ, by Whom we have now received the change.

12 Just as sin entered into the world through one man, and through sin death, so also that death has passed into all men, in that everyone sinned.

13 For sin was in the world before the law, but there was no accounting of it without the Law.

14 Yet death reigned from Adam until Moses, even upon those whose sins were not like the transgression of Adam, who was a type of the One to come.

15 But the free gift was not like the transgression, for if by one transgression many died, much more the grace of God and the gift by grace that is from the One Man, Jesus Christ, abounds unto the multitudes.

16 And the free gift is not like the one who sinned. For the judgment of one was unto condemnation, but the free gift, following many transgressions, brought righteousness.

17 If because of one's trespass death reigned through that one, much more those that receive the abundance of grace and the gift of righteousness shall reign in life through One, Jesus Christ.

18 So then, as through one's transgression, condemnation was to all men, so also through One's act of righteousness, the life that makes righteous is to all men.

19 For as by the disobedience of one man many were made sinners, also then through the obedience of One shall many be made righteous.

20 But, in the meantime, the Law entered in so that the transgression may be abundant, but where sin was abundant, grace was more abundant.

21 So that just as sin reigned unto death, even so also grace reigns through righteousness unto eternal life through Jesus Christ our Lord.

6 What shall we say then? Should we continue in sin that grace may be abundant?

2 Let it not be! How can we who died to sin still live any longer in it?

3 Or are you ignorant that as many of us as were baptized into Christ Jesus were baptized into His death?

4 Therefore, we were buried with Him by baptism into death, that just as Christ was raised up from the dead through the glory of the Father, in this way also we may walk in newness of life.

5 If we have been joined together in the likeness of His death, even so we shall also be in the resurrection,

6 knowing this, that our old man was crucified together with Him, so that the body of sin may be abolished, that we should no longer serve sin.

7 For he who has died has been made righteous from sin.

8 And if we are dead together with Christ, we believe that we shall also live with Him,

9 knowing that Christ, being raised from the dead, dies no more– death has no more dominion over Him.

10 For the death He died He died to sin once for all, but in that He lives He lives to God.

11 In the same way, you also consider yourselves to be truly dead to sin, but alive to God in Christ Jesus our Lord.

12 Therefore, let no sin reign in your mortal body, that you should obey its lust.

13 Do not present your members as instruments of unrighteousness to sin, but present yourselves to God, as alive

from the dead, and your members instruments of righteousness to God.
14For sin shall not have dominion
over you, for you are not under the
Law, but under grace.
15What then, shall we sin because we
are not under the Law but under grace?
Let it not be!
16Do you not know that who you
yield yourself as servants to obey, his
servants you are to whom you obey,
whether sin unto death, or obedience
unto righteousness?
17But thanks be to God because you
were the servants of sin, but by the
grace of God, you have now obeyed
from the heart the blueprint of doctrine delivered to you.
18Now, having been set free from sin,
you became the servants of righteousness.
19I speak as a man because of the
frailty of your flesh. For as you have
yielded your members as slaves to uncleanness and to iniquity unto iniquity,
in the same way now yield your members as servants to righteousness in holiness.
20For when you were servants of sin,
you were free from righteousness.
21Therefore what fruit do you have in
the things that you are now ashamed
of? For the end of those things is death.
22But now, having been set free from
sin, and have become servants to God,
you now have your fruit in holiness,
and the end eternal life.
23For the wages of sin is death, but
the gift of God is eternal life in Jesus
Christ our Lord.

7 Do you not know, brethren– for I
am speaking to those who know
the Law– that the Law has dominion
over a man as long as he lives?
2For a married woman is bound by
the Law to the husband while he lives,
but if the husband dies, there is a release from the law of the husband.
3So then, while the husband lives she
shall be called an adulteress if the
woman has another husband; but if the
husband dies, she is free from the Law
and is not an adulteress while being
with another husband.
4In the same way, my brethren, you
have died to the Law through the body
of Christ. You belong unto another, the
One Who rose from the dead, so that
you may bring forth fruit unto God.
5For when we were in the flesh, the
passions of sin that were by the Law
were at work in our members bringing
forth fruit unto death.
6But now we are released from the
Law, being dead to that which held us,
so that we should serve in newness of
Spirit and not in oldness of letter.
7What then shall we say– that the
Law is sin? By no means! Yet had it not
been for the Law I would have not
known sin. For I would have not
known lust if the Law had not said not
to lust.
8But sin took an opportunity by the
commandment and worked out in me
every lust. For apart from the Law, sin
was dead.
9But I was once alive apart from the
Law. But when the commandment
came, sin revived and I died.
10And the commandment, which was
to life, was found to me death.
11For sin, taking opportunity by the
commandment, deceived me, and by it
slew me.
12So that the Law is holy, and the
commandment is holy and just and
good.
13That which then is good to me has

it become death? May it not be! But sin
producing death through what is good
to me that sin might be shown to be
sin, that through the commandment it
might become exceedingly sinful.
14For we know that the Law is spiritual, but I am fleshly, having been sold
under sin.
15For what I produce I do not understand. For I practice what I do not will,
yet I do what I hate.
16But if I do what I do not will, I consent to the Law that it is good.
17So then now, it is no longer me
producing it, but sin that dwells in me.
18For I know that in me– that is, in
my flesh– dwells no good thing. For to
will is present with me, but to produce
the good I find not.
19For the good I will to do, I do not,
but the evil which I do not will, this I
practice.
20But if I do what I will not to do, it's
no longer me that produces it, but the
sin that dwells in me.
21I find then the Law that when I
would do good, evil is present with me.
22For I delight in the Law of God after the inward man,
23but I see another law in my members warring against the law of my
mind and leading me captive to the law
of sin that is in my members.
24O wretched man that I am! Who
shall deliver me from this body of
death?
25I thank God, through Jesus Christ
our Lord! So then, I myself serve the
law of God with my mind, but the law
of sin with my flesh.

8 There is now no condemnation for
those who are in Christ Jesus, who
walk not after the flesh, but after the
Spirit.
2For the Law of the Spirit of life in
Christ Jesus has freed me from the law
of sin and death.
3For the Law was powerless in that it
was weak through the flesh. God sent
His Son in the likeness of sinful flesh
and concerning sin condemned sin in
the flesh
4that the righteousness of the Law
might be fulfilled in us who walk not
after the flesh but after the Spirit.
5For they who are after the flesh are
the ones who think fleshly, but those
after the Spirit have a spiritual mindset.
6For fleshly thinking is death, but
spiritual thinking is life and peace.
7In as much as fleshly thinking is opposed to God– for it is not subject to
the Law of God, neither indeed can be–
8for those in the flesh are not able to
please God.
9And you are not in the flesh, but in
the Spirit, if indeed the Spirit of God
dwells in you. But if anyone does not
have the Spirit of Christ, this one is not
of Him.
10But if Christ is in you, the body is
dead because of sin, but the Spirit is life
because of righteousness.
11And if the Spirit that raised up Jesus from the dead dwells in you, the
One that raised up Christ from the
dead shall also make alive your body
through the Spirit of Him that dwells in
you.
12Indeed then brethren, we are not in
debt to the flesh to live after the flesh.
13For if you live after the flesh you are
going to die, but if by the Spirit you put
to death the deeds of the body you
shall live.
14For as many as are Spirit-of-God-
led, these are the sons of God.
15You have not received the spirit of
slavery again to fear, but you have re-

ceived the spirit of sonship whereby we cry out, “Abba Father.”

16 It is the Spirit that bears witness with our spirit that we are children of God.

17 And if children, also heirs– God’s heirs and Christ’s co-inheritors– if indeed we suffer, we shall also be glorified together.

18 For I calculate that this that befalls us now for a season is not worthy of the glory that is about to be revealed in us.

19 For the creation eagerly awaits the manifestation of the sons of God.

20 For the creation was subject to futility, not willingly, but because of Him who subjected it in expectation.

21 Also, because the creation herself shall be liberated from the bondage of the corruption into the glorious liberty of the children of God.

22 We also know that all the creation groans and travails together until now.

23 And not only it, but we also– who have the firstfruits of the Spirit– we also ourselves groan within ourselves, eagerly awaiting sonship's redemption of our body.

24 For in this expectation we were saved, but expectation seen is not expectation. For who expects for what he sees?

25 And if we do not see what we expect, then we eagerly await it patiently.

26 And in like manner also, the Spirit helps our weaknesses, for we do not know what we need to pray for, but the Spirit Himself intercedes with inexpressible groanings.

27 But He that searches the heart knows what the thoughts of the Spirit are, because according to God He intercedes on behalf of the holy ones.

28 And we know that to those who love God, all things work together for good to those who are called according to His purpose.

29 Because whom He foreknew, He also predestined to be conformed to the image of His Son, that He might be the first-born among many brethren.

30 Now whom He predestined, these also He called, and whom He called, these also He showed to be righteous– now whom He showed to be righteous, these He also glorified.

31 Therefore what do we say to this? If God is for us, who is against us?

32 He Who spared not His own Son, but handed Him over for us all, how shall He not also with Him freely give us everything?

33 Who shall lay a charge against God’s elect, which God made righteous?

34 Who can condemn? Christ died, and more, has risen, Who is also at the right hand of God, and Who intercedes for us.

35 What shall separate us from the love of Christ: tribulation, or difficulty, or persecution, or famine, or nakedness, or danger, or a sword?

36 As it is written, “Because of You, we are put to death the whole day– considered as sheep for slaughter.”

37 But in all these, we are more than conquerors through the One Who loves us.

38 For we are persuaded that neither death nor life, nor angel nor principalities, nor things present nor things to come, nor powers,

39 neither heights nor depths, nor any other creature shall be able to separate us from the love of God that is in Christ Jesus our Lord!

9 I say the truth in Christ, I lie not, my conscience bearing me witness in the Holy Spirit

2 that I have great heaviness and continual sorrow in my heart.

3 For I have wished myself to be cursed from Christ for my brethren and my kinsmen as pertaining to the flesh

4 who are Israelites, to whom pertains the sonship, and the glory, and the covenants, and the Law that was given, and the service, and the promises,

5 of whom are the fathers and of whom is Christ according to the flesh, Who is God over all, blessed forever: Amen!

6 However, the Word of God has not failed– for not everyone who is of Israel are Israelites.

7 Neither because they are of the seed of Abraham are they all children, but "In Isaac shall your Seed be called."

8 That is, the children of God are not the children of the flesh, but the children of the promise are counted for the seed.

9 For this is the word of promise: "According to this time, I will come, and Sarah shall have a son."

10 And not only that, but also Rebekah had conceived from Isaac our father–

11 for not yet being born or having done anything good or evil (that the purpose of God, which is by election, might stand, not of works, but of Him who calls)–

12 it was said to her, "The greater shall serve the lesser."

13 As it has been written, "Jacob I loved, but Esau I hated."

14 What shall we say then? Is there any unrighteousness with God? May it not be!

15 For He said to Moses, "I will show mercy to whom I show mercy, and will have compassion on whom I have compassion."

16 So then it is not of him that wills, nor of him that runs, but of God Who shows mercy.

17 For the Scripture says to Pharaoh, "For this same thing I raised you up to show in you My power and that My name might be declared throughout all the Earth."

18 So then to whom He wills, He shows mercy, and whom He wills, He hardens.

19 You will say then unto me, "Why yet does He find fault? For who has resisted His will?"

20 On the contrary, O man, who are you to reply against God? Shall the thing formed say to Him Who formed, "Why have You made me like this?"

21 Or doesn't the potter have authority over the clay– out of the same lump to make one vessel unto honor and another unto dishonor?

22 Even if God, willing to show His wrath and to make known His power, endured in much longsuffering the vessels of wrath fitted for destruction,

23 and that He might make known the riches of His glory on the vessels of mercy that He had prepared for His glory,

24 whom also He called us– not only from among the Jews but also from among the nations,

25 as also He said in Hosea, "I will call them that are not My people: 'My people,' and those not beloved: 'beloved.'

26 And it shall come to pass in the place where it was said to them, 'You are not My people,' you shall be called 'the sons of the Living God.'"

27 But Isaiah cries concerning Israel,

"If the number of the sons of Israel should be as the sand of the sea, the remnant shall be saved.

28 For He will finish His Word and cut it short in righteousness, because a thing cut short will the Lord do upon the Earth."

29 And according as Isaiah said before, "Except the Lord of Hosts had left us a seed, we should have become like Sodom, and we should have been made like Gomorrah."

30 What then are we to say? That the Gentiles, who did not follow after righteousness, have attained righteousness– even the righteousness that is of faith.

31 But Israel, who pursued the righteousness of the Law, did not obtain the righteousness of the Law.

32 Why? Because it was not from faith, but as by the works of the Law, for they have stumbled at the stumbling stone.

33 According as it is written, "Behold, I place in Zion a stone of stumbling and a rock of offense, and everyone that believes on Him shall not be ashamed."

10 Brethren, the good pleasure of my own heart's desire and prayer to God on behalf of Israel is for her salvation.

2 For I bear witness to them that they have a zeal for God, but not according to knowledge.

3 For being ignorant of the righteousness of God, and seeking to establish their own righteousness, they have not submitted to the righteousness of God.

4 For Christ is the end of the Law for righteousness to everyone that believes.

5 For Moses writes of the righteousness that is of the Law that the man who practiced those things shall live by them.

6 But the righteousness that is of faith speaks like this: "Say not in your heart, 'Who shall ascend into Heaven?' (that is, to bring Christ down),

7 or, 'Who shall descend into the abyss?' (that is, to bring Christ from death.)"

8 But what does it say? "The word is near you– in your mouth and even in your heart." This is that word of faith that we proclaim.

9 For if you confess with your mouth the Lord Jesus and believe in your heart that God raised Him from the dead, you shall be saved.

10 For the heart believes unto righteousness and the mouth confesses to salvation.

11 For the Scripture says, "Everyone who believes upon Him shall not be ashamed."

12 There is no difference between the Jew and the Greek, for the same Lord of all is rich toward all that call upon Him,

13 for everyone who shall call on the name of the Lord shall be saved.

14 How then shall they call on Him Whom they have not believed? And how shall they believe in Him of Whom they have not heard? And how shall they hear without a preacher?

15 And how shall they preach unless they are sent? For it is written: "How beautiful are the feet of them that proclaim the gospel of peace, that proclaim the gospel of good things."

16 But they have not all obeyed the Gospel. For Isaiah said, "Lord, who has believed our report?"

17 So then faith comes by the report and the report by the Word of God.

18But I say, did they not hear? Yes, their voice went out into all the Earth and their words into the ends of the world.

19But I say, did Israel not know? First Moses says, "I will provoke you to jealousy through those not a nation. Through a foolish nation I will anger you."

20And Isaiah is very bold and says, "I was found by those who were not seeking Me. I appeared to those who did not inquire after Me."

21But to Israel He says, "The whole day I stretched out My hands to a disobedient and contradicting people."

11 I say then, has God cast away His people? May it not be! For I am an Israelite of the seed of Abraham, of the tribe of Benjamin.

2God hath not cast away His people that He knew before. Do you not know what the Scripture says regarding Elijah, how he pleaded with God against Israel saying,

3Lord, they have killed Your prophets and they tore down your altars and I was left alone and they seek my life."?

4But what was said by the divine answer to him? "I have reserved unto Myself 7,000 men who have not bowed the knee to Baal."

5Even so at this time there has been a remnant according to the election of grace.

6And if by grace, then it is not of works, otherwise grace is not grace. But if it is works, it is not grace, otherwise works is not works.

7What then? What Israel seeks it did not obtain, but the elect obtained, and the rest were hardened.

8According as it is written, God gave them a spirit of slumber– eyes that see not, and ears that hear not– unto this day.

9And David says, "Let their table be made a snare, and for a trap, and for a cause of stumbling, and for a reward to them.

10Let their eyes be darkened so their eyes see not, and their backs continually bend."

11I say then, did they stumble that they might fall? May it not be! But by their offense salvation comes to the nations to provoke them to jealousy.

12And if their offense be the riches of the world, and their loss the riches of the nations, how much more their fullness?

13For I speak to you, Gentiles– inasmuch as I am an apostle of the Gentiles I glorify my ministry,

14that if by any means I might provoke my flesh to jealousy, that I might save some among them.

15For if through their rejection the world has reconciliation, what will the acceptance be but life from the dead?

16For if the firstfruit is holy, so also is the whole batch of dough. And if the root is holy, so also are the branches.

17And if some of the branches were broken off, and you, being a wild olive tree, were grafted in among them, and became a partaker of the root and the fatness of the olive tree,

18do not boast against the branches. But if you boast, you are not the root, but the root supports you.

19You will say then, "The branches were broken off that I might be grafted in."

20Good. They are broken off because of unbelief, and you stand by faith. Do not be high-minded, but fear.

21For if God spared not the natural branches, perhaps He will not spare

you either.
22 See then the goodness and severity
of God: upon them that fell, severity,
but upon you, goodness, if you continue in the goodness– otherwise you will
be cut off.
23 Also, if they do not continue in unbelief, they shall be grafted in, for God
is able to graft them in again.
24 For if you, who by nature were cut
out of a wild olive tree, and contrary to
nature were grafted into a good olive
tree, how much more shall these natural branches be grafted into their own
olive tree?
25 For I do not want you to be ignorant of this mystery, brethren (that you
may not be wise in yourselves), that in
part, hardness happened to Israel until
the fullness of the nations are come in,
26 and so all Israel shall be saved. As it
is written, "There shall come out of
Zion the Deliverer, and He shall turn
away ungodliness from Jacob.
27 And this is My covenant unto them
when I shall take away their sins."
28 As concerning the gospel, they are
enemies on your account. But as touching the election, they are beloved for
the Father's sake.
29 For the gifts and callings of God are
irrevocable.
30 For just like also you were once
disobedient to God, but now have been
shown mercy through their disobedience,
31 so also those that are now disobedient to your mercy might also have
mercy shown to them.
32 For God has concluded everyone in
disobedience, that He might have mercy on all.
33 O the depths of the riches both of
the wisdom and knowledge of God!
How unsearchable are His judgments
and His ways unsearchable!
34 For who has known the mind of the
Lord? Or who has become His counselor?
35 Or who has given unto Him and it
shall be repaid?
36 For of Him and through Him and
to Him are all things. To Him be the
glory unto the ages. Amen!

12 Therefore, I exhort you, brethren, through the mercies of
God, that you present your bodies a
living sacrifice, holy, acceptable unto
God, which is your reasonable worship.
2 And do not fashion yourselves after
this age, but be transfigured by the renewing of your mind to prove by you
what is the good and acceptable and
perfect will of God.
3 For I say, through the grace given to
me, to everyone that is among you, do
not think more highly than you ought
to think, but think soberly, as God has
distributed to each one the measure of
faith.
4 For even as we have in one body
many members, but the members do
not all have the same function,
5 so we who are many are one body in
Christ, and so also members one of another.
6 But having different gifts according
to the grace given to us: whether
prophecy according to the proportion
of faith,
7 or ministry in ministry, or he that
teaches in teaching,
8 or he that exhorts in exhortation, he
that imparts with liberality, he that
rules with diligence, and he who shows
mercy with cheerfulness.
9 Have genuine love, hating the evil,
cleaving to the good,
10 loving one another with brotherly

affection, preferentially honoring one another,

11not slothful in diligence, fervent in Spirit, serving the Lord,

12rejoicing in expectation, standing firm in trouble, persistent in prayer,

13communicating to the needs of the holy ones, pursuing hospitality.

14Bless those who persecute you– bless, and never curse!

15Rejoice with those who rejoice. Weep with those who weep.

16Mind the same things toward one another, not high-minded, but go along with the lowly– do not be wise in yourself.

17Do not render evil for evil to anyone. Provide what is right before all men.

18If possible, as to yourselves, be at peace with all men.

19Do not vindicate yourselves, beloved, but endure wrath, for it is written, "'Vengeance is Mine. I will repay,' says the Lord."

20Therefore, "If your enemy hungers, feed him. If he should be thirsty, give him a drink. For in so doing you shall heap coals of fire upon his head."

21Do not be overcome by evil, but overcome evil with good.

13 Let every soul be subject to the higher authorities. For there is no authority but of God. The authorities have been appointed by God.

2So that he who sets himself against the authority resists the ordinances of God. And they that resist shall themselves receive judgment.

3For rulers are not a terror to good works but to evil ones. Do you desire not to be afraid of the authority? Then do good, and you shall have praise from it,

4for it is the minister of God to you for good. But if you do evil, fear– for it does not wear the sword for nothing. For it is the minister of God, an avenger for wrath to him that practices evil.

5Therefore it is necessary to be subject not only on account of wrath but also on account of conscience.

6And even for this cause you pay taxes, for they are God's ministers devoted for the same purpose.

7Therefore, give to everyone their dues: taxes to whom taxes, custom to whom custom, fear to whom fear, honor to whom honor.

8Owe no one anything but to love one another, for he that loves the other fulfills the Law.

9For you shall not commit adultery, you shall not kill, you shall not steal, you shall not bear false witness, you shall not lust, and if there is any other commandment, it is summed up in this word: you shall love your neighbor as yourself.

10Love works no evil to your neighbor. Therefore, love is the fullness of the Law.

11Also knowing that this is the time, it is already the hour to awake out of sleep. For now our salvation is nearer than when we believed.

12The night is far gone, and the day is near. Let us therefore cast aside the works of darkness, and let us be endued with the armor of light.

13Let us walk correctly, as those in the day, not in partying and intoxication, not in sexual immorality and licentiousness, not in strife and envy,

14but be clothed with the Lord Jesus Christ, and make no provision for the flesh to allow for lust.

14 Receive him that is weak in the
faith without quarreling about
opinions.
2 One believes he can eat all things,
but another, being weak, eats herbs.
3 Let him that eats not despise him
who does not eat, and he that does not
eat, let him not judge him that eats, for
God has received him.
4 Who are you to judge another's servant? For to his own master he stands
or falls. And he shall be made to stand,
for God is able to make him stand.
5 One judges a day above another day,
another judges everyday to be alike. Let
each one be fully convinced in his own
mind.
6 He that regards the day, to the Lord
he regards it, and he that does not regard the day, to the Lord he does not
regard it. He that eats, eats to the Lord,
for he gives thanks to God. And he that
does not eat to the Lord, he does not
eat, and gives thanks to the Lord.
7 For none of us lives unto himself,
and no one dies to himself.
8 For both if we live, we should live to
the Lord, and if we die, we should die
to the Lord. Therefore, both if we
should live and if we should die, we are
the Lord's.
9 For unto this Christ both died and
rose, and lived again, that He might
rule both the dead and the living.
10 But why do you then judge your
brother? Or also, why do you despise
your brother? For we shall all stand before the judgment seat of Christ.
11 For it is written, "'As I live,' says the
Lord, 'every knee shall bow to Me and
every tongue shall confess to God.'"
12 So then each of us shall give an account to God concerning himself.
13 Therefore, we should no longer
judge one another, but rather judge
this: do not put an occasion for the
brother to fall or stumble.
14 And I know and am persuaded in
the Lord Jesus that nothing is unclean
of itself– except to the one who considers anything to be unclean, to that one
it is unclean.
15 But if your brother is grieved on
account of meat, you no longer walk
according to love, for with your meat
you destroy him for whom Christ died.
16 Therefore, let not your good be
evil-spoken of.
17 For the Kingdom of God is not
food and drink, but righteousness,
peace, and joy in the Holy Spirit.
18 For he who serves Christ in these
things is well-pleasing to God and approved by men.
19 So then we should pursue the
things of peace and the things for edi-
fying one another.
20 Do not destroy the work of God for
the sake of meat. All things are pure,
but it is evil for that man who through
eating stumbles.
21 It is good to not eat flesh, nor drink
wine, nor have what causes your brother to fall or stumble or be weak.
22 Do you have faith? Have it for
yourself before God. Blessed is he that
does not condemn himself in what he
approves.
23 But he that doubts if he eats has
been condemned, because it is not of
faith, and everything that is not of faith
is sin.

15 Now, we who are strong are in-
debted to bear the weaknesses of
the weak and not to please ourselves.
2 Each of us must please our neighbor
for that which is good unto edification.
3 For also Christ did not please Himself, but as it is written, "The reproach-

es of those who reproach You are fallen on Me."

4For whatever was written beforehand was written for our instruction so that by endurance and by the encouragement of the Scriptures we may have expectation.

5May the God of endurance and encouragement give you understanding with one another according to Christ Jesus,

6so that with one mind and one mouth we may glorify the God and Father of our Lord, Jesus Christ.

7Therefore, receive one another, even as also Christ received you into the glory of God.

8For I tell you: Christ Jesus became a servant of the circumcised on behalf of the truth of God to establish the promises to the fathers,

9and that the Gentiles might glorify God for His mercy– as it is written, "Therefore I will confess You among the Gentiles and sing to Your Name."

10And again, "Rejoice, Gentiles, with His people."

11And again, "Praise the Lord all the Gentiles, and applaud Him all the people."

12And again, Isaiah said, "There shall be a root of Jesse, and He shall arise to rule the nations– in Him shall the nations put their expectation."

13Now the God of expectation fills you with joy and peace in believing that you abound in expectation by the power of the Holy Spirit.

14But I also myself am persuaded of better things concerning you, that you yourselves are also full of goodness, being filled with all knowledge, being able also to admonish one another.

15But I wrote to you more boldly, brethren, in part as a reminder, because of the grace that was given to me by God

16that I should be a minister of Jesus Christ unto the Gentiles, performing the priestly duties of the Gospel of God, that the offering up of the Gentiles might be acceptable, being sanctified by the Holy Spirit.

17I have boasting therefore in Christ Jesus as to the things pertaining to God.

18For I will dare not speak of any of those things that Christ has not worked through me to bring the Gentiles to obedience by word and deed,

19by the power of signs and wonders, by the power of the Spirit of God, so that from Jerusalem and around unto Illyricum I have fully preached the Gospel of Christ!

20And so, being ambitious to preach the Gospel– not where Christ was named, that I not build on another's foundation–

21but according as it is written, "To whom He was not announced, they shall see, and those that have not heard shall understand."

22For this cause, I was hindered many times from coming to you.

23But now no longer having a place in these regions, and having a longing to come to you for many years,

24when I shall go to Spain I will come to you. I trust to see you, passing through, and to be sent on my way from there by you, if I should be first in part satisfied.

25But now I am going to Jerusalem to minister to the holy ones.

26For it has pleased them of Macedonia and Achaia to make a contribution for the poor holy ones who are in Jerusalem.

27For they were pleased, and they are

their debtors. For if the Gentiles shared in their spiritual things, they should also minister to their fleshly things.

28Therefore when I have finished this and have sealed to them this fruit, I will come back by you into Spain.

29And I know that I shall come to you in the fullness of the blessing of the Gospel of Christ when I come.

30But I exhort you, brethren, by our Lord, Jesus Christ, and by the love of the Spirit, to strive together in prayers to God for me,

31that I may be delivered from those of Judea who are disobedient, and that my service for Jerusalem may be acceptable to the holy ones,

32that in my joy I may come to you by the will of God and be refreshed with you.

33And the God of peace be with you all. Amen!

16 I recommend to you Phoebe, our sister, who is a minister of the church in Cenchrea,

2that you receive her in the Lord in a way worthy of the holy ones, and that you may assist her in whatever thing she may need of you– for she has also been the patroness for many, also of myself.

3Greet Priscilla and Aquila, my fellow workers in Christ Jesus,

4who for my life laid down their own neck, who not only I thank, but also the churches of the Gentiles,

5and the church at their house. Greet my dearly-loved Epaenetus, who is the first-fruit for Christ of Achaia.

6Greet Mary, who has labored much for us.

7Greet Andronicus and Junias, my kinsmen and fellow prisoners, who are well-known among the apostles, who were also in Christ before me.

8Greet my dearly-loved Ampliatus in the Lord.

9Greet Urbanus, our fellow worker in Christ and my dearly-loved Stachys.

10Greet Appelles, approved in Christ. Greet those of the household of Aristobulus.

11Greet Herodion, my kinsman. Greet those of the household of Narcissus who are in the Lord.

12Greet Tryphaena and Tryphosa who labor in the Lord. Greet my dearly-loved Persis, who labored much in the Lord.

13Greet Rufus, chosen by the Lord, and his mother and mine.

14Greet Asyncritus, Phlegon, Hermes, Patrobas, Hermas, and the brethren with them.

15Greet Philologus and Julias Nereus and his sister and Olympas and all of the holy ones with them.

16Greet one another with a holy kiss. The churches of Christ greet you.

17Now I implore you brothers, mark those who cause divisions and offenses contrary to the doctrine that you have learned, and turn away from them.

18For such do not serve Jesus Christ our Lord, but their own bellies, and by kind words and praise deceive the hearts of the innocent.

19For your obedience has reached to everyone. Therefore, I rejoice concerning you. But I wish you to be wise to the good but innocent to evil.

20And the God of peace will soon crush Satan under your feet. The grace of our Lord, Jesus Christ, be with you.

21Timotheus, my fellow worker, greets you and Lucius and Jason and Sosipater, my kinsmen.

22Tertius greets you, who wrote this epistle in the Lord.

23Gaius, my host, greets you and the
whole church. Erastus greets you, the
steward of the city, and brother Quar-
tus.
24The grace of our Lord, Jesus Christ,
be with you all. Amen!
25Now to Him Who has power to
strengthen you by my gospel and the
preaching of Jesus Christ according to
the revelation of the mystery kept secret from long ages–
26but now made manifest, and by the
prophetic Scriptures has been made
known to all the nations– according to
the command of the eternal God for
the obedience of faith,
27to the only wise God, to Whom be
glory to the ages through Jesus Christ.
Amen!

THE FIRST EPISTLE OF PAUL THE APOSTLE TO THE
CORINTHIANS

1 Paul, an Apostle, called of Jesus
Christ by the will of God, and
brother Sosthenes,
2 unto the church of God which is at
Corinth, having been made holy in
Christ Jesus, called holy ones with all
those who call on the name of our
Lord, Jesus Christ, in every place, both
theirs and ours.
3 Grace to you, and peace from God
our Father and the Lord Jesus Christ.
4 I always thank my God concerning
you for the grace of God that was given
to you by Jesus Christ,
5 that in all things you are made rich
by Him in all discourse and all knowledge,
6 even as the testimony of Jesus Christ
was confirmed in you,
7 so that you are not lacking in any
spiritual gifts, as you eagerly await the
revelation of our Lord, Jesus Christ,
8 Who will also establish you to the
end, blameless in the day of our Lord,
Jesus Christ.
9 Faithful is God, by Whom you were
called into the fellowship of His Son,
Jesus Christ our Lord.
10 Now I exhort you, brethren, by the
name of our Lord Jesus Christ, that you
all speak the same thing and that there
be no divisions among you– but be knit
together in the same mind and purpose.
11 For it was shown to me, my
brethren, by the house of Chloe, there
are strivings among you.
12 But I say this to each of you that
says, "I am of Paul," and "I am of Apollos," and "I am of Cephas," and "I am of
Christ."
13 Has Christ been divided? Was Paul
crucified for you? Or were you baptized in the name of Paul?
14 I thank God that I did not baptize
any of you except Crispus and Gaius,
15 that none of you should say that I
baptized in my name.
16 I also baptized the house of
Stephanas– as to the rest, I do not
know if I baptized any other.
17 For Christ sent me not to baptize,
but to preach the Gospel– not with
wisdom of words, that the cross of
Christ be not made void.
18 For the word of the cross is foolishness to those who perish, but to those
of us who are saved, it is the power of
God.
19 For it is written, "I will destroy the
wisdom of the wise, and I will bring to
nothing the understanding of the intelligent ones."
20 Where is the wise? Where is the
scribe? Where is the debater of this
age? Didn't God make foolish the wisdom of this world?
21 For since in the wisdom of God, the
world through wisdom knew not God,
it pleased God to save those that believe by the foolishness of preaching.
22 Because also the Jews ask for a sign
and the Greeks seek wisdom,
23 but we preach Christ crucified– to
the Jews, indeed a cause of offense, but
to the Greeks, foolishness.
24 But unto them who are called, both
of Jews and Greeks, Christ is God's
power and God's wisdom.
25 Because the foolishness of God is
wiser than men, and the weakness of
God is stronger than men.
26 For you see your calling, brethren,
that there are not many wise after the
flesh, not many powerful, not many
noble,
27 but God has chosen the foolish
things of the world that He might confound the wise, and God hath chosen
the weak things of the world that He

might confound the mighty things.

28 And God has chosen the despised and insignificant of the world, and the things that are not that He may abolish the things that are,

29 so that all flesh should not boast before Him.

30 But from Him you are in Christ Jesus, Who was made for us wisdom from God, and righteousness, and holiness, and redemption,

31 that according as it is written: He who boasts should boast in the Lord!

2 And I, brethren, when I came to you proclaiming to you the testimony of God, came not in excellency of word or wisdom,

2 for I resolved not to know anything among you except Jesus Christ and Him crucified.

3 And I was with you in weakness, and in fear, and in much trembling.

4 And my word and my preaching were not with persuasive words of human wisdom, but in demonstration of the Spirit and power,

5 that your faith might not be in the wisdom of men, but in the power of God.

6 But we speak wisdom among the perfect, and not the wisdom of this age, nor the rulers of this age, who are coming to an end,

7 but we speak the hidden wisdom of God in a mystery, which God decreed before the ages for our glory,

8 which none of the rulers of this age have known– for if they had known it, they would not have crucified the Lord of glory.

9 But as it is written, "That which eye has not seen, and ear has not heard, and which has not come into the heart of man, which God prepared for those who love Him,"

10 but God has revealed them to us by His Spirit– for the Spirit searches all things, even the depths of God.

11 For who knows the things of men except the spirit of man that is in him? So also the things of God no one knows except the Spirit of God.

12 And we have not received the spirit of the world, but the Spirit that is from God, that we might know the things freely given to us by God,

13 which also we speak, not in words taught of human wisdom, but in those taught by the Holy Spirit, spiritually explaining spiritual things.

14 But the natural man does not receive the things of the Spirit of God, for they are foolishness to him, and he cannot know them, because they are spiritually discerned.

15 But the spiritual one examines all things, but he is examined by no one.

16 For who has known the mind of the Lord? Who shall instruct Him? But we have the mind of Christ.

3 And I could not speak to you, brethren, as unto spiritual ones, but as those merely human, even as babes in Christ.

2 I gave you milk to drink, and not meat, for you were not yet able, but still now you are not able.

3 For you are still merely human. For as long as there is jealousy, strife, and division, are you not merely human and walking like a man?

4 For when one says, "I am of Paul," and another, "I am of Apollos," are you not merely human?

5 Who then is Paul, and who is Apollos, but servants through whom you believed as the Lord assigned to each?

6 I planted, Apollos watered, but God

gave the increase.
7So that neither he that plants is anything, nor he that waters, but God Who
gives the increase.
8But he who plants and he who waters are one, and each shall receive a
reward according to his own labors.
9For we are God's co-laborers– you
are God's field, God's building.
10According to the grace of God that
was given to me as a wise architect, I
have laid the foundation, and another
builds, but let each one take heed how
he builds!
11For no other foundation can be laid
other than the one in place, which is
Christ Jesus.
12Now if anyone builds on this foundation: gold, silver, precious stones,
wood, grass, straw–
13the work of each one will become
visible, for the day will make it known,
because it will be revealed by fire, and
the fire will test what sort of work each
one has done.
14If anyone's work remains that he
built, he shall receive a reward.
15If anyone's work shall be burned up,
he will suffer loss, but he will be saved
from death, but as it were by fire.
16Do you not know that you are the
temple of God and the Spirit of God
dwells in you?
17If any man defiles the temple of
God, God shall destroy him. For the
temple of God is holy, which temple
you are.
18Let no man deceive himself. If anyone among you considers himself to be
wise in this age, let him become foolish
that he may be wise.
19For the wisdom of this world is
foolishness with God. For it is written,
"He takes the wise in their craftiness,"
20and again, "The Lord knows the
reasonings of the wise, that they are
vain."
21So then, let no man boast in men.
For all things are yours:
22whether it be Paul, or Apollos, or
Cephas, or the world, or life, or death,
or present things, or coming things– all
are yours.
23And you are Christ's, and Christ is
God's.

4 So let a man count us as servants
of Christ and stewards of God's
mysteries.
2And as to the rest, it is required of
stewards that they be found faithful.
3But to me it is a very small matter
that I should be judged by you or a day
under man, but I do not judge myself.
4I am not aware of anything by myself, yet I have not been shown righteous by this– it is the Lord that judges
me.
5Therefore judge nothing before the
time until the Lord comes, Who will
both bring to light the hidden things of
darkness and will reveal the counsels of
the heart, and then each one shall have
praise from God.
6These things, brethren, I have ap-
plied to myself and Apollos for you,
that you might learn from us not to
think beyond what is written, that not
one of you be puffed up in favor of one
above the other.
7For what makes you different? And
what do you have that you did not receive? But if you also received it, why
do you boast as though you did not receive it?
8You are already satiated, you are already enriched without us, you have
become kings, and I would that you did
indeed reign, that we might also reign
with you!

9 For I think that God has set forth us,
the apostles, last, as appointed to death.
For we became a spectacle to the world,
both to angels and to men.
10 We are fools on account of Christ,
but you are wise in Christ. We are
weak, but you are strong. You are glorious, but we are without honor.
11 Unto this present hour, we both
hunger and thirst, and are naked, and
are buffeted, and are homeless,
12 and labor, working with our own
hands. Railed at, we bless. Persecuted,
we bear it.
13 Being slandered, we exhort. We
have become like the scum of the
world, the offscouring of all things until now.
14 I do not write these things to shame
you, but as my beloved children I admonish you.
15 For if you should have ten thousand instructors in Christ, yet you do
not have many fathers. For I have begotten you in Christ Jesus through the
gospel.
16 Therefore I exhort you to become
imitators of me.
17 On account of this, I have sent
Timothy to you– Timothy, who is my
beloved and faithful child in the Lord,
who will remind you of my ways that
are in Christ, even as I teach everywhere in every church.
18 Some were puffed up as though I
were not coming to you,
19 but I will come to you shortly, if the
Lord is willing, and I will know not the
talk of them that are puffed up, but the
power.
20 For the Kingdom of God is not in
talk, but in power.
21 What? Do you want me to come to
you with a rod, or in love and the spirit
of meekness?

5 It is commonly reported that there
is sexual immorality among you,
and such sexual immorality that is not
even named among the nations: that
one should have his father's wife!
2 And you are puffed up, and did not
rather mourn that he who did this act
might be taken out of your midst.
3 For I, being absent in the body, but
present in spirit, have already judged
him who did this deed, as though
present,
4 in the name of our Lord Jesus
Christ. When you gather together, and
my spirit, with the power of the Lord
Jesus Christ,
5 deliver such a one to Satan for the
destruction of the flesh that the spirit
might be saved in the day of the Lord
Jesus.
6 Your boasting is not good. Don't you
know that a little leaven leavens the
whole lump?
7 Purge out then the old leaven that
you may be a new lump, as you are unleavened. For Christ our passover was
sacrificed for you,
8 so that we should celebrate the feast
not with old leaven, neither with the
leaven of malice and wickedness, but
with unleavened sincerity and truth.
9 I wrote unto you in the epistle not to
associate with the sexually immoral,
10 Not at all with the sexually immoral
of this world, or with the covetous, or
thieves, or idolaters, since you are obligated to go out to the world!
11 But now I have put it in writing not
to associate with anyone that is called a
brother who is identified as a fornicator, or greedy, or an idolater, or a slanderer, or a drunkard, or a thief– do not
even eat with them!
12 For what is it to me to also judge
those outside? Do you not judge those

that are within?
13 Them that are without, God shall
judge. But you shall remove from
among you that evil person.

6 Dare any of you, having an issue
against another, go to a judge before the unrighteous and not before the
holy ones?
2 Do you not know that the holy ones
shall judge the world? If the world shall
be judged by you, are you not worthy
of these smallest judgments?
3 Do you not know that we shall judge
the angels? How much more the things
of this life?
4 If you have judgment of ordinary
matters, you set them up that are least
esteemed in the church!
5 For I speak this to your shame. Is
there not even a single wise man
among you who shall be able to decide
between his brothers?
6 Instead, brother goes with brother to
a judge, and this before unbelievers!
7 Therefore, now indeed there is a
fault among you that you have lawsuits
among yourselves. Why not rather suffer wrong? Why not rather be defraud-
ed?
8 But you do wrong and defraud, and
these things to your brethren!
9 Or do you not know that the unrighteous shall not inherit the kingdom
of God? Be not deceived, neither sexually immoral, nor idolaters, nor adulterers, nor lesbians, nor homosexuals,
10 nor thieves, nor covetous, nor
drunkards, nor slanderers, nor
swindlers shall inherit the kingdom of
God.
11 And some of you were these
things– but you were washed, but you
were made holy, but you were made
righteous by the name of the Lord Jesus
and by the Spirit of our God.
12 All things are lawful for me, but not
all things are profitable. All things are
lawful for me, but I will not come under the authority of any.
13 Food is for the belly, and the belly
for food, but God shall put an end to
both. But the body is not for sexual
immorality, but for the Lord, and the
Lord for the body.
14 And God both raised up the Lord
and will raise us up by His power.
15 Do you not know that your bodies
are the members of Christ? Shall I take
the members of Christ and make them
members of a harlot? May it not be!
16 Or do you not know that he who is
joined to a harlot is one body? For He
says, "The two shall be one flesh."
17 But he that is joined to the Lord is
one spirit.
18 Flee sexual immorality! Every sin
that a man does is outside the body, but
the fornicator sins against the body itself.
19 Or do you not know that your body
is a temple of the Holy Spirit Who is in
you– Who you have from God– and
you are not your own?
20 You were bought with a price.
Therefore, glorify God in your body
and in your spirit, which are God's.

7 But concerning the things that you
wrote to me: it is good for a man
not to touch a woman.
2 But because of sexual immorality, let
each one have his own wife, and let
each have her own husband.
3 Let the man reward the wife due affection, and likewise also the wife to
the man.
4 The wife does not have authority
over her own body, but the man. And
likewise also the man does not have

authority over his body, but the wife.

5 Do not withhold from one another unless it is by consent for a time, that you may be devoted to fasting and prayer. And again come together in one place, that Satan may not tempt you because of your lack of self-control–

6 but this I say by permission and not by command.

7 For I wish that all men were as I myself, but each man has his own gift from God– one after this manner, another after that.

8 But I say unto the unmarried and to the widows, it is good for them if they remain even as I do.

9 But if they do not have self-control, let them marry, for it is better to marry than to burn.

10 But to the married I command– not I, but the Lord– that the wife not separate from the man.

11 But if she is separated, let her remain unmarried or be reconciled to the man, and let not the man leave the wife.

12 But to the rest, I, not the Lord, say: if any brother has an unbelieving wife, and she consents to dwell with him, let him not leave her.

13 And a woman who has an unbelieving husband, and he consents to dwell with her, let her not leave him.

14 For the unbelieving husband is sanctified by the wife, and the unbelieving wife is sanctified by the husband– otherwise your children are unclean, but now they are holy.

15 But if the unbeliever separates, let him separate. The brother or the sister is not bound in such a case, but God has called us in peace.

16 For who knows, O wife, whether you shall save the man? Or who knows, O man, whether you shall save the wife?

17 Only to each as God has divided, to each as the Lord has called, let him walk. So I order in all the churches.

18 If anyone is called, being circumcised, let him not be uncircumcised. If anyone is called uncircumcised, let him not be circumcised.

19 Circumcision is nothing, and uncircumcision is nothing– but the keeping of the commandments of God.

20 Let each remain in the calling in which he was called.

21 Were you called as a slave? Do not let it be a concern to you. And if, rather, you are able to become free, then make use of it.

22 For he that is in the Lord, being called a slave, is the Lord's freed-man. Also likewise, he that is called, being free, is a slave of Christ.

23 You were bought with a price– be not slaves of men.

24 Each in that which he was called, brethren, in that let him abide with God.

25 But concerning virgins, I have no commandment from the Lord, yet I give my judgment as one that has received mercy from the Lord to be faithful.

26 I suppose that it is good because of the present necessity, that it is good for a man to be so.

27 Are you bound to a wife? Seek not to be released. Have you been released from a wife? Do not seek a wife.

28 And also if you have married, you have not sinned. And if you have married a virgin, she has not sinned. But such shall have tribulation in the flesh– but I am sparing you.

29 This I say, brethren: the time is short. For henceforth, even those who have wives, be as though not having,

30 and they that weep as not weeping, and those rejoicing as not rejoicing, and they that buy as not possessing,

31 and they that use this world as not using it as their own– for the fashion of this world passes away.

32 And I wish you to be without care. The unmarried cares for the things of the Lord: how he shall please the Lord.

33 But he that is married cares for the things of the world: how he might please his wife.

34 There is a difference between a wife and a virgin. The unmarried woman cares for the things of the Lord, that she may be holy both in body and spirit. But she that is married cares for the things of the world: how she might please her husband.

35 And this I say for your own profit, not to cast a snare before you, but for that which is proper and waiting on the Lord without distraction.

36 But if anyone thinks he behaves improperly towards his virgin, if he is beyond his prime, what he wills, let him do. Let him marry– he has not sinned.

37 But he who stands firm in his heart, not having necessity, but has authority over his own will, and has judged in his own heart to keep his virgin, he does well.

38 So then he that gives in marriage does well, but he that does not give in marriage does better.

39 A wife is bound by the Law for as long a time as her husband may live, but if her husband has fallen asleep, she is free to marry whom she wills, only in the Lord.

40 But according to my judgment, she is happier if she should remain, and I think I also have God's Spirit.

8 But concerning things sacrificed to idols, we know that we have all knowledge. Knowledge puffs up, but love builds up.

2 And if anyone thinks to have known anything, he has known nothing as he ought to know it.

3 But if anyone loves God, he is known by Him.

4 Concerning then the eating of things sacrificed to idols, we know that an idol is nothing in the world, and there is no other God except one.

5 For even though there may be gods spoken of– whether in Heaven or on the Earth, as there are many gods and many lords–

6 yet to us there is one God: the Father, of Whom are all things, and we for Him, and one Lord: Jesus Christ, by Whom are all things, and we by Him.

7 But this knowledge is not in everyone– but some, with consciousness of the idol, eat things sacrificed to idols even until now, and their conscience, being weak, is defiled.

8 But meat does not make us acceptable to God– for neither do we have an advantage if we eat, nor do we come short if we do not eat.

9 But take heed unless your authority becomes an occasion for those being weak to stumble.

10 For if anyone sees you who has knowledge eating, shall not the conscience of him who is weak be emboldened to eat those things sacrificed to idols?

11 And by your knowledge, shall the weak brother perish, for whom Christ died?

12 But so sinning against the brethren, and wounding their weak consciences, you sin against Christ.

13 Therefore, if meat offends my

brother, I should not eat meat forever,
that I may not offend my brother.

9 Am I not an apostle? Am I not
free? Have I not seen Jesus Christ
our Lord? Are you not my work in the
Lord?
2 If I am not an apostle to others, yet I
am one to you, for you are the seal of
my apostleship in the Lord.
3 This is my defense to those who examine me.
4 Do we not have authority to eat and
to drink?
5 Do we not have authority to lead
about a sister to wife, as also the other
apostles, and the Lord's brothers, and
Cephas?
6 Or is it only Barnabas and I that do
not have authority to stop working?
7 Who at any time goes to war at his
own expense? Who plants a vineyard
and does not eat of the fruit? Or who
shepherds a flock and does not eat of
the milk?
8 Do I speak these things after the
manner of man? Or does not also the
Law say these things?
9 For it has been written in the law of
Moses, "You shall not muzzle the ox
treading out the grain." Does God have
concern for the oxen,
10 or does He say it altogether because
of us? Because of us it was written, that
he which plows should plow in expectation, and he that treads out the grain
may of his expectation partake in expectation.
11 If we sow to you spiritual things, is
it a great thing if we reap your fleshly
things?
12 If others partake of this authority
over you, can't we? But we did not use
this authority, but we endure all things
lest we should hinder the Gospel of
Christ.
13 Do you not know that those laboring for the temple eat, and those who
attend at the altar are partakers with
the altar?
14 So also the Lord directed that those
who preach the Gospel should live by
the Gospel.
15 But I have used none of these
things. Now I did not write these
things that it should be done this way
to me. For it was better for me to die
than for anyone to make my boasting
void.
16 In that I preach the Gospel, I have
nothing to boast of, for necessity is laid
upon me. But woe to me if I should not
preach the gospel!
17 For if I do this willingly, I have a
reward– but if unwillingly, then an
administration is entrusted to me.
18 What then is my reward? That in
preaching the Gospel, I should make
the Gospel of Christ free of charge, so
as not to use my own authority in the
Gospel.
19 For though I am free from all, yet I
have made myself servant to all men,
that I might win the more.
20 Unto the Jews, I became as a Jew to
win the Jews. To those under the Law
as under the Law, that I might win
those under the Law.
21 To those without law as without law
(not being without law to God, but under the law of Christ), that I might win
those without law.
22 To the weak I became as weak, to
win the weak. To these I become all
things, that I might by all means save
some.
23 And I do this for the sake of the
Gospel, that I might be a partner with
it.
24 Do you not know that those who

run a race all run, but one receives the
prize? Therefore run that you may obtain.
25Now everyone engaged in a contest
is temperate in all things. They do it so
that they might receive a corruptible
crown, but we an incorruptible one.
26I therefore run, not as uncertain–
so I fight, not as one that beats the air–
27but I discipline my body and bring
it into subjection, lest after that I have
preached to others, I myself should be
disqualified.

10 Now brethren, I do not want
you to be ignorant that our fathers were all under a cloud, and all
passed through the sea,
2and all were baptized to Moses in
the cloud and in the sea,
3and all ate the same spiritual meat,
4and all drank of the same spiritual
drink, for they drank of the spiritual
rock that followed them, and that rock
was Christ.
5Yet with many of them, God was not
well-pleased, for they were overthrown
in the wilderness.
6And these things became examples
to us, that we should not desire evil
things as they also desired,
7nor be idolaters as some of them
were. As it is written, "The people sat
down to eat and drink and rose up
again to play."
8Neither should we commit sexual
immorality as some of them committed sexual immorality– and twenty
three thousand fell in one day!
9Neither should we tempt Christ as
also some of them tempted and were
destroyed by the serpents.
10Neither murmur as some of them
murmured and were destroyed by the
destroyer.
11And all these things happened to
them for examples, and were written
for our instruction, upon whom the
ends of the ages have come.
12Therefore, he that thinks he stands,
let him take heed lest he fall.
13No temptation has taken you except that which is of humanity, but
God is faithful, Who shall not allow
you to be tempted beyond your ability,
but will also with the temptation make
an escape so that you are able to endure
it.
14Therefore, my beloved, flee from
idolatry.
15As I speak to the wise, judge what I
say.
16The cup of blessing which we bless:
is it not the fellowship of the blood of
Christ? The bread which we break: is it
not the fellowship of the body of
Christ?
17Because though we are many, we
are one loaf, one body. For we all partake of the one loaf.
18Observe Israel according to the
flesh: Aren't they who eat of the sacrifice partakers of the altar?
19What do I say then– that an idol is
anything, or what is sacrificed to an
idol is anything?
20But what the nations sacrifice to
demons they sacrifice not to God, and
I do not want you to be partakers with
demons.
21You cannot drink of the cup of the
Lord and the cup of demons. You cannot partake of the table of the Lord and
the table of demons.
22Do we provoke the Lord to jealousy? Are we stronger than Him?
23All things are lawful to me, but not
all things are profitable. All things are
lawful to me, but not all things edify.
24Let no man seek his own, but each

one that of the other.
25Everything that is sold in the market, eat, inquiring nothing for the sake
of the conscience,
26for “The Earth is the Lord’s and the
fullness of it.”
27But if any of the unbelieving invite
you and you wish to go, eat whatever is
set before you, inquiring nothing for
the sake of conscience.
28But if anyone says to you, “This is
offered to an idol,” do not eat for the
sake of him that made it known and for
the conscience, for, “The Earth is the
Lord’s and the fullness of it.”
29Conscience I say, not of yourself
but that of the other– for why should
my freedom be judged by another’s
conscience?
30But if I by grace partake, why am I
slandered for that which I give thanks?
31Therefore, whether you eat or you
drink, or whatever you do, do all things
to God’s glory.
32Be without offense to both the Jews
and the Greeks and to the assembly of
God.
33According as I also in all things
please all, not seeking the profit of myself, but that of the many, that they may
be saved.

11 Be imitators of me, just as I also
am of Christ.
2Now I praise you, brethren, that in
all things you have remembered me,
and you keep the traditions just as I
delivered them to you.
3But I wish you to know that the
head of every man is Christ, but the
head of every woman is the man, and
the head of Christ, God.
4Any man praying or prophesying,
having anything on his head, puts to
shame his head.
5But any woman praying or prophesying with the head unveiled puts to
shame her head– for it is the same as
having been shaven.
6If the woman is not veiled, let her
also be shorn. But if it be a shame for a
woman to be shorn or shaven, let her
be veiled.
7For indeed a man should not veil his
head, being the image and glory of
God, but the woman is the glory of
man.
8For the man is not of the woman,
but the woman is of the man.
9For also the man was not created for
the woman, but the woman for the
man.
10Because of this, a woman should
have authority on her head, because of
the angels.
11However, neither is the man without the woman, nor the woman without the man, in the Lord.
12For as the woman is of the man, so
also is the man by the woman, and all
things are of God.
13Judge among yourselves: is it becoming for a woman to pray to God
uncovered?
14Or does not even nature itself teach
you that if a man has long hair, it is a
shame unto him?
15But if a woman has long hair, it is a
glory to her, for the long hair is given
to her in place of a covering.
16But if anyone wants to be quarrel-
some, we have no such custom, nor the
churches of God.
17Now with these instructions I do
not commend you, because when you
come together, it is not for the better,
but for the worse.
18To begin with: when you come together as a church, I hear there are divisions among you, and I partly believe

it.

19For there must also be factions among you that the approved among you may be revealed.

20Therefore, when you come together into one place, it is not to eat the Lord's supper.

21For in eating, each one first takes his own supper– one goes hungry, and the other gets drunk!

22Don't you indeed have houses in which to eat and drink? Or do you despise the church of God, and put them to shame that have not? What should I say to you? Should I praise you in this? I do not praise you.

23For I received from the Lord that which I also delivered to you, that in the night in which the Lord Jesus was delivered up, He took bread.

24And having given thanks, He broke it and said, "Take it and eat. This is My body, which is being broken for you. Do this in remembrance of Me."

25After they had eaten in like manner, He also took the cup, saying, "This is the cup of the New Covenant, which is by My blood. As often you drink this, do it in remembrance of Me."

26For as often as you eat this bread and drink this cup, you proclaim the Lord's death until He comes.

27Therefore, whoever eats this bread or drinks this cup of the Lord unworthily shall be guilty of the body and blood of the Lord.

28But let a man prove himself, and then let him eat of the bread and drink of the cup.

29For he that eats and drinks unworthily eats and drinks judgment to himself, not discerning the body of the Lord.

30Because of this, many among you are weak and sick, and some have died.

31But if we evaluate ourselves, we would not be judged.

32But being judged by the Lord, we are disciplined so that we will not be condemned with the world.

33So then my brethren, when you come together to eat, wait for one another.

34But if anyone is hungry, let him eat at home, so that when you come together it will not be for judgment. And the other things when I come I will set in order.

12 Now concerning the spiritual, brethren, I would not have you to be ignorant.

2You know that you were Gentiles, carried away to the speechless idols, even as you were led.

3For this reason I will inform you that no one speaking by God's Spirit will call Jesus cursed, and without the Holy Spirit no one can say, "Lord Jesus."

4Now there are divisions of gifts, but the same Spirit.

5And there are divisions of ministry, yet the same Lord.

6And there are divisions of activities, but the same God is activating all of these in everyone.

7But to every one is given the manifestation of the Spirit for the good of all.

8For through the Spirit is given a word of wisdom, and to another a word of knowledge according to the Spirit,

9and to another faith by the Spirit, and to another gifts of healings by the same Spirit,

10and to another the operation of powers, and to another prophecy, and to another discerning of spirits, and to others different types of tongues, and to another interpretation of tongues.

11And these are all activated by one and the same Spirit, Who distributes to each one individually according to His will.

12For just as the body is one, yet has many members– and all of the members of the body, being many, are one– so also is the body of Christ.

13For also by one Spirit we are all baptized into one body, whether Jew or Greek, whether slave or free, and all drink of one Spirit.

14For also the body is not one member but many.

15If the foot was to say, "Because I am not the hand, I am not of the body," is it not of the body because of this?

16And if the ear says, "Because I am not an eye, I am not of the body," is it not of the body because of this?

17If the whole body were an eye, where would the hearing be? If the whole were hearing, where would the smelling be?

18But now God placed the members, each one of them, in the body even as He has desired.

19And if they were all one member, where would the body be?

20But now there are many members, but one body.

21And the eye cannot say to the hand, "I have no need of you," or again the head to the feet, "I have no need of you."

22But much more the members of the body, seeming to be weaker, are necessary.

23And those of the body which we think are without honor, upon these we place more abundant honor, and the unattractive has more abundant appeal,

24and our attractive parts have no need. But God has combined together the body, having given more abundant honor to that which is lacking,

25that there may be no division in the body, but that the members have the same care one for another.

26And if one member suffers, all the members suffer. If one member is glorified, all the members rejoice.

27Now you are the body of Christ and members in particular.

28And God set these in the church: first, apostles, second, prophets, third, teachers, after that, works of power, then gifts of healings, helps, governments, diversity of tongues.

29Are all apostles? Are all prophets? Are all teachers? Not all have works of power.

30Do all have gifts of healings? Do all speak with tongues? Does everyone interpret?

31But earnestly strive for these gifts, and still also I will show you an excellent way.

13 If I speak with the tongues of men and angels, but do not have love, I have become as sounding brass or as a clanging cymbal.

2And if I have all prophecy, and know all mysteries, and if I have all knowledge, and if I have all faith so as mountains are removed, but have not love, I am nothing.

3And if I bestow all my goods to feed the poor, and if I deliver up my body that I may be burned, but do not have love, I profit nothing.

4Love has patience, is kind. Love is not envious. Love is not vainglorious, is not puffed up,

5does not act dishonorably, does not seek the things of its own, is not quickly provoked, does not consider evil,

6does not rejoice at unrighteousness,

but rejoices in the truth,

7 conceals all things, believes all things, confident of all things, endures all things.

8 Love never fails. But if prophecies, they shall be done away, if tongues, they shall cease, if knowledge, it shall be done away–

9 for we know in part and we prophesy in part.

10 But when that which is perfect comes, then that which is in part shall be done away.

11 When I was a child, I spoke as a child, I thought as a child, I reasoned as a child– but when I became a man, I put away the things of a child.

12 For we now see obscurely through a glass, but then face-to-face. Now I know in part, but then I shall know as also I am known.

13 Now these three abide: faith, expectation, and divine love, but the greatest of these is divine love.

14 Pursue love and earnestly desire the spiritual and especially that you prophesy.

2 Indeed, he who speaks in tongues speaks not to man but to God, for indeed no one understands, but the Spirit speaks mysteries.

3 But he who prophesies speaks to build up, exhort, and encourage man.

4 The one who speaks in ton-gues strengthens themself, but the one who prophesies strengthens the church.

5 I want all of you to speak with tongues, and more that you prophesy, because he is greater who prophesies than he who speaks with tongues– unless he interprets– that the church may be edified.

6 And now brethren, if I come to you speaking tongues, which of you will benefit unless I speak to you by revelation, or by knowledge, or by prophecy, or by teaching?

7 But yet there are lifeless things giving a sound, whether the flute or the harp. If their distinction of sound is not given, who will recognize that a flute is played or a harp is played?

8 And also, if a trumpet gives an uncertain sound, who can prepare for battle?

9 Also, if you do not give clear words by your tongue, who shall know what was spoken? For you are speaking into the air.

10 There are so many kinds of voices in the world, and none are without a sound.

11 Therefore, if I do not know the power of the sound, the one speaking is a foreigner and my speech is foreign.

12 And therefore, because you are spiritually zealous, seek to have the overflow, that you may build up the church.

13 Therefore, he who speaks in a tongue should pray to put it into words.

14 For indeed, if I pray in tongues, my spirit prays but my mind is unfruitful.

15 What shall be done? I will pray with the Spirit and will pray with the understanding also. I will sing with the Spirit and will sing with the understanding also.

16 Because although you may speak well in the Spirit, how shall they that occupy the place of the unskilled say, “Amen” upon your praise, seeing that what you have spoken is not known?

17 For you truly praise well, but the others are not built up.

18 I thank God that I speak with tongues more than all of you.

19 But in the church I desire to speak

five words with the understanding–
that I may teach the others– than ten-
thousand words with tongues.

20 Brothers, do not be children in
your thinking, but in malice, babies,
and in your thinking be perfect.

21 In the Law, it has been written, “In
another tongue and by other lips I will
speak to these people, and neither in
this way will they listen to Me,” says the
Lord.

22 Therefore tongues is for a sign, not
for those who believe, but the unbeliever– and prophecy is not for the unbeliever, but the believer.

23 Therefore, if the whole church
comes together and everyone speaks
with tongues, and one comes in, unlearned or unbelieving, will they not
say that you are mad?

24 But if all prophesy and an unbeliever or unlearned person enters, then
that one is convinced by all and examined by all,

25 and thereby the secrets of his heart
become manifested, and then falling
down upon his face, worshiping, he declares that God is truly among you.

26 What should be done then, my
brethren, whenever you assemble?
Each one of you has a song of praise, a
teaching, a tongue, a revelation, an interpretation– all to produce a building-
up.

27 If someone speaks in a tongue– after two, or as many as three, and in
turn– then let one put it into words.

28 But if there is no one who can interpret, let him keep silent in the
church, and speak to himself and to
God.

29 Let two or three prophets speak,
and the others judge.

30 And if another sitting by has a revelation, the first keeps silent.

31 For you can all prophesy one-by-
one that all may learn and all may be
exhorted.

32 And the spirits of prophets are subject to prophets.

33 For He is not the God of confusion,
but peace, as in all of the churches of
the holy ones.

34 Let the women in the church keep
silent, for you should not permit them
to talk, but be in submission, as also
the Law says.

35 But if any of them desire to learn,
they shall question their husbands at
home, for it is a shame for women to
talk in church.

36 Or did the Word of God go out
from you? Or did it only reach you?

37 If anyone is thought to be a prophet
or spiritual, acknowledge that what I
write to you is the Lord's commandment.

38 And if anyone is ignorant, let him
be ignorant.

39 So then, my brethren, earnestly desire to prophesy and do not hinder
speaking in tongues.

40 And let all things be done decently
and in order.

15 But brothers, I make known to
you the Gospel that I preached
to you, which you also received, in
which you also stand,

2 through which you are also being
kept safe if you hold fast to the Word
that I preached to you, lest you believed in vain.

3 For in the first place, I delivered
unto you that which I received: how
that Christ died for our sins according
to the Scriptures,

4 and that He was buried, and that He
was raised the third day according to
the Scriptures,

5and that He was seen of Cephas,
then of the twelve.
6After that He was seen by more than
five hundred brethren at once– of
whom many remain unto this day, and
many have fallen asleep.
7After that He appeared to James,
then to all the apostles.
8But last of all, He appeared to me, as
one from an untimely birth.
9For I am the least of all the apostles,
who am not worthy to be called an
apostle, because I persecuted the
church of God.
10But by the grace of God I am what I
am, and His grace given to me has not
been in vain. Rather I labored more
abundantly than all of them, though it
was not I, but the grace of God that was
with me.
11Therefore, whether it was I or they,
so we preached, and so you have believed.
12Now if Christ is preached– how
that He rose from the dead– how can
some among you say that there is no
resurrection of the dead?
13But if there is no resurrection of the
dead, then Christ is not risen.
14But if Christ is not risen, then our
preaching is vain, and your faith is also
vain,
15and we are also found false witnesses of God. For we have testified of
God, how that He raised up Christ,
Whom He did not raise up if the dead
are not raised.
16For if the dead are not raised, then
Christ is not risen,
17and if Christ is not risen, your faith
is useless and you are still in your sins,
18and those who have fallen asleep in
Christ have perished.
19If only in this life we have an expectation in Christ, then we are of all men
most miserable.
20But now Christ has risen from the
dead, having become the first-fruits of
them that have fallen asleep.
21For by a man came death, and by a
man came resurrection from the dead.
22For just like all died by Adam, even
so shall all be made alive by Christ.
23But each in his own order: Christ
the first-fruits, then those who are of
Christ at His coming.
24Then in the end, when He hands
over the Kingdom to God and the Father– when every ruler and every authority and power is abolished,
25(For He must reign until He has put
all enemies under His feet.
26The last enemy that shall be abolished is death.
27For He has subjected all things under His feet. But when it was said, “All
things have been subjected to Him,” it
is evident that He Who subjected all
things under Him is excluded.)
28when all things are subjected to
Him– then shall the Son Himself be in
subjection to Him Who subjected all
things to Him, that God may be all-in-
all.
29For what then shall they do who are
baptized for the dead if the dead are
not raised? Why then are they baptized
for the dead?
30And why are we in danger every
hour?
31I die daily by our boasting which I
have in Christ Jesus our Lord.
32For if I have fought with beasts at
Ephesus after the manner of men, what
profit is it to me if the dead are not
raised? Let us eat and drink, for tomorrow we shall die!
33Be not deceived: evil association
corrupts good morals.
34Righteously awake and sin not, for

some are ignorant of God– I speak this
to your shame.
35 But someone will say, "How are the
dead raised? And with what body do
they come?"
36 Fool! What you sow is not made
alive unless it dies.
37 And that which you sow, you sow
not the body that shall be, but bare
grain– that may be of wheat or of
something else–
38 but God gives it a body according
as He has willed and to each of the
seeds its own body.
39 All flesh is not the same flesh, but
there is one flesh of men, and another
flesh of a beast, and another of fish,
and another of birds.
40 There are heavenly bodies and
earthly bodies, but the heavenly glory
is different than that of the earthly.
41 There is one glory of the sun, and
another glory of the moon, and another glory of the stars, and one star dif-
fers in glory from another star.
42 So also is the resurrection of the
dead. It is sown in corruption and
raised in incorruption.
43 It is sown in dishonor and raised in
glory. It is sown in weakness and raised
in power.
44 It is sown a natural body and raised
a spiritual body. There is a natural
body and there is a spiritual body.
45 So also as it has been written: the
first man, Adam, became a living soul–
the last Adam was a life-giving Spirit.
46 Now the spiritual was not first, but
the natural, then afterwards the spiritual.
47 The first man was made of dust out
of the earth– the second man is the
Lord out of Heaven.
48 As was he who was made of dust,
so also are those made out of dust, and
as the heavenly One, such also are the
heavenly ones.
49 And as we have borne the image of
the one made of dust, we shall also bear
the image of the heavenly.
50 This I say, brethren: that flesh and
blood cannot inherit the Kingdom of
God. Neither can corruption inherit
incorruptibility.
51 Behold I tell you a mystery: we
shall not all sleep, but we shall all be
changed
52 in an instant, in the twinkling of an
eye, at the last trumpet. For the trumpet shall sound, and the dead shall be
raised incorruptible, and we shall be
changed.
53 For this corruptible must put on
incorruptibility, and this mortal must
put on immortality.
54 But when this corruptible shall
have put on incorruptibility and this
mortal shall have put on immortality,
then shall come to pass the word that
has been written, "Death was swallowed up in victory."
55 Death, where is your sting? Hell,
where is your victory?
56 Now the sting of death is sin, and
the power of sin is the Law.
57 But thanks be to God, Who has
given us the victory through Jesus
Christ our Lord!
58 Therefore, my dear brethren, be
steadfast and unmovable, abounding in
the work of the Lord, always knowing
that your labor in the Lord is not in
vain.

16 Now as for the collection for the
holy ones: as I have directed the
churches of Galatia, you should also
do.
2 Every first-of-the-week, let each of
you lay up treasure of whatever he may

have prospered, so that there are no
collections when I come.
3When I arrive, whomever you shall
approve by letters, these I will send to
bring your grace to Jerusalem.
4And if it is suitable for me to go also,
then they shall go with me.
5But I will come to you when I go
through Macedonia, for I will go
through Macedonia.
6It may be that I will stay with you, or
even winter, that you may send me on
my way wherever I may go.
7For I will not see you now in my
passing, but I trust at a certain time to
abide with you, if the Lord permits.
8But I will remain in Ephesus until
Pentecost,
9for a great and effective door has
been opened to me and there are many
adversaries.
10Now, if Timothy comes, see that he
is with you without fear, for he works
the work of the Lord even as I do.
11Do not let anyone despise him, but
send him on his way in peace that he
may come to me– for the brethren and
I look for him.
12And concerning brother Apollos: I
greatly exhorted him that he should go
to you with the brethren, but he was
not at all willing to come now, but he
will come when he has opportunity.
13Keep alert, stand firm in the faith,
be men, and be strong.
14Let all your things be done in love.
15Brethren, you know the house of
Stephanas, how that it is the first-fruits
of Achaia, and that they appointed
themselves to the service of the holy
ones. But I exhort you,
16that you also be subject to such and
to all who work and labor with us.
17And I rejoice at the coming of
Stephanas, Fortunatus, and Achaicus,
because these fill up your lack.
18They have refreshed my spirit and
yours. Therefore, recognize such.
19The churches of Asia greet you.
Aquila and Priscilla greet you much in
the Lord, and so does the church that is
in their house.
20All of the brethren greet you. Greet
one another with a holy kiss.
21The greeting of me, Paul, with my
own hand.
22If any man loves not the Lord Jesus
Christ, the same be accursed! Oh Lord,
come!
23The grace of the Lord Jesus Christ
be with you all.
24My love be with all of you in Christ
Jesus. Amen!

The Second Epistle of Paul the Apostle to the

Corinthians

1 Paul, an apostle of Jesus Christ by the will of God, and brother Timothy, to the church of God that is in Corinth, with all the holy ones who are in the whole of Achaia.

2 Grace to you, and peace from God our Father and the Lord Jesus Christ.

3 Blessed be the God and Father of our Lord Jesus Christ, the Father of compassion, and God of all comfort,

4 who encourages us in all of our tribulations, enabling us to encourage those in every tribulation through the encouragement with which we ourselves are encouraged by God.

5 For as the sufferings of Christ abound toward us in this way, our encouragement through Christ abounds.

6 But if we are troubled, it is for your encouragement and salvation being worked out by the endurance of the same sufferings that we also suffer– if we are encouraged, it is for your encouragement and salvation, and our firm expectation for you,

7 knowing that as you are partners of the sufferings, so also of the encouragement.

8 For we do not desire for you to be ignorant, brethren, of our tribulation that happened unto us in Asia, for we were excessively burdened beyond our power so that we despaired even for our life.

9 But we had in ourselves the sentence of death that we should not trust in ourselves, but in God Who raises the dead,

10 Who delivered us from so great a death and does deliver us, in Whom we trust that He will still deliver.

11 You also join together and help us by prayer, so that many will give thanks for us because of the gift granted to us by many.

12 For our boasting is this, the testimony of our conscience, that in the simplicity and purity of God we have had our conduct in the world and most of all toward you– not in fleshly wisdom, but by the grace of God.

13 For we have written no other things to you except what you read and also know– and I trust that even to the end you shall know–

14 even as you have acknowledged in part that we are your rejoicing, even as you are ours in the day of our Lord Jesus.

15 And in this confidence I had previously wanted to come to you, so that you could have a double benefit,

16 and by you pass through Macedonia and again come to you from Macedonia, and by you to be sent to Judea.

17 Therefore having indeed purposed this, did I use lightness? Or what I purpose, do I purpose according to the flesh that with me there should be yes, yes and no, no.

18 But God is faithful, because our word to you was not yes and no.

19 For the Son of God, Jesus Christ, Who was proclaimed among you by us (by me, Silvanus, and Timothy) was not yes and no,

20 for every promise of God in Him is a Yes, and in Him, Amen, to the glory of God by us.

21 But He Who establishes us with you in Christ and has anointed us is God.

22 And He has sealed us and given us the first installment of the Spirit in our hearts.

23 But I call God as a witness upon my soul that it was to spare you that I did not come to Corinth.

24 We cannot have control over your faith, but are helpers of your joy, for by

faith you stand.

2 For I myself judged this: not to
come again to you in grief.
2For if I also grieve you, who is it that
should make me glad except he who is
grieved by me?
3And I wrote the same to you, lest
coming I might have pain from those
of whom I might rejoice– this confidence I have in all of you: that my joy is
in you all.
4For out of much tribulation and anguish of heart I wrote to you through
many tears, not that you might be
grieved, but that you might know the
abundant love that I have for you.
5If any man has caused grief, the
same has not grieved me, not to be too
severe, but has partly done it to all of
you.
6It is sufficient for such a one that he
was rebuked by many,
7so that now, on the contrary, you
should forgive and encourage, lest such
a one should be swallowed up with
more abundant grief.
8Therefore I exhort you to confirm
love toward him.
9For this also I wrote that I might
know the proof of you, if you are obedient to everything.
10But to whom you forgive anything,
I do also. If I have forgiven anything, I
forgave it for your sakes in the person
of Christ,
11lest Satan should get an advantage,
for we are not ignorant of his inten-
tions.
12Now having come to Troas for the
gospel of Christ– and a door was also
opened to me in the Lord–
13I had no rest in my spirit, because I
did not find Titus my brother, but
taking leave of them, I went out to
Macedonia.
14But thanks be to God, Who always
makes us triumph in Christ and makes
manifest the fragrance of His knowledge through us in every place.
15For we are to God a sweet fragrance
of Christ, to them that are saved and in
them who perish.
16To the one, are we the fragrance of
death unto death, but to the other, the
fragrance of life unto life. And who is
sufficient for these things?
17For we are not, as many, making
gain by corrupting the Word of God,
but in purity, but as of God. Before
God we speak in Christ.

3 Do we begin to prove ourselves
again that we need, as some, letters
of recommendation to you or recommendation from you?
2You are our epistles written in our
hearts, known and read by all men.
3Being revealed that you are epistles
of Christ ministered by us, having been
inscribed, not with ink, but by the Spirit of the Living God– not on tables of
stone, but on fleshly tables of the heart.
4And such confidence we have
through Christ toward God,
5not that we are sufficient of ourselves to think anything as of ourselves,
but our sufficiency is of God,
6Who also has made us qualified
ministers of the New Covenant– not of
the letter, but of the Spirit. For the
letter kills, but the Spirit gives life.
7But also if the ministry of death–
written in letters having been engraved
in stones– was produced in glory, (so
that the children of Israel could not
look into the face of Moses because of
the glory of his face), which is being
abolished,
8how much more will the ministry of

the Spirit be glorious?
9For if there was glory in the ministry of condemnation, much more
does the ministry of righteousness ex-
ceed in glory.
10For even that which was made glorious is not glorious on account of the
surpassing glory.
11For if what was set aside was glorious, how much more glorious is what
remains?
12Seeing then that we have such
hope, we use great plainness of speech.
13And not as Moses, who put a veil
over his face, that the children of Israel
could not steadfastly look to the end of
what is abolished,
14but their minds were blinded– for
until this day remains the same veil un-
taken away in the reading of the Old
Covenant, which veil is done away in
Christ.
15But even unto this day, when Moses
is read, the veil is upon their heart.
16Nevertheless, when it shall turn to
the Lord, the veil shall be taken away.
17Now the Lord is the Spirit, and
where the Spirit of the Lord is, there is
freedom.
18And all of us, with an unveiled face,
beholding the glory of the Lord in a
mirror, are transfigured into the same
image from glory to glory as from the
Spirit of the Lord.

4 Therefore, having this ministry accordingly as we have received mercy, we faint not.
2But we have renounced the hidden
things of shame, neither walking in
trickery nor corrupting the Word of
God, but by manifestation of the truth
approving ourselves to every man's
conscience before God.
3And also, if our gospel is hidden, it
is hidden to those who are perishing,
4in whom the god of this age has
blinded the minds of the unbelieving
lest the light of the glorious gospel of
Christ, Who is the image of God,
should shine unto them.
5For we preach not ourselves, but
Christ Jesus the Lord, and ourselves
your servants for Jesus' sake.
6For it is God, Who commanded the
light to shine out of darkness, Who has
shone in our hearts the light of the
knowledge of the glory of God in the
face of Jesus Christ.
7But we have this treasure in earthen
vessels, that the excellency of the power
may be of God and not of us.
8In every way afflicted, but not restricted; perplexed, but not in doubt;
9persecuted, but not forsaken; cast
down, but not destroyed–
10always bearing about the dying of
the Lord Jesus in the body, that also the
life of Jesus may be manifested in our
body.
11We who live are always delivered to
death because of Jesus, that also the life
of Jesus may be manifested in our mortal flesh.
12So then death works in us but life
in you.
13And having the same Spirit of
faith– accordingly as it has been written, "I believed, therefore I spoke"–
also we believe and therefore also we
speak,
14knowing that He Who raised up the
Lord Jesus shall also raise us up
through Jesus and shall present us with
you.
15For all things are for your sake, that
the abounding grace by the thanksgiving of many may abound to the glory
of God.
16Therefore, we do not weary, for

even though our outward man decays,
the inward man is being renewed day
after day.
17For the momentary light affliction
works out for us an excessively surpassing eternal weight of glory.
18For we do not consider the things
that are seen, but the things not seen.
For the things seen are temporary, but
the things not seen are eternal.

5 For we know that if our earthly
tent-like house were destroyed, we
have a building from God, a house not
made by hands, eternal in the heavens.
2Indeed, for in this dwelling we
groan earnestly, desiring to be clothed
with the one from Heaven.
3And if we are clothed, we shall not
be found naked.
4For indeed while we are in this
tabernacle, we groan, being burdened,
not that we would be unclothed, but
clothed, that mortality might be swallowed up by life!
5Now God Himself has brought this
about for us and has given us the Spirit
as a pledge.
6We therefore have good courage,
and we know that being at home in the
body, we are away from the Lord.
7For we walk by faith, not by sight.
8But we are confident, and also take
great delight in taking leave of the body
to take up residence with the Lord.
9Therefore, we also labor that
whether we are at home or we leave we
may be well-pleasing to Him.
10For we must all appear before the
judgment seat of Christ, that everyone
may receive for the things– whether
good or evil– according to that which
was done in the body.
11Because we know the terror of the
Lord, we try to persuade men. What we
are is well-known to God, and I hope it
is well-known to your conscience.
12For we do not need to prove who
we are again to you. Rather, we are giving you an opportunity to boast about
us and have something to say to those
who boast themselves in a position
rather than in heart.
13For whether we are beside ourselves, it is to God; or whether we are
sober, it is for you.
14For the love of Christ urges us, having judged this: that if One has died for
all, then all have died.
15And He died for all, so that those
who live might not live unto themselves, but to Him who died and has
risen.
16Therefore, from now on, we know
no one after the flesh. Even though we
have known Christ after the flesh, yet
now we know Him no more.
17So then if anyone is in Christ, he is
a new creation, old things have passed
away, and all things have been made
new.
18And all things are of God, Who has
reconciled us unto Himself by Jesus
Christ and has given to us the ministry
of reconciliation.
19For God was in Christ reconciling
the world unto Himself, not counting
their trespasses against them, and has
committed unto us the word of reconciliation.
20So then we are ambassadors for
Christ, since God calls out through us–
we implore you on behalf of Christ to
be reconciled to God.
21For He who knew no sin was made
the sin offering for us so that we may
be the righteousness of God in Him.

6 But also, as working together, we
exhort you that you receive not the

grace of God in vain.

2 For He says, “In an acceptable time I have listened to you, and in a day of salvation I helped you.” Behold, now is the acceptable time. Behold, now is the day of salvation.

3 Let no one give offense in anything, that the ministry not be blamed.

4 But in everything approving themselves as God’s ministers, in much endurance, tribulation, in necessities, in difficulties,

5 in stripes, in imprisonment, in commotions, in labors, in watchings, in fastings,

6 in pureness, in knowledge, in longsufferings, in kindness, in the Holy Spirit, in genuine love,

7 in the word of truth, in the power of God, through the weapons of righteousness on the right hand and left,

8 through glory and dishonor, through evil report and good report, as deceivers but true,

9 as being unknown, but well known, as dying and behold we live, as disciplined and not put to death,

10 as sorrowful but always rejoicing, as poor, but enriching many, as having nothing and possessing all things.

11 Our mouth has been opened to you Corinthians, our hearts enlarged.

12 You are not confined in us, but you are confined in your own affections.

13 But the same response, as to children I speak, be also enlarged.

14 Do not be unequally yoked with unbelievers. For what participation has righteousness and iniquity? And what fellowship has light with darkness?

15 And what agreement has Christ with Belial? Or what part has a believer with an unbeliever?

16 And what union has a temple of God with idols? You are a temple of the living God, accordingly as God said, “I will dwell in them and walk among them, and I will be their God, and they shall be to me a people.”

17 “Therefore, come out from the midst of them and be separate,” says the Lord, “and touch not the unclean thing, and I will receive you,

18 and I will be to you for a Father, and you shall be to Me for sons and daughters,” says the Lord Almighty.

7 Therefore, having these promises, beloved, let us cleanse ourselves from every defilement of the flesh and spirit, perfecting holiness in the fear of God.

2 Receive us– we have wronged no one, we have corrupted no one, we have exploited no one.

3 I say this not to condemn you: for as I have said before, you are in our hearts to die and to live together.

4 Great is my boldness toward you– I boast greatly in you. I have been filled with encouragement. I have exceeding great joy at all our tribulation.

5 For also when we came into Macedonia, our flesh had no rest, but we were troubled in every way– without were contentions and within were fears.

6 But God, Who encourages those who are brought low, encouraged us by Titus’ coming.

7 And not only by his coming, but also by the encouragement with which he was encouraged from you, for he told us your longing and of your mourning and of your zeal for me, so that I rejoiced the more.

8 For if also I grieved you in the epistle I do not regret it– even if I did regret it– for I see that the epistle, if even for an hour, grieved you.

9 Now I did not rejoice that you were
grieved, but that you were grieved to
repentance, for we were grieved according to God, that you might not
suffer loss in anything.
10 For godly grief works repentance to
salvation, not to be regretted, but the
grief of the world works death.
11 For behold, this same thing worked
out in you, to have been grieved according to God– but what a clearing of
yourself, of indignation, of fear, of
longing, of zeal, of vengeance! In every
way you proved yourselves to be pure
in this matter.
12 So then, if I also wrote to you– not
for the sake of him who did wrong, nor
for the sake of him who suffered
wrong– but for the sake that your
earnestness for us might be manifest in
the sight of God.
13 Therefore, we have been encouraged in your encouragement, and
rather more abundantly we rejoice at
the joy of Titus, because his spirit has
been refreshed by all of you.
14 Because I was not put to shame for
anything that I have boasted about you,
but as we have spoken everything to
you in truth, so also our boasting to
Titus was true.
15 And his affections are more abundant towards you, remembering the
obedience of all of you, how you received him with fear and trembling.
16 I rejoice that I may be confident in
everything about you.

8 But we make known to you,
brethren, the grace of God that has
been given to the churches of Macedonia.
2 That in severe testing of tribulation,
their abundance of joy and their deep
poverty abounded to the riches of their
generosity.
3 I bear witness, for according to their
power, and beyond their power, they
were willing of themselves,
4 with much insistence, pleading with
us to receive the grace and the fellowship of the service that was for the
saints.
5 And not only as we expected, but
they also gave themselves first to the
Lord and then, by the will of God, to
us.
6 So we urged Titus that, as he had
begun before, he should also accomplish this grace with you.
7 But even as you abound in everything– in faith, and word, and knowledge, and all diligence, and in love for
us– that also you should abound in this
grace.
8 I do not speak this as a commandment, but rather through the earnestness of others proving the sincerity of
your love.
9 For you know the grace of our Lord
Jesus Christ that, being rich, He became poor for your sake, that through
His poverty you might be rich.
10 And I give a judgment in this– for
this is profitable for you, who not only
began to do it a year ago, but desired to
do it–
11 so now also finish doing it, so that
even as there was an eagerness to desire
it, even so you also complete it out of
what you have.
12 For if a readiness is present, it is acceptable according as anyone may
have, not according to what he does
not have.
13 For it is not that others have relief
while you have distress, but equality–
in the present time your abundance for
their lack,
14 that also their abundance may be

for your lack– so that there should be equality.

15 According as it is written, "He that had much had no increase, and he that had little had no lack."

16 But thanks be to God who put the same diligence for you in the heart of Titus.

17 For he indeed received the exhortation, but being more diligent, he came to you of his own accord.

18 But we sent with him the brother whose praise is in the gospel in all the churches,

19 and not only that, but also chosen by the churches as our fellow traveler with this grace that is administered by us unto the glory of the Lord Himself, and of your readiness.

20 Arranging this, lest any man should blame us in the abundance that is ministered by us.

21 Providing things that are right, not only before the Lord, but also before men.

22 And we sent with them our brother whom we have often proved in many things to be diligent, and now much more diligent by the confidence that is toward you–

23 whether as regards to Titus my partner, and to you a fellow worker, or our brethren and the messengers of the churches, and the glory of Christ.

24 Therefore show, in the presence of the churches, the proof of your love and our boasting about you to them.

9 Now concerning the ministry that is for the saints, it's redundant for me to write to you.

2 For I know your readiness– which, concerning you, I have boasted to the Macedonians that Achaia has been prepared a year ago– and your zeal has provoked a great number.

3 But I sent the brethren, lest our boasting about you should be in vain in this respect and that you, as I have said, may be prepared–

4 lest perhaps, if the Macedonians come, they should find you unprepared and we– I say not you– would be put to shame by the confident boast.

5 Therefore I thought it necessary to exhort the brethren to come beforehand to prepare your promised generosity, so that it might be ready to be a generous gift and not an exploitation.

6 But this I say: he who sows sparingly shall also reap sparingly, but he who sows generously shall reap generously–

7 each according as he has purposed in his heart, not sorrowfully or of necessity, for God loves a cheerful giver.

8 For God is able to make all grace abound unto you, that you will have all sufficiency in all things, that you may have more than enough in every good work.

9 As it has been written, "He scattered abroad, He gave to the poor– His righteousness abides forever."

10 Now He Who supplies seed to him who sows and bread for the eating, may He supply and multiply your sowing, and may He increase your fruits of righteousness.

11 In every way being enriched to all generosity, which works out thanksgiving to God through us,

12 because the service of this ministry not only supplies the need of the saints, but also is overflowing through many thanksgivings to God,

13 through the proof of this service glorifying God for your obedience to the confession of the Gospel of Christ and generosity of the fellowship toward them and toward all,

14 and their deep affection in their prayer for you because of the surpassing grace of God upon you.

15 Now thanks be to God for His unspeakable gift.

10 I, Paul, myself, beseech you by the meekness and gentleness of Christ– who when I am present with you, I am lowly, but am bold toward you being absent.

2 Now I beg you that when I am present I will not have to be bold with that confidence which I consider to be a show of boldness toward those who reason that we walk according to the flesh.

3 For walking in the flesh we do not war after the flesh.

4 For the weapons of our warfare are not fleshly, but powerful through God to demolish strongholds,

5 to destroy thoughts and every arrogant obstacle raised against the knowledge of God, and to take every thought captive to the obedience of Christ,

6 and in readiness to take vengeance on all disobedience when your obedience is fulfilled.

7 Do you look at things according to appearance? If any man is convinced in himself that he is Christ's, let him consider again of himself, that as he is Christ's even so are we Christ's.

8 For if I should boast some more of our authority– which the Lord gave us to edify and not to destroy you– I will not be ashamed.

9 I don't want to appear to be frightening you by means of an epistle.

10 For it is said that his epistles are weighty and strong, but his bodily presence is weak and his speech is despicable.

11 Let such a one consider this: that what we are in word by epistles being absent, such are we also in deeds when present.

12 For we do not dare to rank or compare ourselves with those who are commending themselves, but those who measure themselves among themselves and compare themselves with others lack understanding.

13 Now we will not boast of things beyond measure, but according to the measure of the assignment that God has divided to us, the measure that also reached unto you.

14 For we did not overextend ourselves as if we did not reach to you, for even to you we came with the gospel of Christ.

15 Not boasting of the things beyond measure in the labor of others, but as your faith goes on increasing, our assignment will be abundantly magnified

16 to preach the gospel beyond you, not boasting about what has already been done in another's assignment.

17 But he that boasts, let him boast in the Lord.

18 For it is not the one recommending himself that is approved, but whom the Lord recommends.

11 I would that you bear with me in a little foolishness, but indeed bear with me.

2 For I am jealous over you with the jealousy of God. For I have espoused you to one man, to present you as a chaste virgin to Christ.

3 But I fear, lest as the serpent deceived Eve in his trickery, even so your minds should be corrupted from the simplicity that is in Christ.

4 For if he that comes preaches another Jesus, whom we did not proclaim, or you receive a different Spirit, which

you did not receive, or a different
gospel, which you did not accept, you
did well, bearing with it.
5 For I suppose that I have been behind in nothing of those chief apostles.
6 But even if I were unskilled in
speech, yet not in knowledge; but in
every way made manifest in all things
to you.
7 Or did I commit sin by humbling
myself that you might be exalted because I announced the gospel of God to
you free of charge?
8 I robbed other churches, having received wages to minister to you.
9 And being present with you, and
being in need, I did not burden anyone,
for what was lacking to me, the
brethren who came from Macedonia
supplied. And in all things I kept, and
will keep, myself from being a burden
to you.
10 As the truth of Christ is in me, this
boasting shall not be taken from me in
the regions of Achaia.
11 Why? Because I do not love you?
God knows.
12 But what I do, also I will do, that I
may cut off the opportunity of those
desiring an opportunity to boast that
they may also be found to be as us.
13 For these false apostles are deceitful
workers, disguising themselves as the
apostles of Christ.
14 And it is no wonder, for Satan himself is disguised as an angel of light.
15 Therefore, it is no big thing if his
servants also disguise themselves as
servants of righteousness, of whom the
end shall be according to their works.
16 Again I say, no one should consider
me to be a fool– otherwise receive me
as a fool, that I may also boast a little.
17 What I speak in this confidence of
boasting, I do not speak as the Lord,
but as in foolishness.
18 Since many boast according to the
flesh, I will also boast.
19 For you, being wise, gladly bear
with fools.
20 For you bear with anyone who
brings you into bondage– if anyone devours you, if anyone takes, if anyone
exalts himself, if anyone smites you on
the face.
21 I say this to our shame. We have
been weak. But wherein anyone may be
daring, I speak foolishly, I am also daring.
22 Are they Hebrews? So am I. Are
they Israelites? Are they the seed of
Abraham? So am I.
23 Are they the ministers of Christ? I
speak as a fool, I am more– in labors
more abundantly, in stripes to an extreme degree, in imprisonments more
abundantly, in deaths often.
24 Of the Jews, five times I received
forty lashes minus one.
25 Three times I was beaten with rods.
I was stoned once. I was shipwrecked
three times. I have spent a night and a
day in the deep.
26 In traveling often, in perils of
rivers, in perils of robbers, in perils of
my nation, in perils from nations, in
perils in the city, in perils in the
deserts, in perils on the sea, in perils
among false brethren,
27 in labor and toil, often in sleepless-
ness, in hunger and thirst, often in fastings, in cold and nakedness.
28 And beside these outward things,
on me is the daily pressure, the care
concerning all of the churches.
29 Who is weak and I am not weak?
Who stumbles and I do not burn?
30 If it is necessary to boast, I will
boast about my weakness.
31 The God and Father of our Lord

Jesus Christ, He Who is blessed unto
the ages, knows that I do not lie.
32In Damascus, the governor under
King Aertas was guarding the city of
the Damascenes, desiring to seize me,
33and I was let down in a basket
through a window in the wall and escaped his hand.

12 Indeed, boasting is not benefi-
cial to me, for I will come to visions and revelations of the Lord.
2I knew a man in Christ fourteen
years ago– whether in the body or out
of the body I cannot tell, God knows–
such a one was caught away into the
third heaven.
3And I know such a man– whether in
the body or out of the body I know not,
God knows–
4that he was caught away to Paradise
and heard unutterable sayings that are
not permitted for man to speak.
5Concerning such a one I will boast,
but concerning myself I will not boast,
except about my weakness.
6For if I want to boast, I shall not be a
fool, for I would be telling the truth,
but I forebear, lest anyone should consider me to be above what he sees or
hears of me.
7That I might not be exalted because
of the extraordinary revelation, there
was given to me a thorn in the flesh–
an angel of Satan, that he might buffet
me– that I might not be exalted.
8I implored the Lord three times that
he might depart from me.
9And He said to me, "My grace is sufficient for you, for My power is perfected in weakness." Therefore, most
gladly, I would rather boast in weaknesses, that the power of Christ may
reside upon me.
10Therefore, I take pleasure in weaknesses, in insults, in necessities, in persecutions, in trouble, for Christ. For
when I am weak, then I am powerful.
11I have become a fool boasting. You
forced me, for I should have been en-
dorsed by you, for in nothing was I inferior to the very chief apostles, even
though I am nothing.
12Truly the signs of the apostle were
performed among you in all patience,
in signs and wonders and works of
power.
13For what way were you inferior to
the rest of the churches, except that I
myself did not burden you? Forgive me
for this injustice.
14Now I am ready to come to you a
third time and I will not burden you,
for I do not seek your things but you.
For the children should not store up for
the parents, but the parents for the
children.
15Now I most gladly will spend and
will be spent for your souls, even if loving you more earnestly, I am loved
less.
16But be it so, I myself did not burden
you. I was crafty, you say, and by deceit
got the better of you.
17Did I exploit you by anyone that I
sent to you?
18I urged Titus and sent the brother
with him. Did Titus exploit you? Did
we not walk in the same Spirit?
19Again, do you think that we are
making our defense to you? We speak
before God in Christ Jesus, and all
things for your edification, beloved.
20For I fear, lest perhaps when I come
I should not find you as I desire, and be
found by you such as you would not
desire– lest perhaps strifes, jealousies,
anger, contentions, slanders, gossips,
conceits, insurrections–
21lest again, having come, my God

should humble me before you and I
should have to mourn over many of
those who have sinned and have not
repented over the uncleanness and
sexual immorality and extreme immorality which they practice.

13 Now I come to you the third
time. Let every word be established in the mouth of two or three
witnesses.
2 I have said before when I was
present the second time, and I write
now being absent, saying– to those
who have sinned and to all of the rest–
that if I come again I will not spare.
3 You demand a proof of Christ
speaking in me, which to you was not
weak but mighty among you.
4 For indeed He was crucified in
weakness, but He lives by God's power.
For indeed we are weak in Him, but
among you we shall live with Him by
God's power.
5 Test yourself to see if you are in the
faith. Examine yourself! Do you not
realize that Jesus Christ is in you? Otherwise you are counterfeit!
6 I trust that you will know that we
are not counterfeit.
7 I pray to God that you may do nothing evil, not that we may appear approved, but that you may do what is
right and we be as counterfeit.
8 We can do nothing against the truth,
but for the truth.
9 We are glad when we are weak and
you are strong. But your maturation is
what we also pray for.
10 For this reason I write these things,
being absent from you, that when I am
present I will not use sharpness according to the authority which the Lord has
given me to edify and not to destroy.
11 Finally, brethren, rejoice, be perfect, be encouraged, be of one mind,
live in peace, and the God of love and
peace shall be with you.
12 Greet one another with a holy kiss.
13 All the saints greet you.
14 The grace of our Lord Jesus Christ
and the love of God and the fellowship
of the Holy Ghost be with you all,
Amen.

The second epistle to the Corinthians sent from Philippi, a city in Macedonia, by Titus and Lucas.

The Epistle of Paul the Apostle to the

Galatians

1 Paul, an apostle– not from man nor
by man, but by Jesus Christ and Father God Who raised Him from the
dead–
2 and all the brethren who are with
me, to the churches of Galatia.
3 Grace to you and peace from Father
God and our Lord Jesus Christ,
4 Who gave Himself for our sins in
order to set us free from the present
evil age, according to the will of God
and our Father,
5 to Whom be the glory to the ages of
the ages. Amen.
6 I am astonished at how quickly you
have deserted the One Who called you
in the grace of Christ unto another
gospel.
7 Not that there is another, but some
are confusing you and desire to pervert
the gospel of Christ.
8 But even if we or an angel from
heaven proclaim to you another gospel,
let that one be accursed!
9 As we have said and now say again:
if anyone proclaims another gospel to
you than what you received, let that
one be accursed!
10 Am I now seeking the approval of
man or of God? Or am I trying to
please man? For if I were still pleasing
man, I would not be the servant of
Christ.
11 But I want you to know, brothers:
the Gospel preached by me was not of
man.
12 For I did not receive it from man,
neither was I taught it, but by revelation of Jesus Christ.
13 For you have heard of my way of
life in Judaism: that I violently persecuted the church of God and I tried to
destroy it.
14 Also, I advanced in Judaism beyond
many of my peers that were my own
age, being far more zealous for the tradition of my fathers.
15 But when God was pleased– Who
separated me from my mother's belly
and called me by His grace–
16 to reveal His Son in me that I might
proclaim Him among the Gentiles,
immediately I did not consult with
flesh and blood.
17 Neither did I go up to Jerusalem to
those who were apostles before me, but
I went into Arabia, and afterward I returned to Damascus.
18 Then after three years, I went up to
Jerusalem to visit Peter and stayed with
him for fifteen days.
19 But I did not see any of the other
apostles except James, the Lord's brother.
20 Now the things that I write to you,
behold, in the sight of God, I do not lie.
21 Then I went into the regions of Syria and Cilicia.
22 And I was still unknown by face to
the churches of Judea that are in Christ.
23 They only heard it being said, "The
one who persecuted us now preaches
the faith he once tried to destroy."
24 And they glorified God in me.

2 Then after fourteen years I went up
again into Jerusalem with Barnabas, taking Titus also with me.
2 And I went up by revelation and
communicated to them the gospel I
preach among the nations, but in private to those of reputation, so that I
was not running or had run in vain.
3 But not even Titus, who was with
me, being a Greek, was compelled to be
circumcised.
4 Through these false brethren– who
secretly slipped in to spy out our liberty
which we have in Christ Jesus that they
might bring us into bondage–

5whom we did not yield in submission to for an hour, that the truth of the
gospel might remain with you,
6and from those who were supposed
to be something– whatsoever they were
it makes no difference to me, God does
not regard the person of man– for
those of reputation contributed nothing to me.
7On the contrary, when they saw that
I had been entrusted with the gospel to
the uncircumcised, even as Peter for
the circumcision–
8for He Who worked in Peter to the
apostleship of the circumcision also
worked in me unto the Gentiles–
9and recognizing the grace given me,
James, and Cephas, and John, who
were the recognized pillars, gave to
Barnabas and me the right hand of fellowship that we should go to the Gentiles and they to the circumcision.
10Only that we should remember the
poor, which I was also eager to do.
11But when Peter came to Antioch, I
opposed him to his face, because he
was wrong.
12For until certain ones came from
James, he ate with the Gentiles, but because they came, he withdrew and separated himself, being afraid of the circumcision.
13And other Jews joined in his
hypocrisy, so that even Barnabas was
led away by their hypocrisy.
14But when I saw they were not act-
ing rightly according to the truth of the
gospel, I said to Peter, before them all,
"If you, being a Jew, live like a Gentile
and not like a Jew, then how can you
compel the Gentiles to live like Jews?"
15We are Jews by birth, and not of the
Gentile sinners.
16We know that a man is not made
righteous by the works of the law because they are not through the faith of
Jesus Christ. And we have believed in
Jesus Christ, so that our righteousness
might be by the faith of Christ and not
by law-works, for by the works of the
law no one shall be made righteous.
17But if, while we seek to be made
righteous in Christ, we are also found
to be sinners, is Christ then the minister of sin? It cannot be!
18But if I build again that which I tore
down, I make myself a transgressor.
19For through the law I died to the
law, so that I might live to God.
20I am crucified with Christ. It is no
longer I who lives, but Christ Who
lives in me. And the life that I now live
in the flesh, I live by the faith of the
Son of God, Who loved me and gave
Himself for me.
21I do not invalidate the grace of
God. For if being made righteous
comes through the law, then Christ
died for no reason.

3 O foolish Galatians! Who has be-
witched you against the truth? It
was before your eyes that Jesus Christ
was openly crucified.
2This one thing I want to learn from
you: did you receive the Spirit through
the works of the law or through the report of faith?
3Are you so foolish? Having begun
by the Spirit, are you now perfected by
the flesh?
4Did you suffer so much for nothing,
if indeed it was for nothing?
5Well then, He who supplies you the
Spirit and works works of power
among you, is it through the works of
the law or through the report of faith?
6Just as Abraham believed God and it
was credited to him for righteousness.
7So then, you know that those of

faith are Abraham's sons.

8And the scripture, knowing beforehand that God would make the Gentiles righteous out of faith, proclaimed the gospel to Abraham, "All the Gentiles shall be blessed in you."

9Therefore, those who are of faith are blessed with faithful Abraham.

10For as long as you are of the works of the law, you are under a curse, for it is written, "Cursed is everyone who does not continue in everything written in the book of the law to do them."

11Now it is evident that no one is righteous before God by the law, for the righteous live by faith!

12But the law is not of faith, but the man who observes it lives by it.

13Christ set us free from the curse of the law, being made a curse for us, for it is written, "Cursed is everyone who hangs upon a tree,"

14that the blessing of Abraham might come unto the Gentiles by Christ Jesus, so that we might receive the promise of the Spirit through faith.

15Brothers, I speak according to men: once a man ratifies a covenant, it cannot be nullified nor added to.

16Now to Abraham were the promises made and to his seed. He does not say, "and to the seeds," as of many, but as from one, "and to your Seed," Who is Christ.

17Now I say this: a covenant having been ratified by God in Christ, the law, which came 430 years later, cannot annul it so as to make the promise of no effect.

18For if the inheritance comes from the law, it is no more promise– but God granted it to Abraham through the promise.

19Why the law then? It was added because of transgression, until the Seed should come to whom it has been promised. And it was put into place by angels in the hand of a mediator.

20Now the mediator is not one, but God is One.

21Is the Law against the promises of God? No, for if a law had been given that had power to give life, then righteousness would have indeed come by the Law.

22But the scripture confined everyone under sin, that the promise through faith in Jesus Christ might be given to those who believe.

23Now before the faith came, we were detained, confined under the law until the faith could be revealed.

24Therefore, the law was our guardian until Christ, so that we might be made righteous through faith.

25Now that faith has come, we are no longer under a guardian.

26For all of you are sons of God through the faith in Jesus Christ.

27For as many as were baptized into Christ were clothed with Christ.

28There is no longer Jew or Greek, there is no longer slave or servant, there is no longer male or female, for all of you are one in Christ Jesus.

29And if you are Christ's, then you are Abraham's offspring and are heirs according to the promise.

4 Now I tell you, for as long as an heir is an infant, he is no different from a slave, even though he is lord of all.

2Rather, they are under guard-ians and trustees until the date set by the father.

3So also with us– when we were infants, we were enslaved to the elements of the world,

4but when the fullness of time had

come, God sent His Son to be born of a
woman, born under the law,
5so that those under the law might be
delivered, so that we might receive sonship.
6And because you are sons, God has
sent forth the Spirit of His Son into our
hearts crying out "Abba! Father!"
7Therefore, you are no longer a servant, but a son, and if a son then also
an heir of God through Christ.
8Yet at the time when you did not
know God, you were servants to them
who by nature are not gods.
9And now that you know God, or
rather are known by God, how can you
turn again to the weak and miserable
elements, which you desire to be in
bondage to again?
10You observe months, and times,
and years.
11I am afraid for you, lest somehow I
have labored over you in vain.
12Brethren, I beseech you to be as I
am, for I am also as you are. You have
not wronged me in anything.
13But you know that in weakness of
flesh I preached the Gospel to you at
the first.
14And my trial that I suffered in my
flesh you did not despise, nor rejected
me with contempt, but as an angel of
God you received me as Christ Jesus.
15What then has become of your
happiness? For I bear you record that,
if it had been possible, you would have
plucked out your own eyes and given
them to me.
16So have I become your enemy by
speaking the truth to you?
17They are not rightly zealous of you.
But they desire to exclude you, that you
may be zealous of them.
18But it is good to always be zealous
in something right and not only in my
being present with you.
19My little children of whom I travail
in birth again until Christ is formed in
you:
20I also desired to be present with
you now, and to change my voice, for I
am perplexed about you.
21Tell me, you who desire to be under
the law, do you not hear the law?
22For it is written that Abraham had
two sons, the one by a maid-servant,
and the other by a free woman.
23But the one of the maid-servant
was born according to the flesh, and
the free woman through the promise,
24which things are an allegory. For
these are the two covenants: one from
Mount Sinai– which brought forth
bondage, which is Hagar,
25for Hagar is Mount Sinai in Arabia,
and corresponds to Jerusalem which is
now and is in bondage with her children–
26but Jerusalem which is above is
free, which is the mother of us all.
27For it is written: "Rejoice, O barren
that does not bear. Break forth and cry,
you that have not travailed, for the desolate has many more children than she
who has a husband."
28But we, brethren, like Isaac, are the
children of the promise.
29But, as then– he that was born according to the flesh persecuted him
who was born after the Spirit– so it is
now.
30But what does the scripture say?
Cast out the bond-servant and her son,
for the son of the bond-servant cannot
inherit with the son of the free.
31So then brethren, we are not children of the bond-servant, but of the
free.

5 Stand therefore in the freedom for
which Christ has set us free, and do
not submit again to the yoke of slavery.
2 Listen! I, Paul, am telling you that if
you are circumcised, Christ will be of
no benefit to you.
3 And again I testify to every man
who is being circumcised: he is obligated to do the whole Law.
4 Everyone made righteous by the
Law has cut themselves off from
Christ– you have fallen from grace.
5 For we through the Spirit by faith
eagerly await the expectation of righteousness.
6 For in Christ Jesus neither circumcision nor uncircumcision matters, but
faith working through love.
7 You were running well– who hindered you, persuading you from the
truth?
8 This persuasion is not of Him Who
calls you.
9 A little leaven leavens the whole
lump.
10 I am persuaded of you in the Lord
that you will have no other mind, and
the one who is troubling you will bear
the judgment, whoever he is.
11 But brethren, If I still preach circumcision, why am I being persecuted?
For then the offense of the cross has
been done away with.
12 I would that they who trouble you
would cut themselves off.
13 For brethren, you were called into
freedom, only do not use this freedom
as an occasion for the flesh, but by love
serve one another.
14 For the whole law is fulfilled in one
word: you shall love your neighbor as
yourself.
15 But if you bite and devour one another, take heed that you are not consumed by one another.
16 But I say: walk in the Spirit and you
will not fulfill the lust of the flesh.
17 For fleshly desires are against the
Spirit, and the Spirit is against the
fleshly desires, and these are opposed
to each other so that you would never
do your will.
18 But if you are Spirit-led, you are not
under the Law.
19 Now the works of the flesh are
manifested, which are adultery, sexual
immorality, uncleanness, lascivious-
ness,
20 idolatry, magic, enmity, strife, jealousies, rage, rivalry, dissension, here-
sies,
21 envy, intoxication, reveling, and
things like this– as I have forewarned
you, as also I told you before, that they
who practice such things will not inherit the Kingdom of God.
22 The fruit of the Spirit is love, joy,
peace, long-suffering, kindness, goodness, faith,
23 meekness, self control– against
such things there is no law.
24 And they that belong to Christ have
crucified the flesh with its passions and
lust.
25 If we live in the Spirit, let us keep
rank with the Spirit.
26 We should not become conceited,
provoking one another, envying one
another.

6 Brethren, if any man is taken in
some wrong-doing, you who are
spiritual restore such a one in the spirit
of meekness, considering yourself, lest
you also be tempted.
2 Bear one another's burdens and
thereby fulfill the law of Christ.
3 For if anyone supposes that he is
something, being nothing, he deceives
himself.

4 But let each one prove his own work, then his reason to boast will be in himself alone and not in another.

5 For each one shall bear his own load.

6 Let the one who is taught in the word share in all good things with the one who teaches.

7 Be not deceived: God will not be mocked– for whatever a man sows, that shall he also reap.

8 For he who sows to the flesh shall reap corruption from the flesh, but he who sows to the Spirit shall reap from the Spirit life eternal.

9 But do not be discouraged in doing well, for you shall reap if you do not become weary.

10 So then, when we have an opportunity, we should do good to all, especially those of the household of faith.

11 See how large of a letter I wrote to you with my own hand.

12 As many as desire to make a good showing in the flesh compel you to be circumcised, only that they may not be persecuted for the cross of Christ.

13 For neither they who are being circumcised themselves keep the law, but wish you to be circumcised so that they may boast in your flesh.

14 But may I not boast except in the cross of our Lord Jesus Christ, through Whom the world is crucified to me, and I to the world.

15 For in Christ Jesus neither circumcision is of any force, nor uncircumcision, but a new creation.

16 And as many as shall walk by this rule, peace upon you and mercy, and upon the Israel of God.

17 For the rest, let no one cause trouble for me, for I bear the marks of the Lord Jesus in my body.

18 The grace of our Lord Jesus Christ be with your spirit, brethren. Amen.

THE EPISTLE OF PAUL THE APOSTLE TO THE

EPHESIANS

1 Paul, an apostle of Jesus Christ by the will of God, to the holy ones, which are at Ephesus, and to the faithful in Christ Jesus.

2 Grace and peace to you from God our Father, and from the Lord Jesus Christ.

3 Blessed is the God and Father of our Lord Jesus Christ, who has blessed us in Christ with all spiritual blessings in heaven.

4 Just as He has chosen us in Him before the overthrow of the world, we should be holy and without blemish before Him in love.

5 He predestined us to sonship unto Himself by Jesus Christ, according to the good pleasure of His will,

6 to the glorious praise of His grace, that endowed us with grace in the Beloved,

7 in whom we possess redemption through His blood, the release from trespasses, according to the riches of His grace,

8 which abounds to us in all wisdom and insight.

9 He has made known to us the mystery of His will, according to His good pleasure, which He has set forth in Him,

10 overseeing the fullness of times, to bring together all things in Christ, both which are in Heaven and which are in Earth, in Him–

11 in Whom also we have obtained an inheritance, having been appointed according to the plan of Him who works all things after the counsel of His own will,

12 that we should be to the praise of His glory, who first had confidence in Christ–

13 in Whom you also, when you heard the Word of truth, the gospel of your salvation, in whom, you also believing, were sealed with that Holy Spirit of promise,

14 which is the first installment of our inheritance, as a ransom payment for the purchased possession, unto the praise of His glory.

15 Therefore I also, after I heard of your faith in the Lord Jesus, and love unto all the holy ones,

16 cease not to give thanks for you, making petition for you in my prayers,

17 that the God of our Lord Jesus Christ, the Father of glory, may give unto you the spirit of wisdom and revelation in the knowledge of Him–

18 the eyes of your understanding being enlightened to know the expectation of His calling, and what is the riches of the glory of His inheritance in the holy ones,

19 and what is the exceeding greatness of His power to us who believe, according to the working power of His mighty strength,

20 which He worked in Christ, when He raised Him from the dead, and set Him at His own right hand in the heavens,

21 far above all principality, and authority, and power, and dominion, and every name that is named, not only in this age, but also in the one to come,

22 and has placed all things under His feet, and appointed Him the head over all the church,

23 who is His body, the fullness of Him that fills all in all.

2 But you were dead in your trespasses and sins,

2 according to that which you once walked in, after the age of this world according to the ruler, the authority of the atmosphere, the spirit that now

works in the sons of disobedience.

3 In this we also all conducted ourselves in the desire of our flesh, fulfilling the will of the flesh and of the imagination, and were by nature children of wrath even as others.

4 But God who is rich in mercy through His abundant love with which He has loved us,

5 even when we were dead in trespasses, made us alive together with Christ– by grace you are saved–

6 and has raised us up together, and has made us sit together in the heavens in Christ Jesus,

7 so that throughout the ages to come He might demonstrate the immeasurable riches of His grace in kindness towards us by Christ Jesus.

8 For by grace you are saved through faith, and that not of yourselves– it is the gift of God,

9 not of works, so that none may boast.

10 For we are His workmanship, created in Christ Jesus unto good works, which God ordained that we should walk in them.

11 For this reason remember that you were once Gentiles in the flesh, called uncircumcised by those called circumcised in the flesh made by hands.

12 Because at that time you were separated from Christ, alienated from the citizenship of Israel, and strangers to the covenants of promise, having no hope and without God in this world.

13 But now in Christ Jesus, you who were once far away have been brought near by the blood of Christ.

14 For He is our Peace, Who has made both of us one, and dissolved the enmity, the middle wall of partition, in His flesh,

15 abolishing the Law of commandments in ordinances, so that in Himself He created of the two one new man, making peace,

16 and completely exchanged both to God in one body through the cross, destroying the enmity in Himself,

17 and came proclaiming peace to you that were far away and those that were near.

18 For through Him we are both brought by one Spirit to the Father.

19 Now then, you are no longer foreigners and strangers, but are fellow citizens, holy ones, and of the house of God,

20 built upon the foundation of the apostles and prophets– Christ Jesus Himself being the cornerstone,

21 in Whom the whole building fitted together grows into a holy temple in the Lord,

22 in Whom also you are built together into a habitation of God by the Spirit.

3 For this reason, I, Paul, the servant of Jesus Christ for the sake of you Gentiles,

2 surely you have heard of the grace of God given to me to administer to you,

3 that by revelation He made known to me the mystery as I have briefly written.

4 Thus reading will enable you to perceive my understanding in the mystery of Christ.

5 In other generations it was not made known to the sons of men as it is now revealed by the Spirit to His holy apostles and prophets,

6 that the Gentiles should be co-inheritors and of the same body, and joint partakers of the promise in Christ through the gospel,

7 of which I have become a minister

according to the gift of the grace of God given to me according to the mighty working of His power.

8 To me, who am less than the least of all the holy ones, is this grace given, to announce to the Gentiles the good news of the unfathomable riches of Christ,

9 and to give light to all of the mystery of the fellowship, which has been hidden from the ages in God, Who created everything through Jesus Christ,

10 in order to now make known through the church the manifold wisdom of God to rulers and authorities in the heavens,

11 according to the plan of the ages, which was made in Christ Jesus our Lord,

12 in Whom we have boldness and access by confidence through His faith,

13 on which account you should not lose heart by my tribulation for you, which is your glory.

14 For this reason, I bow my knee to the Father of our Lord Jesus Christ,

15 from Whom the whole family in Heaven and on Earth are named,

16 so that He would grant you according to the riches of His glory, to be strengthened with power by His Spirit in the inner man,

17 that Christ may dwell in your heart by faith, being rooted and grounded in love.

18 So that you may have strength to comprehend, with all the saints, what is the breadth and length and height and depth,

19 and to know the love of Christ that surpasses knowledge so that you may be filled with all the fullness of God.

20 Now to Him Who has the power to do super-abundantly above all that we think or ask according to the power that works in us,

21 unto Him be glory in the church by Jesus Christ, throughout all the generations the age of the ages, amen!

4 I call to you myself, as the prisoner of the Lord, to walk worthy of the calling to which you are called,

2 with all humility and meekness–with longsuffering forbearing one another in love.

3 Giving diligence to keep the oneness of the Spirit in the bond of peace,

4 as one body and one Spirit, just as you are called into one expectation of your calling.

5 One Lord, one faith, one baptism,

6 one God and Father of all, Who is over all, and through all, and in all.

7 And to each of us is given grace, according to the measure of the gift of Christ,

8 on which account He said, "Ascending up on high, He led captivity captive, and gave gifts unto men."

9 Now that He ascended, is it not He that also went down first into the lower parts of the earth?

10 He that descended is also He Who ascended up above all the heavens, so that He might fill all,

11 and He gave the apostles, and the prophets, and the evangelists, and the pastors, and teachers,

12 for the perfecting of the holy ones; for the work of ministry, for the building up of the body of Christ–

13 until we all come to the oneness of faith and the full knowledge of the Son of God, unto a perfect man, to the measure of the maturity of the fullness of Christ,

14 so that we are no longer children tossed by the waves and carried about with every wind of doctrine by the

trickery of men and craft by which
deceivers mislead.
15But speaking the truth in love, we
may grow up into Christ in all things
Who is Himself the Head,
16from whom all the body is joined
and knitted together by every ligament
that provides support, so that each in-
dividual part functions effectively, providing for the growth of the body as it
builds itself up in love.
17This I say then, and testify in the
Lord: you shall no longer walk as also
the Gentiles walk in the vanity of their
mind,
18having their thoughts darkened,
strangers from the life of God through
the ignorance that is in them because
of the callousness of their heart–
19who themselves have lost all
sensitivity are given over to sexual
immorality, to every kind of uncleanness, with a desire for more.
20But you have not learned this from
Christ,
21if you have heard Him and been
taught by Him as the truth is in Jesus.
22You shall lay aside, concerning the
former behavior, the old man, which is
corrupt according to deceitful desires,
23and let your mind be renewed by
the Spirit.
24And be endued with the new man,
which is created after God in righteousness and true holiness.
25For this reason, lay aside lying,
speak the truth everyone with his
neighbor, for we are members one of
another.
26Be angry and sin not– let not the
sun go down on your anger,
27and give no place to the Devil.
28The thief must no longer steal, but
rather labor, doing good work with his
own hands so that he may have something to share with the needy.
29Do not allow a bad word to come
out of your mouth, but instead that
which is good to serve, to edify the
hearer that grace may be supplied.
30And do not grieve the Holy Spirit
of God, by Whom you are sealed unto
the day of redemption.
31Let all bitterness, wrath, anger,
yelling, and slander be lifted from you,
along with all wickedness.
32But having kindness to one
another, being tenderhearted, forgiving
one another even also as God through
Christ has forgiven you.

5 Be then imitators of God as loving
children,
2and walk in love, even as also Christ
loved us and gave Himself over for us,
an offering and sacrifice to God as a
sweet-smelling fragrance.
3But sexual immorality and impurity
of any kind, or covetousness, shall not
be named once among you as true holy
ones.
4Also, obscenity and foolish talking
or joking, which is entirely out of place,
but instead thanksgiving.
5Indeed you recognize and know
this: that all sexual immorality, or impure, or a covetous one, who is an idolater, has no inheritance in the Kingdom of Christ and God.
6Let none deceive you with vain
words, because of these things the
wrath of God comes upon the sons of
disobedience.
7Become not then their co-inheritors.
8Indeed you were once darkness, but
now light in the Lord– walk as children
of light–
9for the fruit of the Spirit is in all
goodness, and righteousness, and
truth,

10proving what is pleasing to the
Lord.
11And have no fellowship with the
unfruitful works of darkness, but
rather reprove it.
12For it is shameful to speak of the
things they do in secret.
13And all things being exposed by the
light are made manifest.
14For everything that reveals is light,
therefore say, "wake up, oh sleeper, and
arise from the dead, and Christ will
shine on you."
15Therefore, watch by what means
you walk accurately, not as unwise but
as wise,
16redeeming the time, for the day is
evil.
17For this reason, do not be foolish,
but understand the will of the Lord.
18And be not intoxicated with wine,
as one unsaved, but be filled with the
Spirit,
19speaking to yourselves in psalms,
and hymns, and spiritual songs, singing
and making melody in your heart to
the Lord,
20giving thanks at all times for all
things to God and the Father in the
name of our Lord Jesus Christ,
21being submitted one to another in
fear of God.
22Wives be in submission to your
own husbands as to the Lord,
23because the man is the head of the
woman, even as also Christ is the Head
of His church, the Savior of the body.
24But even as the church is subject to
Christ, so also the wives to their own
husbands in everything.
25Husbands, love your wives, even as
also Christ loves the church and delivered Himself over for her,
26so that she may be sanctified and
cleansed with the washing of the water
by the word.
27So that He might present to Himself a glorious church, not having spot,
or wrinkle, or any such thing, but that
she should be holy and without blemish.
28So also the men owe it to love their
wives as their own body– he who loves
his wife loves himself.
29For no one ever hated his flesh, but
nourished and cherished her, even as
also the Lord the church.
30For we are members of His body,
31of His flesh and of His bones, "For
this reason a man shall leave his father
and mother, and shall cleave to his
wife, and the two shall become one".
32This is a great mystery, but I speak
as to Christ and to the church.
33Yet still also, everyone should love
his wife as himself, and the wife should
reverence her husband.

6 Children, obey your parents in the
Lord, for this is righteous.
2Honor your father and your mother– this is the first commandment with
promise:
3"So that it will be well for you, and
you shall live a long time upon the
land."
4And fathers, provoke not your children, but bring them up in the discipline and instruction of the Lord.
5Servants, obey your masters according to the flesh with fear and trembling, in singleness of your heart as to
Christ.
6Not just with a show as a man pleas-
er, but as servants of Christ doing the
will of God from the soul.
7Serve with good will as to the Lord
and not men,
8knowing that everyone who shall do
good, the same shall receive of the

Lord, whether servant or free.
9Also, masters, do the same to them–
restrain from threatening, knowing
also that your Master is in Heaven, and
He is no respecter of persons.
10Finally, be strong in the Lord, and
in the strength of His manifest power.
11Be endued with the whole armor of
God so that you can stand against the
craft of the Devil,
12because we are not wrestling
against flesh and blood, but against the
principalities, against the authorities,
against the rulers of this world, the
darkness of this age, against the spiritual iniquity in the heavens.
13Now take up the whole armor of
God, that you may have the ability to
stand in the time of evil, and having
conquered all, stand.
14Stand then, having your loins girded with truth, and endued with the
breastplate of righteousness.
15And bind your feet with the preparation of the gospel of peace.
16In everything taking up the shield
of faith, with which you will be able to
quench all the fiery darts of the wicked.
17And receive the helmet of salvation,
and the sword of the Spirit, which is
the proclamation of God's Word.
18Pray in the Spirit at all times in
every prayer and petition, and through
it stay alert with all persistence and
intercession for all the saints,
19and on my behalf that a word may
be given to me in the opening of my
mouth, by boldly making known the
mystery of the gospel–
20on behalf of which I am an ambassador in bonds, that in it I may speak
boldly even as I ought to speak.
21But that you may also know what I
do, Tychicus, the beloved brother and
faithful servant in the Lord, shall make
known everything to you,
22whom I will send to you so that you
may know how we are doing and encourage your heart.
23Peace to the brethren, and love with
faith from Father God and the Lord
Jesus Christ.
24Grace to all who sincerely love our
Lord Jesus Christ, Amen!

The Epistle of Paul the Apostle to the
Philippians

1 Paul and Timothy, servants of Christ Jesus, to all the holy ones in Christ Jesus who are in Philippi with the bishops and deacons.

2 Grace to you and peace from God our Father and the Lord Jesus Christ.

3 I thank my God upon every remembrance of you,

4 continually, in all my prayers for all of you, making my prayer with joy

5 over your fellowship in the gospel from the first until now.

6 Being confident that He Who began a good work in you will finish it until the day of Jesus Christ.

7 It is righteous for me to think this way of you all, because I hold you in my heart, both in my imprisonment and in the defense and confirmation of the gospel, for you are all fellow-partakers of my grace.

8 For God is my witness how I long after you all in the deepest affections of Jesus Christ.

9 And this I pray: that your love may abound more and more in knowledge and discernment,

10 that you approve what is excellent, that you may be pure and blameless unto the day of Christ,

11 being filled with the fruits of righteousness, which are by Jesus Christ to the glory and praise of God.

12 But I would like you to know, brethren, that these things that happened to me turned out to advance the gospel

13 so that it has become known to the whole imperial guard and all the rest that my imprisonment is for Christ.

14 And most of the brethren in the Lord, becoming more confident by my imprisonment, dare to speak the word of God fearlessly.

15 Some truly preach Christ out of envy and strife, but some also out of good will.

16 Some preach Christ truly out of contention, not sincerely, thinking that they will add affliction to my imprisonment.

17 But others out of love, knowing that I am appointed for a defense for the gospel.

18 What then? Whether in pretense or in truth, Christ is preached– and in that I rejoice and will rejoice.

19 And I know that this shall lead to my deliverance through your prayers and the supply of the Spirit of Jesus Christ.

20 As it is my eager and confident expectation that I will not be ashamed, but in every way confident that now, as always, Christ will be magnified in my body, whether through life or through death.

21 For to me to live is Christ and to die is gain.

22 But if I live in the flesh, this is the fruit of my work, and what I would choose I do not know,

23 for I am pressed by the two desires. For departing and being with Christ is much better,

24 but to remain in the flesh is more necessary for your sake.

25 And being persuaded of this, I know that I shall abide and continue with you all for your advancement and joy of faith,

26 so that in me, through my presence with you again, your boasting may abound in Christ Jesus.

27 Only let your conduct be worthy of the gospel of Christ, so that whether I come and see you, or being absent, hear about you, that you stand unmovable in one Spirit as one soul, contending for the faith of the gospel!

[28]And do not be intimidated in anything by the opposition, which is a clear sign of their destruction, but of your salvation, and this from God.
[29]For it was granted to you for the sake of Christ not only to believe in Him, but to suffer for His sake,
[30]having the same conflict that you saw in me, and now hear of in me.

2 Therefore, if there is any comfort in Christ, if any consolation of love, if any fellowship in the Spirit, if any affection and compassion,
[2]fulfill my joy by thinking the same, having the same love, being one in Spirit, being of one mind.
[3]Do nothing out of selfish ambition or desire for praise, but in humility regarding others better than yourself.
[4]Let each person be more concerned about the interest of others, rather than one's own interest.
[5]Let this mind that was in Christ Jesus be also in you,
[6]Who, being in the form of God, did not consider equality with God as something that could be grasped,
[7]but made Himself void. He took the form of a servant and was made in the likeness of men.
[8]And in form being found as man, he humbled himself and became obedient unto death, even the death of the cross.
[9]Therefore God has highly exalted Him and given to Him a name that is above every name,
[10]that at the name of Jesus, every knee shall bow in heaven and on earth and under the earth.
[11]And every tongue shall confess that Jesus Christ is Lord to the glory of God the Father.
[12]Therefore, my beloved, as you have always obeyed, not as in my presence only, but much more in my absence, work out your own salvation with fear and trembling,
[13]for it is God who works within you both to will and to work according to His own good pleasure.
[14]Do all things without complaining and arguing
[15]so that you may be without blemish and pure, God's perfect children in the midst of a crooked and perverse generation among whom you shine as lights in the world,
[16]holding fast to the word of life so that I may boast in the day of Christ that I did not run in vain nor labor in vain.
[17]Even if I am to be poured out as a drink offering upon the sacrifice and ministry of your faith, I am glad and rejoice with you all.
[18]Likewise you should be glad and rejoice with me.
[19]But my expectation in the Lord Jesus is to send Timothy to you soon, that I also may be encouraged by news of the things concerning you.
[20]For I have no one like-minded who will be genuinely concerned for your welfare,
[21]for they are all seeking things for themselves, not the things of Christ Jesus,
[22]for you know the proof of him: that as a son with a father he has served with me in the Gospel.
[23]Therefore, I expect to send him at once, as soon as I see how things will go with me,
[24]and I am persuaded in the Lord that I myself also will soon come to you.
[25]And I have regarded it necessary to send Epaphroditus to you, my brother,

fellow-worker, and my fellow-soldier, but your messenger and minister to my need,

26 since he was longing after you all, and was also deeply distressed because you heard that he was sick.

27 For indeed he was sick, coming near to death, but God had mercy on him and not only him but also me, that I might not have grief upon grief.

28 Therefore, the more diligently I send him, that when you see him you might rejoice and that I might be less anxious.

29 Therefore, receive him in the Lord with all joy, and hold such in honor,

30 because for the sake of the work of Christ he was near to death, having disregarded his own life, that he might fulfill what you lacked in your service toward me.

3 Rest my brothers, rejoice in the Lord. To write the same thing to you is not irritating to me but is safe for you.

2 Look out for dogs, look out for evil workers, look out for the circumcisers.

3 For we are the circumcision who worship by the Spirit of God, and boast in Christ Jesus, and have no confidence in the flesh.

4 For though I might also have confidence in the flesh, if anyone else thinks to be convinced by the flesh, I the more–

5 circumcised the eighth day, of the nation of Israel, of the tribe of Benjamin, a Hebrew of Hebrews,

6 according to zeal, persecuting the church, concerning the righteousness which is in the Law, blameless.

7 But what things were gain to me I have esteemed loss that I might gain Christ.

8 And what is more, I continue to regard everything as loss for the incomprehensible privilege of knowing Christ Jesus my Lord– for whom I have suffered the loss of everything, and consider it dung, that I might win Christ!

9 And being found in Him, not having my own righteousness from the Law, but that which is through the faith of Christ, righteousness by the faith from God:

10 To know Him and the power of His resurrection and the fellowship of His sufferings, to be conformed to His death.

11 If by any way I may attain to the resurrection of the dead,

12 not as though I had already attained or were already finished, but I pursue, that I might also apprehend, that for which I am apprehended by Christ Jesus.

13 Brethren, I count myself to have not yet apprehended, but one thing I do: forgetting the things that are behind, and stretching forward to the things that are before, I press on toward the goal unto the prize of the high calling of God in Christ Jesus.

14 I passionately pursue the purpose that controls every movement of my life: the crowning award of the high calling of God in Christ Jesus.

15 Therefore, as many as are mature should be of this same mind, and if anyone should think differently, God will also reveal this to you.

16 But in what we have attained, walk by the same rule– be of the same mind.

17 Brethren, be imitators together of me and look for those walking as you have us for examples.

18 For many are walking, of whom I have told you often before and now also tell you weeping– I say these are

enemies of the cross of Christ,
19 whose end is destruction, whose
god is their bellies, and they glory in
their shame, who mind earthly things.
20 For our citizenship is in heaven, the
place from where we look for the Savior, the Lord Jesus Christ,
21 Who will transform our humble
bodies to be conformed to the glory of
His body, according to the working of
His ability, by which He is able to subdue all things to Himself.

4 So then, my beloved and very dear
brethren, you are my joy and
crown. Therefore beloved, stand fast in
the Lord.
2 I plead with you, Euodias, and I
plead with you, Syntyche: be in agreement in the Lord.
3 And I ask you also, true fellow-
workers, help those women who
labored in the gospel with me and
Clement along with my other helpers
whose names are in the Book of Life.
4 Rejoice in the Lord always, and
again, I say: rejoice!
5 Let your gentleness be known to all
men– the Lord is near.
6 Don't be troubled about anything,
but by all petition and prayer with
thanksgiving, let your requests be
made known to God,
7 and the peace of God, which surpasses all understanding, will guard
your heart and your mind in Christ Jesus.
8 Finally brethren, whatever is true,
whatever is honorable, whatever is upright, whatever is pure, whatever is
pleasing, whatever is of good report, if
there be any excellence, if there be anything worthy of praise, think on these
things.
9 And that which you have learned
and received and heard and seen in me,
do, and the God of peace shall be with
you.
10 But now I rejoice in the Lord that at
length you have revived your concern
for me, although also you were concerned about me but lacked opportunity.
11 Not that I speak of lack, for I have
learned whatever I am in to be content.
12 I know how to be brought low and I
know how to abound. In everything
and in all things I have learned the secret of plenty and hunger, abundance
and need.
13 In all things I am strong through
Christ Who strengthens me.
14 But you did well to have fellowship
in my trial.
15 And you Philippians also know that
in the beginning of the gospel, when I
left Macedonia, no church entered into
partnership, with an account of giving
and receiving, except you.
16 Because also in Thessalonica you
sent help twice for my needs.
17 Not that I seek after a gift, but I
seek after fruit that abounds to your
account.
18 But I have all things and abound. I
am well-supplied, having received from
Epaphroditus the things from you– an
odor of a sweet smell, a sacrifice well
pleasing to God.
19 And my God will supply all of your
needs according to His riches in glory
in Christ Jesus.
20 And to our God and Father be glory to the ages of the ages. Amen.
21 Greet every holy one in Christ Jesus. The brethren with me greet you.
22 All the holy ones in Christ Jesus
greet you, especially those of Caesar's
household.
23 The grace of the Lord Jesus Christ
be with you all. Amen.

The Epistle of Paul the Apostle to the
Colossians

1

Paul, an apostle of Jesus Christ
through the will of God, and brother Timothy,
2 to those in Colosse, holy ones and
faithful brethren in Christ. Grace to
you– peace from our Father God and
our Lord Jesus Christ.
3 We give thanks to God, the Father of
our Lord Jesus Christ, praying always
for you,
4 hearing of your faith in Christ Jesus
and love for all the holy ones.
5 For the confidence being stored up
for you in heaven, which you heard before in the word of truth of the gospel,
6 that has come unto you, as also in all
the world, and is bringing forth fruit,
just as in you also, from the day you
heard and knew the grace of God in
truth.
7 Just as you learned from Epapharas,
our beloved fellow-servant, who is a
faithful minister of Christ on your
behalf,
8 who also declared to us your love in
the Spirit.
9 Because of this also, from the day we
heard, we ceased not to pray for you
also, asking that you might be filled
with the knowledge of His will in all
wisdom and spiritual understanding,
10 that you walk worthily of the Lord
in every way being pleasing, being
fruitful in every good work and grow-
ing in the knowledge of God,
11 strengthened with all power according to His glorious might unto all
patience and endurance with joyful-
ness,
12 giving thanks to the Father Who
has made us fit to be partakers of the
inheritance of the saints in light,
13 Who has delivered us from the authority of darkness and translated us
into the Kingdom of His beloved Son,
14 in Whom we have redemption, the
forgiveness of sins,
15 Whose image is that of the invisible
God, first-born of all creation.
16 For by Him, everything in the
heavens and upon the earth was created, the visible and invisible– whether
thrones or dominions or rulers or authorities– everything was created
through Him and for Him.
17 And He is before everything, and
everything was established by Him.
18 And He is the Head of the body, the
church, Who is the beginning, first-
born from the dead, that He may have
first-place in all things.
19 For it was pleasing that in Him all
fullness should dwell,
20 and by Him to completely restore
everything to Him, whether upon the
earth or in the heavens, making peace
through the blood of His cross.
21 And you were once alienated and
enemies in thought by your wicked
works, yet now He has changed
22 in the body of His flesh through
death that you may be able to stand before Him holy and without blemish and
blameless.
23 If you continue on in the faith, firm
and settled, and not being removed
from the confidence of the gospel that
you have heard, which was proclaimed
in all of the creation under the heaven,
of which I, Paul, have become a minister,
24 Who now rejoices in these sufferings over you– and I fill up that which
is lacking of the tribulations of Christ
in my flesh for His body, which is the
church,
25 for which I have become a minister
according to the administration of God
given me for you to fulfill the Word of
God–

26 the mystery that was hidden from the ages and from the generations, but is now made known to His saints,

27 by whom God would make known among the Gentiles what are the riches of the glory, which is Christ in you, the confidence of glory,

28 which we preach, warning every man and teaching every man in all wisdom, that we may present every man perfect in Christ Jesus,

29 to Whom I also labor, contending according to His working that operates in me by power.

2

I would like for you to know that I have had a great conflict for your sake, and for those in Laodicea, and as many as have not seen my face in the flesh,

2 that your hearts might be encouraged, joined together in love and unto all riches of the full assurance of the understanding unto an exact knowledge of the mystery of God and the Father and the Christ,

3 in Whom are hidden all the treasures of wisdom and knowledge.

4 This I say, that you let no one deceive you with persuasive speech.

5 For even if I am absent in the flesh, yet in the spirit I am present with you, rejoicing and beholding your order and the firmness of your faith in Christ.

6 Therefore, as you have received Christ Jesus the Lord, walk in Him,

7 being rooted and built up in Him and established in the faith, abounding in thanksgiving, as you have been taught.

8 Beware that you are not spoiled by philosophies and vain deceits, according to the traditions of men, according to principles of the world, and not according to Christ.

9 For in Him dwells all of the fullness of the Deity bodily.

10 And you are complete in Him, Who is the Head of every ruler and authority,

11 in whom also you were circumcised with a circumcision made without hands in the removal of the body of the sins of the flesh by the circumcision of Christ,

12 being buried with Him by baptism, in Whom also you are raised up through the activity of the faith of God, Who raised Him from the dead.

13 And you, being dead in the trespasses and the uncircumcision of your flesh, He made you alive together with Him, having pardoned all your trespasses,

14 wiping out the certificate of indebtedness, the decrees that were set against us, and took it out of the midst, nailing it to the cross,

15 having stripped the rulers and authorities, exposing them by openly triumphing over them in it.

16 Therefore, let no one judge you in eating and drinking or participating in festivals, or new moons, or Sabbaths.

17 This is a shadow of future things, but the body is of Christ.

18 Let no one rob you of your prize, insisting on self-abasement, a worship of angels, intruding into things which he has not seen– without cause being puffed up from the mind of his flesh.

19 And not holding the Head, from Whom all the body– being supplied and being knit together through the joints and bands– increases with the increase of God.

20 If you died together with Christ from the rudiments of the world, why do you subject yourself to ordinances as living in the world?

21 Do not handle, or taste, or touch,

22 Which all will perish with the using after the religious precepts and teachings of men–

23 Which things indeed have an appearance of wisdom in promoting self-made religion and humility and unsparing treatment of the body, having no value for the indulgence of the flesh.

3

If you then are risen together with Christ, seek those things that are above, where Christ is seated on the right hand of God.

2 Set your affection on things that are above, not on things of this earth.

3 For you died, and your life is hidden with Christ in God.

4 Whenever Christ our life is manifested, then you also shall be manifested with Him in glory.

5 Let your members that are upon the earth be dead then to sexual immorality, uncleanness, inordinate affection, evil desires, and covetousness, which is idolatry–

6 because of these, the wrath of God comes upon the sons of disobedience,

7 in which you also once walked when you lived in them.

8 But now you shall also lay aside all these: wrath, anger, malice, slander, filthy language from your mouth.

9 Do not lie one to another, seeing that the old man has been stripped off with his deeds.

10 And being endued with the new, which is renewed unto a full knowledge after the image of the One Who created Him–

11 where there is neither Greek and Jew, circumcision and uncircumcision, Barbarian, Scythian, slave, nor free, but Christ, Who is all in all–

12 be endued then, as the elect of God, holy and beloved, with deepest inward mercy, kindness, humility, gentleness, long-suffering,

13 being tolerant with one another and gracious to each other. If anyone has a complaint against anyone, just as Christ was gracious to you, so should you also be.

14 And above all of these, love, which is the bond of perfection.

15 And let the peace of God rule your heart, into which you are also called into one body, and be thankful.

16 Let the word of Christ dwell in you richly in all wisdom, teaching and admonishing one another in psalms, in hymns, in spiritual songs, singing with grace in your heart to the Lord.

17 And all that is done in word and in deed, do all in the name of the Lord Jesus, giving thanks to God and the Father through Him.

18 Wives, be submitted to the husbands, as it is proper in the Lord.

19 Husbands, love your wives, and be not bitter toward them.

20 Children, be obedient to your parents in all things, for this is well-pleasing to the Lord.

21 Fathers, do not provoke your children so that they become discouraged.

22 Servants, be obedient to your masters according to the flesh in every way, not with eye-service, as a man-pleaser, but with a generous heart, fearing the Lord.

23 Whatever you may do, work from the soul as to the Lord and not to men,

24 knowing that from the Lord you shall receive the reward, the inheritance serving Christ the Lord.

25 For the one who does wrong shall bear the wrong, and there is no respect of persons.

4 Masters, supply that which is
righteous and fair to your servants,
knowing that you also have a Master in
heaven.
2 Devote yourself to prayer, staying
alert by it with thanksgiving.
3 Also praying for us that God may
open to us a door for the word, to
speak the mystery of Christ, for which
also I am a prisoner,
4 that I may reveal it as I ought to
speak.
5 Walk in wisdom toward them who
are outside, redeeming the time.
6 Let your word always be gracious,
seasoned with salt, that you may know
how to answer everyone.
7 All my affairs shall Tychicus make
known to you, a beloved brother, and
faithful servant, and fellow-laborer in
the Lord,
8 whom I have sent to you for this,
that he may know the things concerning you and comfort your heart.
9 With Onesimus, the faithful and
beloved brother, who is from you, they
shall make known to you all things that
are here.
10 Aristarchus, my fellow prisoner,
greets you. And Mark, the cousin of
Barnabas, about whom you received
orders, if he comes to you, receive him.
11 And Jesus, who is called Justus,
being of the circumcision, these only
are fellow-workers for the Kingdom
of God who have been a comfort to me.
12 Epaphras, who is from you a servant of Jesus Christ, greets you, always
contending on your behalf in prayer
that you may stand perfect and fully
assured in all the will of God.
13 For I bear witness of him that he
has labored much for you and for those
in Laodicea and them in Hierapolis.
14 Luke, the beloved physician, and
Demas, greet you.
15 Greet the brethren in Laodicea, and
Nymphas, and the church in his house.
16 And when this epistle is read
among you, cause that it also be read in
the Laodicean church and that you also
read the one from Laodicea.
17 And say to Archippus, "Take heed
to the ministry that you have received
in the Lord that you fulfill it."
18 The salutation of Paul by my own
hand. Remember my bonds. Grace be
with you. Amen.

The First Epistle of Paul the Apostle to the
Thessalonians

1 Paul and Silvanus and Timothy to
the church of the Thessalonians in
God the Father and the Lord Jesus
Christ– grace to you and peace from
God our Father and the Lord Jesus
Christ.

2 We always give thanks to God for
you all, making mention of you in our
prayers,

3 constantly thinking of your works of
faith, and labor of love, and the persistent expectation of our Lord Jesus
Christ in the presence of our God and
Father,

4 knowing, brethren loved by God,
your election,

5 because our gospel did not come to
you in word only, but also in power,
and in the Holy Spirit, and in full assurance, as you also know who we were
among you for your sake.

6 And you became imitators of us and
of the Lord, having received the word
in much distress and joy of the Holy
Spirit,

7 so that you became examples to all
those who believe in Macedonia and
Achaia.

8 For from you the word of the Lord
rang out, not only in Macedonia and in
Achaia, but also in every place your
faith towards God went out, so that we
have no need to speak of it.

9 For they report to us what sort of
entrance we had among you, and how
you turned to God from idols to serve
the living and true God,

10 and to wait for His Son from heav-
en, Whom He raised from the dead–
Jesus, Who delivers us from the wrath
that is coming.

2 For you yourselves know, brethren,
that our coming to you was not in
vain.

2 Though we suffered and were mistreated in Philippi, as you also know,
we had boldness in our God, declaring
to you the gospel of God in great opposition.

3 For our exhortation was not out of
deceit or of impure motives, nor in
trickery.

4 Rather, as we have also been approved by God to be entrusted with the
gospel, even so we speak, not to please
men, but God, Who examines our
hearts.

5 For neither with flattering words did
we come, as you also know, nor with
motives of greed– God is witness.

6 Neither did we seek praises from
men, nor from you, nor from others,
though we might have made demands
as the apostles of Christ.

7 Rather we were gentle in your midst,
like a nurse cherishing her own children.

8 Having great affection for you, taking delight in imparting to you not
only the gospel of God but also our
own lives, because you have become
dear to us.

9 For remembering, brethren, our labor and toil, for we worked night and
day so that we would not be a burden
to you while we proclaimed the gospel
of God to you.

10 You are witnesses, and God, how
devoted and upright and blameless we
were to you who believe.

11 As you know, like a father with a
child with each one of you, encouraging and admonishing you,

12 and pleading with you to behave
worthily of God, Who has called you to
His own kingdom and glory.

13 Because of this also, we give thanks
to God continually that when you received the word you heard from us, you

received it, not as the word of men, but
as it is in truth: the word of God, which
also works mightily in you who believe.
14For you, brethren, became imitators of the churches of God that are in
Christ Jesus in Judea, because you had
the same suffering also from your own
countrymen as they also did from the
Jews–
15who both killed the Lord Jesus and
their own prophets, and drove us out,
they also do not please God and oppose all men,
16hindering us from speaking to the
Gentiles so that they may be saved,
thus continually filling up their sins.
Now the wrath has finally come down
on them.
17But for us, brothers, being separated from you for a short time in presence, not heart, longing to see your
face with much eagerness.
18For we wanted to come to you, certainly– I, Paul, again and again– but
Satan hindered us.
19For what is our expectation, or joy,
or crown of boasting? Is it not also you
before our Lord Jesus at His coming?
20Oh for you are our glory and joy.

3 Wherefore, being no longer able to
endure, we were happy to be left
alone in Athens.
2And we sent Timothy, our brother
and minister of God, and our fellow-worker in the gospel of Christ, to establish and encourage you concerning
your faith,
3that no one be disturbed by these
tribulations, for yourselves know that
we exist for this.
4For also when we were with you, we
told you beforehand that we were
about to suffer tribulation, even as you
know that it also came to pass.
5Because of this, when I no longer
could endure, I sent to know your faith,
lest in any way the tempter tempted
you and our labor had been in vain.
6But now Timothy has come to us
from you and has brought us the good
news of your faith and love, and that
you always have a good remembrance
of us, longing to see us even as we do
you.
7For this reason, in all our tribulation
and distress, we have been encouraged
by your faith,
8because now we live, if you are
standing fast in the Lord.
9For what thanksgiving can we return unto God for you, for all of the joy
with which we rejoice on account of
you before our God?
10As we ask most earnestly, night and
day, that we may see your face, and
supply the things lacking in your faith.
11Now may our God and Father
Himself, and our Lord Jesus Christ, direct our way to you.
12And the Lord makes you to increase in love one to another and to all
as also we to you,
13so that He may establish your
hearts blameless in holiness before God
and our Father in the coming of Jesus
our Lord with all His holy ones.

4 Finally then, brethren, we ask and
implore you in the Lord Jesus, even
as you received from us how it is necessary for you to walk and please God,
that you walk more and more.
2For you know the instructions that
we gave you through the Lord Jesus.
3For this is the will of God, your
sanctification: that you abstain from
sexual immorality,
4that each of you knows how to control his own vessel in holiness and

honor–
5not with lustful passions, like the
Gentiles who do not know God,
6that no one wrong and exploit his
brother in this matter.
7For God did not call us to moral
impurity, but to holiness.
8Therefore, whoever rejects this rejects not man but God, Who also has
given to us His Holy Spirit.
9Now concerning brotherly love,
there is no need to write to you, for you
yourselves are all taught of God to love
one another.
10For this also you do toward all of
the brethren in the whole of Macedonia, but we implore you to do it more
and more,
11and to have as your ambition to live
quietly and tend your own things, and
to work with your own hands, as we
instructed you,
12so that you may walk properly before outsiders and be dependent on no
one.
13And I do not wish for you to be ignorant, brethren, concerning those
who sleep, that you do not grieve, even
as also the rest who have no expectation.
14For if we believe that Jesus died and
rose again, so also God, through Jesus
Christ, will bring those with Him.
15For this we say to you, by the word
of the Lord, that we who are alive and
remain unto the coming of the Lord
will not precede those who are asleep,
16because the Lord Himself will descend with a shout, with the voice of an
archangel, and with the trumpet of
God, and the dead in Christ shall rise
first.
17Then we who are alive, who remain, shall be caught up together with
them in the clouds for the meeting of
the Lord in the air, and shall always be
with the Lord.
18So exhort one another with these
words.

5 But of the times and seasons,
brethren, you have no need that I
write unto you.
2For you yourselves already perfectly
know that the day of the Lord comes as
a thief in the night.
3For when they shall say, “peace and
safety,” then sudden destruction comes
upon them, as travail on one who is
with child, and they shall not escape.
4But you, brethren, are not of the
darkness that such a day should overtake you as a thief.
5You are all sons of light and sons of
day– we are not of night, nor of darkness.
6So then, we should not sleep, as the
rest also do, but we should watch and
be sober.
7For those who sleep, sleep by night,
and those who have been drunk are
drunk by night.
8But we, being of the day, should be
sober, having put on the breastplate of
faith and love, and the confident expectation of salvation as a helmet.
9For God has not appointed us for
wrath, but to obtain salvation by our
Lord Jesus Christ,
10Who died for us, that whether we
are awake or asleep, we may live together with Him.
11Therefore encourage one another,
and build each other up, even as you
are also doing.
12But we ask you, brethren, to know
those who labor among you, and who
are over you in the Lord and instruct
you,
13and to esteem them very highly in

love for their work's sake. Be at peace
among yourselves.
14But we exhort you, brethren, to
admonish the disorderly, console the
faint-hearted, sustain the weak, and be
patient toward everyone.
15See that no one renders to anyone
evil for evil, but always pursue the
good, both toward one another and
toward all.
16Rejoice always.
17Pray without ceasing.
18In everything give thanks, for this
is the will of God concerning you in
Christ Jesus.
19Do not quench the Spirit.
20Do not despise prophesyings.
21Prove all things. Hold fast to the
good.
22Abstain from every form of evil,
23and the God of peace Himself
makes you holy in every way and complete. And may your entire spirit, and
soul, and body be preserved blameless
unto the coming of our Lord Jesus
Christ.
24Faithful is He Who calls you, Who
will also do it.
25Brethren, pray for us.
26Greet the brethren with a holy kiss.
27I adjure you, by the Lord, that this
epistle be read to all of the holy
brethren.
28The grace of our Lord Jesus Christ
be with you. Amen.

The Second Epistle of Paul the Apostle to the
Thessalonians

1 Paul, Silvanus, and Timothy, to the church of Thessalonica in God the Father and the Lord Jesus Christ.

2 Grace to you and peace from God our Father and the Lord Jesus Christ.

3 We owe it to give thanks to God always for you, brethren, as it is right, because your faith increases beyond measure, and the love of each one of you abounds toward one another,

4 so that we ourselves boast in you in the churches of God because of your patience and faith in all of your persecutions and tribulation that you endure–

5 a proof of the righteous judgment of God to count you worthy of the kingdom of God, for which you also suffer,

6 since it is just with God to pay back tribulation to those afflicting you.

7 And to you who are afflicted, relax with us by the revelation of Jesus Christ from heaven with His mighty angels,

8 in a flame of fire giving vengeance to the ones who do not know God and do not obey the gospel of our Lord Jesus Christ,

9 who will pay the penalty of everlasting destruction from the presence of the Lord and from the glory of His strength

10 when He comes to be glorified in His holy ones and to be admired in all who believe in that day, because you believed our testimony.

11 Unto which we also pray continually for you that our God would count you worthy of the calling and fulfill all the goodness of His good pleasure and work of faith in power,

12 so that the name of our Lord Jesus Christ will be glorified in you, and you in Him, according to the grace of our God and the Lord Jesus Christ.

2 Now we ask you, brethren, on behalf of the coming of our Lord Jesus Christ and our gathering together unto Him,

2 that you should not be quickly shaken in mind and be not troubled, neither by a spirit, nor by word, nor by a letter, as if from us, that the day of Christ has already come.

3 Let no one deceive you in some way, because the apostasy comes first and then the man of sin will be revealed: the son of destruction–

4 he who opposes and exalts himself above all called God or worshiped so as to sit down in the temple of God and declare that he is God.

5 Do you not remember that I told you this while I was still with you?

6 And now you know what holds back the revealing of him in his time.

7 The mystery of iniquity is already at work, but only until the one who restrains is removed.

8 And then the lawless one shall be revealed– whom the Lord shall destroy with the spirit of His mouth and wipe out with the appearance of His coming–

9 who is coming according to the working of Satan in all power and signs and lying wonders,

10 and in all deception of unrighteousness in those being destroyed, because they did not receive the love of the truth in order for them to be saved.

11 And because of this, God will send to them a working of delusion for them to believe the lie,

12 that all may be judged who did not believe the truth but who delighted in unrighteousness.

13 But we owe it to be thankful always to God concerning you, brothers,

beloved by the Lord, because God chose you as first-fruits for salvation by sanctification of the Spirit and belief of the truth,

14 to which He called you through our gospel, to share in the glory of our Lord Jesus Christ.

15 So, then, brothers, stand firm and be strong. Hold the teachings you were taught, whether by word or by our letter.

16 And may our Lord Jesus Christ Himself, and our Father God, Who loves and gives us everlasting encouragement and a good expectation by grace,

17 encourage your hearts, and establish you in every good word and work.

3 Finally, brethren, pray for us, that the word of the Lord may spread rapidly and also be glorified, just as with you,

2 and that we may be delivered from the wicked and evil men, for not every one has faith.

3 But the Lord is faithful Who shall establish you and protect you from the evil.

4 And we have confidence in the Lord regarding you, that you do and will do what we command you.

5 And may the Lord direct your hearts into the love of God and into the perseverance of Christ.

6 And we command you, brethren, in the name of our Lord Jesus Christ that you withdraw yourself from every brother who walks disorderly and not according to the traditions that he received from us.

7 For you yourselves know how it is necessary to imitate us, for we were not disorderly among you.

8 Or what bread did we eat for free? But in toils and labor, night and day, we worked to not be a burden to you.

9 Not because we have no authority, but so that we may provide a model for you to imitate us.

10 For also when we were with you, we commanded you that he who would not work neither should eat.

11 For we hear of those who are among you walking disorderly, not working, but are wasting their time.

12 But such as these we command and exhort by our Lord Jesus Christ that with quietness they work, eating their own bread.

13 But you, brethren, should not weary in well-doing.

14 And if they do not listen to our word by this epistle, mark this one and have no association with him, that he may be ashamed.

15 Yet count not as an enemy, but admonish as a brother.

16 Now may the Lord of peace Himself give you peace always in every way.

17 The greeting of Paul, which is a sign in every epistle, so I write.

18 The grace of our Lord Jesus Christ among all of you. Amen.

THE FIRST EPISTLE OF PAUL THE APOSTLE TO

TIMOTHY

1 Paul, an apostle of the Lord Jesus Christ, according to the command of God our Savior, and of the Lord Jesus Christ our confident expectation.

2 To Timothy, my true child in the faith: grace, mercy, and peace from God our Father and our Lord Jesus Christ.

3 As I urged you to remain at Ephesus, while going to Macedonia, that you might command some not to teach other doctrines,

4 nor to give heed to fables and genealogies, which bring endless questions rather than God's stewardship, which is in faith.

5 But the end of the exhortation is love out of a pure heart, and a good conscience, and genuine faith,

6 from which some have swerved, turning aside to empty talk,

7 desiring to be teachers of the Law, understanding neither what they say nor what they insist.

8 Now we know that the Law is good if anyone uses it lawfully.

9 Knowing this: the Law is not enacted for a righteous person, but for the lawless and rebellious, for the ungodly and sinful, for the unholy and profane, for those who strike their father and mother, for murderers,

10 for fornicators, for homosexuals, for kidnappers, for liars, for perjurers, and for if anything else is contrary to sound doctrine,

11 according to the gospel of the blessed God that I was entrusted with.

12 And I thank Christ Jesus our Lord, Who strengthened me, because He considered me faithful, appointing me to this ministry–

13 formerly being a blasphemer, a persecutor, and a violent one, but I was shown mercy, because, being ignorant, I did it in unbelief.

14 But the grace of our Lord superabounded with faith and love which is in Christ Jesus.

15 Faithful is the word, and worthy of all acceptance, that Christ Jesus came into the world to save sinners, of whom I am first.

16 But for this reason I was shown mercy, that in me first Jesus Christ might show forth every forbearance for a pattern of those who would believe in Him unto eternal life.

17 Now unto the King, eternal, immortal, invisible– to the only wise God: honor and glory to the ages of the ages. Amen!

18 This instruction I commit to you, my child Timothy, according to the prophecies going before you, that by them you may wage a good warfare,

19 holding faith and a good conscience– which some have cast away, making shipwreck their faith–

20 of whom are Hymenaeus and Alexander, who I delivered up to Satan, that they may learn not to blaspheme.

2 I urge you then that first of all, petitions, prayer, intercessions, and giving of thanks be made for all men,

2 for kings, and for all who are in high positions, that we may lead a tranquil and quiet life in all godliness and dignity,

3 for this is good and acceptable before God our Savior,

4 Who desires all men to be saved and to come to the knowledge of the truth.

5 For there is one God and one mediator of God and man: the man, Christ Jesus,

6 Who gave Himself a ransom for all, the testimony in due time,

7 to which I was appointed a preacher

and apostle– I speak the truth in
Christ, I do not lie– a teacher of the nations in faith and truth.
8 I desire that men pray everywhere,
lifting up holy hands without wrath or
quarreling.
9 Similarly the women, with modest
apparel, adorn themselves with mod-
esty and discreetness, not with braided
hair, or gold, or pearls, or costly clothing,
10 but what is becoming of women
professing the fear of God by good
works.
11 Let a woman learn in quietness, in
all subjection.
12 But I do not allow a woman to
teach, nor to have authority over a
man, but to be in quietness,
13 for Adam was formed first, and
then Eve.
14 And Adam was not deceived, but
the woman was deceived and was in
the transgression.
15 But she shall be saved through
child-bearing, if they continue in faith,
and love, and holiness, and self-
control.

3 Faithful is this word: if anyone desires the office of overseer, he as-
pires to a good work.
2 Therefore, an overseer must be
without reproach, the husband of one
wife, sober, discreet, modest, hospitable, able to teach,
3 not addicted to wine, nor violent,
nor greedy of dishonest gain, but gentle, not contentious, nor a lover of
money,
4 one who rules his own house well,
having his children in subjection with
all dignity.
5 For if one does not know how to
rule his own house, how shall he rule
the church of God?
6 Not a novice, lest he be puffed up
and fall into the condemnation of the
Devil.
7 Moreover, he must have a good testimony from those who are outsiders,
lest he fall into reproach and the snare
of the Devil.
8 Deacons in like manner must be
dignified, not double-tongued, not giv-
en to much wine, not greedy for dishonest gain,
9 holding the mystery of the faith in a
pure conscience.
10 And let these also be proven first,
then let them serve as deacons, being
blameless.
11 Their wives in like manner, dignified, not slanderers, sober, faithful in
all things.
12 Let deacons be the husband of one
wife, ruling their own children and
houses well.
13 For those who serve well acquire a
good degree for themselves and much
boldness in the faith which is in Christ
Jesus.
14 These things I write to you– expecting that I will come to you soon,
15 but if I am delayed– so that you
may know how to behave yourself in
the house of God, which is the church
of the living God, the pillar and foundation of truth.
16 And without question, great is the
mystery of godliness: God was manifest in the flesh, declared righteous by
the Spirit, seen by angels, preached to
the Gentiles, believed on in the world,
received up into glory.

4 But the Spirit speaks expressly that
in the latter times some shall depart from the faith, giving heed to deceiving spirits and doctrines of

demons,
2 speaking lies in hypocrisy, having
their own conscience cauterized,
3 forbidding to marry, abstaining
from food, which God created to be
received with thanksgiving by those
who believe and know the truth,
4 because every creature of God is
good, and nothing should be rejected,
being received with thanksgiving–
5 it is consecrated by the word of God
and prayer.
6 Laying these things before the
brethren, you will be a good servant of
Jesus Christ, being trained in the words
of faith and of the good teaching that
you have followed.
7 But refuse the profane and old wives
fables, and exercise yourself toward
godliness.
8 For bodily exercise has a little profit,
but godliness is profitable in every way,
having a promise of life now and of
that which is to come.
9 Faithful is the word and worthy of
all acceptance.
10 For this we both labor and are reproached because we trust in the living
God, Who is the Savior of all men, especially of those who believe.
11 Command and teach these things.
12 Let no one despise your youth, but
be an example of the believers in word,
in conduct, in love, in Spirit, in faith,
and in purity.
13 Until I come, attend yourself to
reading, to exhortation, and to teaching.
14 Do not neglect the gift that is in
you, which was given to you through
prophecy, with the laying on of hands
by the elders.
15 Meditate on these things, be in
them, that your advancement may be
manifest to all.
16 Give heed to yourself and to the
teaching, continuing in them, for doing
this, you will save yourself and them
that hear you.

5

Do not rebuke an elder, but encourage him as you would a father,
younger men as brothers,
2 elder women as mothers, younger as
sisters, with all purity.
3 Honor widows who are truly widows.
4 But if any widow has children or descendants, let them learn to show godliness at home first.
5 Now she is indeed a widow, who
having been left all alone, has her trust
in God, and continues in supplications
and prayers night and day,
6 but she who lives in pleasure is dead
while she lives.
7 Now command these things that
they may be without reproach.
8 But if anyone does not provide for
his own, especially his own household,
he has denied the faith and is worse
than an unbeliever.
9 Let a widow be enrolled, being at
least sixty years old, being the wife of
one man,
10 having a witness of good works, if
she brought up children, if she entertained strangers, if she washed the feet
of the saints, if she brought relief to the
oppressed, if she followed after every
good work.
11 But younger widows refuse, for
when their passions are against Christ,
they will wish to marry,
12 having condemnation, because they
cast off their first faith.
13 Besides that, they also learn to be
idle, going about to the houses– and
not only idle, but also gossipy and
busy-bodies, speaking things that they

should not.

14 So on account of this, I would that the younger ones bear children, rule the house, and give no occasion for the adversary to slander,

15 for some have already turned aside after Satan.

16 If any believing man or believing woman has widows, let them help them, and let not the church be burdened, that the widows indeed might have help.

17 Consider the elders who lead well worthy of double honor, especially those who labor in the word and teaching.

18 For the scripture says, “You shall not muzzle an ox treading out the grain,” and “The workman is worthy of his hire.”

19 Do not receive an accusation against an elder unless there are two or three witnesses.

20 Those that sin examine before everyone, that the rest may also fear.

21 I solemnly testify before God, and the Lord Jesus Christ, and the elect angels, that you keep these things without prejudice, doing nothing by partiality.

22 Do not be quick to lay hands on anyone, nor share in the sins of others– keep yourself pure.

23 No longer drink water only, but use a little wine on account of your stomach and your frequent infirmities.

24 Some men's sins are evident, going before them to judgment, but also some follow after.

25 So also good works are obvious, and those that are otherwise cannot be hidden.

6 As men-servants that are under the yoke, let them esteem their masters worthy of honor, that the name of God and the teaching not be slandered.

2 And they that have believing masters, let them not despise them because they are brethren, but rather let them serve them because they are believers and beloved who are being helped by their good service. These things teach and exhort.

3 If anyone teaches something different and not conforming to the sound words of the Lord Jesus Christ, the doctrine that is according to godliness,

4 he is puffed up, knowing nothing, but rather is sick with cravings for controversy and quarreling over words from which comes envy, strife, blasphemy, evil suspicions,

5 constant friction among men of corrupt minds and destitute of the truth, imagining that gain is godliness– from such separate yourself.

6 But godliness with contentment is great gain.

7 For we brought nothing into this world, and it is evident that we are not able to carry anything out.

8 But let us be satisfied with having food and clothing.

9 But those who desire to be rich fall into temptation and a snare, into many unwise and harmful desires that sink men into destruction and perdition.

10 For the love of money is the root of all evils, which some, having aspired to, were seduced from the faith, and pierced themselves with many woes.

11 But you, oh man of God, flee these things, and pursue righteousness, godliness, faith, love, steadfastness, gentleness.

12 Fight the good fight of faith. Lay hold on eternal life, to which also you were called and did confess a good confession before many witnesses.

13 I charge you before God, Who gives

life to all things, and Christ Jesus, Who
witnessed a good confession before
Pontus Pilate,
14that you keep the commandment,
spotless, without reproach until the appearance of our Lord Jesus Christ,
15Which in its own time shall make
known that He is the blessed and only
Ruler, the King of kings and the Lord
of lords,
16Who alone has immortality,
dwelling in the light that no man can
approach unto, Whom no one has seen
nor is able to see, Who has honor and
everlasting might. Amen!
17Charge those who are rich in this
present age not to be high-minded or
have trust in uncertain riches– but in
the living God, Who gives us all things
richly to enjoy–
18to do good, to be rich in good
works, to be liberal in distribution,
generous,
19treasuring up for themselves a good
foundation for the future, that they
may lay hold on everlasting life.
20Oh Timothy, guard the deposit
committed unto you, turning away
from profane and empty chatter and
oppositions of false knowledge,
21which some, professing, have departed from the faith. Grace be with
you. Amen.

The Second Epistle of Paul the Apostle to

Timothy

1 Paul, an Apostle of Jesus Christ by the will of God, according to the promise of the life in Christ Jesus.

2 To Timothy, my beloved son: grace, mercy and peace from God the Father and Christ Jesus our Lord.

3 I thank God, Whom I serve in a pure conscience from my forefathers, how I have you continually in remembrance in my prayers day and night.

4 Remembering your tears, longing to see you that I may be filled with joy,

5 taking remembrance of the unfeigned faith in you, which first dwelled in your grandmother Lois and in your mother Eunice and I am persuaded also in you.

6 For this cause I remind you to kindle into a flame the gift of God which is in you by the laying on of my hands.

7 For God has not given us a spirit of cowardice, but of power, and of love, and of self-discipline.

8 Therefore you should not be ashamed of the testimony of our Lord, nor of me His prisoner, but share in the suffering of the gospel according to God's power.

9 Who saved us and called us with a holy calling, not according to our works, but according to His own purpose and grace, which was given to us in Christ Jesus before the ages began.

10 But it has now been revealed through the appearance of Jesus Christ, Who abolished death and brought to light life and immortality through the gospel.

11 To which I was appointed a preacher, an apostle and teacher of the nations.

12 For which cause I also suffer these things, but I am not ashamed. For I know in whom I have believed, and am persuaded that He is able to keep that which I have committed unto that day.

13 Follow the example of sound words that you have heard from me, in faith and love which are in Christ Jesus.

14 Keep that precious thing entrusted to you through the Holy Spirit that dwells in you.

15 You know that all who are in Asia turned away from me, among whom are Phygellus and Hermogenes.

16 May the Lord grant mercy to the house of Onesiphorus because he often refreshed me and was not ashamed of my chain.

17 But being in Rome he sought me out more diligently and found me.

18 May the Lord grant him to find mercy from the Lord on that day, and you well know how much he served in Ephesus.

2 Therefore, my son, you be strong in the grace that is in Christ Jesus.

2 And the things that you heard of me with many witnesses, these commit to faithful men who shall be able to teach others also.

3 Therefore, you endure hardship as a good soldier of Jesus Christ.

4 No one serving as a soldier entangles himself with the affairs of this life, that he may please Him who enlisted him to be a soldier.

5 And also, if anyone competes, he is not crowned unless he shall have competed lawfully.

6 The husbandmen who labor must first be a partaker of the fruits.

7 Consider the things that I say, for the Lord shall give you understanding in all things.

8 Remember Jesus Christ of the seed of David was raised from the dead according to my Gospel,

9 in which I endured hardship to the

point of imprisonment as an evil doer,
but the word of God is not bound.
10 Because of this I endure all things
for the sake of the elect, that also they
may obtain salvation which is in Christ
Jesus with eternal glory.
11 Faithful is the word, for if we died
together with Him, we shall also live
together with Him.
12 If we endure, we shall also reign
together– if we deny Him, he will also
deny us.
13 If we are unfaithful, He abides
faithful, he is not able to deny Himself.
14 These things remember, testifying
earnestly before the Lord, not to quarrel about words which are not profitable but destructive to those who
hear.
15 Be diligent to present yourself approved to God, a workman not
ashamed, rightly dividing the word of
truth.
16 But profane and empty babblings
avoid, for they will advance to more
ungodliness.
17 And their word will spread like a
cancer, of whom is Hymenaeus and
Philetus,
18 who as concerning the truth have
departed, saying that the resurrection
has already taken place, and are overturning the faith of some.
19 However, the foundation of God
stands firm, having this seal, "The Lord
knows those that are His" and, "Let
everyone who names the name of
Christ depart from iniquity."
20 In a great house there are not only
vessels of gold and silver, but also of
wood and clay; and some of honor, and
others of dishonor.
21 If then one cleanses themselves
from these things he shall be a vessel
unto honor, consecrated and useful to
the Master, prepared unto every good
work.
22 But flee youthful lusts, and pursue
righteousness, faith, love, and peace
with those who call upon the Lord
from a pure heart.
23 But foolish and uninformed questions refuse, knowing that they shall
breed strife.
24 And a servant of the Lord must not
argue, but be gentle towards all, skillful
to teach, forbearing,
25 correcting those that oppose him in
meekness, if perhaps God may grant
them repentance to the acknowledg-
ment of the truth,
26 and they may come to their senses
out of the snare of the Devil, having
been taken by him to do his will.

3 But know this, in the last days per-
ilous times shall come.
2 For men will be lovers of self, lovers
of money, boasters, arrogant, slanderers, disobedient to parents, unthankful,
unholy,
3 hardhearted, unappeasable, demons,
without self control, brutal, not loving
good,
4 traitors, thoughtless, puffed up,
lovers of pleasure rather than lovers of
God,
5 having a form of godliness, but
denying the power of it. Turn away
from these.
6 For these are they that enter into
houses and lead captive weak women
burdened with sins and led away with
various passions,
7 always learning but never able to
come to the knowledge of the truth.
8 Now, the way that Jannes and Jam-
bres withstood Moses, these also with-
stand the truth, men utterly corrupted
in mind, worthless as regards to the

faith.
9 But they will not progress very far,
for their folly will be fully manifested
to all, as also was that of those.
10 But you have closely followed my
teaching, conduct, purpose, faith, patience, love, endurance,
11 persecution, suffering, such as happened to me in Antioch, in Iconium, in
Lystra, what sort of persecution I endured, and the Lord delivered me out
of it all.
12 And also, all who live godly in
Christ Jesus will be persecuted.
13 But wicked men and imposters will
continue to become worse, deceiving
and being deceived.
14 But as for you, continue in what
you have firmly believed, knowing
from whom you have learned it,
15 and that from a child you have
known the holy scriptures, which are
able to make wise unto salvation
through faith that is in Christ Jesus.
16 All scripture is inspired by God and
is profitable for teaching, for reproof,
for correction, for training in righteousness,
17 so that the man of God may be
qualified, equipped unto every good
work.

4 Therefore, I earnestly testify before
God and the Lord Jesus Christ,
Who is about to judge the living and
the dead according to His appearing
and His kingdom:
2 Proclaim the word, be urgent in season and out of season, rebuke, reprove,
encourage with all patience and teaching.
3 For the time will come when they
will not tolerate sound doctrine, but,
having itching ears, will heap up unto
themselves teachers after their own
lusts.
4 And they will turn their ears away
from the truth and will be turned to
myths.
5 But you be sober in all things, suffer
hardship, do the work of an evangelist,
and fulfill your service.
6 For I am already poured out as a
drink offering and the time for my departure is near.
7 I have fought a good fight, I have
finished my course, I have kept the
faith.
8 Henceforth is laid up for me a
crown of righteousness which the Lord,
the righteous judge, will award to me
on that day.
9 Be diligent to come to me quickly.
10 For Demas has deserted me, having
loved this present age, and has gone to
Thessalonica, Crescens to Galatia, and
Titus to Dalmatia.
11 Luke is alone with me, take Mark to
yourself and bring him to me for he is
useful for service to me.
12 Now I sent Tychicos to Ephesus.
13 The cloak which I left in Troas with
Carpos, bring, and the books, especially the parchments.
14 Alexandria the smith did many evil
things against me, may the Lord render
to him according to his works,
15 whom you also guard against, for
he has insistently stood against our
words.
16 In my first defense no one stood
with me but everyone abandoned me,

may it not be reckoned to them.
17But the Lord stood with me and
strengthened me.
18And the Lord will deliver me from
every wicked work and will preserve
me for His heavenly kingdom, to
Whom be glory to the ages of the ages.
Amen.
19Greet Prisca and Aquila, and the
house of Onesiphorus.
20Erastus remained in Corinth, but
Trophimus I left in Miletus sick.
21Be diligent to come to me before
winter. Eubulus greets you and Pudens
and Linus, and Claudia and all the
brethren.
22The Lord Jesus Christ be with your
spirit. Grace be with you. Amen.

The Epistle of Paul the Apostle to
Titus

1 Paul, a slave of God and an apostle of Jesus Christ, according to the faith of God's elect and knowledge of the truth, which is according to godliness.

2 Through the eager expectation of eternal life, that the trustworthy God has promised before eternal times

3 and has revealed in His own time His word through preaching, which I was entrusted with according to the command of God our Savior.

4 Titus, my true child according to a common faith: grace, mercy, and peace from the Father God and the Lord Jesus Christ our Savior.

5 For this reason I left you behind in Crete, so that which is lacking may be corrected, and that you may appoint elders in the towns as I directed you.

6 If someone is blameless, the husband of one wife, having faithful children, not accused of debauchery or rebelliousness.

7 For a Bishop must be blameless as God's steward, not arrogant, not quick-tempered, not a striker, not greedy of gain.

8 But hospitable, a lover of good, prudent, righteous, devout, self-controlled.

9 Devoted to the teaching of the faithful word so that he may be able to both exhort with teaching, correcting and exposing those who contradict it.

10 For there are also many rebellious, talking nonsense, and deceivers, most of all those of the circumcision.

11 They must be silenced for they are overturning entire households by their teachings; who are not ashamed that they do it for profit.

12 It was one of them, their own prophet, who said Cretes are constant liars, evil beasts, lazy gluttons.

13 This testimony is true, rebuke them severely for this reason, that they may be sound in the faith,

14 paying no attention to Jewish myths and commandments of men who reject the truth.

15 To the pure all things are pure; but to the defiled and unbelieving nothing is pure, but their mind and conscience are corrupt.

16 They profess to know God, but by their works they deny Him, being detestable, and disobedient, and to every good work disqualified.

2 But you speak what is consistent with sound doctrine.

2 Elderly men be temperate, worthy of respect, prudent, healthy in faith, in love and in endurance.

3 Elderly women likewise having reverent behavior, not slanderers, or enslaved to much wine, teaching what is good.

4 That they may teach the younger women to be lovers of husbands, and lovers of children,

5 discreet, chaste, keepers at home, good, subject to their own husbands, that the word of God may not be evil spoken of.

6 The younger men likewise to be discreet.

7 Yourself, in all things, holding forth a pattern of good works: in soundness of teaching, dignity, incorruptible,

8 sound speech that cannot be condemned, that he who opposes you may be ashamed having nothing evil to say concerning you.

9 Servants are to be subject to their own masters, to be well pleasing in everything, not argumentative,

10 not pilfering, but in all good faith showing that they may adorn the doctrine of God your Savior in all things.

11 For the grace of God that brings salvation has appeared to all men.

12 Teaching us that having denied all ungodliness and worldly lust we should live soberly, righteously and godly in this present age,

13 awaiting the blessed expectation and glorious appearing of our great God and Savior Jesus Christ,

14 Who gave Himself for us that He might redeem us from all iniquity and purify to Himself a people for His own possession, zealous of good works.

15 These things speak and exhort and rebuke with all authority, let no one disregard you.

3 Remind them to be subject to rulers and authorities, to be obedient, to be ready for every good work.

2 To speak evil of no one, to not be contentious, gentle to all, showing meekness to all men.

3 For we were also once foolish, disobedient, led astray, serving various lust and pleasures, living in malice and envy, hateful, hating one another,

4 but when the goodness and loving kindness of God our Savior appeared,

5 He saved us, not by works of righteousness that we have done, but according to His mercy, by the washing of regeneration and renewing of the Holy Spirit,

6 which He poured out richly through Jesus Christ our Savior.

7 So that being made righteous by His grace we should be heirs according to the expectation of eternal life.

8 Faithful is the word, and I desire that you insist on these things, that those who have believed may be careful to devote themselves to good works. These things are good and profitable to men.

9 But avoid foolish questions, genealogies and contentions about the law, for they are unprofitable and vain.

10 A man who is a heretic reject after warning him the first and second time,

11 knowing that such a one is perverted and sinful, being condemned of himself.

12 When I shall send Artemas or Tychicus to you, be diligent to come to me in Nicopolis, for I have decided to winter there.

13 Diligently send Zenas the lawyer, and Apollos, that they will have nothing lacking that they need.

14 And let ours also learn to devote themselves to good works and urgent needs that they may not be unfruitful.

15 All those with me greet you, greet those who love us in the faith. Grace be with you all. Amen.

The Epistle of Paul the Apostle to
Philemon

1 Paul, a prisoner of Christ Jesus, and
Timothy our brother, to our beloved
Philemon and our fellow worker.

2 And to the beloved Apphia, and to
Archippus our fellow soldier, and to
the church in your house.

3 Grace to you and peace from God
our Father and the Lord Jesus Christ.

4 I thank my God always for you,
making mention of you in my prayers,

5 hearing of your love and faith,
which you have towards the Lord Jesus
Christ, and towards all of the holy
ones.

6 So that the communication of your
faith may be effectual by the acknowl-
edgment of every good thing that is in
you in Christ Jesus.

7 For we have great thankfulness and
encouragement because of your love,
for the inward affections of the holy
ones have been refreshed by you brother.

8 Therefore, having great boldness in
Christ to command you to do what is
proper,

9 but for love's sake I rather appeal to
you– I, Paul, being older and now the
prisoner of Jesus Christ–

10 I appeal to you for my child Onesimus who I begat in my imprisonment.

11 Formerly he was useless, but now
he is useful to you and to me,

12 whom I am sending back to you,
receive my deepest affections,

13 whom I was desiring to keep with
me, that he might serve me on your
behalf in the gospel in my imprisonment,

14 but I prefer to do nothing without
your consent, so that your goodness
would not be by pressure, but of your
own free will.

15 For perhaps this is why he was separated from you for a time, that you
might have him back forever.

16 No longer as a slave, but above a
slave, a beloved brother, especially to
me, but how much more to you both in
the flesh and in the Lord.

17 So if you consider me a partner,
receive him as you would me.

18 But if in anything he has wronged
you or owes you, put this on my account.

19 I, Paul, wrote this with my own
hand, I will repay it, to say nothing
about you owing me even your own-
self.

20 Yes brother, I want some profit
from you in the Lord, refresh my affections in the Lord.

21 Being persuaded of your obedience
I wrote to you, knowing that you will
do even more than I say.

22 Also, at the same time, prepare for
me lodging, for I expect that through
your prayers I will be given to you.

23 Epapharus, my fellow prisoner in
Christ Jesus, sends greetings to you.

24 Mark, Aristarchus, Demas, and
Luke, my fellow workers.

25 The grace of our Lord Jesus Christ
be with your spirit. Amen.

The Epistle to the
Hebrews

1 God, Who at different times and in
many ways spoke to the fathers by
the Prophets:
2 in these last days has spoken to us
by His Son, Whom He has made heir
of all things, by Whom also He made
the ages.
3 Who being the brightness of His
glory and the exact image of His substance and upholding all things by the
Word of His power, when He had by
Himself purged our sins, He sat down
at the right hand of the majesty on
High.
4 Being so much better than the angels as much as He has inherited a
much more excellent Name than they.
5 For to which of the angels did He
ever say, "You are my Son, today I have
begotten You"? And again, "I will be a
Father to Him, and He will be a Son to
me."
6 And again, when He brought the
first born into the habitation of earth
He said, "Let all of the angels worship
Him."
7 And to the angels He says, "Who
makes His angels spirits and His ministers a flame of fire,"
8 But to the Son, "Your throne, O
God, is to the ages of the ages and the
scepter of uprightness is the scepter of
your Kingdom.
9 You have loved righteousness and
You have hated iniquity, because of this
I have anointed You, God, your God,
with the oil of joy above your companions.
10 And You established the earth in
the beginning, Lord, and the heavens
are the work of your hands.
11 They shall perish, but You continue; and they shall grow old as a garment,
12 and as a robe You shall roll them up
and they will be changed, but You are
the same and Your years shall not
cease."
13 And to which of the angels did He
ever say, "Sit at My right hand until I
place Your enemies as a footstool for
Your feet"?
14 Are they not all ministering spirits,
sent for the service of those who inherit salvation?

2 And because of this it is necessary
for us to more abundantly give
heed to the things that we have heard,
lest at any time we should let them slip
away.
2 For if the word spoken by the angels
was confirmed and every transgression
and disobedience received a just retribution,
3 how shall we escape, if we neglect so
great a salvation? Which began to be
spoken by the Lord, being received by
those who heard, which was confirmed
to us.
4 God testifying, both with miracles
and wonders and many kinds of powers of the Holy Ghost distributed according to His will.
5 For He did not subject the habitation of the earth which is to come to
angels, of which we speak,
6 but one in a certain place witnessed
saying, "What is man that You are
mindful of Him, or the son of man that
You visit him?
7 For You made him, for a short time,
lower than the angels, You crowned
him with glory and honor and set him
over the works of Your hands,
8 You put all things under his feet."
For in subjecting all things to him, you
left nothing unsubjected. But we do not
now see all things subjected to him,
9 but who for a short time was made

lower than the angels, we see Jesus who
because of the suffering of death was
crowned with glory and honor, so that
by the grace of God He might taste
death for everyone.
10In bringing many sons into glory it
was appropriate for Him (for Whom
and by Whom are all things) that the
Captain of their salvation should be
made perfect through suffering.
11For both He who makes holy and
those who are made holy are all of One,
for which cause He is not ashamed to
call them brethren.
12Saying, "I will declare Your Name
to my brethren in the midst of the assembly I will sing praise."
13And again, "I put my trust in Him."
And again, "Behold, I and the children
which God gave me."
14Therefore, since the children have
partaken of flesh and blood, He also
likewise took part in the same that
through death He might destroy the
one who has the power of death– that
is the Devil.
15And might set free those who all of
their lifetime were subject to bondage
through fear of death.
16For He did not take hold of angels,
but He took hold of the seed of Abraham.
17Therefore, He ought in all things to
be made like the brethren, that He
might be a merciful and faithful High
Priest in things relating to God, in order to make propitiation for the sins of
the people.
18For in that He Himself suffered being tempted, He is able to help those
being tempted.

3 Therefore, holy brethren, partakers
of the heavenly calling, consider
the Apostle and High Priest of your
confession, Christ Jesus.
2Being faithful to Him who appointed Him as also Moses was in all of his
house.
3For He has been counted worthy of
more glory than Moses, having much
more honor as the One who built the
house than the house.
4For every house is built by someone;
but He who built all things is God.
5For Moses was indeed faithful in all
his house, as a servant, for a testimony
of things yet to be spoken.
6But Christ, as the Son over His
house, Whose house we are, if indeed
we hold the confidence and the boasting of the trust firm unto the end.
7Therefore, just as the Holy Spirit
says: "Today if you will hear His voice,
8do not harden your hearts as in the
rebellion, in the day of temptation in
the wilderness.
9Where your fathers tested Me,
proved Me, and saw My works for forty
years.
10For this reason I was angry with
that generation, and said, 'They do always err in their hearts, and they did
not know My ways,'
11so I swore in My wrath, they shall
not enter into My rest."
12Take heed, brethren, lest there
should be in any of you a wicked heart
of unbelief in departing from the Living God.
13But encourage yourselves everyday,
as long as it is called today, that none of
you be hardened by the deceitfulness of
sin.
14For we have become partakers of
Christ, if we hold fast the assurance we
began with firm unto the end.
15In that it is said: " Today, if you will
hear His voice, harden not your hearts
as in the rebellion."

16 For some, having heard, disobeyed, but not all who came out of Egypt by Moses.

17 And with whom was He angry with for forty years? Was it not with those who sinned, whose dead bodies fell in the wilderness?

18 And to whom did He swear, they shall not enter into His rest, was it not to those who disobeyed?

19 And we see that they were not able to enter in because of unbelief.

4 Therefore, we should fear lest being left a promise of entering into His rest any of you might come short of it.

2 For truly we have had the gospel preached to us even as they also did. But the report of the word did not profit them because it was not mixed with faith in those who heard it.

3 For we who believe enter into the rest, as He said, "So I swore in My wrath they shall not enter into My rest though the works were done from the overthrow of the world."

4 For where He said concerning the seventh day: "and so God rested on the seventh day from all of His works."

5 And in this place again, "If they shall enter into My rest."

6 Therefore, since it remains for some to enter into it, and those who before heard the gospel did not enter because of disobedience.

7 Again, He appointed in David a certain day, saying, "After so long a time," according as it has been said, "Today, if you will hear His voice harden not your hearts."

8 For if Joshua had given them rest, He would not have afterwards spoken concerning a day.

9 So there remains a sabbath rest to the people of God.

10 For he that is entered into His rest has rested from his works, just as God rested from His own.

11 We should be zealous to enter into that rest, lest anyone should fall after the same example of disobedience.

12 For the Word of God is living, and powerful, and sharper than any double edged sword, piercing even unto the distinction of soul and also spirit, and joint as well as marrow, and is a judge of the thought and intent of the heart.

13 And none of creation is hidden from His sight, but all things are naked and exposed before the eyes of Him who we are accountable to.

14 Therefore, having a Great High Priest who has passed through the heavens, Jesus the Son of God, we should hold fast our confession.

15 For we do not have a High Priest who cannot sympathize with our weaknesses, but Who has been tempted in all things just like we are, yet without sin.

16 We should come with boldness to the throne of grace, that we may receive mercy and may find grace to help in time of need.

5 For every high priest that is taken from among men is appointed for men in things pertaining to God: that he may offer both gifts and sacrifices for sins,

2 who can have forbearance on the ignorant and erring since he himself is also surrounded with weakness,

3 and on account of this weakness, he is obligated to offer for his sins as well as the people.

4 And no one takes this honor unto himself, but he that is called by God, just as Aaron also was.

5 Even so Christ glorified not Himself to be made the High Priest, but He that said unto Him, “You are my Son, this day I have begotten You.”

6 As He also said in another place: “You are a Priest forever according to the order of Melchisedech.”

7 Who in the days of His flesh offered up prayers and supplications with strong crying and tears unto Him that was able to save him from death; and was also heard because He feared.

8 Though He was a Son, He learned obedience from the things which He suffered.

9 And being made perfect, He became the source of eternal salvation to all those who obey him.

10 And is called by God as a High Priest after the order of Melchisedech.

11 Concerning whom we have many things to speak, and hard to explain since you have become dull of hearing.

12 For truly when it is time that you should be teachers, you need someone to teach you again the first principles of the Word of God: and have become such as have need of milk and not of solid food.

13 For everyone that uses milk is unskillful in the word of righteousness, for he is an infant.

14 But solid food belongs to those who are mature, who because of continued use have their senses exercised to discern both good and evil.

6 Therefore, leaving the fundamentals of the Word of Christ, let us go on to maturity, not laying again the foundation of repentance from works of death, and faith towards God,

2 of baptisms, of the doctrine of laying on of hands, and of resurrection of the dead, and eternal judgment.

3 And this we will do if God permits.

4 For it is impossible for those once enlightened and who have tasted of the heavenly gift, and became partakers of the Holy Spirit,

5 and have tasted the good Word of God, and the power of the age to come,

6 and then commit apostasy, to renew them again to repentance, who themselves crucified the Son of God and publicly disgraced Him.

7 For the Earth which drinks in the rain which comes often upon it and brings forth herbs fit for those who tilled it, partakes of the blessing of God.

8 But that which brings forth thorns and thistles is rejected and near to being cursed for which the end is to be burned.

9 But we are persuaded of better things concerning you, brethren, which accompany salvation even though we speak like this.

10 For God is not unrighteous that he should forget your work and labor which you showed towards His Name, having served the holy ones and still serve.

11 But we desire each one of you to show the same diligence of the full assurance of confidence unto the end.

12 So then, do not be sluggish but be followers of them who through faith and patience inherit the promises.

13 For when God made a promise to Abraham, because He had no greater thing to swear by, He swore by Himself.

14 Saying, “Surely blessing I will bless you, and multiplying I will multiply you.”

15 And so having enduring patience, he obtained the promise.

16 Men indeed swear by the greater,

and in all of their disputes an oath is final for confirmation.

17So God, willing more abundantly to show to the heirs the unchangeableness of His plan, He guaranteed it by an oath.

18That by two unchangeable things (in which it was impossible for God to lie) we who have fled for refuge might have a mighty encouragement to hold fast to the confidence set before us.

19Which we have as an anchor of our souls both certain and firm, and enter into that which is within the veil.

20Where Jesus, the forerunner for us has entered, made a High Priest forever after the order of Melchisedech.

7 For this Melchisedec, king of Salem, Priest of the Most High God, who met Abraham– returning from slaughtering the kings– and blessed him.

2To whom also Abraham divided a tenth of all. First being interpreted, "king of righteousness" and then also king of Salem, which is "king of peace."

3Without father, without mother, without a genealogy, with neither beginning of days nor end of life: but is likened unto the Son of God, abides a Priest forever.

4Now consider how great this one was that even the patriarch Abraham gave a tenth of the spoils.

5And they indeed from the sons of Levi, who receive the priesthood, have a commandment to take tithes from the people according to the law, though their brethren came out of the loins of Abraham.

6But the one who has no genealogies from them, has tithed of Abraham, and blessed him who had the promises.

7And without all dispute, the inferior is blessed by the superior.

8And here men that die receive tithes, but there it is witnessed that he lives.

9And so to speak, even Levi who receives tithes paid tithes through Abraham.

10For he was still in the loins of his Father when Melchisedec met him.

11If indeed then fulfillment was through the Levitical priesthood, for the people upon it had received the law, why was there need for another priest to arise according to the order of Melchisedec, and not spoken of according to the order of Aaron?

12For a change of the priesthood demands that there also be a change in the law.

13For he of whom these things are said has shared in another tribe who gave no attendance at the altar.

14For it is known to all that our Lord rose up from Judah, of which tribe Moses said nothing concerning priesthood.

15And yet it is extraordinarily clear that according to the similitude of Melchisedec another priest has risen,

16Who did not come according to the law of a fleshly commandment, but according to the power of an endless life.

17For it is witnessed that You are a Priest forever according to the order of Melchisedec.

18For indeed there has come an annulment of the commandment going before because it is weak and useless.

19For the law could make nothing perfect, but the bringing in of a better expectation by which we draw near to God.

20And accordingly, in as much as it is not apart from taking an oath. For indeed those without an oath have be-

come priests.
21 But with an oath because He said to
Him, “The Lord swore and will not
change His mind, You are a priest forever after the order of Melchisedec.”
22 Jesus has become the guarantee according to a much better covenant.
23 And indeed there are many who
have become priests because by death
they are prevented from continuing.
24 But because He remains forever, He
has an unchanging priesthood.
25 Therefore He is able to completely
save them that come to God by Him,
for He lives on forever to make intercession on their behalf.
26 For such a High Priest is fitting for
us, holy, innocent, undefiled, separate
from sinners and become higher than
the heavens.
27 Who does not have by necessity to
offer sacrifices daily as other High
Priests before Him, first on behalf of
his own sin and then for those of the
people. For this He did once for all,
having offered up Himself.
28 For the law appoints men high
priests who have weakness, but the
word of the oath which is after the law,
“a Son He has perfected forever.”

8 Now the sum of the things being
spoken is that we have such a High
Priest, Who has sat down on the right
hand of the throne of the majesty in the
heavens.
2 A Minister of the Holies, and of the
true tabernacle which the Lord pitched
and not man.
3 For every high priest is appointed to
offer both gifts and sacrifices. Therefore, it was necessary that this One also
have something that He may offer.
4 For indeed if He were on earth, He
would not be a priest, being that there
are priests who offer gifts according to
the law,
5 who serve as a model and shadow of
the heavenlies, according as Moses was
divinely instructed when he was about
to complete the tabernacle, “for see,”
says He, “that you make all things according to the pattern which was
shown you in the mountain.”
6 But now He has obtained a more
excellent ministry, as He is also the
mediator of a much better covenant
which has been established on better
promises.
7 For if the first one was faultless, a
second would have not been sought.
8 For finding fault with them He says,
“behold the days are coming” says the
Lord, “I will make a new covenant with
the house of Judah and with the house
of Israel.
9 Not according to the covenant
which I made with their fathers on the
day I took them by their hand to lead
them out of the land of Egypt, because
they did not continue in my covenant,
and I disregarded them,” says the Lord.
10 “Because this is the covenant that I
will covenant with the house of Israel
after those days” says the Lord. “I will
place my laws into their mind and I
will inscribe them upon their hearts,
and I will be to them for God, and they
shall be to me for a people.
11 And they shall not teach each man
his neighbor and each man his brother,
saying, know the Lord, because all shall
know me from the least unto the greatest,
12 because I will be merciful to their
unrighteousness, and their sins and iniquities I will remember no more.”
13 By speaking of a new, He has made
the first old, and that which grows old
and aged is near to vanishing.

9 And therefore indeed the first tabernacle had regulations of worship and an earthly tabernacle.

2 For a tent was constructed; the first one in which there was the lampstand and the table and the bread of presence, which is called holy.

3 But behind the second curtain is a tabernacle called the Holy of Holies.

4 Having a golden censer and the ark of the covenant, every part completely covered with gold, in which was a golden pot with manna, and the rod of Aaron that budded, and the tables of the covenant.

5 And above it the cherubims of glory, which concerning it is not for now to speak of in detail.

6 Now these things having therefore been prepared, the priests entered at all times into the first tabernacle to accomplish their service.

7 But into the second, the high priest entered alone once a year, not without blood, which he offered for himself and for the people's sins committed in ignorance.

8 By this the Holy Spirit signified that the way into the Holies was not yet revealed so long as the first tabernacle remained standing.

9 Which is symbolic for the present time, in which both gifts and sacrifices were offered that cannot perfect the conscience of him who serves.

10 Consisting only in meats and drinks and different kinds of washings, and ordinances of the flesh, until the time of reformation be imposed.

11 But Christ having become a High Priest of the good things that have come by a greater and more perfect tabernacle, not made by hands, that is not of this creation,

12 neither by the blood of goats and calves, but by His own blood He entered once into the Holy Place, having obtained eternal redemption for us.

13 For if the blood of bulls and of goats, and the sprinkling of the ashes of a heifer, makes one holy that is defiled to the purifying of the flesh,

14 how much more does the blood of Christ (who offered Himself without spot through the eternal Spirit) cleanse our conscience from dead works to serve the Living God?

15 And for this reason He is the mediator of a new covenant, so that by means of death there is redemption for the transgressions under the first covenant, that they which have been called might receive the promise of eternal inheritance.

16 For where there is a covenant, it is necessary for there to be the death of the one who made it.

17 For a covenant becomes effective at death, because while the one who made it is alive it has no power.

18 Therefore, not even the first was ratified without blood.

19 After every commandment according to the law had been spoken to the people by Moses, he took the blood of bull calves, and of goats with water, and scarlet, wool and hyssop, and sprinkled both the book and all of the people.

20 Saying, "this is the blood of the covenant which God has commanded to you."

21 And also in like manner he sprinkled with blood the tabernacle and all of the vessels for ministry.

22 And almost everything is purified with blood according to the law, and without the shedding of blood there is no forgiveness.

23 It was necessary for those things that represent that which is in heaven

to be purified with these, but the heavenlies with better sacrifices than these.

24 For Christ did not enter into the Holies made by hands, which are copies of the true things, but into heaven itself now to appear before the presence of God for us.

25 Neither should He offer himself many times, even as the High Priest had to enter into the Holies year after year with the blood of others,

26 for then it would have been necessary for Him to have suffered often since the overthrow of the world. But now, once, at the end of the ages, He has been manifested for the putting away of sin by the sacrifice of Himself.

27 And just as it is appointed for man to die once and after that comes the judgment,

28 so Christ having been offered once to bear the sins of many shall appear a second time, not for sin, to those who await for deliverance.

10 For the Law was a shadow of good things to come, itself, not being the actual reality, could never with the same sacrifices that are continually every year make those who draw near with them perfect.

2 If it could, would they have not stopped being offered? For the worshipers, having been purified, would have no more conscience of sin.

3 But in these there is a remembrance of sins every year.

4 It is impossible for the blood of bulls and goats to take away sin.

5 Wherefore, coming into the world, He says, "Sacrifice and offering you do not desire, but a body you have prepared for Me.

6 Burnt offerings and sacrifices for sin you did not delight in."

7 Then I said, "Behold I come in the scroll of the book, it is written of Me to do Your will O God."

8 Above saying, "Sacrifice and offering, and burnt offerings, and sacrifices for sin you did not desire nor delighted in," which are offered according to the law.

9 Then He said, "behold I come to do your will O God." He takes away the first that the second may be established.

10 By Whose will we have been made holy through the offering of the body of Jesus Christ once for all.

11 And every priest stands daily ministering, offering the same sacrifices which are never able to take away sins.

12 But He, having offered one sacrifice for all times, He sat down at the right hand of God.

13 Waiting from that time until He places His enemies as a footstool for His feet.

14 For by one offering He has forever perfected those who are made holy.

15 And the Holy Spirit also testifying to us after foretelling,

16 "This is the covenant that I will make for them after those days says the Lord: I will put my laws in their hearts and in their minds I will write them.

17 And their sins and iniquities will I remember no more."

18 Where there is the forgiveness of these there is no more sacrifice for sin.

19 Having boldness therefore brethren to enter into the holiest by the blood of Jesus,

20 by a new and living way that He has consecrated for us through the veil (that is His flesh),

21 and having a Great High Priest over the house of God,

22 let us draw near with a true heart in

full assurance of faith having our hearts sprinkled from an evil conscience, and our bodies washed with pure water.

23 Let us hold fast the confession of our expectation without wavering, for He is faithful that promised.

24 And let us consider one another to stir up love and good works.

25 Not neglecting the assembling of ourselves, as is the habit of some, but exhorting, and with great intensity as you see the day approaching.

26 For if we willingly continue in sin after receiving the knowledge of the truth, there remains no more sacrifice for sin.

27 But a fearful expectation of judgment and fierce fire that will consume the adversaries.

28 Anyone who violated the law of Moses died without mercy by the testimony of two or three.

29 How much worse punishment do you think those are worthy who trampled upon the Son of God, and profaned the blood of the covenant by which they were made holy, and outraged the Spirit of grace?

30 For we know the One Who said, "vengeance is Mine, I will repay, says the Lord" and again "the Lord will judge His people."

31 It is fearful to fall into the hands of a living God.

32 But recall those former days, when you were enlightened, you suffered, enduring many conflicts,

33 being made a spectacle both in reproaches and tribulation, and having become partners with those passing through it.

34 For you sympathized with my bonds and received the plunder of your possessions with joy, knowing that yourselves have a better possession abiding in the heavens.

35 Therefore, cast not away your boldness, which has a great reward.

36 For you have need of endurance that, having done the will of God, you may receive the promise.

37 For yet a little while he who comes will come, and will not delay.

38 But the righteous shall live by faith; and if he draws back, My soul will not delight in him.

39 But we are not of those who draw back to destruction, but of those of faith to the saving of the soul.

11 Now faith is the visible reality of things confidently expected, the proof of things not seen.

2 For by it the elders had a witness.

3 By faith we understand that the ages were prepared by the word of God, so that the visible was made from what is invisible.

4 By faith Abel offered a more excellent sacrifice to God than Cain, through which he obtained witness that he was righteous, God bearing witness to his gift, and by it he still speaks although he is dead.

5 By faith Enoch was taken up, not seeing death, and was not found because God translated him; for before he was translated it was witnessed of him that he pleased God.

6 For without faith it is impossible to be pleasing, for it is necessary for the one who comes near to God to believe that He is and that he is a rewarder of those who seek Him.

7 By faith Noah, being warned concerning things not yet seen, in reverence built an ark to save his house, through which he pronounced sentence on the world, and through the righteousness of faith became heir.

8 By faith Abraham, being called, obeyed. He went out to the place that he would receive as an inheritance, and went out not knowing where he was going.

9 By faith he lived in the land of promise as a stranger, dwelling in tents with Isaac and Jacob, the fellow heirs of his promise.

10 For he was waiting for the city that has foundations, whose designer and builder is God.

11 By faith also Sarah herself received power to conceive seed even when she was beyond the age to give birth, since she esteemed Him faithful who promised.

12 Therefore, also from one, himself being as one dead, were born even as the stars of heaven in multitude and as sand which is by the seashore innumerable.

13 These all died in faith not having received the promise, but seeing them from a distance and having been persuaded, and embracing them, and confessing that they are strangers and sojourners on the Earth.

14 For those who say such things make known that they seek a country.

15 And surely if they were to remember where they had come from, they might have had the opportunity to return.

16 But now they desire a better country, that is, a heavenly one. For this reason God is not ashamed to be called their God, for He prepared for them a city.

17 By faith Abraham, being tried, offered up Isaac and he who had received the promise offered up his only begotten.

18 To whom it was said in Isaac shall your seed be called.

19 Counting that God was able to also raise him from the dead, whom he also received in a figure.

20 By faith Isaac blessed Jacob and Esau concerning things to come.

21 By faith Jacob, dying, leaning upon his staff, worshiped and blessed both of the sons of Joseph.

22 By faith Joseph, dying, gave command concerning the exodus of the sons of Israel, making mention concerning his bones.

23 By faith Moses, having been born, was hidden for three months by his parents because they saw that he was a beautiful child and did not fear the edict of the king.

24 By faith Moses, having become great, refused to be called the son of Pharaoh's daughter,

25 instead choosing to suffer affliction with the people of God rather than the temporary enjoyment of sin,

26 esteeming the reproaches of Christ greater riches than the treasures of Egypt, for he looked to the reward.

27 By faith he left Egypt, not fearing the wrath of the king, for he endured seeing the invisible one.

28 By faith he kept the passover and the sprinkling of blood, lest the destroyer of the firstborn should touch them.

29 By faith, they passed through the Red Sea as through dry land, which the Egyptians attempting were swallowed up.

30 By faith the walls of Jericho fell, having been encircled for seven days.

31 By faith Rahab the harlot did not perish with those who disobeyed because she welcomed the spies with peace.

32 And what more shall I say? For time would fail me to tell of Gideon,

Barak, and also of Samson and Jeph-
thah, also David and Samuel and the
prophets.
33 Who through faith subdued kingdoms, wrought righteousness, obtained
promises, stopped the mouths of lions,
34 quenched the power of fire, escaped the edge of the sword, out of
weakness became strong, became
mighty in war, and put foreign armies
to flight.
35 Women received their dead back to
life again. Others were tortured not ac-
cepting redemption, so that they might
obtain a better resurrection.
36 And others received trials of mock-
ings and scourgings, yes, and moreover
of chains and imprisonment.
37 They were stoned, sawed in two,
they were tempted, they were killed
with the sword, they wandered in
sheepskins and goatskins, being destitute, oppressed, and mistreated,
38 of whom the world was not worthy,
wandering in deserts, in mountains, in
caves and in holes in the earth.
39 And through faith all of these having testified did not receive the promise.
40 God having provided something far
better for us that they should not be
made perfect without us.

12 In that we are surrounded by so
great a cloud of witnesses, let us
lay aside the weight and the sin that
would ensnare us and hold us back,
and run the race with joy.
2 Looking unto Jesus our faith leader
and completer, who for the joy that was
set before Him held onto the cross, de-
testing the shame, then sat down at the
right hand of the throne of God.
3 Consider Him who endured from
sinners great hostilities against Himself
so that you do not weary and faint in
your souls.
4 You have not resisted unto blood,
wrestling against sin.
5 And you have soon forgotten the
exhortation that addresses you as sons:
"My son, despise not the discipline of
the Lord, nor faint being reproved by
Him.
6 For whom the Lord loves He disciplines and scourges every son whom
He receives."
7 If you endure discipline as sons,
God is dealing with you, for what son
does the Father not discipline?
8 But if you are without discipline, of
which all have become partakers, then
you are illegitimate and not sons.
9 Besides we have had fathers in the
flesh who have disciplined us and we
respected them. How much more
should we be submitted to the Father
of spirits and live.
10 For they indeed for a few days disciplined you after what seemed good to
them, but He for our profit, that we
may partake of His holiness.
11 But every discipline for the present
seems to be sorrow and not joy, but afterwards it yields the peaceable fruits of
righteousness to those having been
trained by it.
12 Therefore straighten the hands that
hang down, and the disabled knees.
13 Make straight paths for your feet
unless that which is lame turns you
aside, but rather let it be healed.
14 Pursue peace with everyone, and
the holiness without which no one
shall see the Lord.
15 Looking diligently unless any of
you fall short of the grace of God, lest
any root of bitterness springing up
troubles you and by it many be defiled.
16 Lest there be any fornicator or pro-

fane person, like Esau, who for one
meal sold his birthright.
17You know also that afterwards
when he desired to inherit the blessing,
he was rejected. For he found no place
of repentance although he earnestly
sought it with tears.
18For you have not come to touch the
mount, and a blazing fire, nor to gloom
and darkness and tempest,
19nor to the sound of trumpets and
the voice of words that the hearers rejected that no words should be spoken
to them.
20For they could not bear that which
was commanded: "And if a beast
should touch the mountain it should be
stoned or shot with an arrow."
21And so fearful was the sight that
Moses said, "I am greatly afraid and
tremble."
22But you have come to Mount Zion
and the city of the Living God, the
heavenly Jerusalem and myriads of angels,
23to the joyful gathering and church
of the firstborn which are written in
heaven, and God the judge of all, and
the spirits of the righteous made perfect,
24and to Jesus the mediator of the
New Covenant, and the blood of sprinkling that speaks better things than
Abel!
25Be sure that you do not refuse Him
who is speaking. If they did not escape
when they refused Him who warned
them on earth, how much less will we
if we refuse Him who warns us from
heaven?
26Whose voice then shook the earth
but now He has promised saying, "Yet
once and for all I shake not only the
earth but also the heaven."
27And this, "Yet once and for all,"
signifies the removal of the things that
are shaken, that the things not shaken
may remain.
28Therefore, receiving an unshake-
able kingdom, let us hold on to grace
through which we can serve God ac-
ceptably with reverence and awe.
29For our God is also a consuming
fire.

13 Let brotherly love continue.
2Do not neglect to show hospitality, for by this some have entertained
angels unaware.
3Remember those who are in prison,
as in prison with them; and those who
are mistreated, since you are also in the
body.
4Marriage is honorable in every way
and the bed undefiled, but fornicators
and adulterers God will judge.
5Let the manner of your life be without love for money, be content with
what you have, for He said He will not
leave you nor forsake you.
6So that we may boldly say, "The
Lord is my helper, and I will not be
afraid of what men might do to me."
7Remember your leaders who spoke
to you the word of God, considering
the outcome of their life, imitate their
faith.
8Jesus Christ who is the same yesterday, today, and forever.
9Do not be carried about with
strange and various teachings, for it is
good for the heart to be strengthened
by grace, not by meat, which has not
profited those devoted to them.
10We have an altar which they have
no authority to eat at who serve the
tabernacle.
11For the bodies of those animals,
whose blood is brought into the Holies
by the High Priest for sin, are burned

outside the camp.
12So also Jesus, that He might sanctify the people with His own blood, suffered outside the gate.
13Therefore we should go to Him
outside the camp, bearing His reproach.
14For we do not have an abiding city
here, but we are seeking the one to
come.
15By Him then let us bring the sacrifice of praise continually to God, that is
the fruit of our lips: confessing His
name.
16But of doing good, and fellowship-
ping, do not be forgetful, for with such
sacrifices God is well pleased.
17Obey your leaders and submit to
them as they watch for your soul, as
those who will have to give an account
for you, that they may do so with joy
and not with groaning, for this would
be unprofitable for you.
18Pray for us, for we are persuaded
that we have a good conscience, desiring to conduct ourselves well in all
things
19I urge you to do this more earnestly, so that we may be restored
to you more quickly.
20And the God of peace who brought
again from the dead our Lord Jesus, the
Great Shepherd of the sheep, by the
blood of the everlasting covenant,
21make you perfect in every good
work to do His will, producing in you
that which is well pleasing in His sight
through Jesus Christ: to whom be glory
to the ages of the ages. Amen!
22But I exhort you, brethren, bear
with my words of exhortation for I
have written to you in few words.
23You should know that our brother
Timothy has been released with whom
I shall see you if he comes soon. 24-
Greet all of your leaders and all the
holy ones, those from Italy greet you.
25Grace be with you all– Amen.

The Epistle of
James

1 James, a slave of God and the Lord
Jesus Christ, to the twelve tribes in
the diaspora: Greetings.
2Count it all joy, brothers, when you
fall into various kinds of trials,
3knowing that the testing of your
faith works endurance.
4But let endurance have its perfect
work, that you may be perfect and
complete, falling short in nothing.
5But if any of you lack wisdom, let
him ask of God, Who gives freely and
does not reproach, and it shall be given
to him.
6But let him ask in faith, nothing wavering. For he that wavers is like a wave
of the sea, driven of the wind and
tossed,
7for let not that man suppose that he
shall receive anything from the Lord.
8A double-minded man is unstable in
all of his ways.
9But let the humble brother boast in
his elevation,
10and the rich in his humiliation, because as the flower of the grass he will
pass away.
11For the sun rose with its burning
heat, and dried up the grass, and its
flower fell, and the beauty of its appearance was destroyed. Thus also the
rich in his goings shall wither away.
12Happy is the man who endures
temptation because, having been tested, he shall receive the crown of life,
which the Lord promised to those who
love Him.
13Let no one, being tempted, say, "I
am tempted of God," for God cannot
be tempted by evil, and Himself tempts
no one.
14But each one is tempted, being
drawn away and allured by his own desire.
15Then, desire, having been conceived, gives birth to sin; and sin, having been finished, brings forth death.
16Do not be deceived, my beloved
brethren.
17Every good gift and every perfect
gift is coming down from above, from
the Father of lights, with Whom is no
variation or shadow of turning.
18He chose to give us birth by the
word of truth, so that we would become a kind of firstfruits of His created
things.
19So, my beloved brethren, let every
man be swift to hear, slow to speak,
slow to wrath,
20for man's wrath does not work the
righteousness of God.
21Therefore, lay aside all moral uncleanness and wickedness and receive
in meekness the implanted word,
which is able to save your souls.
22But be doers of the Word and not
hearers only, deceiving yourselves.
23Because if anyone is a hearer of the
Word and not a doer, this one is like a
man who contemplates his natural face
in a mirror.
24For he considers himself and has
gone away and immediately forgets
what he looks like.
25But he that looks into the perfect
law of freedom, and continues in it,
this one having been a doer and not a
forgetful hearer, shall be blessed in his
doings.
26If anyone among you seems to be
religious and does not bridle his
tongue, but deceives his own heart, this
one's religion is vain.
27Pure and undefiled service before
God and the Father is: to care for the
fatherless and the widows in their
trouble and to keep oneself unspotted
from the world.

2

My brethren, do not have partiality in the faith of our Lord of glory, Jesus Christ.

2 For if anyone comes into your synagogue with a gold ring, in bright clothing, but also a poor one, in filthy clothing,

3 and you look favorably on the one who comes wearing the bright clothing, and you say to him, "Sit here," and to the poor you say, "You stand there," or, "Sit at my footstool,"

4 did you not make a distinction among yourselves and become judges with evil thoughts?

5 Listen, my beloved brothers, has not God chosen the poor of this world rich in faith and heirs of the kingdom which He promised to those who love Him?

6 But you dishonor the poor! Do not the rich oppress you and drag you to court?

7 Do they not blaspheme the good name by which you were called?

8 If you fulfill the royal law according to the scripture you do well, "You shall love your neighbor as yourself."

9 But if you show partiality, you are exposed by the law as transgressors.

10 But whoever keeps the whole law, but shall stumble in one thing, becomes guilty for all.

11 For He who said, "Do not commit adultery," also said, "Do not commit murder." Now if you do not commit adultery, but commit murder, you have become a transgressor of the law.

12 So speak and so do as those who are going to be judged by the law of freedom.

13 For judgment is without mercy to him that has not shown mercy, and mercy triumphs over judgment.

14 What good is it, my brothers, if you say you have faith but do not have works? Can that faith save you?

15 Now if a brother or sister be naked and be destitute of daily food,

16 and anyone said to them from among you, "Go in peace and be warmed and filled," but does not give to them the needful things for the body, of what benefit is it?

17 And so faith without works is dead, being by itself.

18 But some will say, "You have faith and I have works." Show me your faith apart from your works, and I will show you my faith by my works.

19 You believe that God is one? You do well, even the demons believe and shudder.

20 But will you know, O vain man, that faith without works is dead?

21 Was not Abraham our father shown to be righteous by works, having offered Isaac his son upon the altar?

22 You see that faith worked with his works, and by the works faith was accomplished.

23 And the scripture was fulfilled which says, "Abraham believed God, and it was accounted to him for righteousness," and he was called the friend of God.

24 You see then that a man is shown to be righteous by works, and not by faith only.

25 And in the same way, was not Rahab the harlot also shown to be righteous by works, having received the messengers and sent them out by another way?

26 Just as the body is dead without the spirit, even so faith without works is dead.

3

Let there not be many teachers among you, my brethren, knowing

that they shall receive the greater
judgment.
2For we all stumble in many ways. If
anyone does not stumble in word, this
one is a perfect man able to bridle his
whole body.
3Behold, we put bits in the horse's
mouth so that they obey us, and we
guide their whole body.
4Behold also the ships, being so large,
driven under strong winds, are guided
by a small rudder whenever the one
who steers has an impulse.
5So also the tongue is a little member
and boasts great things. How large a
forest is set ablaze by a little fire.
6And the tongue is a fire, a world of
unrighteousness. So is the tongue
among our members that it causes the
whole body to be defiled and sets on
fire the course of human existence, and
is set on fire of hell.
7For every species of beast, and of
birds, and of creeping things, and the
things of the sea is subdued and has
been subdued by the human species.
8But the tongue, no man is able to
subdue. It is an uncontrollable evil, full
of deadly poison.
9With it we bless God and the Father,
and with it we curse men, who are
made in the likeness of God.
10Out of the same mouth goes forth
blessings and cursings. These things
should not be, my brethren.
11Does a spring bring forth from the
same opening both sweet and bitter
water?
12My brethren, a fig tree is not able to
produce olives, or a vine figs. So a
fountain is not able to produce sweet
and bitter water.
13Who is wise and understanding
among you? Let him show out of a
good conduct his works in the meekness of wisdom.
14But if you have bitter jealousy and
strife in your heart, do not boast and lie
against the truth.
15This is not the wisdom that comes
down from above, but is earthly, natural, and demonic.
16Where there is jealousy and strife,
there is insurrection and every evil
work.
17But the wisdom that comes from
above is first pure, peaceable, kind,
agreeable, full of mercy and good
fruits, nonjudgmental, and without
hypocrisy.
18And the fruit of righteousness is
sown in peace by those who make
peace.

4 Where do wars and quarrels come
from among you? Is it not from
your pleasures which battle in your
members?
2You desire and have not, so you
murder. You covet and cannot obtain.
You fight and war, and have not, because you ask not.
3You ask, and do not receive, because
you ask evilly, that you may consume it
in your pleasures.
4Adulterers and adulteresses, don't
you know that friendship with the
world is enmity against God? Whosoever will be the friend of the world
makes himself the enemy of God.
5Do you think it meaningless that the
scripture says, "The spirit which dwells
in us has intense envy"?
6But He gives more grace. For this
reason He said: "God opposes the
proud and gives grace to the humble."
7Subject yourself therefore to God,
resist the Devil and he will flee from
you.
8Draw near to God, and He will draw

near to you. Cleanse your hands, sinners, and purify your hearts, you double-minded.

9 Be miserable and mourn and weep. Let your laughter be turned into mourning, and joy into heaviness.

10 Humble yourselves before the Lord, and He will lift you up.

11 Brethren, do not speak against one another. He that speaks against his brother and judges his brother speaks against the law and judges the law. But if you judge the law, you are not a doer of the law, but a judge.

12 One is the lawgiver who is able to save and destroy. Who are you that judges another?

13 Come now, you who say, "Today and tomorrow we will go to such a town, and spend a year, and we will do business, and make money,"

14 yet you do not know what kind of tomorrow you will have. What is your life? For your life is a mist that appears for a little while and then it vanishes.

15 Instead you should say, "If the Lord desires, and we live, we will also do this or that."

16 But now you pride yourself in your arrogance. All such boasting is evil!

17 Therefore, to know to do good and not do it, to him it is sin.

5 Go now you rich and weep, cry aloud over the distresses that are coming on you.

2 Your riches have decayed, your garments have become moth-eaten.

3 Your gold and silver has been eaten away, and their corrosion shall be a witness against you and shall eat your flesh like fire. You have laid up treasure in the last days.

4 Behold the wages of the laborers who mowed your fields, which you have kept back by fraud. The harvesters cry out, and their cries have come into the ears of the Lord of Sabaoth.

5 You lived luxuriously and in self-indulgence upon the earth. You nourished your hearts as in the days of slaughter.

6 You have condemned; you have killed the righteous, he does not resist you.

7 Therefore, brethren, be patient unto the coming of the Lord. Behold the husbandman awaits the precious fruits of the earth, being patient for it until it receives the early and the latter rain.

8 You also, be patient, establish your hearts because the coming of the Lord draws near.

9 Do not grumble against one another, brethren, so that you may not be condemned. Behold, the judge stands at the door.

10 As an example of suffering and patience, my brethren, consider the prophets who spoke in the name of the Lord.

11 Behold we consider them blessed who endured. We have heard of the endurance of Job and we know the end of the Lord, that the Lord is compassionate and merciful.

12 Above all things my brethren do not swear neither by heaven or earth, nor any other oath. But let your yes be yes, and your no be no, that you do not fall into hypocrisy.

13 Is anyone among you suffering hardship? Let him pray. Is anyone cheerful? Let him praise.

14 Is anyone sick among you? Let him call for the elders of the assembly, and let them pray over him and anoint him with oil in the name of the Lord.

15 And the prayer of faith will save the sick, and the Lord will raise him up. If

he has committed sins, it shall be forgiven.
16Confess your offenses one to another and pray for one another that you
may be healed. The supplications of a
righteous man has great power at work.
17Elijah was a man subject to the
same kind of feelings we have, and he
prayed the prayer that it would not
rain, and it did not rain upon the Earth
for three years and six months.
18And again he prayed and the heavens gave rain, and the Earth sprouted
its fruit.
19Brethren, if any among you err
from the truth and anyone brings him
back,
20let him know that anyone who
brings back a sinner from the error of
his ways shall save a soul from death
and cover a multitude of sins.

THE FIRST EPISTLE OF
PETER

1 Peter, an apostle of Jesus Christ, to the elect sojourners of those dispersed: of Pontus, of Galatia, of Cappadocia, of Asia, and of Bithynia.

2 Grace and peace be multiplied to you through the foreknowledge of God the Father by sanctification of the Spirit unto obedience and sprinkling of the blood of Jesus Christ.

3 Blessed be the God and Father of our Lord Jesus Christ, Who according to His abundant mercy has begotten us again into a living expectation through Jesus Christ's resurrection from the dead,

4 into an inheritance; incorruptible, undefiled, and unfading, having been reserved in Heaven for you,

5 who are kept by the power of God through faith in salvation, ready to be revealed in the last time,

6 in Whom you greatly rejoice; though now if need be, for a little while, you are distressed by a great variety of trials,

7 that the testing of your faith, being much more precious than gold that perishes, even though it's tried with fire, may be found unto praise and glory and honor at the appearing of Jesus Christ,

8 Whom having not seen you love; Whom though now you have not looked upon, yet believing you rejoice with joy unspeakable and clothed with splendor,

9 receiving the fulfillment of your faith: the salvation of your soul.

10 Concerning this salvation, prophets searched out and inquired about the grace prophesied to you,

11 searching into what, or what manner of time, the Spirit of Christ within them made plain, testifying beforehand of the sufferings of Christ and the glory that would follow;

12 to whom it was revealed that not unto themselves, but to you they minister the gospel, now announced to you by the Holy Spirit sent from Heaven, which the angels desire to look into.

13 For this reason, gird up the loins of your mind, being sober, completely relying on the grace being brought to you by the revelation of Jesus Christ.

14 As obedient children, not conforming to the former desires in your ignorance.

15 But according to His holy calling, you shall also be holy in every behavior,

16 because it has been written, "Be holy, because I am holy."

17 And if you call on Father, Who without respect of persons judges according to everyone's work, pass the time of your sojourn in fear,

18 knowing that you were not redeemed with corruptible things, such as silver and gold from your vain way of life- the traditions of your fathers,

19 but with the precious blood of Christ, as a blameless and spotless lamb,

20 having been foreordained before the overthrow of the world, but manifested at this last time for you.

21 Who through Him have their faith in God, who raised Him up from the dead and gave Him glory, so that your faith and confidence can be in God.

22 Having purified your souls by obedience to the truth unto unfeigned love, love one another fervently from a pure heart,

23 having been begotten again, not from a corruptible seed, but an imperishable one, through the living and abiding Word of God,

24 because, "All flesh is as grass and all

of the glory as the flower of grass. The
grass dries up, and the flower fades
away,
25 but the Word of the Lord remains
forever;" and this is the Word that has
been proclaimed to you.

2 Therefore, lay aside all evil, all deceit, hypocrisy, envy, and all evil
speaking.
2 As newborn babes, long for the genuine milk of the Word that you may
grow by it,
3 if you have come to know that the
Lord is gracious.
4 To Whom we draw near, a living
stone, rejected by man, but according
to God: elect, precious.
5 We also as living stones are built up
into a spiritual house, a holy priesthood, lifting up spiritual sacrifices, acceptable to God through Jesus Christ.
6 For this reason it is underscored in
the scripture, "Behold, I lay in Zion a
cornerstone, chosen, precious and
those who believe on Him shall not be
ashamed."
7 Therefore, for those who believe, He
is priceless, but to the unbelieving: "the
stone rejected by the builders, the same
has become the head of the corner,"
8 and, "a stumbling stone and a rock
of scandal" for those who, because of
unbelief, stumble at the Word even as
they were appointed.
9 But you are a chosen race, a royal
priesthood, a holy nation, a people for
a treasured possession, that you may
announce the excellencies of the One
Who called you from darkness into His
marvelous light.
10 Who once were not a people, but
now God's people, who had no mercy,
but now have mercy.
11 Beloved I exhort you as strangers
and sojourners; stay away from the
lusts of the flesh which war against the
soul,
12 having your behavior virtuous
among the nations, that even though
they speak evil of you as evil-doers,
seeing these good works they may glorify God in the day of visitation.
13 Submit to every human ordinance
because of the Lord– whether to a king
as supreme,
14 or to governors, as those sent by
him to punish evildoers but to approve
uprightness–
15 because this is the will of God, doing good silences the ignorance of foolish men.
16 As free, and not having freedom as
a covering of wickedness, but as the
servants of God.
17 Honor everyone. Love the brother-
hood. Fear God. Honor the king.
18 House-servants, be subject with all
fear to the masters, not only to the
good and equitable, but also to the
crooked.
19 For this is grace: if on account of
God-consciousness, one endures pain,
suffering wrongfully.
20 For should there be credit if you
endure a beating for having sinned?
But if you do good and endure suffering, you have God's approval.
21 For you are called to this, because
Christ also suffered on your behalf,
leaving you an example, that you
should follow after His footsteps:
22 "Who did not sin, neither was guile
found in His mouth,"
23 Who being insulted, did not insult
in return; suffering, did not threaten–
but handed it over to righteous judgment,
24 Who Himself carried our sins in
His own body upon the tree, so that

being dead to sins, we might live righteously, "by whose wound you were
healed."
25For you were as sheep gone astray,
but now are returned to the Shepherd
and Bishop of your souls.

3 Likewise wives, be submitted to
your own husbands, so that even if
any disobey the Word, they will be won
without the Word through the conduct
of the wives,
2observing that in fear you behave
yourself with purity.
3Of whom let it not be the outward–
braiding of hair, and putting on gold or
worldly garments,
4but the hidden man of the heart, in
the incorruptible, in the gentle and
quiet spirit, which is of great value before God.
5For in this way also, the holy
women, whose expectation was in
God, ordered themselves, being subject
to their own husbands,
6as Sarah listened to Abraham, calling him "lord," to whom you have become children, doing good and not being terrified at any threatening thing.
7The husbands likewise, dwelling together according to knowledge, as with
a weaker vessel, giving honor to the
wife as also heirs together of the grace
of life, that your prayers be not cut off.
8Now finally, everyone be of one
mind: understanding, loving as brothers, compassionate, lowly,
9not returning evil for evil, or abuse
for abuse, but on the contrary, blessing– because you are called to this so
that you might inherit a blessing.
10For he who would love life and see
good days shall restrain his tongue
from evil, even his lips from speaking
deceit.
11Turn away from evil and do good.
Seek peace and pursue it,
12because the Lord's eyes are upon
the righteous and His ears unto their
petitions, but the Lord's face is against
evil-doers!
13And who can harm you if you become imitators of the good,
14but blessed, if you truly suffer because of righteousness– but do not fear
their terror, nor be troubled.
15But sanctify the Lord God in your
heart, and always be prepared to give a
defense to anyone who asks you anything concerning the expectation in
you, with meekness and fear,
16having a good conscience, that if
they speak against you as evil-doers,
they who revile your good behavior in
Christ may be ashamed.
17For it is better, if the will of God
wills, that you suffer for doing good
rather than doing evil,
18because Christ also once suffered
for sin, the righteous on behalf of the
unrighteous, so that He might bring us
to God. Indeed, put to death in the
flesh, but having been made alive in the
Spirit,
19by Whom also, going in, He
preached to those spirits in prison:
20those who disobeyed. When once
the longsuffering of God waited in the
days of Noah, an ark was prepared, into
which a few, that is, eight souls, were
saved by water,
21which also corresponds now to our
salvation: baptism, not the putting
away of filth of flesh, but the answer of
a good conscience toward God by the
resurrection of Jesus Christ,
22Who has gone into Heaven at the
right hand of God– angels and authorities and powers being subject to Him.

4 Seeing that Christ suffered for us
in the flesh, arm yourself with the
same thinking, for he who suffers in
the flesh has ceased from sin,
2so as to not live the rest of your life
in the flesh, in the desires of men, but
the will of God.
3For enough time of our life has been
spent working the will of the gentiles,
having walked in licentiousness, lust,
drunkenness, partying, drinking bouts
and lawless idolatries,
4in which they are surprised that you
do not run with them into the blasphemous excess of the unsaved,
5who shall give account to Him Who
is ready to judge the living and the
dead.
6For this reason, the gospel was also
preached to the dead, that they may be
judged according to men in the flesh,
but live according to God in the Spirit.
7Now the end of all things is near–
therefore be sober and watch through
prayer.
8Above all things, have fervent love
among yourselves, because love will
cover a multitude of sins.
9Use hospitality toward one another
without complaining.
10According as each one has received
a gift, minister one to another as good
stewards of the manifold grace of God.
11If anyone speaks, do so as oracles of
God. If anyone ministers, do so from
out of the strength that God directs
that in all things God may be glorified
through Christ Jesus to Whom be the
glory and might to the ages of the ages.
Amen!
12Beloved, do not be surprised by the
fiery trial that tries you as though a
strange event happened to you.
13Rather, rejoice as partakers of the
sufferings of Christ, that also in the revealing of His glory you may rejoice
with great joy.
14Happy are you if you are reproached for the name of Christ, because the glory and the Spirit of God
rest upon you– on their part He is
blasphemed, but on your part He is
glorified.
15Let none of you suffer as a murderer, or a thief, or an evil-doer, or as a
meddler in the affairs of others–
16but if as a Christian, do not be
ashamed, but in this regard glorify
God,
17because the time of judgment has
begun at the house of God– and if first
with us, what shall the end be of the
disobedient who do not follow the
gospel of God?
18And if the righteous are barely
saved, where will the ungodly and sinners appear?
19Now therefore, those who suffer
according to the will of God commit
their souls to Him by doing good, as to
a Faithful Creator.

5 Therefore, the elders among you I
exhort, being a fellow elder and
witness of the sufferings of Christ and a
partaker of the glory about to be revealed.
2Shepherd the flock of God among
you, taking the oversight– not of necessity, but voluntarily– according to God,
and not eager for base gain, but freely,
3neither as exercising dominion over
the heritage, but as being an example to
the flock.
4And at the appearing of the Chief
Shepherd, you shall receive an unfading crown of glory.
5Likewise younger, obey the elder,
and everyone be subject one to another, and be clothed with humility, be-

cause God battles against anyone who
exalts himself above others, but gives
grace to the lowly.
6Therefore, humble yourself under
the mighty hand of God that you may
be exalted in time,
7casting all of your care upon Him
because He cares for you.
8Think clearly, be alert– your adversary the Devil goes about as a roaring
lion seeking someone to devour,
9whom you must resist firmly in the
faith, knowing that the same sufferings
are accomplished by your brethren
who are in the world.
10And the God of all grace, Who
called you into His eternal glory in
Christ Jesus, after you have suffered a
little, will restore you, establish,
strengthen, set firm.
11To Him be glory and might to the
ages of the ages. Amen!
12I wrote a little to you through your
faithful brother, Silvanus, as I thought
best, exhorting and witnessing this to
be the true grace of God, in which you
stand.
13Those chosen together with you in
Babylon greet you– also Mark, my son.
14Greet one another with a kiss of
love. Peace to all those in Christ Jesus.
Amen!

THE SECOND EPISTLE OF
PETER

1 Simon Peter, a slave and apostle of Jesus Christ, to those equally honored with us, having obtained faith by the righteousness of our God and our Savior, Jesus Christ.

2 Grace to you, and peace multiplied by an exact knowledge of God and Jesus our Lord.

3 As His divine power has given us all things pertaining to life and godliness through the knowledge of the One Who has called us to glory and excellent character,

4 through which precious and exceedingly great promises are given to us, that through these you may be partakers of the divine nature, having escaped from the corruption that is in the world through lust.

5 For this reason, give all diligence to supply by your faith excellence of character, and with excellence of character, knowledge,

6 and with knowledge, self-control, and with self-control, patience, and with patience, godliness,

7 and with godliness, brotherly-kindness, and in brotherly-kindness, love.

8 For these things being in you and abounding, you shall not be barren or unfruitful in the complete knowledge of our Lord, Jesus Christ.

9 For the one in whom these things are not present is blind and short-sighted, forgetting that he was cleansed from his former sins.

10 On account of this, brethren, instead be diligent to make your calling and election sure– for doing these things, you shall never stumble.

11 For in this way, an entrance shall be abundantly supplied to you into the everlasting Kingdom of our Lord and Savior, Jesus Christ.

12 Therefore, I will not neglect to continually remind you concerning these things, although you know and have been established in the present truth.

13 Now, I think it right, that as long as I am in this tabernacle, to stir you up with a reminder,

14 knowing that soon I will put off this tabernacle, just as also our Lord, Jesus Christ, declared to me.

15 And I will also be diligent to cause that you may always have memory of these things after my departure.

16 For we did not follow cleverly-invented fables when we made known to you the power and coming of our Lord, Jesus Christ, but were eye-witnesses of that majesty.

17 For receiving honor and glory from Father God when a voice came to Him from the magnificent glory, "This is My beloved Son in Whom I am well-pleased,"

18 and this voice we heard when it came from Heaven when we were with Him in the holy mount.

19 And we have a more certain word of prophecy that you do well to take hold of as a light shining in a dark place until the day shines through and the morning star arises in your heart.

20 Knowing this first: that every prophecy of Scripture did not come by one's own interpretation.

21 For prophecy did not come at any time by the will of man, but was brought forth by the Holy Spirit as holy men of God spoke.

2 Now there were also false prophets among the people, just as also false teachers shall be among you, who shall sneak in destructive opinions, also resisting the Master Who bought them, bringing upon themselves swift destruction.

2And many shall follow their destructive ways, through which the way of truth will be slandered.

3And by covetously crafted words, they will use you for their own gain, whose judgment shall not wait long, and their destruction shall not slumber.

4For if God spared not the angels who sinned, but put them in chains of darkness, casting them into Hell to be kept for judgment,

5and did not spare the ancient world, but kept Noah, the eighth, a preacher of righteousness, bringing a flood upon a world of ungodliness,

6and overthrowing cities of Sodom and Gomorrah, burning it to ashes, condemned them, setting an example for ungodliness,

7and delivered righteous Lot, who had been worn down by the lawless behavior of the licentious;

8(for the righteous man living among them, seeing and hearing their lawless deeds day after day, tormented his righteous soul);

9then the Lord knows how to deliver the godly from temptation, but the unrighteous are kept to a day of judgment to be punished–

10and most of all, those who walk after the flesh in the lust of defilement and despise authorities: arrogant, self-serving, not afraid to speak evil of glories.

11Whereas angels, being of greater strength and power, do not bring before the Lord a slanderous judgment against them.

12But these as irrational animals according to nature, having been born for capture and destruction, speak evil about things they do not understand, and by their corruption shall perish.

13Doing wrong for an unrighteous wage, taking pleasure in the day of luxury, spots and blemishes, sporting themselves with their own deceptions, feasting with you,

14having eyes full of adultery and that cannot cease from sin, beguile unstable souls, having their hearts exercised in greediness. Accursed children,

15forsaking the right way, wanderers following the way of Balaam of Beor, who loved the wages of unrighteousness,

16but had his iniquity rebuked by a speechless donkey speaking with a man's voice to prevent the prophet's madness.

17These are fountains without water, clouds driven under a hurricane, to whom the darkest darkness is reserved forever.

18For with excessive empty speeches they beguile those– who had escaped from them who live in error– with fleshly lusts and lascivious acts,

19promising them freedom, yet themselves being slaves of corruption– for by whom anyone is overcome, by the same he is enslaved.

20For if these, having escaped the defilement of the world by the knowledge of our Lord and Savior, Jesus Christ, and are again entangled, having been overcome, their last state shall be worse than the first.

21For it would have been better for them not to have fully known the way of righteousness, than knowing, to turn back from the holy commandment delivered to them.

22It has happened to them according to the true proverb: the dog has returned to his own vomit– also, the hog, having been washed, to its filthy wallowing.

3 Beloved, I now write this second epistle, in which I stir up your pure minds by a reminder.

2Remember the word spoken before by the holy prophets and the command of the Lord and Savior by us, the apostles.

3Knowing this first, that in the last day there will be scoffers walking after their own lust,

4and saying, "Where is the promise of His coming? For since the fathers died, all things remain the same from the beginning of creation."

5For they have purposely not taken notice that the heavens were of long ago, and the Earth came out of the water, and afterward, the water was established by the word of God–

6through which the world at that time was utterly destroyed, being inundated with water.

7But the heavens and the Earth that exist now are reserved for fire by His word, kept until a day of judgment and destruction of the ungodly men.

8But beloved, let not this one thing escape you: that one day with the Lord is as a thousand years, and a thousand years as one day.

9The Lord of the promise does not delay as some think it's delayed, but is patient toward us, not willing for anyone to be destroyed, but for all to come to repentance.

10But the Day of the Lord will come as a thief– in which the heavens will pass away with a great noise, and the elements will be destroyed with a fervent heat, and the Earth and the works in it shall be burned up.

11With everything being destroyed in this way, what manner of lifestyle should you have in holiness and godliness,

12expecting and hastening to the coming of the Day of God, through which the heavens, being set on fire, will be destroyed, and the elements will melt with a fervent heat?

13But according to His promise, we look with expectation for a new Heaven and a new Earth in which righteousness dwells.

14Beloved, because you look for these things, be diligent, spotless, and blameless in Him, being found in peace.

15And consider the longsuffering of our Lord for salvation, just as also our beloved brother Paul wrote to you according to the wisdom given to him,

16as also in all his epistles, speaking in them of these things– in which are some things hard to understand, which those who are unstable and unlearned pervert, as also they distort the Scriptures, to their own destruction.

17You then, beloved, knowing this beforehand, beware that you be not led away with the error of iniquity, falling from your own steadfastness.

18But grow in grace and knowledge of our Lord and Savior, Jesus Christ. To Him be glory, both now and forever! Amen!

The First Epistle of
John

1

That which was from the beginning, which we have heard, which we have seen with our eyes, which we have looked upon, and our hands have handled: the Word of Life.

2 And the Life was revealed, and we have seen and bear witness and we proclaim to you that Eternal Life which was with the Father and was revealed to us.

3 What we have seen and heard we proclaim to you, so that you may also have fellowship with us, and indeed our fellowship is with the Father and with His Son Jesus Christ.

4 And these things we write to you that your joy may be full.

5 Now this is the message that we have heard of Him and declare unto you: that God is Light and in Him is no darkness at all.

6 If we say that we have fellowship with Him and walk in darkness, we lie and do not the truth.

7 But if we walk in the Light as He Himself is in the Light, we have fellowship with one another, and the blood of Jesus Christ, His Son, purifies us from all sin.

8 If we should say, "We have no sin," we deceive ourselves, and the truth is not in us.

9 If we should confess our sins, He is faithful and righteous to forgive us of the sins and to cleanse us from all unrighteousness.

10 If we say, "We have not sinned," we make Him a liar, and His Word is not in us.

2

My little children, I write these things to you so that you do not sin. But if anyone sins, we have an Advocate with the Father, Jesus Christ the righteous.

2 And He is the purgation for our sins, and not for ours only, but also for the whole world.

3 And by this we know that we know Him: because we keep His commands.

4 The one who says, "I know Him," but does not keep His commandments, is a liar and the truth is not in him.

5 But whoever keeps His Word, truly in him is the love of God perfected. This is how we know that we are in Him.

6 He that says he abides in Him ought himself to walk also just as He walks.

7 Brethren, this is not a new commandment that I write to you, but an old commandment, which you had from the beginning. The old commandment is the Word that you have heard from the beginning.

8 Again a new commandment I write to you, which is true in Him and in you, because the darkness is past and the true light now shines.

9 He that says he is in the light and hates his brother is still in the darkness, even now.

10 He that loves his brother abides in the light, and there is no occasion of stumbling in him.

11 But he that hates his brother is in the darkness and walks in darkness and does not know where he is going, because the darkness has blinded his eyes.

12 I write to you little children because your sins have been sent away because of His name.

13 I write unto you fathers, because you have known Him Who is from the beginning. I write to you young men, because you have conquered the evil one.

14 I have written unto you littlest children, because you know the Father.

I have written unto you fathers because
you have known Him Who is from the
beginning. I have written unto you
young men, because you are mighty,
and the Word of God dwells in you,
and you have conquered the evil one.
15Do not love the world, nor the
things in the world. If anyone loves the
world, the love of the Father is not in
him.
16Because all that is in the world– the
lust of the flesh, the lust of the eyes,
and the pride of life– is not of the
Father, but is of the world.
17And the world passes away and its
desires, but he who does the will of
God abides forever.
18Littlest children, it is the last time,
and as you have heard, the antichrist
comes and now there are many
antichrists here, whereby we know that
it is the last time.
19They went out from us, but they
were not of us. If they had been of us,
they would have remained with us.
Nevertheless, it is revealed that none of
them are of us.
20And we have an anointing from the
Holy One, and we know everything.
21I have not written because you do
not know the truth, but because you
know it, for there is not one lie that is
of the truth.
22Who is a liar, but he that denies
that Jesus is the Christ? He is an
antichrist that denies the Father and
the Son.
23All that deny the Son do not have
the Father. He who confesses the Son
also has the Father.
24What you have heard from the
beginning, let it dwell in you. If what
you heard from the beginning dwells in
you, then you shall dwell in the Son
and in the Father.
25And this is the promise that He has
promised us: eternal life.
26I write this to you concerning those
who deceive you.
27And the anointing that you have
received from Him dwells in you, (and
you do not need that anyone teach you,
but the anointing teaches you about
everything and is no lie) and just as it
has taught you, you shall dwell in Him.
28And now little children, dwell in
Him, so that when He shall appear you
will have confidence and not be
ashamed before Him at His coming.
29If you know that He is righteous,
you also know that everyone that acts
righteously has been begotten of Him.

3 Look at what amazing love the Father has given to us: that we should
be called the children of God! Therefore the world does not know us, because it did not know Him.
2Beloved, we are now the children of
God. And it has not yet been revealed
what we shall be, but when He is revealed we shall be like Him, because we
shall see Him as He is.
3And everyone that has this expectation in Him purifies himself even as He
is pure.
4Everyone who acts sinfully also does
iniquity, for sin is iniquity.
5And we know that He was revealed
to take away sins, and in Him is no sin.
6Everyone who abides in Him does
not sin. Everyone that sins has not seen
Him nor known Him.
7Little children let no one deceive
you: he who does righteousness is
righteous, just as He is righteous.
8He who acts sinfully is of the Devil
because the Devil sinned from the beginning. For this reason the Son of
God was revealed to destroy the works

of the Devil.
9 Everyone who has been begotten of
God does not sin because His seed
abides in him and he cannot sin, because he is born of God.
10 In this is manifested the children of
God and the children of the Devil:
everyone who does not act righteously
is not of God, nor is he who loves not
his brother.
11 Because this is the message that you
have heard from the beginning: that
you should love one another.
12 Not as Cain who was of the evil one
and murdered his brother. Why did he
murder him? Because his own works
were evil, but his brother's were righteous.
13 And do not be surprised, brethren,
if the world hates you.
14 We know that we have passed from
death to life, because we love the
brethren. He who does not love his
brother abides in death.
15 Everyone who hates his brother is a
murderer, and you know that a murderer does not have eternal life abiding
in him.
16 By this we have known the love of
God: because He laid down His soul
for us, and we owe it to lay down our
soul for the brethren.
17 But he who has this world's living
and sees his brother in need and shuts
off his compassion from him, how does
the love of God dwell in him?
18 Little children, let us not love in
word only, nor with talk only, but in
deed and truth.
19 And by this we know that we are of
the truth and shall assure our hearts
before Him.
20 Because if our heart condemns us,
God is greater than our heart and
knows everything.
21 Beloved, if our heart does not condemn us, then we have confidence before God.
22 And whatever we ask of Him, we
receive, because we keep His commands and do what is pleasing in His
sight.
23 And this is His command: that we
believe on the name of His Son, Jesus
Christ, and love one another as He
commanded us.
24 And he that keeps His commands
dwells in Him, and He in him. And by
this we know that He dwells in us: by
the Spirit Who He gave us.

4 Beloved, believe not every spirit,
but try the spirits, whether they are
from God, because many false prophets
have gone out into the world.
2 By this we know the Spirit of God:
every spirit that confesses that Jesus
Christ is come in the flesh is from God,
3 and every spirit that does not confess Jesus Christ has come in the flesh
is not of God, and this is that antichrist
that you heard would come and now is
already in the world.
4 You are of God, little children, and
have conquered them, because greater
is He that is in you than he that is in
the world.
5 They are of the world– for this reason, they speak from the world and the
world hears them.
6 You are of God– he that knows God
hears us. He who is not of God does
not hear us. By this we know the Spirit
of truth and the spirit of error.
7 Beloved, let us love one another, because he that loves is from God, and
everyone that loves is begotten of God
and knows God.
8 He that does not love does not know
God, for God is love.

9In this the love of God was revealed
in us: because the only begotten Son of
God was sent into the world that we
may live through Him.
10In this is love: not that we loved
God, but that He loved us and sent His
Son to be the purgation for our sins.
11Beloved, if God so loved us, we
ought to love one another.
12No one has ever seen God. If we
love one another, God abides in us and
His love is perfected in us.
13By this we know that we dwell in
Him and He dwells in us: because of
the Spirit that He has given us.
14And we have seen and bear witness
that the Father sent the Son as the Savior of the world.
15Whoever confesses that Jesus is the
Son of God: God dwells in Him, and he
dwells in God.
16And we know and believe the love
that God has in us. God is love, and he
that dwells in love dwells in God, and
God dwells in Him.
17In this the love is perfected within
us: that we may have confidence in the
day of judgment, because as He is, so
are we in this world.
18There is no fear in love. Perfect love
casts out all fear, because fear has torment. Now he who fears is not perfected in love.
19As for us, we love Him because He
first loved us.
20If anyone says that he loves God
and he hates his brother, he is a liar. For
the one who has no love for his brother
whom he has seen cannot love God
Who he has never seen.
21And this is the commandment that
we have from Him: that he who loves
God also loves His brother.

5 Everyone who believes that Jesus is
the Christ has been begotten of
God, and everyone who loves Him
Who begot also loves those begotten of
Him.
2By this we know that we love the
children of God: whenever we love
God and obey His commandments.
3For this is the love of God: that we
keep His commandments, and His
commandments are not burdensome.
4Because everyone who is begotten of
God conquers the world– and this is
the conquering power that conquered
the world: even our faith.
5Who is conquering the world except
the one who believes that Jesus is the
Son of God?
6This is the One who came through
water and blood: Jesus the Christ. Not
by the water only, but by the water and
by the blood– and the Spirit is the witness, because the Spirit is the truth.
7Because there are three who bear
witness in Heaven: the Father, the
Word, and the Holy Spirit, and these
Three are One.
8And there are Three Who bear witness in the Earth: the Spirit, the water,
and the blood– and these three are in
one.
9If we receive the witness of man, the
witness of God is greater, for this is
God's testimony that He testified concerning His Son.
10He that believes on the Son of God
has this witness in himself. He who
does not believe God makes Him a liar,
because he has not believed in the witness that God had witnessed concerning His Son.
11And this is the witness, that God
has given us: eternal life– and this life
is in His Son.
12He who has the Son has life, and he

who does not have the Son of God does
not have life.

13I wrote these things to you who believe on the name of the Son of God–
that you may know that you have eternal life, and that you may believe in the
name of the Son of God.

14And this is the confidence that we
have toward Him: if we ask anything
according to His will, He hears us.

15And if we know that He hears us,
then if we ask, we know that we possess
the requests that we asked of Him.

16If anyone sees his brother sin a sin
not unto death, he shall ask, and he
shall give him life for the sin that is not
unto death. There is a sin unto death– I
do not say that anyone should ask concerning that.

17All unrighteousness is sin, and
there is a sin not unto death.

18We know that everyone that is begotten of God sins not, but the one begotten of God keeps himself and the
evil one cannot touch him.

19We know that we are of God, and
the whole world lies in wickedness.

20We know that the Son of God has
come and given us an understanding:
that we might know Him Who is true.
And we are in Him Who is true: in His
Son, Jesus Christ– this is the true God
and eternal life.

21Little children, keep yourselves
from idols. Amen!

THE SECOND EPISTLE OF
JOHN

1 The Presbyter, to the elect lady and to her children, whom I love in truth, and not only I, but also all those who have known the truth,

2 because the truth abides in us and will be with us forever.

3 For with us there is grace, peace, and mercy from God the Father and from the Lord Jesus Christ, the Son of the Father, in truth and love.

4 I greatly rejoiced that I found your children walking in truth, just as we received a commandment from the Father.

5 And now I ask you Lady– not as writing a new commandment to you, but the one we have had from the beginning– let us love one another.

6 And this is the love: that we walk according to His commandments. This is the commandment, just as you have heard it from the beginning, so that you may walk in it.

7 Because many deceivers have gone out into the world who do not confess that Jesus Christ has come in the flesh– this is the deceiver and the antichrist.

8 You yourselves should watch out that you do not lose what you have worked for– rather receive your full wages.

9 Everyone who transgresses and does not remain in the doctrine of Christ does not have God. Those who abide in the doctrine of Christ also have the Father and the Son.

10 If anyone comes to you and does not bring this doctrine, do not receive him into your house and do not say to him, "Be well."

11 For whoever says to him, "Be well," shares in his evil works.

12 I have much to write to you, but I do not want to with paper and ink– rather, I hope to come to you and talk face-to-face that your joy may be full.

13 The children of your elect sister greet you. Amen.

THE THIRD EPISTLE OF
JOHN

1 The Presbyter, to the beloved Gaius, whom I love in truth.

2 Beloved, all things considered, I pray that you prosper and be in health, even as your soul prospers.

3 I rejoiced greatly when the brethren came and testified of your truth, even as you are walking in truth.

4 I could not have had greater joy than this: to hear that my children are walking in the truth.

5 Beloved, if you work, do it faithfully for the brethren and the strangers,

6 who testify on your behalf of your love for the church– which you do well, sending them on their way worthy of God–

7 who indeed for the sake of the Name go out, taking nothing from the nations.

8 Therefore, we owe it to take such care of them that we may become coworkers with the truth.

9 I wrote to the church, but Diotrephes, who loves to be foremost among them, does not recognize us.

10 Therefore, if I come, I will remember his works that he does: talking nonsense about us with evil words– and not satisfied with this, he does not recognize the brethren; and those who would, he forbids, and casts them out of the church.

11 Beloved, do not imitate what is harmful, but what is good. He that does good is from God– he that does evil things has not seen God.

12 Demetrius is borne witness by everyone, and by the truth itself, and we also bear witness, and you know that our witness is true.

13 I had many things to write to you, but I will not write with ink and pen.

14 Rather, I hope to see you at once, and we shall speak face-to-face. Peace to you. Our friends greet you. Greet the friends by name.

THE EPISTLE OF
JUDE

1 Jude, a servant of Jesus Christ and brother of James, to those made holy by Father God, called and guarded in Jesus Christ.

2 Mercy to you, and peace and love be multiplied.

3 Beloved, having made all haste to write to you concerning the common salvation, I have written to you out of an emergency to urge you to contend for the faith that was once and for all entrusted to the saints.

4 For certain men snuck in, whose condemnation was written about long ago; ungodly men who pervert the grace of our God into licensed immorality, and refuse our only sovereign God and our Lord Jesus Christ.

5 Now I desire to remind you: for you once knew that the Lord, Who saved the people from Egypt, afterward destroyed those who did not believe.

6 Also, those angels who did not keep their proper place, but left their place of habitation, are eternally bound under a hold of darkness until the great day of judgment.

7 As Sodom and Gomorrah and the surrounding cities in the same manner indulged in sexual immorality and pursued unnatural desires, which have set precedence, undergoing the judgment of eternal fire,

8 indeed in the same way these dreamers also defile the flesh, reject authority, and slander glories.

9 But Michael the arch-angel, when contending with the Devil, having disputed about the body of Moses, did not dare bring a slanderous judgment, but said, "The Lord rebukes you!"

10 But these slander the things that they do not understand, and like irrational animals do whatever their depraved instincts dictate; thereby bringing on their own destruction!

11 Woe to them, for they have gone in the way of Cain, poured out themselves to Balaam's error for gain, and perished in Korah's rebellion!

12 These are blemishes in your fellowship of love, while they feast with you, eating without fear, shepherding themselves. Clouds without water, carried about by the winds, dry fruitless trees, twice dead, plucked up by the roots,

13 wild waves of the sea, foaming with their shame, wandering stars for whom the deepest darkness has been reserved forever.

14 Enoch, the seventh from Adam, prophesied about these kinds of people saying, "Behold, the Lord comes with multitudes of His saints

15 to execute judgment on all, and to punish all the ungodly for all the ungodly deeds that they have ungodly committed, and concerning all the harsh things that the ungodly have spoken against Him."

16 These are murmurers and complainers, having gone according to their lusts, and their mouth speaks proud things, flattering others to gain an advantage.

17 But you, beloved, remember the words spoken before by the apostles of our Lord Jesus Christ,

18 for they said to you that in the last time there will be scoffers indulging their own ungodly desires.

19 These are those who cause divisions, carnal ones who do not have the Spirit.

20 But with your most holy faith, beloved, build yourselves up, praying in the Holy Spirit.

21 Keep yourselves in the love of God, receiving the mercy of our Lord Jesus Christ unto eternal life.

[22]Have mercy on some, having discernment–
[23]some save by fear, snatching them
from the fire, hating even the garment
spotted by the flesh.
[24]Now to the One Who is able to
keep you from stumbling and present
you faultless before the presence of His
glory with exceeding joy,
[25]to the only wise God our Savior, be
glory and majesty, power and authority,
both now and throughout all eternity.
Amen.

The Revelation of Jesus Christ

1 The Revelation of Jesus Christ,
which God gave Him to show His
servants what must take place soon.
And He made it known, sending His
messenger to His servant John,

2 who has borne witness to the Word
of God and the testimony of Jesus
Christ of all that he saw.

3 Blessed is he who reads and those
who hear the words of this prophecy
and keep the things written in it, for
the time is near.

4 John to the seven churches that are
in Asia. Grace to you and Peace from
Him who is and was and is to come,
and from the seven spirits that are before His throne.

5 And from Jesus Christ, the faithful
witness, the firstborn from among the
dead, and the ruler of the kings of the
earth– The One Who loves us and has
washed us from our sins with His own
blood,

6 and has made us kings and priests to
God and His Father; glory and might
to Him for ever and ever. Amen.

7 Behold He comes with clouds and
every eye shall see Him, and they
which pierced Him. Yes, and all the
tribes of the earth shall wail on account
of Him, amen.

8 "I am the Alpha and the Omega,
Beginning and Ending," says the Lord,
"Who is and Who was and Who is to
come, the Almighty."

9 I John, also your brother and fellow-
partaker in the tribulation and in the
kingdom and the endurance of Jesus
Christ, was in the island which is called
Patmos because of the Word of God
and because of the testimony of Jesus
Christ.

10 I was in the Spirit on the Lord's day,
and I heard a loud voice as a trumpet
behind me,

11 saying, "I am the Alpha and the
Omega, the first and the last, and what
you see write in a book and send to the
churches which are in Asia: to Ephesus,
and to Smyrna, and to Pergamos, and
to Thyatira, and to Sardis, and to Philadelphia, and to Laodicea.

12 And I turned to see the voice,
which spoke with me, and having
turned I saw seven golden menorahs.

13 And in the midst of the seven
lampstands one like a Son of Man with
a robe reaching to His feet fastened at
the chest with a gold belt.

14 And His head and hair were white
like wool, as white as snow, and His
eyes as a flame of fire.

15 And His feet like fine brass, as if
glowing in a furnace; and His voice as
the voice of many waters.

16 And having in His right hand seven
stars, and a sharp two-edged sword was
going forth out of His mouth, and His
countenance was as the sun shines in
its power.

17 And when I saw Him, I fell at His
feet as dead, and He laid His right hand
upon me, saying to me, "Fear not; I am
the first and the last,

18 and the Living One, and I became
dead, and, behold, I am alive for ever
and ever– Amen– and have the keys of
Hell and of Death.

19 Write the things that you have seen,
and the things that are, and the things
that are about to take place after these
things.

20 The mystery of the seven stars,
which you saw upon my right hand,
and the seven golden lampstands. The
seven stars are the seven messengers of
the seven churches; and the seven
lampstands which you saw are the sev-
en churches."

2 To the messenger in the Ephesian Church write: This is what He says, Who holds the seven stars in His right hand, Who walks in the midst of the seven golden lampstands:

2 “I know your works, and your hard labor, and your endurance, and that you cannot tolerate evil. And you examined those who claim to be apostles, and are not, and found them to be liars.

3 And you have borne, and patiently endured, and you have labored and have not grown weary for My Name.

4 But I have this against you, that you have left your first love.

5 Remember therefore where you have fallen from and do the first works. But if not, I will come to you quickly and I will remove your menorah out of its place, unless you repent.

6 But this you have, that you hate the works of the Nicolaitanes, which I also hate.

7 He that has an ear, let him hear what the Spirit says to the churches. To him that overcomes I will give him to eat from the tree of life, which is in the midst of the paradise of God.”

8 And to the messenger in the Smyrneans church write: “This is what the first and the last says, Who became dead and lives.

9 I know your works and your tribulation and poverty, but you are rich. Also the slander of those who claim to be Jews and are not, but are a synagogue of Satan.

10 The things that you are about to suffer, do not fear at all. Behold, the Devil is about to cast some of you into prison that you may be tried, and you shall have tribulation for ten days. Be faithful unto death, and I will give you a crown of life.

11 He that has an ear, let him hear what the Spirit says to the churches. He that overcomes shall in no way be injured from the second death.”

12 And to the messenger in the Pergamos church write: “this is what He says, Who has the sharp two-edged sword.

13 I know your works and where you dwell, where the throne of Satan is. And you cling to my name and have not denied my faith, even in the days in which Antipas my faithful witness, who was killed among you where Satan dwells.

14 But I have a few things against you, because you have there those who hold to the teachings of Balaam, who taught Balak to cast a stumbling block before the sons of Israel, to eat things sacrificed to idols and to commit sexual immorality.

15 So you also have those holding to the doctrines of the Nicolaitanes, which I hate.

16 Repent, and if not, I am coming to you quickly and I will make war with them by the sword of my mouth.

17 He that has an ear let him hear what the Spirit says to the churches. To him that overcomes I will give to him to eat of the hidden manna. And I will give to him a white stone, and on the stone a new name written, which no one knows except he who receives it.”

18 And to the messenger in the Thyatira church write: “this is what the Son of God says, Who has eyes as a flame of fire and His feet like fine brass.

19 I know your works, love, service, faith and your endurance, and also your last works to be more than your first.

20 But I have a few things against you because you allow that woman Jezebel,

who calls herself a prophetess, to teach and mislead my servants to commit sexual immorality and to eat things sacrificed to idols.

21 And I gave her time that she might repent of her sexual immorality, and she did not repent.

22 Behold, I cast her into a bed, and those who commit adultery with her into great tribulation, unless they repent of their works.

23 And her children I will kill with death, and all of the churches will know that I am the One who searches the minds and the hearts, and I will give to each of you according to your works.

24 But to you I say, and the rest who are in Thyatira, as many as do not have this teaching and who have not known the depths of Satan, such as they express; I will not cast any other burden upon you.

25 But what you have, hold fast until I come.

26 And he that overcomes and he that keeps My works until the end, I will give authority over the nations,

27 and he shall shepherd them with a rod of iron, as vessels of pottery are broken in pieces, just as I also have received from my Father.

28 And I will give him the morning star.

29 He that has an ear let him hear what the Spirit says to the churches."

3 And to the messenger in the Sardis church write: "this is what He says Who has the seven spirits of God and the seven stars. I know your works, that you have a name of being alive, but you are dead.

2 Be watchful! And strengthen the things that remain, which are about to die, for I have not discovered your work to be complete before My God.

3 Remember then how you have received and heard, and keep it and repent. However, if you do not watch, I will come like a thief and you will not know at what hour I will come upon you.

4 You have a few names also in Sardis that have not defiled their garments; and they shall walk with Me in white, because they are worthy.

5 He who overcomes will be clothed in white garments, and I will not blot out his name from the book of life, and I will confess his name before my Father and before His angels.

6 He who has an ear let him hear what the Spirit says to the churches."

7 And to the messenger in the Philadelphia church write; "this is what He Who is Holy and True says, Who has the keys of David, Who opens and no one shuts and Who shuts and no one opens.

8 I know your works, behold I set before you an open door and no one can shut it, because you have a little power, and you have kept my word and not denied My Name.

9 Behold, I will give them from the synagogue of Satan that say they are Jews and are not but are liars; behold, I will make them come then and worship before your feet and they shall know that I have loved you.

10 Because you have kept the word of my endurance, I also shall keep you from the hour of temptation that is about to come upon the whole inhabitants to try the inhabitants upon the earth.

11 Behold, I will come quickly, hold fast what you have so that no one takes your crown.

12 I will make the overcomer a pillar in the temple of My God, and he will never go out anymore. And I will write upon him the name of My God and the Name of the city of My God, the New Jerusalem, which shall come down from Heaven from My God, and My New Name.

13 He who has an ear let him hear what the Spirit says to the churches."

14 And to the messenger in the Laodicea Church write: "this is what the Amen says, the faithful and true witness, the beginning of the creation of God.

15 I know your works, that they are neither cold nor hot. I would that you were cold or hot.

16 Therefore, because you are lukewarm, and are neither hot nor cold, I am about to vomit you out of My Mouth.

17 Because you say that you are wealthy and have become rich and have need of nothing, and do not know that you are wretched and miserable and poor and blind and naked.

18 I counsel you to buy from me gold set on fire in the fire that you may be rich, and white garments that you may be clothed and the shame of your nakedness may not be seen, and rub your eyes with eye salve that you may see.

19 As many as I love, I rebuke and correct. Be zealous then and repent.

20 Behold, I stand at the door and knock, if anyone hears My voice and opens the door, I will come in to him and will dine with him and he with Me.

21 He who overcomes I will give him to sit with Me in My throne, as I also overcame and sat down with My Father in His throne.

22 He who has ears let him hear what the Spirit says to the churches."

4

After these things I looked and saw a door open in Heaven, and the first voice which I heard like a trumpet spoke to me, saying, "Come up here and I will show you what must happen after these things."

2 Immediately I was in the Spirit, and behold a throne was set in Heaven and there was One seated upon the throne.

3 And He who sat there was like the appearance of a jasper and a sardius stone, and a rainbow was around about the throne appearing as an emerald.

4 And around about the throne, twenty-four thrones. And upon the thrones are seated twenty-four elders, dressed in white garments and wearing crowns of gold.

5 And from the throne came forth lightnings and voices and thunders, and seven torches of fire burned before the throne which are the Seven Spirits of God.

6 And in front of the throne was as it were a sea of glass appearing as crystal, and in the midst of the throne and around the throne four living creatures full of eyes in front and in back.

7 And the first of the living creature's resembled a lion, and the second living creature resembled a calf, and the third living creature had the face of a man, and the fourth living creature resembled a flying eagle.

8 And the four living creatures each one of them had six wings they were full of eyes around about and within and they do not rest day and night, saying, "Holy, Holy, Holy, Lord God Almighty, Who is and Who was and Who is to come."

9 And whenever the living creatures give glory and honor and thanks to the

One seated upon the throne, Who lives unto the ages of the ages,

10 the twenty-four elders fall down before the One seated on the throne and worship Him Who lives unto the ages of the ages, and they cast their crowns before the throne, saying,

11 "Worthy is the Lord to receive glory and honor and power, for You have created everything, and by Your will they are and were created."

5 I saw at the right of Him seated upon the throne a book written within and without, sealed up with seven seals.

2 And I saw a mighty angel proclaiming with a loud voice, "Who is worthy to open the book and loose its seals?"

3 And no one was able in Heaven nor upon the earth nor under the earth to open the book nor to look at it.

4 And I wept very much because no one was found worthy to open the book, neither to look at it.

5 And one of the elders said to me, "Do not weep, behold the Lion, being of the tribe of Judah, the Root of David, overcame to open the scroll and to loose the seven seals."

6 And I saw in the midst of the throne and the four living creatures, and in the midst of the elders, a little Lamb standing as though it had been slain, having seven horns and seven eyes, which are the seven Spirits of God, sent into all of the earth.

7 And he came and took the book from the right of the One seated upon the throne.

8 And when he received the book, the four living creatures and the twenty-four elders fell before the little Lamb, each one of them having a harp and a golden bowl full of incense, which are the prayers of the saints.

9 And they sang a new song, saying, "You are worthy to take the book and to open its seals, because You purchased us for God with Your blood from every tribe and language and people and nation,

10 and made us kings and priests to God, and we shall reign upon the earth."

11 And I saw and I heard the voice of many angels around the throne and the living creatures and the elders, and the number of them was ten thousands of ten thousands and thousands of thousands,

12 saying with a great voice, "Worthy is the Lamb that was slain to receive power and riches and wisdom and might and honor and glory and praise."

13 And every creature in heaven and upon the earth and under the earth and upon the seas and in it, I heard all of them saying to Him seated upon the throne and to the Lamb, "Blessings and riches and glory and might unto the ages of the ages."

14 And the four living creatures said, "Amen." And the twenty four elders fell down and worshiped Him who lives unto the ages of ages.

6 And I saw when the Lamb opened one of the seven seals, and I heard one of the four living creatures saying, as with the voice of thunder, "Come and see!"

2 And I saw and beheld a white stallion, and he that was seated upon him had a bow, and to him was given a crown, and he went out conquering also that he may conquer.

3 And when He opened the second seal, I heard the second living creature saying, "Come and see."

4 And out came another horse, red.
And it was given to him that was sitting
on {it} to take peace from the earth,
and that they should slay one another,
and he was given a great sword.
5 And when He opened the third seal
I heard the third living creature saying,
"Come and see." And I saw and beheld
a black horse. And its rider had a balance in his hand.
6 And I heard a voice in the midst of
the four living creatures saying, "A
quart of wheat for a denarius, and three
quarts of barley for a denarius, and do
not harm the oil and the wine."
7 When He opened the fourth seal I
heard the voice of the fourth living
creature saying, "Come and see."
8 And I saw and beheld a pale horse,
and the name of the one sitting on it
was Death, and Hell followed with him.
And authority was given to them over a
fourth of the earth to kill with the
sword, and with famine, and with
death, and by the beast of the earth.
9 And when He opened the fifth seal,
I saw under the altar those that were
slain for the word of God and because
of the testimony which they held.
10 And they cried out with a loud
voice, saying, "How long, O Master,
Holy and True, will You not judge and
avenge our blood on those who dwell
on the earth?"
11 And they were each given white
robes and told to rest a little time, until
their fellow servants and their brothers,
who were about to be killed just as they
had been, should be fulfilled.
12 And I saw when He opened the
sixth seal, and there was a great earthquake. The sun became as black, as
sackcloth made of hair, and the moon
became like blood,
13 And the stars of heaven fell to the
earth, like a fig tree dropping its unripe
figs when a strong wind shakes it.
14 The heavens departed, as a scroll
being rolled up, and every mountain
and island was removed from its place.
15 Then the kings of the earth, the
great, and the rich, the chief captains
and the powerful, and every slave and
every free man, hid themselves in the
caves and among the rocks of the
mountains.
16 And they said to the mountains
and rocks, "Fall on us, and hide us
from the face of Him Who sits on the
throne and from the wrath of the
Lamb,
17 for the day of His great wrath has
come, and who shall be able to stand?"

7 And after this I saw four angels
standing on the four angles of the
earth, holding the four winds of the
earth, that no wind might blow upon
the earth, nor on the sea, nor upon any
tree.
2 And I saw another angel having ascended from the rising sun, having the
seal of the Living God, and he cried
with a loud voice to them whom it was
given to hurt the earth and the sea,
3 saying, "Hurt not the earth, nor the
sea, nor the trees, until we seal the servants of our God upon their
foreheads."
4 And I heard the number of the
sealed, One Hundred and Forty-Four
Thousand out of every tribe of the sons
of Israel.
5 Of the tribe of Judah twelve thousand sealed, out of the tribe of Reuben
twelve thousand sealed, out of the tribe
of Gad twelve thousand sealed,
6 out of the tribe of Asher twelve
thousand sealed, out of the tribe of
Napthalim twelve thousand sealed, out

of the tribe of Manasseh twelve thousand sealed,

7 out of the tribe of Simeon twelve thousand sealed, out of the tribe of Levi twelve thousand sealed, out of the tribe of Issachar twelve thousand sealed,

8 out of the tribe of Zebulun twelve thousand sealed, out of the tribe of Joseph twelve thousand sealed, out of the tribe of Benjamin twelve thousand sealed.

9 After these things I saw a great crowd, which no one was able to number, out of every nation and tribe and people and tongues standing before the throne and before the Lamb, clothed with white robes and palms in their hands,

10 and crying with a loud voice, saying, "Salvation to our God Who sits on the throne, and to the Lamb."

11 And all the angels stood around the throne, and the elders and the four living creatures and they fell upon their faces before the throne and worshiped God,

12 saying, "Amen! Blessings and glory and wisdom and thanksgiving and honor and power and strength to our God to the ages of the ages– Amen."

13 And one of the elders addressed me, saying, "Who are these clothed in white robes, and where have they come from?"

14 And I said to him, "Sir, you know." And he said to me, "These are the ones coming out of great tribulation and they washed their robes and made them white in the blood of the Lamb.

15 Because of this they are before the throne of God and serve Him day and night in His temple, and He who sits on the throne shall tabernacle over them.

16 And they shall not hunger anymore, nor shall they thirst anymore. The sun shall not fall upon them, nor any heat.

17 Because the Lamb which is in the midst of the throne shall shepherd them, and will lead them to living fountains of waters. And God will wipe away every tear from their eyes."

8 And when He opened the seventh seal, there was silence in heaven for about half an hour.

2 And I saw the seven angels who stand before the throne of God, and they were given seven trumpets.

3 And another angel came and stood at the altar, having a golden censer, and a lot of incense was given to him so that he might offer the prayers of all the saints upon the golden altar which was before the throne.

4 And the smoke of the incense went up with the prayers of the saints out of the hand of the angel before God.

5 And the angel took the censer and filled it with fire from the altar and cast it to the earth, and there were voices and thunder and lightning and an earthquake.

6 And the seven angels having the seven trumpets prepared themselves that they might blow their trumpets.

7 And the first angel blew his trumpet, and there was hail and fire mingled with blood, and it was cast upon the earth, and the third of the trees were burnt up, and all green grass was burnt up.

8 And the second angel blew his trumpet, and as a great mountain burning with fire was cast into the sea, and a third of the sea became blood.

9 And a third of the creatures that were in the sea, which have life, died.

And a third of the ships were destroyed.

10 The third angel blew his trumpet, and a great star fell out of heaven burning as a lamp, and it fell upon the third of the rivers and upon the fountains of waters.

11 And the name of the star is called Wormwood; and a third of the waters became wormwood, and many of the men died of the waters because they were made bitter.

12 And the fourth angel blew his trumpet, and a third of the sun was struck and a third of the moon and a third of the stars so that a third of them should be darkened, and a third of the day should not shine and likewise the night.

13 And I saw and heard one angel flying in the midst of heaven, saying with a loud voice, "Woe, woe, woe, to those who dwell in the earth because of the rest of the voices of the trumpet of the three angels who are about to blow their trumpets."

9 The fifth angel sounded his trumpet, and I saw a star falling out of heaven to the earth, and there was given to it the key to the pit of the abyss.

2 He opened the pit of the abyss, and there went up smoke from the pit like a great furnace. The sun and the air were darkened by the smoke from the pit.

3 Then out of the smoke came locusts upon the earth, and they were given power like that of the scorpions of the earth.

4 They were told not to injure the grass of the earth or any green thing or any tree, but only the men that do not have the seal of God on their foreheads.

5 And it was given to them to torment them for five months, but not to kill them, and their torment was like the torment of a scorpion when it stings someone.

6 In those days men will seek death, but will not find it. They shall desire to die, but death will flee from them.

7 The likeness of the locusts were like horses prepared for battle, and on their heads they wore golden crowns; their faces were like human faces.

8 They had hair like the hair of women, and their teeth were like the teeth of lions.

9 They had breastplates like breastplates of iron, and the sound of their wings was like the sound of many horses and chariots running into battle.

10 And they have tails like scorpions, and stingers in their tails, and they have the power to harm men for five months.

11 They have a king over them, the angel of the abyss. His name in Hebrew is Abaddon, and in Greek his name is Apollyon.

12 The first woe has passed. Behold, two woes are still to come after this.

13 Then the sixth angel sounded his trumpet, and I heard a voice from the four horns of the golden altar before God

14 saying to the sixth angel who had the trumpet, "Release the four angels who are bound at the great river Euphrates."

15 The four angels who were prepared for this hour, day, month, and year were released to kill a third of men.

16 And I heard the number of them, the number of the armies on horseback were ten thousand times ten thousand.

17 And I saw the horses in the vision, and those that sat on them had fiery

breastplates, hyacinthine blue, and brimstone like. The heads of the horses were like the heads of lions, and out of their mouths came fire, smoke, and brimstone.

18By these three were killed a third of men; by the fire, the smoke, and the brimstone that came out of their mouths.

19For their power is in their mouth and their tails have heads like serpents, and with them they inflict harm.

20The rest of the men who were not killed by these plagues did not repent from the works of their hands; they did not stop worshiping demons and idols of gold, silver, bronze, stone, and wood, which cannot see, hear, or walk.

21And they did not repent of their murders, nor of their sorceries, sexual immorality, or thefts.

10 And I saw another mighty angel coming down from heaven, clothed in a cloud, and a rainbow upon his head; his face was like the sun, and his feet were like pillars of fire.

2And he had in his hands a little scroll opened. And he placed his right foot on the sea and his left foot on the earth.

3And cried out with a loud voice as a lion roars. When he cried out, the voices of the seven thunders spoke.

4And when the seven thunders spoke, I was about to write. But I heard a voice from heaven saying, "Seal up what the seven thunders have said, and do not write them."

5Then the angel I had seen standing on the sea and on the earth raised his hand to heaven

6and swore by Him who lives forever and ever, Who created Heaven and the things in it, and the earth and the things in it, and the sea and the things in it, and said time shall be no longer;

7but that in the days when the seventh angel is about to sound his trumpet, also the mystery of God would be completed, according to the good news He announced to His servants the prophets.

8And the voice I had heard from Heaven spoke to me again, saying, "Go take the little scroll that is open in the hand of the angel who is standing on the sea and on the earth."

9And I went to the angel, saying to him, "Give me the little scroll." And he said to me, "Take the scroll, and eat it. It will make your stomach bitter, but in your mouth it will be as sweet as honey."

10And I took the scroll from the angel's hand and ate it. And it was in my mouth as sweet as honey, but when I had eaten it, my stomach turned bitter.

11And he said to me, "You must prophesy again about many peoples, nations, tongues, and kings."

11 And I was given a rod like a staff, and I was told, "Rise and measure the temple of God and the altar, and those who worship in it.

2And cast out the courtyard which is outside the temple. Do not measure it, because it has been given to the Nations, and they will trample the holy city for forty-two months.

3And I will give to my two witnesses, and they will prophesy for one thousand two hundred sixty days, clothed in sackcloth."

4These are the two olive trees and the two lampstands that stand before the Lord of the earth.

5And if anyone wants to harm them, fire comes out of their mouth and de-

vours their enemies. And if anyone
wants to harm them, he must be killed
in this way.
6 These have authority to shut up
heaven, so that no rain will fall during
the days of their prophecy. And they
also have authority over the waters to
turn them into blood and to strike the
earth with every plague as often as they
want.
7 And when they have finished their
testimony, the beast that comes up out
of the abyss will wage war against
them, and overcome them and kill
them.
8 Their dead bodies will lie in the
street of the great city, which is spiritually called Sodom and Egypt, where
also our Lord was crucified.
9 And for three and a half days the
peoples, tribes, tongues, and nations
will look at their bodies and refuse to
let them be placed in a tomb.
10 And those who dwell on the earth
will rejoice over them and celebrate
and will send gifts to one another, because these two prophets had tormented them who dwell on the earth.
11 And after three and a half days, the
spirit of life from God entered them,
and they stood on their feet, and great
fear fell upon those who were watching
them.
12 And they heard a loud voice from
Heaven saying to them, “Come up
here.” And they went up to Heaven in
the cloud, and their enemies watched
them.
13 And in that hour there was a great
earthquake, and a tenth of the city fell.
Seven thousand names of men were
killed in the earthquake, and the rest
were terrified and gave glory to the
God of Heaven.
14 The second woe has passed. Behold, the third woe is coming quickly.
15 And the seventh angel sounded his
trumpet, and there were loud voices in
Heaven, saying, “The kingdom of the
world has become the Kingdom of our
Lord and of His Christ, and He will
reign forever and ever.”
16 And the twenty-four elders, who sit
on their thrones before the throne of
God, fell on their faces and worshiped
God,
17 saying, “We give thanks to You, Oh
Lord God Almighty, Who is and Who
was, and Who is coming, because You
have taken Your great power and begun to reign.
18 And the nations were angry, but
Your wrath has come, and the time of
the dead to be judged, and to give reward to Your servants the prophets,
and to Your holy ones and those who
fear Your name, both small and great,
and to destroy those who corrupt the
earth.”
19 And the Temple of God in Heaven
was opened, and the ark of the
covenant was seen in His temple. And
there were lightnings, and voices, and
thunders, and an earthquake and great
hail.

12 And a great sign was seen in
heaven: a woman clothed with
the sun, with the moon under her feet
and a crown of twelve stars on her
head.
2 And she was with child and cried
out in travail and being in pain to give
birth.
3 And another sign was seen in heav-
en: behold, a great fiery red dragon
with seven heads and ten horns, and
seven crowns on his heads.
4 And his tail pulled down a third of
the stars of heaven and cast them to the

earth. And the dragon stands before the woman who was about to give birth, so that when she gives birth he might devour her child.

5 And she gave birth to a son, a male, who is about to shepherd all the nations with a rod of iron, but her child was caught up to God and to his throne.

6 And the woman fled into the wilderness, where she had a place prepared by God that there they should nourish her for one thousand two hundred sixty days.

7 And there was war in the heaven; Michael and his angels made war against the dragon. And the dragon and his angels made war,

8 but they did not prevail, and there was no longer any place found for him in heaven.

9 The great dragon was thrown down, the ancient serpent, who is called the Devil and Satan, the deceiver of the whole world. He was thrown down to the earth, and his angels were thrown down with him.

10 And I heard a loud voice in heaven saying, "Now has come the salvation, power, and Kingdom of our God, and the authority of His Christ. For the accuser of our brothers has been thrown down, who accuses them day and night before our God.

11 And they overcame him by the blood of the Lamb and by the word of their testimony; and they did not love their lives unto death.

12 Because of this rejoice, O heavens and them in the tabernacle! But woe to those who inhabit the earth and the sea! For the Devil has come down to you with great wrath, because he knows that his time is short."

13 When the dragon saw that he had been thrown down to the earth, he persecuted the woman who had given birth to the male.

14 And two great wings of the eagle were given to the woman so that she might fly into the wilderness to her place away from the presence of the serpent, to be nourished there for a time, times, and half a time.

15 And the serpent spewed out of his mouth water like a river after the woman, to sweep her away with a flood.

16 But the earth helped the woman and opened its mouth and swallowed up the river that the dragon had spewed out of his mouth.

17 And the dragon was angry with the woman and went to wage war against the rest of her offspring, who keep the commandments of God and have the testimony of Jesus Christ.

13 And I saw a beast coming up out of the sea that had ten horns and seven heads, with ten crowns on his horns and on his heads the names of blasphemy.

2 And the beast which I saw was like a leopard; its feet were like a bear, and its mouth was like the mouth of a lion. And the dragon gave it his power, his throne, and great authority.

3 And I saw one of its heads as being slain to death. And its mortal wound was healed, and there was wonder in the whole of the earth after the beast.

4 And they worshiped the dragon who had given authority to the beast, and they also worshiped the beast, saying, "Who is like the beast, and who can wage war against it?"

5 And there was given to it a mouth speaking great things and blasphemy and authority was given to it to func-

tion for forty-two months.

6And it opened its mouth to blaspheme against God, to blaspheme His Name and His Tabernacle, and those who tabernacle in heaven.

7And it was given to it to make war with the holy ones and to overcome them, and it was given authority over every tribe, tongue, and nation.

8And all who dwell on the earth worshiped it, those whose names had not been written in the book of life of the Lamb slain from the overthrow of the world.

9If anyone has an ear, let him hear.

10If anyone is to be taken into captivity, into captivity he goes. If anyone is to be slain with the sword, he must with the sword be killed. Here is the endurance and the faith of the holy ones.

11And I saw another beast rising out of the earth and it had two horns like a lamb, but spoke like a dragon.

12And it exercised all the authority of the first beast in its presence, and made the earth and those who dwell in it worship the first beast, whose deadly wound had been healed.

13And it performed great signs, even making fire come down from heaven to earth before men.

14And by the signs that it was permitted to do in the presence of the beast, it deceived those who dwell upon the earth, saying to those who dwell upon the earth to make an image of the first beast, who had the wound from the sword but still lived.

15And it was given to it to give breath to the image of the beast so that also the image of the beast could speak and cause whoever refused to worship the image to be killed.

16And it caused all small and great, rich and poor, free and slave, to receive a mark on their right hand or on their forehead,

17so that no one could buy or sell unless he had the mark, or the name of the beast or the number of its name.

18Here is wisdom: he who has understanding let him calculate the number of the beast, for it is the number of a man; his number is six hundred sixty-six.

14 And I saw and behold the Lamb standing upon Mount Sion and with Him one hundred forty-four thousand, who had his Name of His Father written on their foreheads.

2And I heard a voice from heaven like the voice of many waters and as the voice of great thunder. And I heard a voice of harpists playing their harps.

3And they were singing a new song before the throne and before the four living creatures and the elders. And no one could learn the song except the one hundred forty-four thousand who had been purchased from the earth.

4These are the ones who have not defiled themselves with women, for they are virgins. These are the ones who follow the Lamb wherever he goes. These were purchased from among men as firstfruits to God and the Lamb.

5And in their mouth was found no deceit, for they are blameless before the throne of God.

6And I saw an angel flying in the midst of heaven having the everlasting gospel to preach to those who dwell on the earth, for every nation, tribe, tongue, and people.

7Saying with a loud voice, "Fear God and give him glory, because the hour of his judgment has come and worship him who made heaven and earth, the sea and the fountains of water."

8And another angel followed, saying,
"Fallen is fallen Babylon the great city!
Because she has made all nations drink
of the wine of the fury of her sexual
immorality."
9A third angel followed them, saying
with a loud voice, "If anyone worships
the beast and its image and receives a
mark on his forehead or his hand,
10he too will drink of the wine of the
wrath of God that has been mixed
undiluted in the cup of his anger. He
will be tormented with fire and brimstone in the presence of the holy angels
and in the presence of the Lamb.
11And the smoke of their torment
goes up forever and ever. And there is
no relief day or night for those who
worship the beast and its image or for
anyone who receives the mark of its
name."
12Here is the endurance of the holy
ones, those who keep the commandments of God and the faith of Jesus.
13And I heard a voice from heaven
saying to me, "Write: 'Blessed are the
dead who die in the Lord from now
on.'" "Yes," says the Spirit, "that they
may rest from their labors, and their
works will follow them."
14And I saw, and behold, a white
cloud, and one sitting on the cloud like
the son of man, with a golden crown
on his head and a sharp sickle in his
hand.
15And another angel came out of the
temple, crying out with a loud voice to
him who was sitting on the cloud,
"Take your sickle and reap, because the
hour to reap has come, for the harvest
of the earth is ripe."
16So he who was sitting on the cloud
put forth his sickle upon the earth, and
the earth was reaped.
17And another angel came out of the
temple in heaven; he had a sharp
sickle.
18And another angel who had authority over the fire, came out from the
altar and called out with a loud cry to
him who had the sharp sickle, "Send
your sharp sickle and gather the clus-
ters from the earth, for her grapes are
fully ripe."
19And the angel put forth his sickle to
the earth, and gathered the vintage of
the earth, and threw it into the great
winepress of the wrath of God.
20And the winepress was trodden
outside the city, and blood came out of
the winepress, as high as a horse's bridle, for one thousand six hundred stadia.

15 And I saw another miracle in
the heaven, great and wonder-
ful: seven angels having the seven last
plagues; because in them completed
the wrath of God.
2And I saw as it were a sea of glass
mingled with fire and the overcomers
of the beast and of its image and of its
mark of the number of its name, standing upon the sea of glass having harps
of God.
3And they sang the song of Moses
the servant of God and the song of the
Lamb, saying, "Great and wonderful
are Your works Lord God Almighty;
righteous and true are Your ways, King
of the holy ones.
4Who should not fear You and glorify
Your name O Lord, For You only are
holy; for all the nations shall come and
worship before You for your righteous
deeds are made known."
5And after these things I saw and behold the temple of the tabernacle of
witness was opened in heaven.
6And the seven angels having the

seven plagues came forth out of the Temple, clothed in pure and bright linen and gird around the chest with golden girdles.

7 And one of the four living creatures gave the seven angels the seven golden bowls full of the wrath of God, Who lives forever and ever.

8 And the Temple was filled with smoke from the glory of God and from His power, and no one was able to enter into the Temple until the seven plagues of the seven angels were completed.

16 And I heard a loud voice from out of the Temple, saying to the seven angels, "Go and pour out the bowls of the wrath of God into the earth."

2 And the first one departed and poured out his bowl onto the earth; and there came upon the men an evil and grievous sore who had the mark of the beast, and those who worshiped his image.

3 And the second angel poured out his bowl into the sea; and it became blood, as one dead: and every living soul died in the sea.

4 And the third angel poured out his bowl into the rivers, and into the fountains of waters; and they became blood.

5 And I heard the angel of the waters saying, "Righteous O Lord are You, Who is and Who was and the Holy One, that You have judged these things;

6 because of the blood they poured out of holy ones and of prophets and You have given to them blood to drink, for they are worthy."

7 And I heard another one out of the altar saying, Yes Lord God Almighty, true and righteous are Your judgments.

8 And the fourth angel poured out his bowl upon the sun; and it was given to it to scorch men with fire.

9 And men were scorched with great heat, and they blasphemed the Name of God, who has authority over these plagues and did not repent and give Him glory.

10 And the fifth angel poured out his bowl upon the throne of the beast, and his kingdom became darkened and they gnawed their tongues because of the pain,

11 and blasphemed the God of heaven because of their pain and their sores and did not repent of their works.

12 And the sixth angel poured out his bowl upon the great river Euphrates and its water was dried up so that the way of the king from the rising of the sun might be prepared.

13 and I saw out of the mouth of the dragon, and out of the mouth of the beast, and out of the mouth of the false prophet, three unclean spirits like frogs.

14 For they are demon spirits doing miracles, who go forth to the kings of the earth and the whole earth to assemble them unto the great day of battle of God the Almighty.

15 "Behold, I come as a thief, blessed is he who watches and keeps his garments that he may not walk naked and they see his shame."

16 And He gathered them together to the place which is called in the Hebrew tongue Armageddon.

17 And the seventh angel poured out his bowl into the air and there came out a loud voice from the Temple of Heaven from the throne saying, "it is done."

18 And there were voices and thunders and lightnings and there was a

great earthquake such as was not since
men were upon the earth, so mighty
and so great an earthquake.
19 And the great city was divided into
three parts and the cities of the nations
fell and Babylon the great was remembered before God to give her the cup of
the wine of the wrath of His anger.
20 And every island fled, and the
mountains were not found.
21 And a great hail as of the weight of
a talent came down out of heaven upon
men; and men blasphemed God because of the plague of the hail for exceeding great is the plague.

17 And one of the seven angels
who had the seven bowls came
and spoke with me, saying to me,
"Come here, I will show you the judgment of the great prostitute who sits on
many waters.
2 With whom the kings of the earth
have committed sexual immorality and
those who dwell on the earth were
made drunk with the wine of her sexual immorality."
3 And he carried me away into the
wilderness in the Spirit and I saw a
woman sitting on a scarlet beast that
was full of blasphemous names, and
had seven heads and ten horns.
4 The woman was clothed in purple
and scarlet and adorned with gold, precious stones, and pearls and having in
her hand a golden cup full of abominations and the uncleanness of her sexual
immorality
5 And upon her forehead a mysterious
name was written: "Babylon the great,
the mother of prostitutes and of the
abominations of the earth."
6 And I saw the woman drunk with
the blood of the holy ones, and with
the blood of the witnesses of Jesus. And
having seen her I wondered with great
wonder.
7 But the angel said to me, "Why are
you so amazed?" I will tell you the
mystery of the woman and of the beast
with seven heads and ten horns that
carries her.
8 The beast that you saw was, and is
not, and is about to come up out of the
abyss and go to destruction. And those
who dwell on the earth, whose names
have not been written in the book of
life from the overthrow of the world,
shall wonder when they see the beast
that was and is not and is to come.
9 Here is the mind that has wisdom:
The seven heads are seven mountains
on which the woman sits.
10 And there are seven kings. Five
have fallen, one is, and another has not
yet come; but when he does come, he
must remain for only a little while.
11 The beast that was and is not, is
also an eighth, and is of the seven, and
goes into destruction.
12 The ten horns that you saw are ten
kings who have not yet received a
kingdom, but they will receive authority as kings for one hour with the beast.
13 These have one mind and will give
their power and authority to the beast.
14 These will make war with the
Lamb, but the Lamb will overcome
them because He is the Lord of lords
and King of kings, and those with Him
are called, and chosen, and faithful."
15 And he said to me,"The waters you
saw, where the prostitute sits, are peoples, multitudes, nations, and tongues.
16 And the ten horns which you saw
upon the beast will hate the prostitute
and shall make her desolate and naked;
they will eat her flesh and burn her
with fire.
17 For God has put it into their hearts

to do His purpose by being of one mind and handing over their kingdom to the beast until the words of God are fulfilled.

18And as for the woman that you saw, she is the great city that has dominion over the kings of the earth."

18

And after this I saw an angel coming down from Heaven. He had great authority, and the Earth was illuminated with his glory.

2And he cried out mightily with a loud voice, "Fallen! Fallen is Babylon the great! And has become a dwelling place for demons, a prison for every unclean spirit, and a prison for every unclean and hated bird.

3Because of the wine of the wrath of her sexual immorality all the nations have drunk, and the kings of the earth have committed sexual immorality with her and the merchants of the earth have become rich from the power of her luxury."

4And I heard another voice from heaven saying, "Come out of her, my people, so that you do not participate in her sins, and so that you do not receive of her plagues;

5for her sins follow her as far as heaven, and God has remembered her unrighteousness.

6Render to her as she herself has rendered to you; double to her double according to her works. In the cup that she mixed, mix to her double portion.

7As much as she has glorified herself and lived in luxury, give her the same amount of torment and mourning, for in her heart she says, "I sit enthroned as a queen; I am not a widow and will never see mourning."

8Because of this, her plagues will come in a single day– death, and mourning, and famine. She will be burned up with fire, for mighty is the Lord God Who judges her."

9And the kings of the earth who have committed sexual immorality with her and lived in luxury with her will weep and wail over her when they see the smoke of her burning.

10In fear of her torment they will stand afar off and say, "Woe, woe, the great city, Babylon, the mighty city! For in a single hour your judgment has come."

11And the merchants of the earth will weep and mourn over her, because no one buys their cargo anymore,

12cargo of gold, silver, and precious stones, of pearls, and of fine linen, and of purple, and of silk, and scarlet, all kinds of thyine wood, and of every article of ivory, and every article of most costly wood, bronze, and of iron, and marble;

13and cinnamon, and incense, and ointment and frankincense, and wine, oil, and fine flour, wheat, and cattle, sheep and horses and of chariots, and slaves and souls of men.

14And the ripe fruits of the desire of your soul have departed from you, and all of the fat things and the bright things have departed from you and are lost to you, and you shall never find them.

15The merchants of these things, who became rich from her, will stand far away in fear of her torment, weeping and mourning.

16And saying, "Woe, woe, the great city, which was clothed in fine linen in purple and scarlet, and adorned with gold, and with precious stones and pearls!

17For in one hour such great wealth has been laid waste!" And every shipmaster and seafaring man, sailors and as many as trade by sea, stood far away

18and cried out as they saw the smoke of her burning, saying, “What city is like the great city?”

19They threw dust on their heads and cried out, weeping and mourning, saying, “Woe, woe, the great city, where all who had ships in the sea grew rich from her valuable merchandise! For in one hour she has been made desolate.

20Rejoice over her, O heaven, and you holy ones, apostles, and prophets, for God judged your judgment on her.”

21Then a mighty angel picked up a stone like a great millstone and threw it into the sea, and said, “With violence shall Babylon the great city be thrown down, never to be found again.”

22The voice of harpists, musicians, and flutists, and of trumpeters will never be heard in you again. No craftsman of any trade will ever be found in you again. The sound of a mill will never be heard in you again.

23The light of a lamp will never shine in you again. The voice of the bridegroom and bride will never be heard in you again. For your merchants were the great ones of the earth, for by your sorcery all the nations were deceived.

24And in her was found the blood of prophets and the holy ones, and of all who have been slain on the Earth.”

19 After this I heard a loud voice of a great multitude in heaven, saying, “Hallelujah! Salvation, and glory and honor and power, belong to our God,

2for true and righteous are His judgments; He has judged the great prostitute, who corrupted the earth with her sexual immorality. He has avenged the blood of His servants by her hand.”

3And a second time they said, “Hallelujah! Her smoke goes up forever and ever.”

4And the twenty-four elders and the four living creatures fell down and worshiped God, Who sits on the throne, saying, “Amen. Hallelujah!”

5And a voice came out from the throne, saying, “Praise our God, all you His servants, you who fear Him, both small and great.”

6And I heard as a voice of a great multitude, and as the voice of many waters and as the voice of mighty thunder, saying, “Hallelujah! For the Lord our God the Almighty reigns.

7We should rejoice and be glad and give Him the glory, for the marriage of the Lamb has come, and His wife has made herself ready.

8And it was granted to her to be clothed with fine linen, pure and bright, for the fine linen is the righteousness of the holy ones.”

9And he said to me, “Write: ‘Blessed are those who are called to the marriage supper of the Lamb.’” And he said to me, “These are the true words of God.”

10And I fell at his feet to worship him, but he said to me, “Do not do that! I am a fellow servant of yours, and of your brothers who hold to the testimony of Jesus. Worship God.” For the testimony of Jesus is the spirit of prophecy.

11And I saw heaven opened, and behold, a white horse! And He who sits upon it is called Faithful and True, and in righteousness He judges and makes war.

12His eyes are a flame of fire, and on His head are many crowns, having a name written which no man knows but Himself,

13 and clothed with a garment dipped in blood, and His name is the Word of God.

14 And the armies of heaven were following Him on white horses, clothed in fine linen, white and pure.

15 And out of His mouth came forth a sharp two-edged sword that with it He might strike down the nations, and He shall shepherd them with a rod of iron. And He treads the winepress of the fury of the wrath of God, the Almighty.

16 And He has upon His garment and on His thigh the name written: "King of kings and Lord of lords."

17 And I saw one angel standing in the sun, and he cried out with a loud voice, saying to all the birds that were flying in the midst of heavens, "Come, gather together for the great supper of God,

18 so that you may eat the flesh of kings, the flesh of commanders, the flesh of mighty men, the flesh of horses and their riders, and the flesh of all men, both free and slave, both small and great."

19 And I saw the beast, and the kings of the earth, and their armies gathered together to make war with Him who sits on the horse and with His army.

20 And the beast was taken, and with him the false prophet, who worked miracles before him, by which he deceived those who had received the mark of the beast and those who worshiped his image. And the two were cast alive into the lake of fire that burns with brimstone.

21 The rest were killed by the sword that came out of the mouth of Him who sits upon the horse, and all the birds were filled with their flesh.

20 And I saw an angel descending from heaven, having the key to the abyss and a great chain was in his hand.

2 And he laid hold on the dragon, the ancient serpent, who is the Devil and Satan, and he bound him for a thousand years.

3 And cast him into the abyss and shut and sealed it over him, so that he would no longer deceive the nations until the thousand years were completed. After that he must be released for a short time.

4 And I saw thrones and those that sat upon them, and judgment was to them. And the souls of those who had been beheaded for the testimony of Jesus and for the Word of God. And those who had not worshiped the beast or his image and had not received the mark on their forehead or their hand. And they lived and reigned with Christ for the thousand years.

5 And the rest of the dead did not live again until the thousand years were completed. This is the first resurrection.

6 Blessed and holy is He who has part in the first resurrection, over these the second death has no authority, but they will be priests of God and of Christ, and will reign with Him for a thousand years.

7 And when the thousand years are completed, Satan will be released from his prison,

8 and will go out to deceive the nations that are at the four angles of the earth, Gog and Magog, to gather them for battle; their number is like the sand of the sea.

9 And they went upon the breadth of the Earth and surrounded the camp of the holy ones and the beloved city, and

fire came down out of Heaven from God and devoured them.

10And the Devil, who had deceived them, was cast into the lake of fire and brimstone, where the beast and the false prophet will be tormented day and night forever and ever.

11And I saw a great white throne and Him who sat upon it; from whose face the earth and the heaven fled, and no place was found for them.

12And I saw the dead, great and small, standing before God, and books were opened. And another book was opened, which is the Book of Life. And the dead were judged by what was written in the books, according to their works.

13Then the sea gave up the dead and Death and Hades gave up the dead who were in them, and each person was judged according to his works.

14Then Death and Hades were cast into the lake of fire– this is the second death.

15And if anyone was not found written in the Book of Life, he was thrown into the lake of fire.

21 And I saw a new heaven and a new earth, for the first heaven and the first earth had passed away, and the sea was no more.

2And I John saw the holy city, the new Jerusalem, coming down out of heaven from God, prepared like a bride adorned for her husband.

3And I heard a loud voice from heaven saying, "Behold, the tabernacle of God is with men. And He shall tabernacle with them and they shall be His people and God Himself will be their God.

4And God will wipe away every tear from their eyes. And death will be no more, nor mourning, nor crying, nor pain, for the former things have passed away."

5And He who sits on the throne said, "Behold, I make all things new." And he said to me, "Write, because these words are true and faithful."

6And He said, "It is done. I am the Alpha and the Omega, the beginning and the end. To him who thirsts I will freely give from the fountain of the water of life.

7He who overcomes will inherit all things; and I will be his God, and he will be My son.

8But as for the fearful, and the unbelieving, and the detestable, and the murderers, and the fornicators, and the sorcerers, and the idolaters, and all liars, they shall have their part in the lake that burns with fire and brimstone, which is the second death."

9Then one of the seven angels came to me who had the seven bowls full of the seven final plagues and spoke to me, "Come, I will show you the bride, the Lamb's wife."

10And he carried me away in the Spirit to a great and high mountain and showed me the great city, the holy Jerusalem, coming down out of heaven from God,

11having the glory of God, and her splendor was like a precious stone, like a jasper stone, as crystal.

12Also having a great high wall with twelve gates, and at the gates twelve angels, and on the gates were written the names of the twelve tribes of the sons of Israel.

13On the east three gates, on the north three gates, on the south three gates on the west three gates.

14And the wall of the city had twelve foundations, and in them were the names of the twelve apostles of the Lamb.

15 And the angel who spoke with me had a golden reed to measure the city, and its gates, and its wall.

16 The city is laid out four-square; its length is the same as its width. And he measured the city with the reed to be twelve thousand stadia, the length, the width, and the height are all equal.

17 And he measured its wall- one hundred forty- four cubits according to a man's measurement, which is also an angel's measurement.

18 And the wall was made of jasper, while the city was pure gold, like clear glass.

19 The foundations of the city wall were adorned with every precious stone. The first foundation stone was jasper; the second, sapphire; the third, agate; the fourth, emerald;

20 the fifth, sardonyx; the sixth, carnelian; the seventh, chrysolite; the eighth, beryl; the ninth, topaz; the tenth, chrysoprase; the eleventh, jacinth; and the twelfth, amethyst.

21 And the twelve gates were twelve pearls, each one of the gates was made of a single pearl, and the street of the city was pure gold, like transparent glass.

22 And I did not see a temple in the city, for the Lord God Almighty is its temple, and so is the Lamb.

23 And the city has no need of sun or moon to shine upon it, for the glory of God gives it light, and its lamp is the Lamb.

24 And the saved nations will walk in its light, and the kings of the earth will bring their glory and honor to it.

25 And its gates will never be shut at the end of the day, for no night shall be there.

26 And they will bring the glory and honor of the nations into it.

27 And no unclean thing may enter into it anything that defiles or practices abomination and a lie, but only those whose names are written in the Lamb's Book of Life.

22 And he showed me a river of life of pure water radiant like crystal flowing from the throne of God and the Lamb.

2 In the midst of the city street, and on each side of the river, is the tree of life, bearing twelve kinds of fruit, yielding its fruit each month. And the leaves of the tree are for the healing of the nations.

3 And no longer will there be anything accursed, but the throne of God and of the Lamb will be in the city, and His servants will serve Him.

4 And they will see His face, and His name will be on their foreheads.

5 There will be no night there, and they will not need any lamp or the light of the sun, for the Lord God will give them light, and they will reign forever and ever.

6 And he said to me, "These words are faithful and true. And the Lord, God of the prophets sent his angel to show his servants what must soon take place."

7 "Behold, I am coming quickly. Blessed is he who keeps the words of the prophecy of this book."

8 And I John, am the one who heard and saw these things. And when I heard and saw them, I fell down to worship at the feet of the angel who showed them to me.

9 But he said to me, "Do not do that! I am a fellow servant of yours, and of your brothers the prophets, and of those who keep the words of this book.

Worship God!"
10 And he said to me, "Do not seal up
the words of the prophecy of this book,
for the time is near.
11 Let the unrighteous be unrighteous
still, and the filthy let him be filthy still,
and he that is righteous let him be
righteous still, and he that is holy let
him be holy still.
12 And behold, I am coming quickly,
and My reward is with Me, to render to
each person according to their works.
13 I am the Alpha and the Omega, the
Beginning and the End, the First and
the Last."
14 Blessed are those who keep His
commandments, so that they may have
the authority to the tree of life and may
enter the city by its gates.
15 But outside are the dogs, the sorcerers, the fornicators, the murderers,
the idolaters, and everyone who loves
and practices a lie.
16 I, Jesus, sent My angel to testify to
you about these things in the churches.
I am the Root and Offspring of David,
the Bright Morning Star.
17 The Spirit and the bride say,
"Come." Let the one who hears say,
"Come." Let the one who is thirsty
come, and let the one who is willing
take the water of life freely.
18 For I testify to everyone who hears
the words of the prophecy of this book:
If anyone adds to them, God will add
to him the plagues that are written in
this book.
19 And if anyone takes away from the
words of the book of this prophecy,
God will take away his part from the
Book of Life and in the Holy City, and
those who are written in this book.
20 He who testifies to these things
says, "Yes, I am coming quickly." Amen.
Yes, come Lord Jesus!
21 The grace of the Lord Jesus Christ
be with all. Amen.

PSALMS & PROVERBS

Translated from

Hebrew: Biblia Hebraica Stuttgartensia

PREFACE

The Translation in the Oldest Tradition (TOT) of Psalms and Proverbs is translated from the Biblia Hebraica Stuttgartensia. The BHS is an edition of the Masoretic Text of the Hebrew Bible (The Old Testament).

When originally written the Psalms did not contain chapters or verse numbers, which were added by subsequent transcribers of the ancient poetry. As time progressed a difference in how the chapters and verses in Psalms were numbered came about between the Hebrew Text and the Greek/Latin translations. In most Bibles today (including the TOT) the original Hebrew chapters are maintained, but the verse numbering between modern English translations and the original Hebrew text are not in agreement.

What is considered verse one in the Hebrew text is often separated from the text in modern translations as a title, or attribution. In order to be as close to the original text as possible, the TOT has opted to keep the original verse numberings from the Hebrew text.

For Example

Psalm 7:1-3 (TOT)

[1]Shiggaion of David, which he sang unto Yehovah, concerning Cush, a Benjamite.

[2]Yehovah my God, in You I have taken refuge; save me from all them who pursue me, and deliver me;

[3]lest he tear my soul like a lion, rending it in pieces, while there is none to rescue.

Psalm 7:1-2 (KJV)

(Shiggaion of David, which he sang unto the LORD, concerning the words of Cush the Benjamite.)

[1]O LORD my God, in thee do I put my trust: save me from all them that persecute me, and deliver me:

[2]Lest he tear my soul like a lion, rending it in pieces, while there is none to deliver.

The Book of
Psalms

Psalm 1

1 Blessed is the man who has not
walked in the counsel of the wicked,
nor stood in the way of sinners, nor sat
in the seat of the scornful;
2 but his delight is in the Law of
Yehovah, and in His law he meditates
day and night.
3 And he shall be like a tree planted
by streams of water, that brings forth
its fruit in its season, and whose leaf
will not wither; and in whatever he
does he shall prosper.
4 The wicked are not so, but they are
like the chaff which the wind drives
away.
5 Therefore the wicked shall not stand
in the judgment, nor sinners in the
congregation of the righteous.
6 For Yehovah regards the way of the
righteous, but the way of the wicked
shall perish.

Psalm 2

1 Why are the nations in an uproar?
And why do the people utter foolishness?
2 The kings of the Earth stand up, and
the rulers are closely united together,
against Yehovah, and against His
anointed:
3 "Let us break off their bands, and
cast away their cords from us."
4 He Who sits in Heaven will laugh;
Adonai will mock them.
5 Then will He speak to them in His
wrath, and in His fury terrify them:
6 "I have established My King upon
Zion, My holy mountain."
7 I will tell of the decree: Yehovah said
unto Me: "You are My Son – this day
have I begotten You.
8 Ask of Me, and I will give You the
nations for Your inheritance, and the
ends of the Earth for Your possession.
9 You shall break them with a rod of
iron; like a potter's vessel You shall
shatter them."
10 So then, O kings, be wise. Be
warned, judges of the Earth.
11 Serve Yehovah with fear, and rejoice with trembling.
12 Kiss the Son lest He be angry and
you perish in the way, when suddenly
His wrath is kindled. Happy are all
those who take refuge in Him.

Psalm 3

1 A psalm of David, when he fled
from Absalom his son.
2 Yehovah, how many are my adversaries! There are many who rise up
against me.
3 There are many that say of my soul:
"There is no deliverance for him in
God." Selah.
4 But you, Yehovah, are a shield about
me; my glory and the lifter up of my
head.
5 With my voice I call unto Yehovah
and He answers me out of His holy
mountain. Selah.
6 I lie down and I sleep. I awake, for
Yehovah sustains me.
7 I am not afraid of ten thousands of
people, that have set themselves against
me round about.
8 Arise, Yehovah. Save me, O my God,
for You have struck all my enemies
upon the cheek. You have broken the
teeth of the wicked.
9 Salvation belongs to Yehovah. Your
blessing be upon Your people. Selah.

Psalm 4

1 To the director, with string-music. A
Psalm of David.
2 Answer me when I call, O God of
my righteousness, You Who made
room when I was in distress. Be gra-

cious to me and hear my prayer.
3O sons of men, how long shall my
glory be put to shame, in that you love
emptiness and seek after lies? Selah.
4But know that Yehovah has set apart
the godly man as His own. The Lord
will hear when I call unto Him.
5Tremble and sin not; commune with
your own heart upon your bed, and be
still. Selah.
6Offer the sacrifices of righteousness
and put your trust in Yehovah.
7Many say: "Who will show us
good?" Yehovah, lift up the light of
Your countenance upon us.
8You have put gladness in my heart,
more than when their grain and their
new wine increased.
9 In peace will I both lay down and
sleep; for You, Yehovah, make me dwell
alone in safety.

Psalm 5

1To the director, for the flutes. A
psalm of David.
2Give ear to my words, Yehovah; consider my utterances.
3Respond to the sound of my cry, my
King and my God, for unto You I pray.
4Yehovah, in the morning you shall
hear my voice. In the morning I will
prepare for You and I will watch.
5For You are not a God Who has
pleasure in injustice; evil shall not sojourn with You.
6The foolish will not stand in Your
sight. You hate all workers of iniquity.
7You shall destroy those who speak
lies. The Lord abhors the man of blood
and of deceit.
8But as for me, in the abundance of
Your steadfast love, I will come into
Your house. I will worship toward Your
holy temple in the fear of You.
9Yehovah, lead me in Your righteousness because of my enemies. Make
Your way straight before my face.
10For there is nothing reliable in his
mouth; the inward parts are destruction; the throat an open grave; they
speak deceitfully.
11Destroy them, O God. Let them fall
through their own scheme. Scatter
them because of their many crimes, because they rebel against You.
12All who take refuge in You shall rejoice. Forever we will shout for joy. You
are a shield, and those who love Your
name shall rejoice in You.
13For You will bless the righteous
yourself, Yehovah. You will surround
him with favor as a shield.

Psalm 6

1To the director, with string instruments, according to the Sheminith. A
psalm of David.
2Yehovah, do not rebuke me in Your
anger, nor discipline me in Your wrath.
3Be gracious unto me, Yehovah, for I
am languishing. Heal me, Yehovah, for
my bones are troubled.
4My soul also is very afraid; and You,
Yehovah, how long?
5Return, Yehovah, deliver my soul.
Save me for the sake of Your steadfast
love.
6For in death there is no remembrance of You; in Sheol who will give
You thanks?
7I am weary with my groaning; every
night I flood my bed with my tears; I
drench my couch.
8I waste away because of grief; my
eye grows weak because of all my foes.
9Depart from me, all you workers of
iniquity; for Yehovah has heard the
voice of my weeping.
10Yehovah has heard my supplication;
Yehovah receives my prayer.

11All my enemies shall be ashamed
and very afraid; they shall turn back,
they shall be ashamed suddenly.

Psalm 7

1Shiggaion of David, which he sang
unto Yehovah, concerning Cush, a
Benjamite.
2Yehovah my God, in You I have tak-
en refuge; save me from all them who
pursue me, and deliver me;
3lest he tear my soul like a lion, rending it in pieces, while there is none to
rescue.
4Yehovah my God, if I have done
this; if there be iniquity in my hands;
5if I have requited him who did evil
unto me, or spoiled my adversary unto
emptiness;
6let the enemy pursue my soul, overtake it, and tread my life down to the
Earth; yea, let him lay my glory in the
dust. Selah.
7Arise, Yehovah, in Your anger. Lift
up Yourself in indignation against my
adversaries; yes, awake for me at the
judgment that You have commanded.
8And let the congregation of the
peoples encompass You about, and
over them return on high.
9Yehovah, Who ministers judgment
to the peoples, judge me, Yehovah, according to my righteousness and according to my integrity that is in me.
10Oh that a full measure of evil might
come upon the wicked, and that you
would establish the righteous; for the
righteous God tries the heart and reins.
11My shield is with God, Who saves
the upright in heart.
12God is a righteous judge, yes, a God
that has indignation every day:
13If a man turns not, He will whet
His sword. He has bent His bow and
made it ready.
14He has also prepared for him the
weapons of death, yes, His arrows
which He made sharp.
15Behold, he travails with iniquity;
yes, he conceives mischief, and brings
forth falsehood.
16He has dug a pit, hollowed it, and
fallen into the ditch which he made.
17His mischief shall return upon his
own head, and his violence shall come
down upon his own scalp.
18I will give thanks unto Yehovah according to His righteousness, and will
sing praise to the name of Yehovah
most high.

Psalm 8

1To the director, upon the Gittith. A
Psalm of David.
2Yehovah, our Adonai, how majestic
is Your name in all the Earth, whose
majesty is rehearsed above the heavens?
3Out of the mouth of babes and sucklings You have founded strength, because of Your adversaries; that You
might stop the enemy and adversaries.
4When I behold Your heavens, the
work of Your fingers, the moon and the
stars, which You have established;
5what is man, that You are mindful of
him, and the son of man, that You care
for him?
6Yet You have made him inferior only
to God, and have crowned him with
glory and honor.
7You have made him to have dominion over the works of Your hands; You
have put all things under His feet:
8sheep and oxen – all of them – and
also the beasts of the field;
9the fowl of the air, and the fish of the
sea; whatever passes through the paths
of the seas.
10Yehovah, our Adonai, how majestic

is Your name in all the Earth?

Psalm 9

1To the director upon Muth-labben. A psalm of David.

2I will give thanks, Yehovah. With all my heart I will recount all of Your extraordinary deeds.

3I will rejoice and be extremely joyful in You, I will sing music to your name, most high.

4When my enemies are turned back, they shall stumble and they shall perish at Your presence,

5for you have maintained my cause and my rights. You sat in Your throne judging righteously.

6You have rebuked the nations. You destroyed the wicked. Their names You have blotted out forever and ever.

7The enemies He has completely destroyed. You have plucked up their cities. Forever the remembrance of them has perished.

8And Yehovah dwells forever. He has prepared His throne in judgment.

9He will judge the world in righteousness. He will judge the people in fairness.

10Yehovah will be a fortress to the oppressed, a fortress in time of distress.

11And those who know Your name will trust in You, for You have not forsaken those who seek You, Yehovah.

12Sing to Yehovah, Who dwells in Zion. Proclaim His works among the people.

13For He Who avenges blood has remembered them. He has not forgotten the cry of the humble.

14Be gracious unto me, Yehovah. Behold my affliction at the hands of them who hate me, You who lifts me up from the gates of death;

15that I may tell of all Your praise in the gates of the daughter of Zion, that I may rejoice in Your salvation.

16The nations are sunk down in the pit that they made; in the net which they hid is their own foot taken.

17Yehovah has made Himself known. He has executed judgment. The wicked is snared in the work of his own hands. Higgaion. Selah.

18The wicked shall return to Sheol, all the nations that forget God.

19For the needy shall not always be forgotten, nor the expectation of the poor perish forever.

20Arise, Yehovah, let not man prevail, let the nations be judged before You.

21Set terror over them, Yehovah. Let the nations know they are men. Selah.

Psalm 10

1Why do You stand far off, Yehovah? Why do You hide Yourself in times of trouble?

2Through the arrogance of the wicked, the poor are hotly pursued. They are taken in the devices that they have imagined.

3For the wicked boast of his soul's desire, and the greedy of gain, though he curses and renounces Yehovah.

4The wicked, in the pride of his face, does not inquire. All his thoughts are: “There is no God.”

5His ways prosper at all times; Your judgments are far above, out of his sight. As for all his adversaries, he puffs at them.

6He says in his heart, “I shall not be moved. Throughout all generations I shall not be in adversity.”

7His mouth is full of cursing, deceit, and oppression. Under his tongue is mischief and iniquity.

8He sits in ambush of the villages. In hiding-places he kills the innocent. His

eyes stealthily watch for the helpless.
9 He lies in wait in a hiding-place as a
lion in his covert, He lies in wait that
he may seize the poor. He seizes the
poor when he draws him up in his net.
10 He crouches and he crushes; the
helpless fall into his might.
11 He has said in his heart: "God has
forgotten. He hides His face. He will
never see."
12 Arise, Yehovah. O God, lift up Your
hand. Do not forget the humble.
13 Why does the wicked renounce
God, and say in his heart: "You will not
seek it out"?
14 You have seen, for You behold
trouble and vexation, to take with Your
hand. The helpless commits himself to
You. You have been the helper of the
fatherless.
15 Break the arm of the wicked, and
seek out the wickedness of the evil one,
until none be found.
16 Yehovah is King forever and ever.
The nations have perished from His
land.
17 Yehovah, You have heard the desire
of the humble. You will establish their
heart. You will incline your ear
18 to do justice to the fatherless and
the oppressed, that the man who is of
the Earth may cause terror no more.

Psalm 11

1 For the director of David. In Yehovah I seek refuge. How can you say of
my life, "Flee to your mountain as a
bird"?
2 For behold: the wicked string their
bows – they make ready their arrows
on the string in order to secretly shoot
at the upright in heart.
3 When the foundations are destroyed, what will the righteous do?
4 Yehovah is in His holy palace. Yehovah has His throne in Heaven. His eyes
behold – His pupils examine the sons
of men.
5 Yehovah examines the righteous, but
the wicked and he who does violence
His soul hates.
6 He shall rain upon the wicked coals
of fire, brimstone and a spirit of
scorching heat shall be the portion of
their cup.
7 For righteous Yehovah loves righteousness. His face shall behold the upright.

Psalm 12

1 To the director, on the Sheminith. A
psalm of David.
2 Save us, Yehovah, for the godly have
ceased; for the faithful have vanished
from the sons of men.
3 They speak lies, each man with his
neighbor. With flattering lips and a
double heart they speak.
4 Yehovah shall cut off all the flattering lips, and the tongue that speaks
great things:
5 those who say, "By our tongue we
will prevail, and with our lips. Who
shall lord over us?"
6 "For the oppression of the poor and
for the groaning of the needy, now I
will arise," says Yehovah, "I will set
those in salvation who long for it."
7 The words of Yehovah are pure
words, as silver refined in a furnace of
earth, purified seven times.
8 You, Yehovah, have guarded us. You
have protected us from this generation
forever.
9 The wicked walk about on every
side when the vilest of the sons of men
are exalted.

Psalm 13

1 For the director. A Psalm of David.

2 How long, O LORD, will You forget me? Forever? How long will You hide Your face from me?

3 How long shall I hold counsel in my soul, having sorrow in my heart by day? How long shall my enemy be exalted over me?

4 You consider! Answer me, Yehovah my God; give light to my eyes, lest I sleep death;

5 lest my enemy says: "I have overcome him"; lest my adversaries rejoice when I stumble.

6 But as for me, in Your steadfast love I trust; my heart shall rejoice in Your salvation. I will sing unto the LORD, because He has dealt bountifully with me.

Psalm 14

1 To the director of David. The fool has said in his heart, "There is no God." They are corrupt; they do abominable deeds; there is none who does good.

2 Yehovah looks down from Heaven upon the children of men to see if there are any who inquire, who seek God.

3 They all have gone astray; they were corrupt. There is none who does good – no, not one!

4 "All the workers of iniquity have no knowledge, who eat up My people as they eat bread – they call not upon Yehovah?"

5 See how they greatly tremble, for God is in the righteous generation.

6 You would put to shame the counsel of the poor, but Yehovah is his refuge,

7 Who gives to Israel salvation from Zion of Israel! When Yehovah regathers the fortunes of His people, let Jacob rejoice – let Israel be glad!

Psalm 15

1 A Psalm of David. Yehovah, who shall abide in your tabernacle? Who shall dwell in your holy mountain?

2 He who walks blamelessly, does righteousness, and speaks the truth in his heart,

3 who has no slander upon his tongue, nor does evil to his friend, nor takes up a reproach against his neighbor,

4 in whose eyes a vile one is rejected, but he honors those who fear Yehovah; he who swears to his own hurt and does not change.

5 He does not give his money for interest, nor takes a bribe against the innocent. He who does these things shall never stumble.

Psalm 16

1 Michtam of David. Keep me, O God; for I have taken refuge in You.

2 I said to Yehovah, "Lord, I have no good apart from You."

3 As for the holy ones who are in the Earth, they are the majestic ones in whom is all my delight.

4 They multiply their sorrows who chase after another. I will not pour out their drink-offerings of blood, nor take their names upon my lips.

5 Yehovah, is my chosen portion and my cup. You maintain my lot.

6 The lines have fallen for me in pleasant places – surely I have a delightful inheritance.

7 I will bless Yehovah, Who has given me advice – surely, in the nights He instructs my inward parts.

8 I have set Yehovah always before me, for He is at my right hand; I shall not stumble.

9 Therefore my heart is happy, and my glory rejoices. Surely my flesh dwells in

safety,

10for You will not abandon my soul in Sheol. You will not allow Your godly one to see the pit.

11You make me know the path of life. In Your presence is fullness of joy. At Your right hand are pleasures forevermore.

Psalm 17

1A prayer of David. Hear righteousness, Yehovah. Give heed unto my cry. Give ear unto my prayer from lips without deceit.

2Let my judgment come forth from Your presence – let Your eyes behold integrity.

3You have examined my heart – You have visited it in the night. You have tested me and shall find nothing. I have resolved not to transgress with my mouth.

4As for the deeds of men, by the word of Your lips I have kept myself from the ways of the violent.

5My steps have held fast to Your paths – my feet have not stumbled.

6I call upon You, for You will answer me O God. Incline Your ear unto me – hear my words.

7So wondrous is your steadfast love, O Savior, for those who seek refuge from their enemies at Your right hand.

8Keep me as the apple of your eye. Hide me in the shadow of Your wings,

9from the wicked who lay waste, my mortal enemies who encircle against me.

10Their fat encloses them. With arrogance their mouths speak.

11They surrounded our steps. They set their eyes to cast us down to the ground.

12He is like a lion longing to tear in pieces, and like a young lion crouching in a secret place.

13Stand up, Yehovah. Confront him – make him bow down. With Your sword rescue my soul from the wicked –

14from men, by Your hand, Yehovah, from men of the world – whose portion is in this life. Their bellies You fill with Your treasure. Their children are satisfied, and they leave their abundance to their babies.

15I shall behold Your face in righteousness. I shall be satisfied when I awake with Your likeness.

Psalm 18

1To the director. To a servant of Yehovah, to David, who spoke to Yehovah the words of this song in the day Yehovah delivered him from the grip of all his enemies and from the hand of Saul.

2And he said, “I love you, Yehovah, my strength.

3Yehovah is my cleft in the rock, my fortress, my Rescuer, my God, my rock – in Him I will seek refuge – my shield, and the horn of my salvation; my stronghold.

4I will call Yehovah, worthy of praise! So shall I be saved from my enemies.

5I was encompassed by the bands of death, and the currents of Belial overwhelmed me.

6The bands of Sheol surrounded me – the snares of death came upon me.

7In my distress I called upon Yehovah and unto the God of my salvation. He heard my voice, and my cry for help came before Him – it came into His ears.

8The Earth shook and trembled and the foundation of the mountains shuddered – they shook because of His anger.

9Smoke ascended from His nostrils
and a consuming fire from His mouth.
Glowing coals burned forth from Him.
10He spread apart the heavens and
came down, and a thick cloud was under His feet,
11and He rode upon a cherub and
flew swiftly upon the wings of the
wind.
12He made darkness His covering. All
around Him, His covering was dark
waters of thick clouds
13Out of the brightness of His presence, His clouds passed over hailstones
and coals of fire.
14And Yehovah thundered in the
heavens, and the Most High uttered
His voice, hailstones and coals of fire.
15Then were the channels of waters
discovered, and He uncovered the
foundations of the world – at the rebuke of Yehovah and by the spirit of
the breath of His nostrils.
16And He let loose His arrows and
scattered them, and many bolts of
lightning discomfited them.
17He snatches me away from my
fierce enemy and from those who hated me, for they were too strong for me.
18He delivered me from my enemy,
most strong, and from them who hated
me, for they were too mighty for me.
19They came upon me in the day of
my disaster, but Yehovah was my support.
20He brought me forth also into a
large place. He delivered me because
He delighted in me.
21Yehovah rewarded me according to
my righteousness – according to the
cleanness of my hands has He recom-
pensed me.
22For I have kept the ways of Yehovah, and have not wickedly departed
from my God.
23For all His ordinances were before
me, and I put not away His statutes
from me.
24And I was blameless with Him, and
I kept myself from my iniquity.
25Therefore Yehovah has recom-
pensed me according to my righteousness, according to the cleanness of
my hands in His eyes.
26With the merciful You will show
Yourself merciful, with the upright
man You will show Yourself upright,
27with the pure You will show Yourself pure, and with the crooked You
will show Yourself subtle.
28For You will save the lowly people,
but the haughty eyes You will overthrow.
29For You will light my lamp. Yehovah my God will lighten my darkness.
30For by You I run upon a troop, and
by my God do I scale a wall.
31As for God, His way is perfect. The
word of Yehovah is tried. He is a shield
unto all them who take refuge in Him.
32For who is God except for Yehovah? And who is a rock except for our
God?
33It is God who equips me with
strength and He makes my way perfect.
34He made my feet like the hind and
stood me upon my high places,
35Who trains my hands for war so
that my arm bends a bow of brass.
36You have given me the shield of
Your salvation; and Your right hand
supported me; and your meekness
made me great.
37You have enlarged my steps under
me and my ankles did not slide.
38I pursued my enemies and returned
not again until they were brought to an
end.
39I have smashed them, they are not
able to arise, they have fallen under my

feet.

40For You girded me with strength for the battle and subdued under me those who rose up against me.

41And you gave to me the neck of my enemies, and those who hated me were destroyed.

42They cried for help, but there was none to rescue – unto Yehovah, but He did not answer.

43I crushed them as dust before the wind. Like the mud outside, I cast them out.

44You brought me out from the strife of people. You sat me as the head of the nations. People who I didn't know served me.

45As soon as they heard, they obeyed me – the sons of foreigners feigned obedience to me.

46The sons of the foreigners lost heart and came trembling from their strongholds.

47Yehovah lives, and blessed is my rock, and the God of my salvation be exalted.

48The God Who executed vengeance for me and subdued peoples under me –

49Who rescued me from my enemies also – You lifted me up above those who rose up against me. You saved me from violent men.

50For this I will praise you, Yehovah, among the nations, and sing praises to Your name.

51Great salvation He gives for His king and shows steadfast love for His Messiah, to David and to his seed forever.

Psalm 19

1For the Director. A Psalm of David.

2The heavens make known the glory of God, and the firmament proclaims His handiwork.

3Day unto day pours forth speech, and night unto night makes known knowledge.

4There is no speech, no words, their voices are unheard.

5Their call goes out into all the Earth, and their utterance to the end of the habitable parts. In them He has set a tent there for the sun,

6and he is like a bridegroom coming out of his chamber, and rejoices as a strong one to run his course.

7His place of departure is from the end of the heaven, and his circuit unto the ends of it, and there is nothing hidden from his glow.

8The Law of Yehovah is perfect, reviving the soul. The testimony of Yehovah is sure, making wise the simple.

9The instructions of Yehovah are right, rejoicing the heart. The commandment of Yehovah is clean, enlightening the eyes.

10The fear of Yehovah is pure, enduring forever. The judgments of Yehovah are true and righteous altogether.

11More to be desired are they than gold, even purified gold; sweeter also than the dripping honey from the honeycomb.

12Also Your servant is warned by them. In keeping them there is great reward.

13Who can discern His errors? Clear me from what's hidden.

14Also keep Your servant back from arrogant sins, lest they have dominion over me. Then shall I be blameless, and I shall be innocent from great transgression.

15Let the words of my mouth and the meditation of my heart be acceptable before You, Yehovah, my Rock, and my Redeemer.

Psalm 20

1 To the Director. A song of David.
2 May Yehovah answer you in the day
of trouble. May the name of the God of
Jacob protect you.
3 May He send you help from the
sanctuary, and from Zion may He sustain you.
4 May He remember all of your offerings and your burnt offering. May He
regard you with favor, Selah.
5 May He give to you according to
your heart, and may He fulfill all of
your plans.
6 May we shout for joy in your salvation and in the name of our God! May
Yehovah fulfill all of your petitions.
7 Now I know that Yehovah saves His
anointed one from His holy Heaven
with the power of His right hand.
8 Some in chariots and some in horses, but we boast in the name of Yehovah our God.
9 They collapse and fall, but we rise
up and are relieved.
10 Save, Yehovah! Let the King answer
us in the day that we call.

Psalm 21

1 To the director of music. From
David.
2 In Yehovah's strength the king rejoices, and in Your salvation how greatly he circles in joy!
3 You have given his heart's desire to
him and the request of his lips you
have not withheld.
4 For You set before him the good
blessings, You will set upon his head a
crown of pure gold.
5 He asks life of You – You gave it to
him – length of days eternal and forever.
6 Great is his glory through Your salvation. Majesty and splendor you have
set upon him.
7 For You have set blessings upon him
forever. You shall make him rejoice
with the joy of Your presence.
8 For the king trusted in Yehovah, and
in the lovingkindness of the Most High
he will not swerve.
9 Your hand shall find all Your enemies. Your right hand shall find those
who hate You.
10 You shall set them as in a fiery
furnace at the time of Yehovah's
presence – His anger engulfed them
and His fire devoured them.
11 You shall destroy their offspring
from the Earth and their seed from the
sons of men.
12 For they plotted a revolt against
You. They thought up devices but
could not carry them out.
13 But You will put them to flight.
With Your bowstring You shall aim at
their faces.
14 Be exalted, O Yehovah, in Your own
strength. We will sing and praise Your
power.

Psalm 22

1 To the Director. According to the
doe of the dawn. A song of David.
2 My God, my God, why have You
forsaken me, so far from saving me;
words of my groanings.
3 O my God, I call by day, but You do
not answer; and at night, but there is
no rest for me.
4 Yet You are holy, enthroned on the
praises of Israel.
5 Our fathers trusted in You – they
trusted, and You rescued them.
6 They cried to You, and You saved
them. They trusted You and were not
ashamed.
7 But I am a worm and no man,
scorned by mankind and despised by

the people.
8All who see me mock me. They stick
out their lips – they shake their head.
9"Let him commit himself unto
Yehovah! Let Him rescue him! Let Him
deliver him, seeing He delights in
him!"
10For You are He Who took me out of
the womb. You made me trust when I
was upon my mother's breasts.
11Upon You I have been cast from my
birth. You are my God from my mother's womb.
12Be not far from me, for trouble is
near – for there is none to help.
13Many bulls have surrounded me.
Strong bulls of Bashan have surrounded me.
14They open widely their mou-ths
against me like a ravenous and roaring
lion.
15I am poured out like water, and all
my bones are out of joint. My heart has
become like wax. It is melted in my innermost parts.
16My strength is dried up like a pot-
sherd, and My tongue cleaves to My
throat, and You lay me in the dust of
death.
17For dogs have encompassed me. A
company of evil-doers have enclosed
Me. Like a lion, they are at my hands
and my feet.
18I may count all my bones. They
look and gloat over me.
19They part my garments among
them, and for my vesture they cast lots.
20But You, Yehovah, be not far off. O
You my strength, hasten to help me.
21Deliver me from the sword; my
soul from the hand of the dog.
22Save me from the lion's mouth.
Make me triumph over the horns of
wild oxen.
23I will declare Your name to my
brethren. I will sing praise.
24You who fear Yehovah: praise Him.
All the seed of Jacob: glorify Him. And
be in awe of Him, all the seed of Israel.
25For He has not despised nor looked
down on the suffering of the poor, nor
has He hid His face from him; but
when he cried unto Him, He heard.
26From You are my praise in the great
congregation. I will pay my vows before them who fear Him.
27The humble shall eat and be satisfied. They who seek after Yehovah shall
praise Him. May your heart live forever!
28All the ends of the Earth shall remember and turn to Yehovah, and all
the families of the nations shall bow
down before You.
29For the kingdom is Yehovah's, and
He is the ruler over the nations.
30All the fat ones of the Earth shall
eat and bow down. All they who go
down to the dust shall kneel before
Him, and none can keep alive his own
soul.
31A seed shall serve Him – it shall be
counted to the Lord for a generation.
32They shall come and proclaim His
righteousness to a people born that He
has done it.

Psalm 23

1A song of David. Yehovah is my
Shepherd. I shall not lack.
2In green meadows He will make me
lie down. Near still waters He will
guide me.
3My soul He refreshes. He leads me
into entrenchments of righteousness
for the sake of His name.
4Even though I should walk in the
valley of the shadow of death, I will
fear no evil for You are with me. Your
rod and Your staff will comfort me.

5You prepare a table before me in front of my adversaries. You anoint my head with oil. My cup overflows.

6Surely goodness and lovingkindness shall pursue me all the days of my life, and I shall dwell in the house of Yehovah for days without end.

Psalm 24

1A Song of David. The Earth is Yehovah's and the fullness of it; the world and the inhabitants in it.

2For He founded it upon the waters and established it upon the rivers.

3Who shall ascend into the mountain of Yehovah? And who shall stand in the place of His holiness?

4The one with clean hands and a pure heart, who has not lifted up his soul to vanity nor sworn deceitfully:

5He shall lift up blessings from Yehovah and righteousness from the God of his salvation.

6This is Jacob, the generation that resorts to Him, who seeks Your face. Selah.

7Lift up your heads, O ye gates, and be ye lifted up, ye everlasting doors; that the King of glory shall come in.

8'Who is the King of glory?' 'Yehovah strong and mighty, Yehovah mighty in battle.'

9Lift up your heads, O ye gates, yes, lift them up, you everlasting doors; that the King of glory shall come in.

10'Who then is the King of glory?' 'Yehovah of hosts; He is the King of glory.' Selah

Psalm 25

1From David. Yehovah, unto You I lift up my soul.

2My God in you I trust let me not be ashamed let not my enemies triumph over me.

3Also all who wait for you shall not be ashamed; ashamed shall be the vainly deceitful.

4Yehovah cause me to know your ways teach me your paths.

5Lead me in your faithfulness and teach me, for you are the God of my salvation it is you I invoke all the day.

6Remember your compassions Yehovah and your loving kindnesses for they are from everlasting.

7The sins of my youth and the transgressions, do not remember according to your own loving kindness. Remember me on account of your goodness Yehovah.

8Good and right is Yehovah therefore He shows sinners His way.

9He will guide the humble in judgment and He will teach the humble His way.

10All the ways of Yehovah are lovingkindness and truth to those who keep His covenant and His testimonies.

11For Your name's sake, Yehovah, pardon my iniquity, for it is great.

12What man is he who fears Yehovah? He will instruct him in the way that He should choose.

13His soul shall be in prosperity, and his seed shall inherit the land.

14The secret of Yehovah is with those who fear Him – and His covenant, to make them know it.

15My eyes are ever toward Yehovah, for He will bring forth my feet out of the net.

16Turn to me and be gracious to me, for I am solitary and afflicted.

17The troubles of my heart are enlarged. O bring me out of my distresses!

18See my affliction and my travail, and forgive all my sins.

19Consider how many are my enemies and the cruel hatred with which they hate me.

20 O keep my soul, and deliver me! Let me not be ashamed, for I have taken refuge in You.

21 Let integrity and uprightness preserve me, because I wait for You.

22 Redeem Israel, O God, out of all his troubles.

Psalm 26

1 Of David. Judge me, Yehovah, for I have walked in my purity, and I have trusted in Yehovah without wavering.

2 Examine me, Yehovah, and try me. Test the depths of my being and my heart.

3 For your lovingkindness is before my eyes, and I have walked in Your truth.

4 I have not sat with men of falsehood, nor will I go in with hypocrites.

5 I hate the assembly of evil-doers, and will not sit with the wicked.

6 I will wash my hands in innocence. So will I encompass Your altar, Yehovah,

7 to cause the voice of thanksgiving to be heard and to recount all Your wondrous works.

8 Yehovah, I love the dwelling of Your house and the place where Your glory tabernacles.

9 Do not destroy my soul with sinners, nor my life with men of blood,

10 in whose hands is an evil plan, and their right hand is full of bribes.

11 But as for me, I will walk in my purity. Redeem me, and be gracious to me.

12 My foot stands in an even place. In the congregations will I bless Yehovah.

Psalm 27

1 Of David. Yehovah is my light and my salvation – whom shall I fear? Yehovah is the stronghold of my life – of whom shall I be afraid?

2 When evil-doers came near to eat up my flesh – even my adversaries and my enemies against me – they stumbled and fell.

3 Though an army encamp against me, I shall not fear. Though war rise up against me, in this I am confident.

4 One thing I have asked of Yehovah, that will I seek after: that I may dwell in the house of Yehovah all the days of my life, to behold the beauty of Yehovah, and inquire in His temple.

5 For He will hide me in His shelter in the day of evil. He hides me in the hiding place of His tent. He exalts me upon the rock.

6 And now shall my head be exalted above my enemies round about me, and I will offer in His tabernacle sacrifices with shouts of joy. I will sing. I will praise Yehovah.

7 Hear, Yehovah, when I call with my voice, and be gracious unto me, and answer me.

8 He says to my heart, "Discover My face." Your face, Yehovah, will I discover.

9 Do not hide Your face from me. Put not Your servant away in anger. You have been my help. Cast me not off, nor forsake me, O God of my salvation.

10 For though my father and my mother have forsaken me, Yehovah will take me up.

11 Teach me Your way, Yehovah, and lead me in an even path because of them who lie in wait for me.

12 Deliver me not over to the will of my adversaries, for false witnesses are risen up against me, and such as breathe out violence.

13 If I had not believed to look upon

the goodness of Yehovah in the land of the living!
14Wait on Yehovah, be strong, and let your heart take courage. Yes, wait for Yehovah.

Psalm 28

1Of David. To You, Yehovah, do I call. My Rock, do not be silent to me. If You are silent to me, I become like them who go down into the pit.
2Hear the voice of my pleadings when I cry to you for help – when I lift up my hands toward Your Holy of Holies.
3Carry me not away with the wicked, and with the workers of iniquity who speak peace with their neighbors but evil is in their hearts.
4Give them according to their deeds and according to the evil of their deeds. Give them after the work of their hands. Give back to them their due reward.
5Because they give no regard to the works of Yehovah or to the works of His hands, He will tear them down and He will not rebuild them.
6Blessed be Yehovah, because He has heard the voice of my pleadings.
7Yehovah is my strength and my shield. In Him has my heart trusted, and I am helped. So my heart triumphs, and with my song I will praise Him.
8Yehovah is a strength to them, and He is a stronghold of salvation to His anointed.
9Save Your people, and bless Your inheritance, and be their Shepherd, and carry them forever.

Psalm 29

1A Psalm of David. Give to Yehovah, O you sons of God. Give to Yehovah glory and strength.
2Give to Yehovah the glory of His name. Worship Yehovah in the majesty of holiness.
3The voice of Yehovah is upon the waters. The God of glory thunders. Yehovah is upon many waters.
4The voice of Yehovah is powerful. The voice of Yehovah is majestic.
5The voice of Yehovah breaks the cedars. Yehovah breaks the cedars of Lebanon.
6He also makes them leap like a calf – Lebanon and Sirion like a young wild bull.
7The voice of Yehovah flashes forth flames of fire.
8The voice of Yehovah shakes the wilderness. Yehovah shakes the wilderness of Kadesh.
9The voice of Yehovah makes the deer give birth and strips the forests. And in His temple, all say, “Glory!”
10Yehovah sat upon the flood, and Yehovah sits as King forever.
11Yehovah will give strength to His people. Yehovah will bless His people with peace.

Psalm 30

1A Psalm. A Song at the dedication of the house. Of David.
2I will exalt You, Yehovah, for You have raised me up, and my enemies have not rejoiced over me.
3Yehovah my God, I called to You for help, and You healed me.
4Yehovah, You brought up my soul from Sheol. You kept me alive from going down to the pit.
5Sing praise unto Yehovah, His godly ones, and give thanks to His holy remembrance.
6His anger is for a moment – His favor is for a lifetime. Weeping may tarry

for the night, but in the morning: joy!

7Now I had said in my security, “I shall never be moved.”

8You have established, Yehovah, in Your favor, my mountain as a stronghold. You hid Your face. I was afraid.

9To You, Yehovah, did I call, and to Yehovah I implore for grace:

10“What profit is there in my blood when I go down to the pit? Shall the dust praise You? Shall it declare Your truth?

11Hear, Yehovah, and be gracious to me. Yehovah, be my Helper.”

12You have turned my mourning into dancing. You removed my sackcloth and clothed me with gladness,

13so that my glory may sing praise to You and not be silent. O Yehovah my God, I will give thanks to You forever.

Psalm 31

1For the Conductor. A Psalm of David.

2In You, Yehovah, have I taken refuge. Let me never be ashamed. In Your righteousness, deliver me.

3Incline Your ear to me. Rescue me quickly. Be to me a rock of refuge – a strong fortress – to save me.

4For You are my rock and my fortress, so for Your name's sake lead me and guide me.

5Bring me out of the net that they have hid for me, for You are my stronghold.

6Into Your hand I commit my spirit. You have redeemed me, Yehovah, God of truth.

7I hate those who regard worthless idols, but I trust in You, Yehovah.

8I will shout and rejoice in Your lovingkindness, for You have seen my affliction. You have known of the troubles of my soul,

9and You have not given me over into the hand of the enemy. You have set my feet in a broad place.

10Be gracious to me, Yehovah, for I am in distress. My eye is wasted with sorrow – my soul and my belly.

11For my life is spent in sorrow, and my years in sighing. My strength stumbles because of my iniquity, and my bones waste away.

12Because of all my adversaries, I have become a reproach, and more to my neighbors, and a dread to my acquaintance. They that see me in the street flee from me.

13I am forgotten as one dead, out of mind. I am like a broken vessel.

14For I have heard the rumor of many – horror on every side – as they conspire together against me. They have plotted to take my soul.

15But I have trusted in You, Yehovah. I have said, “You are my God.”

16My times are in Your hand. Deliver me from the hand of my enemies and from my persecutors.

17Let Your face shine upon Your servant. Save me in Your lovingkindness.

18Yehovah, let me not be ashamed, for I have called upon You. Let the wicked be ashamed. Let them wail in Sheol.

19Let lying lips be silenced, which speak against the righteous with arrogance and contempt.

20Oh how abundant is Your goodness, which You have laid up for them who fear You, which You perform for them who take refuge in You, in the sight of the sons of men!

21You hide them in the hiding place: Your presence, from the slander of man. You keep them in a shelter from the strife of tongues.

22Blessed be Yehovah, for He has

shown His wondrous lovingkindness to me in a besieged city.

23 As for me, I said in my haste, “I am cut off from before Your eyes.” However, You heard the voice of my pleading when I cried to You for help.

24 Love Yehovah, all you His godly ones. Yehovah preserves the faithful and abundantly repays him who acts arrogantly.

25 Be strong and strengthen your heart all who wait for Yehovah.

Chapter 32

1 Of David. A Maschil. Blessed is the one whose transgressions are taken away and sin is covered.

2 Blessed is the man to whom Yehovah does not impute iniquity and in whose spirit there is no deceit.

3 When I remained silent, my bones wore out with groanings all day.

4 For day and night Your hand was heavy upon me. My vigor was dried up in the heat of summer. Selah.

5 I made known my sin to You and I did not conceal my iniquity. I said, "I will confess to the Lord the most high my transgressions," and You took away the punishment of my sin.

6 Therefore, let everyone who is godly pray to You in the time when You may be found. In the flood of great waters they shall not reach you.

7 You are my hiding place. You keep me from distress. You surround me with shouts of deliverance. Selah.

8 “I will instruct you and direct you in the way you must go. I will guide you with my eyes.

9 Do not be as the horse or as the mule: without discernment. With bridle and rein his straps hold him, else he comes not near you.

10 Many sorrows shall be to the wicked, but those who trust in Yehovah will be surrounded by His lovingkindness.

11 Rejoice in Yehovah and shout for joy, you righteous, and give a ringing cry all you upright in heart.

Psalm 33

1 Rejoice in Yehovah, O you righteous. Songs of praise are beautiful for the upright.

2 Give thanks to Yehovah with the lyre. With the harp of ten strings sing praise to Him.

3 Sing to Him a new song. Play skillfully with a war cry of joy!

4 For the word of Yehovah is upright, and all His work is in faithfulness.

5 He loves righteousness and justice. The Earth is full of the lovingkindness of Yehovah.

6 By the word of Yehovah were the heavens made – and all the host of them by the breath of His mouth.

7 He gathered the waters of the sea together as a heap – He laid up the depths in storehouses.

8 Let all the Earth fear Yehovah. Let all the inhabitants of the land be afraid of Him.

9 For He spoke, and it was. He commanded, and it stood.

10 Yehovah brings to nothing the counsel of the nations – He frustrates the thoughts of the peoples.

11 The counsel of Yehovah stands forever – the thoughts of His heart to all generations.

12 Blessed is the nation whose God is Yehovah – the people whom He has chosen for His own inheritance.

13 Yehovah looks from Heaven – He sees all the sons of men;

14 From the place of His habitation He gazes upon all who dwell in the Earth;

[15]He Who fashioned their hearts alike considers all their doings.
[16]A king is not saved by the multitude of his strength. A mighty man is not delivered by great strength.
[17]A horse is a vain thing for deliverance – by its great power it cannot save.
[18]Behold, the eye of Yehovah is toward them who fear Him, toward them who wait for His lovingkindness,
[19]to deliver their souls from death, and to keep them alive in famine.
[20]Our soul has waited for Yehovah. He is our help and our shield.
[21]For in Him does our heart rejoice, because we have trusted in His holy name.
[22]Let Your lovingkindness, Yehovah, be upon us, accordingly as we have waited for You.

Psalm 34

[1]Of David. When he changed his behavior before Abimelech, who drove him away, and he departed.
[2]I will bless Yehovah at all times. His praise will continually be in my mouth.
[3]My soul shall make its boast in Yehovah. The humble shall hear thereof and be glad.
[4]O magnify Yehovah with me, and let us exalt His name together.
[5]I sought Yehovah, and He answered me and delivered me from all my fears.
[6]They looked to Him and their faces shine – they are never put to shame.
[7]This poor one called, and Yehovah heard and saved him from all his trouble.
[8]The Angel of Yehovah encamps all around those who fear Him, and He rescues them.
[9]Taste and see that Yehovah is good. Happy is the man who takes refuge in Him.
[10]O fear Yehovah, you His holy ones, for there is no lack for them who fear Him.
[11]The young lions do lack and suffer hunger, but they who seek Yehovah will not be deprived of any good thing.
[12]Come, you children, hearken unto me – I will teach you the fear of Yehovah.
[13]Who is the man who desires life and loves days that he may see good?
[14]Keep your tongue from evil and your lips from speaking guile.
[15]Depart from evil and do good – seek peace and pursue it.
[16]The eyes of Yehovah are toward the righteous, and His ears are open to their cry.
[17]The face of Yehovah is against those who do evil, to cut off the remembrance of them from the Earth.
[18]They cried out, and Yehovah heard and delivered them out of all their troubles.
[19]Yehovah is near to them of a broken heart and saves such as are of a contrite spirit.
[20]Many are the disasters of the righteous, but Yehovah delivers him out of them all.
[21]He keeps all his bones – not one of them is broken.
[22]Evil shall slay the wicked, and they who hate the righteous shall be condemned.
[23]Yehovah redeems the soul of His servants, and none of them who take refuge in Him shall be condemned.

Psalm 35

[1]A psalm of David. Yehovah, strive with those who strive with me – fight against those who fight against me.
[2]Take hold of shield and buckler, and rise up to my help.

3 Draw out also the spear and the battle-ax against those who pursue me. Say unto my soul, "I am Your salvation."

4 Let them be ashamed and brought to confusion who seek after my soul. Let them be turned back and be confused who devise my hurt.

5 Let them be as chaff before the wind, the Angel of Yehovah thrusting them.

6 Let their way be dark and slippery, the Angel of Yehovah pursuing them.

7 For without cause they have hidden a pit for me, even their net. Without cause have they dug for my soul.

8 Let destruction come upon him without him knowing, and let his net that he has hidden catch him. With destruction let him fall into it.

9 And my soul shall rejoice in Yehovah – it shall be glad in His salvation.

10 All my bones shall say, "Yehovah, who is like unto You, who delivers the weak from him who is too strong for him? Yes, the weak and the needy from him who robs?"

11 Violent witnesses rise up. They ask me things that I do not know.

12 They repay me evil for good, bereaving my soul.

13 But as for me, when they were sick, my clothing was sackcloth. I afflicted my soul with fasting. May my prayer return into my own bosom.

14 I went about as though it had been my friend or my brother. I bowed down mournfully, as one who mourns for his mother.

15 But when I stumble, they rejoice and gather themselves together – the injured ones gather themselves together against me, and those whom I know not: they tear and are not silent.

16 With profane mockeries, they gnash against me with their teeth.

17 Yehovah, how long will You look on? Rescue my soul from their destruction – my life from the lions.

18 I will give You thanks in the great congregation – a mighty praise to You among many people.

19 Let not those who are wrongfully my enemies rejoice over me, nor let them wink with the eye who hate me without a cause.

20 For they speak not of peace, but they conceive words of deceit against those who are at rest in the land.

21 Yes, they open their mouths wide against me. They say: "Aha! Aha! Our eye has seen it!"

22 You have seen, Yehovah. Do not be silent, Lord. Be not far from me.

23 Stir up and awake to my judgment, even unto my cause, my God and my Lord.

24 Judge me, Yehovah, my God, according to Your righteousness, and let them not rejoice over me.

25 Let them not say in their heart, "Aha, we have our desire!" Let them not say, "We have swallowed him up."

26 Let them be ashamed and confused together who rejoice at my hurt. Let them be clothed with shame and dishonor who magnify themselves against me.

27 Let them shout for joy and be glad who delight in my righteousness. Yes, let them say continually, "Yehovah be magnified, who delights in the peace of His servant."

28 And my tongue shall speak of Your righteousness, and of Your praise all the day.

Psalm 36

1 For the Conductor. Of David, the servant of Yehovah.

2 The rebellious wicked utters in the
midst of his heart – there is no fear of
God before his eyes.
3 For he flatters himself in his own
eyes until his iniquity is found and he
is hated.
4 The words of his mouth are iniquity
and deceit. He has left off to be wise, to
do good.
5 He devises iniquity upon his bed.
He sets himself in a way that is not
good. He does not abhor evil.
6 Your lovingkindness, Yehovah, is in
the heavens – Your faithfulness reaches
unto the clouds.
7 Your righteousness is like the
mighty mountains – Your judgments
are like the great deep. You preserve
man and beast, Yehovah.
8 How precious is Your lovingkindness, O God! And the children of men
take refuge in the shadow of Your
wings.
9 They are abundantly satisfied with
the fatness of Your house, and You
make them drink of the river of Your
pleasures.
10 For with You is the fountain of life.
In Your light, we see light.
11 O continue Your lovingkindness
unto those who know You, and Your
righteousness to the upright in heart.
12 Let not the foot of pride overtake
me, and let not the hand of the wicked
drive me away.
13 There are the workers of iniquity
fallen – they are thrust down and are
not able to rise.

Psalm 37

1 To David, do not be worried because of evildoers nor be envious because of the workers of iniquity.
2 For they shall quickly wither as the
grass and fade as the green grass.
3 Trust in Yehovah and do good dwell
in the land and feed on faithfulness.
4 And delight in Yehovah and He shall
give you the petitions of your heart.
5 Commit your way to Yehovah and
trust in Him and He shall bring it to
pass.
6 And He shall bring forth your righteousness as a light and your judgment
as the noonday.
7 Be still before Yehovah and tremble
before Him. Do not worry about him
who prospers in his ways because of
the man who devises a plot.
8 Cease from anger and forsake wrath
do not worry because of evil.
9 For evildoers shall be cut off but
those that wait on Yehovah shall inherit
the earth.
10 And yet a little while and the
wicked shall be no more and you shall
not be able to discern their place.
11 But the meek shall inherit the earth
and delight themselves in the abundance of peace.
12 The wicked plot against the righteous and grind on them with their
teeth.
13 Yehovah shall laugh at him for He
sees that his day is coming!
14 The wicked have drawn their
sword, they have bent their bows to
cast down the meek and the needy to
butcher the upright way.
15 Their swords shall enter into their
own hearts and their bows broken in
pieces.
16 The little of the righteous is better
than the abundance of many wicked.
17 The arms of the wicked shall be
broken but Yehovah shall uphold the
righteous.
18 Yehovah knows the days of the perfect and their inheritance shall be forever.

[19]They shall not be ashamed in the
evil time and in the days of famine they
shall be satisfied.
[20]But the wicked shall perish and the
enemies of Yehovah shall be as the fat
of lambs consumed into smoke, consumed.
[21]The wicked borrow, and do not repay; but the righteous deals graciously,
and gives.
[22]For such as are blessed of Him shall
inherit the land; and they that are
cursed of Him shall be cut off.
[23]The steps of a good man are ordered of Yehovah.
[24]Though he fall he shall not be cast
down for Yehovah holds His hand.
[25]I have been young, and now am
old; yet I have not seen the righteous
forsaken, nor his seed begging bread.
[26]All the day long he deals graciously,
and lends; and his seed is blessed.
[27]Depart from evil, and do good; and
dwell for evermore.
[28]For Yehovah loves judgment and
will not forsake His godly ones. They
are preserved forever.
[29]The righteous shall inherit the land,
and dwell therein for ever.
[30]The mouth of the righteous utters
wisdom, and his tongue speaks justice.
[31]The law of his God is in his heart;
none of his steps slide.
[32]The wicked watch the righteous
and seek to slay him.
[33]Yehovah will not leave him in his
hand nor condemn him when he is
judged.
[34]Wait upon Yehovah, and keep His
way, and He will exalt you to inherit
the land; when the wicked are cut off,
you shall see it.
[35]I have seen the wicked in great
power, and spreading himself like a
leafy tree in its native soil.
[36]But one passed by, and lo, he was
not; yes, I sought him, but he could not
be found.
[37]Mark the perfect, and behold the
upright; for there is a future for the
man of peace
[38]But transgressors shall be destroyed
together; the future of the wicked shall
be cut off.
[39]The salvation of the righteous is of
Yehovah, He is their strength in the
time of trouble.
[40]And Yehovah shall help them and
rescue them. He shall rescue them
from the wicked and save them, because they trust in him.

Psalm 38

[1]A Psalm of David, to remember
[2]Yehovah, rebuke me not in Your
anger; neither chasten me in Your
wrath.
[3]For Your arrows are gone deep into
me, and Your hand has come down
upon me.
[4]There is no soundness in my flesh
because of Your indignation; neither is
there any health in my bones because
of my sin.
[5]For mine iniquities are gone over
my head; as a heavy burden they are
too heavy for me.
[6]My wounds stink, they fester, because of my foolishness.
[7]I am bent and bowed down greatly;
I go mourning all the day.
[8]For my loins are filled with burning;
and there is no soundness in my flesh.
[9]I am weak and crushed; I groan because of the moaning of my heart.
[10]Yehovah, all my desire is before
You; and my sighing is not hidden
from You.
[11]My heart throbs, my strength fails
me; as for the light of my eyes, it also is

gone from me.
12My friends and my companions
stand aloof from my plague; and my
kinsmen stand far off.
13They also that seek after my life lay
snares for me; and they that seek my
hurt speak crafty devices, and utter deceits all the day.
14But I am as a deaf man, I hear not;
and I am as a dumb man that opens
not his mouth.
15Yes, I have become as a man that
hears not, and in whose mouth are no
arguments.
16For in You, Yehovah, do I hope; You
will answer, Lord my God.
17For I said: 'Lest they rejoice over
me; when my foot slips, they magnify
themselves against me.'
18For I am ready to stumble, and my
pain is continually before me.
19For I do declare mine iniquity; I am
full of care because of my sin.
20But mine enemies are strong in
health; and they that hate me wrongfully are multiplied.
21They also that repay evil for good
are adversaries unto me, because I follow the thing that is good.
22Forsake me not, Yehovah; O my
God, be not far from me.
23Make haste to help me, Lord of my
salvation.

Psalm 39

1For the Conductor, for Jeduthun. A
Psalm of David
2I said: 'I will take heed to my ways,
that I sin not with my tongue; I will
keep a watch upon my mouth, while
the wicked is before me.
3I was dumb with silence; I held my
peace, had no comfort; and my pain
was held in check.
4My heart waxed hot within me;
while I was sighing, the fire kindled;
then I spoke with my tongue:
5Yehovah, make me know my end,
and the measure of my days, what it is;
let me know how transient.
6Behold, You have made my days as
hand-breadth; and my age is as nothing
before You; surely every man at his best
estate is altogether vanity. Selah
7Surely man walks as a mere image;
surely for vanity they are in turmoil; he
heaps up, and knows not who shall
gather them.
8And now, Lord, what do I wait for?
My hope is in You.
9Deliver me from all my transgressions; do not make me the reproach of
the base.
10I am dumb, I do not open my
mouth; because You have done it.
11Remove Your stroke from me; I am
consumed by the blow of Your hand.
12With rebukes do you chasten man
for iniquity, and like a moth You make
his beauty to consume away; surely
every man is vanity. Selah
13Hear my prayer, Yehovah, and give
ear unto my cry; keep not silence at my
tears; for I am a stranger with You, a
sojourner, as all my fathers were.
14Look away from me, that I may
take comfort, before I go from here,
and be no more.'

Psalm 40

1To the chief musician a song of
David,
2Wait, I have waited for Yehovah and
he reached out to me and heard my cry
for help.
3He brought me up from a roaring
pit from the miry clay and He caused
my feet to stand upon a cleft in a rock
He made firm my steps.
4And He has put a new song of praise

in my mouth unto our God. Many shall
see it and they shall fear and they shall
trust in Yehovah.
5 Blessed is the man whose confidence is in Yehovah and does not turn
unto arrogance nor swerve to lies.
6 Many are your wondrous works
Yehovah my God and your thoughts
towards us there is none to be compared with You. If I were to tell or
speak they are too numerous to recount.
7 Sacrifices and offerings you did not
delight, my ears you unstopped. Whole
burnt offerings and sin offerings you
did not require.
8 Then I said, behold I come in the
scroll of the book that is written of me.
9 I delight to do our will, my God for
your law is in the midst of my inward
parts.
10 I have preached righteousness in
the great congregation behold I have
not refrained my lips Yehovah you
know this.
11 Your righteousness I have not hid
within my heart. I have declared Your
faithfulness and Your salvation. I have
not hidden your steadfast love and
your truth from the great congregation.
12 Yehovah you shall not withhold
your mercies from me; your steadfast
love and your truth shall continually
keep me.
13 For evils surround me until there is
no numbering them. My iniquities
reach unto me until I have no ability to
look up. They are more in number than
the hairs of my head and so my heart
fails me.
14 Be pleased, Yehovah, to deliver me;
Yehovah, make haste to help me.
15 Let them be ashamed and confused
together that seek after my soul to
sweep it away; let them be turned
backward and brought to dishonor that
delight in my hurt.
16 Let them be appalled by reason of
their shame that say unto me: 'Aha,
aha.'
17 Let all those that seek You rejoice
and be glad in You; let such as love
Your salvation say continually: 'Yehovah be magnified.'
18 But, as for me, that am poor and
needy, the Lord will consider it unto
me; You are my help and my deliverer;
O my God, do not delay.

Psalm 41

1 For the Conductor. A Psalm of
David
2 Happy is he that considers the poor;
Yehovah will deliver him in the day of
evil.
3 Yehovah protects him, and keeps
him alive, called blessed in the land;
and You do not deliver him to the will
of his enemies.
4 Yehovah sustain him upon the bed
of illness; You will make all of his lying
down in his sickness change.
5 I said: 'Yehovah, be gracious to me;
heal my soul; for I have sinned against
You.'
6 My enemies say in malice of me:
'When shall he die, and his name perish?'
7 And if one comes to see me, he has
empty words; his heart assembles iniquity to itself; when he goes abroad, he
speaks of it.
8 All that hate me whisper together
against me, against me do they devise
my hurt:
9 'An evil thing cleaves fast to him;
and where he lies, he shall not rise up.'
10 Yes, my own familiar friend, in
whom I trusted, who did eat of my
bread, has lifted up his heel against me.

11But You, Yehovah, be gracious unto me, and raise me up, that I may repay them.

12By this I know that You delight in me, that my enemy does not triumph over me.

13And as for me, You uphold me because of my integrity, and set me before Your face forever.

14Blessed be Yehovah, the God of Israel, from everlasting and to everlasting. Amen, and Amen.

Psalm 42

1For the Conductor; Maschil of the sons of Korah

2As the deer pants for the water brooks, so my soul pants after You, O God.

3My soul thirsts for God, for the living God: 'When shall I come and appear before God?'

4My tears have been my food day and night, while they say unto me all the day: 'Where is your God?'

5These things I remember, and pour out my soul within me, how I passed on with the multitude, and led them to the house of God, with the voice of joy and praise, a multitude keeping a festival.

6Why are you cast down, O my soul? and why do you moan within me? Hope in God; for I shall yet praise Him for the salvation before Him.

7O my God, my soul is cast down within me; therefore do I remember You from the land of Jordan, and the Hermons, from the hill Mizar.

8Deep calls unto deep at the voice of Your water spouts; all Your waves and Your billows are gone over me.

9By day Yehovah will command His lovingkindness, and in the night His song shall be with me, even a prayer unto the God of my life.

10I will say unto God my Rock: 'Why have You forgotten me? Why do I go mourning under the oppression of the enemy?'

11As with a crushing in my bones, my adversaries taunt me; while they say unto me all the day: 'Where is Your God?'

12Why are you cast down, O my soul? Why do you moan within me? Hope in God; for I shall yet praise Him, for the salvation before my God.

Psalm 43

1Be my judge, O God, and plead my cause against an ungodly nation; O rescue me from the deceitful and unjust man.

2For You are the God of my strength; why have You cast me off? Why do I go mourning under the oppression of the enemy?

3O send out Your light and Your truth; let them lead me; let them bring me unto Your holy mountain, and to Your dwelling-places.

4Then will I go unto the altar of God, unto God my exceeding joy and praise You upon the harp, O God, my God.

5Why are you cast down, O my soul? Why do you moan within me? Hope in God; for I shall yet praise Him, for the salvation before my God.

Psalm 44

1For the Conductor; of the sons of Korah. Maschil

2O God, we have heard with our ears, our fathers have told us; a work You did in their days, in the days of old.

3You with Your hand drive out the nations, and planted them in it; You broke the peoples, and spread them abroad

4 For they did not gain possession of the land with their swords and their own arm did not save them. For your right hand and your arm and the light of your face for you favored them.

5 You are my King, O God; command the salvation of Jacob.

6 Through You do we push down our adversaries; through Your name do we tread them under that rise up against us.

7 For I trust not in my bow, neither can my sword save me.

8 But You have saved us from our adversaries, and have put them to shame that hate us.

9 In God we boast all day long and your name forever we praise, Selah

10 Yet You have cast off, and brought us to confusion; and do not go out with our armies.

11 You make us to turn back from the adversary; and they that hate us spoil at their will.

12 You have given us like sheep to be eaten; and have scattered us among the nations.

13 You sell Your people for small gains, and have not set their prices high.

14 You make us a reproach to our neighbors, a scorn and a derision to them that are round about us.

15 You make us a byword among the nations, a shaking of the head among the peoples.

16 All the day is my confusion before me, and the shame of my face has covered me,

17 For the voice of him that reproaches and blasphemes; by reason of the enemy and the revengeful.

18 All this has come upon us; yet have we not forgotten You, nor have we been false to Your covenant.

19 Our heart is not turned back, neither have our steps declined from Your path;

20 Though You have crushed us into a place of jackals, and covered us with the shadow of death.

21 If we had forgotten the name of our God, or spread forth our hands to a strange god;

22 Would not God search this out? For He knows the secrets of the heart.

23 No, but for Your sake we are killed all the day; we are accounted as sheep for the slaughter.

24 Awake, why do you sleep Yehovah? Stir up Yourself, cast us not off forever.

25 Why hide Your face, and forget our affliction and our oppression?

26 For our soul is bowed down to the dust; our belly cleaves unto the earth.

27 Arise for our help, and redeem us for Your mercy's sake.

Psalm 45

1 For the Conductor; upon Shoshannim; of the sons of Korah. Maschil. A Song of love

2 My heart is stirred with a good word. I shall declare my work to the king, my tongue is like the pen of an expert writer.

3 You are more beautiful than the sons of man. Grace is poured upon your lips therefore God has blessed you forever!

4 Gird your sword upon your side Mighty One, your glory and your majesty.

5 And in Your majesty prosper, ride on, in behalf of truth and meekness and righteousness; and let Your right hand teach You tremendous things.

6 Your arrows are sharp, the people fall under You, into the heart of the king's enemies.

7 Your throne given of God is for ever

and ever; a scepter of uprightness is the scepter of Your kingdom.

8You have loved righteousness, and hated wickedness; therefore God, Your God, has anointed You with the oil of gladness above Your friends.

9Myrrh, and aloes, and cassia are all Your garments; out of ivory palaces stringed instruments have made You glad.

10Daughters of kings stand among your ladies of honor; at your right hand stands the queen in gold of Ophir.

11'Listen, O daughter, and consider, and incline your ear; forget also your own people, and your father's house;

12So shall the king desire your beauty; for he is your lord; and do homage unto him.

13And daughter of Tyre with gifts the rich from among the people will seek your favor.'

14All glorious is the king's daughter within her chamber; her raiment is gold woven robes.

15She shall be led unto the king in many colored robes; the virgins her companions in her train being brought unto you.

16They shall be led with gladness and rejoicing; they shall enter into the king's palace.

17In place of your fathers shall be your sons, whom you shall make princes in all the land.

18I will make your name to be remembered in all generations; therefore shall the people praise you for ever and ever.

Psalm 46

1To the Conductor of the sons of Korah a song upon Alamoth

2God is our refuge and strength very present in distress.

3Therefore we will not be afraid of the changes in the earth or in its shaking the mountains into the heart of the seas.

4Though its waters rage and foam its mountains heave with its swelling Selah.

5There is a river whose streams make glad the city of God the holy tabernacles of the Most High.

6God is in the midst of her she shall not be shaken God will help her at the break of dawn.

7The nations rage, the kingdoms shake, he uttered His voice the earth melted

8Yehovah of host is with us the God of Jacob is our security Selah.

9Come behold the works of Yehovah what desolation He has made in the earth.

10He makes wars to cease throughout the earth He breaks the bow and snaps the spear He burns the chariots in the fire.

11Be still and know that I am God exalted among the nations exalted in the earth.

12Yehovah of host is with us the God of Jacob is our security Selah.

Psalm 47

1For the Conductor; a Psalm for the sons of Korah

2All you people clap your hands, shout to God with a voice of shouting for joy!

3For Yehovah Most High causes trembling, a great King over all the earth.

4He shall subdue the people, putting the nations under our feet.

5He chooses our inheritance for us, the pride of Jacob whom He loves. Selah

6God is gone up in joyous shouting,
Yehovah in the sound of the shofar.
7Sing praises to God, sing praises;
sing praises unto our King, sing praises.
8For God is the King of all the earth;
sing praises in a skillful song.
9God reigns over the nations; God
sits upon the throne of His holiness.
10The princes of the peoples are gathered together, the people of the God of Abraham; for unto God belong the shields of the earth; He is highly exalted.

Psalm 48

1A Song; a Psalm of the sons of Korah
2Great is Yehovah, and greatly to be
praised, in the city of our God, His holy mountain,
3Beautiful for situation, the joy of the
whole earth; even Mount Zion, the far north, the city of the great King.
4God in her towers has made Himself
known as a sure defense.
5For lo, the kings assembled themselves, they came onward together.
6They saw, straightway they were
amazed; they were afraid, they hastened away.
7Trembling took hold of them there,
pangs, as of a woman in travail.
8With the east wind You break the
ships of Tarshish.
9As we have heard, so have we seen
in the city of Yehovah of hosts, in the city of our God, God establishes it forever. Selah
10We have thought on Your lovingkindness, O God, in the midst of Your temple.
11As is Your name, O God, so is Your
praise unto the ends of the earth; Your right hand is full of righteousness.
12Let mount Zion be glad, let the
daughters of Judah rejoice, because of Your judgments.
13Walk about Zion, and go round
about her; count the towers thereof.
14Mark well her ramparts, traverse
her towers; that you may tell it to the generation following.
15For such is God, our God, forever
and ever; He will guide us eternally.

Psalm 49

1To the director to the sons of Korah
a Psalm
2People everywhere hear this, all inhabitants of the world listen!
3Also sons of Adam, sons of men together rich and poor.
4My mouth shall speak wisdom and
the utterance of my heart insight.
5I will bend my ear to a parable. I will
open my dark sayings upon a string instrument.
6Why should I be afraid in the days
of evil or the iniquity of slanderers that surround me.
7They trust in their wealth and in the
multitude of their riches they boast.
8Alas no man can ever redeem himself nor pay to God His ransom price.
9For the ransom of their souls is precious forever ceasing.
10That he should continue to live forever and never see the Pit.
11For he sees that wise men die, the
fool and the brutish together perish, and leave their wealth to others.
12Their inward thought is, that their
houses shall continue for ever, and their dwelling places to all generations; they call their lands after their own names.
13But man cannot abide in his pomp;
he is like the beasts that perish.
14This is their fate-stupidity, and

those after them who approve their sayings. Selah

15 Like sheep they are appointed for Sheol; death shall be their shepherd; and the upright shall have dominion over them in the morning; and their form shall be for Sheol to wear away their habitation.

16 But God will redeem my soul from the power of Sheol; for He shall receive me. Selah

17 Do not be afraid when one becomes rich, when the wealth of his house is increased;

18 For when he dies he shall carry nothing away; his wealth shall not descend after him.

19 Though while he lived he blessed his soul: 'Men will praise you, when you do well for yourself';

20 You will go to the generation of your fathers forever; they will not see light.

21 Man in his pomp does not discern; he is like the beasts that perish.

Psalm 50

1 A Psalm of Asaph. Yehovah, God, has spoken, and called the earth from the rising of the sun unto the going down thereof.

2 Out of Zion, the perfection of beauty, God has shone forth.

3 Our God comes, and does not keep silence; a fire devours before Him, and round about Him are mighty storms.

4 He calls to the heavens above, and to the earth, that He may judge His people:

5 'Gather My godly ones together unto Me; those that have made a covenant with Me by sacrifice.'

6 And the heavens declare His righteousness; for God, He is judge. Selah

7 'Hear, O My people, and I will speak; O Israel, and I will testify against you: God, your God, am I.

8 I will not reprove you for your sacrifices; and your burnt offerings are continually before Me.

9 I will take no bullock out of your house, nor he-goats out of your folds.

10 For every beast of the forest is Mine, and the cattle upon a thousand hills.

11 I know all the fowls of the mountains; and the wild beasts of the field are Mine.

12 If I were hungry, I would not tell you; for the world is Mine, and the fulness thereof. 13 Do I eat the flesh of bulls, or drink the blood of goats?

14 Offer unto God the sacrifice of thanksgiving; and pay your vows unto the Most High;

15 And call upon Me in the day of trouble; I will deliver you, and you shall honor Me.'

16 But unto the wicked God says: 'What right do you have to recite My statutes, or take My covenant in upon your lips?

17 Seeing you hate discipline, and cast My words behind you.

18 When you saw a thief, you had company with him, and with adulterers was your portion.

19 You give free reign to your mouth for evil, and your tongue frames deceit.

20 You sit and speak against your brother; you slander your own mother's son.

21 These things you have done, and I have kept silent? You have thought that I was altogether such a one as yourself; but I will reprove you, and set the charge before your eyes.

22 Now consider this, you that forget God, unless I tear in pieces, and there be none to deliver.

23He that offers thanksgiving honors me and he who orders his way I will show Him the salvation of God.

Psalm 51

1For the Leader. A Psalm of David

2When Nathan the prophet came unto him, after he had gone in to Bath-sheba

3Be gracious unto me, O God, according to Your lovingkindness; according to the multitude of Your compassions blot out my transgressions.

4Wash me thoroughly from my iniquity, and cleanse me from my sin.

5For I know my transgressions; and my sin is ever before me.

6Against You, You only, have I sinned, and done that which is evil in Your sight; that You may be shown righteous when You speak, and pure when You judge.

7Behold, I was brought forth in iniquity, and in sin did my mother conceive me.

8Behold, You desire truth in the inward parts; make me, therefore, to know wisdom in my hidden parts..

9Purge me with hyssop, and I shall be clean; wash me, and I shall be whiter than snow.

10Make me to hear joy and gladness; that the bones which You have crushed may rejoice.

11Hide Your face from my sins, and blot out all my iniquities.

12Create me a clean heart, O God; and renew a steadfast spirit within me.

13Cast me not away from Your presence; and take not Your Holy Spirit from me.

14Restore unto me the joy of Your salvation; and let a willing spirit uphold me.

15Then will I teach transgressors Your ways; and sinners shall return unto You.

16Deliver me from bloodguiltiness, O God, You God of my salvation; so shall my tongue shout for joy of Your righteousness.

17O Lord, open my lips; and my mouth shall declare Your praise.

18For You delight not in sacrifice, else would I give it; You have no pleasure in burnt-offering.

19The sacrifices of God are a broken spirit; a broken and a contrite heart, O God, You will not despise.

20Do good in Your good pleasure unto Zion; build the walls of Jerusalem.

21Then will You delight in the sacrifices of righteousness, in burnt-offering and whole offering; then will they offer bullocks upon Your altar.

Psalm 52

1For the Conductor. Maschil of David

2When Doeg the Edomite came and told Saul, and said unto him: 'David has come to the house of Ahimelech.

3Why do you boast yourself of evil, O mighty one? The lovingkindness of God is all the day long.

4Your tongue devises destruction; like a sharp razor, working treachery.

5You love evil more than good; falsehood rather than speaking righteousness. Selah

6You love all devouring words, the deceitful tongue.

7God will likewise break you forever, He will take you up, and pluck you out of your tent, and root you out of the land of the living. Selah

8The righteous also shall see, and fear, and shall laugh at him:

9'Lo, this is the man that did not make God his stronghold; but trusted

in the abundance of his riches, but
sought safety in his wickedness.'
10But I am like a green olive tree in
the house of my God. I will trust in His
lovingkindness forever and ever.
11I will give You thanks forever, because You have done it; and I will wait
for Your name, for it is good, in the
presence of Your godly ones.

Psalm 53

1For the Conductor; upon Mahalath.
Maschil of David
2The fool has said in his heart: 'There
is no God'; they are corrupt, and have
done abominable iniquity; none does
good.
3God looked from heaven upon the
children of men, to see if there were
any wise, that seek after God.
4Every one of them has turned, they
are all filthy; there is none that does
good, not even one
5'They have no understanding who
work iniquity, who eat up My people as
they eat bread, and call not upon God.'
6There are they in great terror, where
there was no terror; for God has scattered the bones of him that encamp
against you; You have put them to
shame, because God has rejected them.
7Oh that the salvation of Israel were
come out of Zion! When God turns the
captivity of His people, let Jacob rejoice, let Israel be glad.

Psalm 54

1For the Conductor; with string-music. Maschil of David
2When the Ziphites came and said to
Saul: 'Is not David hiding among us?
3O God, save me by Your name, and
vindicate me by Your might.
4O God, hear my prayer; listen to the
words of my mouth.
5For strangers have risen up against
me, and violent men seek after my soul;
they have not set God before them. Selah
6Behold, God is my helper; the Lord
is for me as the upholder of my soul.
7He will return the evil unto my enemies; in your faithfulness destroy
them.
8With a freewill-offering I will sacrifice unto You; I will praise Your name,
Yehovah, for it is good.
9For He has delivered me out of
every trouble; and my eye has looked
upon my enemies.

Psalm 55

1For the Conductor; with string-music. Maschil of David
2O God, listen to my prayer; and hide
not from my supplication.
3Attend unto me, and answer me; I
am overcome by my trouble, and I am
distraught;
4Because of the voice of the enemy,
because of the oppression of the
wicked; for they cast mischief upon me,
and in anger they persecute me.
5My heart is in anguish within me;
and the terrors of death have fallen
upon me.
6Fear and trembling came upon me,
and horror overwhelmed me.
7And I said: 'Oh that I had wings like
a dove! then would I fly away, and be at
rest.
8Lo, then I would flee away, I would
lodge in the wilderness. Selah
9I would hasten to shelter from the
raging wind and tempest.'
10Destroy, O Lord, and confuse their
tongue; for I have seen violence and
strife in the city.
11Day and night they go about it
upon the walls; iniquity also and mis-

chief are within it.
[12]Wickedness is within it; oppression
and guile depart not from her marketplace.
[13]For it was not an enemy that reproached me, then I could bear it; it
was not one who hated me who magnified himself against me, then I could
have hid myself from him.
[14]But it was you, a man mine equal,
my companion, and my familiar friend;
[15]We took sweet counsel together, in
the house of God we walked with the
multitude.
[16]May death beguile them, let them
go down alive into the Sheol; for evil is
in their dwelling, and within them.
[17]As for me, I will call upon God; and
Yehovah will save me.
[18]Evening and morning and at noon I
will pray and cry aloud and you shall
hear my voice
[19]He has redeemed my soul in peace
from the battle that I waged; for there
were many against me.
[20]God will hear, and humble them,
even He that is enthroned of old, Selah,
for there is no change, and they do not
fear God.
[21]He stretched out his hands against
those that were at peace with him; he
has profaned his covenant.
[22]Smoother than cream was his
mouth, but he had war in his heart; his
words were softer than oil, yet they
were drawn swords.
[23]Cast your burden upon the LORD,
and He will sustain you; He will never
permit the righteous to stumble
[24]But You, O God, will bring them
down into the well pit; men of blood
and deceit shall not live out half their
days; but I, I will trust in You.

Psalm 56

[1]For the Conductor; upon Jonath-
elem-rehokim. Of David; a Michtam;
when the Philistines took him in Gath
[2]Show favor to me, O God, for man
would swallow me up; He fights against
me all day, oppressing me.
[3]My enemies would swallow me up
all day; for there are many that fight
against me proudly.
[4]The day I am afraid, I will trust in
You.
[5]In God I will praise His word, in
God I will trust, I will not fear what
flesh can do to me.
[6]All day they seek to dispel my
words; all their thoughts are against me
for evil.
[7]They gather themselves together,
they hide themselves, they mark my
steps; as they wait for my soul.
[8]For iniquity carry them away; in
anger bring down the people, O God.
[9]You have counted my tossings; put
my tears into Your bottle; are they not
in Your book?
[10]Then shall mine enemies turn back
on the day that I call; this I know, that
God is for me.
[11]In God, I will praise His word, in
Yehovah, I will praise His word.
[12]In God do I trust, I will not be
afraid; what can man do unto me?
[13]Your vows are upon me, O God; I
will render thanksgiving unto You.
[14]For You have delivered my soul
from death; Have You not delivered my
feet from stumbling? that I may walk
before God in the light of the living.

Psalm 57

[1]For the Conductor; Al-tashheth. of
David; Michtam; when he fled from
Saul, in the cave
[2]Be gracious unto me, O God, be

gracious unto me, for in You has my soul taken refuge; and in the shadow of Your wings will I take refuge, until destruction passes over.

3 I will cry to God Most High; to God who accomplishes it for me.

4 He will send from heaven, and save me, He will confuse those who would swallow me up; Selah. God shall send forth His lovingkindness and His faithfulness.

5 My soul is among lions, I lie down among them that are aflame; even the sons of men, whose teeth are spears and arrows, and their tongue a sharp sword.

6 Be exalted, O God, above the heavens; Your glory be above all the earth.

7 They have set a net for my steps, my soul is bowed down; they have dug a pit before me, but they have fallen into it. Selah

8 My heart is steadfast, O God, my heart is steadfast; I will sing, and make a melody.

9 Awake, my glory; awake, psaltery and harp; I will awake the dawn.

10 I will praise You, O Lord, among the peoples; I will sing praises to You among the nations.

11 For Your lovingkindness is great unto the heavens, and Your faithfulness unto the skies.

12 Be exalted, O God, above the heavens; Your glory be above all the earth.

Psalm 58

1 For the Conductor; Al-tashheth. of David; Michtam

2 Do you indeed speak as a righteous company? Do you judge the sons of men uprightly?

3 Yes, in heart you work malice; you weigh out in the earth the violence of your hands.

4 The wicked are estranged from the womb; from the belly they err speaking lies.

5 Their venom is like the venom of a serpent; they are like the deaf adder that stops her ear;

6 Which does not respond to the voice of magicians, charming cunningly.

7 Break their teeth, O God, in their mouth; break out the fangs of the young lions, Yehovah.

8 Let them melt away as water that runs away; when he aims his arrows, let them be as though they were cut off.

9 Let them be as a snail which melts and passes away; like the untimely birth that never sees the sun.

10 Sooner than your cooking pots can feel the thorns, let them be as life, let them be as anger, carried off.

11 The righteous shall rejoice when he sees the vengeance; he shall wash his feet in the blood of the wicked.

12 And men shall say: 'Truly there is a reward for the righteous; truly there is a God that judges in the Earth.'

Psalm 59

1 For the Conductor; Al-tashheth. Of David; Michtam; when Saul sent them to watch the house to kill him.

2 Deliver me from my enemies, O my God; set me on high from them that rise up against me.

3 Deliver me from the workers of iniquity, and save me from the men of blood.

4 For, lo, they lie in wait for my soul; fierce men band themselves against me; not for my transgression, nor for my sin, Yehovah.

5 Without my fault, they run and prepare themselves; awake to help me, and behold.

6 And You, Yehovah God of hosts, the God of Israel, awake to punish all the nations; show no mercy to any iniquitous traitors. Selah

7 They return in the evening, they howl like a dog, and go around the city.

8 Behold, they bellow with their mouth; swords are in their lips: 'For who hears?'

9 But You, Yehovah, shall laugh at them; You shall have all the nations in derision.

10 Because of his strength, I will wait for You; for God is my fortress.

11 The God of my lovingkindness will go in front of me; God will let me gaze upon mine adversaries.

12 Do not kill them, lest my people forget, make them wander to and fro by Your power, and bring them down, O Lord our shield.

13 For the sin of their mouth, and the words of their lips, let them even be taken in their pride, and for cursing and lying which they speak.

14 Consume them in wrath, consume them, that they be no more; and let them know that God rules in Jacob, unto the ends of the earth. Selah

15 And they return at evening, they howl like a dog, and go round about the city;

16 They roam around to devour, and they growl if they do not have their fill.

17 I will sing of your might and rejoice in the morning because of your lovingkindness for you have been my defense and refuge in the day of my trouble

18 O my strength, unto You will I sing praises; for God is my fortress, the God of my lovingkindness.

Psalm 60

1 For the Conductor; upon Shushan Eduth; Michtam of David, to teach

2 when he strove with Aram-naharaim and with Aram-zobah, and Joab returned, and smote of Edom in the Valley of Salt twelve thousand

3 O God, You have rejected us, broken us down; been angry; O restore us.

4 You have made the land to shake, split it open; heal the breaches; for it totters.

5 You have made Your people see hard things; made us drink the wine of staggering.

6 You have given a banner to them that fear You, that it may be displayed in front of the bow. Selah

7 That Your beloved may be delivered, save with Your right hand, and answer us.

8 God spoke in His holiness, that I would exult; that I would divide Shechem, and measure the valley of Succoth.

9 Gilead is mine, and Manasseh is mine; Ephraim also is the defense of my head; Judah is my scepter.

10 Moab is my washpot; upon Edom do I cast my shoe; Philistia, shout because of me!

11 Who will bring me into the fortified city? Who will lead me unto Edom?

12 Have you not rejected us, O God? And You do not go out, O God, with our armies.

13 Grant us help against our oppressors; for vain is the help of man.

14 Through God we shall do valiantly; for He it is that will tread down our adversaries.

Psalm 61

1 For the Conductor; with stri-ng-music- of David

2 Hear my cry, O God; attend unto my

prayer.
3 From the end of the earth will I call
unto You, when my heart faints; lead
me in the rock that is higher than I.
4 For You have been a refuge for me, a
strong tower in the face of the enemy.
5 I will dwell in Your Tent forever; I
will take refuge under the shelter of
Your wings. Selah
6 For You, O God, have heard my
vows; You have given heritage to those
that fear Your name.
7 May You add days unto the king's
days! May his years be as many generation after generation.
8 May he be enthroned before God
forever! Appoint lovingkindness and
faithfulness, that they may preserve
him.
9 So will I sing praise unto Your name
forever, that I may perform my vows
day after day.

Psalm 62

1 For the Conductor; for Jeduthun. A
Psalm of David
2 Only for God does my soul wait in
stillness; my salvation comes from
Him.
3 He only is my rock and my salvation, my refuge, I shall not be greatly
moved.
4 How long will you set upon a man,
that you may slay him, all of you, as a
leaning wall, a tottering fence?
5 They only devise to thrust him
down from his height, delighting in
lies; they bless with their mouth, but
they curse inwardly. Selah
6 Only for God wait in stillness, my
soul; for from Him comes my hope.
7 He only is my rock and my salvation, my high tower, I shall not be
moved.
8 On God is my salvation and my glory, my mighty rock, and my refuge, is
in God.
9 Trust in Him at all times people;
pour out your heart before Him; God is
a refuge for us. Selah
10 Surely the sons of men are lying
vanities, the sons of men in a balance-
they are altogether vanity.
11 Put no trust in extortion, and put
no vain hope in robbery; if riches increase, do not set your heart on them.
12 God has spoken once, twice have I
heard this: that strength belongs unto
God;
13 Also unto You, O Lord, is lovingkindness; for You render to every
man according to his work

Psalm 63

1 A Psalm of David, when he was in
the wilderness of Judah
2 O God, you are my God; early will I
seek you. My soul thirsts for you, my
flesh longs for you as in a dry and
thirsty land where there is no water.
3 To see your power and Your glory,
so as I have seen you in the sanctuary.
4 For Your lovingkindness is better
than life; my lips shall praise You.
5 So will I bless You as I live; in Your
name will I lift up my hands.
6 My soul is satisfied as with marrow
and fatness; and my lips praise You
with joyful lips;
7 When I remember You upon my
couch, and meditate on You in the
night-watches.
8 For You have been my help, and in
the shadow of Your wings I sing for joy.
9 My soul cleaves to You; Your right
hand takes hold of me.
10 But those that seek my soul, to destroy it, shall go into the lowest parts of
the earth.
11 They shall be given over to the

power of the sword; they shall be a prey
for jackals.
12But the king shall rejoice in God;
every one that swears by Him shall
boast; for the mouth of them that speak
lies shall be stopped.

Psalm 64

1For the Conductor. A Psalm of
David
2Hear my voice, O God, in my complaint; preserve my life from the terror
of the enemy.
3Hide me from the secret plots of the
wicked; from the insurrection of the
workers of iniquity;
4Who sharpen their tongue like a
sword, and have aimed their arrow, a
poisoned word;
5That they may shoot in secret places
at the perfect; suddenly they shoot at
him without fear.
6They encourage one another in an
evil purpose; they talk of laying snares
secretly; asking, who can see them.
7They search out iniquities, we have
thought out a plot one cunningly conceived of the depths of heart and of the
inner man.
8But God shoots at them with an arrow and suddenly they are wounded.
9So they make their own tongue
stumble upon themselves; all that see
them shake their head.
10And all men fear; and they declare
the work of God, and ponder what He
has done.
11The righteous rejoice in Yehovah,
and take refuge in Him; and all the upright in heart they shall praise

Psalm 65

1For the Conductor. A Psalm. A Song
of David
2Praise waits for You, O God, in
Zion; and unto You the vow is performed.
3He who hears prayer, unto You all
flesh comes.
4The tale of iniquities prevails against
me; our transgressions, You will purge
them away.
5Blessed is the man whom You
choose, and bring near, that he may
dwell in Your courts; may we be satisfied with the goodness of Your house,
Your holy temple!
6With wondrous works You answer
us in righteousness, O God of our salvation; You are the confidence of all the
ends of the earth, and the furthest seas;
7Who by Your strength has established mountains, being girded with
might;
8Who calms the roaring of the seas,
the roaring of their waves, and the tumult of the people;
9So that those that dwell in the uttermost parts stand in awe of Your
signs; You make the going forth of the
morning and evening to rejoice.
10You visit the earth and give it
abundance, You greatly enrich her,
with the river of God that is full of water; You provide them grain, for so You
prepared her.
11Saturating her furrows, settling the
ridges, with showers softening it. You
bless its growth.
12You crown the year with Your
goodness; and Your camps drip fatness.
13The pastures of the wilderness drip;
and the hills are girded with joy.
14The meadows are clothed with
flocks; the valleys also are covered over
with grain; they shout for joy, and they
sing.

Psalm 66

1For the Conductor. A Song, a Psalm.
Shout unto God, all the earth;

2 Sing unto the glory of His name; make His praise glorious.

3 Say unto God: ‘How awesome is Your work! Through the greatness of Your power shall Your enemies dwindle away before You.

4 All the earth shall worship You, and shall sing praises unto You; they shall sing praises to Your name.’ Selah

5 Come, and see the works of God; He is awesome – His deeds among the sons men.

6 He turned the sea into dry land; they went through the river on foot; there we rejoiced in Him!

7 Who rules by His might for ever; His eyes keep watch upon the nations; let not the rebellious exalt themselves. Selah

8 Bless our God, you people, and make the voice of His praise to be heard;

9 Who has set our soul in life, and has not allowed our foot to slip,

10 For You, O God, have tried us; You have refined us, as silver is refined.

11 You brought us into the hold; You laid constraint upon our loins.

12 You have caused men to ride over our heads; we went through fire and through water; but You brought us out unto abundance.

13 I will come into Your house with burnt-offerings, I will fulfill my vows to You,

14 Which my lips have uttered, and my mouth spoke, when I was in trouble.

15 I will offer unto You burnt-offerings of fatlings, with the smoke of rams; I will offer bullocks with he-goats. Selah

16 Come, and hearken, all you that fear God, and I will declare what He has done for my soul.

17 I cried unto Him with my mouth, and He was lifted high with my tongue.

18 If I had regarded iniquity in my heart, the Lord would not hear;

19 Truly God has heard; He has attended to the voice of my prayer.

20 Blessed be God, who has not turned away my prayer, nor His mercy from me.

Psalm 67

1 For the Conductor; with string-music. A Psalm, a Song

2 God be gracious unto us, and bless us; may He cause His face to shine toward us; Selah

3 That Your way may be known upon earth, Your salvation among all nations.

4 Let the people give thanks unto You, O God; let the people give thanks unto You, all of them.

5 O let the nations be glad and shout for joy; for You will judge the people with uprightness, and lead the nations upon earth. Selah

6 Let the people give thanks unto You, O God; let the people give thanks unto You, all of them.

7 The earth has yielded her increase; may God, our own God, bless us.

8 God has blessed us; and let all the ends of the earth fear Him.

Psalm 68

1 For the Conductor. A Psalm of David, a Song

2 Let God arise, let His enemies be scattered; and let those that hate Him flee before Him.

3 As smoke is driven away, so drive them away; as wax melts before the fire, so let the wicked perish at the presence of God.

4 But let the righteous rejoice, let

them be glad before God; yes, let them
rejoice with gladness.
5Sing unto God, sing praises to His
name; Him who rides upon the heights
through the desert, whose name is the
Yah; and be glad before Him.
6A father of the fatherless, and a
judge of the widows, is God in His holy
habitation.
7God makes the desolate dwell in a
household; He brings out the prisoners
into prosperity; but the rebellious dwell
in a scorched land.
8O God, when You went out before
Your people, when You marched
through the wilderness; Selah
9The earth trembled, the heavens
also poured down rain at the presence
of God; even on Sinai at the presence of
God, the God of Israel.
10You poured down an abundance of
rain, O God; when Your inheritance
was weary, You established it.
11Your flock settled in it; You provided in Your goodness for the needy, O
God.
12The Lord gives the word; Great is
the host that proclaims it.
13Kings of armies flee, they flee; and
she that tarries at home divides the
spoil.
14Though you lie among the sheepfolds, the wings of the dove are covered
with silver, and her pinions with the
shimmer of gold.
15When the Almighty scatters kings
there it shall snow in Zalmon.
16A mountain of God is the mountain of Bashan; a mountain of peaks is
the mountain of Bashan.
17Why do you look with envy, you
mountains of peaks, at the mountain
which God has desired for His abode?
Yes, Yehovah will dwell there forever.
18The chariots of God are ten thousands, even thousands upon thousands;
the Lord is among them, as in Sinai, in
holiness.
19You have ascended on high, You
have led captivity captive; You have received gifts among men, even the rebellious that Yah God might dwell
there.
20Blessed be the Lord, day by day He
bears our burden, even the God who is
our salvation. Selah
21God is unto us a God of deliver-
ances; and unto Yehovah the Lord belongs the issues of death.
22Surely God will shatter the head of
His enemies, the hairy scalp of him
that walks in his guiltiness.
23The Lord said: 'I will bring them
back from Bashan, I will bring them
back from the depths of the sea;
24That your foot may wade through
blood, that the tongue of thy dogs may
have its portion from your enemies.'
25They see Your goings, O God, even
the goings of my God, my King, in holiness.
26The singers go before, the players of
instruments last, in the midst of
damsels playing timbrels.
27Bless God in the great congregation, Yehovah, from the fountain of Israel.
28There is Benjamin, the youngest,
ruling them, the princes of Judah, their
council the princes of Zebulun, the
princes of Naphtali.
29Your God has commanded your
strength; strengthen O God, that which
you have done for us.
30Because of Your temple at Jerusalem, there kings shall bring
presents unto You.
31Rebuke the wild beast of the reeds,
the herd of bulls, with the calves of the
peoples, trampling after pieces of silver;

He has scattered the people that delight
in striving!
32Nobles shall come out of Egypt;
Ethiopia shall hasten to stretch out her
hands unto God.
33Sing unto God, you kingdoms of
the earth; O sing praises unto the Lord;
Selah
34To Him that rides upon the heavens, the ancient heavens, lo, he sends
forth His voice, a mighty voice.
35Ascribe strength unto God; His
majesty is over Israel, and His strength
is in the skies.
36God you are awesome out of your
holy places; the God of Israel, He gives
strength and power unto the people;
blessed be God.

Psalm 69

1For the Conductor; upon Shoshannim, of David
2Save me, O God; for the waters are
come unto the soul.
3I am sunk in deep mire, where I am
not able to stand; I have come into
deep waters, and the flood overwhelmed me.
4I am weary of my crying; my throat
is dried; mine eyes fail while I wait for
my God.
5They that hate me without a cause
are more than the hairs of my head;
they that would cut me off, being mine
enemies wrongfully, are many; should I
restore that which I took not away?
6O God, You know my folly; and my
trespasses are not hid from You.
7Let not them that wait for You be
ashamed through me, O Lord GOD of
hosts; let not those that seek You be
brought to confusion through me, O
God of Israel.
8Because for Your sake I have born
reproach; confusion has covered my
face
9I am become a stranger unto my
brethren, and an alien unto my mother's children.
10For the zeal of your house has eaten
me up and the reproaches of your reproaches have fallen on me.
11And I wept with my soul fasting,
and that became unto me a reproach.
12I made sackcloth also my garment,
and I became a byword unto them.
13They that sit in the gate talk of me;
and I am the song of the drunkards.
14But as for me, let my prayer be unto
You, O LORD, in an acceptable time; O
God, in the abundance of Your mercy,
answer me with the truth of Your salvation.
15Deliver me out of the mire, and let
me not sink; let me be delivered from
them that hate me, and out of the deep
waters.
16Let not the waterflood overwhelm
me, neither let the deep swallow me up;
and let not the pit shut her mouth
upon me.
17Answer me, O LORD, for Your
mercy is good; according to the multitude of Your compassions turn unto
me.
18And hide not Your face from Your
servant; for I am in distress; answer me
speedily.
19Draw near unto my soul, and redeem it; ransom me because of my enemies.
20You know my reproach, and my
shame, and my confusion; mine adversaries are all before You.
21Reproach has broken my heart; and
I am sore sick; and I looked for some to
show compassion, but there was none;
and for comforters, but I found none.
22Yes, they put poison into my food;
and in my thirst they gave me vinegar

to drink.
23 Let their table before them become
a snare; and when they are in peace, let
it become a trap.
24 Let their eyes be darkened, that
they see not; and make their loins continually to totter.
25 Pour out Your indignation upon
them, and let the fierceness of Your
anger overtake them.
26 Let their encampment be desolate;
let none dwell in their tents.
27 For they persecute him whom You
have smitten; and they tell of the pain
of those whom You have wounded.
28 Add iniquity unto their iniquity;
and let them not come into Your righteousness.
29 Let them be blotted out of the book
of the living, and not be written with
the righteous.
30 But I am afflicted and in pain; let
Your salvation, O God, set me up on
high.
31 I will praise the name of God with a
song, and will magnify Him with
thanksgiving.
32 And it shall please Yehovah better
than a bullock that has horns and
hoofs.
33 The humble shall see it, and be
glad; you that seek after God, let your
heart revive.
34 For Yehovah hearkens unto the
needy, and despises not His prisoners.
35 Let heaven and earth praise Him,
the seas, and every thing that moves
therein.
36 For God will save Zion, and build
the cities of Judah; and they shall abide
there, and have it in possession.
37 The seed also of His servants shall
inherit it; and they that love His name
shall dwell therein.

Psalm 70

1 For the Conductor. of David; to
make remembrance.
2 O God, to deliver me, Yehovah, to
help me, make haste.
3 Let them be ashamed and put to
confusion that seek after my soul; let
them be turned back and brought to
dishonor that delight in my hurt.
4 Let them be turned back because of
their shame that say: 'Aha, aha.'
5 Let them all rejoice and be glad in
You that seek You; and let those who
love Your salvation say continually:
'great is God'
6 But I am poor and needy; O God,
make haste to me; You are my help and
my deliverer; Yehovah, tarry not.

Psalm 71

1 In You, Yehovah, have I taken
refuge; let me never be ashamed.
2 In Your righteousness deliver me,
and rescue me; incline Your ear unto
me, and save me.
3 Be to me a rock, a hiding place
where I may continually come, You
have commanded to save me; for You
are my shelter and my fortress.
4 O my God, rescue me out of the
hand of the wicked, out of the grasp of
the unjust and cruel.
5 For You are my expectation; O Lord
Yehovah, my trust from my youth.
6 Upon You have I relied from the
belly; You are He that took me out of
my mother's womb; In you is my praise
continually.
7 I have become a sign unto many;
and you are my strong refuge.
8 Your praise shall fill my mouth, all
the day your splendor.
9 Cast me not away in the time of old
age; when my strength fails, do not
leave me.

10 For my enemies speak against me,
and they that watch for my soul take
counsel together,
11 Saying: 'God has abandoned him;
pursue and take him; for there is none
to deliver.'
12 O God, be not far from me; O my
God, hurry to help me.
13 Let them be ashamed and consumed that accuse my soul; let them be
covered with reproach and confusion
that seek to hurt me.
14 And I will continually wait, and will
praise You more and more.
15 My mouth will recount Your righteousness, and of Your salvation all the
day; for I do not know their number.
16 I will come with Your mighty acts,
O Lord Yehovah; I will make mention
of Your righteousness, even of Yours
only.
17 O God, You have taught me from
my youth; and until now do I declare
Your miraculous works.
18 And even unto old age and gray
hairs, O God, do not forsake me; until I
have declared Your strength unto the
next generation, Your might to every
one that is to come.
19 Your righteousness O God which
reaches unto heights; You who have
done great things, O God, who is like
You?
20 You, who have made me see many
and sore troubles, will make me alive
again, and bring me up again from the
depths of the earth.
21 You will increase my greatness, and
turn and comfort me.
22 I also will give thanks unto You
with the psaltery, for your faithfulness
O my God; I will sing praises unto You
with the lyre, O Holy One of Israel.
23 My lips shall shout for joy when I
sing praises unto You; and my soul,
which You have redeemed.
24 My tongue also shall recount Your
righteousness all the day; for they are
ashamed, for they are confused, that
seek to hurt me.

Psalm 72

1 Of Solomon. Give the king Your
judgments, O God, and Your righteousness unto the king's son;
2 May he judge Your people with
righteousness, and Your poor with justice.
3 Let the mountains bear peace to the
people, and the hills, in righteousness.
4 May he judge the poor of the people,
and save the children of the needy, and
crush the oppressor.
5 They shall fear You while the sun
endures, and so long as the moon,
throughout all generations.
6 May He come down like rain upon
the mown grass, as showers that water
the earth.
7 In His days let the righteous flourish, and abundance of peace, till the
moon be no more. 8 May He have dominion also from sea to sea, and from
the river unto the ends of the earth.
9 Let them who dwell in the wilderness bow before Him; and His enemies
lick the dust.
10 The kings of Tarshish and of the
isles shall render tribute; the kings of
Sheba and Seba shall offer gifts.
11 Yes, all kings shall bow down before
Him; all nations shall serve Him.
12 For He will deliver the needy when
He cries for help; and the poor, and
him that has no helper.
13 He will have pity on the weak and
needy, and the souls of the needy He
will save.
14 He will redeem their soul from oppression and violence, and precious

will their blood be in His sight;
15 And he shall live, and shall be given
the gold of Sheba, that shall pray for
him continually, yes, bless him all the
day.
16 May there be an abundance of
grain in the land upon the top of the
mountains; may his fruit wave like
Lebanon; and may they blossom from
the city like grass of the earth.
17 May His name endure for ever; may
His name continue as long as the sun;
may they bless themselves by Him; may
all nations call Him happy.
18 Blessed Yehovah God, the God of
Israel, who only does miraculous
things;
19 And blessed be His glorious name
for ever; and let the whole earth be
filled with His glory. Amen, and Amen.
20 The prayers of David the son of
Jesse are ended.

Psalm 73

1 A Psalm of Asaph. Surely God is
good to Israel, even to such as are pure
in heart.
2 But as for me, my feet were almost
gone; my steps had nearly slipped.
3 For I was envious of the arrogant,
when I saw the prosperity of the
wicked.
4 For there are no pangs at their
death, and their body is sound.
5 They are not in the trouble of man;
neither are they plagued like men.
6 Therefore pride is as a chain about
their neck; violence covers them as a
garment.
7 Their eyes stand out from fatness;
they have gone beyond the imaginations of their heart.
8 They scoff, and in wickedness utter
oppression; they speak as if there were
none on high.
9 They have set their mouth against
the heavens, and their tongue walks
through the earth.
10 Therefore His people return here;
and waters of fullness are drained out
by them.
11 And they say: 'How does God
know? And is there knowledge in the
Most High?'
12 Behold, such are the wicked; and
they that are always at ease increase
riches.
13 Surely in vain have I cleansed my
heart, and washed my hands in inno-
cency;
14 For all the day have I been plagued,
and my chastisement came every
morning.
15 If I had said: 'I will speak thus', behold, I had been faithless to the generation of Your children.
16 And when I pondered how I might
know this, it was wearisome in mine
eyes;
17 Until I entered into the sanctuary of
God, and considered their end.
18 Surely You set them in slippery
places; You hurled them down to utter
ruin.
19 How are they become a desolation
in a moment! They are wholly consumed by terrors.
20 As a dream when one awakes, so, O
Lord, when You arouse Yourself, You
will despise their semblance.
21 For my heart was in a ferment, and
I was pricked in my reins.
22 But I was brutish, and ignorant; I
was as a beast before You.
23 Nevertheless I am continually with
You; You hold my right hand.
24 You will guide me with Your counsel, and afterward receive me with glory.
25 Who do I have in heaven but you

and I desire none on the earth.
26My flesh and my heart fails; but
God is the rock of my heart and my
portion forever.
27For, lo, they that go far from You
shall perish; You destroy all them that
go astray from You.
28But as for me, the nearness of God
is my good; I have made the Lord God
my refuge, that I may tell of all Your
works.

Psalm 74

1Maschil of Asaph. O God, why have
you cast us off forever? Why does Your
anger smoke against the flock of Your
pasture?
2Remember Your congregation,
which You have purchased in ancient
times, which You have redeemed to be
the tribe of Your inheritance; and
mount Zion, wherein You have dwelled
3Lift up Your steps because of the
perpetual ruins, even all the evil that
the enemy has done in the sanctuary.
4Your enemies roared in the midst of
Your meeting-place; they have set up
their own signs for signs.
5Observed as coming to a high place
with axes in a thicket of trees.
6And now all the carved work thereof
together they strike down with hatchet
and hammers.
7They have set Your sanctuary on
fire; they have profaned the dwelling-
place of Your name even to the ground.
8They said in their heart: 'Let us
make havoc of them altogether'; they
have burned up all the meeting-places
of God in the land.
9We do not see our signs; there is no
longer a prophet among us and known
among us who knows how long.
10How long, O God, shall the oppressor reproach? Shall the enemy blaspheme Your name forever?
11Why do You withdraw Your hand,
even Your right hand? Draw it out of
Your bosom and consume them.
12Yet God is my King of old, working
salvation in the midst of the earth.
13You broke the sea in pieces by Your
strength; You shattered the heads of the
sea-monsters in the waters.
14You crush the heads of leviathan,
You gave him to be food to those in-
habiting the wilderness.
15You cleave fountains and brooks;
You dry up ever-flowing rivers.
16Yours is the day, Yours also the
night; You have established luminary
and sun.
17You have set all the borders of the
earth; You have made summer and
winter.
18Remember this, how the enemy has
reproached Yehovah, and how a foolish
people have blasphemed Your name.
19O deliver not the soul of Your tur-
tle-dove unto the wild beast; forget not
the life of Your poor forever.
20Look upon the covenant; for the
dark places of the land are full of the
habitations of violence.
21O let not the oppressed return
ashamed; let the poor and needy praise
Your name.
22Arise, O God, plead Your own
cause; remember Your reproach from
the foolish all the day.
23Forget not the voice of Your adversaries, the roar of those that rise up
against You which ascend continually.

Psalm 75

1For the Conductor, Do not destroy.
A Psalm of Asaph, a Song
2We give thanks unto You, O God,
we give thanks, and Your name is near;
they declare Your wondrous works.

3 ‘Because I set the appointed time, I Myself will judge uprightly.

4 When the earth and all the inhabitants thereof are swerving, I Myself steady the pillars of it.’ Selah

5 I say unto the foolish: ‘don’t be foolish’; and to the wicked: ‘do not exalt your horn.’

6 Do not exalt your horn on high, speaking with an arrogant neck.

7 For neither from the east, nor from the west, nor yet from the wilderness, is exaltation.

8 For God is judge; He makes low, and exalts.

9 For in the hand of Yehovah there is a cup, of foaming wine, full of mixture, and surely He pours out the sediments, all the wicked of the earth shall drain them, and drink them.

10 But as for me, I will declare for ever, I will sing praises to the God of Jacob.

11 All the horns of the wicked I will cut off; but the horns of the righteous shall be lifted up.

Psalm 76

1 For the Conductor; with string-music. A Psalm of Asaph, a Song.

2 In Judah is God known; His name is great in Israel.

3 In Shalem also is set His tabernacle, and His dwelling-place in Zion.

4 There He broke the fiery arrows of the bow; the shield, and the sword, and the battle. Selah

5 You are shining and majestic, from the mountains of prey.

6 The stout-hearted are spoiled, they sleep their sleep; and none of the mighty men have found their hands.

7 At Your rebuke, O God of Jacob, they are in deep sleep, both chariot and horse.

8 You, even You, are to be feared; and who may stand in Your sight when once You are angry?

9 From heaven you caused judgment to be heard; the earth feared, and was still,

10 When God arose to judgment, to save all the humble of the earth. Selah

11 Surely the wrath of man shall praise You; the residue of wrath You shall wear.

12 Vow, and pay unto Yehovah your God; let all that are round about Him bring gifts to Him that is to be feared;

13 He diminishes the spirit of princes; He is terrible to the kings of the earth.

Psalm 77

1 For the Conductor; for Jeduthun. A Psalm of Asaph.

2 I cried unto God with my voice; my voice unto God, that He may hear me.

3 In the day of my trouble I seek the Lord; with my hand lifted up in the night without wearying; my soul refuses to be comforted.

4 I remember God and I moan; I meditate and my spirit faints. Selah

5 You hold the eyelids of my eyes; I am troubled, and cannot speak.

6 I have pondered the days of old, the years of ancient times.

7 I remembrance my music in the night; I will commune with mine own heart; and my spirit makes diligent search:

8 ‘Will the Lord cast off forever? And will He be favorable no more?

9 Is His mercy clean gone forever? Has His promise come to an end forevermore?

10 Has God forgotten to be gracious? Has He in anger shut up his compassions?’ Selah

11 And I say: ‘This is my weakness, that the right hand of the Most High

could change.

12 I will make mention of the deeds of Yehovah; yes, I will remember Your wonders of old

13 I will meditate also upon all Your work, and muse on Your doings.'

14 O God, Your way is in holiness; who is a great god like unto God?

15 You are the God that does wonders; You have made known Your strength among the peoples.

16 You have with Your arm redeemed Your people, the sons of Jacob and Joseph. Selah

17 The waters saw You, O God; the waters saw You, they were in pain; the depths also trembled.

18 The clouds flooded forth waters; the skies sent out a sound; Your arrows also went abroad.

19 The voice of Your thunder was in the whirlwind; the lightning lit up the world; the earth trembled and shook.

20 Your way was in the sea, and Your path in the great waters, and Your footsteps were not known.

21 You led Your people like a flock, by the hand of Moses and Aaron.

Psalm 78

1 Maschil of Asaph. Give ear, O my people, to my teaching; incline your ears to the words of my mouth.

2 I will open my mouth with a parable; I will utter dark sayings concerning days of old;

3 That which we have heard and known, and our fathers have told us,

4 We will not hide from their sons, recounting to the generation to come the praises of Yehovah, and His strength, and His wondrous works that He has done.

5 For He established a testimony in Jacob, and appointed a law in Israel, which He commanded our fathers, that they should make them known to their children;

6 That the generation to come might know them, even the children that should be born; who should arise and tell them to their children,

7 That they might put their confidence in God, and not forget the works of God, but keep His commandments;

8 And might not be as their fathers, a stubborn and rebellious generation; a generation whose heart was not steadfast, and whose spirit was not faithful to God.

9 The children of Ephraim were archers handling the bow that turned back on the day of battle.

10 They kept not the covenant of God, and refused to walk in His law;

11 And they forgot His works, and His miracles that He had shown them.

12 He did marvelous things in the sight of their fathers, in the land of Egypt, in the field of Zoan.

13 He split the sea, and caused them to pass through; and He made the waters to stand as a heap.

14 By day He led them with a cloud, and all the night with a light of fire.

15 He split rocks in the wilderness, and gave them drink abundantly as out of the great deep.

16 He brought streams also out of the cliff, and caused waters to run down like rivers.

17 And still they continued to sin against Him, to rebel against the Most High in the desert.

18 And they tested God in their heart by demanding food for their appetite.

19 And they spoke against God; they said: 'Can God prepare a table in the wilderness?

20 Behold, He smote the rock, that wa-

ters gushed out, and rivers poured
down; can He give bread also? or will
He provide flesh for His people?'
21Therefore Yehovah heard, and He
was infuriated; and a fire was kindled
against Jacob, and anger also went up
against Israel;
22Because they did not believe in
God, and did not trust in His salvation.
23And He commanded the skies
above, and opened the gates of heaven;
24And He caused manna to rain upon
them for food, and gave them the grain
of heaven.
25Man did eat the bread of the
mighty; He sent them food to the full.
26He caused the east wind to set forth
in heaven; and by His power He
brought on the south wind.
27He caused flesh also to rain upon
them as the dust, and winged fowl as
the sand of the seas;
28And He let it fall in the midst of
their camp, round about their dwellings.
29So they did eat, and were well filled;
and He gave them that which they desired.
30They had not yet turned aside from
their desire, their food was still in their
mouths,
31When the anger of God rose
against them, and slew the fattest of
them, and smote down the young men
of Israel.
32In spite of all this they still sinned,
and believed not in His wondrous
works.
33Therefore He finished their days as
a breath, and their years in terror.
34When He slew them, then they
would seek after Him, and return and
look for God.
35And they remembered that God
was their Rock, and the Most High
God their redeemer.
36But they beguiled Him with their
mouth, and lied unto Him with their
tongue.
37For their heart was not right with
Him, neither were they faithful in His
covenant.
38But He, being full of compassion,
covered iniquity, and did not destroy;
and many times He turned back His
anger, and did not stir up all His fury.
39So He remembered that they were
but flesh, a wind that passes away, that
does not return.
40How often did they rebel against
Him in the wilderness, and grieve Him
in the desert!
41And again they tried God, and
grieved the Holy One of Israel.
42They remembered not His hand,
the day when He redeemed them from
their enemy.
43How He set His signs in Egypt, and
His wonders in the field of Zoan;
44And turned their rivers into blood,
so that they could not drink their
streams.
45He sent among them swarms of
flies, which devoured them; and frogs,
which destroyed them.
46He gave also their increase unto the
caterpillar, and their labour unto the
locust.
47He destroyed their vines with hail,
and their sycamore-trees with frost.
48He gave over their cattle to the hail,
and their flocks to fiery thunderbolts.
49He sent forth upon them the
fierceness of His anger, fury, and indignation, and trouble, sending destroying angels.
50He leveled a path for His anger; He
spared not their soul from death, but
gave their life over to the pestilence;
51And smote all the first-born in

Egypt, the first of their strength in the
tents of Ham;
52Then He led out His own people
like sheep, and guided them in the
wilderness like a flock.
53And He led them safely, and they
feared not; but the sea covered their
enemies.
54And He brought them to His holy
border, to the mountain, which His
right hand had acquired.
55He drove out the nations before
them, and divided to them for an inheritance by line, and made the tribes
of Israel to dwell in their tents.
56Yet they tried and provoked God,
the Most High, and did not keep His
testimonies;
57But turned back, and dealt treach-
erously like their fathers; they twisted
as a slack bow.
58For they provoked Him with their
high places, and made Him jealous
with their graven images.
59God heard, and was furious, and
He utterly rejected Israel;
60And He abandoned the tabernacle
of Shiloh, the tent to dwell among men;
61And delivered His strength into
captivity, and His splendor into the
hand of the oppressor.
62He gave His people over unto the
sword; and was furious with His inheritance.
63His young men were consumed by
fire; and his virgins were not praised.
64His priests fell by the sword; and
their widows made no lamentation.
65Then the Lord awoke as one asleep,
like a mighty man shouting from wine.
66And He smote His oppressors
backward; He put upon them a perpetual reproach.
67He abhorred the tent of Joseph, and
did not chose Ephraim;
68But chose the tribe of Judah, the
mount Zion which He loved.
69And He built His sanctuary like the
heights, like the earth which He hath
founded for ever.
70He chose David also His servant,
and took him from the sheepfolds;
71From following the nursing ewes.
He brought him, to be shepherd over
Jacob His people, and Israel His inheritance.
72So he shepherded them according
to the integrity of his heart; and led
them by the skillfulness of his hands.

Psalm 79

1A Psalm of Asaph. O God, the hea-
then are come into Your inheritance;
they have defiled Your holy temple;
they have made Jerusalem into heaps.
2They have given the dead bodies of
Your servants to be food unto the fowls
of the heaven, the flesh of Your godly
ones unto the beasts of the earth.
3They have poured out their blood
like water round about Jerusalem, with
none to bury them.
4We are become a disgrace to our
neighbors, scorned and mocked by
them that are round about us.
5How long, Yehovah, will You be angry forever? How long will Your jealousy burn like fire?
6Pour out Your wrath upon the nations that do not know You, and upon
the kingdoms that do not call upon
Your name.
7For they have devoured Jacob, and
laid waste his habitation.
8Do not remember against us our
former iniquities; let Your compassions
quickly come to meet us; for we are
brought very low.
9Help us, O God of our salvation, for
the glory of Your name; and deliver us,

and cover our sins, for Your name's sake.

10 Wherefore should the nations say: 'Where is their God?' Let it be made known among the nations before our eyes the avenging of Your servants' blood that was poured out.

11 Let the groaning of the prisoner come before You; according to the greatness of Your arm spare the sons appointed to death;

12 And return unto our neighbors sevenfold into their bosom their reproach, with which they have reproached You, O Lord.

13 So we Your people and the flock of Your pasture will give You thanks forever; we will tell of Your praise generation after generation.

Psalm 80

1 For the Conductor; upon Shoshannim. A testimony. A psalm of Asaph.

2 Give ear, O Shepherd of Israel, You that leads Joseph like a flock; enthroned upon the cherubim, shine forth.

3 Before Ephraim and Benjamin and Manasseh, stir up Your might, and come to save us.

4 O God, restore us; and cause Your face to shine, and we shall be saved.

5 Yehovah God of hosts, how long will You smoke against the prayer of Your people?

6 You have fed them with the bread of tears, and given them tears to drink in large measure.

7 You make us a strife unto our neighbors; and our enemies mock among themselves.

8 O God of hosts, return to us; and cause Your face to shine, and we shall be saved.

9 You plucked up a vine out of Egypt; You expelled the nations, and planted it.

10 You cleared a place before it, and it took deep root, and filled the land.

11 The mountains were covered with the shadow of it, and the mighty cedars with its branches.

12 She sent out her branches unto the sea, and her shoots unto the river.

13 Why have You broken down her walls, so that all that pass by pick her?

14 The boar of the forest devours her, the wild creatures of the field feed on her.

15 O God of hosts, return, we pray; look from heaven, and behold, and be mindful of this vine,

16 And of the stock which Your right hand has planted, and the son that You made strong for Yourself.

17 She is burned with fire, she is cut down; they perish at the rebuke of Your countenance.

18 Let Your hand be upon the man of Your right hand, upon the son of man whom You made strong for Yourself.

19 Then we shall not turn back from You; quicken us, and we will call upon Your name.

20 Yehovah God of hosts, return to us; cause Your face to shine, and we shall be saved.

Psalm 81

1 For the Conductor; upon the Gittith, of Asaph.

2 Sing for joy to God our strength; shout unto the God of Jacob.

3 Lift up the song, and strike the Tambourine, the pleasant lyre with the string instrument.

4 Blow the Shofar in the new moon, in the day of the feast.

5 For it is a statute for Israel, a decision of the God of Jacob.

6He placed it a statute in Joseph,
when He went out against the land of
Egypt. I heard a language I did not
know:
7'I removed his shoulder from the
burden; His hands were freed from the
basket.
8You call in trouble, and I rescued
you; I answered you in the secret place
of thunder; I tested you at the waters of
Meribah. Selah
9Hear, O My people, and I will admonish you: O Israel, if you would
hearken unto Me!
10There shall not be a strange god in
you; neither shall you bow down to a
foreign god.
11I am Yehovah your God, who
brought you up out of the land of
Egypt; open your mouth wide, and I
will fill it.
12But My people did not listen to My
voice; and Israel did not yield to Me.
13So I let them go in the stubborn-
ness of their heart, they walked in their
own counsels.
14Oh that My people would listen
unto Me, that Israel would walk in My
ways!
15I would soon subdue their enemies,
and turn My hand against their adversaries.
16The haters of Yehovah would cringe
before Him; and it would be that way
forever.
17And he would feed him from the
bounty of wheat; and I would satisfy
you with honey from a rock.'

Psalm 82

1A Psalm of Asaph. God stands in
the congregation of God; in the midst
of God He shall judge.
2'How long will you-all judge per-
versely, and have respect for the
wicked? Selah
3Judge the poor and fatherless; do
righteously to the humble and weak.
4Rescue the poor and needy; deliver
them out of the hand of the wicked.
5They know not, nor do they understand; they go about in darkness; all the
foundations of the Earth shall be shak-
en.
6I said: You are gods, and all of you
sons of the Most High.
7Surely you shall die like men, and
fall like one of the princes.'
8Arise, O God, judge the Earth; for
You shall possess all the nations.

Psalm 83

1A Song, a psalm of Asaph.
2O God, do not rest; do not keep
silent, and do not be still, O God.
3For, behold, Your enemies roar; and
they that hate You have lifted up the
head.
4They cunningly scheme against
Your people, and they plot against Your
protected ones.
5They say: 'Come, and let us wipe
them out from being a nation; that the
name of Israel may be remembered no
more.'
6For they have resolved in their
heart; a covenant against you, they
shall cut you off;
7The tents of Edom and the Ish-
maelites; Moab, and the Hagrites;
8Gebal, and Ammon, and Amalek;
Philistia with the inhabitants of Tyre;
9Assyria also is joined with them;
they have been an arm to the children
of Lot. Selah
10Do unto them as unto Midian; as to
Sisera, as to Jabin, at the brook Kishon;
11Who were destroyed at En-dor;
they became as dung for the Earth.
12Make their nobles like Oreb and

Zeeb, and like Zebah and Zalmunna all
their princes;
13Who said: 'Let us take to ourselves
in possession the habitations of God.'
14O my God, make them like the
whirling dust; as stubble before the
wind.
15As the fire that burns the forest,
and as the flame that sets the mountains ablaze;
16So pursue them with Your tempest,
and scare them with Your storm.
17Fill their faces with shame; that
they may seek Your name, O Lord.
18Let them be ashamed and afraid
forever; and let them be abashed and
perish;
19That they may know that it is You
alone whose name is the Lord, the
Most High over all the Earth.

Psalm 84

1For the Conductor; upon the Gittit.
A Psalm of the sons of Korah
2How beloved are Your tabernacles,
O Yehovah of hosts!
3My soul longs, and also faints for the
courts of Yehovah; my heart and my
flesh shouts for joy unto the living
God.
4Also, the sparrow has found a house,
and the swallow a nest for herself,
where she may lay her young; Your altars, O Yehovah of hosts, my King, and
my God.
5Blessed are they that dwell in Your
house, they are ever praising You. Selah
6Blessed is the man whose strength is
in You; in whose heart are the highways.
7Passing through the valley of Baca
they make it a place of springs; yes, the
early rain covers it with blessings.
8They go from strength to strength,
each appear before God in Zion.
9O Yehovah God of hosts, hear my
prayer; give ear, O God of Jacob. Selah.
10Behold, O God our shield, and look
upon the face of Your anointed.
11For a day in Your courts is better
than a thousand; I had rather stand at
the threshold of the house of my God,
than to dwell in the tents of wickedness.
12For Yehovah God is a sun and a
shield Yehovah gives grace and glory
He will not withhold any good thing
from those who walk uprightly.
13O Yehovah of hosts, blessed is the
man who trusts in You.

Psalm 85

1For the Conductor. A Psalm of the
sons of Korah.
2Yehovah, You have been favorable
unto Your land, You have turned the
captivity of Jacob.
3You took away the iniquity of Your
people, You have covered all their sin.
Selah
4You have withdrawn all Your wrath;
You have turned from Your burning
anger.
5Restore us, O God of our salvation,
and put away Your vexation with us.
6Will You be angry with us forever?
Will You draw out Your anger generations after generation?
7Will You not revive us again, that
Your people may rejoice in You?
8Show us Your mercy, Yehovah, and
grant us Your salvation.
9I will hear what God Yehovah will
speak; for He will speak peace unto His
people, and to His holy ones; but let
them not turn back to folly.
10Surely His salvation is near them
that fear Him; that glory may dwell in
our land.
11Lovingkindness and truth are met

together; righteousness and peace have
kissed.
12 Truth springs out of the earth; and
righteousness has looked down from
heaven.
13 Also, Yehovah will give that which
is good; and our land will give her produce.
14 Righteousness shall go before Him,
and shall make His steps a pathway.

Psalm 86

1 A Prayer of David. Incline Your ear,
Yehovah, and answer me; for I am poor
and needy.
2 Keep my soul, for I am godly; You
are my God, save Your servant who
trusts in you.
3 Be gracious unto me, O Adon; for
unto You I cry all day.
4 Rejoice the soul of Your servant; for
unto You, Adon, do I lift up my soul.
5 For You, Adon, are good, and ready
to pardon, and plenteous in lovingkindness to all who call on You.
6 Give ear, Yehovah, to my prayer; and
attend unto the voice of my supplications.
7 In the day of my distress I call to
You; for You will answer me.
8 There is none like unto You among
the gods, O Adon, and there are no
works like Yours.
9 All nations whom You have made
shall come and shall bow themselves
before You, O Adon; and they shall glorify Your name.
10 For You are great, and do miraculous things; You are God alone.
11 Teach me, Yehovah, Your way, that
I may walk in Your truth; unite my
heart to fear Your name.
12 I will praise You, O Adonay my
God, with my whole heart; and I will
glorify Your name for evermore.
13 For great is Your lovingkindness
toward me; and You have delivered my
soul from the lowest Hell.
14 O God, the insolent are risen up
against me, and the company of ruth-
less men have sought after my soul, and
have not set You before them.
15 But You, O Adon, are a God full of
mercy and gracious, slow to anger, and
plenteous in lovingkindness and truth.
16 O turn unto me, and be gracious to
me; give Your strength unto Your servant, and save the son of Your hand-
maid.
17 Work in my behalf a sign for good;
and they that hate me shall see it, and
be ashamed, because You, Yehovah
have helped me, and comforted me.

Psalm 87

1 A Psalm of the sons of Korah; a
Song. His foundation is in the holy
mountains.
2 Yehovah loves the gates of Zion
more than all the dwellings of Jacob.
3 Glorious things are spoken of You,
O city of God. Selah
4 'I will make mention of Rahab and
Babylon as among them that know Me;
behold Philistia, and Tyre, with Ethiopia; this one was born there,' and the
Most High will establish her
5 But of Zion it shall be said: 'This
man and that was born in her; and the
Most High Himself doth establish her.'
6 Yehovah shall count in the register
of the peoples: 'This one was born
there.' Selah
7 And singers like dancers, all my
springs are in You.

Psalm 88

1 A Song, a Psalm of the sons of Korah; for the Conductor; upon Mahalath
Leannoth. Maschil of Heman the

Ezrahite.

2 Yehovah, God of my salvation, a time I cried in the night before You,

3 Let my prayer come before You, incline Your ear unto my lamentation.

4 For my soul is filled with misery, and my life reaches to Sheol.

5 I am counted with them that go down into the pit; I am become as a man that has no help;

6 Free among the dead, like the slain that lie in the grave, whom You remember no more; and they are cut off from Your hand.

7 You have laid me in the lowest pit, in the depths, in dark places.

8 Your wrath lies hard upon me, and all Your waves break over me, You overwhelm. Selah

9 You have put my acquaintance far from me; You have made me an abomination unto them; I am shut up, and I cannot escape.

10 Mine eye languishes from my affliction; I have called upon You, Yehovah, every day, I have spread forth my hands unto You.

11 Will You work wonders for the dead? Or shall the ghost of the dead arise and give You thanks? Selah

12 Shall Your lovingkindness be declared in the grave? or Your faithfulness in destruction?

13 Shall Thy wonders be known in the dark? and Thy righteousness in the land of forgetfulness?

14 And as for me, unto You Yehovah, do I cry, and in the morning my prayer come to meet You.

15 Yehovah why do You reject my soul? You hide Your face from me.

16 I am afflicted and close to death from my youth up; I have suffered Your terrors, I am helpless.

17 Your anger is gone over me; Your terrors have cut me off.

18 They surrounded me like waters all day; they go around upon me altogether.

19 You have caused both lover and friend to shun me and my acquaintance into darkness.

Psalm 89

1 Maschil of Ethan the Ezrahite

2 I will sing of the lovingkindness of Yehovah forever; with my mouth will I make known Your faithfulness to all generations.

3 For I have said: ‘Forever is lovingkindness built; Your faithfulness is established in the heavens.

4 I have cut a covenant with My chosen, I have sworn unto David My servant:

5 Forever will I establish your seed, and build up your throne to all generations.’ Selah

6 So shall the heavens praise Your wonders, Yehovah, Your faithfulness also in the assembly of the holy ones

7 For who in the skies can be compared unto Yehovah, who among the sons of might can be likened unto the Yehovah,

8 God is greatly to be feared through the council of His holy ones, and to be feared by all who are around about Him.

9 Yehovah God of hosts, who is a mighty one, like unto You, Yehovah? And Your faithfulness is round about You.

10 You rule the proud swelling of the sea; when the waves thereof arise, You still them.

11 You crushed Rahab, as one that is slain; You scatter Your enemies with the arm of Your strength.

12 Yours are the heavens, Yours is also

the earth; the world and the fulness
thereof, You have founded them.
13The north and the south, You have
created them; Tabor and Hermon rejoice in Your name.
14Yours is an arm with might; strong
is Your hand, and exalted is Your right
hand.
15Righteousness and judgment is the
foundation of your throne mercy and
truth shall go before your presence.
16Happy are the people who know
the joyful shout; they walk, Yehovah, in
the light of Your countenance.
17In Your name they rejoice all the
day; and through Your righteousness
are they exalted.
18For You are the glory of their
strength; and in Your favor our horn is
exalted.
19For of Yehovah is our shield; and
the Holy One of Israel is our king.
20Then You spoke in a vision to Your
godly ones, and said: ‘I have laid help
upon one that is mighty; I have exalted
one chosen out of the people.
21I have found David My servant;
with My holy oil have I anointed him;
22With whom My hand shall be established; Mine arm also shall
strengthen him.
23The enemy shall not exact from
him; nor the son of wickedness afflict
him.
24And I will beat to pieces his adversaries before him, and smite them that
hate him.
25But My faithfulness and My mercy
shall be with him; and through My
name shall his horn be exalted.
26I will set his hand also on the sea,
and his right hand on the rivers.
27He shall call unto Me: You are my
Father, my God, and the rock of my
salvation.
28I also will appoint him firstborn,
the highest of the kings of the earth.
29Forever will I keep for him My
mercy, and My covenant shall stand
fast with him.
30His seed also will I make to endure
forever, and his throne as the days of
heaven.
31If his children forsake My law, and
do not walk in My ordinances;
32If they profane My statutes, and do
not keep My commandments;
33Then will I visit their transgression
with the rod, and their iniquity with
strokes.
34But My mercy I will not break off
from him, nor will I be false to My
faithfulness.
35My covenant will I not profane, nor
alter that which is gone out of My lips.
36Once have I sworn by My holiness:
Surely I will not be false unto David;
37His seed shall endure forever, and
his throne as the sun before Me.
38It shall be established forever as the
moon; and be steadfast as the witness
in sky.’ Selah.
39But You have cast off and rejected,
You have been angry with Your anointed.
40You have abhorred the co-venant of
Your servant; You have profaned his
crown even to the ground.
41You have broken down all his
fences; You have brought his strongholds to ruin.
42All who pass by the way spoil him;
he has become a taunt to his neighbors.
43You have exalted the right hand of
his adversaries; You have made all his
enemies to rejoice.
44Yes, You turn back the edge of his
sword, and have not made him to stand
in the battle.
45You have removed his purity, and

cast his throne down to the earth.
46You have shortened the days of his
youth; You have covered him with
shame. Selah
47How long, Yehovah, will You hide?
forever? How long shall Your wrath
burn like fire?
48I remember my duration of life; on
account of what vanity have You created all the sons of men.
49What man is he that lives and shall
not see death, that shall deliver his soul
from the power of the grave? Selah
50Where are Your former mercies, O
Lord, which You swore unto David in
Your faithfulness?
51Remember, Lord, the reproach of
Your servants; how I do bear in my bosom so many peoples;
52Wherewith Your enemies have reproached, Yehovah, wherewith they
have reproached the footsteps of Your
anointed.
53Blessed be Yehovah for evermore.
Amen, and Amen!

Psalm 90

1A Prayer of Moses the man of God.
Lord, You have been our dwelling-
place in all generations.
2Before the mountains were brought
forth, or ever You had formed the earth
and the inhabited earth, even from
everlasting to everlasting, You are God.
3You turn man to dust; and say: 'Return, you sons of Adam.'
4For a thousand years in Your sight
are a day, as yesterday when it is past,
and as a watch in the night.
5You carry them away as with a
flood; they are as a sleep; in the morning they are like grass which grows up.
6In the morning it flourishes, and
grows up; in the evening it is cut down,
and withers.
7For we are consumed in Your anger,
and by Your wrath we are overwhelmed
8You have set our iniquities before
You, our secret in the light of Your
presence.
9For all our days are passed away in
Your fury; we bring our years to an end
as a tale.
10The days of our years are seventy
years and by reason of strength eighty
years; yet is their pride but travail and
vanity; for it is speedily gone, and we
fly away.
11Who knows the power of Your
anger, and according to Your fear Your
fury.
12So teach us to number our days,
that we may invite a heart of wisdom.
13Return, Yehovah; how long? And
have pity upon Your servants.
14O satisfy us in the morning with
Your mercy; that we may rejoice and be
glad all our days.
15Make us glad according to the days
wherein You have afflicted us, according to the years wherein we have seen
evil.
16Let Your work appear unto Your
servants, and Your splendor upon their
children.
17And let the beauty of the Lord our
God be upon us; establish also upon us
the work of our hands; the work of our
hands establish it.

Psalm 91

1He who dwells in the secret place of
the Most High shall abide under the
shadow of the Almighty.
2I will say of the LORD, my refuge
and my fortress: my God; in Him I
trust.
3For He will deliver you from the
snare of the fowler and from the de-

struction of the pestilence.
4He shall cover you with His pinions, and under His wings you will take refuge: His truth shall be your shield and buckler.
5You shall not be afraid of the terror by night; nor of the arrow that flies by day;
6or for the pestilence that walks in darkness; nor for the destruction that devastates at noonday.
7A thousand shall fall at your side, And ten thousand at your right hand; But it shall not come near you.
8Only with your eyes shall you behold And see the retribution of the wicked.
9Because you have made the LORD, who is my refuge, Even the most High, your habitation;
10There no evil shall be allowed to happen to you, Neither shall any plague come near your tent.
11For he will give his angels charge over you, To keep you in all your ways.
12They shall bear you up in their hands, So that you do not smash your foot against a stone.
13You shall tread upon the lion and cobra: The young lion and the dragon you shall trample.
14Because he cleaves to my love I will rescue him: I will set him on high, because he has known my name.
15He calls me and I will answer him: I will be with him in trouble; I will deliver him and honor him.
16With long life will I satisfy him, And show him my salvation.

Psalm 92

1A Psalm, a Song for the sabbath day.
2It is a good thing to give thanks unto Yehovah, and to sing praises unto Your name, O Most High;
3To declare Your lovingkindness in the morning, and Your faithfulness in the night,
4With an instrument of ten strings, and with the harp; and with the melody of a lyre.
5For You, Yehovah, have made me rejoice through Your work; in the works of Your hands I will shout.
6How great are Your works, Yehovah! Your thoughts are very deep.
7A brutish man knows not, nor does a fool understand this.
8Although the wicked sprout like grass, and all the workers of iniquity flourish; they will be destroyed forever.
9But You, Yehovah, are on high forever.
10For, behold, Your enemies, Yehovah, for, behold, Your enemies shall perish: all the workers of iniquity shall be scattered.
11But You have exalted my horn like the wild-ox; I am anointed with fresh oil.
12My eye also has looked on my foes, my ears have heard the evil-doers that rise up against me.
13The righteous shall flourish like the palm-tree; he shall grow like a cedar in Lebanon.
14Planted in the house of Yehovah, they shall flourish in the courts of our God.
15They shall still bring forth fruit in old age; they shall be fresh and full of sap:
16To declare that Yehovah is upright, my Rock, in whom there is no iniquity.

Psalm 93

1Yehovah reigns; He is clothed with majesty. Yehovah is clothed with strength- He has girded Himself. The inhabitable world is firmly established, it cannot be moved.

2 Your throne is established from then, you are from everlasting.

3 Floods have lifted up O Yehovah, floods have lifted up their roaring sound, floods have lifted up their pounding.

4 The thunder of many waters , the mighty waves of the sea, Yehovah on high is Mighty.

5 Your testimonies are very sure, Yehovah! Holiness belongs to your house, for as long as there are days.

Psalm 94

1 Oh Yehovah God to Whom vengeance belongs, to You God Whom vengeance belongs, shine forth.

2 Lift up Yourself, Judge of the Earth; render recompense to the proud.

3 Yehovah, how long shall the wicked, how long shall the wicked triumph?

4 They gush out their words arrogantly; all the workers of iniquity boast.

5 They crush Your people Yehovah, and afflict Your inheritance.

6 The widow and the stranger they slay, and murder the fatherless.

7 And they say: 'Yah will not see, neither will the God of Jacob pay attention.'

8 Consider, you brutish among the people; and you fools, when will ye understand?

9 He Who planted the ear, shall He not hear? He Who formed the eye, shall He not behold?

10 He Who disciplines nations, shall not He correct – even He Who teaches man knowledge?

11 Yehovah knows the thoughts of man, that they are vanity.

12 Blessed is the man whom You, Yah, discipline and teach out of Your Law;

13 that You may give him rest from the days of evil until the pit is dug for the wicked.

14 For Yehovah will not forsake His people, nor will He forsake His inheritance.

15 For righteousness shall return unto judgment, and all the upright in heart shall follow it.

16 Who will rise up for me against the evil-doers? Who will stand up for me against the workers of iniquity?

17 Unless Yehovah had been my help, my soul had soon dwelt in silence.

18 If I say: 'My foot slips', Your lovingkindness, Yehovah, holds me up.

19 When my cares are many within me, Your comforts delight my soul.

20 Shall the throne of wickedness have fellowship with You, Who frames mischief by statute?

21 They gather themselves together against the soul of the righteous, and condemn innocent blood.

22 But Yehovah has been my high tower, and my God, the rock of my refuge.

23 And He has brought upon them their own iniquity, and will destroy them in their own evil; Yehovah our God will destroy them.

Psalm 95

1 O come, let us sing for joy to Yehovah; let us shout for joy to the Rock of our salvation.

2 Let us come before His presence with thanksgiving, let us shout for joy unto Him with songs.

3 For the Yehovah is a great God, and a great King above all gods;

4 In whose hand are the depths of the earth; the heights of the mountains are His.

5 The sea is His, for He made it; and His hands formed the dry land.

6O come, let us bow down and bend the knee, let us bless before the LORD our Maker;

7For He is our God, and we are the people of His pasture, and the flock of His hand. Today, if you hearken to His voice!

8'Harden not your heart, as at Meribah, as in the day of Massah in the wilderness;

9When your fathers tried Me, proved Me, even though they saw My work.

10For forty years was I wearied with that generation, and said: It is a people that do err in their heart, and they have not known My ways;

11Which I swore in My wrath, that they should not enter into My rest.'

Psalm 96

1O sing unto Yehovah a new song; sing unto Yehovah, all the Earth.

2Sing unto the Yehovah, bless His name; proclaim from day to day His salvation.

3Declare His glory among the nations, His wonderful works among all the peoples.

4For great is Yehovah, and greatly to be praised; He is to be feared above all gods.

5For all the gods of the peoples are idols; but Yehovah made the heavens.

6Honor and majesty are before Him; strength and beauty are in His sanctuary.

7Ascribe unto the Yehovah, you families of the peoples, ascribe unto Yehovah glory and strength.

8Ascribe unto the Yehovah the glory of His name; lift to Him an offering, and come into His courts

9Worship Yehovah in the splendor of holiness, tremble before Him all the Earth.

10Say among the nations: 'Yehovah reigns.' The world also is established that it cannot be moved; He will judge the peoples with equity.

11Let the heavens rejoice, and let the earth be glad; let the sea roar, and the fulness thereof;

12Let the field be joyful and all that is therein; then shall all the trees of the forest sing for joy;

13Before the Yehovah, for He is come; for He is come to judge the Earth; He will judge the world with righteousness, and the peoples in His faithfulness.

Psalm 97

1Yehovah reigns; let the earth rejoice; let the multitude of isles be glad.

2Clouds and thick darkness are round about Him; righteousness and judgment are the foundation of His throne.

3A fire goes before Him, and burns up His adversaries round about.

4His lightnings light up the world; the Earth saw, and trembled.

5The mountains melted like wax at the presence of Yehovah, at the presence of the Lord of the whole Earth.

6The heavens declared His righteousness, and all the people saw His glory.

7Be ashamed all those who serve graven images, that boast themselves of things of vanity; bow down to Him, all you gods.

8Zion heard and was glad, and the daughters of Judah rejoiced; because of Your judgments, Yehovah.

9For You, Yehovah, are most high above all the earth; You are exalted far above all gods.

10O you that love YaHoWaH (the Lord), hate evil; He preserves the souls of His holy ones; He delivered them out of the hand of the wicked.

11 Light is sown for the righteous, and gladness for the upright in heart.

12 Rejoice in Yehovah, you righteous; and give thanks at the remembrance of His Holiness.

Psalm 98

1 A psalm. O sing unto Yehovah a new song; for He has done wonderful things; His right hand, and His holy arm, has brought salvation.

2 Yehovah has made known His salvation; His righteousness He has revealed in the sight of the nations.

3 He has remembered His lovingkindness and His faithfulness toward the house of Israel; all the ends of the earth have seen the salvation of our God.

4 Shout unto Yehovah, all the earth; break forth and sing for joy, yes, sing praises.

5 Sing praises unto Yehovah with the harp; with the harp and the voice of melody.

6 With trumpets and sound of the horn shout before the King, Yehovah.

7 Let the sea roar, and the fulness thereof; the world, and they that dwell therein;

8 Let the floods clap their hands; let the mountains sing for joy together;

9 Before the LORD, for He is come to judge the earth; He will judge the world with righteousness, and the peoples with equity.

Psalm 99

1 Yehovah reigns; let the people tremble; He is enthroned upon the cherubim; let the earth quake.

2 Yehovah is great in Zion; and He is high above all the people.

3 Let them praise Your great and awesome name; Holy is He.

4 Also the Kings strength loves justice—You have established uprightness, you execute judgment and righteousness in Jacob.

5 Exalt Yehovah our God, and worship at His footstool; Holy is He.

6 Moses and Aaron among His priests, and Samuel calling upon His name, They called upon Yehovah, and He answered them.

7 He spoke unto them in the pillar of cloud; they kept His testimonies, and the statute that He gave them.

8 Yehovah our God, You answer them; a forgiving God were You unto them, though You took vengeance of their misdeeds.

9 Exalt Yehovah our God, and worship at His holy hill; for Yehovah our God is holy.

Psalm 100

1 A Song of Praise- Make a joyful shout all the Earth!

2 Serve Yehovah with rejoicing come before His presence with shouts of joy!

3 Know that Yehovah He is God; it is He that has made us, and not we ourselves, His people, and the flock of His pasture.

4 Enter into His gates with thanksgiving, His courts with praise. Be thankful unto Him, bless His name.

5 For Yehovah is good; His lovingkindness is forever; and His faithfulness unto all generations.

Psalm 101

1 A song of David, I will sing to you of your lovingkindness and judgments Yehovah, I will sing praise.

2 I will behave myself wisely in a way that is blameless. When will you come

to me? I will walk in the midst of my house with a perfect heart.

3 I will set no wicked thing before my eyes. I hate the works of rebellion – none of it shall cleave to me.

4 A perverse heart shall depart from me; I will know no evil thing.

5 Whoever slanders his neighbor in secret, him will I destroy; whoever is haughty of eye and proud of heart, him I will not suffer.

6 My eyes are upon the faithful of the land, that they may dwell with Me; he who walks perfect in the way, he shall minister unto Me.

7 He who does deceitful things shall not dwell within My house. He who tells lies shall not tarry in My sight.

8 Morning by morning will I destroy all the wicked of the land; to cut off all the workers of iniquity from the city of Yehovah.

Psalm 102

1 A prayer of the afflicted, when he faints, and pours out his complaint before Yehovah.

2 Yehovah, hear my prayer, and let my cry come unto You.

3 Hide not Your face from me in the day of my distress; incline Your ear unto me; in the day when I call, answer me speedily.

4 For my days are consumed like smoke, and my bones are burned as a hearth.

5 My heart is smitten like grass, and withered; for I forget to eat my bread.

6 Because of the voice of my sighing my bones cleave to my flesh.

7 I am like a crane of the wilderness; I am become as an owl of the waste places.

8 I watch, and am become like a sparrow that is alone upon the housetop.

9 Mine enemies taunt me all day; those who deride me do curse by me.

10 For I have eaten ashes like bread, and mingled my drink with weeping,

11 From the face of Your anger and Your wrath You have taken me up, and cast me away.

12 My days are like a lengthening shadow; and I am withered like grass.

13 But You, Yehovah, sit enthroned forever; and Your remembrance to all generations.

14 You will arise, and have compassion upon Zion; for it is time to be gracious unto her, for the appointed time has come.

15 For Your servants take pleasure in her stones, and favor her dust.

16 So the nations will fear the name of Yehovah, and all the kings of the earth Your glory;

17 When Yehovah has built up Zion, He appeared in His glory;

18 When He regarded the prayer of the destitute, and not despised their prayer.

19 This shall be written for the generation to come; and a people which shall be created shall praise Yah.

20 For He has looked down from the height of His sanctuary; from heaven did Yehovah behold the earth;

21 To hear the groaning of the prisoner; to set free the sons of death;

22 That men may declare the name of Yehovah in Zion, and His praise in Jerusalem;

23 When the peoples are gathered together, and the kingdoms, to serve Yehovah.

24 He weakened my strength in the way; He shortened my days.

25 I say: 'O my God, take me not away in the midst of my days, You whose years endure through-out all genera-

tions.
26Of old You lay the foundation of
the earth; and the heavens are the work
of Your hands.
27They shall perish, but You shall endure; yes, all of them shall wax old like
a garment; as a vesture You shall
change them, and they shall pass away;
28But You are the same, and Your
years have no end.
29The children of Your servants shall
dwell securely, and their seed shall be
established before You.'

Psalm 103

1Of David. Bless Yehovah, O my soul;
and all that is within me, bless His holy
name.
2Bless Yehovah, O my soul, and forget not all His benefits;
3Who pardons all your iniquities and
heals all your diseases.
4Who redeemed your life from destruction; who encompassed you with
lovingkindness and tender mercies;
5Who satisfies your ornaments with
good things; so that your youth is renewed like the eagle.
6Yehovah does righteousness, and
acts of justice for all that are oppressed.
7He made known His ways unto
Moses, His doings unto the children of
Israel.
8Yehovah is compassionate and gracious, slow to anger, and plenteous in
mercy.
9He will not always contend; neither
will He keep His anger forever.
10He has not dealt with us after our
sins, nor rewarded us according to our
iniquities.
11For as the heaven is high above the
earth, so great is His mercy toward
them that fear Him.
12As far as the east is from the west,
so far has He removed our transgressions from us.
13Like as a father has compassion
upon his children, so Yehovah has
compassion upon them that fear Him.
14For He knows our frame; He remembers that we are dust.
15As for man, his days are as grass; as
a flower of the field, so he flourishes.
16For the wind passes over it, and it is
gone; and the place thereof knows it no
more.
17But the lovingkindness of Yehovah
is from everlasting to everlasting upon
them that fear Him, and His righteousness unto children's children;
18To those who keep His covenant,
and to those that remember His instructions to do them.
19Yehovah has established His throne
in the heavens; and His kingdom rules
over all.
20Bless Yehovah, you angels of His,
you mighty in strength, that fulfill His
Word,hearkening unto the voice of His
word.
21Bless Yehovah, all His hosts; you
ministers of His, that do His pleasure.
22Bless Yehovah, all His works, in all
places of His dominion; bless Yehovah,
O my soul.

Psalm 104

1Bless Yehovah, O my soul. Yehovah
my God, You are very great; You are
clothed with honor and majesty.
2You are covered with light as with a
garment, who spread out the heavens
like a curtain;
3Who laid the beams of His upper
chambers in the waters, who make the
clouds His chariot, who walks upon the
wings of the wind;
4Who makes winds Your messengers,
the flaming fire Your ministers.

5Who established the earth upon its
foundations, that it should not be
moved forever and ever;
6You cover it with the deep as with a
vesture; the waters stood above the
mountains.
7From Your rebuke they fled, From
the voice of Your thunder they hastened away.
8The mountains rose, the valleys
sank down—unto the place which You
had founded for them;
9You set a bound which they should
not pass over, that they might not return to cover the earth.
10Who sent forth springs into the valleys; they run between the mountains;
11They give drink to every beast of
the field, the wild donkeys quench
their thirst.
12Beside them dwell the fowl of the
heaven, from among the branches they
sing.
13Who water the mountains from
Your upper chambers; the earth is full
of the fruit of Your works.
14Who causes the grass to spring up
for the cattle, and herb for the service
of man; to bring forth bread out of the
earth,
15And wine that makes glad the heart
of man, making the face brighter than
oil, and bread that stays man's heart.
16The trees of Yehovah have their fill,
the cedars of Lebanon, which He has
planted;
17Wherein the birds make their nests;
as for the stork, the fir-trees are her
house.
18The high mountains are for the
wild goats; the rocks are a refuge for
the badgers.
19Who appointed the moon for seasons; the sun knows his going down.
20You make darkness, and it is night,
wherein all the beasts of the forest
creep forth.
21The young lions roar after their
prey, and seek their food from God.
22The sun arises, they slink away, and
couch in their dens.
23Man goes forth unto his work and
to his labor until the evening.
24How manifold are Your works,
Yehovah! In wisdom You have made
them all; the earth is full of Your riches.
25The sea, great and wide, which
teams with innumerable living things,
both small and great.
26There go the ships; there is
leviathan, whom You formed to play
therein.
27All of them wait for You, that You
may give them their food in due season.
28You give it unto them, they gather
it; You open Your hand, they are satisfied with good.
29You hide Your face, they are horri-
fied; You withdraw their breath, they
perish, and return to their dust.
30You send forth Your Spirit, they are
created; and You renew the face of the
earth.
31May the glory of Yehovah endure
forever; let Yehovah rejoice in His
works!
32Who looks on the earth, and it
trembles; He touches the mountains,
and they smoke.
33I will sing unto Yehovah as long as I
live; I will sing praise to my God while
I have any being.
34Let my meditation be sweet unto
Him; as for me, I will rejoice in Yehovah.
35Let sinners cease out of the earth,
and let the wicked be no more. Bless
Yehovah, O my soul. Hallelu Yah.

Psalm 105

1 O give thanks unto Yehovah, call upon His name; make known His deeds among the peoples.

2 Sing unto Him, sing praises unto Him; speak ye of all His marvelous works.

3 Boast in His holy name; let the heart of them rejoice that seek Yehovah.

4 Seek Yehovah and His stre-ngth; seek His face continually.

5 Remember His marvelous works that He has done, His signs, and the judgments of His mouth;

6 Seed of Abraham His servant, children of Jacob, His chosen ones.

7 He is Yehovah our God; His judgments are in all the earth.

8 He has remembered His cov-enant forever, the word which He commanded to a thousand generations;

9 Which He cut with Abraham, and His oath unto Isaac;

10 And He established it unto Jacob for a statute, to Israel for an everlasting covenant;

11 Saying: 'to you I will give the land of Canaan, the lot of your inheritance.'

12 When they were but few in number. very few, and sojourners in it,

13 And when they went about from nation to nation, from one kingdom to another people,

14 He allowed no man to oppress them, and for their sake He reproved kings:

15 'Touch not Mine anointed ones, and do My prophets no harm.'

16 And He called a famine upon the land; He broke the whole staff of bread.

17 He sent a man before them, sold as a slave, Joseph.

18 They hurt his feet with fetters, iron came upon his soul.

19 Until the time that his word came, a word of Yehovah tried him.

20 The king sent and released him; even the ruler of the peoples, and set him free.

21 He made him lord of his house, and ruler of all his possessions;

22 To bind his princes at his pleasure, and teach his elders wisdom.

23 Israel also came into Egypt; and Jacob sojourned in the land of Ham.

24 And He increased His people greatly, and made them too numerous for their adversaries.

25 He turned their heart to hate His people, to deal craftily with His servants.

26 He sent Moses His servant, and Aaron whom He had chosen.

27 They showed His signs among them, and wonders in the land of Ham.

28 He sent darkness, and it was dark; and they rebelled not against His word.

29 He turned their waters into blood, and slew their fish.

30 Their land swarmed with frogs, in the chambers of their kings.

31 He spoke, and there came swarms of flies, and gnats in all their borders.

32 He gave them hail for rain, and flaming fire in their land.

33 He smote their vines also and their fig-trees; and broke the trees of their borders.

34 He spoke, and the locust came, and the young locust without number,

35 And did eat up every herb in their land, and did eat up the fruit of their ground.

36 He smote also all the first-born in their land, the first-fruits of all their strength.

37 And He brought them forth with silver and gold; and there was none that was feeble among His tribes.

38 Egypt was glad when they depart-

ed; for the fear of them had fallen upon
them.
39He spread a cloud for a covering;
and fire to give light in the night.
40They asked, and He brought quails,
and gave them in plenty the bread of
heaven.
41He opened the rock, and waters
gushed out; they ran, a river in the dry
places.
42For He remembered His holy word
unto Abraham His servant;
43And He brought forth His people
with joy, His chosen ones with singing.
44And He gave them the lands of the
nations, and they took the labor of the
peoples in possession;
45That they might keep His statutes,
and observe His laws. Hallelujah.

Psalm 106

1Halelu Yah! Give thanks unto the
Yehovah; for He is good; for His lovingkindness endures forever.
2Who can express the mighty acts of
Yehovah, or make all His praise to be
heard?
3Blessed are they that keep judgment,
that do righteousness at all times.
4Remember me, Yehovah, when You
favor Your people; visit me in Your salvation;
5That I may behold the goodness of
Your chosen, that I may rejoice in the
gladness of Your nation, that I may glory with Your inheritance.
6We have sinned like our fathers, we
have done iniquity, we have done
wickedly.
7Our fathers in Egypt gave no heed
unto Your wonders; they did not remember the abundance of Your lovingkindness; but were rebellious at the
sea, even at the Red Sea.
8Still He saved them for His name's
sake, that He might make His mighty
power to be known.
9And He rebuked the Red Sea, and it
was dried up; and He led them through
the depths, as through a wilderness.
10And He saved them from the hand
of him that hated them, and redeemed
them from the hand of the enemy.
11And the waters covered their enemies; there was not one of them left.
12Then believed they His words; they
sang His praise.
13They soon forgot His works; they
did not wait for His advise;
14But lusted exceedingly in the
wilderness, and tested God in the
desert.
15And He gave them their request;
but sent leanness into their soul.
16They were jealous also of Moses in
the camp, and of Aaron the holy one of
Yehovah.
17The earth opened and swallowed
up Dathan, and covered the company
of Abiram.
18And a fire broke out in their company; the flame burned up the wicked.
19They made a calf in Horeb, and
worshiped a molten image.
20And they exchanged their glory for
the likeness of an ox that eats grass.
21They forgot God their Saviour, who
had done great things in Egypt;
22Wondrous works in the land of
Ham, frightening things by the Red
Sea.
23And He said He would destroy
them, but Moses His chosen stood before Him in the breach, to turn away
His wrath, from destroying them.
24And they rejected the pleasant land,
they did not believe His word;
25And they complained in their tents,
they would not listen to the voice of
Yehovah.

26 And He raised His hand to them, to cause them to fall in the wilderness;

27 And that He would cast out their seed among the nations, and scatter them in the lands.

28 They joined themselves also unto Baal of Peor, and ate the sacrifices of the dead.

29 And they provoked Him with their doings, and the plague broke in upon them.

30 Then stood up Phinehas, and interceded and held back the plague.

31 And that was counted to him for righteousness, from generation to generation, forever.

32 They angered Him also at the waters of Meribah, and it went bad with Moses because of them;

33 For they provoked his spirit, and he spoke thoughtlessly with his lips.

34 They did not destroy the peoples, as Yehovah had told them;

35 But mingled themselves with the nations, and learned their works;

36 And they served their idols, which became a snare unto them;

37 Yes, they sacrificed their sons and their daughters unto demons,

38 And shed innocent blood, the blood of their sons and of their daughters, which they sacrificed unto the idols of Canaan; and the land was polluted with blood.

39 And were defiled with their works, and played the harlot in their deeds.

40 And the anger of Yehovah kindled against His people, and He detested His inheritance.

41 And He gave them into the hand of the nations; and those that hated them ruled over them.

42 Their enemies also oppressed them, and they were subdued under their power.

43 Many times did He deliver them; but they were rebellious in their plan, and sank low through their iniquity.

44 But He looked upon their distress, when He heard their singing;

45 And He remembered for them His covenant, and repented according to the multitude of His lovingkindnesses.

46 He made them also to be pitied of all those that carried them captive.

47 Save us, Yehovah our God, and gather us from among the nations, that we may give thanks unto Your Holy Name, that we may triumph in Your praise.

48 Blessed is Yehovah, the God of Israel, from everlasting even to everlasting, and let all the people say: ‘Amen.’ Halelu Yah.

Psalm 107

1 Give thanks unto Yehovah, for He is good, for His lovingkindness endures forever.’

2 So let the redeemed of Yehovah say, whom He has redeemed from the hand of the adversary;

3 And gathered them out of the lands, from the east and from the west, from the north and from the sea.

4 They wandered in the wilderness in a desert way; they found no city of habitation.

5 Hungry and thirsty, their soul fainted in them.

6 Then they cried unto Yehovah in their trouble, and He delivered them out of their distress.

7 And He led them by the upright way, that they might go to a city of habitation.

8 Let them give thanks unto Yehovah for His lovingkindness, and for His wonderful works to the children of men!

9For He has satisfied the longing
soul, and the hungry soul He has filled
with good.
10Such as sat in darkness and in the
shadow of death, being bound in affliction and iron–
11Because they rebelled against the
words of God, and despised the counsel of the Most High.
12Therefore He bowed down their
heart with toil, they stumbled, and
there was none to help.
13They cried unto Yehovah in their
trouble, and He saved them out of their
distresses.
14He brought them out of darkness
and the shadow of death, and broke
their bands in pieces.
15Let them give thanks unto Yehovah
for His mercy, and for His wonderful
works to the children of men!
16For He has broken the gates of
brass, and cut the bars of iron in pieces.
17Fools because of the way of their
transgression, are afflicted because of
their iniquities.
18Their souls loathed any kind of
food, until they touched the gates of
death.
19They cried unto Yehovah in their
distress, and He saved them;
20He sent His word, and healed them,
and delivered them from their graves.
21Give thanks unto Yehovah for His
lovingkindness, and for His wonderful
works to the children of men!
22And let them sacrifice the sacrifices
of thanksgiving, and declare His deeds
with singing.
23They go down to the sea in ships
that do business in great waters.
24These saw the works of Yehovah,
and His wonders in the deep;
25For He said stormy wind, and they
rose up, and lifted up the waves thereof;
26They mounted up to the heaven,
they went down to the deeps; their soul
melted away because of evil;
27They reeled to and fro, and stag-
gered like a drunken man, and all their
wisdom was swallowed up.
28They cried unto Yehovah in their
trouble, and He brought them out of
their distresses.
29He made the storm calm, and
waves were hushed.
30Then were they glad because they
were quiet, and He led them unto their
desired harbor.
31Let them give thanks unto Yehovah
for His lovingkindness, and for His
wonderful works to the children of
men!
32Let them lift Him high also in the
assembly of the people, and praise Him
in the seat of the elders.
33He changed rivers to a desert, and
waters to a thirsty ground;
34A fruitful land to a salt waste, for
the wickedness of them that dwell in it.
35He changed a wilderness into a
pool of water, and a dry land into waters.
36And there He makes the hungry to
dwell, and they establish a city of habitation;
37And sow fields, and plant vine-
yards, which yield a fruitful harvest.
38He blessed them also, so that they
are multiplied greatly, and their cattle
he does not decrease.
39And, they are diminished and
brought low through oppression of evil
and sorrow.
40He pours contempt upon princes,
and causes them to wander in the
waste, where there is no way.
41And He sets the needy on high
from affliction, and makes his families

like a flock.
[42]The upright see it, and are glad; and all iniquity stops her mouth.
[43]Who is wise, let him keep these things, and let them understand the lovingkindness of Yehovah.

Psalm 108

[1]A Song, a Psalm of David
[2]My heart is fixed O God; I will sing, yes, I will sing praises, even with my glory.
[3]Awake, harp and lyre; I will awake the dawn.
[4]I will praise You, among the people, Yehovah; and I will sing praises unto You among the tribes.
[5]For Your lovingkindness is great above the heavens, and Your truth reaches unto the skies.
[6]Lifted high above the heavens, O God; and Your glory above all the earth.
[7]That Your beloved may be delivered, save with Your right hand, and answer me.
[8]God spoke in His holiness, I shall rejoice; that I would divide Shechem, and I will measure out the valley of Succoth.
[9]Gilead is mine, Manasseh is mine; Ephraim is the protection of my head; Judah is my sceptre.
[10]Moab is my washpot; upon Edom do I cast my shoe; over Philistia do I shout.
[11]Who will bring me into the fortified city? Who will lead me into Edom?
[12]Have You not cast us off, O God? and do not go out with our hosts O God?
[13]Give us help against the enemy; for vain is the help of man.
[14]Through God we shall do valiantly; for He it is that will tread down our enemies.

Psalm 109

[1]For the Conductor. A Psalm of David. O God of my praise, keep not silence;
[2]For the mouth of the wicked and the mouth of deceit they have opened against me; they have spoken unto me with a lying tongue.
[3]They surrounded me with words of hatred, and fought against me without a cause.
[4]In return for my love they are my adversaries; but I am praying.
[5]And they have laid upon me evil for good, and hatred for my love:
[6]'Set a wicked man over him; and let an adversary stand at his right hand.
[7]When he is judged, let him go forth condemned; and let his prayer be turned into sin.
[8]Let his days be few; let another take his charge.
[9]Let his children be fatherless, and his wife a widow.
[10]Let his children be vaga-bonds, and beg; and let them seek their bread out of their desolate places.
[11]Let the creditor seize all that he has; and let strangers plunder all of his labour.
[12]Let there be none to extend lovingkindness unto him; neither let there be any to pity his fatherless children.
[13]Let his descendants be cut off; in the generation following let their name be destroyed.
[14]Let the iniquity of his fathers be brought to remembrance unto Yehovah; and let not the sin of his mother be destroyed.
[15]Let them be before Yehovah continually, that He may cut off the memory of them from the earth.

16 Because he remembered not to do lovingkindness, but pursued the poor and needy man, and the broken in heart to their death

17 And he loved cursing, and it came upon him; and he delighted not in blessing, and it is far from him.

18 He clothed himself with cursing as his coat, and it is come into his inward parts like water, and like oil into his bones.

19 Let it be unto him as the garment which he clothes himself and as a belt with which he wears continually.'

20 This is the reward of my accusers from Yehovah, and those who speak evil against my soul.

21 But You, Yehovah my Lord, do for me for Your name's sake; because Your lovingkindness is good, deliver me.

22 For I am poor and needy, and my heart is pierced within me.

23 I am gone like a shadow stretched out; I am shaken off like the locust.

24 My knees are weak through fasting; and my flesh has become gaunt

25 I am become also a disgrace to them; when they see me, they shake their head.

26 Help me, Yehovah my God; O save me according to Your lovingkindness;

27 That they may know that this is Your hand; that You, Yehovah, have done it.

28 Let them curse, but You bless; when they arise, they shall be ashamed, but Your servant shall rejoice.

29 My adversaries shall be clothed with dishonor, and shall put on their own shame as a mantle.

30 I will greatly praise Yehovah with my mouth; and in the midst of the multitude I will boast in Him.

31 Because He stands at the right hand of the needy, to save him from them that judge his soul.

Psalm 110

1 A Song of David. Yahovah said to my Lord, "Sit at My right hand until I make Your enemies a stool for your feet."

2 Yahoah shall send from Zion the rod of your strength; rule in the midst of your enemies.

3 Your people shall be willing in the day of Your power in the splendor of holiness from the womb of the morning: you have the dew of your youth.

4 Yehovah has sworn, and will not repent: 'You are a priest forever after the manner of Mel-chizedek.'

5 The Lord at Your right hand will crush kings in the day of His wrath.

6 He will judge among the nations; He fills it with dead bodies, He crushes the head over a wide land.

7 He shall drink from the river on the way– therefore He shall be exalted as the head.

Psalm 111

1 Halelu Yah! I will give thanks unto Yehovah with my whole heart, in the council of the upright, and in the congregation.

2 The works of Yehovah are great, sought out of all them that have delight in them.

3 His work is glory and majesty; and His righteousness endures forever.

4 He has made a memorial for His wonderful works; Yehovah is gracious and full of compassion.

5 He has given food unto them that fear Him; He will ever be mindful of His covenant.

6 He has declared to His people the power of His works, in giving them the heritage of the nations.

7The works of His hands are truth and justice; all His precepts are sure.

8They are established for ever and ever, they are done in truth and uprightness.

9He has sent redemption unto His people; He has commanded His covenant forever; Holy and awesome is His name.

10The fear of Yehovah is the beginning of wisdom; a good understanding have all they that do them; His praise endures for ever.

Psalm 112

1Halelu Yah! Happy is the man that fears Yehovah, that delights greatly in His commandments.

2Mighty upon the Earth shall his children be – the generation of the upright shall be blessed.

3Wealth and riches are in his house and his righteousness remains forever.

4Unto the upright He shines as a light in the darkness, gracious, merciful, and righteous.

5Well is it with the man that deals graciously and lends, and conducts his affairs with justice.

6For he shall never be moved; the righteous shall be in everlasting remembrance.

7He shall not be afraid of evil reports; his heart is steadfast, trusting in Yehovah.

8His heart is established, he shall not be afraid, until he gaze upon his adversaries.

9He has scattered abroad, he has given to the needy; his righteousness endures forever; his horn shall be exalted in honour.

10The wicked shall see it, and be vexed; he shall gnash his teeth, and melt away; the desire of the wicked shall perish.

Psalm 113

1HaleluYah! Praise, servants of Yehovah, praise the name of Yehovah.

2Blessed be the name of Yehovah from this time forth and forever.

3From the rising of the sun unto the going down thereof Yehovah's name is to be praised.

4Yehovah is high above all nations, His glory is above the heavens.

5Who is like unto Yehovah our God, that is enthroned on high,

6That looks down upon heaven and upon the earth?

7Who raises up the poor out of the dust, and lifts up the needy out of the dunghill;

8That He may set him with princes, even with the princes of His people.

9Who makes the barren woman to dwell in her house as a joyful mother of children. Halelu Yah!

Psalm 114

1When Israel came forth out of Egypt, the house of Jacob from a people of strange language;

2Judah became His sanctuary, Israel His dominion.

3The sea saw it, and fled; the Jordan turned backward.

4The mountains skipped like rams, the hills like lambs.

5What ails you, O sea, that you flee? Jordan, that you turn backward?

6Mountains that you skip like rams; you hills, like lambs?

7Tremble earth, at the presence of the Lord, at the presence of the God of Jacob;

8Who turned the rock into a pool of water, the flint into a fountain of waters.

Psalm 115

1Not unto us, Yehovah, not unto us,
but unto Your name give glory, for
Your lovingkindness, and for Your
truth's sake.
2Why should the nations say: 'Where
is their God now?'
3But our God is in the heavens;
whatever pleased Him He has done.
4Their idols are silver and gold, the
work of men's hands.
5They have mouths, but they speak
not; they have eyes, but they see not;
6They have ears, but they hear not;
they have noses, but they smell not;
7They have hands, but they handle
not; they have feet, but they walk not;
neither do they speak with their throat.
8They that make them shall be like
unto them; yes, every one that trusts in
them.
9O Israel, trust in Yehovah! He is
their help and their shield!
10O house of Aaron, trust in Yehovah! He is their help and their shield!
11You that fear Yehovah, trust in
Yehovah! He is their help and their
shield.
12Yehovah has been mindful of us,
He will bless—He will bless the house
of Israel; He will bless the house of
Aaron.
13He will bless them that fear Yehovah, both small and great.
14Yehovah increase you more and
more, you and your children.
15Blessed are you of Yehovah who
made heaven and earth.
16The heavens are the heavens of
Yehovah; but the earth has He given to
the children of men.
17The dead do not praise Yehovah,
neither any that go down into silence;
18But we will bless Yehovah from this
time forth and forever. Halelu Yah!

Psalm 116

1I love that Yehovah should hear my
voice and my supplications.
2Because He has inclined His ear
unto me, therefore will I call upon Him
all my days.
3The cords of death swirled around
me, and the pains of Sheol took hold of
me; trouble and sorrow found me.
4But I called upon the name of Yehovah: O please, Yehovah, save my soul.
5Yahovah, You are gracious and
righteous, and our God of mercy.
6Yehovah preserves the simple; I was
brought low, and He rescued me.
7Return, O my soul, unto your rest-
ing place; for Yehovah has dealt bountifully with you
8You have delivered my soul from
death, my eyes from tears, and my feet
from stumbling.
9I shall walk before Yehovah in the
lands of the living.
10I trusted when I spoke: 'I am greatly afflicted.'
11I said in my haste: 'All men are
liars.'
12How can I repay Yehovah for all
His benefits toward me?
13I will lift up the cup of salvation,
and call upon the name of Yehovah.
14My vows will I pay unto Yehovah,
in the presence of all His people.
15Precious in the eyes of Yehovah is
the death of His saints.
16Please, Yehovah, for I am Your servant; I am Your servant, the son of
Your handmaid; You have unlocked my
chains
17I will sacrifice the sacrifice of
thanksgiving to You, and will call upon
the name of Yehovah.
18I will fulfill my vows unto Yehovah,
in the presence of all His people;
19In the courts of Yehovah's house, in

the midst of you, O Jerusalem. Halelu
Yah!

Psalm 117

1Praise Yehovah, all you nations; glorify Him, all you peoples.
2For His mercy is great toward us;
and the truth of Yehovah endures forever. Halelu Yah!

Psalm 118

1Give thanks unto Yehovah, for He is
good, for His mercy endures forever.
2So let Israel now say, for His mercy
endures forever,
3So let the house of Aaron now say,
for His mercy endures forever.
4So let them now that fear Yehovah
say, for His mercy endures forever.
5Out of my anguish I called upon
Yah; Yah answered me in a large place.
6Yehovah is for me; I will not fear;
what man can do to me?
7Yehovah is for me as my helper; and
I shall look upon them that hate me.
8It is better to take refuge in Yehovah
than to trust in man.
9It is better to take refuge in Yehovah
than to trust in princes.
10All nations surrounded me; in the
name of Yehovah I will cut them off.
11They surround me, even they surrounded me; in the name of Yehovah I
will cut them off.
12They surrounded me like bees; they
were quenched as the fire of thorns; in
the name of Yehovah I will cut them
off.
13You pushed me hard that I might
fall; but Yehovah helped me.
14Yah is my strength and song; and
He has become my salvation.
15The voice of rejoicing and salvation
is in the tents of the righteous; the right
hand of Yehovah does valiantly.
16The right hand of Yehovah is lifted
high; the right hand of Yehovah does
valiantly.
17I shall not die, but live, and declare
the works of Yah.
18Yah has severely disciplined me; but
He has not given me over unto death.
19Open to me the gates of righteousness; I will enter into them, I will
give thanks unto Yah.
20This is the gate of Yehovah the
righteous shall enter into it.
21I will praise You, for You have answered me, and have become my salvation.
22The stone which the builders rejected has become the chief cornerstone.
23This is Yehovah's doing; it is marvelous in our eyes.
24This is the day Yehovah made – we
will rejoice and be glad in Him!
25We beseech You, Yehovah, save
now! We beseech You, Yehovah, make
us now to prosper!
26Blessed be he that comes in the
name of Yehovah; we bless you out of
the house of Yehovah.
27Yehovah is God, and has given us
light; bind the festival procession with
boughs, even unto the horns of the altar.
28You are my God, and I will give
thanks unto You; You are my God, I
will lift You high.
29O give thanks unto Yehovah, for He
is good, for His lovingkindness endures
forever.

Psalm 119

א ALEPH

1Blessed are those whose ways are
blameless who walk in the law of Yehovah.
2Blessed are those who keep His tes-

timonies and seek Him with a whole
heart.
3They also do no iniquity they walk
in His ways.
4You have commanded your instructions to be kept diligently.
5Oh that my ways may be steadfast to
keep your statutes.
6Then I shall not be ashamed having
gazed upon all your commandments.
7I will praise you with an upright
heart when I learn your righteous
judgements.
8I will keep your statutes do not utterly forsake me.

ב BET

9By what shall a young man keep his
way pure? By watching according to
Your word.
10With my whole heart I have sought
You; O let me not go astray from Your
commandments.
11Your word have I hid in my heart,
that I might not sin against You.
12Blessed are You, Yehovah; teach me
Your statutes.
13With my lips I have recounted all of
the judgments of Your mouth.
14I have rejoiced in the way of Your
testimonies, as much as in all riches.
15I will meditate in Your instructions,
and have respect unto Your ways.
16I will delight myself in Your
statutes; I will not neglect Your word.

ג GIMEL

17Deal bountifully with Your servant
that I may live, and I will keep Your
word.
18Open my eyes, that I may behold
wondrous things out of Your law.
19I am a sojourner in the earth; Do
not hide Your commandments from
me.
20My soul is overwhelmed for the
longing that it has for Your judgments
at all times.
21You have rebuked the proud that
are cursed, that go astray from Your
commandments.
22Roll away from me reproach and
contempt; for I have kept Your testimonies.
23Even though princes sit and talk
against me, Your servant meditates in
Your statutes.
24Also, Your testimonies are my delight, they are my counsellors.

ד DALETH

25My soul cleaves unto the dust; revive me according to Your word.
26I recounted my ways, and You answer me; teach me Your statutes.
27Make me to understand the way of
Your instructions, that I may meditate
in Your wondrous works.
28My soul sheds tears of sorrow; sustain me according unto Your word.
29Remove from me the way of lies;
and Your law give graciously.
30I have chosen the way of faithfulness; Your judgments I desire.
31I cleave to Your testimonies; Yehovah, put me not to shame.
32I will run the way of Your commandments, for You enlarge my heart.

ה HE

33Teach me, Yehovah, the way of
Your statutes; and I will keep it to the
end.
34Give me understanding, that I observe Your law and keep it with my
whole heart.
35Lead me in the path of Your commandments; for in Him I delight.
36Draw my heart unto Your testimonies, and not to gain.

37 Turn away my eyes from beholding vanity, and give me life in Your ways.

38 Confirm Your word unto Your servant, which pertains unto Your fear.

39 Turn away my reproach which I dread; for Your judgments are good.

40 Behold, I have longed after Your instructions; make me alive in Your righteousness.

ו VAV

41 And let Your lovingkindness come to me, Yehovah, Your salvation, according to Your word;

42 And I shall have an answer for him who reproaches me, for I trust in Your word.

43 And take not the very word of truth out of my mouth; for I wait on Your commandments.

44 And I will keep Your law continually forever and ever.

45 And I will walk at ease, for I have sought Your instructions.

46 And I will also speak of Your testimonies before kings, and will not be ashamed.

47 And I will take joy in Your commandments, which I have loved.

48 And I will lift up my hands also unto Your commandments, which I have loved; and I will meditate in Your statutes.

ז ZAIN

49 Remember the word unto Your servant, in which you cause me to hope.

50 This is my comfort in my affliction, that Your word has qiven me life.

51 The proud have utterly mocked me; yet I have not turned aside from Your law.

52 I have remembered Your judgments from of old, Yehovah, and have comforted myself.

53 Burning indignation has taken hold of me, because of the wicked that forsake Your law.

54 Your statutes have been my songs in the house of my pilgrimage.

55 I have remembered Your name in the night Yehovah, and have kept Your law.

56 This I have had, that I have kept Your instructions.

ח CHETH

57 Yehovah is my portion, I have said I will keep Your words.

58 I have sought your face with my whole heart; be gracious unto me according to Your word.

59 I considered my ways, and turned my feet unto Your testimonies.

60 I hurry, and do not delay, to keep Your commandments.

61 The cords of the wicked bind me; I do not forget Your law.

62 At midnight I will rise to give thanks unto You because of Your righteous judgments.

63 I am a companion of all them that fear You, and of them that keep your instructions.

64 The earth, O Lord, is full of Your lovingkindness; teach me Your statutes.

ט TET

65 You have dealt well with Your servant, Yehovah, according to your word.

66 Teach me good discernment and understanding; for I have believed Your commandments.

67 Before I was afflicted, I erred; but now I keep Your word.

68 You are good, and do good; teach me Your statutes.

69 The proud smear me with lies; but I will keep Your instructions with my

whole heart.

70 Their heart is insensitive like fat; I take joy in Your law.

71 It is good for me that I have been afflicted, in order that I might learn Your statutes.

72 The law of Your mouth is better to me than thousands of gold and silver.

י YOD

73 Your hands made me and fashioned me; give me understanding, that I may learn Your commandments.

74 They that fear You shall see me and rejoice, because I have hope in Your word.

75 I know, Yehovah, that Your judgments are righteous, and that in faithfulness You have afflicted me.

76 Let, I pray, your lovingkindness comfort me, according to Your word to your servant.

77 Let Your tender mercies come unto me, that I may live; for Your law is my delight.

78 Let the proud be ashamed, for they have wronged me with lies; but I will meditate in Your instructions.

79 Let those that fear You return unto me, and they that know Your testimonies.

80 Let my heart be blameless in Your statutes, that I may not be ashamed.

כ CAPH

81 My soul pines for Your salvation; I hope in Your word.

82 My eyes long for Your word, saying: 'When will You comfort me?'

83 For I am become like a wine-skin in the smoke; yet I do not forget Your statutes.

84 How many are the days of Your servant? When will You execute judgment on them that persecute me?

85 The proud have dug pits for me, which is not according to Your law.

86 All Your commandments are faithful; they persecute me falsely; help me.

87 They had almost destroyed me upon earth; but as for me, I forsook not Your Instructions.

88 According to Your lovingkindness make me live, and I will observe the testimony of Your mouth.

ל LAMED

89 Forever, Yehovah, Your word is settled in heaven.

90 Your faithfulness is unto all generations; You have established the earth, and it stands.

91 By Your ordinances they stand today; for all are Your servants.

92 Unless Your law had been my delight, I would have perished in my affliction.

93 I will never forget Your Instructions; for with them You have made me alive.

94 I am Yours, save me; for I have sought your instructions.

95 The wicked have waited for me to destroy me; I will consider Your testimonies.

96 I have seen a limit to every good thing; but Your commandment is exceeding wide.

מ MEM

97 O how I love Your law! It is my meditation all day.

98 Your commandments make me wiser than my enemies: for they are ever with me.

99 I have more understanding than all my teachers; for Your testimonies are my meditation.

100 I understand more than my elders, because I have kept Your instruction.

101 have refrained my feet from every
evil way, in order that I might keep
Your Word.
102I have not turned aside from Your
judgments; for You have taught me.
103How sweet are Your words unto
my taste! Like honey to my mouth!
104From Your instruction I get understanding; therefore I hate every false
way.

נ NUN

105Your Word is a lamp unto my feet,
and a light unto my path.
106I have sworn, and have confirmed
it, to keep Your righteous judgments.
107I am afflicted very much; revive
me, Yehovah, according unto Your
word.
108Yehovah be pleased I pray with the
freewill-offerings of my mouth, and
teach me Your judgments.
109My soul is in my hand continually
and I have not forgotten Your law.
110The wicked laid a snare for me; but
I have not wandered from Your instruction.
111Your testimonies are my inheritance forever; for they are the rejoicing
of my heart.
112I have inclined my heart to perform Your statutes forever, at the end of
every step.

ס SAMECH

113I hate double mindedness; but
Your Law I love.
114You are my hiding place and my
shield; I hope in Your Word.
115Remove wickedness from me; that
I may keep the commandments of my
God.
116Uphold me according to Your
Word, that I may live; and put me not
to shame in my hope.
117Support me and I shall be saved;
and I will pay attention to Your statutes
continually.
118Reject all who have gone astray
from Your statutes; for their deceit is
falsehood.
119You destroy all the wicked of the
earth like dross; therefore I love Your
testimonies. 120 My flesh trembles for
fear of You; and I am afraid of Your
judgments.

ע AIN

121I have done judgment and righteousness; leave me not to mine oppressors.
122Be surety for Your servant for
good; let not the proud oppress me.
123Mine eyes fail for Your salvation,
and for Your righteous word.
124Do with Your servant according
unto Your lovingkindness, and teach
me Your statutes.
125I am Your servant, give me understanding, that I may know Your testimonies.
126It is time for Yehovah to work;
they have made void Your law.
127Therefore I love Your commandments above gold, yea, above refined
gold.
128For all the instructions I consider
truly right; every false way I hate.

פ PE

129Your testimonies are wonderful;
therefore my soul keeps them.
130The revelation of Your words gives
light; it gives understanding unto the
simple.
131I opened wide my mouth, and
panted; for I longed for Your commandments.
132Turn towards me, and be gracious
unto me, as judgment towards those

who love Your name.

133 Order my footsteps by Your word; and let not any iniquity have dominion over me.

134 Redeem me from the oppression of Adam, and I will keep Your instructions.

135 Cause Your face to shine upon Your servant; and teach me Your statutes.

136 My eyes run down with rivers of water, because they do not observe Your law.

צ TZADE

137 Righteous are You, Yehovah, and upright are Your judgments.

138 You have commanded Your testimonies in righteousness and exceeding faithfulness.

139 My zeal has consumed me, because my foes have forgotten Your words.

140 Your word is tried to the uttermost, and Your servant loves it.

141 I am small and despised; yet have I not forgotten Your instructions.

142 Your righteousness is an everlasting righteousness, and Your law is true.

143 Trouble and anguish have overtaken me; yet Your commandments are my delight.

144 Your testimonies are righteous forever; give me understanding, and I shall live.

ק KOPH

145 I have called with my whole heart; answer me, Yehovah; I will keep Your statutes.

146 I have called You, save me, and I will keep Your testimonies.

147 I rose early at dawn, and cried for help; I hoped in Your word.

148 Mine eyes look toward you in the night-watches, that I might meditate in Your word.

149 Hear my voice according unto Your lovingkindness; Yehovah, according to Your judgments let me live.

150 They draw near that follow after wickedness; they are far from Your law.

151 You are near Yehovah; and all Your commandments are truth.

152 Of old have I known from Your testimonies that You have founded them forever.

ר RESH

153 See my affliction, and rescue me; for I do not neglect Your law

154 Plead my cause, and redeem me; quicken according to your word, give me life.

155 Salvation is far from the wicked; for they do not seek Your statutes.

156 Many are your mercies Yehovah; according to Your judgments give me life.

157 Many are my persecutors and mine adversaries; yet have I not turned aside from Your testimonies.

158 I beheld them that were faithless, and was grieved; because they did not observe Your word.

159 See how I love Your instructions Yehovah; give me life according to Your lovingkindness.

160 Your word is the sum of truth and all your righteous judgments are forever.

ש SHIN

161 Princes have persecuted me without a cause; but my heart stands in awe of Your words.

162 I rejoice at Your word, as one that finds great spoil.

163 I hate and abhor falsehood; I love Your law.

164Seven times a day do I praise You,
because of Your righteous judgments.
165Great peace have they that love
Your law; and there is no stumbling for
them.
166I have hoped for Your salvation,
Yehovah, and have done Your commandments.
167My soul has observed Your testimonies; and I love them exceedingly.
168I have observed Your instructions
and Your testimonies; for all my ways
are before You.

ת TAV

169Let my cry come near before You,
Yehovah; give me understanding according to Your word.
170Let my supplication come before
You; deliver me according to Your
word.
171My lips shall bubble up with
praise: because You teach me Your
statutes.
172My tongue shall sing of Your word;
for all Your commandments are righteousness.
173Let Your hand be ready to help me;
for I have chosen Your instructions.
174I have longed for Your salvation,
Yehovah; and Your law is my delight.
175Let my soul live, and it shall praise
You; and let Your judgments help me.
176I have gone astray like a lost sheep;
seek Your servant; for I have not forgotten Your commandments.

Psalm 120

1A Song of Ascents. In my distress I
called unto Yehovah, and He answered
me.
2Yehovah, deliver my soul from lying
lips, from a deceitful tongue.
3What shall be given unto you, and
what shall be done more unto you, you
deceitful tongue?
4Sharp arrows of the mighty, with
coals of broom.
5Woe is me, that I sojourn with
Meshech, that I dwell beside the tents
of Kedar!
6My soul has long had her dwelling
with him that hates peace.
7I am for peace; but when I speak,
they are for war.

Psalm 121

1A Song of Ascents. I will lift up
mine eyes unto the mountains: from
where shall my help come?
2My help comes from Yehovah, who
made heaven and earth.
3He will not allow your foot to be
moved; He that keeps you will not
slumber.
4Behold, He that keeps Israel does
not slumber or sleep.
5Yehovah is your keeper; Yehovah is
your shade at your right hand.
6The sun shall not smite you by day,
nor the moon by night.
7Yehovah shall keep you from all evil;
He shall keep your soul.
8Yehovah shall guard your going out
and your coming in, from this time
forth and forever.

Psalm 122

1A Song of Ascents; of David. I rejoiced when they said unto me: 'Let us
go unto the house of Yehovah.
2Our feet are standing within your
gates, O Jerusalem;
3Jerusalem, that is built as a city that
is compact together;
4Whither the tribes went up, even the
tribes of the Yehovah, as a testimony
unto Israel, to give thanks unto the
name of Yehovah.
5For there were set thrones for judg-

ment, the thrones of the house of David.

6 Pray for the peace of Jeru-salem; may they prosper that love you.

7 Peace be within your walls, and prosperity within your palaces.

8 For my brethren and companions' sakes, I will now say: 'Peace be within you.'

9 For the sake of the house of Yehovah our God I will seek your good.

Psalm 123

1 A Song of Ascents. Unto You I lift up mine eyes, O You that are enthroned in the heavens.

2 Behold, as the eyes of servants unto the hand of their master, as the eyes of a maiden unto the hand of her mistress; so our eyes look unto Yehovah our God, until He be gracious unto us.

3 Be gracious unto us, Yehovah, be gracious unto us; for we have had enough with contempt.

4 Our soul has had enough with the scorning of those that are at ease, and with the contempt of the proud oppressors.

Psalm 124

1 A Song of Ascents; of David. 'If it had not been Yehovah who was for us', let Israel now say;

2 'If it had not been Yehovah who was for us, when man rose up against us,

3 Then they had swallowed us up alive, when their wrath was kindled against us;

4 Then the waters had overwhelmed us, the stream had gone over our soul;

5 Then the proud waters had gone over our soul.'

6 Blessed be Yehovah, who has not given us as a prey to their teeth.

7 Our soul is escaped as a bird out of the snare of the fowlers; the snare is broken, and we are escaped.

8 Our help is in the name of Yehovah, who made heaven and earth.

Psalm 125

1 A song of ascent. They who put their trust in Yehovah will be as Mount Zion, which cannot be shaken, but abides forever.

2 As the mountains are round about Jerusalem, so Yehovah is round about His people, from this time forth and forever.

3 For the rod of wickedness shall not rest upon the lot of the righteous; unless the righteous put forth their hands unto iniquity.

4 Do good, Yehovah, unto the good, and to them that are upright in their hearts.

5 But as for such as turn aside unto their crooked ways, Yehovah will lead them away with the workers of iniquity. Peace be upon Israel.

Psalm 126

1 A Song of Ascents. When Yehovah brought back those that returned to Zion, we were like unto them that dream.

2 Then was our mouth filled with laughter, and our tongue with singing; then said they among the nations: 'Yehovah has done great things with them.'

3 Yehovah has done great things with us; we rejoice!

4 Turn our captivity, Yehovah, as the streams in the dry land.

5 They that sow in tears shall reap in joy.

6 Though he goes on his way weeping that bears the measure of seed, he shall come home with joy, bearing his

sheaves.

Psalm 127

1 A Song of Ascents; of Solomon. Except Yehovah build the house, they labor in vain that build it; except Yehovah keep the city, the watchman wakes but in vain.

2 It is vain for you that you rise early, and sit up late, you that eat the bread of toil; so He gives unto His beloved sleep.

3 Behold, children are a heritage of Yehovah; the fruit of the womb is a reward.

4 As arrows in the hand of a mighty man, so are the children of one's youth.

5 Happy is the man that has his quiver full of them; they shall not be put to shame, when they speak with their enemies in the gate.

Psalm 128

1 A Song of Ascents. Happy is everyone who fears Yehovah, who walks in His ways.

2 When you eat the labor of your hands, you shall be happy, and it shall be well with you.

3 Your wife shall be as a fruitful vine, in the innermost parts of your house; your children like olive plants round about your table.

4 Behold, surely this man shall be blessed who fears Yehovah.

5 Yehovah bless you out of Zion; that you see the good of Jeru-salem all the days of your life;

6 And see your children's children. Peace be upon Israel!

Psalm 129

1 A Song of Ascents. 'Much have they afflicted me from my youth up,' let Israel now say;

2 'Much have they afflicted me from my youth up; but they have not prevailed against me.

3 The plowers plowed upon my back; they made long their furrows.

4 Yehovah is righteous; He has cut asunder the cords of the wicked.'

5 Let them be ashamed and turned backward, all they that hate Zion.

6 Let them be as the grass upon the housetops, which withers before it springs up;

7 With which the reaper does not fill his hand, nor he that binds sheaves his bosom.

8 Neither do they that go by say: 'The blessing of Yehovah be upon you; we bless you in the name of Yehovah.'

Psalm 130

1 A Song of Ascents. Out of the depths have I called You, Yehovah.

2 Lord, hearken unto my voice; let Your ears be attentive to the voice of my supplications.

3 If You, Yehovah, should mark iniquities, O Lord, who could stand?

4 For with You there is forgiveness, that You may be feared.

5 I wait for Yehovah, my soul does wait, and in His word do I hope.

6 My soul waits for the Lord, more than watchmen for the morning; yes, more than watchmen for the morning.

7 O Israel, wait on Yehovah; for with Yehovah there is mercy, and with Him is plenteous redemption.

8 And He will redeem Israel from all his iniquities.

Psalm 131

1 A Song of Ascents; of David. Yehovah, my heart is not haughty, nor my eyes lofty; neither do I exercise myself in things too great, or in things too wonderful for me.

2 Surely I have stilled and quieted my soul; like a weaned child with his mother; my soul is with me like a weaned child.

3 O Israel, wait on Yehovah from this time forth and forever.

Psalm 132

1 A Song of Ascents. Yehovah, remember all the afflictions of David;

2 How he swore unto Yehovah, and vowed unto the Mighty One of Jacob:

3 'Surely I will not come into the tent of my house, nor go up into the bed that is spread for me;

4 I will not give sleep to mine eyes, nor slumber to mine eyelids;

5 Until I find out a place for Yehovah, a dwelling-place for the Mighty One of Jacob.'

6 Behold, we heard of it as being in Ephrath; we found it in the field of the wood.

7 Let us go into His dwelling-place; let us worship at His footstool.

8 Arise, Yehovah, unto Your resting-place; You, and the ark of Your strength.

9 Let Your priests be clothed with righteousness; and let Your holy ones shout for joy.

10 For Your servant David's sake do not turn away the face of Your anointed.

11 Yehovah swore unto David in truth; He will not turn back from it: 'Of the fruit of your body will I set upon your throne.

12 If your children keep My covenant and My testimony that I shall teach them, their children also forever shall sit upon your throne.'

13 For Yehovah has chosen Zion; He has desired it for His habitation:

14 'This is My resting-place forever; here will I dwell; for I have desired it.

15 I will abundantly bless her provision; I will satisfy her poor with bread.

16 Her priests also will I clothe with salvation; and her holy ones shall shout aloud for joy.

17 There will I make a horn to shoot up unto David, there have I ordered a lamp for My anointed.

18 His enemies will I clothe with shame; but upon him, his crown shall shine.'

Psalm 133

1 A Song of Ascents; of David. Behold, how good and how pleasant it is for brethren to dwell together in unity!

2 It is like the precious oil upon the head, coming down upon the beard; even Aaron's beard, that comes down upon the collar of his garments;

3 Like the dew of Hermon, that comes down upon the mountains of Zion; for there Yehovah commanded the blessing, even life forever.

Psalm 134

1 A Song of Ascents. Behold, bless Yehovah, all you servants of Yehovah, who stand by night in the house of Yehovah..

2 Lift up your hands in the holy place, and bless Yehovah.

3 Yehovah bless you out of Zion; even He that made heaven and earth.

Psalm 135

1 Halelu Yah. Praise the name of Yehovah; give praise, O you servants of Yehovah,

2 You that stand in the house of Yehovah, in the courts of the house of our God.

3 Praise Yehovah, for Yehovah is good; sing praises unto His name, for it is

pleasant.
[4]For Yehovah has chosen Jacob for
Himself, and Israel for His own treasure.
[5]For I know that Yehovah is great,
and that our Lord is above all gods.
[6]Whatever Yehovah delighted, that
has He done, in heaven and in earth, in
the seas and in all deeps;
[7]Who caused the storm clouds to ascend from the ends of the earth; He
makes lightning for the rain; He brings
forth the wind out of His treasuries.
[8]Who smote the first-born of Egypt,
both man and beast.
[9]He sent signs and wonders into the
midst of you, O Egypt, upon Pharaoh,
and upon all his servants.
[10]Who smote many nations, and slew
mighty kings:
[11]Sihon king of the Amorites, and Og
king of Bashan, and all the kingdoms of
Canaan;
[12]And gave their land for a heritage, a
heritage unto Israel His people.
[13]Yehovah, Your name endures forever; your memorial, Yehovah, throughout all generations.
[14]For Yehovah will judge His people,
and repent Himself for His servants.
[15]The idols of the nations are silver
and gold, the work of men's hands.
[16]They have mouths, but they speak
not; they have eyes, but they see not;
[17]They have ears, but they hear not;
neither is there any breath in their
mouths.
[18]They that make them shall be like
unto them; yes, every one that trusts in
them.
[19]O house of Israel, bless Yehovah; O
house of Aaron, bless Yehovah;
[20]O house of Levi, bless Yehovah; you
that fear Yehovah, bless Yehovah.
[21]Blessed be Yehovah out of Zion,
who dwells at Jerusalem. Halleluyah.

Psalm 136

[1]O give thanks unto Yehovah, for He
is good, for His mercy endures forever.
[2]O give thanks unto the God of gods,
for His mercy endures forever.
[3]O give thanks unto the Lord of
lords, for His mercy endures forever.
[4]To Him who alone does great wonders, for His mercy endures forever.
[5]To Him that by understanding made
the heavens, for His mercy endures
forever.
[6]To Him that spread out the earth
upon the waters, for His mercy endures
forever.
[7]To Him that made great lights, for
His mercy endures forever;
[8]The sun to rule by day, for His mercy endures forever;
[9]The moon and stars to rule by night,
for His mercy endures forever.
[10]To Him that smote Egypt in their
first-born, for His mercy endures forever;
[11]And brought out Israel from among
them, for His mercy endures forever;
[12]With a strong hand, and with an
outstretched arm, for His mercy endures forever.
[13]To Him who divided the Red Sea in
sunder, for His mercy endures forever;
[14]And made Israel to pass through
the midst of it, for His mercy endures
forever;
[15]But overthrew Pharaoh and his
host in the Red Sea, for His mercy endures forever.
[16]To Him that led His people through
the wilderness, for His mercy endures
forever.
[17]To Him that smote great kings; for
His mercy endures forever;
[18]And slew mighty kings, for His

mercy endures forever.

19Sihon king of the Amorites, for His mercy endures forever;

20And Og king of Bashan, for His mercy endures forever;

21And gave their land for a heritage, for His mercy endures forever;

22Even a heritage unto Israel His servant, for His mercy endures forever.

23Who remembered us in our low estate, for His mercy endures forever;

24And has delivered us from our adversaries, for His mercy endures forever.

25Who gives food to all flesh, for His mercy endures forever.

26O give thanks unto the God of heaven, for His mercy endures forever.

Psalm 137

1By the rivers of Babylon, there we sat down, and, we wept, when we remembered Zion.

2Upon the willows in the midst thereof we hung up our harps.

3For there they that led us captive asked of us words of a song, and our tormentors asked of us mirth: 'Sing us one of the songs of Zion.'

4How shall we sing Yehovah's song in a foreign land?

5If I forget you, O Jerusalem, let my right hand forget her cunning.

6Let my tongue cleave to the roof of my mouth, if I do not remember you; if I set not Jerusalem above my chiefest joy.

7Remember, Yehovah, against the children of Edom the day of Jerusalem; who said: 'Raze it, raze it, even to the foundation thereof.'

8O daughter of Babylon, that is to be destroyed; happy shall he be, that repays you as you have served us.

9Happy shall he be, that takes and dashes your little ones against the rock

Psalm 138

1Of David, I will give thanks to You with all my heart. In the presence of God I will sing praise.

2I will bow down toward Your holy temple, and give thanks unto Your name for Your mercy and for Your truth; for You have magnified Your word above all Your name.

3In the day that I called, You answered me; You encouraged me in my soul with strength.

4All the kings of the Earth shall give You thanks, Yehovah, for they have heard the words of Your mouth.

5Yea, they shall sing of the ways of Yehovah; for great is the glory of Yehovah.

6For though Yehovah be high, yet He regards the lowly, and the haughty He knows from afar.

7Though I walk in the midst of trouble, You quicken me; You stretch forth Your hand against the wrath of mine enemies, and Your right hand saves me.

8Yehovah will accomplish that which concerns me; Your mercy, Yehovah, endures for ever; forsake not the work of Your own hands.

Psalm 139

1A song of David to the directors Yehovah you have searched me and you know.

2You know when I sit down and when I rise up you discern my thoughts that are far away.

3My wandering and my lying down you winnow and you are familiar with all of my ways.

4For there is not an utterance in my tongue but lo Yehovah you know it all.

5You have surrounded me in front

and behind and you have placed your hand upon me.

6 This knowledge is incomprehensible to me it is beyond what I can grasp.

7 Whither shall I go from Your spirit? or whither shall I flee from Your presence?

8 If I ascend up into heaven, You are there; if I make my bed in hell, behold, You are there.

9 If I take the wings of the morning, and dwell in the uttermost parts of the sea;

10 Even there would Your hand lead me, and Your right hand would hold me.

11 And if I say: 'Surely the darkness shall envelop me, and the light about me shall be night';

12 Even the darkness is not too dark for You, but the night shines as the day; the darkness is even as the light.

13 For You have made my reins; You have knit me together in my mother's womb.

14 I will give thanks unto You, for I am fearfully and wonderfully made; wonderful are Your works; and that my soul knows right well.

15 My frame was not hidden from You, when I was made in secret, and curiously wrought in the lowest parts of the earth.

16 Your eyes did see my unformed substance, and in Your book they were all written—even the days that were fashioned, when as yet there was none of them.

17 How precious are Your thoughts unto me, O God! How great is the sum of them!

18 If I would count them, they are more in number than the sand; were I to come to the end of them, I would still be with You.

19 Surely You will slay the wicked, O God–depart from me therefore, you men of blood;

20 Who utter Your name with wicked thought, they take it for falsehood, even Your enemies–

21 Do not I hate them, Yehovah, that hate You? And do not I strive with those who rise up against You?

22 I hate them with utmost hatred; I count them mine enemies.

23 Search me God and know my heart examine me and know my thoughts.

24 See if there are any offensive ways in me and lead me in the way everlasting.

Psalm 140

1 For the Leader. A Psalm of David.

2 Deliver me, Yehovah, from the evil man; preserve me from the violent man;

3 Who devise evil things in their heart; every day do they stir up wars.

4 They have sharpened their tongue like a serpent; vipers' venom is under their lips. Selah

5 Keep me, Yehovah, from the hands of the wicked; preserve me from the violent man; who has purposed to make my steps slip.

6 The proud have hid a snare for me, and cords; they have spread a net by the wayside; they have set gins for me. Selah

7 I have said unto Yehovah: 'You are my God'; give ear, Yehovah, unto the voice of my supplications.

8 O God the Lord, the strength of my salvation, who has covered my head in the day of battle,

9 Grant not, Yehovah, the desires of the wicked; further not his evil device, so that they exalt themselves. Selah

10 As for the heads of those that com-

pass me about, let the mischief of their own lips cover them.

11 Let burning coals fall upon them; let them be cast into the fire, into deep pits, that they rise not up again.

12 A slanderer shall not be established in the earth; the violent and evil man shall be hunted with thrust upon thrust.

13 I know that Yehovah will maintain the cause of the poor, and the rights of the needy.

14 Surely the righteous shall give thanks unto Your name; the upright shall dwell in Your presence.

Psalm 141

1 A Psalm of David Yehovah, I have called You; hasten to me, hear my call when I call to you.

2 Let my prayer be set before you as incense and the lifting up of my hands as the evening sacrifice.

3 Lord put a watch on my mouth, keep the door of my lips.

4 Let not my heart be opened to any evil thing to perform any act of wickedness and let me not eat of their delights.

5 Let the righteous smite me in kindness, and correct me; let not my head refuse choice oil; for my prayer will continue against their wickedness.

6 Their judges are thrown down by the sides of the rock; and they shall hear my words, that they are sweet.

7 As when one cleaves and breaks up the Earth, our bones are scattered at the grave's mouth.

8 For my eyes are unto You, O God the Lord; in You have I taken refuge, pour not out my soul.

9 Keep me from the snare which they have laid for me, and from the gins of the workers of iniquity.

10 Let the wicked fall into their own nets, while I escape.

Psalm 142

1 Maschil of David, when he was in the cave; a prayer.

2 With my voice I cry unto Yehovah; with my voice I make supplication unto Yehovah.

3 I pour out my complaint before Him, I declare before Him my trouble;

4 When my spirit faints within me–You know my path–in the way wherein I walk they have hidden a snare for me.

5 Look on my right hand, and see, for there is no man that knows me; I have no way to flee; no man cares for my soul.

6 I have cried unto You, Yehovah; I have said: 'You are my refuge, my portion in the land of the living.'

7 Attend unto my cry; for I am brought very low; deliver me from my persecutors; for they are too strong for me.

8 Bring my soul out of prison, that I may give thanks unto Your name; the righteous shall crown themselves because of me; for You will deal bountifully with me.

Psalm 143

1 A Psalm of David, Yehovah hear my prayer, hear my supplication, in Your faithfulness answer me in Your righteousness.

2 And do not enter into judgment with your servant; for of all the living, none are righteous in your presence.

3 For the enemy has persecuted my soul; he has crushed my life down to the ground; he has made me to dwell in darkness, as those that have been long dead.

4 And my spirit faints within me; my

heart within me is appalled.

5 I remember the days of old; I meditate on all Your actions; I meditate on the work of Your hands.

6 I spread forth my hands unto You; my soul is after You, as a weary land. Selah

7 Answer me speedily, Yehovah, my spirit fails; do not hide Your face from me; lest I become like them that go down into the pit.

8 Cause me to hear Your lovingkindness in the morning, for in You do I trust; cause me to know the way wherein I should walk, for unto You have I lifted up my soul.

9 Deliver me from my enemies, Yehovah; with You have I hidden myself.

10 Teach me to do Your will, for You are my God; let Your good Spirit lead me in an even land.

11 For Your name's sake, Yehovah, quicken me; in Your righteousness bring my soul out of trouble.

12 And in Your lovingkindness cut off mine enemies, and destroy all the adversaries of my soul; for I am Your servant.

Psalm 144

1 To David. Blessed be Yehovah my Rock, who trains my hands for war, and my fingers to fight

2 My lovingkindness, and my fortress, my high tower, and my deliverer; my shield, and He in whom I take refuge; who subdues my people under me.

3 Yehovah, what is man, that You take knowledge of him? or the son of man, that You make account of him?

4 Man is like unto a breath; his days are as a shadow that passes away.

5 Yehovah, bow the heavens, and come down; touch the mountains, that they may smoke.

6 Cast forth lightning, and scatter them; send out Your arrows, and rout them.

7 Stretch out Your hands from on high; rescue me, and deliver me out of many waters, out of the hand of strangers;

8 Whose mouth speaks falsehood, and their right hand is a right hand of lying.

9 O God, I will sing a new song unto You, upon a psaltery of ten strings will I sing praises unto You;

10 Who gives salvation unto kings, who rescues David Your servant from the hurtful sword.

11 Rescue me, and deliver me out of the hand of strangers, whose mouth speaks falsehood, and their right hand is a right hand of lying.

12 We whose sons are as plants grown up in their youth; whose daughters are as corner-pillars carved after the fashion of a palace;

13 Whose garners are full, affording all manner of store; whose sheep increase by thousands and ten thousands in our fields;

14 Whose oxen are well laden; with no breach, and no going forth, and no outcry in our broad places;

15 Happy are the people that are in such a case. Yea, happy are the people whose God is still Yehovah.

Psalm 145

1 I exalt You my God the king! And I will bless Your name forever and ever.

2 I will bless You every day and I will praise Your name forever and ever.

3 Great is Yehovah and greatly to be praised and His greatness is beyond searching out.

4 Generation to generation shall sing the praise of what you have done and tell of your greatness.

5 My words will be about the majesty of your splendorous glory and your wonders I will declare.

6 And of your awesome might I will speak and of your greatness I will recount.

7 They will gush remembering your abundant goodness and they will shout of your righteousness.

8 Gracious and merciful is Yehovah, long suffering and great in lovingkindness.

9 Yehovah is good to all and His compassion is upon all of His works.

10 All your works shall thank you Yehovah, and your holy ones shall bless you.

11 They will speak of the glory of your kingdom and their words will be of your might;

12 To make known to the sons of Adam His exploits and the glorious majesty of His kingdom.

13 Your kingdom is a kingdom for all eternities and your dominion is throughout every generation.

14 Yehovah you sustain all those who fall and you lift up all who are bowed down.

15 The eyes of all wait upon you and you give them their food in every season.

16 You open your hand and satisfy the desire of every living thing.

17 Yehovah is righteous in all of His ways and holy in all of His works.

18 Yehovah is close to all who call upon Him, to everyone who calls to Him in faithfulness.

19 He will perform the desire of those who fear Him and He will hear their cry and rescue them.

20 Yehovah protects all those who love Him but He will destroy all the wicked.

21 My mouth will speak praise to Yehovah– and all flesh shall praise His holy name.

Psalm 146

1 Hallelu Yah. Praise Yehovah, O my soul.

2 I will praise Yehovah while I live; I will sing praises unto my God while I have my being.

3 Put not your trust in princes, nor in the son of man, in whom there is no help.

4 His breath goes forth, he returns to his dust; in that very day his thoughts perish.

5 Happy is he whose help is the God of Jacob, whose hope is in Yehovah his God,

6 Who made heaven and earth, the sea, and all that is in them; who keeps truth for ever;

7 Who executes justice for the oppressed; who gives bread to the hungry. Yehovah looses the prisoners;

8 Yehovah opens the eyes of the blind; Yehovah raises up them that are bowed down; Yehovah loves the righteous;

9 Yehovah preserves the strangers; He upholds the fatherless and the widow; but the way of the wicked He makes crooked.

10 Yehovah will reign forever, Your God, O Zion, unto all generations. Hallelu Yah.

Psalm 147

1 Hallelu Yah; for it is good to sing praises unto our God; for it is pleasant, and praise is comely.

2 Yehovah builds up Jerusalem, He gathers together the dispersed of Israel;

3 Who heals the broken in heart, and binds up their wounds.

4 He counts the number of the stars; He gives them all their names.

5Great is our Lord, and mighty in
power; His understanding is infinite.
6Yehovah upholds the humble; He
brings the wicked down to the ground.
7Sing unto Yehovah with thanksgiving, sing praises upon the harp unto
our God;
8Who covers the heaven with clouds,
who prepares rain for the earth, who
makes the mountains spring with grass.
9He gives to the beast his food, and
to the young ravens which cry.
10He delights not in the strength of
the horse; He takes no pleasure in the
legs of a man.
11Yehovah takes pleasure in those
that fear Him, in those that wait for His
mercy.
12Glorify Yehovah, O Jerusalem;
praise your God, O Zion.
13For He has made strong the bars of
your gates; He has blessed your children within you.
14He makes your borders peace; He
gives you in plenty the fat of wheat.
15He sends out His commandment
upon earth; His word runs very swiftly.
16He gives snow like wool; He scatters the hoar-frost like ashes.
17He cast forth His ice like crumbs;
who can stand before His cold?
18He sends forth His word, and melts
them; He causes His wind to blow, and
the waters flow.
19He declares His word unto Jacob,
His statutes and His ordinances unto
Israel.
20He has not dealt so with any nation;
and as for His ordinances, they have
not known them. Hallelu Yah.

Psalm 148

1Praise Yah, praise Yehovah from the
heavens, praise Him in the heights.
2Praise Him all his angels, praise
Him all his host.
3Praise Him sun and moon, praise
Him all stars of light.
4Praise Him heaven of the heavens,
and water which is above the heavens.
5Let them praise the name of Yehovah for He commanded and they were
created.
6And He established them forever
and ever; He gave a decree, and it shall
not pass away.
7Praise Yehovah from the earth, sea
creatures and all deeps.
8Fire and hail, snow and thick fog,
stormy wind performing His Word.
9The mountains and hills, fruit trees
and all cedars.
10Kings of the Earth all nations

Psalm 149

1HalleluYah! Sing to Yehovah! Sing a
new song! Praise Him in the assembly
of the godly!
2Let Israel rejoice in Him Who made
them. The sons of Zion shout for joy
over their King!
3Let them praise His name in the
dance. With the tambourine and the
harp, let them make music.
4For Yehovah takes pleasure in His
people. He will beautify the meek with
salvation.
5Let the godly rejoice in glory, let
them cry out for joy upon their beds.
6Let the high praises of God be in
your mouth and a two-edged sword in
your hand
7to execute vengeance upon the nations and punishment upon the people.
8To bind their kings with fetters their
nobles with iron fetters,
9to execute the judgments written:
this honor He has given to all His godly
ones. Hallelu Yah!

Psalm 150

1HalleluYah. Praise God in His sanctuary; praise Him in the firmament of
His power.
2Praise Him for His mighty acts;
praise Him according to His abundant
greatness.
3Praise Him with the blast of the
horn; praise Him with the psaltery and
harp.
4Praise Him with the timbrel and
dance; praise Him with stringed instruments and the pipe.
5Praise Him with the loud-sounding
cymbals; praise Him with the shouts of
cymbals.
6Let everything that has breath praise
Yehovah. Hallelu Yah!

The Proverbs

1 The proverbs of Solomon the son of
David, king of Israel;
2To know wisdom and instruction; to
perceive the words of understanding;
3To receive the discipline of wisdom,
righteousness, judgment, and uprightness;
4To give discernment to the simple,
to the young man knowledge and
discretion;
5A wise one hears, and in-creases in
learning, and the one of understanding
will acquire counsels;
6To understand a proverb, and its
elusive sayings; the words of the wise,
and their riddles.
7The fear of Yehovah is the beginning
of knowledge; but the foolish despise
wisdom and instruction.
8Hear, my son, the instruction of
your father, and forsake not the law of
your mother;
9For they are an ornament of grace
unto your head, and necklace about
your neck.
10My son, if sinners entice you, do
not consent.
11If they say: 'Go with us, let us lie in
wait for blood, let us ambush the
innocent without cause;
12Let us swallow them up alive as
Sheol, and whole, as those that go
down into the pit;
13We shall find all precious wealth,
we shall fill our houses with spoil;
14Cast in your lot among us; let us all
have one purse'—
15My son, do not walk in the way
with them, keep your foot from their
path;
16For their feet run to evil, and they
are hurrying to shed blood.
17For in vain the net is spread in the
sight of any bird;
18And these lie in wait for their own
blood, they ambush their own souls.
19So are the ways of everyone who
gets ill gotten gain; it takes away the
soul of the owners.
20Wisdom shouts in the places
outside, she utters her voice in the
streets;
21She calls at the most prominent
noisy gathering places, at the entrances
of the gates, in the city, she speaks her
words:
22How long, you simple ones, will
you love being simple? Scoffers delight
in their scorning, and fools hate
knowledge?
23Turn at my reproof; behold, I will
pour out my Spirit to you, I will make
known my words to you.
24Because I called, and you refused, I
have stretched out my hand, and you
would not obey,
25But you have ignored all my
counsel, and would not have my
reproof;
26I also, will laugh in your calamity, I
will mock when your fear comes;
27When your fear comes as a storm,
and your calamity as a whirlwind;
when trouble and distress come upon
you.
28Then they will call to me, but I will
not answer, they will seek me diligently,
but they will not find me.
29For they hated knowledge, and did
not choose the fear of Yehovah;
30They would not agree with my
counsel, they despised all my reproof.
31Therefore shall they eat of the fruit
of their ways, and be filled with their
own devices.
32For the turning away of the simple
will kill them, and the complacency of
fools shall destroy them.
33But the one who listens to me shall
dwell securely, and will be at ease

without fear of evil.'

2 My son, if you will receive my
words, and treasure my commandments with you;
2To cause your ear to bow to wisdom
and incline your heart to discernment.
3Because if you call for understanding, and raise your voice for
discernment;
4If you seek her as silver, and search
for her as for hid treasures;
5Then shall you understand the fear
of Yehovah, and find the know-ledge of
God.
6For Yehovah gives wisdom; from
His mouth: knowledge and discernment.
7He treasures up abiding wisdom for
the upright, He is a shield to them that
walk blameless;
8That He may guard the paths of
judgment, and preserve the way of His
godly ones.
9Then shall you understand righteousness and judgment, and uprightness,
yes, every good path.
10For wisdom shall enter into your
heart, and knowledge shall be pleasant
to your soul;
11Discretion shall watch over you,
discernment shall guard you;
12To deliver you from the way of evil,
from the men that speak deceitful
things;
13Who abandon the ways of uprightness, to walk in the ways of
darkness;
14Who rejoice to do evil, and delight
in the perversity of evil;
15Whose paths are crooked and who
are devious in their ways;
16To deliver you from the strange
woman, even from the smooth words
of a foreign woman;
17That abandons the companion of
her youth, and forgets the covenant of
her God.
18For her house sinks down unto
death, and her path unto the dead;
19All that go in to her, none return,
neither do they regain the paths of life;
20That you may walk in the good
way, and keep the way of the righteous.
21For the upright shall dwell in the
land, and the blameless shall remain in
it.
22But the wicked shall be cut off from
the land, and the unfaithful shall be
plucked up out of it.

3 My son do not forget my law and
guard your heart with my commandments;
2they will add to you length of days
and years of life and peace.
3You shall not forsake lovingkindness
and truth bind them upon your neck,
write them upon the table of your heart
4And find favor and a good understanding in the eyes of God and man.
5Trust in Yehovah with all your heart
and do not rely on your own
understanding
6Know Him in all of your ways and
He will direct your paths.
7Do not be wise in your own eyes,
fear Yehovah and turn away from evil.
8And it shall be health to your navel
and refreshment to your bones.
9Honor Yehovah with your wealth
and the firstfruits of all your increase.
10And your storehouse shall be filled
with plenty and your wine vats will
overflow with new wine.
11My son, do not despise the chas-
tening of Yehovah, neither resent His
correction;
12For whom Yehovah loves He
corrects, even as a father the son in

whom he delights.

13 Blessed is the man that finds wisdom, and the man that gets understanding.

14 For the gain of it is better than the gain of silver, and the profit of fine gold.

15 She is more precious than jewels; and all the things you desire cannot be compared to her.

16 Length of days is in her right hand; in her left hand are riches and honor;

17 her ways are ways of pleasantness, and all her paths are peace.

18 She is a tree of life to them that lay hold on her, and happy are those who hold her fast.

19 Yehovah founded the earth by wisdom; by understanding He established the heavens.

20 By His knowledge the deep broke forth and the clouds dropped down the dew.

21 My son, let not them depart from your eyes; keep sound wisdom and discretion;

22 So shall they be life unto your soul, and grace to your neck.

23 Then you shall walk securely on your way, and your foot will not stumble.

24 When you lie down, you shall not be afraid; and, you shall lie down, and your sleep shall be sweet.

25 do not be afraid of sudden terror, neither of the destruction of the wicked, when it comes;

26 For Yehovah will be your confidence, and will keep your foot from being caught.

27 Withhold not good from him to whom it is due, when it is in the power of your hand to do it.

28 Say not unto your neighbor: 'Go, and come again, and tomorrow I will give'; when you have it by you.

29 Devise not evil against your neighbor, seeing he dwells trustingly by you.

30 Do not strive with a man without a reason, if he has done you no harm.

31 Do not envy the man of violence, and choose none of his ways.

32 For the deceitful are an abomination to Yehovah; but His secret is with the upright.

33 The curse of Yehovah is in the house of the wicked; but He blesses the habitation of the righteous.

34 Surely He scorns the scorners, but unto the humble He gives grace.

35 The wise will inherit glory; but fools are promoted to shame.

4 Sons hear the instruction of a father, and listen attentively to know understanding.

2 For I give you good doctrine; do not forsake my teaching.

3 For I was a son unto my father, tender and an only one in the sight of my mother.

4 And he taught me, and said unto me: 'Take hold of my words with your heart, keep my commandments, and live;

5 Acquire wisdom, Acquire understanding; do not forget, do not turn away from the words of my mouth;

6 Do not forsake her, and she will keep you; love her, and she will preserve you.

7 The chief thing is wisdom; lay hold of wisdom, and with all that you acquire lay hold of understanding.

8 Exalt her, and she will lift you up; embrace her and she will honor you.

9 She will place a crown of grace on your head; and bestow on you a crown of splendor.'

10 Hear, O my son, and receive my

words; and the years of your life shall
be many.
11I have taught you in the way of
wisdom; I have led you in the direction
of uprightness.
12When you walk your step shall not
be impeded and if you run you shall
not stumble.
13Seize her discipline, don't let her
go; keep her, for she is your life.
14Do not enter the way of the wicked,
and you who are upright do not go in
the way of evil.
15Avoid it, pass not by it; turn from it,
and pass on.
16For they cannot sleep, unless they
have done evil; and their sleep is taken
away, unless they have caused someone
to stumble.
17For they eat the bread of wickedness, and drink the wine of violence.
18But the way of the righteous is as a
shining light, that continues to shine
unto the perfect day.
19The way of the wicked is as deep
darkness; they know not at what they
stumble.
20My son, be attentive to my words;
incline your ear unto my sayings.
21Do not let them depart from your
eyes; keep them in the midst of your
heart.
22For they are life unto those that
find them, and health to all their flesh.
23With all watchfulness guard your
heart; for out of it are the issues of life.
24Put away from you a deceitful
mouth, and corrupt lips put far from
you.
25Look straight forward with your
eyes, and let your eyelids be straight
before you.
26Level out the direction of your feet,
and all your ways will be established.
27Turn not to the right nor to the left;
remove your foot from evil.

5 My son, listen to my wisdom;
stretch out your ear to my understanding;
2That you may keep discretion, and
your lips may preserve knowledge.
3For the lips of a strange woman
drop honey, and her mouth is
smoother than oil;
4But her end is bitter as wormwood,
sharp as a two-edged sword.
5Her feet go down to death; her steps
take hold on Sheol;
6She does not consider the way of
life, she does not know that her
direction of life has wandered.
7Now, you children, listen to me, and
do not turn from the words of my
mouth.
8Remove your way far from her, and
do not come near the door of her
house;
9Lest you give your splendor to
others, and your years to the cruel
ones;
10Lest strangers be filled with your
strength, and your labors be in the
house of an alien;
11And you moan, when your end
comes, when your flesh and your body
are consumed,
12And say: 'How have I hated
instruction, and my heart despised
reproof;
13Neither have I hearkened to the
voice of my teachers, nor inclined my
ear to them that instructed me!
14I was almost in total ruin in
the midst of the congregation and
assembly.'
15Drink water out of your own
cistern, and running water out of your
own well.
16Should your springs be dispersed

abroad, like courses of water in the streets?

17Let them be yours alone, and not strangers.

18Let your fountain be blessed; and have joy with the wife of your youth.

19A lovely hind and a graceful doe, let her breasts satisfy you at all times; with her love be always ravished.

20My son, why then will you be ravished with a strange woman, and embrace the bosom of an alien?

21For the ways of man are before the eyes of Yehovah, and He makes all his paths level.

22The wicked shall be ensnared with his own iniquities and he shall be held with the cords of his sin.

23He shall die for lack of instruction; and in the greatness of his folly he shall go astray.

6 My son, if you become surety for your neighbor, if you have struck your hands for a stranger,

2You are snared by the words of your mouth, you are caught by the words of your mouth,

3Do this my son, and deliver yourself, seeing you have come into the hands of your neighbor; go, humble yourself, and be bold with your neighbor.

4Give no sleep to your eyes, nor slumber to your eyelids.

5Deliver yourself as a gazelle from the hand, and as a bird from the hand of the fowler.

6Go to the ant, you sluggard; consider her ways, and be wise;

7Which having no leader, over-seer, or ruler,

8She prepares her bread in the summer, and gathers her food in the harvest.

9How long will you sleep, O sluggard? When will you arise out of your sleep?

10'A Little sleep, a little slumber, a little folding of the hands to lie down'

11So shall your poverty come as a traveler and your lack as an armed man.

12A base man, a man of iniquity, is he that walks with a deceitful mouth;

13That winks with his eyes, signals with his feet, that points with his fingers;

14Perversity is in his heart, he devises evil continually; he sows discord.

15Therefore shall his calamity come suddenly; in a moment he shall be broken, without remedy.

16These six things Yehovah hates, and seven are an abomination unto His Soul:

17Haughty eyes, a lying tongue, and hands that shed innocent blood;

18A heart that devises wicked thoughts feet that are swift in running to evil;

19A false witness that breathes out lies, and he that sows discord among brethren.

20My son, keep the commandment of your father, and forsake not the law of your mother;

21Bind them continually upon your heart, tie them about your neck.

22When you walk, it shall lead you, when you lie down, it shall watch over you; and when you awake, it shall talk with you.

23For the commandment is a lamp, and the teaching is light, and reproofs of instruction are the way of life;

24To keep you from the evil woman, from the smoothness of the foreign tongue.

25Desire not after her beauty in your heart; neither let her captivate you with

her eyelashes.
26For the price of a harlot a man is
brought to a loaf of bread, but a
married woman hunts for the precious
life.
27Can a man take fire in his bosom,
and his clothes not be burned?
28Or can one walk upon hot coals,
and his feet not be scorched?
29So he that goes into his neighbor's
wife; whosoever touches her shall not
go un-punished.
30Men do not despise a thief, if he
steal to satisfy his soul when he is
hungry;
31But if he be found, he must pay
sevenfold, he must give all the
substance of his house.
32He that commits adultery with a
woman lacks reason; he that does it
will destroy his own soul.
33Wounds and shame shall he get,
and his disgrace will not be wiped
away.
34For jealousy makes a man furious,
and he will not show mercy when he
takes revenge.
35He will not accept any bribe; nor be
appeased, though you give many gifts.

7 My son, keep my words, and lay up
my commandments with you.
2Keep my commandments and live,
and my teaching as the pupil of your
eye.
3Bind them upon your fingers, write
them upon the table of your heart.
4Say unto wisdom: 'You are my sister,
and call understanding your kins-
woman;
5That they may keep you from the
strange woman, from the foreign
woman that makes smooth her words.
6For at the window of my house I
looked through my window;
7And I beheld among the thoughtless
ones, I discerned among the youths, a
young man void of understanding,
8Passing through the street near her
corner, and he went the way to her
house;
9In the twilight, in the evening of the
day, in the blackness of night and the
darkness.
10And, behold, there met him a
woman with the attire of a harlot, and
subtle of heart.
11She is riotous and rebellious, her
feet abide not in her house;
12Now she is in the streets, now in
the broad places, and lies in wait at
every corner.
13So she caught him, and kissed him,
and with an impudent face she said
unto him:
14'Sacrifices of peace-offerings were
due from me; this day I have paid my
vows.
15Therefore I came out to meet you,
to seek your face, and I have found you.
16I have decked my couch with
coverlets, with striped clothes of the
yarn of Egypt.
17I have perfumed my bed with
myrrh, aloes, and cinnamon.
18Come, let us take our fill of love
until the morning; let us enjoy
ourselves with love.
19For my husband is not at home, he
is gone on a long journey;
20He has taken the bag of money
with him; he will come home at the full
moon.'
21She deceives him with her sed-
uctive speech she causes him to yield,
with the seductiveness of her lips she
compels him away.
22He goes after her at once as an ox
that goes to the slaughter, or as one in
chains to the correction of the fool;

23 Until an arrow strikes through his liver; as a bird hastens to the snare, and does not know that it is for his soul.

24 Now sons, listen to me, and pay attention to the words of my mouth.

25 Do not let your heart turn aside to her ways, do not stray in her paths.

26 For she has cast down many dead; and she has killed a mighty host.

27 Her house is the way to Sheol, going down to the chambers of death.

8 Does not wisdom call, and understanding put forth her voice?

2 In the top of high places by the way, where the paths meet, she stands;

3 Beside the gates, at the entry of the city, at the coming in at the doors, she cries aloud:

4 'Unto you, O men, I call, and my voice is to the sons of men.

5 O you thoughtless, understand prudence, and, you fools, be of an understanding heart.

6 Hear, for I will speak excellent things, and the opening of my lips shall be right things. 7 For my mouth shall recite truth, and wickedness is an abomination to my lips.

8 All the words of my mouth are in righteousness, there is nothing twisted or deceitful in them.

9 They are all right to him that understands, and upright to them that find knowledge.

10 Receive my instruction, and not silver, and knowledge rather than choice gold.

11 For wisdom is better than jewels, and all things desired cannot be compared to her.

12 I wisdom dwell with prudent insight, and I discover discretion and knowledge.

13 The fear of Yehovah is to hate evil; pride, and arrogance, and the evil way, and the deceitful mouth, do I hate.

14 Counsel is mine, and sound wisdom; I am understanding, power is mine.

15 By me kings reign, and rulers decree righteousness.

16 By me princes rule, and nobles, even all the righteous judges.

17 I love them that love me, and those that seek me earnestly shall find me

18 Riches and glory are with me enduring wealth and righteousness.

19 My fruit is better than gold, yes fine gold; and my produce is better than choice silver.

20 I walk in the way of righteousness, in the midst of the paths of judgment;

21 That I may cause those that love me to inherit substance, and that I may fill their treasuries.

22 Yehovah possessed me from the beginning of His way, from His works of old.

23 I was poured out from everlasting, at the first from the ancient times of the earth

24 When there were no depths, I was brought forth; when there were no fountains abounding with water.

25 Before the mountains were shaped, before the hills was I brought forth;

26 While as yet He had not made the earth, nor the fields, nor the beginning of the dust of the world.

27 When He established the heavens, I was there; when He drew a circle upon the face of the deep,

28 When He made firm the skies above, when the fountains of the deep showed their might,

29 When He gave to the sea His decree, that the waters should not transgress His commandment, when He appointed the foundations of the

earth;
[30]Then I was at His side, I was a Master workman and I was a delight day by day always rejoicing before Him,
[31]Rejoicing in His habitable earth, and my delights are with the sons of men.
[32]Now therefore, sons, listen to me; for they are happy that keep my ways.
[33]Hear instruction, and be wise, and refuse it not.
[34]Happy is the man that hearkens to me, watching daily at my gates, waiting at the posts of my doors.
[35]For whoso finds me finds life, and obtains the favor of Yehovah.
[36]But he that sins against me wrongs his own soul; all they that hate me love death.'

9 Wisdom has built her house, she has dug out her seven pillars;
[2]She has slaughtered her fatlings, she has mixed her wine; she has also set her table.
[3]She has sent out her maidens, she calls, upon the highest places of the city:
[4]'Whoso is thoughtless, let him turn in here'; as for him that lacks sense, she says to him:
[5]'Come, eat my bread, and drink the wine which I have mixed.
[6]Forsake all thoughtlessness, and live; and walk in the way of understanding.
[7]He that rebukes a scoffer will get abused, and he that rebukes a wicked man, it becomes to him a blot.
[8]Do not correct a scoffer, or he will hate you; correct a wise man, and he will love you.
[9]Give to a wise man, and he will be yet wiser; teach a righteous man, and he will increase in learning.
[10]The fear of Yehovah is the beginning of wisdom, and the knowledge of the holy ones is understanding.
[11]For by me your days shall be multiplied, and the years of your life shall be increased.
[12]If you are wise, you are wise for yourself; and if you scorn, you alone shall bear it.'
[13]A foolish woman is riotous; she is thoughtless, and knows nothing.
[14]And she sits at the door of her house, on a seat in the high places of the town,
[15]To call to those who pass by, who are going straight on their paths.
[16]'Whoever is thoughtless, let him turn in here'; and for the one who lacks sense, she says to him:
[17]'Stolen waters are sweet, and bread eaten in secret is pleasant.'
[18]But he knows not that the dead are there; that her guests are in the depths of Sheol.

10 The proverbs of Solomon. A wise son makes a glad father; but a foolish son is the grief of his mother.
[2]Treasures of wickedness profit nothing; but righteousness delivers from death.
[3]Yehovah will not suffer the soul of the righteous to famish; but He thrust away the desire of the wicked.
[4]He will become poor through slacking off; but the hand of the diligent shall make rich.
[5]A wise son gathers in summer; but a son that does shamefully sleeps in harvest.
[6]Blessings are upon the head of the righteous; but the mouth of the wicked conceals violence.
[7]The memory of the righteous shall

be for a blessing; but the name of the wicked shall be forgotten.

8The wise in heart will receive commandments; but one with foolish lips shall fall.

9He that walks uprightly walks securely; but he who perverts his ways shall be found out.

10He that winks with the eye causes sorrow; and the one with foolish lips shall fall.

11The mouth of the righteous is a fountain of life; but the mouth of the wicked conceals violence.

12Hatred stirs up strife; but love covers all transgressions.

13In the lips of him that has discernment wisdom is found; but a rod is for the back of him that lacks sense.

14Wise men lay up knowledge; but the mouth of the foolish is an imminent ruin.

15The rich man's wealth is his strong city; the ruin of the poor is their poverty.

16The wages of the righteous is life; the increase of the wicked is sin.

17He who listens to instruction is on the path of life; but he that forsakes reproof is in error.

18He that hides hatred is of lying lips; and he who brings forth slander is a fool.

19In the multitude of words there is no lack of transgression; but he that refrains his lips is wise.

20The tongue of the righteous is as choice silver; the heart of the wicked is of little worth.

21The lips of the righteous feed many; but the foolish die for lack of sense.

22The blessings of Yehovah causes one to become rich and no sorrow is added with it.

23As a fool takes pleasure in doing wickedness, a man of wisdom does understanding.

24What the wicked fears will come upon him; and the desire of the righteous shall be granted.

25When the whirlwind passes, the wicked are no more; but the righteous is an everlasting foundation.

26Like vinegar to the teeth, and like smoke to the eyes, so is the sluggard to them that send him.

27The fear of Yehovah adds days; but the years of the wicked are cut short.

28The expectation of the righteous is joy; but the hope of the wicked shall perish.

29The way of Yehovah is a stronghold to the blameless, but ruin to the workers of iniquity.

30The righteous shall never be moved; but the wicked shall not inhabit the land.

31The mouth of the righteous buds with wisdom; but the perverse tongue shall be cut off.

32The lips of the righteous know what is acceptable; but the mouth of the wicked is all perversity.

11 A false balance is an abomination to Yehovah; but a correct weight is His delight.

2Pride comes and then comes shame but with humility comes wisdom.

3The integrity of the upright shall guide them; but the perverseness of the unfaithful destroys them.

4Riches do not profit on the day of wrath; but righteousness delivers from death.

5The righteousness of the blameless shall make straight his way; but the wicked shall fall by his wickedness.

[6]The righteousness of the upright
shall deliver them; but the unfaithful
shall be trapped in their evil desires.
[7]When a wicked man dies his
expectation shall perish, and the hope
of strength perishes.
[8]The righteous are delivered out of
trouble, and the wicked come into it
instead.
[9]With his mouth the godless man
destroys his neighbor; but through
knowledge shall the righteous be
delivered.
[10]When it goes well with the
righteous, the city triumphs; and when
the wicked perish, there is rejoicing
[11]By the blessing of the upright a city
is exalted; but it is overthrown by the
mouth of the wicked.
[12]He that despises his neighbor lacks
sense; but a man of understanding
holds his peace.
[13]He that goes about as a talebearer
reveals secrets; but he that is of a
faithful spirit conceals a matter.
[14]Where there is no wise direction, a
people fall; but in the multitude of
counsellors there is deliverance.
[15]He that is surety for a stranger
suffers harm; he who spurns pledging
shall be secure.
[16]A gracious woman obtains honor;
and strong men obtain riches.
[17]The merciful man does good to his
own soul; but he that is cruel troubles
his own flesh.
[18]The wicked earns deceitful wages;
but he that sows righteousness has a
sure reward.
[19]Stedfast righteousness tends to life;
but he that pursues evil his death.
[20]They that are perverse in heart are
an abomination to Yehovah; but such
as are blameless in their way are His
delight.
[21]Hand to hand the evil man shall
not be unpunished; but the seed of the
righteous shall be delivered.
[22]As a ring of gold in a swine's snout,
so is a fair woman that turns aside
from discretion.
[23]The desire of the righteous is only
good; but the expectation of the wicked
is wrath.
[24]There is that scatter, and yet
increases; and there is that which
withholds more than is necessary, but it
tends only to want.
[25]The soul who blesses shall be made
fat, and the one who gives drink shall
also be refreshed.
[26]He that withholds corn, the people
shall curse him; but blessing shall be
upon the head of him that sells it.
[27]He that diligently seeks good seeks
favor; but he that searches for evil, it
shall come unto him.
[28]He that trusts in his riches shall fall;
but the righteous shall flourish like a
green leaf.
[29]He that troubles his own house
shall inherit the wind; and the foolish
shall be servant to the wise of heart.
[30]The fruit of the righteous is a tree
of life; and he that is wise wins souls.
[31]Behold, the righteous shall be
repaid in the earth; how much more
the wicked and the sinner!

12 Whoso loves knowledge loves
correction; but he that is brutish
hates reproof.
[2]A good man shall obtain the favor of
Yehovah; but the wicked will He
condemn.
[3]A man shall not be established by
wickedness; but the root of the
righteous shall never be moved.
[4]A virtuous woman is a crown to her
husband; but she that does shamefully

is rotten in his bones.
5The thoughts of the righteous are
just; but the counsels of the wicked are
deceit.
6The words of the wicked are to lie in
wait for blood; but the mouth of the
upright shall deliver them.
7The wicked are overthrown, and are
not; but the house of the righteous shall
stand.
8A man shall be praised for good
sense; but he that is of a twisted heart
shall be despised.
9Better is he that is lightly esteemed,
and has a servant, than he that plays
the great man, and lacks bread.
10A righteous man regards the life of
his beast; but the tender mercies of the
wicked are cruel.
11He that tills his ground shall have
plenty of bread; but he that follows
after vain things is void of understanding.
12The wicked desire the plunder of
evil; but the root of the righteous yields
fruit.
13In the transgression of the lips the
evil man is snared; but the righteous
escape from trouble.
14From the fruit of man's mouth he is
satisfied with good, and the work of
man's hands returns to him.
15The way of a fool is upright in his
own eyes; but he that is wise listens to
counsel.
16A fool's vexation is known at once;
but a prudent man conceals shame.
17He that breathes forth truth speaks
righteousness; but a false witness
deceit.
18There is blunt speaking that pierces
as a dagger but the tongue of the wise
restores.
19Truthful lips shall be established
forever; but a lying tongue for a
moment.
20Deceit is engraved in the heart of
those that devise evil; but those who
plan good is joyous peace.
21There is no evil that will befall the
righteous; but the wicked are filled
with evil.
22Lying lips are an abomination to
Yehovah; but they that deal truly are
His delight.
23A prudent man conceals knowledge; but the heart of fools proclaims
foolishness.
24The hand of the diligent shall rule;
but the slothful shall be under tribute.
25The heart of a man is bowed down
by concern; but a good word makes it
glad.
26The righteous guides his friend; but
the way of the wicked leads them
astray.
27The slothful man does not have
prey to roast; but the diligent man has
precious wealth.
28In the way of righteousness is life,
and in its pathway there is no death.

13 A wise son is instructed by his
father; but a scorner does not
hear rebuke.
2A man shall eat good from the fruit
of his mouth; but the soul of the
faithless is violence.
3He who guards his mouth keeps his
soul; the one who opens wide his lips
ruins it.
4The soul of the sluggard desires, and
has nothing; but the soul of the diligent
becomes fat..
5A righteous man hates a lying word;
but the wicked are vile and disgraceful.
6Righteousness protects him whose
way is blameless; but wickedness
overthrows the sinner.
7There is one who pretends to be

rich, yet has nothing; there is one who pretends to be poor, yet has great wealth.

8 A man ransoms his soul with his riches; but the poor hear no threats.

9 The light of the righteous rejoices; but the lamp of the wicked shall be put out.

10 By pride comes only strife; but wisdom is to those who seek counsel.

11 Wealth gotten by vanity shall be diminished; but he that gathers little by little shall increase.

12 Hope deferred makes the heart sick; but desire fulfilled is a tree of life.

13 Whoever despises the word brings destruction on himself; but he that fears the commandment shall be rewarded.

14 The teaching of the wise is a fountain of life, to depart from the snares of death.

15 Good insight gives favor; but the way of the faithless is unchanging.

16 All who are prudent act with knowledge; but a fool exposes folly.

17 A wicked messenger falls into evil; but a faithful ambassador brings healing.

18 Poverty and shame shall be to him that refuses instruction; but he that regards reproof shall be honored.

19 The desire fulfilled is sweet to the soul; and it is an abomination to fools to depart from evil.

20 He that walks with wise men shall be wise; but the companion of fools shall pay for it.

21 Evil pursues sinners; but to the righteous good shall be repaid.

22 A good man leaves an inheritance to his children's children; and the wealth of the sinner is laid up for the righteous.

23 The untilled ground of the poor has much food; but swept away by injustice.

24 He that spares the rod hates his son; but he that loves him seeks to instruct him.

25 The righteous eats to the satisfying of his soul; but the belly of the wicked shall want.

14 Every wise woman builds her house; but the foolish pluck it down with her hands.

2 He that walks in his up-rightness fears Yehovah; but he that is perverse in his ways despises Him.

3 In the mouth of the foolish is a rod of pride; but the lips of the wise shall preserve them.

4 Where no oxen are, the crib is clean; but an abundance of harvest comes from the strength of the ox.

5 A faithful witness will not lie; but a false witness breathes forth lies.

6 A scorner seeks wisdom, and does not find it; but knowledge is easy unto him that has understanding.

7 Go from the presence of a foolish man, for you will not learn the speech of knowledge.

8 The wisdom of the prudent is to look well to his way; but the folly of fools is deceit.

9 Fools mock at guilt; but among the upright is favor..

10 The heart knows its own bitterness; and a stranger does not share its joy.

11 The house of the wicked shall be overthrown; but the tent of the upright shall flourish.

12 There is a way before man that seems right, but the end of it is the ways of death.

13 Even in laughter the heart aches; and the end of joy is heaviness.

14 The one drawing back in heart shall

be filled with his own ways; a good man from his deeds.

15 The thoughtless believe every word; one of understanding ponders his steps.

16 A wise man fears, and departs from evil; but the fool rages and falls.

17 One who is quick tempered acts foolishly; and a man of discretion is hated.

18 The thoughtless inherit folly; but the prudent are crowned with knowledge.

19 The evil bow before the good, and the wicked bow at the gates of the righteous.

20 The poor are hated even of his own neighbors; but the rich are liked by many.

21 He that despises his neighbor sins; but he that is gracious unto the humble, he is blessed.

22 Shall they not go astray that devise evil? But lovingkindness and truth shall be for them that plan good.

23 In all toil there is profit; but by the talk of the lips there is only poverty.

24 The crown of the wise is their riches; but the folly of fools is folly.

25 A true witness delivers souls; but he that speaks lies is deceitful.

26 In the fear of Yehovah a man has a strong confidence; and his children shall have a place of refuge.

27 The fear of Yehovah is a fountain of life, to depart from the snares of death.

28 In the multitude of people is the king's glory; but without a nation a prince is ruined.

29 The one that is slow to anger is of great understanding; but he that is hasty of spirit exalts folly.

30 A calm heart is the life of the flesh; but envy is the rottenness of the bones.

31 He that oppresses the poor blasphemes his Maker; but he that is gracious unto the needy honors Him.

32 The wicked is thrust down in his misfortune; but the righteous, even when he is brought to death, has hope.

33 Wisdom rests in the heart of him that has understanding; but it is not known in the midst of a fool.

34 Righteousness exalts a nation; but sin is a reproach to any people.

35 The king's favor is toward a servant who has insight; but his wrath strikes him that is shameful.

15 A soft answer turns away wrath; but a grievous word stirs up anger.

2 The tongue of the wise uses knowledge properly; but the mouth of fools pour out foolishness.

3 The eyes of Yehovah are in every place, keeping watch upon the evil and the good.

4 A soothing tongue is a tree of life; but perverseness harms the spirit.

5 A fool despises his father's correction; but he who heeds reproof is prudent.

6 In the house of the righteous is much treasure; but in the revenues of the wicked is trouble.

7 The lips of the wise disperse knowledge; not so with the heart of the foolish.

8 The sacrifice of the wicked is an abomination to Yehovah; but the prayer of the upright is His delight.

9 The way of the wicked is an abomination to Yehovah; but He loves him that follows after righteousness.

10 There is severe correction for him that forsakes the way; and he that hates reproof shall die.

11 Sheol and Abaddon are in front of Yehovah; how much more the hearts of

the children of men!
12A scorner does not like to be
rebuked; he will not go unto the wise.
13A joyful heart makes a pleasing
face; but a sorrowful heart crushes the
spirit.
14The heart of him who has understanding seeks knowledge; but the
mouth of fools feeds on foolishness.
15All the days of the afflicted are bad;
but goodness of heart is a continual
feast.
16Better is little with the fear of
Yehovah, than great treasure and
turmoil with it.
17Better is a meal of herbs with love
there, than a fattened steer and hatred
with it.
18A hot tempered man stirs up strife;
but he that is slow to anger quiets
contention.
19The way of the lazy person is like a
hedge of thorns; but the path of the
upright is even.
20A wise son makes a glad father; but
a foolish man despises his mother.
21Foolishness is joyful to him that
lacks sense; but a man of understanding walks straight.
22Plans go wrong without counsel;
but in the multitude of advisors they
succeed.
23It is joyful when a man's mouth
delivers the answers, and how good is a
word in due season.
24The way of life is above to the wise:
that they may depart from Sheol
beneath.
25Yehovah will tear down the house
of the proud; but He will establish the
border of the widow.
26The thoughts of wickedness are an
abomination to Yehovah; but pure
words are beautiful.
27He that is greedy of ill-gotten gain
troubles his own house; but he that
hates bribes shall live.
28The heart of the righteous studies
to answer; but the mouth of the wicked
pours out evil things.
29Yehovah is far from the wicked; but
He hears the prayer of the righteous.
30The light of the eyes rejoices the
heart; and a good report makes the
bones fat.
31The ear that listens to life giving
reproof lodges among the wise.
32He that refuses correction despises
his own soul; but he that hearkens to
reproof gets sense.
33The fear of Yehovah is the
instruction of wisdom; and before
honor goes humility.

16 To man belongs the plans of the
heart, but the answer of the
tongue is from Yehovah.
2All the ways of a man are clean in
his own eyes; but Yehovah examines
the spirits.
3Commit your works unto Yehovah,
and your thoughts shall be established.
4Yehovah has prepared everything to
its purpose, and also the wicked for the
day of trouble.
5Every one that is arrogant in heart is
an abomination to Yehovah; hand to
hand! He shall not be unpunished.
6By lovingkindness and truth
iniquity is atoned; and by the fear of
Yehovah men depart from evil.
7When a man's ways please Yehovah,
He makes even his enemies to be at
peace with him.
8Better is a little with righteousness
than great revenues with injustice.
9A man's heart plans his way; but
Yehovah directs his steps.
10An oracle is in the lips of the king;
his mouth will not be unfaithful in

judgment.
11 A just balance and scales are
Yehovah's; and all the weights in the
bag are His work.
12 It is an abomination to kings to
commit wickedness; for by righteousness the throne is established.
13 Righteous lips are the delight of
kings; and they love him that speaks
right.
14 The wrath of a king is as messengers of death; but a wise man will
appease it.
15 In the light of the king's countenance is life; and his favor is as a cloud
of the latter rain.
16 How much better is it to get
wisdom than gold! To get understanding is preferable to silver.
17 The highway of the upright is to
depart from evil; he that keeps his way
preserves his soul.
18 Pride goes before destruction, and
a haughty spirit before a fall.
19 Better it is to be of a lowly spirit
with the humble, than to divide the
spoil with the proud.
20 He who has the insight of the word
shall find good; and he who trusts in
Yehovah, is blessed.
21 The wise in heart is called a man of
understanding; and the sweetness of
the lips increases learning.
22 Prudence is a fountain of life unto
him that has it; but folly is the
chastisement of fools.
23 The heart of the wise teaches his
mouth, and adds learning to his lips.
24 Pleasant words are like a honeycomb, sweet to the soul, and health to
the bones.
25 There is a way before man that
seems right, but the end of it is the way
of death
26 A soul's appetite works for him, for
his mouth urges him on.
27 An ungodly man digs up evil, and
in his lips are like a burning fire.
28 A froward man spreads strife; and a
whisperer separates familiar friends.
29 A man of violence deceives his
neighbor, and leads him into a way that
is not good.
30 He that shuts his eyes, it is to devise
perverse things; puckering the lips he
brings evil to pass.
31 The gray hair is a crown of
splendor it is found in the way of
righteousness.
32 He that is slow to anger is better
than the mighty; and he that rules his
spirit than he that takes a city.
33 The lot is cast into the lap; but from
Yehovah is all judgment.

17 Better is a dry morsel and
quietness with it, than a house
full of feasting with strife.
2 A servant that deals wisely shall
have rule over a son that deals
shamefully, and shall have part of the
inheritance among the brethren.
3 The refining pot is for silver, and the
furnace for gold; but Yehovah examines
the hearts.
4 The wicked listen to evil lips; and a
liar obeys a malicious tongue.
5 He who mocks the poor treats his
Maker with contempt; and he that
rejoices at calamity shall not be
unpunished.
6 Children's children are the crown of
old men; and the glory of children are
their fathers.
7 Excellent lips are not suited to a
fool; much less lying lips a prince.
8 A gift is as a precious stone in the
eyes of him that has it; wherever he
turns, he prospers.
9 He that covers a transgression seeks

love; but he that harps on a matter estranges a familiar friend.

10 A rebuke enters deeper into a man of understanding than a hundred stripes into a fool.

11 A rebellious man seeks only evil; therefore a cruel messenger shall be sent against him.

12 Let a bear robbed of her whelps meet a man, rather than a fool in his folly.

13 Whoso rewards evil for good, evil shall not depart from his house.

14 The beginning of strife is as when one lets out water; therefore leave off contention, before the quarrel breaks out.

15 He that justifies the wicked, and he that condemns the righteous, even they both are an abomination to Yehovah.

16 Wherefore is there a price in the hand of a fool to buy wisdom, seeing he hath no understanding?

17 A friend loves at all times, and a brother is born for adversity.

18 A man void of understanding is he that strikes hands, and becomes surety in the presence of his neighbor.

19 He loves transgression that loves strife; he that exalts his gate seeks destruction.

20 He that has a crooked heart finds no good; and he that has a perverse tongue falls into evil.

21 He that begets a fool gets sorrow; and the father of a fool has no joy.

22 A joyful heart is good medicine; but a broken spirit dries the bones.

23 The wicked takes a bribe out of the bosom, to pervert the ways of judgment.

24 Wisdom is before him that has understanding; but the eyes of a fool are in the ends of the earth.

25 A foolish son is vexation to his father, and bitterness to her that bore him.

26 To punish also the righteous is not good, nor to strike the noble for their uprightness.

27 He that spares his words has knowledge; and he that husbands his spirit is a man of discernment.

28 Even a fool, when he holds his peace, is counted wise; and he that shuts his lips is esteemed as a man of understanding.

18 He that separates himself seeks his own desire, and is hostile against all sound wisdom.

2 A fool has no desire in discernment, but only that his heart may reveal itself.

3 When the wicked comes, there also comes contempt, and with insult reproach.

4 The words of a man's mouth are as deep waters; a gushing stream, a fountain of wisdom.

5 It is not good to lift up a wicked man, to turn aside the righteous in judgment.

6 A fool's lips bring strife, and his mouth calls for a beating.

7 A fool's mouth is his ruin, and his lips are the snare of his soul.

8 The words of a whisperer are as dainty morsels, and they go down into the innermost parts of the belly.

9 Even one that is slack in his work is brother to him who destroys.

10 The name of Yehovah is a strong tower: the righteous run in and are inaccessible.

11 The rich man's wealth is his strong city, and as a high wall in his own delusion.

12 Before destruction a man's heart is haughty, but humility comes before honor.

13 He that gives answer before he
hears, it is folly and confusion unto
him.
14 The spirit of a man will endure his
infirmity; but a broken spirit who can
bear?
15 The understanding heart acquires
knowledge; and the ear of the wise
seeks knowledge.
16 A man's gift makes room for him,
and brings him before the great ones.
17 At first the cause seems righteous;
until his neighbor comes and examines
him.
18 The lot causes strife to cease, and
decides between powerful contenders.
19 An offended brother is like a strong
city; and contentions like the bars of a
castle.
20 A man's belly shall be filled with the
fruit of his mouth; with the produce of
his lips he shall be satisfied.
21 Death and life are in the hand of
the tongue; and those who love it will
eat its fruit.
22 He who finds a wife finds good,
and obtains favor from Yehovah.
23 The poor speak supplications; but
the rich man answers roughly.
24 A man's friends come to ruin; but
there is a love that sticks closer than a
brother.

19 Better is the poor that walks
blameless than he who is
perverse in speech and is a fool.
2 Also, a soul without know-ledge is
not good; and he that hurries with his
feet sins.
3 The foolishness of a man perverts
his way; and his heart rages against
Yehovah.
4 Wealth brings many friends; but a
poor man is separated from his friends.
5 A false witness shall not be
unpunished; and he that speaks lies
shall not escape.
6 Many seek the presence of a giver;
and every man is a friend to him that
gives gifts.
7 All the brothers of the poor do hate
him; how much more do his friends go
far from him! He pursues them with
words but they are not.
8 He that acquires a heart loves his
own soul; he that keeps under-standing
shall find good.
9 A false witness shall not be
unpunished; and he that speaks lies
shall be destroyed.
10 Delight is not fitting for a fool;
much less for a servant to have rule
over princes.
11 A prudent man is slow to anger and
it is his honor to overlook an offense.
12 The king's wrath is as the roaring of
a lion; but his favor is as dew upon the
grass.
13 A foolish son is the calamity of his
father; and the contentions of a wife are
a continual dropping.
14 House and wealth are the inheritance of fathers; but a prudent wife is
from Yehovah.
15 Laziness casts into a deep sleep; and
the idle soul shall suffer hunger.
16 He that keeps the commandment
keeps his soul; but he that despises His
ways shall die.
17 He that is gracious unto the poor
lends unto Yehovah; and what he has
done will He repay unto him.
18 Chasten your son, for there is hope;
but set not your soul on his
destruction.
19 A man of great wrath shall suffer
punishment; if you deliver him you
must do it again
20 Hear counsel, and receive discipline, that you may be wise in your

latter end.
21 There are many plans in the heart
of a man; but the counsel of Yehovah, it
shall stand.
22 The desire of a man is his lovingkindness; and a poor man is better
than a liar.
23 The fear of Yehovah tends to life;
and he shall abide satisfied, he shall not
be visited with evil.
24 The sluggard buries his hand in the
dish, and will not so much as bring it
back to his mouth.
25 Strike a scorner, the simple will
become prudent; and when one that
has understanding is rebuked, he will
understand knowledge.
26 A son that deals shamefully and
reproachfully will do violence to his
father, and chase away his mother.
27 Cease, my son, to hear the instruction that causes you to go astray
from the words of knowledge.
28 An ungodly witness mocks judgment; and the mouth of the wicked
devours iniquity.
29 Judgments are prepared for scorners, and a beating for the back of
fools.

20 Wine is a mocker, strong drink
is riotous; and whoever staggers
from it is not wise.
2 The terror of a king is as the roaring
of a lion: he that provokes him to anger
forfeits his life.
3 It is a glory for a man to keep away
from strife; but every fool will be
quarreling.
4 The sluggard will not plow when
winter sets in; therefore he shall beg in
harvest, and have nothing.
5 Counsel in the heart of man is like
deep water; but a man of understanding will draw it out.
6 Most men will proclaim every one
his own goodness; but a faithful man
who can find?
7 He that walks in his integrity is a
righteous man, happy are his children
after him.
8 A king that sits on the throne of
judgment scatters away all evil with his
eyes.
9 Who can say: 'I have made my heart
clean, I am pure from my sin'?
10 Divers weights, and divers measures, both of them alike are an
abomination to Yehovah.
11 Even a child is known by his
doings, whether his work be pure, and
whether it be right.
12 The hearing ear, and the seeing eye,
Yehovah has made both of them.
13 Love not sleep, lest you be
dispossessed; open your eyes, and you
shall have bread in plenty.
14 'It is bad, it is bad', says the buyer;
but when he is gone his way, then he
boasts.
15 There is gold, and a multitude of
rubies; but the lips of knowledge are a
precious jewel.
16 Take his garment that is surety for a
stranger; and hold him in pledge that is
surety for an alien woman.
17 Bread of falsehood is sweet to a
man; but afterwards his mouth shall be
filled with gravel.
18 Every purpose is established by
counsel; and war is carried out with
good advice.
19 He that goes about as a talebearer
reveals secrets; therefore meddle not
with him that opens wide his lips.
20 Whoso curses his father or his
mother, his lamp shall be put out in the
blackest darkness.
21 An estate may be gotten hastily at
the beginning; but the end thereof shall

not be blessed.
22Say not: 'I will repay evil'; wait for
Yehovah, and He will save you.
23Diverse weights are an abomination
to Yehovah; and a false balance is not
good.
24A man's goings are of Yehovah; how
then can a man understand his way?
25It is a snare to a man to rashly say:
'Holy', and after he vows to reconsider.
26A wise king sifts the wicked, and
turns the wheel over them.
27The spirit of man is the lamp of
Yehovah, searching all the inward
parts.
28Mercy and truth preserve the king;
and his throne is upheld by mercy.
29The glory of young men is their
strength; and the beauty of old men is
the grey head.
30Sharp wounds cleanse away evil; so
do stripes that reach the inward parts.

21 The king's heart is in the hand
of Yehovah as streams of waters:
He turns it wherever He wills.
2Every way of a man is right in his
own eyes; but Yehovah ponders the
hearts.
3To do righteousness and justice is
chosen by Yehovah rather than
sacrifice.
4Haughty eyes, and a proud heart is
sin, it is the lantern of the wicked.
5The thoughts of the diligent tend
only to abundance; but every one that
is hasty tends only to lack.
6The getting of treasures by a lying
tongue is a fleeting vapor and a snare
of death.
7The violence of the wicked shall
drag them away; because they refuse to
do right.
8The way of man is crooked and
strange; but as for the pure, his deed is
upright.
9It is better to dwell in a corner of the
housetop, than sharing a house with a
woman of strife.
10The soul of the wicked desires evil;
his neighbor finds no favor in his eyes.
11When the scorner is punished, the
thoughtless is made wise; and when the
wise is instructed, he receives knowledge.
12The righteous one considers the
house of the wicked; the wicked are
overthrown to their ruin.
13Whoso stops his ears at the cry of
the poor, he also shall cry himself, but
shall not be answered.
14A gift in secret pacifies anger, and a
present in the bosom strong wrath.
15It is a joy to the righteous to do
justice, but ruin to the workers of
iniquity.
16The man that strays out of the way
of understanding shall rest in the
congregation of the dead.
17He that loves pleasure shall be a
poor man; he that loves wine and oil
shall not be rich.
18The wicked is a ransom for the
righteous; and the unfaithful for the
upright ones.
19It is better to dwell in a desert land,
than with a contentious and angry
woman.
20There is desirable treasure and oil
in the dwelling of the wise; but a
foolish man swallows it up.
21He that pursues righteousness and
lovingkindness finds life, prosperity,
and glory.
22A wise man scales the city of the
mighty, and brings down the stronghold wherein it trusts.
23He who guards his mouth and his
tongue guards his soul from troubles.
24Scoffer is the name of a proud and

haughty man, he acts in the rage of arrogance.

25The slothful one's desire kills him; because his hands refuse to work,

26he covets greedily all day; but the righteous gives and spares not.

27The sacrifice of the wicked is an abomination; how much more, when he brings it with the proceeds of wickedness?

28A false witness shall perish; but the man that obeys shall speak forever.

29A wicked man hardens his face; but as for the upright, he looks well to his way.

30There is no wisdom nor understanding nor counsel against Yehovah.

31The horse is prepared against the day of battle; but victory is of Yehovah.

22 Choose a name rather than great riches, and good favor rather than silver and gold.

2The rich and the poor meet together —Yehovah is the maker of them all.

3A prudent man sees the evil, and hides himself; but the thoughtless pass on, and suffer for it.

4The reward for humility is the fear of Yehovah: wealth, glory and life!

5Thorns and snares are in the way of the crooked; he that guards his soul keeps far from them.

6Train up a child in the way he should go, and even when he is old, he will not depart from it.

7The rich rule over the poor, and the borrower is a servant to the lender.

8He that sows iniquity shall reap misery; and the rod of his fury shall fail.

9He who has a good eye shall be blessed; for he gives of his bread to the poor.

10Cast out the scorner, and contention will go out; yes, strife and shame will cease.

11He that loves pureness of heart, that has grace in his lips, the king shall be his friend.

12The eyes of Yehovah preserve him that has knowledge, but He overthrows the words of the treacherous one.

13The sluggard says: 'There is a lion without; I shall be slain in the streets.'

14The mouth of strange women is a deep pit: he that is abhorred of Yehovah shall fall therein.

15Foolishness is bound up in the heart of a child; but the rod of correction shall drive it far from him.

16The one who oppresses the poor to gain increase; and he who gives to the rich will come to poverty.

17Incline your ear, and hear the words of the wise, and apply your heart unto my knowledge,

18for it is a pleasant thing if you keep them within you; let them be established altogether upon your lips.

19That your trust may be in Yehovah, I have made them known to you this day, even to you.

20Have not I written unto you excellent things of counsels and knowledge;

21That I might make you know the certainty of the words of truth, that you might bring back words of truth to them that send you?

22Rob not the weak, because he is weak, neither crush the poor in the gate;

23For Yehovah will plead their cause, and plunder those who plunder them.

24Make no friendship with a man that is given to anger; neither go with a wrathful man;

25unless you learn his ways, and get a snare to your soul.

26Be not of them that strike hands, or
of them that are sureties for debts;
27If you do not have the ability to pay,
why should he take away your bed
from under you?
28Remove not the ancient landmark,
which your fathers have set.
29See a man diligent in his business?
he shall stand before kings; he shall not
stand before obscure men.

23 When you sit to eat with a ruler,
you should really understand
what is before you;
2And put a knife to your throat, if
you are a man given to appetite.
3Do not desire his delicacies; for they
are deceitful food.
4Do not weary yourself to be rich;
cease from your own understanding.
5When your eyes blink it is gone; for
it surely makes to itself wings like an
eagle and flies to heaven.
6Do not eat the bread of him that has
an evil eye, neither desire his delicacies;
7For as one who has calculated in his
own soul, so is he: 'Eat and drink', he
says to you; but his heart is not with
you.
8The morsel which you have eaten
you shall vomit up, and destroy your
pleasant words.
9Do not speak in the ears of a fool;
for he will despise the insight of your
words.
10Do not remove the ancient boundaries; nor enter the fields of the
orphans;
11For their Redeemer is strong; He
will contend with you on their behalf.
12Bring your heart to discipline, and
your ears to the words of knowledge.
13Do not hold back discipline from
your boy; for though you strike him
with the rod, he will not die.
14You strike him with the rod, and
will deliver his soul from Sheol.
15My son, if your heart is wise, my
heart will also be glad;
16My reins will rejoice, when your
lips speak right things.
17Do not let your heart envy sinners,
but be in the fear of Yehovah every day;
18For surely there is a future; and
your hope shall not be cut off.
19Hear, my son, and be wise, and
guide your heart in the way.
20Do not be among those who are
drunk with wine; among gluttonous
eaters of meat;
21For the drunkard and the glutton
shall come to poverty; and laziness
shall clothe a man with rags.
22Hear your father who beget you,
and do not despise your mother when
she is old.
23Buy the truth, and sell it not; also
wisdom, discipline, and understanding.
24The father of the righteous will
greatly rejoice; and he that begets a
wise child will have joy in him.
25Let your father and your mother be
glad, and let her that bore you rejoice.
26My son, give me your heart, and let
your eyes favor my ways.
27For a prostitute is a deep pit; and a
foreign woman is a narrow well.
28She also lies in wait as a robber, and
increases the un-faithful among men.
29Who has Woe? Who has sorrow?
Who has strife? Who has anguish?
Who has wounds without cause? Who
has dimness of eyes?
30They that tarry long at the wine;
they that go to try mixed wine.
31Look not upon the wine when it is
red, when it gives its color in the cup,
when it glides down smoothly;
32Finally it bites like a serpent, and
stings like a viper.

33 Your eyes shall see strange things, and your heart shall speak perversity.

34 You will be as one that lies down in the midst of the sea, or as he that lies upon the top of a mast.

35 'They have struck me, and I did not feel it, they have beaten me, and I knew it not; when shall I awake? I will seek it yet again.'

24 Do not be jealous of evil men, neither desire to be with them.

2 For their heart studies destruction, and their lips talk of mischief.

3 Through wisdom a house is built; and by understanding it is established;

4 And by knowledge your chambers shall be filled with all precious wealth and pleasant things.

5 A wise man is strong; yes, a man of knowledge increases strength.

6 For with wise advice you shall make war; and in the multitude of counsellors there is victory.

7 Wisdom is too high for the fool; he opens not his mouth in the gate.

8 He that devises to do evil, men shall call him a schemer.

9 The shameful behavior of foolishness is sin; and the scorner is an abomination to men.

10 If you faint in the day of adversity, your strength is small.

11 Deliver them that are drawn unto death; and those that are ready to be slain rescue.

12 If you say: 'Behold, we knew it not,' does not He that weighs the hearts consider it? And He that preserves your soul, does He not know it? And shall He not render to every man according to his works?

13 My son, eat honey, for it is good, and the honeycomb is sweet to your taste;

14 So let your soul know wisdom; when you have found it, then shall there be a future, and your hope shall not be cut off.

15 Lie not in wait, O wicked man, against the dwelling of the righteous, spoil not his resting-place;

16 For a righteous man falls seven times, and rises up again, but the wicked stumble under adversity.

17 Rejoice not when your enemy falls, and let not your heart be glad when he stumbles;

18 Lest Yehovah see it, and it displeases Him, and He turns away His wrath from him.

19 Fret not yourself because of evildoers, neither be envious at the wicked;

20 For there will be no future to the evil man, the lamp of the wicked shall be put out.

21 My son, fear Yehovah and the king, and meddle not with them that are given to change;

22 For their calamity shall rise suddenly; and who knows the ruin from them both?

23 These also are sayings of the wise. To have respect of persons in judgment is not good.

24 He that says unto the wicked: 'You are righteous', peoples shall curse him, nations shall abhor him;

25 But to them that decide justly shall be delight, and a good blessing shall come upon them.

26 He kisses the lips that gives a right answer.

27 Prepare your work without, and make it fit for yourself in the field; and afterwards build your house.

28 Do not be a witness against your neighbor without cause; and do not deceive with your lips.

29 Say not: ‘I will do so to him as he has done to me; I will render to the man according to his work.’

30 I went by the field of a slothful man, and by the vineyard of the man lacking heart;

31 And, lo, it was all grown over with thistles, the face of it was covered with nettles, and the stone wall thereof was broken down.

32 Then I beheld, and set it to my heart; I saw, and took instruction.

33 ‘Yet a little sleep, a little slumber, a little folding of the hands to sleep’—

34 So shall your poverty come as a runner, and your want as an armed man.

25 These also are proverbs of Solomon, which the men of Hezekiah king of Judah transmitted.

2 It is the glory of God to conceal a matter; but the glory of kings is to search out a matter.

3 The heaven for height, and the earth for depth, and the heart of kings is unsearchable.

4 Take away the dross from the silver, and there comes out a vessel for the refiner;

5 Take away the wicked from before the king, and his throne shall be established in righteousness.

6 Do not honor yourself in the presence of the king, and do not stand in the place of great men;

7 For it is better that one says to you: ‘Come up here’, than that you should be put lower in the presence of the prince, whom your eyes have seen.

8 Do not go out quickly to quarrel, unless you do not know what to do afterwards, when your neighbor has disgraced you.

9 Make your complaint with your neighbor, do not reveal it to another;

10 Unless he that hears rep-roaches you, and your bad reputation has no end.

11 A word spoken at the appropriate time is like apples of gold in settings of silver.

12 As a ring of gold, and an ornament of fine gold, so is a wise reprover to an obedient ear.

13 As the coolness of snow, so a faithful messenger to the one who sends him on the day of harvest; for he refreshes the soul of his master.

14 Like clouds and wind without rain, so is he that boasts himself falsely of a gift.

15 By longsuffering is a ruler persuaded, and a soft tongue breaks the bone.

16 Have you found honey? eat just enough, unless you are too satisfied, and vomit it.

17 Let your foot be seldom in your neighbor’s house; unless he be tired of you, and hate you.

18 A man that bears false witness against his neighbor is a maul, a sword, and a sharp arrow.

19 Confidence in an unfaithful one in a time of trouble is like a broken tooth, and a foot out of joint.

20 As one that takes off a garment in cold weather, and as vinegar upon nitre, so is he that sings a song to a heavy heart.

21 If your enemy is hungry, give him bread to eat, and if he is thirsty, give him water to drink;

22 For you will heap coals of fire upon his head, and Yehovah will reward you.

23 The north wind brings rain, and a backbiting tongue an angry countenance.

24 It is better to dwell in a corner of

the housetop, than in a house in common with a woman of strife.

25 As cold waters to a thirsty soul, so is good news from a far country.

26 As a muddied spring, and a corrupted fountain, so is a righteous man who gives way to the wicked.

27 It is not good to eat much honey; so it is to search out their own glory is not glory.

28 Like a city broken down without a wall, so is he whose spirit is without self control.

26 As snow in summer, and as rain in harvest, so honor is not fitting for a fool.

2 As the wandering bird, as the flying swallow, so the curse that is causeless shall not come.

3 A whip for the horse, a bridle for the donkey, and a rod for the back of fools.

4 Do not answer a fool acc-ording to his folly, otherwise you will also be like him.

5 Answer a fool according to his folly, otherwise he will be wise in his own eyes.

6 He that sends a message by the hand of a fool cuts off his own feet, and drinks violence.

7 The legs of the lame are useless; so is a proverb in the mouth of fools.

8 As one who binds a stone in a sling, so is he that gives honor to a fool.

9 As a thorn that goes up into the hand of a drunkard, so is a parable in the mouth of fools.

10 He who hires a fool and hires one passing by wounds everyone.

11 As a dog that returns to his vomit, so a fool repeats his folly.

12 See a man wise in his own eyes? there is more hope of a fool than of him.

13 The sluggard says: 'There is a fierce lion in the way; there's a lion in the square.'

14 As the door turns upon its hinges, a sluggard turns on his bed.

15 The sluggard buries his hand in the dish; and is too lazy to bring it back to his mouth.

16 The sluggard is wiser in his own eyes than seven that can answer discreetly.

17 He that passes by and becomes furious in a quarrel that's not his own, is like one that takes a dog by the ears.

18 As a madman who throws fiery darts, arrows, and death;

19 So is the man that deceives his neighbor, and says: 'I am joking?'

20 Where there is no wood, the fire goes out; and where there is no talebearer, contention ceases.

21 As coals are to burning coals, and wood to fire; so is a contentious man to kindle strife.

22 The words of a whisperer are as tasty morsels, and they go down into the innermost parts of the belly.

23 Silver dross laid over a clay vessel is like glowing lips and a wicked heart

24 He who hates pretends with his lips, but inwardly holds deceit.

25 When he speaks graciously, don't believe him; for there are seven abominations in his heart.

26 Though he covers his hatred by deceit, his wickedness shall be revealed before the congregation.

27 He who digs a pit will fall into it; and he that rolls a stone, it shall return upon him.

28 A lying tongue hates those that are crushed by it; and a flattering mouth works ruin.

27 Boast not yourself of tomorrow; for you do not know what a day may bring.

2Let another man praise you, and not your own mouth; a stranger, and not your own lips.

3A stone is heavy, and the sand weighty; but a fool is heavier than them both.

4Wrath is cruel, and anger is overwhelming; but who is able to stand before jealousy?

5Better is open rebuke than secret love.

6Faithful are the wounds of a loved one; but many are the kisses of one who hates.

7The soul who is full tramples over honeycomb; but to the hungry soul every bitter thing is sweet.

8As a bird that wanders from her nest, so is a man that wanders from his place.

9Oil and perfume rejoice the heart; so does the sweetness of soul advice by a friend.

10Don't forsake your friend, or your father's friend; and do not go to your brother's house in the day of your disaster; better is a neighbor that is near than a brother far off.

11My son, be wise, and make my heart rejoice, that I may answer him that treats me with contempt.

12The prudent one sees the evil, and hides; but the thoughtless pass on, and pay for it

13Take his garment which is surety for a stranger; and hold him in pledge that is surety for a strange woman.

14He that blesses his neighbor with a loud voice, rising early in the morning, it shall be counted a curse to him.

15A constant dripping on a rainy day and a woman of strife are alike;

16Restraining her is to restrain the wind, or to hold oil by his right hand.

17Iron sharpens iron; so a man sharpens the countenance of his neighbor.

18The one who keeps his fig tree shall eat the fruit; and he that guards his master shall be honored.

19As in water face reflects face, so the heart of man to man.

20Sheol and destruction are never satisfied; so the eyes of man are never satisfied.

21The refining pot is for silver, and the furnace for gold, and a man is tried by his praise.

22Though you grind a fool in a mortar along with grain you will not remove his foolishness..

23Be diligent to know the state of your flocks, and set your heart on your herds;

24For riches are not forever; and does the crown endure unto all generations?

25When the hay is mown, and the tender grass shows itself, and the herbs of the mountains are gathered;

26The lambs will be for your clothing, and the goats the price for a field.

27And there will be enough goats' milk for your food, for the food of your household; and provision for your maidens.

28 The wicked flee when no man pursues; but the righteous are as confident as a fierce lion.

2For the transgression of a land many are the princes; but it will continue long by a man of understanding and knowledge.

3A poor man that oppresses the weak is like a sweeping rain which leaves no bread.

4They that forsake the law praise the

wicked; but they that keep the law contend with them.

5 Evil men do not understand judgment; but they that seek Yehovah understand all things.

6 Better is the poor that walks in his blamelessness, than he that is perverse in his ways, though he be rich.

7 A son of understanding ob-serves the law; but he that is a friend of gluttons shames his father.

8 He that increases his wealth by interest and usury, gathers it for him that is gracious to the poor.

9 He that turns away his ear from hearing the law, his prayer is also an abomination.

10 He who misleads the upright in an evil way, he shall fall himself into his own pit; but the blameless shall inherit good.

11 The rich man is wise in his own eyes; but the poor that has understanding searches him out.

12 When the righteous rejoice, there is great beauty; but when the wicked rise, men hide themselves

13 He that covers his transgressions shall not prosper; but whoso confesses and forsakes them shall have mercy.

14 Blessed is the man who trembles continually; but he that hardens his heart shall fall into evil.

15 A wicked ruler over poor people is as a roaring lion, and a ravenous bear.

16 A ruler that lacks discern-ment is also a great oppressor; but he that hates unjust gain shall prolong his days.

17 A man burdened with the blood of any person shall flee to the pit; let no one help him.

18 He who walks blameless shall be saved; but he that is perverse in his ways shall fall at once.

19 He that tills his ground shall be filled with bread; but he that pursues vain things shall be filled with poverty.

20 A faithful man shall abound with blessings; but he that makes haste to be rich shall not be unpunished.

21 To show partiality is not good; for a man will transgress for a piece of bread.

22 He that has an evil eye hastens after wealth, and knows not that poverty shall come upon him.

23 He that rebukes a man shall in the end find more favor than he that flatters with the tongue.

24 He who robs his father or his mother, and says: 'It is no trans-gression', he is companion to the man who destroys.

25 A greedy spirit stirs up strife; but he that puts his trust in Yehovah shall thrive.

26 He that trusts in his own heart is a fool; but he who walks in wisdom shall be saved.

27 He that gives unto the poor shall not lack; but he that hides his eyes will be cursed profusely.

28 When the wicked rise, men hide themselves; but when they perish, the righteous increase.

29 A man who is often reproved hardens his neck shall suddenly be broken and that without remedy.

2 When the righteous increase, the people rejoice; but when the wicked rule, the people groan.

3 A man who loves wisdom causes his father's heart to rejoice but he that keeps company with harlots wastes his wealth.

4 By judgement a king establishes the land; but a man who accepts bribes destroys it.

5 A man who flatters his neighbor spreads a net for his steps.

6An evil man is snared in his
transgression but the righteous shout
and rejoice.
7The righteous know the rights of the
poor; the wicked does not understand
such knowledge.
8Scornful men inflame a city; but
wise men turn away wrath.
9If a wise man contends with a
foolish man, whether he be angry or
laugh, there will be no rest.
10The men of blood hate the one who
is blameless; and as for the upright,
they seek his soul.
11A fool spends all his spirit; but a
wise man quietly holds it back.
12If a ruler hearkens to false-hood, all
his servants are wicked.
13The poor man and the oppressor
meet together; Yehovah gives light to
the eyes of them both.
14The king that faithfully judges the
poor, his throne shall be established
forever.
15The rod and reproof give wisdom;
but a child left to himself causes shame
to his mother.
16When the wicked increase, transgression increases; but the righteous
shall see their fall.
17Correct your son, and he will give
you rest; he will give delight unto your
soul.
18With no revelation the people run
wild but happy is he who keeps the
law .
19A slave will not be corrected by
words; for though he under-stands,
there will be no response.
20Do you see a man that is hasty in
his words? There is more hope for a
fool than for him.
21He that pampers his servant from a
child, afterwards he will be arrogant
22An angry man stirs up strife, and a
wrathful man abounds in transgression.
23A man's pride shall bring him low;
but he that is of a lowly spirit shall
attain to honor.
24He who is partnered with a thief
hates his own soul: he hears the curse
and says nothing.
25The terror of man brings a snare;
but whoso puts his trust in Yehovah
shall be exalted.
26Many seek the ruler's favor; but a
man's judgment comes from Yehovah.
27An unjust man is an abomination
to the righteous; and he that is upright
in the way is an abomination to the
wicked.

30 The words of Agur the son of
Jakeh; the burden. The man
said unto Ithiel, unto Ithiel and Ucal:
2I am too stupid to be a man, and
have not the understanding of a man;
3And I have not learned wisdom, but
I do know the Holy One.
4Who has ascended up into heaven,
and come down? Who has gathered the
wind in his fists? Who has bound the
waters in his garment? Who has
established all the ends of the earth?
What is his name, and what is his Son's
name, if you know?
5Every word of God is tried; He is a
shield unto them that take refuge in
Him.
6Do not add to His words, unless He
reproves you, and you are found to be a
liar.
7I have asked two things of you; do
not deny me of them before I die:
8Remove far from me falsehood and
lies; give me neither poverty nor riches;
feed me with my share of bread;
9Lest I be full, and deny, and say:
'Who is Yehovah?' Or lest I be

disinherited, and steal, and profane the
name of my God.
10Do not slander a servant to his
master, unless he curses you, and you
are found guilty.
11There is a generation that curses
their father, and does not bless their
mother.
12There is a generation that are pure
in their own eyes, and yet are not
washed from their filthiness.
13There is a generation, Oh how lofty
are their eyes! and their eyelids are
lifted up.
14There is a generation whose teeth
are as swords, and their great teeth as
knives, to devour the poor from off the
earth, and the needy from among men.
15The leech has two daughters: 'Give,
give.' There are three things that are
never satisfied, yes, four that say not:
'Enough':
16Sheol; and the barren womb; the
earth that is not satisfied with water;
and the fire that saith not: 'Enough.'
17The eye that mocks his father, and
scoffs to obey his mother, the crows of
the valley shall pick it out, and the
young vultures shall eat it.
18There are three things which are
too wonderful for me, yes, four which I
know not:
19The way of an eagle in the air; the
way of a serpent upon a rock; the way
of a ship in the midst of the sea; and
the way of a man with a young woman.
20So is the way of an adulterous
woman; she eats, and wipes her mouth,
and says: 'I have done no wickedness.'
21Under three things the earth
quakes, and for four it cannot endure:
22Under a slave when he reigns; and a
fool when he is filled with food;
23Under a hated woman when she
gets a husband; and a hand-maid that
is heir to her mistress.
24There are four things which are
little upon the earth, but they are
exceeding wise:
25The ants are not a strong people,
yet they provide their food in the
summer;
26The rock-badgers are not a strong
people, yet they make their houses in
the rock;
27The locusts have no king, yet they
all go out in ranks;
28The lizard you can catch with your
hands, yet it is in kings' palaces.
29There are three things which are
impressive in their walk, four which are
impressive in move-ment:
30The lion, which is mightiest among
beasts, and does not turn away for any;
31The strutting rooster; the he-goat
and the king with an army.
32If you have done foolishly in
exalting yourself, or if you have devised
something, lay your hand on your
mouth.
33For the churning of milk brings
forth curd, and the wringing of the
nose brings forth blood; so the pressing
of anger brings forth strife.

31 The words of king Lemuel; the
burden his mother had when
she corrected him.
2Oh my son? and oh son of my
womb? O son of my vows?
3Do not give your strength to
women, or your ways to that which
destroys kings.
4O Lemuel it is absolutely not for
kings to drink wine: nor for princes to
desire strong drink'
5Lest they drink, and forget what is
decreed, and pervert the judgment of
all the afflicted.
6Give strong drink unto him that is

dying, and wine unto the bitter in soul;
7Let him drink, and forget his
poverty, and not remember his misery
anymore.
8Open your mouth for the speechless, in the cause of all the children
of the needy.
9Open your mouth, judge righteously, and plead the cause of the poor
and needy.
10Who can find a woman of valor?
her value is far above precious jewels.
11Her husband's heart safely trusts in
her, and he has no lack of gain.
12She does him good and not evil all
the days of her life.
13She seeks wool and flax, and works
willingly with her hands.
14She is like the merchant-ships; she
brings her food from afar.
15She rises also while it is yet night,
and gives food to her household, and a
portion to her maidens.
16She considers a field, and buys it;
with the fruit of her hands she plants a
vineyard.
17She girds her loins with strength,
and strengthens her arms.
18She perceives that her merchandise is good; her lamp does not go
out at night.
19She lays her hands to the distaff,
and her hands hold the spindle.
20She stretches out her hand to the
afflicted; she puts forth her hands to
the poor.
21She is not afraid of the snow for her
household; for all her household are
clothed with scarlet.
22She makes coverings for herself; her
clothing is fine linen and purple.
23Her husband is known in the gates,
where he sits among the elders of the
land.
24She makes linen garments and sells
them; and delivers belts to the
merchant.
25Strength and dignity are her
clothing; and she laughs at the time to
come.
26She opens her mouth in wisdom;
and the law of loving-kindness is on
her tongue.
27She looks after the ways of her
household, and does not eat the bread
of idleness.
28Her children rise up, and call her
blessed; and her husband praises her:
29'Many daughters have done
valiantly, but you excel them all.'
30Grace is deceitful, and beauty is
meaningless; but a woman that fears
Yehovah, she shall be praised.
31Give her of the fruit of her hands;
and let her works praise her in the
gates

www.ingramcontent.com/pod-product-compliance
Lightning Source LLC
LaVergne TN
LVHW081321110826
845149LV00007B/1563

* 9 7 9 8 9 9 4 4 0 9 8 1 7 *